The New Humanities Reader

The New Humanities Reader

FOURTH EDITION

RICHARD E. MILLER
Rutgers University

KURT SPELLMEYER
Rutgers University

WADSWORTH
CENGAGE Learning™

Australia • Brazil • Japan • Korea • Mexico • Singapore • Spain • United Kingdom • United States

WADSWORTH
CENGAGE Learning™

**The New Humanities Reader,
Fourth Edition**
Richard E. Miller and Kurt
Spellmeyer

Publisher/Executive Editor:
Lyn Uhl

Acquisitions Editor: Kate Derrick

Senior Development Editor:
Leslie Taggart

Senior Assistant Editor: Kelli
Strieby

Editorial Assistant: Elizabeth
Reny

Media Editor: Cara Douglass-
Graff

Associate Media Editor: Janine
Tangney

Marketing Director: Jason Sakos

Marketing Coordinator:
Ryan Ahern

Marketing Communications
Manager: Stacey Purviance

Content Project Management:
PreMediaGlobal

Art Director: Jill Ort

Print Buyer: Betsy Donaghey

Rights Acquisitions Specialist—
Text: Katie Huha

Rights Acquisitions Specialist—
Image: Jennifer Meyer Dare

Cover Designer: Lisa Devenish

Cover Image: GettyImages.com

Compositor: PreMediaGlobal

For product information and
technology assistance, contact us at **Cengage Learning
Customer & Sales Support, 1-800-354-9706**

For permission to use material from this text or product,
submit all requests online at **www.cengage.com/permissions**
Further permissions questions can be e-mailed to
permissionrequest@cengage.com

Library of Congress Control Number: 2010940925

ISBN-13: 978-0-495-91286-6

ISBN-10: 0-495-91286-7

Wadsworth
20 Channel Center Street
Boston, MA 02210
USA

Cengage Learning is a leading provider of customized learning solutions with office locations around the globe, including Singapore, the United Kingdom, Australia, Mexico, Brazil, and Japan. Locate your local office at **international.cengage.com/region**

Cengage Learning products are represented in Canada by Nelson Education, Ltd.

For your course and learning solutions, visit **www.cengage.com**

Purchase any of our products at your local college store or at our preferred online store **www.cengagebrain.com**

Instructors: Please visit **login.cengage.com** and log in to access instructor-specific resources.

Printed in the United States of America
2 3 4 5 14 13 12 11

Contents

Thematic Contents   xi

Preface   xv

Reading and Writing About the New Humanities   xix

LEILA AHMED, On Becoming an Arab   1

An Egyptian scholar describes her evolving sense of what it means to be an Arab within the context of the transformation of Egypt from a British colony into a sovereign Arab nation.

KAREN ARMSTRONG, *Homo religiosus*   21

Is God a father? Is heaven a place? Do we have immortal souls? None of these questions, Armstrong maintains, were important to religion in the past. Instead, for tens of thousands of years, religion was seen as an art of consciousness designed to restore our natural sense of connection to the world.

JONATHAN BOYARIN, Waiting for a Jew: Marginal Redemption at the Eighth Street Shul   44

A first-person account of the author's disenchantment with the Jewish tradition of his childhood, followed by his personal reinvention of Jewishness after an odyssey through a postmodern world of multiple perspectives and beliefs.

NICHOLAS CARR, Is Google Making Us Stupid?   66

When it first arrived, the World Wide Web was supposed to revolutionize society. The unrestricted flows of information would produce a population more articulate and informed than any that existed before. But now we learn that the Web is changing us in ways that might actually do damage to our capacity for sustained thought.

SUSAN FALUDI, The Naked Citadel   77

A reporter describes the legal battle—and the cultural meltdown—that ensues when The Citadel, an all-male military academy, admits its first female recruit.

CAROLINE FRASER, Rewilding North America   110

Generations of conservationists have tried to isolate a shrinking wilderness from the rising human tide. Today it appears that this strategy has been a disaster for nature itself. Saving the natural world is going to require taking down the barriers that separate wilderness from civilization.

DANIEL GILBERT, Immune to Reality   132

Despite the tens of thousands of hours we spend pursuing the American Dream, recent research in psychology demonstrates that we often prove surprisingly inept when we try to predict what will make us happy. Is fulfillment just an accident?

MALCOLM GLADWELL, The Power of Context: Bernie Goetz and the Rise and Fall of New York City Crime   151

Why is it that in matters of human behavior, change is so hard to predict? According to Malcolm Gladwell, a journalist and social critic, we seldom see the real causes of social change because we pay too much attention to the big picture. Instead, we need to start with the little things.

STEVEN JOHNSON, The Myth of the Ant Queen   168

Do complex systems like ant colonies and megacities have a collective intelligence greater than the intelligence of their individual members? If the answer is "Yes," then can we ever know where our systems are taking us?

CHRISTINE KENNEALLY, You Have Gestures   186

Where does language begin? Do animals have access to language? What is the significance of the fact that humans point but apes don't? Kenneally teases apart the differences between human gestures and gestures in the animal kingdom to show how language is present and active long before a human child begins to speak.

JON KRAKAUER, *Selections from* Into the Wild   202

Searching for the fundamentals of life, a young man named Christopher McCandless sets off into Alaska's backcountry. There he dies, apparently of starvation. Was he a fool, or does his journey bear witness to courage, curiosity, and other admirable traits?

BETH LOFFREDA, *Selections from* Losing Matt Shepard: Life and Politics in the Aftermath of Anti-Gay Murder   224

In Laramie, Wyoming, the murder of a gay college student puts the town under the media microscope. From one perspective, we see citizens struggling to spin their public image. From another perspective, we might be able to detect the first signs of genuine cultural change.

AZAR NAFISI, *Selections from* Reading Lolita in Tehran: A Memoir in Books   247

Can art be more powerful than a dictatorship? This is the question posed by an account of a women's reading group in the days following the establishment of the Islamic Republic of Iran.

TIM O'BRIEN, How to Tell a True War Story   268

When applied to the reality of war, words like *honor, valor, courage,* and *sacrifice* may be profoundly dishonest. O'Brien's short story asks its readers to take another look at a subject that no one can claim to understand fully, not even those who have found themselves in the thick of battle.

JUHANI PALLASMAA, *Selections from* The Eyes of the Skin: Architecture and the Senses   281

Buildings typically are designed to appeal to the eye, but Pallasmaa argues that the best of them appeal to all five senses. The tyranny of the eye has led us to an architectural desert, but a revolution in design could create spaces that make us feel thrillingly alive.

OLIVER SACKS, The Mind's Eye: What the Blind See   302

For more than a century, people have believed that the structure of the brain was fixed at birth and more or less unchangeable thereafter. But the writings of people who have lost their sight suggest that the brain can rewire itself to a degree that scientists have only started to recognize.

CHARLES SIEBERT, An Elephant Crackup?   320

The phenomenon known as Human-Elephant Conflict—as measured by events where elephants destroy villages and crops, attacking and killing humans—is on the rise. Elephants, who travel in herds and mourn their dead, are profoundly social creatures. The collapse of elephant culture, brought on by predation, stress, and trauma, may point to what lies ahead for human culture.

Peter Singer and Jim Mason, Meat and Milk Factories   337

Most of the meat, poultry, pork, milk, and eggs that Americans eat comes from massive factory farms where animals live sedentary, medicated lives before being slaughtered. The environmental consequences of this approach are familiar to many, but Singer and Mason underscore the ethical consequences of turning a blind eye to the suffering of animals.

Michael Specter, A Life of Its Own   363

Experts foresee that the building blocks of life will soon be available commercially, while children in elementary school will compete to invent the cutest new animals and plants. Fabricating living creatures seems to be the ultimate in creativity. But given the condition of the world today, are we ready for that power?

Martha Stout, When I Woke Up Tuesday Morning, It Was Friday   380

The term *divided consciousness* refers to those times when we withdraw mentally from the world around us. Daydreams and other forms of subjective escape often help us to keep our mental balance by shutting out events when they threaten to be over-whelming. But when does our power to shut things out begin to close the door on sanity itself?

Deborah Tannen, The Roots of Debate in Education and the Hope of Dialogue   401

Anyone who watches the presidential debates or listens to talk radio can see that Americans love to argue. But the truth is that the winner in any debate may prove to be mistaken, while the loser may fail to communicate information that everyone could benefit from hearing. According to linguist Deborah Tannen, there has to be a better way.

Edward Tenner, Another Look Back, and a Look Ahead   432

Technological innovations happen in response to problems, but each innovation ends up producing a series of new problems in turn—which require new innovations, which produce new problems once again, apparently ad infinitum. Is all of this change self-defeating? While admitting that technology has "revenge effects," Edward Tenner makes the case that progress is no illusion.

Robert Thurman, Wisdom   459

Losing one's sense of self or having an empty self is typically imagined to be a fate worse than death. But Robert Thurman, an expert on the Buddhism of Tibet, argues that we have misjudged the experience of "no self," which is not a dark corridor to oblivion, but the road to what he calls "infinite life."

JEAN TWENGE, An Army of One: *Me*   476
What it means to have a self has changed over the course of the past thirty years. While Baby Boomers set out to transform the world, Generation Me seeks out fun as the highest value and promotes self-esteem as the greatest good. Drawing on data taken from 1.3 million young people, Twenge argues that this obsessive focus on the self is not just bad for society, it's also bad for the individual.

JANINE R. WEDEL, Confidence Men and Their Flex Lives   502
For the last twenty years, the "entrepreneur" has been a cultural icon—the lone visionary who could step outside the box. But now Wedel shows us the mythology's dark side: a shadow elite who play many roles at once—diplomat, business leader, media spokesman, political insider. While claiming impartiality, the new breed pursues its partisan goals, and its personal enrichment.

Eight Sample Assignment Sequences   526
Credits   533
Author and Title Index   535

Thematic Contents

Making Sense of Violence

LEILA AHMED, On Becoming an Arab 1

DANIEL GILBERT, Immune to Reality 132

MALCOLM GLADWELL, The Power of Context: Bernie Goetz and the Rise and Fall of New York City Crime 151

BETH LOFFREDA, *Selections from* Losing Matt Shepard: Life and Politics in the Aftermath of Anti-Gay Murder 224

TIM O'BRIEN, How to Tell a True War Story 268

CHARLES SIEBERT, "An Elephant Crackup?" 320

World Religion and World Secularity

KAREN ARMSTRONG, Homo religiosus 21

LEILA AHMED, On Becoming an Arab 1

JONATHAN BOYARIN, Waiting for a Jew: Marginal Redemption at the Eighth Street Shul 44

AZAR NAFISI, *Selections from* Reading Lolita in Tehran: A Memoir in Books 247

JUHANI PALLASMAA, *Excerpts from* The Eyes of the Skin: Architecture and the Senses 281

ROBERT THURMAN, Wisdom 459

Education: Learning, Conforming, Knowing

JONATHAN BOYARIN, Waiting for a Jew: Marginal Redemption at the Eighth Street Shul 44

NICHOLAS CARR, Is Google Making Us Stupid?   66

SUSAN FALUDI, The Naked Citadel   77

JON KRAKAUER, *Selections from* Into the Wild   202

AZAR NAFISI, *Selections from* Reading Lolita in Tehran: A Memoir in Books   247

DEBORAH TANNEN: The Roots of Debate in Education and the Hope
   of Dialogue   401

The Future of the Environment

CAROLINE FRASER, Rewilding North America   110

STEVEN JOHNSON, The Myth of the Ant Queen   168

JON KRAKAUER, *Selections from* Into the Wild   202

CHARLES SIEBERT, "An Elephant Crackup?"   320

MICHAEL SPECTER, A Life of Its Own   363

JEAN TWENGE, An Army of One: *Me*   476

Health and Healing

KAREN ARMSTRONG, Homo religiosus   21

OLIVER SACKS, The Mind's Eye: What the Blind See   302

CHARLES SIEBERT, An Elephant Crackup?   320

MARTHA STOUT, When I Woke Up Tuesday Morning, It Was Friday   380

ROBERT THURMAN, Wisdom   459

JEAN TWENGE, An Army of One: *Me*   476

Gender

SUSAN FALUDI, The Naked Citadel   77

JON KRAKAUER, *Selections from* Into the Wild   202

BETH LOFFREDA, *Selections from* Losing Matt Shepard: Life and Politics in the
   Aftermath of Anti-Gay Murder   224

AZAR NAFISI, *Selections from* Reading Lolita in Tehran: A Memoir in Books   247

TIM O'BRIEN, How to Tell a True War Story   268

DEBORAH TANNEN: The Roots of Debate in Education and the Hope
   of Dialogue   401

Art and the Making of Meaning

DANIEL GILBERT, Immune to Reality   132

CHRISTINE KENNEALLY, You Have Gestures   186

AZAR NAFISI, *Selections from* Reading Lolita in Tehran: A Memoir in Books   247

TIM O'BRIEN, How to Tell a True War Story   268

JUHANI PALLASMAA, *Excerpts from* The Eyes of the Skin: Architecture and the Senses   281

EDWARD TENNER, Another Look Back, and a Look Ahead   432

Economics, Inequality, and Justice

SUSAN FALUDI, The Naked Citadel   77

MALCOLM GLADWELL, The Power of Context: Bernie Goetz and the Rise and Fall of New York City Crime   151

AZAR NAFISI, *Selections from* Reading Lolita in Tehran: A Memoir in Books   247

PETER SINGER AND JIM MASON, Meat and Milk Factories   337

MICHAEL SPECTER, A Life of Its Own   363

JANINE WEDEL, Confidence Men and their Flex Lives   502

Culture and Performance

SUSAN FALUDI, The Naked Citadel   77

MALCOLM GLADWELL, The Power of Context: Bernie Goetz and the Rise and Fall of New York City Crime   151

CHRISTINE KENNEALLY, You Have Gestures   186

AZAR NAFISI, *Selections from* Reading Lolita in Tehran: A Memoir in Books   247

JUHANI PALLASMAA, *Excerpts from* The Eyes of the Skin: Architecture and the Senses   281

DEBORAH TANNEN: The Roots of Debate in Education and the Hope of Dialogue   401

The Future of Democracy

NICHOLAS CARR, Is Google Making Us Stupid?   66

SUSAN FALUDI, The Naked Citadel   77

BETH LOFFREDA, *Selections from* Losing Matt Shepard: Life and Politics in the Aftermath of Anti-Gay Murder   224

MICHAEL SPECTER, A Life of Its Own   363

DEBORAH TANNEN: The Roots of Debate in Education and the Hope of Dialogue   401

JANINE R. WEDEL, Confidence Men and their Flex Lives   502

Preface

This book is based on a single idea that might seem far from revolutionary: students starting college should write about nonfiction that explores in a thoughtful way the major issues of their time. Although the university itself has changed—some would say past all recognition—most people even now would accept the value of such reading for young adults in transit from their home communities to a larger and often confusing world. One claim that universities have always made is that higher education has the power to impart a broader view, if not a magic key to the universe, then at least a few useful paradigms that can make events more coherent in some way. And now, in the twenty-first century, most of those paradigms circulate through the medium of nonfiction prose.

Indeed, the prose argument could be described as the major genre of our time, enjoying the same pride of place held by poetry in the Renaissance or by novels in the nineteenth century. If the goal is to change how people live by changing how they think, then the prose argument simply has no rivals. Simone de Beauvoir's *The Second Sex* went beyond a critique of inequality by insisting that women have the power to create their own identities, independent of male desires. *Silent Spring*, the book that pushed into public view the environmental crisis, qualifies as a prose argument, and so does *An Inconvenient Truth*, which has indirectly or directly reached millions of people around the world. Whether we are readers of *Foreign Affairs*, *Harper's*, *Science*, or *JAMA*, we look to nonfiction prose when we need to navigate the complexities of politics, health, the arts, management, history, computer science or engineering. Civic life in general and culture broadly speaking become legible for us only when they find expression in the sentences and paragraphs of arguments that might range from ten or fifteen pages to hundreds.

In a period that we might call the "Age of Nonfiction," teaching prose should not be seen as a revolutionary act—and yet, remarkably, it is. We might find it shocking when we stop to reflect that throughout the whole of their high school years, most young Americans never cast eyes on anything of the kind.

Only textbooks—for commercial reasons aimed well below the level of the target audience—supplement the literary works that students read. Convention and bureaucracy combine to ensure that Huck Finn and Holden Caulfield dominate a space for inquiry which might be shared with world events, new technologies, and changes in a market system rigged to ensure that most young Americans start their adult lives hopelessly in debt. Needless to say, literary art has enormous value, but educators in the English speaking world have too readily assumed that discourse in a more "philosophical" vein lies beyond the reach of ordinary minds, who can't get any thinking done without vivid imagery and lively narrative.

An even larger impediment to change is a prejudice still more deeply engrained in the culture of the humanities themselves. No one in the humanities needs to be argued into seeing the past as "another country"— remote, difficult to understand, essential to retrieve, and quite unlike the "now." But this belief presupposes a transparency that the present moment can never possess. Nothing is more mysterious to us—more unstable, enigmatic, multifaceted, dangerous, and blind—than the period we are living through. Only in retrospect can it assume the apparent fixity of a "period," with neat boundaries and a clear trajectory that emerge from interpretation done from a safe, detached, retrospective vantage point. Of all the "other countries" we will ever know, the present is the most "other" of them all, and yet we have treated it as obvious and unworthy of the attention that accrues to the most abstruse details of times long gone. Naturally, an understanding of the past is essential for an intelligent response to the here-and-now, but why have the humanities so willingly postponed the encounter with contemporary life? The question becomes still more troubling when we recognize how little freedom people have for study and reflection once their energies are channeled into work and family. If an investigation of the here-and-now never happens in a course we teach, then it probably won't happen at all.

Of course, future web designers might read *Wired*; future business people might pore over *Business Week*; aspiring directors of museums are likely to cast an eye from time to time over the pages of *ArtForum*. But as for reading outside one's likely métier, that's a far less likely scenario, especially now, when universities have backed away from a commitment to the goal of broad general knowledge. The one place within the university—and perhaps within our whole culture—where connective thinking can create a coherent "world" from all the disarray might be English 101, the first-year writing class taken by most undergraduates. No matter how students and faculty look at English 101, it can be understood as the only course whose concern is nearly universal: not this or that specific knowledge but the way that meaning itself gets made and communicated. And precisely because the explosive growth of knowledge has produced an explosive growth of ignorance, learning how to make meaning would appear to be more important than ever.

Yet even in English 101, change is impeded by the weight of the past and by the image of students starting college as incapable of wading through twenty-five pages from *Harper's* or the *New York Times Magazine*. And this attitude persists even though tenth graders somehow find a way to cope with the challenges of Shakespeare's plays, and even though the students in English 101 might be doing physics that same term or reading Max Weber for some other class. But this book imagines students differently—as quite ready for complex arguments if supported by the proper scaffolding. It sees teachers too in a different light, as agile generalists well qualified to introduce the world of living ideas, which is, after all, the world where writing really matters.

In order to furnish more "scaffolding," a revised Introduction, "Reading and Writing about the New Humanities," now provides students with specific advice about how to read creatively, make synthetic links between the texts, explore discontinuities, and develop a position.

New sequenced assignments at the end of the book offer faculty and students questions they can use as starting points to explore connections between essays and to think creatively about positioning their own ideas in the ensuing conversation.

Nearly 25% of the readings are new to this edition. New readings from across the disciplines include excerpts from three important books published in 2009: Karen Armstrong's *The Case for God*; Caroline Fraser's *Rewilding the World: Dispatches from the Conservation Revolution*; and Janine R. Wedel's *Shadow Elite: How the World's New Power Brokers Undermine Democracy, Government, and the Free Market*. In an excerpt from his classic of architectural theory, *The Eyes of the Skin: Architecture and the Senses*, Juhani Pallasmaa discusses the overemphasis of the visual in modern architecture. In an article from the *Atlantic*, Nicholas Carr asks, "Is Google Making Us Stupid?" while in the *New Yorker* Michael Specter's "A Life of Its Own" reviews the field of synthetic biology.

To those colleagues who have contributed to this enterprise, we would like to offer our heartfelt thanks for responding to questionnaires and helping us determine the shape of this book over its four editions:

Dan Bauer, Georgia College and State University; Tisha Bender, Rutgers University; Manuel Betancourt, Rutgers University; Lynn Z. Bloom, University of Connecticut, Storrs; Barbara B. Booker, Pasco-Hernando Community College; Kirk Branch, Montana State University; John C. Brereton, Boston Athenaeum; Susan E. Carlisle, Boston University; Suzanne Diamond, Youngstown State University; Lisa Fluet, Boston College; Maureen Fonts, University of Miami; Melora Giardetti, Simpson College; Andrew Green, University of Miami; Alfred E. Guy, Jr., Yale University; Andrew Haggerty, Broome Community College; Paul Hammond, Rutgers University; Susanmarie Harrington, Indiana University-Purdue University, Indianapolis; Brian Hayter, Grossmont College; Jessica Hedges, Rutgers University; Deborah H. Holdstein, Governors State University; Joanna Johnson, University of Miami; Deborah Kirkman, University of Kentucky; Thomas C. Laughner, University of Notre Dame; Jennifer Lee, University of Pittsburgh; Jenna Lewis, Rutgers University; Gina L. Maranto, University of Miami; Trinyan Mariano, Rutgers University; Stephen M. North, SUNY, Albany; Judith Gatton Prats, University of Kentucky; Thomas Recchio, University of Connecticut; Gail Shivel, Florida International University; Jermey Smyczek, University of North Carolina, Wilmington; Tony Spicer, Eastern Michigan University; Roberta J. Stagnaro, San Diego State University; Gordon P. Thomas, University of Idaho; Anna Tripp, California State University,

Northridge; Mark Vareschi, Rutgers University; Paul Yeoh, Rutgers University; and Sue Zabowksi, University of Miami.

At Rutgers, students who used the previous edition of this book participated in a series of focus groups conducted by editors from Cengage. Thanks to each of them for sharing their thoughts about how we could improve the book.

Jamaal Brown

Mary Conlon

Cassandra Dass

Cynthia Fereno

Keith Flyer

Jennifer Hellman

Isha Kalwani

Binni Kunvarjee

Aysha Lakhani

Ruth Lee

Irvin Martinez

Saif Mohamed

Alexandra Murtha

Patrick O'Connell

Kathleen Oroho

Dhara Patel

Julie Patel

Michael Pinkard

Tara Rabinowitz

Sanjeev Rai

Pearl Shah

Jenna Sholk

Shin Yang Pai

Eric Wai-Kit Yip

ZhenZhen Zheng

Faisal Zoa

—Kurt Spellmeyer and Richard E. Miller

Reading and Writing About the New Humanities

This book probably differs from many you have encountered, at least those that you have encountered in school. Generally, the books taught in school tell their audience how or what to think, but ours has a different purpose. We wanted to put in your hands a book that would encourage you to think for yourself, and to do your thinking while you read and write about some of the most important issues of our time. Genetic engineering, the impact of the Internet, environmental breakdown, sweeping cultural change—these are just a few of the issues we address.

The articles and essays collected here touch on subjects as diverse as the mental health of elephants and the practice of Tibetan meditation, but these subjects in and of themselves aren't the real point of the book. The real point is thinking, and we believe that thinking in our time needs to assume a new and more appropriate form. In the last hundred years our world has seen changes more rapid and profound than those witnessed in the previous millennium. From the media we get daily reports on subjects our great-grandparents might have found absolutely incomprehensible: breakthroughs in nanotechnology; mergers of U.S. firms with partners overseas; the covert spread of nuclear weapons that could annihilate all humanity; a new account of the universe in the first seconds after the Big Bang; melting polar icecaps and rising seas; a growing gap between the poor and the mega-rich, while the middle class slowly withers away. Such events are truly without precedent.

We need a new kind of thinking because we live in world defined primarily by possibilities, and possibilities go hand in hand with risk and unintended consequences. The globalized economy could lead mankind to a future where poverty will become a relic of the past, or the whole planet could be transformed into a sweatshop run by an owner class sequestered behind high walls and indifferent to the suffering of ordinary people. The Web could produce a Renaissance of popular empowerment and solidarity, or it could degrade all forms of communication, ushering in a new Dark Age of vulgarity and mass ignorance. Cultures long divided by geography might greet one another with open arms, or we could see a clash of civilizations that would unleash the worst instincts of all. Unlike the problems from your textbooks in school, the questions arising from events in our time don't have answers hidden in the teacher's edition. The best educated, most experienced people can't predict with any certainty how the next century will turn out. Even expertise is not good enough because the questions we face now are more complex than any ever faced before. Globalization, to take one good example, is not just the concern of economists, or historians, or anthropologists. Instead, it is an issue for all of them together—and for everybody else as well. The degradation of the biosphere is not exclusively the property of environmental science, but also a matter for political theory, sociology, and economics.

The complexity and open-endedness of the big problems in our time require us to work hard to devise new understandings of ourselves and the world. One purpose of this book is to provide a forum for these understandings to emerge. Perhaps it may seem strange that we would entertain such lofty goals in a course designed for undergraduates. Surely the experts are better equipped than students just beginning their careers at college or the university. But this assumption might be unjustified. While the forms of expertise available today clearly have enormous value, most of the current academic disciplines were created more than a century ago, and the divisions of knowledge on which they are based reflect the needs of a very different era. It is worth remembering that in 1900 gas-powered cars were a new technology, while airplanes and radios had yet to be invented. Scientists still wrestled with the structure of the atom. The British Empire dominated three-fourths of the globe, and "culture" meant the traditions of Western Europe's elite, never more than one-tenth of one percent of the population of that region. In a certain sense, the current generation of college students and teachers needs to reinvent the university itself, not by replacing one department with another, but by forging broad connections across areas of knowledge that still remain in relative isolation. Forging these connections is the "new way of thinking" that we had in mind when we created this book.

NEW HUMANITIES FOR NEW TIMES: THE SEARCH FOR COHERENCE

Probably some readers will be surprised by the absence of material from the traditional humanities: poems and plays, photographs of paintings and statues, excerpts from great works of philosophy such as Plato's *Republic* and Descartes's *Discourse on Method*. Clearly, no one should leave unread Aristotle, Shakespeare, or Toni Morrison. And anyone unfamiliar with Leonardo da Vinci, Frida Kahlo, Thelonious Monk, and Georgia O'Keeffe has missed a priceless opportunity. Yet this book grows out of our belief that the humanities today must reach further than in centuries past. Without consciously intending to, humanists might have contributed to the decline of their own enterprise. One could even argue their devotion to the past led them to neglect the future. Humanists have often been quite willing to leave real-world concerns to other fields, devoting themselves primarily to passive contemplation, aesthetic escape, and the production of criticism few people ever read. Consequently, outside the university many people see the humanities as entertainment or sheer snobbery. At the same time, business and science reign supreme as the only real truth.

If the humanities are going to survive, they must be understood in a new way: not as a particular area of knowledge but as the human dimension of *all* knowledge. Engineering may lie well outside the boundaries of the old humanities, but it enters the domain of the New Humanities when we turn, as Edward Tenner does, to the unintended consequences of innovations that seemed benign when they arrived but were responsible for catastrophes. Once we define the humanities this way—as the human dimension of all knowledge—it may come as a surprise to observe that some of our foremost humanists work in fields quite far removed from English, History, and Philosophy. Oliver Sacks, one of the writers in this collection, is a world-renowned neurologist whose case histories have helped reveal the brain's deeper mysteries while humanizing patients who suffer from mental illnesses, cranial injuries, and neurological disorders. Juhani Pallasmaa, an architect, has tried to revolutionize his field by encouraging his colleagues to reflect on the ways the built environment can deaden our senses or bring them to life.

The New Humanities, as represented by this book, enlarge the arena of human concern in another way as well. They invite us to take academic knowledge beyond the confines of the university. In a certain sense, this operation requires that we all become our own teachers: we have to discover in our own lives—our problems, values, dreams, goals, and commitments—an organizing principle that cannot be found in any single curriculum. The great, unspoken secret of the university is that the curriculum has no center: specialization makes sure of that. Historians write primarily for historians; literary critics for other critics. As we shuttle back and forth between the disciplines, the only coherence we will ever find is the coherence we construct for ourselves. Under these conditions, the New Humanities can teach us a different way of using knowledge, a way of thinking that connects many disparate fields of study.

Specialized learning in the disciplines typically deals with the "how," but it often leaves unanswered the "why." There has never been a course called "Life 101," and given the persistence of specialization, such a course will probably never exist. But something important will be missing if we leave the "why" questions unexplored. Should we continue to pursue a technological utopia? Does modern science mean the end of religion? Is social inequality an acceptable price to pay for economic growth? Any attempt to answer these questions requires specialized knowledge, yet knowledge alone is not enough. Because a cogent, well-informed case can be made on either side of almost every issue, the source of our ultimate commitments has to be found in our own lives. The "why" questions shape these commitments because they address our most basic relations to other people and the world. In different ways, such questions ask how we ourselves will choose to think and act. No expert can choose on our behalf, because no expert can live our lives for us or define what our experience should mean.

The coherence missing from the curriculum is not a quality of knowledge itself. When it emerges, that coherence comes instead from our own creative activity. Again and again, we need to make connections between separate areas of knowledge, and between formal knowledge and our personal experience. But even after we have created this coherence, it will still be incomplete because there is always something more to learn, something that remains unconnected. We might think of coherence, then, not as a goal we can finally reach but as an ideal worth pursuing throughout the course of our lives. Needless to say, cynicism and fragmentation are always options, too, and they require no special effort. One could easily live as though nothing and no one mattered, but in such a case, learning and living become exercises in futility. The New Humanities offer a better path.

KNOWLEDGE IN DEPTH AND KNOWLEDGE OF THE WORLD

As everyone understands, formal education has been carefully designed to keep the disciplines separate. In economics classes, we typically read economics; in history classes, we read history. This approach allows information to be conveyed in small, efficiently managed packages. We can divide, say, biology from chemistry, and then we can divide biology into vertebrate and invertebrate, and chemistry into organic and inorganic. We start with the general and move to the particular: ideally, we learn in depth, with increasing mastery of details that become more and more refined. At the end of the semester, if everything goes well, we can distinguish between an ecosystem and a niche, a polymer and a plastic, a neo-Kantian and a neo-Hegelian. We can contrast Hawthorne's treatment of the outsider with Salinger's, or we can explain the debate about whether slavery or states' rights actually caused the Civil War.

Knowledge in depth is indispensable. But it can also produce a sense of disconnection, the impression that education is an empty ritual without real-world consequences beyond getting a grade or fulfilling a requirement. In the classroom, we learn to calculate sine and cosine without ever discovering how these calculations might be used and why they were invented. Searching for symbols in a poem or a short story becomes a mental exercise on par with doing a crossword puzzle. Instead of reflecting on why events have happened and how they get remembered and recorded, we refine our ability to recapitulate strings of dates and names. At its worst, learning in depth can produce a strange disconnect: the purpose of learning becomes learning itself, while activity in the real world grows more and more difficult to imagine. As students reach the final years of high school, they may grasp vaguely that they should have read *Hamlet*, be able to identify *The Declaration of Independence*, and explain how photosynthesis has influenced the shape of leaves, but in response to an actual tragedy—an environmental disaster or a war—they might feel unqualified to speak and completely at a loss about what to do.

College-level learning can offer a reprieve from this predicament by giving students greater freedom to choose what they will study, and in many cases the subjects they select are closely related to their real-world goals. But even with this newfound freedom, the problem of disconnection crops up in other ways. After years of hard work, a student who has mastered electrical engineering may still leave college poorly informed about the global economy in which most engineers now do their work. Students well versed in Renaissance drama or the history of World War I can understand the past quite well, but they might find the events of their own time incomprehensible. The problem of disconnection could arise long before you graduate. The student who sets out to memorize facts from, say, a social psychology text may find that these facts grow increasingly stale. Easily memorized one day, they are quickly forgotten the next. The risk of knowledge in depth is that we lose our sense of the larger world and we forget that a field like psychology, for all its current sophistication, began with people just like us asking somewhat clumsy questions about how the mind might work. Ironically, the more we treat an area of knowledge as a reality in itself, the less we may be able to understand and use what we have supposedly learned.

There is another kind of knowledge we create when we ask ourselves how our learning applies to the world outside the classroom. This line of questioning is more complex than it might seem initially because the larger world is never simply waiting there. All knowledge starts with parts and fragments, even our knowledge of the private lives we know in most detail. To each of us, our private life may seem complete, just as a field like psychology can seem to explain everything once we are immersed in its methods and facts. But this sense of completeness is an illusion produced by the limits of our perspective. Beyond the reach of what we know here and now, nothing might seem important. We begin to get a glimpse of the larger world only when we shift our focus from one reality to another: only then can we become aware of the deficiencies in our prior certainties, and only then are we able to think in new and revealing ways. This movement from the known to the unknown is the essence of all learning; indeed, the most successful learners are generally those who have developed the highest tolerance for not knowing—those who continue to question and explore issues beyond their own areas of specialization, entertaining alternatives that others might find unimaginable.

Knowledge itself can be defined in many ways: as a quantity of information, as technical expertise, as cultivated taste, as a special kind of self-awareness. Various as these definitions might appear, they share an underlying commonality. Whatever the form that knowledge takes, it always emerges from a process that we might describe as **connecting**. The eighteenth-century English scientist Sir Isaac Newton, who first understood the relations between force, mass, and acceleration, might have been inspired by the need to connect his groundbreaking scientific work with his deeply held convictions about the rational perfection of

God and His Creation. Many other notable thinkers have also found inspiration through connection. About two hundred years after Newton sparked a scientific revolution, a young lawyer born in India, Mohandas K. Gandhi, drew on Henry David Thoreau's *Civil Disobedience,* written in support of abolitionists just before the Civil War, to launch a campaign of passive resistance against the racist government of South Africa. Two years before Gandhi spent his first term in jail as a political prisoner, a French artist and intellectual, Marcel Duchamps, shocked the art world with a painting—*Nude Descending a Staircase*—inspired by scientific photographs of athletes in motion. Whether we are talking about physics or political systems, epidemiology or art, knowledge by its very nature brings together disconnected worlds of thought and action.

CREATIVE READING I : THE PROSPECTIVE VIEW

The selections in this book were chosen specifically with creative reading in mind. Our assumption is that the humanities should do more than preserve information or give professors an opportunity to demonstrate their brilliance. After all, studies have consistently shown that people retain little of what they are taught unless they put that knowledge to some kind of use. At its best, higher learning offers beginners the chance to do what more accomplished thinkers do: beyond receiving knowledge, beginners too should have a hand in its creation. The articles and book chapters collected here offer many opportunities for this kind of creativity. It's true that the selections often pose challenges—sometimes because they are long and complex, sometimes because they draw on specialized knowledge, and sometimes because they introduce unusual ways of seeing. But those challenges are also opportunities: they ask the reader to become an active co-creator with the writer.

Creative reading has begun once we move from the specific details of a text to what it might mean as a whole. When we try to understand challenging material, we won't get far by following along, word by word and detail by detail. As we read we also need to ask ourselves what the writer's larger point might be and how each small step makes a contribution to the entire argument. When Fraser starts "Rewilding North America" with the story of a five-year old female wolf, few of us might be able to foresee the direction her account will finally take. But we can begin with a **prospective view**—a guess at the argument that potentially lies ahead. As we read further we might be surprised that the wolf's story gets left behind and we are suddenly plunged into debates among population scientists about the fate of ecosystems that become cut off from the outside world. Actually a dramatic shift like this—from wolves to academic debates—is quite typical of complex thought, and skillful readers are the ones who know how to keep revising their prospective views as they move ahead. Working with a complex text means shifting back and forth from each additional part to the whole as we imagine it, revising prospectively until finally we arrive at a reading that seems to include everything we've learned.

One way to test your understanding of a text after you have finished reading it is to look for key words or major ideas and ask how they fit with your prospective view. Here, for example, is a question we pose in the "Questions for Reading" that follows up on Fraser's account of rewilding:

> The key to understanding Fraser's argument is the term "connectivity." Re-read the selection in order to take note of all the different forms of connectivity you find, not only in the natural world but also in culture and society.

A question like this is designed to find out how well you have managed to create a comprehensive understanding of the text. Unless you test your understanding in this way, you might assume that simply having read the words automatically confers a working knowledge when in reality what you really know might be quite fragmentary. But each time you expand your prospective view by looking carefully at a text's details, you draw closer to the kind of mastery that accomplished readers can achieve.

CREATIVE READING II: INTERPRETATION AND
THE RETROSPECTIVE VIEW

The fact that reading is so commonplace should not lead us to overlook just how complicated it can really get. The act of reading starts with nothing more than marks of ink printed on a page, and those marks cannot tell us anything in and of themselves. But when you read with a prospective view, you are actually creating a text that exists only after you have done the work. The reader's job, however, does not end there. Once reading with a prospective view has created a coherent text, the **meaning** of that text still remains unclear because what we call "meaning" actually depends on the connections we are able to make within the text itself or between one text and another text. Meaning is a product of interpretation, and interpretation demands from us another form of creative reading: the search for a **retrospective view**. If "prospective" means "looking forward," "retrospective" means looking back. The most basic form of interpretation starts when we isolate one part of a text—even if it's only a sentence—and we use it as a frame or window through which we can take a second look at the entire text.

Consider, for example, the first sentence of Jonathan Boyarin's "Waiting for a Jew." "My story begins in a community," he writes, "with an illusion of wholeness." The account that follows this first sentence grows increasingly complex, weaving together many twists and turns that might seem related only tangentially. The Boyarin family leaves Farmingdale, New Jersey, moving to the suburbs where Jewish life plays a far less important role. Then, when Boyarin goes to Oregon for college, he feels overwhelmed by an environment in which Judaism seems marginal—not unwelcome but simply out of sight. A student friend from Long Island helps keep alive his interest in the "Jewish mentality," and after graduation he heads East again, where he decides that he will pursue a Ph.D. in anthropology. From there, Boyarin's world broadens out to include several trips to France and encounters with the nearly lost traditions of old Jewish New York.

If we try to explain what Boyarin meant to do in writing "Waiting for a Jew," we could simply say that he wanted to tell the story of his changing involvement with various aspects of Jewish life. But if we try to say *how* these views have changed, and what the meaning of his narrative might be, one place to start would be with that first sentence: "My story begins in a community, with an illusion of wholeness." We don't have to start there but if we do, we will make a remarkable discovery. The sentence will become like a window through which we can see the meaning we were looking for. Probably every detail in the account can be connected in some way to this key phrase "the illusion of wholeness." Sometimes the events that Boyarin recalls appear to underscore the word *illusion,* confirming the irreparable loss of the community in which he had grown up. But other moments in his narrative might speak directly to the sense of *wholeness* and the persistence of communities of shared belief in the midst of a larger world made up of unbelievers along with those who believe very different things in very different ways. Explicitly Boyarin's text makes no such points, but implicitly the point lies within the realm of possibility, and by making it we become interpreters who give meaning to the text in much the same way as prospective reading first made the text coherent.

CREATIVE READING III: CONNECTIVE THINKING AND THE SEARCH FOR A SHARED HORIZON

The simplest form of interpretation links one part of a text to other parts. But what about connections to other texts? These connections are especially important because no one's world is entirely defined by the perspective or "horizon" of any single text alone. Indeed, there is far more to Boyarin himself than his essay is able to express, however complex and many-layered it might be. Because no one lives in a one-text world, the truths we learn in reading "Waiting for a Jew" cannot be confined to the pages of the book. As soon as we read something for another class, or we engage in conversations with our friends, all sorts of possible connections will begin to compete for realization. The different texts that we encounter in our lives might come to us from worlds of experience far removed from ours, but once they have entered into our own lives, we need to bring them all together in a way that creates a **shared horizon**, a greater, more inclusive coherence.

One great tragedy of formal education is that it often works against this shared horizon by promoting imitative thinking: we learn to reproduce information made and organized by someone else. Imitative thinking presupposes the sufficiency of knowledge in its present state, and it preserves the separateness of different texts and differing realities. But this separateness cannot be maintained except at the cost of a greater incoherence in our lives, individually and collectively. Maybe the lecture in English class today contradicted a point made yesterday in anthropology. Or perhaps an assigned article describes an aspect of the social world in a way that we find incomplete, biased, or flatly incorrect. On occasions like these, when we encounter the limits of knowledge, imitative thinking cannot help us; instead, we are obliged to think connectively—to think *across texts* rather than thinking only from within them.

Connective thinking calls for another kind of interpretation. Instead of starting with one part of a text and using it as a window from which to re-view the rest, we can use it as a window to begin a retrospective reading of another text. We might turn once again, for instance, to Boyarin's opening sentence: "My story begins in a community, with an illusion of wholeness." But now this sentence could become the window through which we undertake a retrospective reading of Susan Faludi's "The Naked Citadel," which involves the early and failed attempts to integrate young women applicants into an all-male military college founded soon after the Civil War. At first glance the two texts might appear as completely unrelated as any two could be. One deals with the religious odyssey of a Jewish anthropologist, the other with the forces of change overtaking the identity of American men. And yet when we start to read retrospectively, a shared horizon can emerge. The easiest way to search for that horizon would be to find a passage from Faludi that makes a point central to her argument. One passage, which occurs early on, describes the responses of some of the cadets when asked by their professor in Western Civilization how they felt about the first woman student, who had been admitted but eventually left after she could no longer tolerate the hostile atmosphere:

> Weighing heaviest on the cadets' minds, it turned out, was the preservation of the all-male communal bathroom. The sharing of the stall-less showers and the stall-less toilets is "at the heart of the Citadel experience," according to more than one cadet.... Another cadet said, "I know it sounds trivial, but all of us in one shower, it's like we're all one, we're all the same."

Clearly this passage has nothing to do with Jewish life in Farmingdale, New Jersey, but it still says something quite important about "community," its loss, and the threats to its "wholeness," real and imaginary. The community in this case is composed of students who fear the mere presence of young women will undermine their school's most cherished traditions, including the "oneness" that they have felt in a completely all-male milieu. And while that oneness seems real to the cadets, readers will need to look carefully to see if Faludi argues—or implies—that this wholeness is an "illusion." Even if Faludi remains silent on the score, when we use Boyarin as our window on the text, we will need to make a judgment one way or another if we really want to bring the two texts into a single, coherent world.

The connections between Boyarin's first sentence and Faludi's narrative are not exhausted by this example. We might find other connections by looking at additional passages, and eventually, as we work through the new connections, we might discover that a larger point or implication has begun to emerge—such as an overarching view of the Citadel as a "community." An overarching view of this kind seldom emerges right away. More often it requires all the usual ingredients of creativity: concentration, patience, hard work, some luck, and a good deal of time. For a nerve-wracking interval, the individual connections might appear disjointed, even contradictory, but then, suddenly, a larger view may present itself—like the pattern in a Persian carpet we unroll a few inches at a time.

Of course some passages in Faludi's account might not connect in a meaningful way to Boyarin's opening sentence. Initially, a connection might look promising, but then we could discover that it leads to a dead end. It's possible to spend many frustrating hours following connections that eventually lead nowhere. But this is precisely what thinking involves: forging new connections where none exist now. Imitation means letting others do that work and sitting back to admire the results; creativity means taking risks. Some of the risks we take will truly surprise us with their spectacular results, while others may prove quite disappointing. Both risk and failure, on occasion, are the price of creative reading—the price of discovery.

Some people are convinced that creativity cannot be taught at all, but we believe it can be taught and learned by asking readers to forge connections between texts that might appear unrelated at first glance. Many of the questions you will find in this book seem to push hard in that direction. One question, for example, asks you to work out the connections between Charles Siebert's report on the fate of elephants in Africa today and Edward Tenner's brilliant argument about the self-correcting nature of technology even after terrible disasters. Elephants and the sinking of the Titanic seem to belong to different universes, but we are asking you to undertake what all creativity involves—venturing beyond the familiar.

PROSPECTIVE WRITING

Imitative thinking goes hand in hand with writing to tell—writing for the purpose of showing a command of existing knowledge. In American schools, the classic example of writing to tell is the venerable book report. Like imitative thinking, writing to tell has its appropriate place. Connective thinking calls, however, for a different approach which might be described as **prospective writing**. Just as you can read prospectively, looking for a larger coherence behind all the individual details, so you can write without knowing from the start where your ideas will lead. A good example of writing of this kind is "The Mind's Eye," by Oliver Sacks. Because Sacks is a neurologist, an Oxford-trained physician as well as a professor of medicine—we might have expected him to begin with some of the answers he has found in his four decades of research. Instead he set out with a question that sounds startling in its simplicity: "to what extent are we ... shaped, predetermined, by our brains, and to what extent do we shape our own brains?" In attempting to think through this question, Sacks might have drawn on research by other specialists in fields like chemistry, genetics, and neuroanatomy. He might have taped electrodes to the heads of volunteers or studied their brains with an MRI machine. These are certainly legitimate ways of responding to the question, but the sources Sacks prefers to use are the first person narratives written by people who have gone blind but then adapted to the loss of sight in a variety of creative ways.

Perhaps the question that Sacks poses—Do our brains shape us, or do we shape our brains?—has followed him from the earliest years of his career as a scientist. Or perhaps he framed the question only after he had read the books mentioned in his essay. But no matter how his project began, what seems certain is that these accounts called into doubt much that Sacks had once assumed about the development of the brain. On the one hand, his training led him to suppose that the tasks assigned to the regions of the brain were essentially unalterable after childhood. On the other hand, the writer's accounts he read strongly suggested to him that our brains can rebuild themselves—that our brains are capable of significant change throughout adult life. We cannot know exactly what inspired Sacks, but surely one powerful motive was the profound discontinuity between his old assumptions and the new evidence. Facing that discontinuity, Sacks was prepared to take a risk—to put his old assumptions to the test.

From time immemorial, teachers of English have told their students to begin the task of writing only when they clearly know what they intend to say. But these instructions have always expressed more fantasy than truth. Typically, a thesis or argument will remain fairly vague until we have done a great deal of prospective writing. Discontinuities lead us to the search for a shared horizon, and from this shared horizon new questions come. Then, provided we are willing to push far enough, a coherent thesis will begin to emerge, not all at once in a grand sweep but with one insight building on the next. At some point, these insights will cohere—the pattern in the carpet once again. Retrospectively we can recognize the direction of our thoughts, a direction writing itself has revealed. We write, stop, and assess where our writing has gone. Only then are we ready to revise, and to convey our discoveries to others in the form of a well-crafted presentation.

In order for an author like Sacks to become a source for our own writing, we need to start with a question that his work leaves unresolved, at least partially. If human brains are inherently as flexible as he suggests, then why do people generally seem so similar in their outlooks and behavior? Could it be that education, not biology, has made us all the same? If in the future we abolish formal schooling, would our mental lives become far less uniform than they appear to be now? Of course, each of us is free to conclude that our basic human nature will never change, regardless of changes in our brains, and in that case we might choose to brush aside the implications of Sacks's ideas. But these ideas might nudge us to rethink a number of our presuppositions. If events are actually capable of changing the structure of our brains, then perhaps we are doing serious damage when we spend countless hours glued to TV shows that routinely push their viewers into emotions like greed, envy, anger, and contempt. Instead, should we care for our mental health as much as we care for our bodies through diet and exercise? As we explore questions like this one, we might also draw on Martha Stout's discussion of the way the brain responds to psychological trauma. Or we might make some fruitful connections to Robert Thurman's ideas about the pursuit of wisdom. Ultimately, through prospective writing, we start to develop a thesis of our own.

DEVELOPING A THESIS: FROM PROSPECTIVE
TO RETROSPECTIVE WRITING

A thesis is not exactly an argument in the ordinary sense of the word. In everyday speech, the term *argument* suggests an adversarial stance: with great vehemence we might argue for, or against, synthetic biology of the kind that Michael Specter describes. "Making an argument" tends to mean deciding ahead of time what you think and then looking for "support" to back up your points. There is, however, another way. Instead of simply taking sides in an existing opposition, each of us can move beyond such debates, which are often hackneyed and overly simplistic, in order to say something genuinely new. To do so is to imagine ourselves in a different light, not as combatants slugging it out but as engaged participants in an ongoing conversation. Even if we read a writer with distaste, what matters most are the questions raised, not the answers given. Precisely because the search for a thesis starts with some degree of uncertainty, it demands a willingness on our part to suspend judgment and pursue ideas wherever they might lead. Remember, however, that this pursuit does not require our complete assent or unwavering commitment. We can always entertain and explore ideas that we will eventually reject.

The writing process closely parallels the process of reading. Once readers have created a sense of the text through prospective reading, they can go on to view it retrospectively in the search for meaning. Much the same holds true for writing in its different stages. We might consider the first few drafts to be essentially prospective. As we explore possible connections and see how they unfold, we will notice that the process has carried us in unforeseen directions, some highly productive and some cul-de-sacs. But a later stage in the process requires that we move from a preliminary draft, replete with loose ends and promising connections, to become the interpreter of all the work we've done. Retrospective writing is interpretive because it tries to tease out the implicit meaning, which it develops further and refines. If the first drafts are exploratory, the final draft is meant to present the writer's discoveries in a way that will conform to the reader's expectations. A thesis statement, logical organization, transitions, and well-structured paragraphs are all tools at our disposal for an effective public presentation.

Let's suppose we start writing with the idea that Chris McCandless, the young man whose travels are retraced by Jon Krakauer, was spoiled and self-deceiving. But when we turn to Caroline Fraser's account of rewilding in North America, our opinion of McCandless may grow less firm and distinct. As we write, our thinking could lose its way and we might realize, after three or four pages, that we have contradicted ourselves. McCandless's behavior might now seem justified, even commendable. Instead of treating this change in our position as a failure or a lapse, we should appreciate its value as a genuine discovery, which we could achieve only after a great deal of hard work. When revising we should not try to conceal or erase the evidence of such a fruitful redirection in our thinking. By doing so we would actually suppress the great discovery we have made.

The genre most familiar to students starting college is the "five paragraph essay" they learn to compose throughout their high school years. The first paragraph should present the main idea. Three body paragraphs should elaborate, and the final paragraph should sum up the main idea yet again. This format was designed to give beginners some control over a process that can become overwhelming with its sheer complexity. But this virtue is also the greatest defect of the five paragraph model. None of the selections in the *New Humanities Reader* look remotely like the kind of essay students write while they are in high school. Not only do most of the selections connect with many areas of knowledge at once, but they offer thinking far more many-layered and nuanced than the high school format could allow. Instead of pounding home a single idea, they guide the reader through a journey of the mind that typically has many twists and turns, that takes two steps forward and one step back, that entertains alternative possibilities and, at times, answers criticisms. Instead of suppressing complexity, the writers embrace it as the source of a deeper understanding. In your own writing you can learn to do the same.

THE SPIRIT OF THE NEW HUMANITIES

Because we can learn from everything, no one should fear making mistakes. We should never forget that the greatest thinkers of every age have often been refuted later, whereas ordinary people have sometimes lived more wisely than they were given credit for. Not so long ago, the best-educated Europeans believed that all celestial bodies beyond the moon were eternal and changeless. Professors taught that matter in every form could be reduced to the basic elements of earth, air, fire, and water. Medical experts sternly warned against the perils of regular bathing and eating whole grains. In sexual reproduction, men were supposed to contribute the blueprint, while women provided the raw material. One could spend a lifetime enumerating the follies that have passed for knowledge. And when we pause to consider such a checkered history, we might decide that education is itself a folly.

But maybe not. Instead of expecting knowledge to be true once and for all, we might try to see it as pragmatic and provisional, always subject to revision given further evidence or new circumstances. In our society today, the sciences may offer the best example of this experimentalist attitude, but some philosophers and artists of every generation have also refused the twin consolations of dogmatism and disillusionment. In the years ahead, our society will face many challenges—environmental, social, cultural, economic, and political—that are sure to seem overwhelming. Given the high level of uncertainty that has become a constant feature of our lives, people may be drawn to ideologies that promise truths exempt from all revision and insulated from the challenges of diversity. If this book does nothing else, we hope that it will offer an alternative more compatible with the values espoused by the readings we have chosen: trust in the world and trust in ourselves.

The New Humanities Reader

LEILA AHMED

LEILA AHMED, THE author of *A Border Passage: From Cairo to America—A Woman's Journey* (1999), has spent her life contending with issues of identity. Coming of age in Cairo during a period of political tumult, Ahmed witnessed the transformation of Egypt from a British colony into a sovereign Arab nation. The multilingual, multicultural family life that she knew—English and French were spoken at home, and a cosmopolitan Yugoslavian nanny introduced her to many different cultures through language and food—came increasingly into conflict with the young Egyptian nation's attempts to carve out a discrete cultural identity. Ahmed found herself struggling in particular with the "living Islam" she inherited from the women in her family and the strict, patriarchal "official Islam" that was woven into the self-understanding of the Egyptian nation.

Drawn from *A Border Passage*, "On Becoming an Arab" charts the emergence of the Arab League as a political association. It also provides a record of Ahmed's conflicted feelings as she is told that she is an Arab and that this identity supersedes her prior understanding of herself as an Egyptian. For Ahmed, her experience is representative of how the process of developing an Arab identity "unsettled and undercut the old understanding of who we were and silently excluded people who had been included in the old definition of Egyptian" (244). Writing the book, and this section in particular, was a way for Ahmed to come to "understand the history [she]'d lived through." As Ahmed's personal and political history demonstrates, markers of identity are neither perfectly separate nor completely intertwined, but rather always in play.

Ahmed left Egypt to pursue her education and to fashion her identity as a scholar at Cambridge University's Girton College; she has since been elected a lifetime member of Clare Hall at Cambridge. After receiving her doctorate in 1981, she taught Near Eastern studies at the University of Massachusetts–Amherst. She continues to cross borders in her academic career, having been appointed the first-ever professor of women's studies at Harvard Divinity School, where she is currently the Victor S. Thomas Professor of Divinity. Prior to writing *A Border Passage*, Ahmed published her influential work *Women and Gender in Islam* (1992), which focuses on the range of relationships that Muslim women have to the Islamic religion.

Ahmed, Leila. "On Becoming an Arab." *A Border Passage: From Cairo to America—A Woman's Journey.* New York: Farrar, Straus and Giroux, 1999. 243–70.

Quotations come from "On Becoming an Arab" as well as an interview with Ahmed available at <http://us.penguingroup.com/static/rguides/us/border_passage.html>.

On Becoming an Arab

I remember the very day that I became colored.

—ZORA NEALE HURSTON

The teacher called on me to read. I started haltingly. She began interrupting me, correcting me, quietly at first but gradually, as I stumbled on, with more and more irritation, leaving her desk now to stand over me and pounce on every mistake I made. She was an irascible woman, and I had not prepared my homework.

"You're an Arab!" she finally screamed at me. "An Arab! And you don't know your own language!"

"I am not an Arab!" I said, suddenly furious myself. "I am Egyptian! And anyway we don't speak like this!" And I banged my book shut.

"Read!"

I sat on stonily, arms folded.

"Read!"

I didn't move.

She struck me across the face. The moment afterward seemed to go on forever, like something in slow motion.

I was twelve and I'd never been hit before by a teacher and never slapped across the face by anyone. Miss Nabih, the teacher, was a Palestinian. A refugee.

The year was 1952, the year of the revolution. What Miss Nabih was doing to me in class the government was doing to us through the media. I remember how I hated that incessant rhetoric. *Al-qawmiyya al-Arabiyya! Al-Uraba! Nahnu al-Arab!* Arab nationalism! Arabness! We the Arabs! Even now, just remembering those words, I feel again a surge of mingled irritation and resentment. Propaganda *is* unpleasant. And one could not escape it. The moment one turned on the radio, there it was: military songs, nationalistic songs, and endless, endless speeches in that frenetic, crazed voice of exhortation. In public places, in the street, it filled the air, blaring at one from the grocery, the newsstand, the café, the garage, for it became patriotic to have it on at full volume.

Imagine what it would be like if, say, the British or French were incessantly told, with nobody allowed to contest, question, or protest, that they were now European and only European. European! European! European! And endless songs about it. But for us it was actually worse and certainly more complicated. Its equivalent would be if the British or French were being told that they were white. White! White! White! Because the new definition of who we were unsettled and undercut the old understanding of who we were and silently excluded people who had been included in the old definition of Egyptian. Copts, for example, were not Arab. In fact, they were Copts precisely because they had refused to convert to the religion of the Arabs and had refused, unlike us Muslims, to intermarry with Arabs. As a result, Copts (members of the ancient Christian church of Egypt) were the only truly indigenous inhabitants of Egypt and as such, in our home anyway and in the notion of Egypt with which I grew up, Copts had a very special place in the country. In the new definition of us, however, they were included as speakers of Arabic but they were not at the heart of the definition in the way that we were.

But of course the people who were most directly, although as yet only implicitly, being excluded by the redefinition were the Jews of Egypt, for the whole point of the revolutionary government's harping insistence that we were Arab, in those first years following the founding of Israel, and following the takeover of Egypt's government by New Men with a new vision and new commitments, was to proclaim our unequivocal alignments: on the side of the Palestinians and Arabs and against Israel, against Zionism. Ever since, this issue has been the key issue determining the different emphases Egypt's leaders have placed on its identity. If they have proclaimed insistently and emphatically (as Nasser did) that we were Arab, it has meant that we would take a confrontational, unyielding line on Israel and that we would "never deal with the Zionists." If we were Egyptians above all (Sadat), then we could talk, negotiate.

Our new identity proclaimed openly our opposition to Israel and Zionism—and proclaimed implicitly our opposition to the "Zionists" in our midst, Egyptian Jews. For although explicitly Zionism was distinguished from Jewishness, an undercurrent meaning "Jewish" was also contained in the word. The word "Arab," emerging at this moment to define our identity, silently carried within it its polar opposite—Zionist/Jew—without which hidden, silent connotation, it actually had no meaning. For the whole purpose of its emergence now was precisely to tell us of our new alignments and realignments in relation to both terms, Arab and Jew.

Jews and Copts were not, to me, abstractions. They were people my parents knew and saw and talked about, and they were my brothers' friends and my sister's and my own, including my best friend, Joyce. I am sure I sensed these insidious, subterranean shifts and rearrangements of our feelings that this new bludgeoning propaganda was effecting, or trying to effect, in us. And I am sure that this, as well as the sheer hatefulness of being endlessly subjected to propaganda, was part of the reason I so much disliked and resisted the idea that I was an Arab.

Nor was it only through the media that the government was pressuring us into acceptance of its broad political agenda and coercing us into being Arab. For this was the era, too, of growing political repression and of the proliferation of the *mukhabarat*, the secret police—the era when political opponents and people suspected of being disloyal to the revolution were being jailed or disappearing. In this atmosphere, being disloyal to the revolution and to the Arab cause (being, as it were, un-Arab) became as charged and dangerous for Egyptians as being un-American was for Americans in the McCarthy era.

The propaganda worked on me and on others. To question our Arabness and all that our Arabness implied became unthinkable. Only despicable, unprincipled traitors would do such a thing. And it is with this complicated legacy that my own sense of identity as Egyptian and as Arab is entangled.

The following pages recount a personal odyssey through the politics, emotions, and history of our becoming Arab. For no matter how carefully I examined my memories and feelings, they remained opaque until I took this journey into history and into the history of the world of my childhood. These pages both describe the information that I discovered and pieced together—some of it quite surprising and even shocking to me—and trace the process and voyage of discovery itself and my new understandings of my past.

Thinking back to the incident with which I began this chapter, I asked myself what this scene between me and Miss Nabih told me about my parents and family, from whom, certainly, I got my understanding of what it meant to be Egyptian. Why was it that I was so stubborn, so convinced that I was Egyptian and not Arab, definitely not Arab? Presumably this was what my parents thought, but why? Was this a class issue? Were they part of some elite milieu which imagined they were Egyptian while "the masses" knew all along that they were Arabs? When, in fact, did Egyptians become Arab—or have we always been Arab?

The answer to this question, which I assumed I would find simply by looking up a book or two on the history of Egypt, actually took quite a lot of detective work, for it was not clearly or fully addressed in any of the books where I had expected to find it. It felt as if I had embarked in search of some esoteric secret. In the last few years there has begun to be a scholarship piecing together the history of the rise of Arab nationalism, but as regards Egypt, it is a history as yet only barely sketched in.

The story, anyway, begins in Syria, in the late nineteenth century, where the idea of an Arab identity and Arab nationalism first arose. Prior to this, "Arab" had referred throughout the Middle East only to the inhabitants of Arabia and to bedouins of the region's deserts. It was among the Christians of Syria, and in particular among a group of Syrian men who had attended French missionary schools, that the idea of Arab nationalism first appeared, in part as a movement of literary and cultural revival and in part as a way of mobilizing both Christian and Muslim Syrians to throw off the domination of the Islamic Ottoman Empire.

Egyptians, who in that era were preoccupied with getting rid of the British, not the Ottomans, were either uninterested in or positively hostile to this strange Syrian idea of an Arab identity. Mustapha Kamil, the leading nationalist of the day in Egypt, strongly pro-Ottoman and pro-Islamic, denounced Arab nationalism as an idea invented and fomented by the Europeans to hasten the destruction of the Ottoman Empire. And paranoid though Kamil's notion sounds, there may have been some truth to it. Historical records suggest that British officials were indeed already encouraging and supporting the idea of Arabism even before World War I (that they did so during the war is well known).

Well into the first decades of this century, neither the self-defined new Arabs nor the Egyptians themselves thought that this new identity had anything to do with Egyptians. For example, in 1913 an Arab conference was organized in Paris. When an Egyptian who was attending as an observer asked permission to speak, he was refused on the grounds that the floor was open only to Arabs.

During World War I, the idea of Arab nationalism emerged again as an important idea—and again as an idea mobilizing people against the Turks and their Islamic Empire. This time it took the form of the British-instigated "Arab revolt," led by T. E. Lawrence. (The fact that this famous revolt was led by an Englishman makes obvious, of course, Britain's political interest in promoting Arabism as a way of fighting the Ottoman Empire and bringing about its final dissolution.) Once more, as with the Syrian form of Arab nationalism, not only were Egyptians not part of this movement, they were, if anything, inclined to be sympathetic to the other side. For one thing, this Arab movement now involved mainly the Arabs of Arabia and nomadic tribal Arabs, people whom Egyptians regarded as even more different from themselves than the Syrians. The distinction between settled and nomad is, in the Middle East, one of the fundamental divides. For Egyptians it is a distinction that has marked off their society from that of "the Arabs" (Arabians, nomads) since the beginning of their civilization.

In addition, these Arabs were fighting *with* the hated British, the oppressors of Egypt, and *against* the Islamic Empire and the caliph of Islam. Egypt's Khedive Abbas had been sent into exile by the British for his open sympathies with the Turks and the Islamic Empire, and so also had the leader of the Nationalist Party, Mohamad Farid. The Egyptian writer Naguib Mahfouz, in his novel *Bain al-Qasrain (Palace Walk)*, set in World War I, portrays his characters, the "common folk" of Egypt, as praying for the return of Abbas and for the Turks to "emerge victorious" and as declaring that "the most important thing of all is that we get rid of the English nightmare" and that the caliphate return to its former glory. Aware of popular sentiment in Egypt, the British took care to represent the Arab revolt to Egyptians as a rebellion not against the caliph but against the "impious, godless" Young Turks who were oppressing "the Arabs."

At the end of the war the British invited the leaders of the Arabs to the Versailles conference but refused to permit the Egyptian leaders to attend. Still, the Arabs reaped no benefits. In a series of treaties the European powers (Britain and France) dismantled the Ottoman Empire and distributed among themselves its former territories. For the British, having induced the Arabs to fight with them against the Turks by promising them independence, had also signed a secret treaty with the French (the Sykes-Picot agreement) undertaking to divide between them after the war "the spoils of the Ottoman Empire." Formalizing their control over the territories that they had just captured from the Ottomans, France took Syria and divided it into two countries, Lebanon and Syria, and Britain took Iraq and Palestine. Britain was, of course, already occupying Egypt. Similarly the Balfour Declaration, promising Palestine, a land obviously with its own inhabitants, to people living elsewhere—designating it a national homeland for the Jews—had been issued earlier, in 1917, when the British first captured Palestine. (There were, of course, Jews as well as Muslims and Christians among the population of Palestine when the British captured it, but it was not out of concern for Palestinian Jews that the British now declared Palestine a homeland for the Jews but rather—as is well known—in response to the desires and hopes of European Jewry for a homeland in Palestine.)

Some of this I knew already. I knew about T. E. Lawrence and the Arab revolt, and I had known in a general way that Arab nationalism was a recent idea. But only now, putting together the Christian and missionary-inspired origins of Arab nationalism in Syria and the use the British made of the idea to mobilize the "Arabs" against the Ottomans, did I realize the extent to which Arab nationalism had emerged as a way of opposing the Islamic Empire. And only now did I realize the extent to which Egypt had not only *not* been Arab but actually had been mostly on the opposite side to that of the Arabs. The exiled khedive and political leaders of Egypt supported the Ottomans and hated the British, and so apparently did the "masses." And even the modernizing intellectuals, who wanted political independence from the Ottomans, had all their cultural, intellectual, and personal ties with Turks and with Istanbul, which many of them regularly visited.

And so already my understanding of Egypt and its relation to the Arabs was beginning to shift. Already I was beginning to feel that the world was not as I had assumed it to be and its seas and continents not after all where I had thought they were. Still, whatever internal shifts and readjustments were involved for me in what I had learned thus far, they were nothing to the geologic shifts and turmoil and upheaval that I would find myself flung up or cast down by as I read on, trying to piece together what happened next—and reading now about the history of the Jews in Egypt and about Egypt's relations to Zionism and the Palestinians.

Eventually things would calm down. Eventually I would come to see that these facts, too, were part of the history of Egypt and that after all they fitted quite intelligibly into that history. But to begin with, with almost every new detail I learned I found myself precipitated into a state of general agitation, my feelings running the gamut of shock, disbelief, shame, despair, and exhilaration— why exhilaration?—and finally, finally understanding. Physically I could not sit still, I could only read a paragraph or two at a time, at least whenever I stumbled upon one or the other of these, to me, completely mind-blowing facts. I'd jump up and walk and walk, repeating to myself whatever it was I'd just read. Egyptians, I'd be rushing around saying to myself, joined their Zionist friends in Cairo and Alexandria to celebrate the Balfour Declaration? There were Zionist associations in Cairo and Alexandria then? It was okay in Egypt to be a Zionist? The governor of Alexandria, Ahmad Ziyour Pasha—later prime minister of Egypt— went to a party in the city celebrating the Balfour Declaration that culminated in their sending a telegram to Lord Balfour to thank him?

Hours and hours and days of this, then, would be interspersed with enormous, crashing, paralyzing anxieties at the very thought of writing about Arabness. There was no question I couldn't do it. I'd just have to leave it out. Just forget it—Arab, not Arab—just forget it. It was much too complicated. How could I possibly deal with all this history?

The first Jewish flag to fly over Jerusalem after its capture by the British was made in Egypt? Joseph Cicurel of the house of Cicurel (a department store I remembered from my childhood, the Harrods of Cairo) had had it made in his Alexandria workshops. Cicurel was president of the Zionist association of Cairo. And at the same time he was an Egyptian nationalist? He was also a trustee of the Bank of Egypt, the bank founded by the Muslim nationalist Talaat Harb with the object of wresting control of the Egyptian economy from Europeans and placing it in Egyptian hands. The same was true of Leon Castro, the vice president of the same Zionist association and likewise an Egyptian nationalist. A member of the Wafd, the party leading the struggle for independence from the British, he was also a friend and staunch supporter of Saad Zaghloul, leader of the Wafd and *the* hero of the Egyptian nationalist struggle.

On and on, more such extraordinary facts about Egyptians' relationship to Zionism—and also to the Palestinians. The Egyptian government sent a representative—we are now in 1925—to the celebrations for the inauguration of the Hebrew University in Jerusalem. This representative was none other than Ahmad Lutfi al-Sayyid, the editor of *al-Jarida*, the paper that shaped the political consciousness of a generation of Egyptians—my father's generation—and the man who would later facilitate women's entry into the Egyptian University. In the late 1920s and early 1930s, when Palestinians began publishing a paper in Egypt advocating their cause, the Egyptian government several times closed the paper down and banned the publication of "Palestinian propaganda." And in the wake of conflict over the Wailing Wall and Muslim fears about rights of access to the al-Aqsa mosque, also in the early 1930s, it even banned the invocation of the name of Palestine in mosques on Fridays. Meanwhile several Zionist papers continued publication and Zionism was not banned.

Reading such facts as these and observing my own feelings and the paralyzing anxiety I felt at the mere thought of writing about such things, I came to conclude that this sort of information did not ordinarily figure in history books on Egypt precisely because, according to the political alignments of our day, alignments that we consider to be entirely obvious and natural, they seemed so shamefully unpatriotic, and so disloyal and unfeeling toward the Palestinians.

In the ensuing days I would begin to understand how it was that Egyptian attitudes had been so profoundly different from what they are today, and I would come to understand also my own connection to that past and the ways in which it was interwoven with my own early life. But even then, even when I'd understood all this, I would still find myself completely stalled and unable to imagine how I could possibly write about these things.

Still feeling totally paralyzed, I began to analyze my paralysis as a product probably of my having internalized the taboos against questioning Arabness that had been part, after all, of my adolescence. But this insight—if it was an insight—did me no good. I was still perfectly capable of silencing myself without any external prohibitions.

Quite a number of remarkable Egyptians, I discovered along the way, had been suspected or accused of being either too pro-Jewish, too conciliatory, and too weak on Zionism or deficient in their Arabness or their loyalty to Arabness. Among those whose actions or words or positions one way or another laid them open to such charges were Saad Zaghloul, hero of Egyptian nationalism. And Taha Husain and Tewfik al-Hakim and Naguib Mahfouz, three of Egypt's finest writers. Major figures in the country's history. The equivalent in American terms would be to find that Harry Truman, William Faulkner, F. Scott Fitzgerald, and Eugene O'Neill had all been suspected of un-American inclinations. And of course there was Anwar

Sadat, gunned down in part for his retreat—and all that such a retreat implied—from Nasser's position as to Egypt's fundamental Arabness.

But knowing this made no difference either. Nothing unfroze me.

Then one evening as I was walking home, something began to shift. I am not sure quite why or how things began to change but I know that the shift was connected to, or, more exactly, was the direct outcome of, the preceding perfectly pleasant but uneventful few hours. I was in Cambridge for the year on a fellowship (it was here that I pursued and pieced together this history) and had gone out to hear a talk by the Lebanese novelist Hanan al-Shaykh. She'd come down from London to speak at the Oriental Studies Faculty. Hanan was already there when I arrived and rose to greet me, which took me by surprise: we had met only once, briefly and in a crowd, and I hadn't expected her to recognize me. It had felt good, I realized, sitting down and looking around me, to be recognized and to be greeted in the way that, in the world in which I had once lived, one automatically greeted people—or at least other women. The room was more crowded than it had been for the previous lecturers. Aside from Tareef and Bassim, who were the professors at the Oriental Faculty, and some students, the audience did not seem the usual academic crowd that I'd seen at other lectures. Hanan's reputation had clearly drawn out from wherever they were in their separate spaces a good number of the town's Arab and, I guessed from their looks, specifically Lebanese community. There were several older people there, many of them women, living, for whatever reason, in this exile. Here now to honor one of their own, to take pride in her, to listen to her words—and to remember.

Hanan, a slight, beautiful woman, began to read in a clear, soft voice and the room fell quiet, a look of intentness and pleasure and anticipation already on people's faces. Her paper, about how she became a writer, was full of evocations of the streets and cafés of Beirut, and of its dusty, cluttered, narrow bookshops, and of her youthful discoveries of the classics of contemporary Arabic literature, and of poetry read and heard and ideas exchanged under the apple trees. It began, almost at once, to work its enchantment. As the minutes passed, the faces around me grew perceptibly happier, mellower, more relaxed. Even Bassim and Tareef, sitting facing me on either side of her—dear colleagues both but men who, as I knew, were somewhat skeptical of the fame of Arab women writers—were looking mellow and happy and relaxed. They had clearly been won over.

I found myself thinking enviously that this was what I would like to be writing, something that would affirm my community in exile. Something that would remind its members of how lovely our lives, our countries, our ways are. How lovely our literature. What a fine thing, whatever it is people say of us, what a fine thing it is, in spite of them all, to be Arab; what a wonderful heritage we have. Something that would sustain them. Sustain us. What wouldn't I give, I sat there thinking, listening to her quote Arab poets, to have had that in my past, all that wealth of Arabic literature that nurtured her as writer; what wouldn't I give now to have all those poets and writers to remember and write about and remind people of? I loved the lines she was quoting—but I appreciated them, I realized, only the way I might the poetry of a foreign tongue that I only somewhat knew. They did not have for me the resonances of lines learned long ago. Nor, of course, since they were in literary

Arabic, did they have the charge and redolence and burdened evocativeness of a language spoken in childhood and youth and in love and anger and just in the ordinary moments of living. But on the other hand they didn't have that wealth and redolence for her, either. Even though she clearly loved the literature and language and was herself a fine Arabic writer, for her too it was a language she had not spoken in childhood and did not speak now. Nobody speaks literary Arabic— or maybe just some pedant somewhere.

We went afterward—Hanan, Tareef, Bassim, Zeeba (another colleague), and I—for drinks at King's. The mood of the lecture stayed with us, our talk pleasant, relaxed, easy. At some point Hanan asked me what I was working on. I was vague, evasive, guilty. I even lied a little. "I'm looking at Egypt's history," I said, "twentieth century." And then for the rest of the evening I felt guilty, sitting there like a Judas among these friends. I felt like a betrayer. Was it even imaginable that I could have responded, sitting there among them—two Lebanese, one Palestinian, one Iranian, three of the four of them having been made homeless one way or another by Israeli aggression or by some spin-off of that conflict—was it conceivable that I could say, "Well, actually I am looking into this whole question of the Arabness of Egyptian identity, I am trying to really look at it, deconstruct it. You see, I remember ..." It was completely unimaginable, impossible, inconceivable.

I felt like a betrayer.

Coming out onto King's Parade, afterwards, the night suddenly balmy, the street almost empty though it wasn't that late, people's voices carrying clear, loud, the way they do sometimes on summer nights—but not usually now, in winter, winter on the point of turning to spring—I walked on homeward, down Senate House Passage and along the narrow road onto the bridge. There was a crescent moon over the trees in a deep, deep sky.

I did feel kin, of course, and I did feel that I was among people who were, in some quite real sense, my community. But was this because of "Arabness"? Was I, for instance, really likely to feel more kin, more at home, with someone from Saudi Arabia than with someone, say, from Istanbul? I doubted it. (Saudis speak Arabic, Turks don't.) This, though, was not the issue now. I realized that my feelings of being completely prohibited from writing about Arabness were not, or not only, a response to old prohibitions or a fear of breaking some mental taboo internalized in adolescence. No, my fear that I would, in this act of unraveling, cross over the line into betrayal was about real, not abstract betrayal. I'd been so set on this act of unraveling, this taking apart of the notion of Arabness. It had seemed to me so essential, so necessary to understanding what it was that I'd lived through, and essential and necessary also to freeing myself from the unbearable lies that I'd forever felt trapped in. Essential and necessary in one sense, and yet to proceed would inevitably, as it now felt, take me over the line into betrayal. And so, thinking about it now, from the context of having been with people I liked and felt in some sense kin with, I wondered what it could possibly matter, when weighed against the reality of people's being driven from their homes or penned into impossible lives, that I had felt myself coerced into being something that I did not feel I was. A small, trivial nothing of a detail to put up with as a way of conveying to them solidarity and support.

"But I am not here to betray," I said, waiting at the traffic lights. Had I said it out loud? I looked around—there was nobody there anyway.

I am not here to betray. I just do not want to live any longer with a lie about who I am. I don't want any longer to live with lies and manipulations, I can't stand to be caught up like this forever in other people's inventions, imputations, false constructions of who I am—what I think, believe, feel, or ought to think or believe or feel.

But how—if I don't directly address this—how will I ever free myself from lies?

If I didn't live where I live, I thought to myself, if I were still living in Egypt, I probably wouldn't feel that it was so absolutely necessary to extricate myself from this enmeshment of lies. In Egypt the sense of falseness and coercion would be there in a political sense, but at least in ordinary daily life I'd be just another Egyptian, whereas in the West it's impossible for me ever to escape, forget this false constructed Arabness. It's almost always somehow there, the notion that I am Arab, in any and every interaction. And sometimes it's quite grossly and offensively present, depending on how bigoted or ignorant the person I am confronting is.

But this is a problem, I realized now, arising out of *their* notion of Arab, the Western, not the Arab, notion of Arab. So there are two different notions of Arab that I am trapped in—both false, both heavily weighted and cargoed with another and silent freight. Both imputing to me feelings and beliefs that aren't mine. They overlap in some ways, but they are not, I am sure, identical. But this was a piece of the puzzle—the fact that there were two different notions of Arab—that for the moment I would have to defer figuring out.

Anyway, the long and short of it is that I am not here to betray. I am taking apart the notion of Arabness and following out the history of when and how we became Arab just to know—not with the object of, or as code for, the betrayal of anybody. For Egyptians to debate or question their Arabness ("search" for their identity) is usually code, as I realize now, for debating the extent of our responsibility toward the Palestinians. And it is accordingly read by Arabs and by Egyptians as a covert way of advocating either support for or abandonment of the Palestinians. But my own exploration of the question here is not code for anything. My sole object here is only to see things, as clearly and exactly as I know how, for what they are. And to free myself of lies. And so in any case one reason that Zionism was permitted to be overtly present in Egypt in the late 1920s and early 1930s and that prominent members of the government and of the governing classes were sympathetic to Zionism was that Egyptians seemed not to know what is obvious to us in hindsight—that making Palestine into a homeland for the Jews would eventually entail the expulsion and dispossession of the Palestinians. There had as yet been no large-scale immigration of Europeans to Palestine and, at the end of the 1910s and through most of the 1920s, when troubles broke out intermittently in Palestine the government and media in Egypt typically reacted by exhorting the Jews and Muslims and Christians of Palestine to work together to find a peaceful solution, offering themselves as mediators, and worrying that this reprehensible interreligious, intercommunal violence would spread to their own country. Because of this last concern, newspapers (or at least some newspapers) and the government responded to news of outbreaks of violence in Palestine by reiterating their own total commitment to preserving religious pluralism, and the government in addition took such measures as banning Palestinian "propaganda"—in fear that interreligious hostilities and in particular anti-Jewish violence, as yet unknown in Egypt, would spread to their own land.

For, as of 1918, the modernizing intellectuals and their party, the Wafd, had begun to become the uncontested political leaders of the nation. And in the early twenties their political goals and platform—democracy, a constitution guaranteeing, among other things, the rights of the individual, pluralism, and an implicit secularism committed to the equal rights of all Egyptians, regardless of religion—won the support of the nation in a landslide election that carried small villages as well as major cities. These goals, conceived and defined by the country's political and intellectual leadership, received the endorsement of the populace as a whole.

Egypt's experiment in democracy would be conducted under difficult circumstances. The British, refusing to grant Egypt complete independence, retained important powers and sometimes interfered outright in the democratic process, at one point later forcing Egypt's king, literally at gunpoint (surrounding his palace with their tanks), to appoint the prime minister they wanted. The king, for his part, plotted to wrest power back from the government to himself. Despite these difficulties the country did make political progress and there were even some exhilarating times and significant achievements, among them the promulgation of a constitution in 1923, Article 3 of which granted equal rights to all Egyptians, "without distinction of race, language, or religion." The same principles were reiterated in Egypt's Nationality Laws, which went into effect in 1929 with the formal dissolution of the Ottoman Empire and the replacement of Ottoman citizenship with a brand-new nationality, the Egyptian nationality. These principles and a commitment to Egypt as a multireligious community were furthermore made clear and visible to all in the composition of the government. When, in 1924, Zaghloul became Egypt's first elected prime minister, Jews as well as Copts served in his cabinet—and indeed both Jews and Copts would continue to serve in the Egyptian government in the following decades.

As all this shows, then, not only was the country's political leadership deeply committed to the goal of preserving Egypt as a pluralist society; in addition, Jews were integrally part of the community of Egypt and of its political and cultural leadership, and they were the friends and colleagues and co-workers of Muslim and Coptic Egyptians. Then there were other factors, too, influencing how Egyptians related to the issue of Palestine. Most obviously, there were no Palestinians then (or very few) in Egypt and certainly there was no historical community of Palestinians as there was a historical Jewish community. In this era about half the Jewish community of Egypt—a community of about 75,000—were Egyptian Jews. The rest were recent immigrants from other territories of the Ottoman Empire and from Europe. (These latter often looked down on the local Jewish community, particularly the Jewish working classes, who were indistinguishable in culture and ways from working-class Muslims and Copts. Middle- and upper-class Jews, like Copts and Muslims of their class, were fast becoming Europeanized.)

And then finally there was the fact that Egyptians at this point did not (and at any class level) see themselves as Arab or as having any special connection with the Arabs, nor did they think that they had any particular interest in or special responsibility for what transpired in Palestine.

Egyptian attitudes began to shift toward a sympathy with the Palestinians in the thirties, as the situation in Palestine began to change when, with the rise of Fascism in Europe, European Jewish immigration to Palestine increased enormously. Palestinian political activism also increased. Through the thirties Palestinian strikes and rebellions against the British and their struggles with Zionists were constantly in the news. By the late thirties the Palestinians had won the sympathies of Egyptians. Fund-raisers and various other events in support of Palestine and in aid of Palestinian relief were held at all class levels, including by Huda Shaarawi's Feminist Union, among the first associations to organize a regionwide conference in support of the Palestinians.

Most important, in terms of publicizing the situation of Palestinians and mobilizing popular support for them, the Muslim Brotherhood, dedicated to instituting an Islamic government in Egypt and to freeing all Muslim lands from imperialists, vigorously took up the Palestinian cause. It began to hold protest demonstrations on Balfour Day and to address the issue of Palestine in Friday sermons.

It was these sorts of activities that, as I mentioned earlier, the government had been attempting to suppress, out of its commitment to a pluralist Egypt and its desire to prevent the spread of interreligious strife. And the government continued through the thirties to try to suppress inflammatory pro-Palestinian activities and to keep Egypt out of direct involvement in the question of Palestine. This was the position assumed not only by the Wafd when it was in power but by the several governments formed by different parties in this era. This view represented, in other words, the consensus position of the governing classes across party lines. And so a rift began to form in Egypt on the issue of Palestine, not on the matter of sympathy for the Palestinians but as to what Egypt's political involvement should be: a rift, initially, not so much between the governing classes and the "masses" as between the government and governing classes on the one hand and the Brotherhood on the other.

Through the thirties the demonstrations the Brotherhood organized grew steadily more massive, and they began to take the direction that the government had, all along, feared they would take. In 1936, the Brotherhood called for a boycott of Jewish businesses. In the same year, the first anti-Jewish graffiti to be reported in Egypt appeared in Port Said. In 1938, police clashed with Brotherhood demonstrators—some of whom were shouting "Down with the Jews"— and tried to prevent them from entering the Jewish quarter of Old Cairo.

It was in the thirties that a few intellectuals—two or three men to begin with, all of whom had links with the Arabs—began to express the idea that Egypt should align itself with the Arabs and regard itself as Arab. But it was probably the emphasis the Muslim Brotherhood now placed on this idea that helped spread it most effectively. While the government had emphasized Egypt's heritage as quintessentially and indissolubly multicultural (Pharaonic, Mediterranean, and Islamic, as they put it in those days) as a way of legitimizing its determined emphasis on pluralism as a fundamental goal for this country, the Brotherhood countered by asserting that Islam and only Islam constituted Egypt's defining identity. It was Islam, they declared, that had saved Egypt from its pagan past (thereby conveniently erasing from history the fact that the majority of Egyptians had been Christian at the time of the Muslim invasion)—an Islam brought to the country, they stressed, by the Arabs. All Egyptians, therefore, and all Muslims owed a particular debt to the Arabs and had an obligation to help liberate Arab lands from infidel imperialists.

By the end of the thirties the popularity of the Palestinian cause and the growing influence of the Brotherhood were forcing the government and dominant political parties to slant their message differently. In 1939, a prominent member of the Wafd made headlines by writing an article declaring "Egypt is Arab!"

Through World War II overt political activism and demonstrations were banned under the Emergencies Act. When they resumed after the war, the pro-Palestinian demonstrations organized by the Muslim Brotherhood took the course of ever greater intercommunal tensions and anti-Jewish violence that the government and the different political parties had all along feared. Huge demonstrations held on Balfour Day in 1945 and again in 1947 spilled over into violent attacks on Jews and now on any other group deemed "foreign." Jewish, European, and Coptic shops were looted, and synagogues and Catholic, Greek Orthodox, and Coptic churches and schools vandalized. One synagogue was set on fire.

The unraveling of that old world and its society are just dimly part of the fabric of my own memories.

I remember being at play in the garden one dusk when the news came that al-Na'rashi, the prime minister, had been shot. *"Atalu al-Na'rashi!"* They killed al-Na'rashi! "They," I know now, were the Muslim Brothers. There was somberness then in our home. My parents, I believe, knew the Na'rashis. But not only somberness—there was something electric, still there even now in my memory, about how they uttered the words and how they spoke of this death. Now I imagine them saying to one another, the adults, living through these crises and troubled times, what next for the country, what next?

And I remember the midnight-blue paper on the windows, purplish when the daylight came through it, during the 1948 war with Israel, and being woken in the night and taken downstairs to the entree, a room with no windows and only a heavy glass and ironwork door, where everyone was gathered in the darkness, talking, listening to the bombs fall.

This was a few months before the assassination of Na'rashi (al-Nuqrashi)—as the history books, not my memory, tell me.

And then, in retaliation for Na'rashi's murder, Hasan al-Banna, the founder of the Muslim Brotherhood and its Supreme Guide, was gunned down. This I do not remember. The Muslim Brotherhood, by now an enormously powerful organization in the country with a vast membership and its own secret military units, was engaged through the forties in a terrorist and counterterrorist war with the political establishment. Al-Banna died in the hospital to which he was brought and where, by order of King Farouk, he was given no medical treatment.

It was by order of Farouk, too, that Egypt went to war with Israel. After the United Nations resolution to partition Palestine and Israel's declaration of statehood in 1948, the Egyptian political establishment—both government and opposition—had favored a cautious response, a verbal, not a military, response. But Farouk harbored dreams, now that the Ottoman Empire was gone, of having himself declared caliph of Islam. He worried that, if Egypt did not go to war now, King Abdullah of Jordan, who had declared that Jordan would go to war, would reap glory on the battlefield and put an end to his own dreams. And so, pre-empting the Egyptian government's decision and in violation of the constitution, he ordered military units to cross into Palestine. After the fact, the government hastily convened a meeting to bestow a semblance of legality on the king's orders. The opposition, however, and in particular the Liberal Constitutionalists—who (as the history books put it), out of a "narrow Egyptian secular nationalism," were "most impervious to Palestinian appeals"—were fiercely critical of this government action.

But of course it was not that Farouk had been pervious to Palestinian appeals. Nor was it only Farouk for whom from now on taking up the Palestinian cause was essentially an avenue to the fulfillment of his political ambitions. While Na'rashi was making speeches cautioning against a hasty military response, Hasan al-Banna was declaring in mosques the Muslim Brotherhood's readiness for a jihad against the Zionists. But he, too, was in reality furthering his own cause. In the forties the Brotherhood, historians have speculated, had a trained secret army of about 75,000 men. But they reportedly sent to the Palestine campaign just 600. The movement was hoping, say historians, to reserve most of its secret units for its Egyptian war—its war on the cities of Egypt.

By this point, that is, Palestine and the Palestinian cause had begun to be what they have been ever since in the politics of the Arab world: an issue that the Middle East's villains and heroes would use to manipulate people's sympathies and to further their own political ends and fantasies of power—with what costs or benefits to the Palestinian people only the Palestinians themselves can say.

Where did my parents stand in all this? I don't know. I was too young and do not remember. It would be quite impossible for me to have grasped what they said enough to be able to say, now, they said this or believed that.

And yet also now I think I know.

But the evidence I have is so vague, so insubstantial, so inconclusive. Some things I do know and do remember beyond a shadow of a doubt. For instance, I know that they definitely did not like the Muslim Brothers. I don't remember any particular thing that they said about them, but I remember this as a general feeling. And I remember that a man who was a relative by marriage (a younger man beholden in some way, looking in some way to my father) was a Muslim Brother and that he emerged from prison at some point (still, now, in the days of King Farouk) and that he had tuberculosis and that he came to our house and that my father, making clear to him (and evidently to all of us) his total disapproval of his politics, helped him get treatment.

I don't remember in any way that I would now be able to reproduce what my parents were saying as they lived through these wrenching times in the history of Egypt. But I was there, obviously, and heard them talk and no doubt in some sense absorbed what they were saying. And they *were* people who talked politics. Over lunch when my father came home from work and on weekends when we were home from school and joined our parents. Over tea and the papers in the early morning, sitting in my mother's huge bed, where we half listened to them talk.

What exactly was the content of that grief and somberness that descended over our home and the feeling of charged tension that I remember when Na'rashi was shot? What exactly did they say to each other? And what did they say when al-Banna was shot—and allowed to die, untreated, by order of the king?

That's another thing I incontrovertibly know and remember: they did not like King Farouk.

And what did they say when there were riots in Egypt and attacks on synagogues and churches? And what did they say as we sat in the dark in the entree, listening to the sound of distant bombs and anti-aircraft fire and then a nearer, louder, more frightening explosion? What were they saying about the war with Israel? Could they have been among those who condemned the king for getting us into this war? Could they have been among those who, like the government opposition, condemned the government for "lending any semblance of legitimacy" to the king's action? Could they have been among those who, like the Liberal Constitutionalists, out of a "narrow Egyptian secular nationalism" opposed the war? Could they have been among those "impervious to Palestinian appeals" who believed that Egypt should not go to war with Israel? Could they have been among those for whom grief about what was happening to Egypt overrode and took priority over what was happening to the Palestinians?

Though I do not remember their words, I would have picked up the import of what they were saying, and their attitudes would certainly have shaped my responses to whatever I encountered at school.

Including, of course, Miss Nabih.

I did not know, until I read into this history and learned what I have here set down, that there had been Egyptians—perfectly ordinary, decent, upright, principled citizens of Egypt, not disloyal, unpatriotic, unfeeling people—who believed in something else, some other idea of Egypt and its society and future, and who openly argued against getting involved in supporting the Palestinians and going to war with Israel.

My parents were the people that they were. Of the class that they were, the milieu that they were, the era that they were. And they had the feelings and beliefs about Egypt that they had, and the hopes for Egypt that they had. Not indifference toward the Palestinians and their sufferings, nor commitment to some "narrow Egyptian secular nationalism," but quite simply loyalty to their own community and to the people—Copts, Jews, and Muslims—who made up that community had been what my parents had steadfastly held on to and had refused to be moved from. Loyalty to their actual community—over and above some fictive, politically created community that the politicians ordered them to be loyal to. And, yes, their overall position reflected too their particular hopes for Egypt, and their commitment to what we today call "pluralism." But "pluralism" after all is merely a modern version of what had been, in another world, another era, their tradition and heritage, from generation to generation to generation, in Cairo and Alexandria and Spain and Morocco and Istanbul.

And so this, then, had been the source of those moments of inexplicable exhilaration in the midst of turbulence—my beginning to glimpse finally what had been the history and prehistory of my own conflicted feelings. They taught me so well, instilled in me so deeply their notion of what it was to be Egyptian, that I still mourn and am always still and all over again filled with an enormous sense of loss at the thought of the destruction of the multireligious Egyptian community that I knew. And still now news of intercommunal violence in Egypt and of attacks on Copts (there are no Jews now) and of attacks on Muslims too, of course—but it is the Copts who are the beleaguered community—is almost the bleakest news I know of coming out of there.

In 1941, Anthony Eden, the British foreign minister, proposed the creation of an Arab League, to include Egypt. This British proposal precipitated an intense debate that polarized Egyptians. Was Egypt Arab? Mediterranean? Pharaonic? Britain had put forward the idea as a counterproposal to an idea that Iraq had been advancing: the creation of a federated Arab state, to consist of Iraq, Syria, Jordan, and Palestine. Such a federation, should it occur, could lead to the rise of a formidable new power in the Middle East, and this was something Britain did not want. It was something Egypt did not want, either. As the region began to adjust to the disappearance of Turkey as the center of empire and the newly emergent countries began to vie for regional dominance, Egypt—at that point the richest, most developed, and most populous nation in the region—had no intention of ceding power and influence to Iraq or Jordan or to any federation of these. Thus, in 1943, the Egyptian government agreed to the British proposal and the Arab League was formed in 1945.

And so here we are in 1945, and Egypt, for reasons of regional strategy, officially becomes an Arab country, although not as yet exclusively Arab, as it would become under Nasser. And again, curiously, Britain played the role of instigator, and of midwife, as it were, to the birth of yet another Arab nation. Once more, as with its leadership of the Arab revolt, Britain's purpose in urging Egypt to define itself as Arab was, of course, the furtherance of British political interests.

It was as if we had become Arab, and all the region gradually had become Arab (when, once, only Arabia had been Arab), because the Europeans saw us as Arabs—all of us as just Arabs. And because, to serve their own political interests and in pursuit of their own ends—the dismantling of the Ottoman Empire, the acquisition of new colonial territories, retaining control of territories under their mandate—it was strategically and politically useful to them, in this particular era in history, to define us, and to have us define ourselves, as Arabs. And gradually over this era we had all complied, imagining this, correctly or not, to be in our own interest, too.

The Europeans were defining us and we, falling in with their ideas, agreed to define ourselves as Arab in the dictionary sense: "a member of the Semitic people of the Arabian peninsula; a member of an Arabic-speaking people." But the Europeans were also defining us as Arab in quite another sense. Just as with the word "African"—"a native or inhabitant of Africa; a person of immediate or remote African ancestry; esp: Negro"—there is no trace in the dictionary definition of the word's pejorative connotations. There is nothing here of what anyone who has heard of O. J. Simpson or *The Bell Curve* or who knows anything about American history *knows* what that word means. This is the case also with the word "Arab," which similarly comes, in European tongues, internally loaded in the negative.

Such words carry within them entire landscapes, entire histories.

The European powers defined us as "Arab" in this other sense by what they did. They defined us as "Arab" in this sense when they made an agreement with Sheikh Abdullah and those who fought alongside Lawrence, promising them independence—and then broke the agreement. They defined us as "Arab" at the peace conferences of Versailles and Sèvres when they dealt with Middle Eastern territories as mere spoils of the Ottoman Empire, to be divided between France and Britain as booty, bargaining with one another for this bit or that, drawing lines and borders on their maps with little concern for the people and lands they were carving up. And they defined us as "Arab" when they designated an already inhabited land as a homeland for people living, then, elsewhere. They defined us as "Arab" when they led Egyptians to believe that in return for neutrality during the war they would get independence—and failed to keep their promise and exiled leaders and fired on demonstrators who dared protest. They defined us as "Arab" when they set aside the results of elections and forced the appointment of their chosen prime minister.

"Arabs" meant people with whom you made treaties that you did not have to honor, arabs being by definition people of a lesser humanity and there being no need to honor treaties with people of lesser humanity. It meant people whose lands you could carve up and apportion as you wished, because they were of a lesser humanity. It meant people whose democracies you could obstruct at will, because you did not have to behave justly toward people of a lesser humanity. And what could mere arabs, anyway, know of democracy and democratic process?

Until now, all who had come to this land of Egypt—Greeks, Romans, Arabs, Turks—had known that they were coming to a place of civilization. All, until now, had come knowing that they had as much to learn here as to teach, as much to take, in terms of knowledge and ways of understanding and of living, as to give. That, until now, was how it had been.

The Europeans began writing their meaning of the word "arab" freely and indiscriminately all over the Middle East from about 1918 on, when the region as a whole fell into their hands. Prior to this, during their rule in Egypt, that meaning of the word had occasionally surfaced—at Dinshwai, for instance—but it had not been the dominant, consistent hallmark of their conduct.

And so in those years they scribbled their meaning of "arab" all over the landscape, in their acts and in the lines they drew on maps, tracing out their meaning in a script at once cryptic and universal: as cryptic and universal as the mark of a snake or the trail of deer on a blank page of snow.

And in time, quite soon, their meaning of the word "arab" would enter our meaning of it, too. Not etymologically, in the way that dictionaries trace meanings through transformations from word to word to word. No. It entered it corrosively, changing it from within, as if the European meaning were a kind of virus eating up the inside of the word "Arab," replacing it with itself—leaving it unchanged on the outside. Think of what it did to the words "African," "Africa": somehow, somehow, loading those words in the negative.

The European meaning of "arab," then, hollowed out our word, replacing it entirely with itself. Except that now ours is their meaning of the word "arab" in reverse. Like "black" and "Black," as in "Black is beautiful."

It is this sense of "arab," the European sense, with its cargo of negativities, that I, living in the West, so often encounter and feel myself trapped in. This is the meaning of "arab," still very much alive, still very much around, that prompted me, for instance, to quickly hide my Arabic newspaper in my shopping bag so that people would not know I was Arab—and so react to me, possibly, in some bigoted fashion, as people all too commonly do when they discover I am Arab. Like the man—more extreme than usual—who spat at me on the bus in Cambridge when I was a student: smiling at first, asking me if I was Israeli, and then, leaning toward me, seeing that the medallion I wore was after all Arabic, spitting right at me. And it is the meaning of "arab" that is there in my students' understanding when, as they grow more at ease with me, they disarmingly reveal that they would never have thought of calling me an Arab until I had called myself one, because, until then, they had thought the word was an insult. And it is there in the countless microaggressions (as the noted author and legal scholar Patricia Williams calls them) that ordinarily and daily are part of the fabric of living for those of us in the West who belong to a "race" charged, in this culture, in the negative.

And it is there in the meanings threading Western books and films and newspapers and so on. I, like many I know who are Arab, never go to a film in which I know that Arabs or Muslims figure. Naturally—why would I want to subject myself to the lies and racism that all too often are part of such things? This goes, too, for popular books on Arabs—their very popularity is usually an index of the fact that they are filled with bigotries and dehumanizations masquerading as truth.

But it would be another generation, not my parents' generation, not the generation who had grown up admiring European civilization, who would come to see clearly and to decipher for themselves what it was that the Europeans had scrawled across the landscape.

Nasser, born in 1917 and coming to consciousness, then, entirely after the watershed year of 1918, was perhaps among the first to figure out (for he was, whatever his flaws, an astute man) the meaning of what they had traced there— and to respond to it by crystallizing the identity "arab" into its obverse, "Arab," although even he, as I discovered to my surprise, fully grasped that he was Arab only a few years before I got slapped for not knowing that I was Arab. For Nasser seems to have understood that he was Arab precisely by intently studying the marks and runes the imperialists had made upon the landscape. Reflecting himself on when it was exactly that he understood that he was Arab, he singles out the study of the recent history of the region, and above all (he repeatedly returns to this) the history of Palestine, as critical to his understanding of himself as an Arab. He wrote in his *Philosophy of the Revolution:* "As far as I am concerned I remember the first elements of Arab consciousness began to filter into my mind as a student in secondary school, when I went out with my fellow schoolboys ... every year as a protest against the Balfour Declaration whereby England gave the Jews a national home usurped unjustly from its legal owners. When I asked myself at the time," Nasser goes on, "why I left my school so enthusiastically and why I was angry for this land which I never saw I could not find an answer except the echoes of sentiment." Gradually "a form of comprehension" began when he studied "the Palestine campaigns and the history of the region in general" in military college, and finally that comprehension crystallized "when the Palestine crisis loomed on the horizon."

"When I asked myself … why I was so angry." Anger, as Nasser's own choice of words makes clear, was the key emotion in the early formation of his nascent identity as an Arab.

Spring is here.

The crocuses are out on the Backs. Rivulets of blue, all along the pathways, vividest, vividest blue, and gashes and splashes of it on the verges and under the trees.

Why then, walking through this, did I suddenly feel this sense of loss—measureless, measureless loss—sweep through me?

And so that, O my daughter, is what happened. That, in those years, is what happened to us.

QUESTIONS FOR MAKING CONNECTIONS
WITHIN THE READING

1. How many definitions of the word *Arab* does Ahmed provide in "On Becoming an Arab"? Construct a chart that tracks the changes in the meaning of *arab* and *Arab* over time. Why did Ahmed reject the name in the 1950s and why does she accept it now?

2. Ahmed states repeatedly in her piece that she is "not here to betray." One could argue that repeating this declaration is a clear sign that Ahmed is concerned that she will be read as betraying someone or some cause. Whom is she worried about betraying? And why does she feel that her search for her own identity might appear to justify the charge of betrayal?

3. What role does Palestine play in Ahmed's project of defining the contemporary meanings of *Arab* and *Egyptian*?

QUESTIONS FOR WRITING

1. Ahmed describes her project as "a personal odyssey through the politics, emotions, and history of our becoming Arab." Why does she include emotions as part of her project? Where do you see emotion surfacing in her argument? Are there places where you would say that emotions are shaping her argument? What role should the emotions play in research on the formation of the self in history?

2. Ahmed's story begins with a slap and ends with "a sense of loss—measureless, measureless loss…." What would you say Ahmed has learned by the end of her odyssey? Is her lesson one that applies to people generally or only to expatriates?

QUESTIONS FOR MAKING CONNECTIONS
BETWEEN READINGS

1. In Ahmed's narrative, she documents the changing meaning of *Arab* over time, pointing to a moment when the word "silently carried within it its polar opposite—Zionist/Jew—without which hidden, silent connotation it actually had no meaning." Later in her account, Ahmed reports that "[t]he European meaning of 'arab' hollowed out our word, replacing it entirely with itself." Does Ahmed find herself caught in one version of the "argument culture" that Deborah Tannen describes in "The Roots of Debate in Education and the Hope for Dialogue"? What roles do conflict and dialogue play in the identity formation of an individual? A nation?

2. Both Ahmed and Jonathan Boyarin are concerned with locating the self in time, and both are concerned with memory and loss. Their methods for pursuing their shared interests diverge, however, as do their writing styles and their conclusions: Ahmed closes with "a sense of loss—measureless, measureless loss," while Boyarin ends with "the marginal redemption of one Jew." How do you account for these differences? What might those who are not Jews or Arabs learn from the journeys of these two writers? Write an essay where you discuss what, if anything, can be learned from reading about another's search for identity.

KAREN ARMSTRONG

In 1981, Karen Armstrong published *Through the Narrow Gate,* a controversial account of her experience as a Sister of the Society of the Holy Child Jesus, a Roman Catholic order. Armstrong left the convent and the Church in 1972, "wearied by religion" and "worn out by years of struggle," and then spent the intervening years pursuing a doctorate in literature and teaching at an English girls' school. Although her first book was a milestone, Armstrong has described her life's real turning point as a series of trips she made to Jerusalem beginning in 1982. Shocked by Israel's invasion of Lebanon and also by the Palestinians' intifada, Armstrong found herself questioning just how accurately most Westerners— herself included—understood the lives and beliefs of Muslims in the Middle East.

Convinced that the West was "posing as a tolerant and compassionate society and yet passing judgments from a position of extreme ignorance and irrationality," Armstrong set out to help rectify cross-cultural misperceptions and religious misunderstandings. She has written a number of books that explore relations among Judaism, Christianity, and Islam, including *Holy War: The Crusades and their Impact on Today's World* (1991); *Mohammed: A Biography of the Prophet* (1992); and *Islam: A Short History* (2000). She has also written a biography, *Buddha* (2001), and *The Battle for God* (2000), an account of the rise of fundamentalism in modern societies.

The selection that follows comes from *The Case for God* (2009), in which Armstrong, a self-described "freelance monotheist," responds to the writings of "New Atheists" Richard Dawkins, Daniel C. Dennett, Sam Harris, Victor J. Stenger, and Christopher Hitchens. Armstrong makes the case that their view of religion has been shaped by the very fundamentalism they reject. Dawkins, for example, assumes that religion rests on faith in "a superhuman, supernatural intelligence who deliberately designed and created the universe and everything in it." Today this view of God is accepted by hundreds of millions of believers, yet Armstrong argues that in earlier times, religion was understood quite differently— as *mythos,* a symbolic language meant to transform our consciousness and our ways of being. As she told an interviewer in 2008, she sees religion as "poetry":

> Now a poet spends a great deal of time listening to his unconscious, and slowly calling up a poem word by word, phrase by phrase, until

Armstrong, Karen. "Homo religiosus." *The Case for God* (New York: Alfred A. Knopf, 2009). 3–26.

Biographical information and opening quotations are taken from http://www.islamfortoday.com/karenarmstrong.htm; the middle quotation is from www.washington-report.org/backissues/0293/9302038.htm. The quotation from Richard Dawkins appears on p. 304 of *The Case for God.* The final quotation is drawn from http://speakingoffaith.publicradio.org/programs/armstrong/transcript.shtml.

something beautiful is brought forth, we hope, into the world that changes people's perceptions. And we respond to a poem emotionally. And I think we should take as great a care when we write our theology as we would if we were writing such a poem … because I do see religion as a kind of art form.

■ ■

Homo religiosus

When the guide switches off his flashlight in the underground caverns of Lascaux in the Dordogne, the effect is overwhelming. "The senses suddenly are wiped out," one visitor recalled, "the millennia drop away … You were never in darker darkness in your life. It was—I don't know, just a complete knockout. You don't know whether you are looking north, south, east, or west. All orientation is gone, and you are in a darkness that never saw the sun." Normal daylight consciousness extinguished, you feel a "timeless dissociation from every concern and requirement of the upper world that you have left behind."[1] Before reaching the first of the caves decorated by our Palaeolithic ancestors in the Stone Age, seventeen thousand years ago, visitors have to stumble for some eighty feet down a sloping tunnel, sixty-five feet below ground level, penetrating ever more deeply into the bowels of the earth. Then the guide suddenly turns the beam of his flashlight onto the ceiling, and the painted animals seem to emerge from the depths of the rock. A strange beast with gravid belly and long pointed horns walks behind a line of wild cattle, horses, deer, and bulls that seem simultaneously in motion and at rest.

In all there are about six hundred frescoes and fifteen hundred engravings in the Lascaux labyrinth. There is a powerful bellowing black stag, a leaping cow, and a procession of horses moving in the opposite direction. At the entrance to another long passage known as the Nave, a frieze of elegant deer has been painted above a rocky ledge so that they appear to be swimming. We see these images far more clearly than the Palaeolithic artists did, since they had to work by the light of small flickering lamps, perched precariously on scaffolding that has left holes in the surface of the wall. They often painted new pictures over old images, even though there was ample space nearby. It seems that location was crucial and that, for reasons we cannot fathom, some places were deemed more suitable than others. The subject matter was also governed by rules that we can never hope to understand. The artists selected only a few of the species known to them, and there are no pictures of the reindeer on which they relied for food.[2] Animals are consistently paired—oxen and bison with horses, bison with mammoths—in combinations that would not occur in real life.[3] Lascaux is not unique. There are about three hundred decorated caves in this region of southern France and northern Spain. In some the artwork is more elementary, but in all these caverns the imagery and layout are basically the same. The earliest site, at Grosse Chauvet, dates from about 30,000 BCE, a time when *Homo sapiens* seems to have undergone an abrupt evolutionary change in this locality. There was a dramatic rise in population, which may have resulted in social tension. Some historians believe that the cave art records a "corpus of socially constructed rituals ... for conflict control ... pictorially encoded for storage and transmission through generations."[4] But the paintings also express an intensely aesthetic appreciation of the natural world. Here we have the earliest known evidence of an ideological system, which remained in place for some twenty thousand years, after which the caves fell into disuse in about 9000 BCE.[5]

It is now generally agreed that these labyrinths were sacred places for the performance of some kind of ritual. Some historians have argued that their purpose was purely pragmatic, but their upkeep alone would have required an immense amount of unproductive labor. Some of these sites were so deep that it took hours to reach their innermost core. Visiting the caves was dangerous, exhausting, uneconomical, and time-consuming. The general consensus is that the caves were sanctuaries and that, as in any temple, their iconography reflected a vision that was radically different from that of the outside world.[6] We do not build temples like this in the modern West. Our worldview is predominantly rational, and we think more easily in concepts than images. We find it hard enough to decode the symbolism of a medieval cathedral such as the one in Chartres, so these Palaeolithic shrines offer an almost insurmountable challenge.

But there are a few clues to aid our understanding. A remarkable picture, dated to about 12,000 BCE, in a cave at Lascaux known as the Crypt because it is even deeper than the other caverns, depicts a large bison that has been eviscerated by a spear thrust through its hindquarters. Lying in front of the wounded beast is a man, drawn in a far more rudimentary style than the animals, with arms outstretched, phallus erect, and wearing what seems to be a bird mask; his staff, which lies on the ground nearby, is also topped by a bird's head. This seems to be an illustration of a well-known legend and could have been the founding myth of the sanctuary. The same scene appears on an engraved reindeer horn at nearby Villars and on a sculpted block in a cliff shelter at Roc de Sers near Limoges, which is five thousand years older than the Lascaux painting.[7] Fifty-five similar images in the other caves and three more Palaeolithic rock drawings in Africa have been found, all showing men confronting animals in a state of trance with upraised arms.[8] They are probably shamans.

We know that shamanism developed in Africa and Europe during the Palaeolithic period and that it spread to Siberia and thence to America and Australia, where the shaman is still the chief religious practitioner among the indigenous hunting peoples. Even though they have inevitably been influenced by neighboring civilizations, many of the original structures of these societies, which were arrested at a stage similar to that of the Palaeolithic, remained intact until the late nineteenth century.[9] Today there is a remarkable continuity in the descriptions of the shaman's ecstatic flight all the way from Siberia, through the Americas to Tierra del Fuego:[10] he swoons during a public stance and believes that he flies through the air to consult the gods about the location of game. In these traditional societies, hunters do not feel that the species are distinct or permanent categories: men can become animals and animals human. Shamans have bird and animal guardians and can converse with the beasts that are revered as messengers of higher powers.[11] The shaman's vision gives meaning to the hunting and killing of animals on which these societies depend.

The hunters feel profoundly uneasy about slaughtering the beasts, who are their friends and patrons, and to assuage this anxiety, they surround the hunt with taboos and prohibitions. They say that long ago the animals made a covenant with humankind and now a god known as the Animal Master regularly sends flocks from the lower world to be killed on the hunting plains, because the hunters promised to perform the rites that will give them posthumous life. Hunters often abstain from sex before an expedition, hunt in a state of ritual purity, and feel a deep empathy with their prey. In the Kalahari Desert, where wood is scarce, the Bushmen have to rely on light weapons that can only graze the skin, so they anoint their arrows with a lethal poison that kills the animal very slowly. A tribesman has to remain with his victim, crying when it cries and participating symbolically in its death throes. Other tribes identify with their prey by donning animal costumes. After stripping the meat from the bones, some reconstruct their kill by laying out its skeleton and pelt; others bury these inedible remains, symbolically restoring the beast to the netherworld from which it came.[12]

The hunters of the Palaeolithic age may have had a similar worldview. Some of the myths and rites they devised appear to have survived in the traditions of later, literate cultures. Animal sacrifice, for example, the central rite of nearly every religious system in antiquity, preserved prehistoric hunting ceremonies and continued to honor a beast that gave its life for the sake of humankind.[13] One of the functions of ritual is to evoke an anxiety in such a way that the community is forced to confront and control it. From the very beginning, it seems, religious life was rooted in acknowledgment of the tragic fact that life depends upon the destruction of other creatures.

The Palaeolithic caves may have been the scene of similar rites. Some of the paintings include dancing men dressed as animals. The Bushmen say that their own rock paintings depict "the world behind this one that we see with our eyes," which the shamans visit during their mystical flights.[14] They smear the walls of the caves with the blood, excrement, and fat of their kill in order to restore it, symbolically, to the earth; animal blood and fat were ingredients of the Palaeolithic paints, and the act of painting itself could have been a ritual of restoration.[15] The images may depict the eternal, archetypal animals that take temporary physical form in the upper world.[16] All ancient religion was based on what has been called the perennial philosophy, because it was present in some form in so many premodern cultures. It sees every single person, object, or experience as a replica of a reality in a sacred world that is more effective and enduring than our own.[17] When an Australian Aborigine hunts his prey, he feels wholly at one with First Hunter, caught up in a richer and more potent reality that makes him feel fully alive and complete.[18] Maybe the hunters of Lascaux re-enacted the archetypal hunt in the caves amid these paintings of the eternal hunting ground before they left their tribe to embark on the perilous quest for food.[19]

We can, of course, only speculate. Some scholars believe that these caverns were likely to have been used for the initiation ceremonies that marked the adolescent boy's rite of passage from childhood to maturity. This type of initiation was crucial in ancient religion and is still practiced in traditional societies today.[20] When they reach puberty, boys are taken from their mothers and put through frightening ordeals that transform them into men. The tribe cannot afford the luxury of allowing an adolescent to "find himself" Western-style; he has to relinquish the dependency of infancy and assume the burdens of adulthood overnight. To this end, boys are incarcerated in tombs, buried in the earth, informed that they are about to be eaten by a monster, flogged, circumcised, and tattooed. If the initiation is properly conducted, a youth will be forced to reach for inner resources that he did not know he possessed. Psychologists tell us that the terror of such an experience causes a regressive disorganization of the personality that, if skillfully handled, can lead to a constructive reorganization of the young man's powers. He has faced death, come out the other side, and is now psychologically prepared to risk his life for his people.

But the purpose of the ritual is not simply to turn him into an efficient killing machine; rather, it is to train him to kill in the sacred manner. A boy is usually introduced to the more esoteric mythology of his tribe during his initiation. He first hears about the Animal Master, the covenant, the magnanimity of the beasts, and the rituals that will restore his life while he is undergoing these traumatic rites. In these extraordinary circumstances, separated from everything familiar, he is pushed into a new state of consciousness that enables him to appreciate the profound bond that links hunter and prey in their common struggle for survival. This is not the kind of knowledge we acquire by purely logical deliberations, but is akin to the understanding derived from art. A poem, a play, or, indeed, a great painting has the power to change our perception in ways that we may not be able to explain logically but that seem incontestably true. We find that things that appear distinct to the rational eye are in some way profoundly connected or that a perfectly commonplace object—a chair, a sunflower, or a pair of boots—has numinous significance. Art involves our emotions, but if it is to be more than a superficial epiphany, this new insight must go deeper than feelings that are, by their very nature, ephemeral.

If the historians are right about the function of the Lascaux caves, religion and art were inseparable from the very beginning. Like art, religion is an attempt to construct meaning in the face of the relentless pain and injustice of life. As meaning-seeking creatures, men and women fall very easily into despair. They have created religions and works of art to help them find value in their lives, despite all the dispiriting evidence to the contrary. The initiation experience also shows that a myth, like that of the Animal Master, derives much of its meaning from the ritualized context in which it is imparted.[21] It may not be empirically true, it may defy the laws of logic, but a good myth will tell us something valuable about the human predicament. Like any work of art, a myth will make no sense unless we open ourselves to it wholeheartedly and allow it to change us. If we hold ourselves aloof, it will remain opaque, incomprehensible, and even ridiculous.

Religion is hard work. Its insights are not self-evident and have to be cultivated in the same way as an appreciation of art, music, or poetry must be developed. The intense effort required is especially evident in the underground labyrinth of Trois Frères at Ariège in the Pyrenees. Doctor Herbert Kuhn, who visited the site in 1926, twelve years after its discovery, described the frightening experience of crawling through the tunnel—scarcely a foot high in some places—that leads to the heart of this magnificent Palaeolithic sanctuary. "I felt as though I were creeping through a coffin," he recalled. "My heart is pounding and it is difficult to breathe. It is terrible to have the roof so close to one's head." He could hear the other members of his party groaning as they struggled through the darkness, and when they finally arrived in the vast underground hall, it felt "like a redemption."[22] They found themselves gazing at a wall covered in spectacular engravings: mammoths, bison, wild horses, wolverines, and musk oxen; darts flying everywhere; blood spurting from the mouths of the bears; and a human figure clad in animal skin playing a flute. Dominating the scene was a large painted figure, half man, half beast, who fixed his huge, penetrating eyes on the visitors. Was this the Animal Master? Or did this hybrid creature symbolize the underlying unity of animal and human, natural and divine?

A boy would not be expected to "believe" in the Animal Master before he entered the caves. But at the culmination of his ordeal, this image would have made a powerful impression; for hours he had, perhaps, fought his way through nearly a mile of convoluted passages to the accompaniment of "songs, cries, noises or mysterious objects thrown from no one knows where," special effects that would have been "easy to arrange in such a place."[23] In archaic thinking, there is no concept of the supernatural, no huge gulf separating human and divine. If a priest donned the sacred regalia of an animal pelt to impersonate the Animal Master, he became a temporary manifestation of that divine power.[24] These rituals were not the expression of a "belief" that had to be accepted in blind faith. As the German scholar Walter Burkert explains, it is pointless to look for an idea or doctrine *behind* a rite. In the premodern world, ritual was not the product of religious ideas; on the contrary, these ideas were the product of ritual.[25] *Homo religiosus* is pragmatic in this sense only; if a ritual no longer evokes a profound conviction of life's ultimate value, he simply abandons it. But for twenty thousand years, the hunters of the region continued to thread their way through the dangerous pathways of Trois Frères in order to bring their mythology—whatever it was—to life. They must have found the effort worthwhile or they would, without a backward glance, have given it up.

Religion was not something tacked on to the human condition, an optional extra imposed on people by unscrupulous priests. The desire to cultivate a sense of the transcendent may be *the* defining human characteristic. In about 9000 BCE, when human beings developed agriculture and were no longer dependent on animal meat, the old hunting rites lost some of their appeal and people ceased to visit the caves. But they did not discard religion altogether. Instead they developed a new set of myths and rituals based on the fecundity of the soil that filled the men and women of the Neolithic age with religious awe.[26] Tilling the fields became a ritual that replaced the hunt, and the nurturing Earth took the place of the Animal Master. Before the modern period, most men and women were naturally inclined to religion and they were prepared to work at it. Today many of us are no longer willing to make this effort, so the old myths seem arbitrary, remote, and incredible.

Like art, the truths of religion require the disciplined cultivation of a different mode of consciousness. The cave experience always began with the disorientation of utter darkness, which annihilated normal habits of mind. Human beings are so constituted that periodically they seek out *ekstasis,* a "stepping outside" the norm. Today people who no longer find it in a religious setting resort to other outlets: music, dance, art, sex, drugs, or sport. We make a point of seeking out these experiences that touch us deeply within and lift us momentarily beyond ourselves. At such times, we feel that we inhabit our humanity more fully than usual and experience an enhancement of being.

Lascaux may seem impossibly distant from modern religious practice, but we cannot understand either the nature of the religious quest or our current religious predicament unless we appreciate the spirituality that emerged quite early in the history of *Homo religiosus* and continued to animate the major confessional traditions until the early modern period, when an entirely different kind of religiosity emerged in the West during the seventeenth century. To do that we must examine a number of core principles that will be of fundamental importance to our story.

The first concerns the nature of the ultimate reality—later called God, Nirvana, Brahman, or Dao. In a rocky overhang at Laussel, near Lascaux, there is a small stone relief that is seventeen thousand years old and was created at about the same time as the earliest of the nearby cave paintings. It depicts a woman holding a curved bison's horn above her head so that it immediately suggests the rising, crescent moon; her right hand lies on her pregnancy. By this time, people had begun to observe the phases of the moon for practical purposes, but their religion had little or nothing to do with this protoscientific observation of the physical cosmos.[27] Instead, material reality was symbolic of an unseen dimension of existence. The little Venus of Laussel already suggests an association between the moon, the female cycle, and human reproduction. In many parts of the world, the moon was linked symbolically with a number of apparently unrelated phenomena: women, water, vegetation, serpents, and fertility. What they all have in common is the regenerative power of life that is continually able to renew itself. Everything could so easily lapse into nothingness, yet each year after the death of winter, trees sprout new leaves, the moon wanes but always waxes brilliantly once more, and the serpent, a universal symbol of initiation, sloughs off its old withered skin and comes forth gleaming and fresh.[28] The female also manifested this inexhaustible power. Ancient hunters revered a goddess known as the Great Mother. In large stone reliefs at Çatalhüyük in Turkey, she is shown giving birth, flanked by boars' skulls and bulls' horns—relics of a successful hunt. While hunters and animals died in the grim struggle for survival, the female was endlessly productive of new life.[29]

Perhaps these ancient societies were trying to express their sense of what the German philosopher Martin Heidegger (1899–1976) called "Being," a fundamental energy that supports and animates everything that exists. Being is transcendent. You could not see, touch, or hear it but could only watch it at work in the people, objects, and natural forces around you. From the documents of later Neolithic and pastoral societies, we know that Being rather than *a* being was revered as the ultimate sacred power. It was impossible to define or describe because Being is all-encompassing and our minds are only equipped to deal with particular beings, which can merely participate in it in a restricted manner. But certain objects became eloquent symbols of the power of Being, which sustained and shone through them with particular clarity. A stone or a rock (frequent symbols of the sacred) expressed the stability and durability of Being; the moon, its power of endless renewal; the sky, its towering transcendence, ubiquity, and universality.[30] None of these symbols was worshipped for and in itself. People did not bow down and worship a rock *tout court*; the rock was simply a focus that directed their attention to the mysterious essence of life. Being bound all things together; humans, animals, plants, insects, stars, and birds all shared the divine life that sustained the entire cosmos. We know, for example, that the ancient Aryan tribes, who had lived on the Caucasian steppes since about 4500 BCE, revered an invisible, impersonal force within themselves and all other natural phenomena. Everything was a manifestation of this all-pervading "Spirit" (Sanskrit: *manya*).[31]

There was, therefore, no belief in a single supreme being in the ancient world. Any such creature could only be *a* being—bigger and better than anything else, perhaps, but still a finite, incomplete reality. People felt it natural to imagine a race of spiritual beings of a higher nature than themselves that they called "gods." There were, after all, many unseen forces at work in the world—wind, heat, emotion, and air—that were often identified with the various deities. The Aryan god Agni, for example, *was* the fire that had transformed human life, and as a personalized god symbolized the deep affinity people felt with these sacred forces. The Aryans called their gods "the shining ones" *(devas)* because Spirit shone through them more brightly than through mortal creatures, but these gods had no control over the world: they were not omniscient and were obliged, like everything else, to submit to the transcendent order that kept everything in existence, set the stars on their courses, made the seasons follow each other, and compelled the seas to remain within bounds.[32]

By the tenth century BCE, when some of the Aryans had settled in the Indian subcontinent, they gave a new name to the ultimate reality. Brahman was the unseen principle that enabled all things to grow and flourish. It was a power that was higher, deeper, and more fundamental than the gods. Because it transcended the limitations of personality, it would be entirely inappropriate to pray to Brahman or expect it to answer your prayers. Brahman was the sacred energy that held all the disparate elements of the world together and prevented it from falling apart. Brahman had an infinitely greater degree of reality than mortal creatures, whose lives were limited by ignorance, sickness, pain, and death.[33] You could never define Brahman because language refers only to individual beings and Brahman was "the All"; it was everything that existed, as well as the inner meaning of all existence.

Even though human beings could not think about the Brahman, they had intimations of it in the hymns of the Rig Veda, the most important of the Aryan scriptures. Unlike the hunters of Lascaux, the Aryans do not seem to have thought readily in images. One of their chief symbols of the divine was sound, whose power and intangible quality seemed a particularly apt embodiment of the all-pervasive Brahman. When the priest chanted the Vedic hymns, the music filled the air and entered the consciousness of the congregation so that they felt surrounded by and infused with divinity. These hymns, revealed to ancient "seers" *(rishis),* did not speak of doctrines that the faithful were obliged to believe, but referred to the old myths in an allusive, riddling fashion because the truth they were trying to convey could not be contained in a neatly logical presentation. Their beauty shocked the audience into a state of awe, wonder, fear, and delight. They had to puzzle out the underlying significance of these paradoxical poems that yoked together apparently unrelated things, just as the hidden Brahman pulled the disparate elements of the universe into a coherent whole.[34]

During the tenth century, the Brahmin priests developed the Brahmodya competition, which would become a model of authentic religious discourse.[35] The contestants began by going on a retreat in the forest, where they performed spiritual exercises, such as fasting and breath control, that concentrated their minds and induced a different type of consciousness. Then the contest could begin. Its goal was to find a verbal formula to define the Brahman, in the process pushing language as far as it could go, until it finally broke down and people became vividly aware of the ineffable, the other. The challenger asked an enigmatic question, and his opponent had to reply in a way that was apt but equally inscrutable. The winner was the contestant who reduced his opponents to silence—and in that moment of silence, when language revealed its inadequacy, the Brahman was present; it became manifest only in the stunning realization of the impotence of speech.

The ultimate reality was not a personalized god, therefore, but a transcendent mystery that could never be plumbed. The Chinese called it the Dao, the fundamental "Way" of the cosmos. Because it comprised the whole of reality, the Dao had no qualities, no form; it could be experienced but never seen; it was not a god; it predated heaven and earth and was beyond divinity. You could not say anything about the Dao, because it transcended ordinary categories: it was more ancient than antiquity and yet it was not old; because it went far beyond any form of "existence" known to humans, it was neither being nor nonbeing.[36] It contained all the myriad patterns, forms, and potential that made the world the way it was and guided the endless flux of change and becoming that we see all around us. It existed at a point where all the distinctions that characterize our normal modes of thought became irrelevant.

In the Middle East, the region in which the Western monotheisms would develop, there was a similar notion of the ultimate. In Mesopotamia, the

Akkadian word for "divinity" was *ilam,* a radiant power that transcended any particular deity. The gods were not the source of *ilam* but, like everything else, could only reflect it. The chief characteristic of this "divinity" was *ellu* ("holiness"), a word that had connotations of "brightness," "purity," and "luminosity." The gods were called the "holy ones" because their symbolic stories, effigies, and cults evoked the radiance of *ellu* within their worshippers. The people of Israel called their patronal deity, the "holy one" of Israel, Elohim, a Hebrew variant on *ellu* that summed up everything that the divine could mean for human beings. But holiness was not confined to the gods. Anything that came into contact with divinity could become holy too: a priest, a king, or a temple—even the sacred utensils of the cult. In the Middle East, people would have found it far too constricting to limit *ilam* to a single god; instead, they imagined a Divine Assembly, a council of gods of many different ranks, who worked together to sustain the cosmos and expressed the multifaceted complexity of the sacred.[37]

People felt a yearning for the absolute, intuited its presence all around them, and went to great lengths to cultivate their sense of this transcendence in creative rituals. But they also felt estranged from it. Almost every culture has developed a myth of a lost paradise from which men and women were ejected at the beginning of time. It expressed an inchoate conviction that life was not *meant* to be so fragmented, hard, and full of pain. There *must* have been a time when people had enjoyed a greater share in the fullness of being and had not been subject to sorrow, disease, bereavement, loneliness, old age, and death. This nostalgia informed the cult of "sacred geography," one of the oldest and most universal religious ideas. Certain places that stood out in some way from the norm—like the labyrinthine caverns of the Dordogne—seemed to speak of "something else."[38] The sacred place was one of the earliest and most ubiquitous symbols of the divine. It was a sacred "center" that brought heaven and earth together and where the divine potency seemed particularly effective.

A popular image, found in many cultures, imagined this fructifying, sacred energy welling up like a spring from these focal places and flowing, in four sacred rivers, to the four quarters of the earth. People would settle only in sites where the sacred had once become manifest because they wanted to live as closely as possible to the wellsprings of being and become as whole and complete as they had been before they were ejected from paradise.

This brings us to the second principle of premodern religion. Religious discourse was not intended to be understood literally because it was only possible to speak about a reality that transcended language in symbolic terms. The story of the lost paradise was a myth, not a factual account of a historical event People were not expected to "believe" it in the abstract; like any *mythos,* it depended upon the rituals associated with the cult of a particular holy place to make what it signified a reality in the lives of participants.

The same applies to the creation myth that was central to ancient religion and has now become controversial in the Western world because the Genesis story seems to clash with modern science. But until the early modern period, nobody read a cosmology as a literal account of the origins of life. In the ancient world, it was inspired by an acute sense of the contingency and frailty of existence. Why had anything come into being at all, when there could so easily have been nothing? There has never been a simple or even a possible answer to this question, but people continue to ask it, pushing their minds to the limit of what we can know. One of the earliest and most universal of the ancient cosmologies is particularly instructive to us today. It was thought that one of the gods, known as the "High God" or "Sky God" because he dwelt in the farthest reaches of the heavens, had single-handedly created heaven and earth.[39] The Aryans called him Dyaeus Pitr, the Chinese Tian ("Heaven"), the Arabians Allah ("*the* God"), and the Syrians El Elyon ("Most High God"). But the High God proved to be an unviable deity, and his myth was jettisoned.

It suffered from an internal contradiction. How could a mere being—even such a lofty one—be responsible for being itself? As if in response to this objection, people tried to elevate the High God to a special plane. He was considered too exalted for an ordinary cult: no sacrifices were performed in his honor; he had no priests, no temples, and virtually no mythology of his own. People called on him in an emergency, but otherwise he scarcely ever impinged on their daily lives. Reduced to a mere explanation—to what would later be called First Cause or Prime Mover—he became *Deus otiosus,* a "useless" or "superfluous" deity, and gradually faded from the consciousness of his people. In most mythologies, the High God is often depicted as a passive, helpless figure; unable to control events, he retreats to the periphery of the pantheon and finally fades away. Today some of the indigenous peoples—Pygmies, Aboriginal Australians, and Fuegians—also speak of a High God who created heaven and earth, but, they tell anthropologists, he has died or disappeared; he "no longer cares" and "has gone far away from us."[40]

No god can survive unless he or she is actualized by the practical activity of ritual, and people often turn against gods who fail to deliver. The High God is often mythologically deposed, sometimes violently, by a younger generation of more dynamic deities—gods of storm, grain, or war—who symbolized relevant, important realities. In Greek *mythos,* the High God Uranus ("Heaven") was brutally castrated by his son Kronos. Later Kronos himself was overthrown by his own son Zeus, head of the younger gods, who lived more accessibly on Mount Olympus. In our own day, the God of the monotheistic tradition has often degenerated into a High God. The rites and practices that once made him a persuasive symbol of the sacred are no longer effective, and people have stopped participating in them. He has therefore become *otiosus,* an etiolated reality who for all intents and purposes has indeed died or "gone away."

In the ancient world, the High God myth was replaced by more relevant creation stories that were never regarded as factual. As one of the later hymns of the Rig Veda insists, nobody—not even the highest *deva*—could explain how something had issued from nothing.[41] A good creation myth did not describe an event in the distant past but told people something essential about the present. It reminded them that things often had to get worse before they got better, that creativity demanded self-sacrifice and heroic struggle, and that everybody had to work hard to preserve the energies of the cosmos and establish society on a sound foundation. A creation story was primarily therapeutic. People wanted to tap into the massive implosion of energy that had—somehow—brought the world we know into being, so they would recite a creation myth when they were in need of an infusion of sacred potency: during a political crisis, at a sickbed, or when they were building a new house. The creation myth was often re-enacted during the New Year ceremonies, when the old year was ebbing away. Nobody felt obliged to "believe" in a particular cosmology; indeed, each culture usually had several creation stories, each of which had its own lesson to impart, and people thought nothing of making up a new one if their circumstances changed.

Once people had abandoned the myth of the High God, there was no concept of creation "out of nothing" (*ex nihilo*) in the ancient world. A god could only assist a creative process that was already well under way. In the tenth century, another Indian *rishi* suggested that the world had been set in motion by a primordial sacrifice—something that made sense in India, where new vegetation was often seen to sprout from a rotting tree so that it was not unnatural to think of death resulting in new life. The *rishi* imagined the Purusha ("Person"), the first, archetypal human being, striding of his own free will to the place of sacrifice and allowing the gods to put him to death; thence everything—animals, horses, cattle, heaven, earth, sun, moon, and even some of the gods—emerged from his corpse.[42] This *mythos* encapsulated an important truth: we are at our most creative when we do not cling to our selfhood but are prepared to give ourselves away.

The cosmology was not influenced by current scientific speculation because it was exploring the interior rather than the external world. The priests of Mesopotamia undertook the first successful astronomical observations, noting that the seven celestial bodies they sighted—later known as Sun, Moon, Mercury, Venus, Mars, Jupiter, and Saturn—moved in an apparently circular path through the constellations. But the chief inspiration behind their creation myth was their pioneering town planning.[43] The first cities had been established in Sumer in the Fertile Crescent in about 3500 BCE; it was an enterprise that required enormous courage and perseverance, as time and time again, the mud-brick buildings were swept away by the flooding of the Tigris and the Euphrates. Constantly it seemed that the Sumerians' fragile urban civilization would sink back into the old rural barbarism, so the city needed a regular infusion of sacred energy. And yet it seemed such an extraordinary achievement that the city was extolled as a holy place. Babylon was the "Gate of the gods" *(Babi-lani),* where heaven and earth could meet; it re-created the lost paradise, and the ziggurat, or temple tower, of Esagila replicated the cosmic mountain or the sacred tree, which the first men and women had climbed to meet their gods.[44]

It is difficult to understand the creation story in Genesis without reference to the Mesopotamian creation hymn known from its opening words as the *Enuma Elish*. This poem begins by describing the evolution of the gods from primordial sacred matter and their subsequent creation of heaven and earth, but it is also a meditation on contemporary Mesopotamia. The raw material of the universe, from which the gods emerge, is a sloppy, undefined substance—very like the silty soil of the region. The first gods—Tiamat, the primal Ocean; Apsu, the "Abyss"; and Mummu, "Womb" of chaos—were inseparable from the elements and shared the inertia of aboriginal barbarism and the formlessness of chaos: "When sweet and bitter mingled together, no reed was plaited, no rushes muddied the water, the gods were nameless, natureless, futureless."[45] But new gods emerged, each pair more distinct than the last, culminating in the splendid Marduk, the Sun God and the most developed specimen of the divine species. But Marduk could not establish the cosmos until he had overcome the sluggish torpor of Tiamat in a tremendous battle. Finally he stood astride Tiamat's massive carcass, split her in two to make heaven and earth, and created the first man by mixing the blood of one of the defeated gods with a handful of dust. After this triumph, the gods could build the city of Babylon and establish the ritual "from which the universe receives its structure, the hidden world is made plain, and the gods assigned their places."[46]

There was no ontological gulf separating these gods from the rest of the cosmos; everything had emerged from the same sacred stuff. All beings shared the same predicament and had to participate in a ceaseless battle against the destructive lethargy of chaos. There were similar tales in neighboring Syria, where Baal, god of storm and life-giving rain, had to fight the sea dragon Lotan, symbol of chaos, Yam, the primal sea, and Mot, god of sterility, in order to establish civilized life.[47] The Israelites also told stories of their god Yahweh slaying sea monsters to order the cosmos.[48] In Babylon, the *Enuma Elish* was chanted on the fourth day of the New Year festival in Esagila, a re-enactment that symbolically continued the process Marduk had begun and that activated this sacred energy. There was a ritualized mock battle and a saturnalia that re-created the lawlessness of chaos. In archaic spirituality, a symbolic return to the formless "nothingness" of the beginning was indispensable to any new creation.[49] It was possible to move forward only if you had the courage to let go of the present, unsatisfactory state of affairs, sink back into the potent confusion of the beginning, and begin again.

As life became more settled, people had the leisure to develop a more interior spirituality. The Indian Aryans, always in the vanguard of religious change, pioneered this trend, achieving the groundbreaking discovery that the Brahman, being itself, was also the ground of the human psyche. The transcendent was neither external nor alien to humanity, but the two were inextricably connected. This insight would become central to the religious quest in all the major traditions. In the early Upanishads, composed in the seventh century BCE, the search for this sacred Self *(atman)* became central to Vedic spirituality. The Upanishadic sages did not ask their disciples to "believe" this but put them through an initiation whereby they discovered it for themselves in a series of spiritual exercises that made them look at the world differently. This practically acquired knowledge brought with it a joyous liberation from fear and anxiety.

We have a precious glimpse of the way this initiation was carried out in the Chandogya Upanishad. Here the great sage Uddalaka Aruni slowly and patiently brings this saving insight to birth within his son Shvetaketu and has him perform a series of tasks. In the most famous of these experiments, Shvetaketu had to leave a lump of salt in a beaker of water overnight and found, of course, that even though the salt had dissolved, the water still tasted salty. "You, of course, did not see it there, son," Uddalaka pointed out, "yet it was always right there." So too was the invisible Brahman, essence and inner self of the entire world. "And you are *that,* Shvetaketu."[50] Like the salt, the

Brahman could not be seen but was manifest in every single living thing. It was the subtle essence in the tiny banyan seed, from which a giant tree would grow, yet when Shvetaketu dissected the seed, he could not see anything at all. The Brahman was also the sap in every part of the tree that gave it life, and yet it could never be pinned down or analyzed.[51] All things shared the same essence, but most people did not realize this. They imagined they were unique and special and clung to these particularities—often with extreme anxiety and expenditure of effort. But in reality these qualities were no more durable than rivers that flowed into the same sea. Once they had merged, they became "just the ocean," and no longer asserted their individuality by insisting "I am that river," "I am this river." "In exactly the same way, son," Uddalaka persisted, "when all these creatures reach the Existent, they are not aware that: 'We are reaching the Existent.'" Whether they were tigers, wolves, or gnats, they all merged into Brahman. To hold on to the mundane self, therefore, was a delusion that led inescapably to pain, frustration, and confusion, which one could escape only by acquiring the deep, liberating knowledge that the Brahman was their atman, the truest thing about them.[52]

The Upanishadic sages were among the first to articulate another of the universal principles of religion—one that had already been touched upon in the Purusha myth. The truths of religion are accessible only when you are prepared to get rid of the selfishness, greed, and self-preoccupation that, perhaps inevitably, are ingrained in our thoughts and behavior but are also the source of so much of our pain. The Greeks would call this process *kenosis*, "emptying." Once you gave up the nervous craving to promote yourself, denigrate others, draw attention to your unique and special qualities, and ensure that you were first in the pecking order, you experienced an immense peace. The first Upanishads were written at a time when the Aryan communities were in the early stages of urbanization; *logos* had enabled them to master their environment. But the sages reminded them that there were some things—old age, sickness, and death—that they could not control; things—such as their essential self—that lay beyond their intellectual grasp. When, as a result of carefully crafted spiritual exercises, people learned not only to accept but to embrace this unknowing, they found that they experienced a sense of release.

The sages began to explore the complexities of the human psyche with remarkable sophistication; they had discovered the unconscious long before Freud. But the atman, the deepest core of their personality, eluded them. Precisely *because* it was identical with the Brahman, it was indefinable. The atman had nothing to do with our normal psycho-mental states and bore no resemblance to anything in our ordinary experience, so you could speak of it only in negative terms. As the seventh-century sage Yajnavalkya explained: "About this Self [atman] one can only say 'not ... not' [neti ... neti]."[53]

> You can't see the Seer who does the seeing. You can't hear the Hearer who does the hearing; you can't think with the Thinker who does the thinking; and you can't perceive the Perceiver who does the perceiving. This Self within the All [Brahman] is this *atman* of yours.[54]

Like the Brahmodya, any discussion of the atman in the Upanishads always ended in silence, the numinous acknowledgment that the ultimate reality was beyond the competence of language.

Authentic religious discourse could not lead to clear, distinct, and empirically verified truth. Like the Brahman, the atman was "ungraspable." You could define something only when you saw it as separate from yourself. But "when the Whole [Brahman] has become a person's very self, then who is there for him to see and by what means? Who is there for me to think of and by what means?"[55] But if you learned to "realize" the truth that your most authentic "Self was identical with Brahman, you understood that it too was "beyond hunger and thirst, sorrow and delusion, old age and death."[56] You could not achieve this insight by rational logic. You had to acquire the knack of thinking outside the ordinary "lowercase" self, and like any craft or skill, this required long, hard, dedicated practice.

One of the principal technologies that enabled people to achieve this self-forgetfulness was yoga.[57] Unlike the yoga practiced in Western gyms today, it was not an aerobic exercise but a systematic breakdown of instinctive behavior and normal thought patterns. It was mentally demanding and, initially, physically painful. The yogin had to do the opposite of what came naturally. He sat so still that he seemed more like a plant or a statue than a human being; he controlled his respiration, one of the most automatic and essential of our physical functions, until he acquired the ability to exist for long periods without breathing at all. He learned to silence the thoughts that coursed through his mind and concentrate "on one point" for hours at a time. If he persevered, he found that he achieved a dissolution of ordinary consciousness that extracted the "I" from his thinking.

To this day, yogins find that these disciplines, which have measurable physical and neurological effects, evoke a sense of calm, harmony, and equanimity that is comparable to the effect of music. There is a feeling of expansiveness and bliss, which yogins regard as entirely natural, possible for anybody who has the talent and application. As the "I" disappears, the most humdrum objects reveal wholly unexpected qualities since they are no longer viewed through the distorting filter of one's own egotistic needs and desires. When she meditated on the teachings of her guru, a yogin did not simply accept them notionally but experienced them so vividly that her knowledge was, as the texts say, "direct"; bypassing the logical processes like any practically acquired skill, it had become part of her inner world.[58]

But yoga also had an ethical dimension. A beginner was not allowed to perform a single yogic exercise until he had completed an intensive moral program. Top of the list of its requirements was *ahimsa*, "nonviolence." A yogin must not swat a mosquito, make an irritable gesture, or speak unkindly to others but should maintain constant affability to all, even the most annoying monk in the community. Until his guru was satisfied that this had become second nature, a yogin could not even sit in the yogic position. A great deal of the aggression, frustration, hostility, and rage that mars our peace of mind is the result of thwarted egotism, but when the aspiring yogin became proficient in this selfless equanimity, the texts tell us that he would experience "indescribable joy."[59] Their experience of yoga led the sages to devise a new creation myth.

In the beginning, there was only a single Person, who looked around him and discovered that he was alone. In this way, he became aware of himself and cried: "Here I am!" Thus the "I," the ego principle, was born. Immediately the Person became afraid, because we instinctively feel that we must protect the fragile ego from anything that threatens it, but when the Person remembered that because he was alone, there was no such threat, his fear left him. But he was lonely, so he split his body in two to create a man and a woman, who together gave birth to every single being in the cosmos "down to the very ants." And the Person realized that even though he was no longer alone, there was still nothing to fear. Was he not identical with Brahman, the All? He was one with all the things that he had made; indeed, he was himself his own creation.[60] He had even created the gods, who were essentially a part of himself.[61]

Even now, if a man knows "I am *brahman*" in this way, he becomes this whole world. Not even the gods are able to prevent it, for he becomes their very self [atman]. So when a man venerates another deity, thinking, "He is one, and I am another," he does not understand.[62] This insight, Yajnavalkya explained, brought with it a joy comparable to that of sexual intercourse, when one loses all sense of duality and is "oblivious to everything within or without."[63] But you would not have this experience unless you had performed the yogic exercises. Other traditions would also find that these fundamental principles were indispensable: Buddhism, Jainism, Confucianism, and Daoism, as well as the three monotheistic faiths of Judaism, Christianity, and Islam. Each had its own unique genius and distinctive vision, each its peculiar flaws. But on these central principles they would all agree. Religion was not a notional matter. The Buddha, for example, had little time for theological speculation. One of his monks was a philosopher manqué and, instead of getting on with his yoga, constantly pestered the Buddha about metaphysical questions: Was there a god? Had the world been created in time or had it always existed? The Buddha told him that he was like a man who had been shot with a poisoned arrow and refused medical treatment until he had discovered the name of his assailant and what village he came from. He would die before he got this perfectly useless information. What difference would it make to discover that a god had created the world? Pain, hatred, grief, and sorrow would still exist. These issues were fascinating, but the Buddha refused to discuss them because they were irrelevant: "My disciples, they will not help you, they are not useful in the quest for holiness; they do not lead to peace and to the direct knowledge of Nirvana."[64]

The Buddha always refused to define Nirvana, because it could not be understood notionally and would be inexplicable to anybody who did not undertake his practical regimen of meditation and compassion. But anybody who did commit him- or herself to the Buddhist way of life could attain Nirvana, which was an entirely natural state.[65] Sometimes, however, Buddhists would speak of Nirvana using the same kind of imagery as monotheists use for God: it was the "Truth," the "Other Shore," "Peace," the "Everlasting," and "the Beyond." Nirvana was a still center that gave meaning to life, an oasis of calm, and a source of strength that you discovered in the depths of your own being. In purely mundane terms, it was "nothing," because it corresponded to no reality that we could recognize in our ego-dominated existence. But those who had managed to find this sacred peace discovered that they lived an immeasurably richer life.[66] There was no question of "believing" in the existence of Nirvana or taking it "on faith." The Buddha had no time for abstract doctrinal formulations divorced from action. Indeed, to accept a dogma on somebody else's authority was what he called "unskillful" or "unhelpful" (akusala). It could not lead to enlightenment because it amounted to an abdication of personal responsibility. Faith meant trust that Nirvana existed and a determination to realize it by every practical means in one's power.

Nirvana was the natural result of a life lived according to the Buddha's doctrine of anatta ("no self"), which was not simply a metaphysical principle but, like all his teachings, a program of action. Anatta required Buddhists to behave day by day, hour by hour, as though the self did not exist. Thoughts of "self" not only led to "unhelpful" (akusala) preoccupation with "me" and "mine," but also to envy, hatred of rivals, conceit, pride, cruelty, and—when the self felt under threat—violence. As a monk became expert in cultivating this dispassion, he no longer interjected his ego into passing mental states but learned to regard his fears and desires as transient and remote phenomena. He was then ripe for enlightenment: "His greed fades away, and once his cravings disappear, he experiences the release of the mind."[67] The texts indicate that when the Buddha's first disciples heard about anatta, their hearts were filled with joy and they immediately experienced Nirvana. To live beyond the reach of hatred, greed, and anxieties about our status proved to be a profound relief.

By far the best way of achieving anatta was compassion, the ability to feel with the other, which required that one dethrone the self from the center of one's world and put another there. Compassion would become the central practice of the religious quest. One of the first people to make it crystal clear that holiness was inseparable from altruism was the Chinese sage Confucius (551–479 BCE). He preferred not to speak about the divine because it lay beyond the competence of language, and theological chatter was a distraction from the real business of religion.[68] He used to say: "My Way has one thread that runs right through it." There were no abstruse metaphysics; everything always came back to the importance of treating others with absolute respect.[69] It was epitomized in the Golden Rule, which, he said, his disciples should practice "all day and every day":[70] "Never do to others what you would not like them to do to you."[71] They should look into their own hearts, discover what gave them pain, and then refuse under any circumstance whatsoever to inflict that pain on anybody else.

Religion was a matter of doing rather than thinking. The traditional rituals of China enabled an individual to burnish and refine his humanity so that he became a junzi, a "mature person." A junzi was not born but crafted; he had to work on himself as a sculptor shaped a rough stone and made it a thing of beauty. "How can I achieve this?" asked Yan Hui, Confucius's most talented disciple. It was simple, Confucius replied: "Curb your ego and surrender to ritual (li)."[72] A junzi must submit every detail of his life to the ancient rites of consideration and respect for others. This was the answer to China's political problems: "If a ruler could curb his ego and submit to li for a single day, everyone under Heaven would respond to his goodness."[73]

The practice of the Golden Rule "all day and every day" would bring human beings into the state that Confucius called *ren,* a word that would later be described as "benevolence" but that Confucius himself refused to define because it could be understood only by somebody who had acquired it. He preferred to remain silent about what lay at the end of the religious journey. The practice of *ren* was an end in itself; it was itself the transcendence you sought. Yan Hui expressed this beautifully when he spoke of the endless struggle to achieve *ren* "with a deep sigh."

> The more I strain my gaze towards it, the higher it soars. The deeper I bore down into it, the harder it becomes. I see it in front, but suddenly it is behind. Step by step, the Master skil[l]fully lures one on. He has broadened me with culture, restrained me with ritual. Even if I wanted to stop, I could not. Just when I feel that I have exhausted every resource, something seems to rise up, standing over me sharp and clear. Yet though I long to pursue it, I can find no way of getting to it at all.[74]

Living a compassionate, empathetic life took Yan Hui beyond himself, giving him momentary glimpses of a sacred reality that was not unlike the "God" worshipped by monotheists. It was both immanent and transcendent: it welled up from within but was also experienced as an external presence "standing over me sharp and clear."

Religion as defined by the great sages of India, China, and the Middle East was not a notional activity but a practical one; it did not require belief in a set of doctrines but rather hard, disciplined work, without which any religious teaching remained opaque and incredible. The ultimate reality was not a Supreme Being—an idea that was quite alien to the religious sensibility of antiquity; it was an all-encompassing, wholly transcendent reality that lay beyond neat doctrinal formulations. So religious discourse should not attempt to impart clear information about the divine but should lead to an appreciation of the limits of language and understanding. The ultimate was not alien to human beings but inseparable from our humanity. It could not be accessed by rational, discursive thought but required a carefully cultivated state of mind and the abnegation of selfishness.

NOTES

1. Joseph Campbell, *Primitive Mythology: The Masks of God,* rev. ed. (New York, 1988), p. 305; Joseph Campbell with Bill Moyers, *The Power of Myth* (New York, 1988), p. 79.

2. André Leroi-Gourhan, *Treasures of Prehistoric Art* (New York, n.d.), p. 112. This rules out the suggestion that the paintings were simply a form of hunting magic.

3. Ibid., p. 118.

4. John E. Pfeiffer, *The Creative Explosion* (New York, 1982), p. viii.

5. André Leroi-Gourhan, *Les religions préhistorique: Paléolithique* (Paris, 1964), pp. 83–84; Mircea Eliade, *A History of Religious Ideas,* 3 vols., trans. Willard R. Trask (Chicago and London, 1978, 1982, 1985), 1:16.

6. Joseph Campbell, *Historical Atlas of World Mythologies*, 2 vols. (New York, 1988), 1,1:58.

7. Ibid., 1,1:65.

8. Leo Frobenius, *Kulturgeschichte Africas* (Zurich, 1933), pp. 131–32; Campbell, *Primitive Mythology*, p. 300.

9. Mircea Eliade, *History of Religious Ideas*, 1:24.

10. Joseph Campbell with Bill Moyers, *Power of Myth*, pp. 85–87.

11. Ibid., pp. 72–79; *Historical Atlas*, 1,1:48–49; Mircea Eliade, *History of Religious Ideas*, 1:7–8.

12. Walter Burkert, *Homo Necans: The Anthropology of Ancient Greek Sacrificial Ritual and Myth*, trans. Peter Bing (Berkeley, Los Angeles, and London, 1983), pp. 16–22.

13. Walter Burkert, *Structure and History in Greek Mythology and Ritual* (Berkeley, Los Angeles, and London, 1980), pp. 54–56; Walter Burkert, *Homo Necans*, pp. 42–45.

14. Joseph Campbell, *Historical Atlas*, 1, 2:xiii.

15. Ibid., 1,1:93.

16. Joseph Campbell, *Primitive Mythology*, p. 66.

17. Mircea Eliade, *The Myth of the Eternal Return, or Cosmos and History*, trans. Willard R. Trask (Princeton, N.J., 1954), pp. 1–34.

18. Huston Smith, *The World's Religions*, rev. ed. (New York, 1991), p. 367.

19. Mircea Eliade, *History of Religious Ideas*, 1:17.

20. Mircea Eliade, *Birth and Rebirth: The Religious Meanings of Initiation in Human Cultures* (New York, 1958); Mircea Eliade, *Myths, Dreams and Mysteries: The Encounter between Contemporary Faiths and Archaic Realities*, trans. Philip Mairet (London, 1960), pp. 194–226; Joseph Campbell with Bill Moyers, *Power of Myth*, pp. 81–85.

21. Mircea Eliade, *Myths, Dreams*, p. 225.

22. Herbert Kuhn, *Auf den Spuren des Eiszeitmenschen* (Wiesbaden, 1953), pp. 88–89; Joseph Campbell, *Primitive Mythology*, pp. 307–8.

23. Abbé Henri Breuil, *Four Hundred Centuries of Cave Art* (Montignac, France, 1952), pp. 170–71.

24. Joseph Campbell, *Primitive Mythology*, p. 311.

25. Walter Burkert, *Homo Necans*, pp. 27–34.

26. Mircea Eliade, *Patterns in Comparative Religion*, trans. Rosemary Sheed (London, 1958), pp. 331–43.

27. Alexander Marshack, "Lunar Notations on Upper Palaeolithic Remains," *Scientia* 146 (1964).

28. Mircea Eliade, *Patterns in Comparative Religion*, pp. 146–85.

29. Walter Burkert, *Homo Necans*, pp. 78–82.

30. Mircea Eliade, *Patterns in Comparative Religion*, pp. 1–124, 216–39.

31. Mary Boyce, *Zoroastrians: Their Religious Beliefs and Practices*, 2nd ed. (London and New York, 2001), p. 2; Peter Clark, *Zoroastrians: An Introduction to an Ancient Faith* (Brighton and Portland, Ore., 1998), p. 18.

32. Mary Boyce, *Zoroastrians*, pp. 9–11.

33. Jan Gonda, *Change and Continuity in Indian Religion* (The Hague, 1965), p. 200; Louis Renou, "Sur la notion de *brahman*," *Journal Asiatique* 237 (1949).

34. Louis Renou, *Religions of Ancient India* (London, 1953), pp. 10, 16–18; Michael Witzel, "Vedas and Upanishads" in Gavin Flood, ed., *The Blackwell Companion to Hinduism* (Oxford, 2003), pp. 70–71.

35. J. C. Heesterman, *The Inner Conflict of Tradition: Essays in Indian Ritual, Kingship and Society* (Chicago and London, 1985), pp. 70–72, 126.

36. Zhuangzi, *The Book of Zhuangzi*, 6:29–31.

37. Mark S. Smith, *The Origins of Biblical Monotheism: Israel's Polytheistic Background and the Ugaritic Texts* (New York and London, 2001), pp. 41–79.

38. Mircea Eliade, *Patterns in Comparative Religion*, pp. 367–88; Mircea Eliade, *The Sacred and the Profane: The Nature of Religion*, trans. Willard R. Trask (New York, 1959), pp. 50–54, 64; Mircea Eliade, *Images and Symbols: Studies in Religious Symbolism*, trans. Philip Mairet (Princeton, N.J., 1991), pp. 37–56.

39. Mircea Eliade, *Patterns in Comparative Religion*, pp. 38–63; Mircea Eliade, *Myths, Dreams*, pp. 172–78; Wilhelm Schmidt, *The Origin of the Idea of God* (New York, 1912), passim.

40. Mircea Eliade, *The Sacred and the Profane*, pp. 120–25.

41. Rig Veda 10.129.

42. Rig Veda 10.90.

43. Gwendolyn Leick, *Mesopotamia: The Invention of the City* (London, 2.001), p. 268.

44. Thorkild Jacobsen, "The Cosmos as State," In H. and H. A. Frankfort, eds., *The Intellectual Adventure of Ancient Man: An Essay on the Speculative Thought in the Ancient Near East* (Chicago, 1946), pp. 186–97.

45. "The Babylonian Creation" 1.1 in N. K. Sanders, trans. and ed., *Poems of Heaven and Hell from Ancient Mesopotamia* (London, 1971).

46. *Enuma Elish* 6.19, In Sanders, *Poems of Heaven and Hell*.

47. E. O. James, *The Ancient Gods* (London, 1960), pp. 87–90.

48. Psalms 89:10–13; 93:1–4; Isaiah 27:1; Job 7:12; 9:8; 26:12; 38:7.

49. Mircea Eliade, *Myths, Dreams*, pp. 80–81.

50. Chandogya Upanishad (CU) 6.13; my italics. All quotations from the Upanishads are from Patrick Olivelle, trans. and ed., *Upanisads* (Oxford and New York, 1996).

51. CU6.11–12.

52. CU6.10.

53. Brhadaranyaka Upanishad (BU) 4.5.15.

54. BU3.4.

55. BU4.5.13–15.

56. BU 3.5.1.

57. Mircea Eliade, *Yoga, Immortality and Freedom*, trans. Willard R. Trask (New York, 1958).

58. Women participated in Upanishadic spirituality and, later, in Buddhist practice.

59. Patanjali, Yoga Sutra 2.42, in Eliade, *Yoga*, p. 52.

60. BU 1.4.1–5.

61. BU 1.4.6.

62. BU 1.4.10.

63. BU 4.3.21.

64. Samyutta Nikaya 53:31. The quotations from the Pali Canon of Buddhist scriptures are my own version of the texts cited.

65. Sutta–Nipata 43:1–44.

66. Majjima Nikaya 29.

67. *Vinaya:* Mahavagga 1.6.

68. Confucius, Analects 17.19. Unless otherwise stated, quotations from the Analects are taken from Arthur Waley, trans. and ed., *The Analects of Confucius* (New York, 1992).

69. Analects 4.15.

70. Analects 15.23.

71. Ibid.

72. Analects 12.1. Translation suggested by Benjamin I. Schwartz, *The World of Thought in Ancient China* (Cambridge, Mass., and London, 1985), p. 77.

73. Ibid.

74. Analects 9.10.

QUESTIONS FOR MAKING CONNECTIONS
WITHIN THE READING

1. In "Homo religiosus," Armstrong takes us back to the roots of religion in the Paleolithic era. The portrait she paints might surprise many readers. In "archaic thinking," she argues, "there [was] no concept of the supernatural, no huge gulf separating human and divine." There was "no belief in a single supreme being," and indeed belief itself was beside the point because religion was openly understood as a myth, not a literal truth. Re-read the chapter and carefully note the many differences between religion then and religion now. Next, go back and look for the continuities. In spite of the differences, would you say that much of the Paleolithic legacy survives to this day? Can we conclude that religion has become more mature and sophisticated, or is it possible that we have lost touch with what religion actually represents? Where does Armstrong herself seem to stand on this final question?

2. Whether we are looking at the Middle East, ancient China, or the culture of Aryan peoples who came off the steppes and settled in India, Armstrong insists that religion has been "a matter of doing rather than thinking." But what exactly does she mean by "doing"? What kinds of activities might religion have entailed in ancient times? Start with the ancient shamans whose activities are hinted at by the frescos at Chauvet, and then follow the historical thread until you reach Heidegger. Clearly, religious activities are meant to enhance ordinary life, but at the same time they appear to involve forms of behavior that are quite distinct from everyday existence. How do the mundane and the sacred interact in the history of religious "doing"?

3. One central concern of "Homo Religiosus" is the self in its connections to the universe as a whole. Even though religion in our time is quite commonly understood in terms of a personal relationship with God, Armstrong emphasizes the importance of what the ancient Greeks called *ekstasis*, a "stepping outside the norm," and *kenosis,* the "emptying" of the self. In what way does self-emptying connect the individual with the "sacred energy" of the universe? How might the experience of "nothingness" make people more alive and creative? What gets lost, in Armstrong's view, when we imagine the "ultimate reality" as a "Supreme Being"?

QUESTIONS FOR WRITING

1. According to Armstrong, "All ancient religion was based on what has been called the perennial philosophy, because it was present in some form in so many premodern cultures." To support this claim she looks at religion among such disparate groups as the Australian Aborigines, the ancient Aryans and Chinese, the peoples of the Middle East, and the ancient Greeks. While their belief systems can appear quite dissimilar today, Armstrong points to underlying commonalities. For example, just as the Aryans thought of their gods as *devas* or shining ones, so the forerunners of the Abrahamic faiths—Judaism, Christianity, and Islam—used the world *ilam*, meaning "radiant power," to describe their own deities. What are the implications of these parallels? Have we put so great an emphasis on the differences that we have lost touch with the greater unity? What factors might explain the emphasis on such differences?

2. One theme of Armstrong's recent work has been the distinction between two forms of knowing that she calls *logos* and *mythos.* "Logos" describes a kind of truth that strives for objectivity through the use of critical reason, while "mythos" describes a truth whose purpose is to overcome our subjective sense of separateness from the world and other living beings. Though past societies understood the distinction between the two, Armstrong contends that in our time both skeptics and religious people treat *mythos* as a set of objective claims. After reading "Homo religiosus," would you say that *mythos* should have a place in our lives today? Is it really possible for us to keep *mythos* separate from *logos*? How might the two become confused, and what dangers might rise from confusing them?

QUESTIONS FOR MAKING CONNECTIONS
BETWEEN READINGS

1. In "Waiting for a Jew," Jonathan Boyarin describes the sense of "wholeness" that came from living in a Jewish community in Farmingdale, New Jersey. That sense of wholeness was lost, however, when his family left Farmingdale

and moved to a new town where Jewish observance seemed much less important to the other Jews they met. How would Armstrong explain the sense of wholeness that Boyarin experienced, and how would she explain the feeling of loss? In what ways might Armstrong's chapter help us understand Boyarin's inner journey after college—especially why he later comes to see the wholeness of his childhood as an "illusion"?

2. Armstrong sees religion as "matter of doing" rather than a matter of allegiance to unchanging beliefs. Re-read her chapter and carefully note the many different forms of "doing" she explores, from ritual sacrifice to yoga. In what sense might we understand premodern religion as a form of psychotherapy of the kind practiced today by Martha Stout, author of "When I Woke Up Tuesday Morning, It Was Friday"? Were religious practices possibly designed to overcome dissociated states and the pathologies that they cause? Or does religion actually encourage dissociation? If the answer to this last question is yes, what might be the purpose of turning away from the here and now, at least temporarily?

JONATHAN BOYARIN

JONATHAN BOYARIN IS an anthropologist and an ethnographer who has studied the lifestyle and culture of Jews all over the world. Although the discipline of anthropology originally arose as a way for outsiders to study and understand foreign cultures, the anthropology that Boyarin practices is of a different sort: he is providing an insider's view of cultures and traditions that are, in some ways, his own. For this reason, Boyarin's fieldwork on Jewish identity and tradition in Paris, New York, and Jerusalem is not simply descriptive; instead it is aimed at both defining and preserving Jewish culture. Boyarin's research has led him to participate in the effort to revive the Yiddish language as an advocate and as a translator, and his work provides a record of the role that Jewish intellectuals and religious leaders have played in the development of Western civilization. But as "Waiting for a Jew" also chronicles, Boyarin improvises on this history, inventing a "funky Orthodox" Jewish identity for himself.

Considered one of America's most original thinkers about Jewish culture, Boyarin has written extensively about the roles that history, memory, and geography have played in the formation of Jewish life. In books that include *A Storm from Paradise: The Politics of Jewish Memory* (1992), *Thinking in Jewish* (1996), and *Jewishness and the Human Dimension* (2008), Boyarin asks his readers to consider whether or not there is such a thing as an "essential" Jewish identity. This question is especially complex because many people have come to see collective identity as a cause of conflict and enormous suffering, and they believe that the best future for humankind lies with a universalism that rejects us-and-them distinctions. Boyarin sympathizes with this view, but he argues that identity for marginalized groups plays a very different role than it does for those groups that are dominant. As he puts it in *Remapping Memory: The Politics of TimeSpace* (1994), "For people who are somehow part of a dominant group, any assertions of essence are ipso facto products and reproducers of the system of domination. For subaltern groups, however, essentialism is resistance, the insistence on the 'right' of the group actually to exist." As "Waiting for a Jew" documents, answering the question "Who are you?" is not as simple as it might seem, for the answer requires that one first consider the histories, traditions, and communal experiences that have made identity possible.

Boyarin, Jonathan. "Waiting for a Jew: Marginal Redemption at the Eighth Street Shul." *Thinking in Jewish*. Chicago: University of Chicago Press, 1996. 8–34.

Waiting for a Jew

Marginal Redemption at the Eighth Street Shul

My story begins in a community, with an illusion of wholeness. I am between the age when consciousness begins and the age of ten, when my family leaves the community and my illusion is shattered. Our family lives on the edge of the Pine Barrens in Farmingdale, New Jersey, along with hundreds of other families of Jewish chicken farmers who have come from Europe and New York City in several waves, beginning just after World War I.

Among the farmers are present and former Communists, Bundists, Labor Zionists, German refugees who arrived in the 1930s, and Polish survivors of concentration camps. These, however, are not the distinctions I make among them as a child. Johannes Fabian has shown us that when we write ethnography we inevitably trap those about whom we write into a hypostatic, categorical, grammatical "present" (Fabian 1983). An autobiographer has the same power over the memory of himself and those he knew in prior times as the fieldworker who later obliterates the narrative aspect of his encounter with his subjects—the power to deny their autonomy in hindsight.[1] Those of the farming community whom I will later remember, I know therefore by their own names and places: my grandparents closer to Farmingdale proper; the Silbers off on Yellowbrook Road, with a tree nursery now instead of chickens; the Lindauers, stubbornly maintaining an egg-packing and -distribution business, while others find different ways to earn a living.

My child's world is not exclusively Jewish, nor am I brought up to regard it as such. Across our road and down a few hundred yards is a tiny house built by Jewish farmers when they first came to settle here. It is now, incredibly, occupied by a black family of ten. Next to them lives an equally poor and large white family. Shortly before we leave Farmingdale, the old Jew in the farm next to ours passes away, and the property passes to a Japanese businessman. The young men he hires live in the farmhouse, growing oriental vegetables on the open field and bonsai in a converted chicken coop, and they introduce me to the game of Go. The nearest Jewish household is that of my great-uncle Yisroel and his wife, Helen, the third house to the right of ours.

Yet we are near the heart of Jewish life in Farmingdale. Half a mile—but no, it must be less—down Peskin's Lane (the name my grandfather Israel Boyarin gave to what was a dirt road in the 1930s) is the Farmingdale Jewish Community Center, on the next plot of land after Uncle Yisroel's house. Just past the community center is the farm that once belonged to my father's uncle Peskin, the first Jew in Farmingdale. Fifteen years after Peskin's death, the bodies of two gangsters were found buried on the farm. The local papers noted: "Mr. Peskin was not available for comment."

Our own farm consists of eleven acres. Facing the road is the house my grandfather built, with a large front lawn and an apple tree in back. Farther back, four large chicken coops mark the slope of a hill ending in our field, behind which woods conceal the tiny Manasquan River. The field, well fertilized by chickens allowed to scratch freely on it during the day, is leased each summer by a dirt farmer who grows corn. My father has joined the insurance agency begun by my mother, and they have gotten rid of the birds. The coops stand empty by my fourth birthday. One day, though, while a friend and I chase each other through the coops in play, we are startled by a pair of chickens. Their presence in the stillness and the faint smell of ancient manure is inexplicable and unforgettable. Thus, on the abandoned farm, my first memories are tinged with a sense of traces, of mystery, of loss. Do all who eventually become anthropologists have this experience in some form, at some time in their early lives?

My mother's turn to business is wise: chicken farming as the basis for the community's livelihood is quickly becoming untenable. Nor is it surprising, as she had given up a career as a chemist to come live with my father on the farm—thus taking part in the process of Jewish dispersal from the immigrants' urban centers, which in the last quarter of the century would be mirrored by a shrinking of Jewish communities in small towns and a reconsolidation of the Orthodox centers. My mother's father, an Orthodox Jew from a leading Lithuanian rabbinical family, has struggled to learn English well and has gone into the insurance business himself. After his death, my mother tells me that he had originally resisted her desire to marry the son of a Jewish socialist, but he consented when he met my father's father's father, a Lubavitcher Hasid named Mordechai.

My grandfather's concern for his daughter's future as an observant Jew was well founded. The Sabbath is marked in our family only on Friday nights: by my mother's candle-lighting, and her chicken soup in winter; by the challah; by the presence of my grandfather. We do not keep kosher, nor do we go to shul on *shabbes*.

The Jewish Community Center—with its various functions as social and meeting hall, synagogue, and school—is nevertheless a focus of our family's life. Most of the ten or so other children in these classes I see at other times during the week as well, either in public school or playing at one another's homes. I am there three times each week, first for Sunday school, and then for Hebrew school on Tuesday and Thursday afternoons. This odd distinction is no doubt a practical one since some parents do not choose to send their children three times a week. But since Sunday school was first a Christian institution, it also reflects an accommodation to Christian church patterns, as evidenced by the fact that Sundays are devoted to teaching stories of the Bible. One Sunday school teacher we have in our kindergarten year captivates me with his skill in making these stories come to life, as when he imitates the distress of an Egyptian waking up to find his bed covered with frogs.

Another teacher, a young woman with a severe manner and a heavy black wig, the wife of a member of the Orthodox yeshiva in Lakewood, later causes general misery because of her inability to understand children, although I will eventually appreciate the prayers she teaches us to read. One time I come in to Hebrew school immediately after yet another in a series of martyred family dogs has been run over in front of our house. Her attempt to comfort me is like some malicious parody of Talmudic reasoning: "You shouldn't be so upset about an animal. If a chicken and a person both fell down a well, which one would you save first?"

In addition to this somewhat haphazard religious training, there is the local chapter of Habonim, the Labor Zionist Youth Organization, to which my older brother and sister belong. I tag along and am tolerated by their peers. Once I am given a minor role in a stage performance by the chapter. Though I am too young to remember quite what it is about, the phrase *komets-aleph:aw* stands in my memory.

Later I will learn that this phrase occurs in a famous and sentimental Yiddish folksong. It is the first letter of the Hebrew alphabet, the first thing countless generations of Jewish children have been taught. Here is an unusual case in which a traditional lesson—how to pronounce the alphabet—is successfully inculcated in the secularized framework of a dramatic performance about the traditional setting. Perhaps this is because of the necessary rehearsals, in which I must have heard, as the song puts it, "once more, over and over again, *komets-aleph:aw*." The memory reinforces my later preference for this older, European pronunciation of the Hebrew vowels, my sense of the Israeli *kamets-aleph:ah* as inauthentic.

Also memorable at the Jewish Community Center is the annual barbecue run by the Young Couples' Club. Though my father will assure me in an interview years later that its association with the Fourth of July was purely a matter of convenience, the atmosphere is certainly one of festival, even including "sacrifices" and "altars": My father and his friends set up huge charcoal pits with cement blocks, and broil vast amounts of chicken; corn is boiled in aluminum garbage cans to go with it.[2] For the children, a Purimlike element of riotous excess is added: This one time each year, we are allowed to drink as much soda as we want. One year "wild," blond-haired Richie L., whose parents have a luncheonette booth for a kitchen table and an attic filled with antiques, claims to drink fourteen bottles, thus adding to the mystique he holds for me.

But it is the days when the Community Center becomes a synagogue that leave the strongest impression on my memory. There must be services every Saturday morning, but I am completely unaware of them. What I will remember are the holidays: Purim, Rosh Hashanah, Yom Kippur, Simchas Torah, and a crowd of people who just a few years later will never be there again. On the fall holidays, the shul is full of movement, impatience, noise, and warmth. Except for a few moments such as the shofar blowing, we children are free to come and go: By the steps in front, tossing the juicy, poisonous red berries of a yew that was planted, I am told, in memory of my brother Aaron, whom I never knew; inside the main doors, to look left at Walter Tenenbaum wrapped in a *tallis* that covers his head, standing at a lectern by the Ark of the Torah as he leads the service, or to look right, along the first long row of folding chairs for our fathers; thence a few rows back to where our mothers sit separately from the men, although unlike most synagogues that look and sound as traditional as this one, there is no *mekhitse*, no barrier between women and men; and finally out through the side door and down a flight of wooden steps to the monkey bars, into the ditch where one miraculous day we found and drank an intact bottle of orange soda, or into the kitchen, social room, and classroom in the basement. Once each year we children are the center of attention, as we huddle under a huge tallis in front of the Ark on Simchas Torah to be blessed.

In classic ethnographies of hunting-and-gathering groups, landscapes are described as personalized, integral elements of culture. This was true of the landscape of my childhood friendships, which today is as obliterated as any *shtetl* in Eastern Europe. Any marginal group in mass society may be subject without warning to the loss of its cultural landscape, and therefore those who are able to create portable landscapes for themselves are the most likely to endure.

The Jews have been doing so for thousands of years; the Simchas Torah tallis can stand in front of any Ark, and the original Ark, in the biblical account, was itself transported from station to station in the desert. Yet the members of a community are orphaned when the naïve intimacy of a living environment is torn away from them. Such a break appears often in Jewish literature—significantly with the emphasis not forward on the beginning of adulthood, as in the European *Bildungsroman*, but rather on the end of childhood.[3]

I suddenly discover the distance between the world and myself at the end of August in 1966. When my parents pick me up from camp, they take me to a new house. For the last time, we attend high holiday services in Farmingdale. It is the only time we will ever drive there, and our family's friends no longer join us during the afternoon break on Yom Kippur for a surreptitious glass of tea and a slice of challah. Farmingdale is no longer home, and though our new house is only ten miles away, it is another world.

We live now in an almost exclusively white, middle-class suburb with many Jews, but our older, brick house is isolated on a block of working-class cubes. While neighbors my age play football in our yard, I often retreat to my room and console myself with sports books for preadolescents. My new and bewildering sense of marginality leads me to develop an exquisite self-consciousness. It is manifested in an almost constant internal dialogue, which keeps me company and will interfere with my adolescent sexuality.

Ostracism is often the fate of a new kid on the block, and it may last longer when his family is Jewish and his home better than those on either side. There is a custom in this part of New Jersey of tolerating petty vandalism on "mischief night," the night before Halloween. Pumpkins are smashed, and we, along with other unpopular families on the block, have the windows of our cars and house smeared with soap. One Halloween I wake up to see graffiti chalked in bold letters on the sidewalk in front of our house: "Jon the Jew, a real one too." My father summons the kids next door—whom we suspect of being the authors—to scrape the words off the sidewalk, as I burn with shame.

He and I never discuss the incident, but later I will compare it with a memory of Freud's. As a child, he was walking with his father, when a gentile knocked his father's hat off. Rather than confronting the man, Freud's father meekly bent over to pick up the hat, and his son's humiliation persisted into adulthood (Bakan 1958; D. Boyarin 1997). The moral is that a victim is likely to view any response as adding insult to injury. In my case, as my father asserts the American principle of equality and "teaches a lesson" to my occasional and vindictive playmates by forcing them to erase what they have written, I feel as though he is inviting them to write the words again, this time making me watch my own degradation.

The new synagogue my parents join is only a partial refuge. It exemplifies the difference between a shul and a temple. Everything in Farmingdale had faced inward: little concern was paid for praying in unison, and though the *shammes* would bang his hand on the table for silence, he was seldom heeded; even the cantor was alone with God, facing away from everyone else, rather than performing for the congregation. Calling a synagogue a temple, by contrast, is doubly revealing. On the one hand, it indicates a striving for the majesty of the ancient House in Jerusalem. On the other hand, just like the English term used to designate it, its trappings are borrowed from the Christian world, down to the black robes worn by the rabbi and cantor.

These robes lack the warm mystery of Walter Tenenbaum's tallis. The responsive readings of Psalms in English seem ridiculously artificial to me from the first. And my mother, who still comes only on the holidays though I sometimes drag my father to temple on Friday nights, complains of the rabbi's long-winded sermons and yearns aloud for the intimate conversations along the back wall of the Farmingdale Jewish Community Center.

Unlike some, I do not leave the synagogue immediately after my bar mitzvah. I teach the blessings of the Haftorah to two reluctant boys a year younger than me. I briefly experience religious inspiration, and for perhaps two weeks put on *tefillin* every morning. But the atmosphere is hollow, and the emptiness breeds cynicism in me in my teens.

The coldness of the building itself is symptomatic of the lack of sustenance I sense there. The pretense and bad taste of modern American synagogues are well-known yet puzzling phenomena that deserve a sociological explanation of their own. Even the walls of the temple are dead concrete blocks, in contrast to the wood of the Farmingdale Jewish Community Center. Services are held in a "sanctuary," unlike the room at the Community Center where activities as varied as dances and political meetings were conducted when services were not being held. Aside from any question of Jewish law, there is a loss of community marked by the fact that everyone drives to the temple rather than walking. It is a place separated from the home, without the strong and patient webs spun by leisurely strolling conversations to and from a shul.

Most generally, the temple is victim to the general alienation of the suburbs. What happens or fails to happen there is dependent on what the people who come there expect from each other. Those who belong (there are vastly more "members" than regular attendees) seem bound primarily by a vague desire to have Jewish grandchildren. The poor rabbi, typical of Conservative congregations, seems hired to be a stand-in Jew, to observe all the laws and contain all knowledge they don't have the time for. They are not bound to each other Jewish religious ways, nor do they share the common interests of everyday life—the same livelihood or language- –that helped to make a complete community in Farmingdale.

I go off to college and slowly discover that my dismissal of Judaism leaves me isolated, with few resources. I had realized my individual difference on leaving Farmingdale. Now, much more removed from a Jewish environment than ever before, I become aware of my inescapable Jewishness. In the small northwestern college of my dreams, everyone around me seems "American" and different, though I have never thought of myself as anything but American. Even in the humanities curriculum on which the school prides itself, Jewish civilization is absent. It is as though Western cultural history were just a triumphant straight line from the Greeks to Augustine and Michelangelo (with his horned Moses and uncircumcised David), confusion setting in at last only with Marx and Freud.

Five years too late to benefit me, a Jewish Studies position will in fact be established at the college. Such positions are usually funded by Jewish individuals or organizations, and hence they represent the growing acculturation (not assimilation) of Jews into American academic life. The fact that they are regarded as legitimate by the academic community, however, is part of a reintegration of Jewish thought into the concept of Western humanities. Jewish ethnographers can contribute to this movement—for example, by elucidating the dialectic of tradition and change as worked out in communities facing vastly different historical challenges. We may then move beyond efforts to explain the explosive presence of Jews in post-Enlightenment intellectual life as a result of their "primitive" encounter with "civility" (Cuddihy 1974) to explore how the Jewish belief that "Creation as the (active) speech or writing of God posits first of all that the Universe is essentially intelligible" (Faur 1986: 7) provided a pathway from Torah to a restless, unifying modern impulse in the natural and social sciences.

Such notions are far beyond me as an undergraduate. At my college in the 1970s, the social scientists in their separate departments strive to separate themselves from their "objects of study"; the humanists treasure the peace of their cloisters; the artists, knowing they are intellectually suspect, cultivate a cliquish sense of superiority; and there is none of the give-and-take between learning and everyday experience that I have come to associate with the best of Jewish scholarship.

I find a friend, a Jew from Long Island, and we begin to teach each other that we need to cultivate our Jewishness. We discuss the "Jewish mentality" of modern thinkers, and paraphrasing Lenny Bruce's category of the *goyish*, sarcastically reject all that is "white." "I am not 'white,'" my friend Martin proudly postures, "I am a Semite." Meanwhile, reflecting on my own dismissal of suburban Judaism, I decide not to end willingly an almost endless chain of Jewish cultural transmission. I stake my future on the assumption that a tradition so old and varied must contain the seeds of a worthwhile life for me, and decide to begin to acquire them through study.

Besides, my reading as a student of anthropology leads me to reason that if I concentrate on Jewish culture, no one will accuse me of cultural imperialism (see Gough 1968). No doubt others in my generation who choose to do fieldwork with Jews are motivated by similar considerations. Jewish anthropologists as a class are privileged to belong to the world of academic discourse, and to have an entrée into a variety of unique communities that maintain cultural frameworks in opposition to mass society.

Something deeper than Marxist critiques of anthropology draws me to Yiddish in particular. Before I left Farmingdale, my best friend had been a child of survivors from Lemberg. I remember being at his house once, and asking with a sense of wonder: "Ralph, do you really know Yiddish?"

Ralph told me that although he understood the language—which his parents still spoke to him—he had never learned to speak it. Still, I was impressed that he knew this secret code. And now that I am finished with college and looking to find my own way home, Yiddish seems to be the nearest link to which I can attach myself. It is the key to a sense of the life of the *shtetl,* that Jewish dreamtime that I inevitably associate with my lost Farmingdale.

The Farmingdale community has, by this point, completely disintegrated: Virtually no Jews in that part of New Jersey earn their living as chicken farmers anymore. Many of those who have gone into business have moved to nearby towns like Lakewood. The Torah scrolls of the Community Center have been ceremoniously transferred to a new synagogue near housing developments on the highway between Farmingdale and Lakewood. I have never considered becoming a chicken farmer myself.

So, when I finish my college courses, without waiting for graduation, I flee back to New York. "Flee": No one chases me out of Portland, Oregon, God forbid! "Back": The city, though a magnet and a refuge, has never been my home before. Yet for three years I have shaped my identity in opposition to the "American" world around me, and I have reverted, along with my close friends, to what we imagine is an authentic New York accent—the "deses" and "doses" that were drilled out of my parents' repertoire in the days when New York public school teachers had to pass elocution exams.

Rejecting suburban Judaism, belatedly pursuing the image of the sixties' counterculture to the Pacific Northwest, and self-consciously affecting a "New York Jew" style were all successive attempts to shape a personal identity. In each case, the identity strategy was in opposition to the prevailing conventions of the immediate social order. Similarly, opposition to their parents' perceived bourgeois complacency may underlie the involvement of young people with Judaism. Yet as Dominique Schnapper has noted (1983), for young, intellectual Jews becoming involved in Jewish religion, politics, or culture, there can be no question of canceling out prior experience and "becoming traditional." In fact, this is true even of the most seemingly Orthodox and insular Jewish communities. There is a difference between learning about great rabbis of the past through meetings with Jewish graybeards who knew them, and through reading about their merits in the Williamsburg newspaper *Der Yid.*

Of course, not only Jews are in the position of reconstituting interrupted tradition (cf. Clifford 1986: 116 ff.). But since they have been in the business of reshaping tradition in a dialogue with written texts for thousands of years, Jews may benefit more directly than others from learning about what other

Jews are doing with their common tradition. It is conceivable that individuals may choose to adopt traits from other communities or even join those communities based on what they read in ethnographies. Whether such cultural borrowings and recombinations are effected in an "authentic" manner will depend less on precedent than on the degree of self-confident cultural generosity that results.

Arriving in New York, I adopt a knitted yarmulke, although my hair still falls below my shoulders. I immediately begin a nine-week summer course in Yiddish at Columbia, and it seems as though the language were being brought out from deep inside me. When I go to visit my parents on weekends, my father remembers words he'd never noticed forgetting. When I take the IRT after class back down to the Village, it seems as if everybody on the train is speaking Yiddish. Most important for my sense of identity, phrases here and there in my own internal dialogue are now in Yiddish, and I find I can reflect on myself with a gentle irony that was never available to me in English.

Then, after my first year in graduate school, I am off to Europe the following summer, courtesy of my parents. I arrive at the Gare du Nord in Paris with the address of a friend and without a word of French. I am spotted wearing my yarmulke by a young North African Jew who makes me understand, in broken English, that he studies at the Lubavitch yeshiva in Paris. He buys me a Paris guidebook and sets me on my way in the Metro. At the end of the summer, this meeting will stand as the first in a set of Parisian reactions to my yarmulke which crystallize in my memory:

—The reaction of the generous young Trotskyist with whom my friend had grown close and with whom I stayed for two weeks. She could see the yarmulke only as a symbol of Jewish nationalism and argued bitterly that it was inherently reactionary;

—Of a young North African Jew, selling carpets at the flea market at Clignoncourt, who grabbed my arm and cried, "*Haver! Haver!* Brother Jew!";

—Of another young man, minding a booth outside one of the great department stores, who asked me if I were Orthodox, and interrupted my complicated response to explain that, although he was Orthodox himself, he was afraid to wear a yarmulke in the street;

—Of an old man at the American Express office who spoke to me in Yiddish and complained that the recent North African migrants dominated the Jewish communal organizations, and that there was no place for a Polish Jew to go.

Those first, fragmentary encounters are my fieldwork juvenilia. In assuming the yarmulke, I perhaps do not stop to consider that neither my actions nor my knowledge match the standards that it symbolically represents. But it works effectively, almost dangerously, as a two-way sensor, inducing Jews to present themselves to me and forcing me to try to understand how I am reflected in their eyes.

Externally, I learn many things about the situation of French Jewry. From the patent discomfort my non-Jewish Trotskyist friend feels at my display of Jewish specificity, I gain some sense of the conflicts young French Jews—coming out of the universalist, antihistorical revolutionary apogee of May 1968—must have felt years later when they first began to distinguish themselves from their comrades and view the world from the vantage point of their specific history. From the young street peddlers, I learn about how much riskier public proclamation of oneself as a Jew is perceived as being in Paris than in New York, and a concomitant depth of instant identification of one Jew with another. My meeting with the old Polish Jew at the American Express office hints at the dynamics of dominant and declining ethnic groups within the Jewish community, so vastly different from those dynamics in the United States.

Internally, I begin to understand that an identifiably Jewish headcovering places its own claims on the one who wears it. The longer it stays put, the more its power to keep him out of non-kosher restaurants grows. More important, people want to know who he is as a Jew. And if he does not know, the desire for peace of mind will spur further his effort to shape an identity.

Returning from Paris, I find an apartment at Second Avenue and Fifth Street in Manhattan. I tell people, "After three generations, my family has finally made it back to the Lower East Side." In fact, none of my grandparents lived on the East Side for a long time after immigrating, even though my mother tells me she regrets having missed the Yiddish theater on Second Avenue during her girlhood. By the time I move in, there is no Yiddish theater left. The former Ratner's dairy restaurant on Second Avenue, where, I'm told, Trotsky was a lousy tipper, is now a supermarket. Though sometimes one still sees a white newspaper truck with the word *Forverts* in lovely blue Hebrew letters on its side drive by late at night, this neighborhood has been the East Village since the sixties, and I think of it as such.

A new friend, who devotes his time to a frustrating effort to rescue Lower East Side synagogues, tells me of a shul still in use on an otherwise abandoned block east of Tompkins Square Park. Though my friend has never been inside, he is sure that I will be welcomed, since such an isolated congregation must be looking for new blood.

The place is called the Eighth Street Shul, but its full name is Kehilas Bnei Moshe Yakov Anshei Zavichost veZosmer—Congregation Children of Moses and Jacob, People of Zavichost and Zosmer. It is owned by a *landsmanshaft* (hometown society) founded by émigrés and refugees from two towns in south central Poland. No one born in either town prays regularly at the shul now, and only one or two of the congregants are actually members of the society.

The shul is located in the center of what New York Latinos call "Loisaida"—an area bounded by Avenue A on the east, Avenue D on the west, Houston Street on the south, and Fourteenth Street on the north. Once the blocks up to Tenth Street were almost exclusively Jewish, and on nearly every one stood a synagogue or a religious school. Now two of those former synagogues stand abandoned, several more have become churches, and the rest have disappeared.

Eighth Street is a typical and not especially distinguished example of turn-of-the-century Lower East Side synagogue architecture.[4] It consists of five levels. The lowest contains a cranky and inadequate boiler. The second is the *besmedresh*, or study room, which was destroyed by a suspicious fire in August 1982. The third level is the main sanctuary, long and narrow like the tenements among which it was tucked when it was built. Two rows of simple pews are separated by an aisle, which is interrupted in the center of the room by the raised table from which the weekly Torah portion is read. At the very front is the Ark, surrounded by partially destroyed wooden carvings that are the most artistic aspect of the shul. The walls are decorated with representations of the traditional Jewish signs for the zodiac; the two in front on the left have been obliterated by water damage from the leaky roof. Covering most of this level, with roughly an eight-foot opening extending toward the back, is the women's gallery. The gallery is constructed in such a way that it is easier for women sitting on opposite sides of the opening to converse with one another than to see what the men are doing downstairs. Finally, upstairs from the women's gallery is an unused and cramped apartment that was once occupied by the shul's caretaker. In the roof behind it, an opening that was a skylight until there was a break-in is now covered with a solid wooden framework, allowing neither light nor vandals to enter.

Avenues B and C, which mark off the block, were once lively commercial streets with mostly Jewish storekeepers. There were also several smaller streets lined with tenements, right up to the edge of the East River. When the FDR Drive was built along the river, all the streets east of Avenue D disappeared, the tenements on the remaining available land were replaced by municipal housing, and the stores declined rapidly. During the same years, a massive middle-class housing cooperative, funded by a government mortgage, was built along Grand Street one mile to the south. Many of the remaining Jewish families moved into those houses, leaving virtually no Jews in the immediate area of the Eighth Street Shul.

Yet a minyan has continued to meet there every Saturday morning, with virtually no interruptions, throughout the years of the neighborhood's decline, while the block served as the Lower East Side's heaviest "shopping street" for hard drugs. It has lasted into the present, when buildings all around it are being speculated upon and renovated by both squatters and powerful real estate interests. It appears that until recently the main reason for this continuity was a felicitous rivalry between two men who were unwilling to abandon the synagogue because their fathers had both been presidents of it at one time. Perhaps if there had been only one, he would have given up and made peace with his conscience. Perhaps if the two men had naturally been friends, they could have agreed to sell the building and officially merge their society with another still functioning further south in the neighborhood. If they had been able to agree on anything besides continuing to come to the shul, the shul might not have survived this long.

The first time I walk in, a clean-shaven, compact man in his sixties—younger than several of the congregants, who number perhaps seventeen in all—hurries forward to greet me. What's my name? Where do I live? Where am I from originally? And where do I usually go to pray on shabbes? His name is Moshe Fogel, and he sees to it that I am called to the Torah, the honor accorded any guest who comes for the first time, without asking any questions as to his level of religious observance. Later, an older member explains to me: "Once upon a time, you wouldn't get called to the Torah unless you kept kosher and observed shabbes." Now, Moish prefers simply to leave those matters undiscussed.

The history of the East Side as a place where all types of Jews have lived together reinforces his discretion. Externalities such as proper or improper clothing are not essential criteria for participation. This is true of the entire Orthodox community on the East Side and has even become part of its mystique. Rabbi Reuven Feinstein, head of the Staten Island branch of the East Broadway–based yeshiva, Tifereth Jerusalem, noted in a recent speech the common reaction in Boro Park and other thriving Orthodox centers to the nonconformist dress of East Side visitors: "It's okay, you're from the East Side." The president at Eighth Street still wears a traditional *gartl* when he prays, a belt worn over his jacket to separate the pure from the base parts of his body, and no one has suggested that such old customs are out of place today. But partly because the older members at the Eighth Street Shul walked through the East Village in the 1960s and knew there were many young Jews among the longhairs—even if they were horrified at the thought—they were willing to include in the minyan a young man in the neighborhood who, when he first came, wore dreadlocks under a Rastafarian-style knitted cap. It is also doubtless true that at that time there was no other Orthodox synagogue anywhere that he would have contemplated entering.

By contrast, it is impossible for any Jew raised in the middle of secular society (including a Jewish anthropologist) to join a traditionalist community without giving up major parts of his or her identity. The ways in which a researcher of contemporary Hasidic life "becomes a Hasid" are much more dramatic than the way in which one becomes a regular at Eighth Street—but they are probably more transient as well. In order to gain the confidence of the traditionalist communities, the fieldworker has to give the impression, whether implicitly or explicitly, that he or she is likely eventually to accept their standards in all areas of life (Belcove-Shalin 1988). All one has to do at Eighth Street is agree to come back—"a little earlier next time, if possible."

Two things will draw me back to join this congregation, occasionally referred to as "those holy souls who *daven* in the middle of the jungle." The first pull is the memory of Farmingdale: the Ashkenazic accents and melodies (though here they are Polish, whereas Walter Tenenbaum had prayed in his native Lithuanian accent); the smell of herring on the old men's breath and hands; the burning sensation of whiskey, which I must have tasted surreptitiously at the conclusion of Yom Kippur one year in Farmingdale.

The second thing that draws me, though I do not come every week, is a feeling that I am needed and missed when I am absent. It's hard for me to get up early on Saturday mornings, after being out late Friday nights. It still seems like a sacrifice, as though I were stealing part of my weekend from myself. If I arrive in time for the *Shema*, about half an hour into the service, I congratulate myself on my devotion. The summer before I marry, in 1981, I hardly come at all. When I go with my brother to meet Moshe Fogel at the shul and give him the provisions for the kiddush I am giving to celebrate my upcoming wedding, I tell Dan that I usually arrive "around nine-thirty," to which Moish retorts: "Even when you used to come, you didn't show up at nine-thirty!" Though he says it with a smile, a message comes through clearly: If I want to claim to belong, I should attend regularly and arrive on time. Although I am always welcome, only if I can be counted on am I part of the minyan. The dependence of Jews on each other—a theme running through biblical and rabbinic literature—is pressingly literal at Eighth Street.

Meanwhile, my feelings about Paris coalesce into a plan. I know I want to live there for a time, but only if I will be among Jews. Since I am at the point in my graduate school career when I must find a dissertation topic, I decide to look for fieldwork situations with Jews in Paris. I make an exploratory visit with my fiancée, Elissa. Will she agree to a pause in her own career to follow me on this project? Will the organizations of Polish Jewish immigrants whom I have chosen to study be willing to have me study them?

The answer is yes to both questions. Speaking Yiddish and appearing as a nice young Jewish couple seem to be the critical elements in our success. We are invited to sit in on board meetings, negotiations aimed at the reunification of societies split by political differences for over half a century. I am struck by the fact that these immigrants seem so much more marked by their political identification than the East European Jews I've met in New York. Also, I am impressed at the number of societies remaining in a country that has suffered Nazi occupation and that historically has shown little tolerance for immigrant cultural identifications.

But I am drawn not so much by the differences between these Yiddish speakers and those I know in New York as by encountering them in an environment that is otherwise so foreign. Speaking Yiddish to people with whom I have no other common language confirms its legitimacy and reinforces the sense of a distinctive Jewish identity that is shared between generations. I go for a trial interview of one activist, who is disappointed that I didn't bring "the girl," Elissa, along with me. When he discovers to my embarrassment that I have been secretly taping the interview, he is flattered.

Just before leaving Paris, Elissa and I climb the steps of Sacré Coeur. The cathedral itself is an ungracious mass, and the city looks gray and undifferentiated below us. I experience a moment of vertigo, as if I could tumble off Montmartre and drown. Part of my dream of Paris, "capital of the nineteenth century," is an infantile fantasy of becoming a universal intellectual—to be free both of the special knowledge and of the limitations of my knowledge that follow on my personal history. Yet I know I cannot come to Paris and immediately move among its confident, cliquish intellectual elite. Even less will I ever have contact with that "quintessentially French" petite bourgeoisie typified by the stolid Inspector Maigret. My first place will be with the immigrants, whose appearance, strange language, and crowded quarters provided material for unkind portraits by Maigret's creator, Simenon, in the 1930s.[5] If I am unable to come to see Paris as they have seen it, if I cannot make out of a shared marginality a niche in the city for myself, I will be lost, as much as the "lost generation," and in a most unromantic way.

During the two years between our decision to spend a year in Paris and the beginning of that year, I attend the Eighth Street Shul more and more regularly, and Elissa occasionally joins me. Gradually, my feelings when I miss a week shift from guilt to regret. One shabbes, waking up late but not wanting to miss attending altogether, I arrive just in time for the kiddush, to the general amusement of the entire minyan. One February morning I wake up to see snow falling and force myself to go outside against my will, knowing that on a day like this I am truly needed.

Other incidents illustrate the gap in assumptions between myself and the other congregants. I try to bring friends into the shul, partly because it makes me more comfortable, and partly to build up the congregation. A friend whose hair and demeanor reflect his love of reggae music and his connections with Jamaican Rastafarians comes along one Yom Kippur. We reach the point in the service when pious men, remembering the priests in the days of the Temple, descend to their knees and touch their foreheads to the floor. Since no one wants to soil his good pants on the dirty floor, sheets of newspaper are provided as protection. Reb Simcha Taubenfeld, the senior member of the congregation, approaches my friend with newspaper in hand and asks in his heavy Yiddish accent: "Do you fall down?" The look of bewilderment on my friend's face graphically illustrates the term "frame of reference."

Another week, the same friend, failing to observe the discretion with regard to the expression of political opinions that I have learned to adopt at shul, gets into a bitter argument over the Palestinian question. Fishel Mandel, a social worker and one of the younger members of the congregation, calls me during the week to convey the message that "despite our political differences, your friend is still welcome."

After our wedding, I attend virtually every week. When Elissa comes, she is doubly welcome, since the only other woman who attends regularly is Goldie Brown, Moish Fogel's sister. Though Goldie doesn't complain about being isolated in the women's gallery one flight above the men, she seconds Elissa's suggestion that a mekhitse be set up downstairs. The suggestion gets nowhere, however: it would entail displacing one of the regular members of the congregation from his usual seat, and though there is no lack of available places (I myself usually wander from front to back during the course of the service), he refuses to consider moving.

I reason that I will have more of a voice concerning questions such as the seating of women if I formalize my relationship to the shul by becoming a member. My timid announcement that I would like to do so meets with initial confusion on the part of the older members of the society present. Then Fishel, ever the mediator and interpreter, explains to me that the shul is not organized like a suburban synagogue: "There's a *chevra*, a society, that owns the shul. In order to join, you have to be *shomer mitzves*, you have to keep kosher and strictly observe the Sabbath."

I drop my request. Shiye the president reassures me with a speech in his usual roundabout style to the effect that belonging to the chevra is a separate question from being a member of the minyan: "They send their money in from New Jersey and Long Island, but the shul couldn't exist without the people that actually come to pray here."

Meanwhile, our plans to go to Paris proceed. Our travel plans become a topic for discussion over kiddush at shul. One of the older, Polish-born members tells us for the first time that he lived in Paris for nine years after the war. We ask him why he came to America, and he answers, "*Vern a frantsoyz iz shver* [It's hard to become a Frenchman]," both to obtain citizenship and to be accepted by neighbors.

At the end of the summer, we expect to give a farewell kiddush at the shul. A few days before shabbes, I get a phone call from Moish Fogel: "Don't get things for kiddush. We won't be able to daven at Eighth Street for a while. There's been a fire. Thank God, the Torah scrolls were rescued, but it's going to take a while to repair the damage." It is two weeks after Tisha B'Av, the fast commemorating the destruction of the Temple in Jerusalem.

Leaving New York without saying goodbye to the shul and its congregation, we fly overnight to Brussels and immediately *shlep* (the word "drag" would not do the burden justice) our seven heavy suitcases onto a Paris train. Arriving again at the Gare du Nord, I think of the thousands of Polish Jews who were greeted at the station in the twenties and thirties by fellow immigrants eager to hire workers. As soon as we get off the train, Elissa immediately "gets involved," demanding the credentials of two men who claim to be policemen and attempt to "confiscate" a carpet two Moroccan immigrants are carrying. Upon Elissa's challenge, the "policemen" demur.

We practice our French on the cab driver: I explain to him why we've come to Paris. He warns us that we shouldn't tell strangers we're Jewish. It is only a few weeks since the terrorist attack on Goldenberg's restaurant, and no one knows when the next anti-Semitic attack may come. I reply that if I hadn't said we were Jewish, we wouldn't have found out he was a Jew as well, adding that in New York the names of taxi drivers are posted inside the cabs. He says he wouldn't like that at all.

So we receive an early warning that ethnicity in Paris is not celebrated publicly as it is in New York, nor are ethnic mannerisms and phrases so prevalent as a deliberate element of personal style. This is the repressive underside of marginality. It appears wherever the individual or community think it is better not to flaunt their distinctiveness, even if they cannot fully participate in the host culture. It leads to suspicion and silence, to the taxi driver's desire for anonymity.

Arriving at our rented apartment, we meet our neighbor Isabel, who will be our only non-Jewish friend during the year in Paris, and who later explains that meeting us has helped dispel her prejudices about Jews. Over the next few days, we introduce ourselves to Jewish storekeepers in the neighborhood: Guy, the Tunisian kosher butcher; Chanah, the Polish baker's wife; Leon, the deli man from Lublin, who insists he didn't learn Yiddish until he came to Paris.

We have a harder time finding a synagogue where we feel at home. For Rosh Hashanah and Yom Kippur, we have purchased tickets at one of the "official" synagogues run by the Consistoire, the recognized religious body of French Jewry set up under Napoleon. Most synagogues run by the Consistoire are named after the streets on which they're located. Meeting a Hasid on the street, I ask him whether he happens to know when Rosh Hashanah services begin at "Notre Dame de Nazareth." He grimaces and makes as if spitting: "Don't say that name, *ptu ptu ptu!*"

The synagogue is strange to us as well. Most of the crowd seems if anything more secular than most American Jews, who go to the synagogue only on the high holidays. Many teenagers wear jeans or miniskirts. Because of the fear of terrorism, everyone is frisked on entering. Inside, the synagogue is picturesque with its nineteenth-century pseudo-Moorish motifs; when it was built, Offenbach was the choirmaster. Yet it is as religiously dissatisfying as the suburban American temple I used to attend. The services seem to be conducted in a traditional manner, but it is hard to tell from among the noisy throng in back. The *shammes,* as a representative of the government, wears a Napoleonic hat, and the rabbi delivers his sermon from a high pulpit.

After Yom Kippur, I think idly about the need to find a more comfortable shul, and when I hear about an East European–style minyan within walking distance, I consider going on Simchas Torah. Watching television reports of terrorist attacks on Simchas Torah in other European capitals, I am consumed with shame at my own apathy, and thus I walk a kilometer or two to find the synagogue on the rue Basfroi the following shabbes.

Going in, I am first shown into a side room, where men are reciting incomprehensible prayers with strange and beautiful melodies. Eventually I realize that they are North African Jews, and I venture into the main room to ask, "Is there an Ashkenazic minyan here?"

The man I ask replies in French, "We're not racists here! We're all Jews!" at which his friend points out:

"The young man spoke to you in Yiddish!" Continuing in Yiddish, he explains that while everyone is welcome in the main synagogue, the services there are in fact Ashkenazic, and so some of the North African men prefer to pray in their own style in the smaller room.

Gradually I settle in, though I have trouble following the prayers in the beginning. Remembering a particular turn in the melody for the reader's repetition of the Amidah that the president at Eighth Street uses, I listen for it from the cantor here at the rue Basfroi and hear a satisfying similarity in his voice. I feel like a new immigrant coming to his *landsmanshaft*'s shul to hear the melodies from his town.

Throughout our year in Paris, I attend this synagogue about as frequently as I had gone to Eighth Street at first. Although the congregation is not unfriendly, no one invites me home for lunch, partly out of French reserve, and perhaps also because it is clear that I'm not very observant. I feel "unobservant" here in another sense: I do not register the vast store of information obviously available here about the interaction of religious Jews from different ethnic backgrounds. It escapes me, as though I were "off duty." In contrast to my feelings at Eighth Street, I am not motivated by the desire to make myself a regular here. And this is not my fieldwork situation: nothing external moves me to push my way through socially, to find out who these people really are and let them see me as well.

The Jews I encounter in the course of my research belong to an entirely different crowd. The *landsmanshaftn* to which they belong are secular organizations.

If I wanted to observe the Sabbath closely, it would be difficult for me to do my fieldwork. The immigrants hold many meetings on Saturdays, including a series of *shabbes-shmuesn*, afternoon discussions at which the main focus this year is the war in Lebanon.

I mention to one of my informants that I sometimes go to the synagogue. "I admire that," he responds. "I can't go back to the synagogue now. I've been away too long; it's too late for me." Toward the end of the year, we invite an autodidact historian of the immigrant community to dinner on Friday night and ask him to say the blessing over the challah. "I can't," he refuses, and will not explain further. Though his intellectual curiosity has led him to become friendly with us, and he is considering doing research on the resurgence of Orthodoxy among French Jews, his critical stance vis-à-vis his own secularist movement is insufficient to allow him to accept this religious honor. Enjoying the possibilities offered by marginality is sometimes impossible for those who are neither young nor well educated and who have often been deceived in their wholehearted commitments.

Throughout the year, Elissa has been growing stricter regarding *kashres*. She refuses to eat nonkosher meat and will order only fish in restaurants. She articulates our shared impression that Jewish secularism has failed to create everyday lifeways that can be transmitted from generation to generation, and that any lasting Judaism must be grounded in Jewish law and learning. Before parting for the summer—she to study Yiddish at Oxford, I to Jerusalem, to acquire the Hebrew that I will need to learn about Jewish law—we discuss the level of observance we want to adopt on our return to New York, but we come to no decision.

Elissa and I meet at the end of the summer in Los Angeles, for the bar mitzvah of her twin cousins. I am uncomfortable riding on shabbes; after spending an entire summer in Jerusalem, for the first time, it seems like a violation of myself. The roast beef sandwich I eat at the reception is the first nonkosher food I've eaten since leaving Paris.

Thus, without having made a formal declaration, I join Elissa in observing kashres (save for occasional lapses that I call my "*treyf* of the month club" and that become less and less frequent), and she joins me in keeping shabbes, albeit with some reluctance. Preparing to fulfill a promise made in a dream I had while in Paris, I take a further step: At the beginning of November, I begin attending daily services at another East Side shul and thus putting on tefillin again. One of my mother's cousins at the Telshe Yeshiva in Cleveland—whom I have never met—told me in the dream that I would always be welcome there, and I responded that if I got there, I would put on tefillin every day from then on. Later in November, Elissa and I fly to Cleveland for the weekend. Though we are welcomed warmly, it is clear that the rabbis and *rebetsins* at the yeshiva hoped for something more Jewish from me, the great-grandson of the Rosh Yeshiva's second wife, Miriam.

We return to the Eighth Street Shul as well, which has been secured and repaired sufficiently to make it usable once again. There are changes. Old Mr. Klapholz, with whom I hardly had exchanged a word, has passed away. Fishel's uncle Mr. Hochbaum, a congregant for half a century, no longer attends, since he is unable to walk all the way from Grand Street. On the other hand, my long-haired friend has moved into the neighborhood and attends regularly. Two of the younger members of the congregation have small children now, and they must go to a shul where there are other children for their son and daughter to play with. In February, our oldest member passes away, and after Shavuot, another member moves to Jerusalem. Two more young men eventually begin coming regularly and bring along their infant children. Now, in June 1986, the shul has thirteen regular male attendees. I am no longer free to sleep late on Saturday mornings, and fortunately I no longer want to.

All of this, to the extent it is of my own making, is the result of a search to realize that fragile illusion of wholeness which was destroyed when my family and almost all the others left Farmingdale. I will hazard a guess that Jewish anthropologists—perhaps anthropologists in general—are motivated by a sense of loss. Yet the seamless image of community is inevitably a child's image. We cannot regain what is lost, if only because it never existed as we remember it. Nothing in society is quite as harmonious as it seemed to me then, and I later learned about bitter political struggles that had taken place in Farmingdale, just as they had among the immigrants in Paris.

Our strategy, rather, should be to attempt to understand what it is we miss and need, which is available in still-living communities in another form. The image of wholeness which we share is foreshadowed by communities all of us stem from, however many generations back, and it can serve as a guide in the search for the reciprocal relationships of autonomous adulthood.

Anthropology is a tool for mediating between the self and the community. It has helped me to come to belong at the Eighth Street Shul: to withhold my opinions when it seems necessary, without feeling the guilt of self-compromise; to accept instruction and gentle reprimands with good humor; to believe it is worthwhile preserving something that might otherwise disappear. But belonging at Eighth Street does not mean that I have dissolved myself into an ideal Orthodox Jew. If I attempted to do so, I would be unable to continue being an anthropologist. If I fit into any category, it may be what my friend Kugelmass calls the "funky Orthodox": that is, those who participate in the community but whose interests and values are not confined to the Orthodox world. In fact, there are no ideal Orthodox Jews at Eighth Street; it is our respective quirks that provide the *raison d'être* of this haphazard but now intentional once-a-week community.

The fact that I have found a religious community that needs me because of its marginality and will tolerate me because of a generosity born of tradition is what I mean by the marginal redemption of one Jew. Likewise, if the shul survives, it will be because of its very marginality, because of the many individuals who have recognized the creative possibilities of a situation that demands that they create a new unity, while allowing each of them to retain their otherness. Isn't this the dream of anthropologists? Whether attempting to communicate knowledge between different Jewish communities, or between communities much more distant in tradition and empathy, we are messengers. We spend our own lives in moving back and forth among the worlds of others. As we do so, in order to avoid getting lost along the way, we must become cultural pioneers, learning to "get hold of our *trans*cultural selves" (Wolff 1970: 40). Communities on the edge of mass society, or even on the fringes of ethnic enclaves, seem to be among the most congenial fields in which to do so.

Let me finish with a parable:

Two Jews can afford to be fastidious about the dress, comportment, and erudition of a third. It gives them something to gossip about and identify against. Ten healthy Jews can have a similar luxury; an eleventh means competition for the ritual honors. It's nine Jews who are the most tolerant, as I learned one forlorn shabbes at Eighth Street. It was almost ten o'clock, and there was no minyan. Since everyone seemed content to wait patiently, I assumed that someone else had promised to come, and asked, who are we waiting for?"

"A *yid*," our oldest member replied without hesitation.

Eventually a Jew came along.

NOTES

1. Compare Pierre Bourdieu's critique of the structuralist theory of "reciprocal" gift exchange: "Even if reversibility [i.e., the assumption that gifts entail counter-gifts of equivalent value] is the objective truth of the discrete acts which ordinary experience knows in discrete form and calls gift exchanges, it is not the whole truth of a practice which could not exist if it were consciously perceived in accordance with the model. The temporal structure of gift exchange, which objectivism ignores, is what makes possible the coexistence of two opposing truths, which defines the full truth of the gift" (1977: 6).

    Similarly, in a narrative such as this one, because I, as author, already know the ending, it may seem as though each successive element fits into those that precede and follow it in such a way that their necessity is perfectly known. Actually my aim is to show how the background that nurtured me shaped in part my unpredictable responses to situations that in themselves were historically rather than culturally determined. See my conclusion, where I refer to one of the communities I now participate in as "haphazard but intentional."

2. Even if it was no more than a matter of convenience, this annual event demonstrates Jonathan Woocher's point that American Jewish "civil religion expects Jews to take advantage of the opportunities which America provides, and to use them to help fulfill their Jewish responsibilities" (1985: 161).

3. This may seem an outrageously loose claim, and I am quite willing to be proven wrong by literary scholars. But compare the conclusion of James Joyce's *Portrait of the Artist as a Young Man:*

    > Mother is putting my new secondhand clothes in order. She prays now, she says, that I may learn in my own life and away from home and friends what the heart is and what it feels. Amen. So be it. Welcome, O life! I go to encounter for the millionth time the reality of experience and to forge in the smithy of my soul the uncreated conscience of my race.
    > (1968: 252–53)

with the end of Moshe Szulsztein's memoir of a Polish Jewish childhood:

> When the truck was already fairly far along Warsaw Street and Kurow
> was barely visible, two more relatives appeared in a great rush, wanting to
> take their leave. These were my grandfather's pair of pigeons. The pi-
> geons knew me, and I knew them. I loved them, and perhaps they loved
> me as well ... But the truck is stronger than they are, it drives and drives
> further and further away from Kurow. My poor pigeons can't keep up,
> they remain behind ... Before they disappear altogether from my view I
> still discern them within the distant evening cloud, two small flying silver
> dots, one a bit behind the other. That, I know, is the male, and the sec-
> ond, a bit in front, is the female. (1982: 352)

4. For photographs of Eighth Street and other Lower East Side shuls, both surviving
   and abandoned, see Fine and Wolfe (1978).

5. "In every corner, in every little patch of darkness, up the blind alleys and the
   corridors, one could sense the presence of a swarming mass of humanity, a sly,
   shameful life. Shadows slunk along the walls. The stores were selling goods
   unknown to French people even by name" (Simenon 1963: 45).

REFERENCES

Bakan, David. 1958. *Sigmund Freud and the Jewish Mystical Tradition*. Princeton, N.J.: Van
  Nostrand.

Belcove-Shalin, Janet. 1988. "Becoming More of an Eskimo." In *Between Two Worlds:
  Ethnographic Essays on American Jews*. 77–98. Ithaca: Cornell University Press.

Bourdieu, Pierre. 1977. *Outline of a Theory of Practice*. Cambridge: Cambridge University
  Press.

Boyarin, Daniel. 1997. *Judaism as a Gender*. Berkeley: University of California Press.

Clifford, James. 1986. "On Ethnographic Allegory." In *Writing Culture: The Poetics and
  Politics of Ethnography*, ed. James Clifford and George Marcus. 98–121. Berkeley:
  University of California Press.

Cuddihy, John. 1974. *The Ordeal of Civility: Freud, Marx, Lévi-Strauss and the Jewish
  Struggle with Modernity*. New York: Basic Books.

Fabian, Johannes. 1983. *Time and the Other*. New York: Columbia University Press.

Faur, José. 1986. *Golden Doves with Silver Dots*. Bloomington: Indiana University Press.

Fine, Jo Renée, and Gerard Wolfe. 1978. *The Synagogues of New York's Lower East Side*.
  New York: Washington Mews Books.

Gough, Kathleen. 1968. "Anthropology and Imperialism." *Monthly Review* 19: 12–27.

Joyce, James. 1968 [1916]. *Portrait of the Artist as a Young Man*. New York: Viking Press.

Schnapper, Dominique. 1983. *Jewish Identities in France: An Analysis of Contemporary
  French Jewry*, trans. Arthur Goldhammer. Chicago: University of Chicago Press.

Simenon, Georges. 1963. *Maigret and the Enigmatic Left*, ed. Daphne Woodward. New
  York: Penguin Books.

Szulsztein, Moshe. 1982. *Dort vu mayn vig iz geshtanen*. Paris: Published by a Committee.

Wolff, Kurt. 1970. "The Sociology of Knowledge and Sociological Theory." In *The Sociology of Sociology,* ed. Larry T. Reynolds and Janice M. Reynolds. 31–67. New York: David McKay.

Woocher, Jonathan. 1985. "Sacred Survival." *Judaism* 34 (2): 151–62.

QUESTIONS FOR MAKING CONNECTIONS
WITHIN THE READING

1. When Jonathan Boyarin describes his childhood in Farmingdale, New Jersey, he takes us into a world of Jewish traditions and references that may be unfamiliar to some readers. Indeed, Boyarin's essay is concerned, in part, with tracing the author's efforts to grow more familiar with and gain a greater understanding of his own traditions. In the process, he describes many different kinds of Jews: an Orthodox Jew, a Jewish socialist, a Lubavitcher Hasid, an observant Jew, Zionists, and Jews who have been acculturated into American academic life, to name a few. What are the differences between the groups that Boyarin identifies? Why is he drawn to one group more than another?

2. "Waiting for a Jew" opens with the statement, "My story begins in a community...." What is the difference between an essay and a story? Why has Boyarin elected to tell his fellow anthropologists a story? What are the major events or pieces of this story? Is this a story that has a point? A moral? An argument?

3. The subtitle Boyarin has selected for his essay is "Marginal Redemption at the Eighth Street Shul." What is "marginal redemption"? What is it that gets redeemed in "Waiting for a Jew"?

QUESTIONS FOR WRITING

1. "[O]n the abandoned farm," Boyarin writes, "my first memories are tinged with a sense of traces, of mystery, of loss. Do all who eventually become anthropologists have this experience in some form, at some time in their early lives?" In posing this question, Boyarin suggests that there might be a connection between anthropology and a sense of loss. What might this connection be? In what ways has Boyarin's own research been shaped by this sense of loss?

2. Boyarin believes that "[a]ny marginal group in mass society may be subject without warning to the loss of its cultural landscape, and therefore those who are able to create portable landscapes for themselves are the most likely to endure." What is the difference between a "cultural landscape" and a "portable landscape"? At the end of Boyarin's story, what kind of landscape does he inhabit?

QUESTIONS FOR MAKING CONNECTIONS
BETWEEN READINGS

1. Leila Ahmed and Jonathan Boyarin can both be considered insiders, part of the very cultures they are studying. Are they both insiders in the same way, though? What difference does it make whether a culture is studied by insiders or outsiders? Write an essay in which you explore what it means to be a member of a culture. Consider the role that self-reflection plays in either establishing or limiting memberships in the cultures that Ahmed and Boyarin describe.

2. In "The Myth of the Ant Queen," Steven Johnson argues that complex systems have an intelligence of their own. And he suggests that as such systems develop, the individuals involved—whether humans or ants—may remain largely oblivious to the larger patterns of change. Individuals may assume they are doing one sort of thing, but the system as a whole is doing something else. Does Boyarin appear to share this way of thinking? Is culture also a complex system that unfolds in directions the individual actors might not always control or even understand fully? When we look at cultural change as exemplified by Boyarin's religious odyssey, does that change appear to be directed by a "unified, top-down" intelligence, or does it take place from the bottom up as a result of individual choices made by many different people? Are some cultures, institutions, and religions organized differently—that is, in a more top-down way?

NICHOLAS CARR

Perhaps with some justification, contemporary critics of technology often get dismissed as "Luddites"—a reference to a movement of British artisans who tried to halt mechanized manufacturing in the nineteenth century. Yet one of those critics, Nicholas Carr, is anything but backward-looking. A former executive editor of the *Harvard Business Review* and a member of the steering board for the World Economic Forum's cloud computing project, Carr is an astute inside observer of technological change. More than many writers on the subject of the Web, who tend to praise it hyperbolically, he has been able to step back and ask about its larger and less positive implications. In his book *The Big Switch* (2008), Carr disputes the notion that the Web is inherently democratic. While admitting that the rise of the PC brought about a temporary flourishing of individual creativity, he alleges that this freedom has been lost with the shift away from PCs to the Net—and the client-server system that increasingly enables corporations and bureaucrats to reassert their accustomed mastery over worker-citizens. He writes that as the "pages of the World Wide Web turn into the unified and programmable database of the World Wide Computer ... a powerful new kind of control becomes possible." A site like Facebook might appear to provide endless opportunities for individual expression and networking among friends, but this "sharing" can actually erode the boundaries essential to personal freedom, mental health, and civility.

One important strain of all Carr's work is a critique of "techno–utopianism," the idea that technological change will automatically have positive results. As he recognizes in an earlier book, *Does IT Matter?* (2004), the advantages of a new technology tend to get exaggerated the first time they are trotted out. Gradually, he reasons, the Net will become ordinary and predictable, like the plumbing in our homes or the highway system. The pace of innovation will slow down and businesses will have to look elsewhere for their competitive advantage. Recently Carr's thinking has taken a new turn, as he has examined the cognitive effects of the Net on its users. In a widely circulated article, "Is Google Making Us Stupid?," and in the book that followed, *The Shallows* (2010), Carr argues that the "media are not just passive channels of information. They supply the stuff

Carr, Nicholas. "Is Google Making Us Stupid? What the Internet is Doing to Our Brains," *The Atlantic*, July/August 2008. http://www.theatlantic.com/magazine/archive/2008/07/is-google-making-us-stupid/6868.
Biographical information is drawn from http://www.nicholasgcarr.com/index.shtml.
The quotation in the first paragraph is from http://www.nicholasgcarr.com/bigswitch/excerpt3.shtml. The observation about Facebook comes from http://www.britannica.com/blogs/2009/01/sharing-is-creepy/.

of thought, but they also shape the process of thought." And he alleges that the Net is changing thought today in a way that makes it increasingly shallow—that is, unreflecting and blandly standardized. "Once," he writes, "I was a scuba diver in a sea of words. Now I zip along the surface like a guy on a Jet Ski."

■ ■

Is Google Making Us Stupid?

"Dave, stop. Stop, will you? Stop, Dave. Will you stop, Dave?" So the super-computer HAL pleads with the implacable astronaut Dave Bowman in a famous and weirdly poignant scene toward the end of Stanley Kubrick's *2001: A Space Odyssey*. Bowman, having nearly been sent to a deep-space death by the mal-functioning machine, is calmly, coldly disconnecting the memory circuits that control its artificial brain. "Dave, my mind is going," HAL says, forlornly. "I can feel it. I can feel it." I can feel it, too. Over the past few years I've had an uncomfortable sense that someone, or something, has been tinkering with my brain, remapping the neural circuitry, reprogramming the memory. My mind isn't going—so far as I can tell—but it's changing. I'm not thinking the way I used to think. I can feel it most strongly when I'm reading. Immersing myself in a book or a lengthy article used to be easy. My mind would get caught up in the narrative or the turns of the argument, and I'd spend hours strolling through long stretches of prose. That's rarely the case anymore. Now my concentration often starts to drift after two or three pages. I get fidgety, lose the thread, begin looking for something else to do. I feel as if I'm always dragging my wayward brain back to the text. The deep reading that used to come naturally has become a struggle.

I think I know what's going on. For more than a decade now, I've been spending a lot of time online, searching and surfing and sometimes adding to the great databases of the Internet. The Web has been a godsend to me as a writer. Research that once required days in the stacks or periodical rooms of libraries can now be done in minutes. A few Google searches, some quick clicks on hyperlinks, and I've got the telltale fact or pithy quote I was after. Even when I'm not working, I'm as likely as not to be foraging in the Web's info-thickets, reading and writing e-mails, scanning headlines and blog posts, watching videos and listening to podcasts, or just tripping from link to link to link. (Unlike foot-notes, to which they're sometimes likened, hyperlinks don't merely point to re-lated works; they propel you toward them.)

For me, as for others, the Net is becoming a universal medium, the conduit for most of the information that flows through my eyes and ears and into my mind. The advantages of having immediate access to such an incredibly rich store of information are many, and they've been widely described and duly applauded. "The perfect recall of silicon memory," *Wired's* Clive Thompson has written, "can be an enormous boon to thinking." But that boon comes at a price. As the media theorist Marshall McLuhan pointed out in the 1960s, media are not just passive channels of information. They supply the stuff of thought, but they also shape the process of thought. And what the Net seems to be doing is chipping away my capacity for concentration and contemplation. My mind now expects to take in information the way the Net distributes it—in a swiftly moving stream of particles. Once I was a scuba diver in the sea of words. Now I zip along the surface like a guy on a Jet Ski.

I'm not the only one. When I mention my troubles with reading to friends and acquaintances—literary types, most of them—many say they're having similar experiences. The more they use the Web, the more they have to fight to stay focused on long pieces of writing. Some of the bloggers I follow have also begun mentioning the phenomenon. Scott Karp, who writes a blog about online media, recently confessed that he has stopped reading books altogether. "I was a lit major in college, and used to be [a] voracious book reader," he wrote. "What happened?" He speculates on the answer: "What if I do all my reading on the web not so much because the way I read has changed, i.e. I'm just seeking convenience, but because the way I *think* has changed?"

Bruce Friedman, who blogs regularly about the use of computers in medicine, has also described how the Internet has altered his mental habits. "I now have almost totally lost the ability to read and absorb a longish article on the web or in print," he wrote earlier this year, A pathologist who has long been on the faculty of the University of Michigan Medical School, Friedman elaborated on his comment in a telephone conversation with me. His thinking, he said, has taken on a "staccato" quality, reflecting the way he quickly scans short passages of text from many sources online. "I can't read *War and Peace* anymore," he admitted. "I've lost the ability to do that. Even a blog post of more than three or four paragraphs is too much to absorb. I skim it."

Anecdotes alone don't prove much. And we still await the long-term neurological and psychological experiments that will provide a definitive picture of how Internet use affects cognition. But a recently published study of online research habits conducted by scholars from University College London suggests that we may well be in the midst of a sea change in the way we read and think. As part of the five-year research program, the scholars examined computer logs documenting the behavior of visitors to two popular research sites, one operated by the British Library and one by a U.K. educational consortium, that provide access to journal articles, e-books, and other sources of written information. They found that people using the sites exhibited "a form of skimming activity," hopping from one source to another and rarely returning to any source they'd already visited. They would typically read no more than one or two pages of an article or book before they would "bounce" out to another site. Sometimes they'd save a long article, but there's no evidence that they ever went back and actually read it. The authors of the study report:

> It is clear that users are not reading online in the traditional sense; indeed there are signs that new forms of "reading" are emerging as users "power browse" horizontally through titles, contents pages and abstracts going for quick wins. It almost seems that they go online to avoid reading in the traditional sense.

Thanks to the ubiquity of text on the Internet, not to mention the popularity of text-messaging on cell phones, we may well be reading more today than we did in the 1970s or 1980s, when television was our medium of choice. But it's a different kind of reading, and behind it lies a different kind of thinking—perhaps even a new sense of the self. "We are not only *what* we read," says Maryanne Wolf, a developmental psychologist at Tufts University and the author of *Proust and the Squid: The Story and Science of the Reading Brain*. "We are *how* we read." Wolf worries that the style of reading promoted by the Net, a style that puts "efficiency" and "immediacy" above all else, may be weakening our capacity for the kind of deep reading that emerged when an earlier technology, the printing press, made long and complex works of prose commonplace. When we read online, she says, we tend to become "mere decoders of information." Our ability to interpret text, to make the rich mental connections that form when we read deeply and without distraction, remains largely disengaged.

Reading, explains Wolf, is not an instinctive skill for human beings. It's not etched into our genes the way speech is. We have to teach our minds how to translate the symbolic characters we see into the language we understand. And the media or other technologies we use in learning and practicing the craft of reading play an important part in shaping the neural circuits inside our brains. Experiments demonstrate that readers of ideograms, such as the Chinese, develop a mental circuitry for reading that is very different from the circuitry found in those of us whose written language employs an alphabet. The variations extend across many regions of the brain, including those that govern such essential cognitive functions as memory and the interpretation of visual and auditory stimuli. We can expect as well that the circuits woven by our use of the Net will be different from those woven by our reading of books and other printed works.

Sometime in 1882, Friedrich Nietzsche bought a typewriter—a Malling-Hansen Writing Ball, to be precise. His vision was failing, and keeping his eyes focused on a page had become exhausting and painful, often bringing on crushing headaches. He had been forced to curtail his writing, and he feared that he would soon have to give it up. The typewriter rescued him, at least for a time. Once he had mastered touch-typing, he was able to write with his eyes closed, using only the tips of his fingers. Words could once again flow from his mind to the page.

But the machine had a subtler effect on his work. One of Nietzsche's friends, a composer, noticed a change in the style of his writing. His already terse prose had become even tighter, more telegraphic. "Perhaps you will through this instrument even take to a new idiom," the friend wrote in a letter, noting that, in his own work, his "'thoughts' in music and language often depend on the quality of pen and paper."

"You are right," Nietzsche replied, "our writing equipment takes part in the forming of our thoughts." Under the sway of the machine, writes the German media scholar Friedrich A. Kittler, Nietzsche's prose "changed from arguments to aphorisms, from thoughts to puns, from rhetoric to telegram style."

The human brain is almost infinitely malleable. People used to think that our mental meshwork, the dense connections formed among the 100 billion or so neurons inside our skulls, was largely fixed by the time we reached adulthood. But brain researchers have discovered that that's not the case. James Olds, a professor of neuroscience who directs the Krasnow Institute for Advanced Study at George Mason University, says that even the adult mind "is very plastic." Nerve cells routinely break old connections and form new ones. "The brain," according to Olds, "has the ability to reprogram itself on the fly, altering the way it functions."

As we use what the sociologist Daniel Bell has called our "intellectual technologies"—the tools that extend our mental rather than our physical capacities—we inevitably begin to take on the qualities of those technologies. The mechanical clock, which came into common use in the 14th century, provides a compelling example. In *Technics and Civilization,* the historian and cultural critic Lewis Mumford described how the clock "disassociated time from human events and helped create the belief in an independent world of mathematically measurable sequences." The "abstract framework of divided time" became "the point of reference for both action and thought."

The clock's methodical ticking helped bring into being the scientific mind and the scientific man. But it also took something away. As the late MIT computer scientist Joseph Weizenbaum observed in his 1976 book *Computer Power and Human Reason: From Judgment to Calculation,* the conception of the world that emerged from the widespread use of timekeeping instruments "remains an impoverished version of the older one, for it rests on a rejection of those direct experiences that formed the basis for, and indeed constituted, the old reality." In deciding when to eat, to work, to sleep, to rise, we stopped listening to our senses and started obeying the clock.

The process of adapting to new intellectual technologies is reflected in the changing metaphors we use to explain ourselves to ourselves. When the mechanical clock arrived, people began thinking of their brains as operating "like clockwork." Today, in the age of software, we have come to think of them as operating "like computers." But the changes, neuroscience tells us, go much deeper than metaphor. Thanks to our brain's plasticity, the adaptation occurs also at a biological level.

The Internet promises to have particularly far-reaching effects on cognition. In a paper published in 1936, the British mathematician Alan Turing proved that a digital computer, which at the time existed only as a theoretical machine, could be programmed to perform the function of any other information-processing device. And that's what we're seeing today. The Internet, an immeasurably powerful computing system, is subsuming most of our other intellectual technologies.

It's becoming our map and our clock, our printing press and our typewriter, our calculator and our telephone, and our radio and TV.

When the Net absorbs a medium, that medium is re-created in the Net's image. It injects the medium's content with hyperlinks, blinking ads, and other digital gewgaws, and it surrounds the content with the content of all the other media it has absorbed. A new e-mail message, for instance, may announce its arrival as we're glancing over the latest headlines at a newspaper's site. The result is to scatter our attention and diffuse our concentration.

The Net's influence doesn't end at the edges of a computer screen, either. As people's minds become attuned to the crazy quilt of Internet media, traditional media have to adapt to the audience's new expectations. Television programs add text crawls and pop-up ads, and magazines and newspapers shorten their articles, introduce capsule summaries, and crowd their pages with easy-to-browse info-snippets. When, in March of this year, *The New York Times* decided to devote the second and third pages of every edition to article abstracts, its design director, Tom Bodkin, explained that the "shortcuts" would give harried readers a quick "taste" of the day's news, sparing them the "less efficient" method of actually turning the pages and reading the articles. Old media have little choice but to play by the new-media rules.

Never has a communications system played so many roles in our lives—or exerted such broad influence over our thoughts—as the Internet does today. Yet for all that's been written about the Net, there's been little consideration of how, exactly, it's reprogramming us. The Net's intellectual ethic remains obscure.

About the same time that Nietzsche started using his typewriter, an earnest young man named Frederick Winslow Taylor carried a stopwatch into the Midvale steel plant in Philadelphia and began a historic series of experiments aimed at improving the efficiency of the plant's machinists. With the approval of Midvale's owners, he recruited a group of factory hands, set them to work on various metalworking machines, and recorded and timed their every movement as well as the operations of the machines. By breaking down every job into a sequence of small, discrete steps and then testing different ways of performing each one, Taylor created a set of precise instructions—an "algorithm," we might say today—for how each worker should work. Midvale's employees grumbled about the strict new regime, claiming that it turned them into little more than automatons, but the factory's productivity soared.

More than a hundred years after the invention of the steam engine, the Industrial Revolution had at last found its philosophy and its philosopher. Taylor's tight industrial choreography—his "system," as he liked to call it—was embraced by manufacturers throughout the country and, in time, around the world. Seeking maximum speed, maximum efficiency, and maximum output, factory owners used time-and-motion studies to organize their work and configure the jobs of their workers. The goal, as Taylor defined it in his celebrated 1911 treatise *The Principles of Scientific Management,* was to identify and adopt, for every job, the "one best method" of work, and thereby to effect "the gradual substitution of science for rule of thumb throughout the mechanic arts." Once his system was applied to all acts of manual labor, Taylor assured his followers, it would bring about a restructuring not only of industry but of society, creating a Utopia of perfect efficiency. "In the past the man has been first," he declared. "In the future the system must be first."

Taylor's system is still very much with us; it remains the ethic of industrial manufacturing. And now, thanks to the growing power that computer engineers and software coders wield over our intellectual lives, Taylor's ethic is beginning to govern the realm of the mind as well. The Internet is a machine designed for the efficient and automated collection, transmission, and manipulation of information, and its legions of programmers are intent on finding the "one best method"—the perfect algorithm—to carry out every mental movement of what we've come to describe as "knowledge work." Google's headquarters in Mountain View, California—the Googleplex—is the Internet's high church, and the religion—practiced inside its walls is Taylorism. Google, says its chief executive, Eric Schmidt, is "a company that's founded around the science of measurement," and it is striving to "systematize everything" it does. Drawing on the terabytes of behavioral data it collects through its search engine and other sites, it carries out thousands of experiments a day, according to the *Harvard Business Review,* and it uses the results to refine the algorithms that increasingly control how people find information and extract meaning from it. What Taylor did for the work of the hand, Google is doing for the work of the mind. The company has declared that its mission is "to organize the world's information and make it universally accessible and useful." It seeks to develop "the perfect search engine," which it defines as something that "understands exactly what you mean and gives you back exactly what you want." In Google's view, information is a kind of commodity, a utilitarian resource that can be mined and processed with industrial efficiency. The more pieces of information we can "access" and the faster we can extract their gist, the more productive we become as thinkers.

Where does it end? Sergey Brin and Larry Page, the gifted young men who founded Google while pursuing doctoral degrees in computer science at Stanford, speak frequently of their desire to turn their search engine into an artificial intelligence, a HAL-like machine that might be connected directly to our brains. "The ultimate search engine is something as smart as people—or smarter," Page said in a speech a few years back. "For us, working on search is a way to work on artificial intelligence." In a 2004 interview with *Newsweek,* Brin said, "Certainly if you had all the world's information directly attached to your brain, or an artificial brain that was smarter than your brain, you'd be better off." Last year, Page told a convention of scientists that Google is "really trying to build artificial intelligence and to do it on a large scale."

Such an ambition is a natural one, even an admirable one, for a pair of math whizzes with vast quantities of cash at their disposal and a small army of computer scientists in their employ. A fundamentally scientific enterprise, Google is motivated by a desire to use technology, in Eric Schmidt's words, "to solve problems that have never been solved before," and artificial intelligence is the hardest problem out there. Why wouldn't Brin and Page want to be the ones to crack it?

Still, their easy assumption that we'd all "be better off" if our brains were supplemented, or even replaced, by an artificial intelligence is unsettling. It suggests a belief that intelligence is the output of a mechanical process, a series of discrete steps that can be isolated, measured, and optimized. In Google's world, the world we enter when we go online, there's little place for the fuzziness of contemplation. Ambiguity is not an opening for insight but a bug to be fixed. The human brain is just an outdated computer that needs a faster processor and a bigger hard drive.

The idea that our minds should operate as high-speed data-processing machines is not only built into the workings of the Internet, it is the network's reigning business model as well. The faster we surf across the Web—the more links we click and pages we view—the more opportunities Google and other companies gain to collect information about us and to feed us advertisements. Most of the proprietors of the commercial Internet have a financial stake in collecting the crumbs of data we leave behind as we flit from link to link—the more crumbs, the better. The last thing these companies want is to encourage leisurely reading or slow, concentrated thought. It's in their economic interest to drive us to distraction.

Maybe I'm just a worrywart. Just as there's a tendency to glorify technological progress, there's a countertendency to expect the worst of every new tool or machine. In Plato's *Phaedrus,* Socrates bemoaned the development of writing. He feared that as people came to rely on the written word as a substitute for the knowledge they used to carry inside their heads, they would, in the words of one of the dialogue's characters, "cease to exercise their memory and become forgetful." And because they would be able to "receive a quantity of information without proper instruction," they would "be thought very knowledgeable when they are for the most part quite ignorant." They would be "filled with the conceit of wisdom instead of real wisdom." Socrates wasn't wrong—the new technology did often have the effects he feared—but he was shortsighted. He couldn't foresee the many ways that writing and reading would serve to spread information, spur fresh ideas, and expand human knowledge (if not wisdom).

The arrival of Gutenberg's printing press in the 15th century set off another round of teeth gnashing. The Italian humanist Hieronimo Squarciafico worried that the easy availability of books would lead to intellectual laziness, making men "less studious" and weakening their minds. Others argued that cheaply printed books and broadsheets would undermine religious authority, demean the work of scholars and scribes, and spread sedition and debauchery. As New York University professor Clay Shirky notes, "Most of the arguments made against the printing press were correct, even prescient." But, again, the doomsayers were unable to imagine the myriad blessings that the printed word would deliver. So, yes, you should be skeptical of my skepticism. Perhaps those who dismiss critics of the Internet as Luddites or nostalgists will be proved correct, and from our hyperactive, data-stoked minds will spring a golden age of intellectual discovery and universal wisdom. Then again, the Net isn't the alphabet, and although it may replace the printing press, it produces something altogether different. The kind of deep reading that a sequence of printed pages promotes is valuable not just for the knowledge we acquire from the author's words but for the intellectual vibrations those words set off within our own minds. In the quiet spaces opened up by the sustained, undistracted reading of a book, or by any other act of contemplation, for that matter, we make our own associations, draw our own inferences and analogies, foster our own ideas. Deep reading, as Maryanne Wolf argues, is indistinguishable from deep thinking. If we lose those quiet spaces, or fill them up with "content," we will sacrifice something important not only in ourselves but in our culture. In a recent essay the playwright Richard Foreman eloquently described what's at stake:

> I come from a tradition of Western culture, in which the ideal (my ideal) was the complex, dense and "cathedral-like" structure of the highly educated and articulate personality—a man or woman who carried inside themselves [sic] a personally constructed and unique version of the entire heritage of the West. [But now] I see within us all (myself included) the replacement of complex inner density with a new kind of self—evolving under the pressure of information overload and the technology of the "instantly available."

As we are drained of our "inner repertory of dense cultural inheritance," Foreman concluded, we risk turning into "'pancake people'—spread wide and thin as we connect with that vast network of information accessed by the mere touch of a button."

I'm haunted by that scene in *2001*. What makes it so poignant, and so weird, is the computer's emotional response to the disassembly of its mind: its despair as one circuit after another goes dark, its childlike pleading with the astronaut—"I can feel it. I can feel it, I'm afraid"—and its final reversion to what can only be called a state of innocence. HAL's outpouring of feeling contrasts with the emotionlessness that characterizes the human figures in the film, who go about their business with an almost robotic efficiency. Their thoughts and actions feel scripted, as if they're following the steps of an algorithm. In the world of *2001,* people have become so machine-like that the most human character turns out to be a machine. That's the essence of Kubrick's dark prophecy: as we come to rely on computers to mediate our understanding of the world, it is our own intelligence that flattens into artificial intelligence.

QUESTIONS FOR MAKING CONNECTIONS
WITHIN THE READING

1. At various points in his essay Carr employs the term "deep reading" to describe an alternative to the sort of reading that people do online. Indeed, Carr's own essay might be understood as an example of writing that encourages deep reading. Carefully retrace Carr's entire argument, noting where the phrase "deep reading" appears. When it does, is Carr merely restating a point he has already made, or is he adding something that extends his previous insights? Is his essay meant to make a single argument, or is he

trying to demonstrate a process of questioning that might go on even after the act of reading is done?

2. One striking element of Carr's argument is his use of illustrative anecdotes. For example, he devotes two paragraphs to the German philosopher Nietzsche's experience with learning to type. Later, Carr recaps in some detail the ideas of several theorists who have explored the way mechanical clocks changed how people think. Still later he recounts the enormous influence of Taylor's experiment with "scientific management." What are the relationships among these anecdotes? If Carr simply wants to make the point that technology shapes our mental processing, why does he choose examples from the past?

3. As Carr develops his argument, he weaves together citations—the words and ideas of many different writers, from journalists, programmers, and scientists to philosophers, historians, and sociologists. What function do these citations serve other than to assure his readers that Carr has received a very broad education? What do Carr's citations tell us about the way his own thinking has developed? How might the cited writers have helped him to think more carefully than any single person could manage by himself? At what points do you see the thinking of others, and at what points does Carr seem to begin thinking independently?

QUESTIONS FOR WRITING

1. It is relatively easy to map out the differences between deep reading and the "foraging" behavior that the internet promotes. But what consequences might follow from the Net's emergence as a "universal medium"? What might be the costs of this total dominance, if it ever comes to pass? Increasingly, music and the visual arts as well as forms of written communication all get siphoned through the Net. What are the benefits of multiple conduits for knowledge—books, magazines, newspapers, radio, vinyl records, movies, even phones—and what would we lose if this diversity were absent? Compare, for example, sitting in a movie theater with watching the same film online. Remember to explore the larger contexts as well—that is, the physical and social environments in which information circulates.

2. Even while we create technology, it is also re-creating us. What can be learned from Carr's essay about the complex relations between technology and the human race? Is it an illusion to assume that humans are in control, or that we can somehow remain unchanged no matter what we do? Even though a massive amount of evidence—from history as well as contemporary science—suggests that our nature is so pliable that new technologies can deeply change us, why do you think we tend to remain unconvinced? Has a belief in a singular "human nature" and a permanent "core self" kept us from responding to dangers that should have been obvious by now? Even

though the benefits of the Net might outweigh the costs, how can we detect its potential problems before they become gravely destructive? Finally, is it actually impossible to control the growth of new technology, or is the belief in unstoppable change a modern-day superstition?

QUESTIONS FOR MAKING CONNECTIONS
BETWEEN TEXTS

1. In rather different ways, both Carr and Oliver Sacks are part of a larger cultural shift: a turning away from the "mind" to the "brain" as the key term for understanding ourselves. Since ancient times, philosophers have written on the mind and on faculties like reason and imagination, which they saw as unchanging and universal. By contrast, the brain is now understood to be highly "plastic"—that is, subject to deep changes in the way it operates, depending on the environment. In what ways might this shift from mind to brain transform how we view human nature? On the basis of your reading of Sacks and Carr, would you say a fixed "human nature" exists at all?

2. In "Immune to Reality," Daniel Gilbert makes an argument about the complexity of human motivations, arguing that "people are typically unaware of the reasons why they are doing what they are doing." He means that we often overlook our real motives, which are largely unconscious, preferring to make up reasons that seem to fit with our conscious assumptions and beliefs. Often the result is unhappiness, even when we get exactly what we want. Using Gilbert as your starting point, take a second look at the promise of the Net, and then compare it to the reality. When we sing the praises of this new technology, are we actually engaged in what Gilbert calls "cooking the facts"? Does Carr's essay support the view that the Net has been wildly oversold?

SUSAN FALUDI

PULITZER PRIZE–WINNING journalist Susan Faludi first became interested in writing about feminism in the fifth grade, when she polled her classmates to determine their feelings about the Vietnam War and legalized abortion. In the furor that followed Faludi's release of data showing her peers' liberal attitudes, Faludi came to realize, as she put it in an interview, "the power that you could have as a feminist writer. Not being the loudest person on the block, not being one who regularly interrupted in class or caused a scene, I discovered that through writing I could make my views heard, and I could actually create change."

The daughter of a Hungarian immigrant who survived the holocaust, Faludi was raised in Queens and attended Harvard, where she studied literature and American history. After graduating in 1981, Faludi worked for a number of newspapers, including the *New York Times* and the *Wall Street Journal*, before devoting her time to writing *Backlash: The Undeclared War Against American Women* (1991), a study of the media's assault on feminism. The following year, *Backlash* won the National Book Critics Circle Award for general nonfiction and made Faludi into a household name. She appeared on the cover of *Time* magazine with Gloria Steinem and, almost overnight, became a national spokesperson on women's rights and the future of feminism.

While doing research for *Backlash*, Faludi began to wonder why the men who opposed women's progress were so angry. In setting out to understand this anger, Faludi interviewed men's groups sex workers in the pornography industry, union members, the unemployed, and other disenfranchised males. "The Naked Citadel," which presents Faludi's investigation into why male cadets were so enraged by the admission of women into the military academy, is one part of this project, and has since been incorporated into Faludi's second book, *Stiffed: The Betrayal of the American Man* (1999). The surprising thesis of *Stiffed* is that men, too, have suffered during the recent social upheavals because the work that many of them did in the past is no longer held in high regard or even readily available because of the loss of manufacturing jobs. Faludi's most recent book, *The Terror Dream: Fear and Fantasy in Post-9/11 America* (2007), returns to the issues of gender and social upheaval. While "The Naked Citadel" explores antifeminist attitudes in a time of peace, *The Terror Dream* charts the difficulties facing feminism in a time of war. Faludi concludes in this book that the

Faludi, Susan. "The Naked Citadel." *The New Yorker*, September 5, 1994. 62–81.
Quotations come from Brian Lamb's interview with Susan Faludi on Booknotes, October 25, 1992 <http://www.booknotes.org/transcripts/10096.htm> and Kate Melloy's interview with Susan Faludi, "Feminist Author Susan Faludi Preaches Male Inclusion" <http://www.kollegeville.com/kampus/faludi.htm>.

September 11 attacks have created further challenges for feminism by ushering in an era of hysterical insistence on traditional roles for men and women: the men are summoned to protect, while the women must be passively defended. In spite of this predicament, Faludi holds out hope for a society where men and women can work together cooperatively and on equal footing. But she also believes that "[t]o revive a genuine feminism, we must disconnect feminism from the individual pursuit of happiness and reconnect it with the individual desire for social responsibility: the basic human need and joy to be part of a larger, meaningful struggle, which engages the entire society."

The Naked Citadel

Along the edges of the quad, in the gutters, the freshman cadets were squaring their corners. The "knobs," as they are called for their nearly hairless doorknob pates, aren't allowed to step on the lawn of the broad parade ground, which is trimmed close, as if to match their shorn heads. Keeping off the grass is one of many prohibitions that obtain at The Citadel, a public military college on Charleston's Ashley River. Another is the rule that so many of the cadets say brought them to this Moorish-style, gated campus: Girls keep out.

The campus has a dreamy, flattened quality, with its primary colors, checkerboard courtyards, and storybook-castle barracks. It feels more like an architect's rendering of a campus—almost preternaturally clean, orderly, antiseptic—than the messy real thing. I stood at the far end of the quad, at the academic hall's front steps, and watched the cadets make their herky-jerky perpendicular turns as they drew closer for the first day of class. They walked by stiffly, their faces heat-blotched and vulnerable, and as they passed each in turn shifted his eyes downward. I followed one line of boys into a classroom, a Western Civ class—except, of course, they weren't really boys at all. These were college men, manly recruits to an elite military college whose virile exploits were mythicized in best-selling novels by Calder Willingham and Pat Conroy, both Citadel alumni. So why did I expect their voices to crack when they spoke for the first time? Partly, it was the grammar-schoolish taking of attendance, compulsory at The Citadel. Multiple absences can lead to "tours," hours of marching back and forth in the courtyard with a pinless rifle over one shoulder; or to "cons," confinement to one's room.

But mostly it was the young men themselves, with their doughy faces and twitching limbs, who gave me the urge to babysit. Despite their enrollment in a college long considered "the big bad macho school" (as a former R.O.T.C. commander, Major General Robert E. Wagner, once put it), the cadets lacked the swagger and knowingness of big men on campus. They perched tentatively on their chairs, their hands arranged in a dutiful clasp on their desktops, as if they were expecting a ruler slap to the knuckles. A few dared to glance over at the female visitor, but whenever they made eye contact they averted their gaze and color stained their cheeks.

"As many of you probably know," their teacher said, "this was almost the day the first woman joined The Citadel." The cadets continued to study their polished shoes. "How do you, in fact, feel about whether women should be allowed to attend?"

Silence reigned. Maybe the cadets felt the question put them in an awkward spot. Not only was their teacher in favor of admitting women to The Citadel's Corps of Cadets, the teacher *was* a woman. Indeed, Professor Jane Bishop seemed to be in the strange situation of calling in an air strike on her own position. It was the first day of fall classes in the 1993–94 academic year at The Citadel, and she was broaching the question of the hour. But this incongruity wasn't limited to her classroom. From the moment I stepped onto the school's campus, I had been struck by an unexpected circumstance: though an all-male institution—an institution, moreover, whose singular mission was "making men"—The Citadel was by no means free of women. Female teachers were improving cadets' minds, female administrators were keeping their records, and an all-female (and all-black) staff served the meals in the mess hall. There was also the fact that female students made up seventy-seven percent of the enrollment of the evening school, and many other female students attended summer school with the cadets. What about them? Of course, summer school and evening school aren't part of the military college proper. Cadets don't attend the evening school; and as Major Rick Mill, The Citadel's public-relations director, notes, those cadets who attend the summer school "aren't wearing their uniforms."

Today they were, and so was their teacher. All permanent instructors, regardless of their sex (about fifteen percent are women), wear uniforms as part of their required affiliation with a largely ceremonial outfit once known as the South Carolina Unorganized Militia, and still called by the unfortunate acronym SCUM. Bishop wore hers with what seemed like a deliberate air of disarray.

The cadets' uniforms were considerably tidier—testament to the efficacy of the famous cadet shirt tuck, a maneuver akin to hospital-corners bedmaking and so exacting a cadet cannot perform it without assistance. Even so, the gray cadet uniform, with the big black stripe down the side of the pants and the nametag above the left breast, is the sort more often seen on high-school band members than on fighting soldiers.

"Remember," Bishop prodded them, "speech is free in the classroom."

At last, a cadet unclasped and raised a hand. "Well, I'd have no problem with her in the day program, but she can't join the Corps."

"She," as everyone there knew, was Shannon Faulkner, the woman who had challenged the school's hundred-and-fifty-year-old all-male policy by omitting reference to her sex from her application and winning acceptance to the

Corps of Cadets earlier that year—acceptance that was rescinded once the administrators discovered their error. Faulkner's attempt to gain entrance then shifted from the admissions office to the courts. She was allowed under court order to attend day classes during the spring semester of 1994, the first woman to do so. On July 22nd, a United States District Court ruled that The Citadel must admit Faulkner into the Corps of Cadets proper; three weeks later, the Fourth United States Circuit Court of Appeals granted The Citadel a stay pending appeal.

Yet why shouldn't she be permitted into the Corps, Bishop pressed. One of her students recited the fitness requirement—forty-five pushups and fifty-five sit-ups in two-minute sets, and a two-mile run in sixteen minutes. But the administration made passing the fitness test a requirement for graduation only *after* Shannon Faulkner filed suit. An alumnus recounted in court that many upperclassmen he knew who had failed the test skipped the punitive morning run and "sat around and ate doughnuts." Another of Bishop's students cited the shaved-head rule. But this, too, seemed a minor point. A woman cadet could conceivably get a buzz cut. Sinéad O'Connor had done it, Bishop pointed out, without undue injury to her career. And, anyway, after freshman year the men no longer get their heads shaved. Other deprivations of freshman year were invoked: having to "brace" on demand—that is, assume a stance in which a knob stands very erect and tucks in his chin until it puckers up like a rooster's wattle—and having to greet every upperclassman's bellowed command and rebuke with "Sir, yes sir!" or "Sir, no sir!" or "Sir, no excuse sir!" But women, obviously, aren't incapable of obeisance; one might even say they have a long history of it.

Weighing heaviest on the cadets' minds, it turned out, was the preservation of the all-male communal bathroom. The sharing of the stall-less showers and stall-less toilets is "at the heart of the Citadel experience," according to more than one cadet. The men bathe as a group; they walk to the shower down the open galleries, in full view of the courtyard below, and do so, one cadet said, in "nothing but our bathrobes" or "even without any clothes." Another cadet said, "I know it sounds trivial, but all of us in one shower, it's like we're all one, we're all the same, and—I don't know—you feel like you're exposed, but you feel safe. You know these guys are going to be your friends for life." His voice trailed off. "I just can't explain it but when they take that away, it's over. This place will be ruined."

"If women come here, they'll have to put up window shades in all the rooms," a cadet said. "Think of all the windows in the barracks. That could be eight thousand, nine thousand dollars. You've got to look at the costs."

At the end of the hour, the cadets filed out and resumed their double-time jog along the gutters—and their place in the "fourth-class system." This "system" is a nine-month regimen of small and large indignities intended to "strip" each young recruit of his original identity and remold him into the "Whole Man," a vaguely defined ideal, half Christian soldier, half Dale Carnegie junior executive. As a knob explained it to me, "We're all suffering together. It's how we bond." Another knob said, "It's a strange analogy, but it's almost like a P.O.W. camp."

Freshmen are in the "fourth-class system," a regimen to "strip" each recruit of his identity and remold him into the "Whole Man." Illustration by Mark Zingarelli, originally published in *The New Yorker*. © Mark Zingarelli/House of Zing

One cadet dawdled, glancing nervously around, then sidled up to me. He spoke in a near whisper, and what he had to say had nothing to do with lavatory etiquette or military tradition. "The great majority of the guys here are very misogynistic," he said. "All they talk about is how girls are pigs and sluts."

I asked him to explain at greater length. He agonized. "I have to keep quiet," he said, but he finally agreed to meet me later, in an out-of-the-way spot on the upper floor of the student-activities center. He rejoined his class-mates with that distinctive knob march, "the march of the puppets," as a profes-sor described it to me later. It was a gait caused in some cases, I was told, by the most conscientious cadets' efforts to keep their shirts perfectly straight with the help of garters—one end of the garter clipped to the shirttail, the other end to the socks.

As I waited for my cadet informant, I decided to kill an hour on the vast parade ground, where the Corps of Cadets marches every Friday afternoon in full dress uniforms, and where, according to an old school brochure, "manhood meets mastery." This is a paramilitary display, not a military one. Despite the regalia and officer ranks, and despite its notoriously fierce military discipline ("To discipline is to teach" is the motto emblazoned on one of the school's books of regulations), this is a military academy by self-designation only. Unlike the federal service academies—West Point, Annapolis, the Air Force Academy—The Citadel has no connection with the United States Armed Forces (other than its R.O.T.C. program and its employment of some active and retired officers). Its grounds are adorned with dusty and decommissioned military hardware—a Sherman tank, a submarine's torpedo-loading hatch, a Phantom jet named Annette, two cannons named Betsy and Lizzie. In most cases, the weapons, in-cluding the pinless M-14s the cadets carry, are inoperative. The mouths of the various cannons are stuffed with cement—all except those of Betsy and Lizzie, which are fired during parades, but carefully aimed high enough so that their powder does not dust the crenellated barracks. The overall effect is that of a theme park for post–Cold War kids.

The hokeyness and childlike innocence of the scene—the stage-prop artil-lery, the toy-soldier clip-clop of the cadets as they squared their corners—were endearing, in a Lost Boys sort of way, and I strolled over to the student-activities center for my rendezvous with my cadet informant thinking that The Citadel's version of martial culture was not so menacing after all. The cadet was not in evidence. I spent the next thirty minutes prowling the halls, which were lined with portraits of stern-faced "generals" (I couldn't tell which were United States military and which were SCUM), and examining ads on the student bulletin board for items like "Save the Males" bumper stickers. I tried to reach the cadet's room by phone—women aren't admitted into the barracks—but he was not there. A bit thoughtlessly, I left a message with an upperclassman and headed toward town.

At my hotel, the receptionist handed me a message from my vanished cadet. "Please, don't ever call here again!" it read. The phone clerk peered at me curi-ously. "Sorry about that exclamation mark, but he seemed quite distraught," she said. "His voice was shaking."

What brought a young man to an all-male preserve in the last decade of the twentieth century, anyway? What was going on outside the academy gates that impelled thousands of boys, Southern and Northern alike (about a fifth of its student body of about two thousand are Yankees), to seek refuge behind a pair of corroding cannons?

"The forces arrayed against us," an attorney named Robert Patterson declared in a February, 1994, court hearing, consider his military academy to be "some big-game animal to be hunted down, tracked, caught, badgered, and killed so that some lawyer or some organization can go back up and hang a trophy on a wall in an office." Patterson was defending not The Citadel but the Virginia Military Institute, which is the only other public military academy in the United States that does not admit women, and which was involved in a similar sex-discrimination suit. (Three months later, Patterson, a V.M.I. alumnus, returned to court to defend The Citadel.) "I will say this, Your Honor," he went on. "This quest by these people constitutes the longest and most expensive publicly financed safari in the annals of big-game hunting."

The Citadel's administration has fought the female hunters with a legal arsenal of nearly a million dollars and with dour, tight-lipped determination, which has only increased with time. The Citadel's president, Claudius Elmer (Bud) Watts III, who is a retired Air Force lieutenant general and a second-generation Citadel alumnus, views Shannon Faulkner's legal efforts as an enemy invasion, placing his young troops "under attack." "The Citadel is in this to the end," he pronounced at a press conference held in the spring of 1994 on the parade ground, his feet planted between Betsy and Lizzie, his uniform decked with ribbons, and his chin tucked in, as is his custom, as if in a permanent brace position.

Later, in his living room, surrounded by coffee-table books on football, Watts told me firmly, "You cannot put a male and a female on that same playing field," though he couldn't say exactly why. Of his own Citadel years he conceded, "I've not the foggiest notion if it would have been different" had women attended. He was just glad there were no female cadets then; otherwise, he said, the cadets would have faced "a different form of intimidation—not wanting to be embarrassed in front of a girl."

Faulkner has been opposed not only by many Citadel staff and alumni but—at least, publicly—by almost all the current cadets. They say that her presence in the Corps would absolutely destroy a basic quality of their experience as Citadel men. She would be what one Citadel defender called in his court deposition "a toxic kind of virus." Tellingly, even before the United States District Court judge enjoined The Citadel to admit Faulkner to the Corps of Cadets for the fall of 1994, and before the injunction was set aside, the administration announced its selection of her living quarters: the infirmary.

Cadets cite a number of reasons that women would have a deleterious effect on the Corps of Cadets, and the reasons are repeated so often as to be easily predictable, though their expression can be novel. "Studies show—I can't cite them, but studies show that males learn better when females aren't there," one cadet explained to me (a curious sentiment at a school where a knob motto about grades is "2.0 and Go"). "If a girl was here, I'd be concerned not to look foolish. If you're a shy student, you won't be as inhibited." Another cadet said, "See, you don't have to impress them here. You're free." From a third: "Where does it end? Will we have unisex bathrooms?" But among the reasons most frequently heard for repelling Faulkner at the gate is this: "She would be destroying a long and proud tradition."

The masculine traditions of West Point and Annapolis were also closely guarded by their male denizens, but the resistance to women joining their ranks was nowhere near as fierce and filled with doomsday rhetoric as The Citadel's efforts to repel feminine interlopers. At Norwich University, a private military college in Northfield, Vermont, that voluntarily opened its barracks to women in 1974, two years before the federal service academies, the administration actually made an effort to recruit and accommodate women. "There was no storm of protest," said a Norwich spokeswoman, Judy Clauson. But then, "it was a time when there were so many rules that were being loosened." The Air Force veteran Linnea Westberg, who was one of the eight women in Norwich's first coed class, recalled, of her integration into its corps, that "ninety-five percent of the male cadets were fine, especially the freshmen, who didn't know any different." Westberg said she was baffled by the intensity of The Citadel's opposition to women in its corps. "It's hard for me to believe it's still an issue."

"The Citadel is a living museum to the way things used to be," John Drennan, a Citadel graduate and a public defender in Charleston, told me one day during The Citadel's legal proceedings. But how, exactly, did things use to be? The cadets and the alumni of the school, along with those protesting against its exclusionary policies, envision its military tradition above all. And The Citadel once did have a strong military aspect: it was formed as an arsenal in 1822 in response to a slave revolt purportedly planned by the freed Charleston slave Denmark Vesey, which, though it was foiled, aroused widespread alarm in the region. Yet twenty years later the guns and the gold braid became mere adornment as The Citadel turned into an industrial school of domestic and practical skills. Union troops shut down The Citadel at the end of the Civil War, but it was reinvented and reopened in 1882, after the Union's Reconstruction officials had thoroughly stripped the school of all military muscle. Its new mission was to reinvigorate the masculinity of the South by showing its men how to compete with the business and industrial skills of the Yankee carpetbaggers, who were believed to be much better prepared than the sons of Dixie to enter the Darwinian fray of modern commerce. John Peyre Thomas, who ran The Citadel from 1882 to 1885, wrote of the need to teach spoiled plantation boys the rudiments of self-reliance. "It must be admitted that the institution of African slavery, in many respects, affected injuriously the white youth of the South," he wrote. "Reared from infancy to manhood with servants at his command to bring his water, brush his shoes, saddle his horse, and, in fine, to minister to his personal wants, the average Southern boy grew up in some points of character dependent, and lazy, and inefficient. He was found, too, wanting in those habits of order and system that come from the necessity, in man, to economize time and labor."

What makes the school's Reconstruction-era mission important is that in so many ways it remains current; the masculine and industrial culture of our age and that of the conquered South may have more in common than we care to imagine. Again, we are at a psychic and economic crisis point for manhood. And, again, the gun issues hide the butter issues: the bombast masks a deep insecurity about employment and usefulness in a world where gentleman soldiers are an anachronism and a graduate with gentleman's Cs may find himself busing tables at Wendy's.

The uncertain prospects of Citadel graduates are worsened by military downsizing. Only about a third of recent graduates entered the military—a figure that has fallen steeply since the mid-seventies, when half of The Citadel's graduating class routinely took a service commission. News of Shannon Faulkner's court case competed in the Charleston *Post & Courier* with news of the shutting down of the local shipyards and decommissionings from the local military installations.

The night before the closing arguments in Faulkner's suit, I had dinner at the on-campus home of Philippe and Linda Ross, who have both taught at The Citadel. Philippe, the head of the Biology Department, had just completed his first round of moonlighting as a "retraining" instructor at the Charleston Naval Shipyard. He had been prepping laid-off nuclear engineers to enter one of the few growth industries in the area—toxic-waste management. Facing a room filled with desperate men each day had been a dispiriting experience, he said. He recalled the plea of a middle-aged engineer, thrust out of the service after twenty-six years: "All I want to do is work." Linda Ross, who was then teaching psychology at The Citadel, looked across the table with a pained expression. "That whole idea that if a young man went to college he could make a decent living and buy a house, and maybe even a boat, just does not hold anymore," she said softly. "There's a Citadel graduate working as a cashier at the grocery store. And the one thing these young men felt they could count on was that if things got hard they could always go into the military. No more. And they are bitter and angry."

In the fall of 1991, Michael Lake, a freshman, decided to leave The Citadel. He had undergone weeks of bruising encounters with upperclassmen—encounters that included being knocked down with a rifle butt and beaten in the dark by a pack of cadets. Incidents of hazing became so violent that, in a school where publicly criticizing the alma mater is virtually an act of treason, several athletes told their stories to *Sports Illustrated*. Much of the violence was aimed at star freshman athletes: a member of the cycling team was forced to hang by his fingers over a sword poised two inches below his testicles; a placekicker had his head dunked in water twenty times until he was unconscious; a linebacker was forced to swallow his chewing tobacco and tormented until, he said later, "I was unable even to speak clearly in my classes." It was a time when the Churchill Society, a literary club reportedly containing a white-supremacist faction, was organized on campus. It was a time when the local chapter of the National Association for the Advancement of Colored People urged a federal investigation into a pair of racial incidents on the school's campus: the appearance of a noose over the bed of a black freshman who had earlier refused to sing "Dixie," and the shooting and wounding of a black cadet by a sniper who was never identified. (A few years earlier, upperclassmen wearing Klan-like costumes left a charred paper cross in the room of a black cadet.) And it was a time when a leader of the Junior Sword Drill, a unit of cadet sword-bearers, leaped off a five-foot dresser onto the head of a prostrate cadet, then left him in a pool of blood in a barracks hall. According to one cadet, a lacrosse-team member returning from an away game at three in the morning stumbled upon the victim's unconscious body, his face split open, jaw and nose broken, mouth a jack-o'-lantern of missing teeth.

One night, at about 2 A.M., high-ranking cadets trapped a raccoon in the barracks and began to stab it with a knife. Beau Turner, a student at the school, was awakened by the young men's yelling. "My roommate and I went out there to try and stop it," Turner recalled, "but we were too late." Accounts of the episode vary. In a widely circulated version (which was referred to in a faculty member's testimony), the cadets chanted, "Kill the bitch! Kill the bitch!" as they tortured the raccoon to death.

In October 1993, two upperclassmen burst into the room of two freshmen and reportedly kneed them in the genitals, pulled out some of their chest hair, and beat them up. They were arrested on charges of assault and battery, and agreed to a program of counseling and community service, which would wipe clean their records. They withdrew from The Citadel, in lieu of expulsion, the spokesman Major Rick Mill said.

One of the offending cadets, Adrian Baer, told me that he and the other accused sophomore, Jeremy Leckie, did indeed come back from drinking, burst into the knobs' room after 10 P.M., and "repeatedly struck them in the chest and stomach" and bruised one of them in the face, but he denied having kicked them in the groin and yanked out chest hair. He said that what he did was common procedure—and no different from the "motivational" treatment he had received as a knob at the hands of a senior who came into *his* room. They entered the freshmen's room, Baer explained, because they viewed one of the occupants as "a problem" knob who "needed some extra motivation." Baer elaborated: "His pinkie on his right hand wouldn't completely close when he went to salute. He caught a lot of heat for that, of course, because it's a military school; it's important to salute properly." The strict rule that upperclassmen not fraternize with knobs, he said, meant that they couldn't simply counsel the freshman kindly. "If we just sat down and said, 'Listen, guy, we have a little problem,' that would be fraternization. And more important, knobs would lose respect for upperclassmen. It's a lot of denial on the part of officials at The Citadel about hazing," Baer said. "They don't want to believe it goes on." Leckie's father, Timothy Rinaldi, said that while he believed his son "was definitely in the wrong," he felt The Citadel's fourth-class system bred such behavior. "They help build this monster," he said of The Citadel. "The monster gets up off the table and starts walking through town—and now Dr. Frankenstein wants to shoot it."

Needless to say, not every cadet embraces the climate of cruelty; the nocturnal maulings likely frighten as many cadets as they enthrall. But the group mentality that pervades The Citadel assures that any desire on the part of a cadet to speak out about the mounting violence will usually be squelched by the threat of ostracism and shame. While group rule typifies many institutions, military and civilian, that place a premium on conformity, the power and authoritarianism of the peer group at The Citadel is exceptional because the college gives a handful of older students leave to "govern" the others as they see fit. (A lone officer provided by the military, who sleeps in a wing off one of the dorms, seldom interferes.) This is a situation that, over the years, an occasional school official has challenged, without success. A former assistant commandant for discipline, Army Lieutenant Colonel T. Nugent Courvoisie, recalled that he "begged" the school's president back in the sixties to place more military officers—and ones who were more mature—in the barracks, but his appeals went unheeded. Discipline and punishment in the dorms is in the hands of the student-run regimental command, and ascendancy in this hierarchy is not always predicated on compassion for one's fellow man. In consequence, the tyranny of the few buys the silence of the many.

This unofficial pact of silence could, of course, be challenged by the Citadel officialdom. On a number of occasions over the past three decades—most recently when some particularly brutal incidents found their way into the media—The Citadel has commissioned "studies." But when the administration does go on the offensive, its animus is primarily directed not at miscreant cadets but at the "unfair" media, which are "victimizing" the institution by publicizing the bad behavior of its boys.

In recent years, enough bad news leaked out locally to become a public-relations nightmare, and the school appointed a committee of Citadel loyalists to assess the situation. Even the loyalists concluded, in a January 1992 report, that the practice of physical abuse of freshmen, along with food and sleep deprivation, had gotten out of hand. As a result, Major Mill told me, The Citadel ordered upperclassmen to stop using pushups as a "disciplinary tool" on individual cadets. "That was the most important one" of the reforms prompted by the report, Mill said. Other reforms were adopted: for example, freshmen would no longer be compelled to deliver mail to upperclassmen after their evening study hours, thus reducing opportunities for hazing; freshmen would at least officially—no longer be compelled to "brace" in the mess hall. At the same time, the report declared that it "wholeheartedly endorses the concept of the fourth-class system," which it called "essential to the attainment of college objectives and the development of the Citadel man."

Institutions that boast of their insularity, whether convents or military academies, are commonly pictured in the public imagination as static, unchanging abstractions, isolated from the ebb and flow of current events. But these edifices are rarely as otherworldly as their guardians might wish; indeed, in the case of The Citadel, its bricked-off culture has functioned more as a barometer of national anxieties than as a garrison against them. The militaristic tendencies within the Corps seem to vary inversely with the esteem in which the American soldier is held in the larger society. In times when the nation has been caught up in a socially acceptable conflict, one in which its soldiers return as heroes greeted by tickertape parades, The Citadel has loosened its militaristic harness, or even removed it altogether. Thus, during perhaps the most accept-able war in American history, the Second World War, the fourth-class system of knob humiliation was all but discontinued. Upperclassmen couldn't even order a knob to brace. The changes began largely in response to the demands of the real military for soldiers they could use in a modern war. "The War Department and the Navy Department were asking R.O.T.C. to do less dril-ling, more calculus," Jamie Moore, a professor of history at The Citadel and a former member of the United States Army's Historical Advisory Committee, told me. "The Citadel dismantled its fourth-class system because it was getting in the way of their military training." The changes didn't seem to interfere with the school's production of Whole Men; on the contrary, an extraordinary percentage of The Citadel's most distinguished graduates come from these years, among them United States Senator Ernest (Fritz) Hollings; Alvah Chapman, Jr., the former chief executive of Knight-Ridder; and South Carolina's former governor John C. West.

The kinder, gentler culture of the Second World War–era Citadel survived well into the next decade. Although a new fourth-class system was soon estab-lished, it remained relatively benign. "We didn't have the yelling we have to-day," Colonel Harvey Dick, class of '53 and now a member of The Citadel's governing body, recalled. "They didn't even shave the freshmen's heads."

The postwar years also brought the admission of women to the summer program, and without the hand-wringing provoked by Shannon Faulkner's application. "WOMEN INVADE CITADEL CLASSES FIRST TIME IN SCHOOL'S HISTORY," the Charleston daily noted back on page 16 of its June 21, 1949, edition. "Most male students took the advent of the 'amazons' in their stride," the paper reported cheerfully. "Only the younger ones seemed at all uneasy. Professors and instructors were downright glad to see women in their classes."

The Vietnam War, needless to say, did not inspire the same mood of relax-ation on campus. "The fourth-class system was very physical," Wallace West, the admissions director who was an undergraduate at The Citadel during the Vietnam War years, said. "When I was there, there was no true emphasis on academics, or on positive leadership. It was who could be worked to physical exhaustion." Alumni from those years recounted being beaten with sticks, coat hangers, and rifle butts. That was, of course, the era that inspired Pat Conroy's novel *The Lords of Discipline*, a tale of horrific hazing, directed with special virulence against the school's first African-American cadet. "They just tortured us," Conroy recalled from his home in Beaufort, South Carolina. "It taught me the exact kind of man I didn't want to be," he added.

In 1968, the administration appointed a committee to investigate the vio-lence. The committee issued a report that, like its 1992 successor, concluded "there have been significant and extensive abuses to the [fourth-class] system." And, with its strong recommendation that hazing result in expulsion, the report seemed to promise a more pacific future on campus.

In the past decade and a half, however, the record of violence and cruelty at The Citadel has attracted increasing notice, even as the armed forces have been racked by downsizing and scandal. The Citadel president during much of this era, Major General James A. Grimsley, Jr., declined to discuss this or any other aspect of campus life during his tenure. "I don't do interviews," he said. "Thank you for calling, young lady." He then hung up. Others have been less reticent.

Thirteen years before Vice-Admiral James B. Stockdale consented to be Ross Perot's running mate, he took on what turned out to be an even more thankless task: fighting brutal forms of hazing at The Citadel. In 1979, Stockdale, who had graduated from Annapolis, was chosen to be The Citadel's president because of his status as a genuine military hero: he had survived eight years as a P.O.W. in Vietnam. This hero failed to see the point of manufactured adversity. In an afterword to the book *In Love and War*, a collaboration between Stockdale and his wife, Sybil, he wrote that there was "something mean and out of control about the regime I had just inherited."

On his first day in the president's office, Stockdale opened a desk drawer and discovered "what turned out to be Pandora's box," he wrote. "From the top down, what was written on the papers I took out of the desk drawers—and conversations with some of their authors—was enough to break anybody's heart." Among them was a letter from an infuriated father who wanted to know what had happened to his son "to change him from a levelheaded, optimistic, aggressive individual to a fatigued, irrational, confused and bitter one." He also found copies of memos from The Citadel's staff physician complaining repeatedly of (as Stockdale recalled) "excessive hospitalization"—such as the case of a knob who had suffered intestinal bleeding and was later brought back to the infirmary, having been exercised to unconsciousness. Stockdale sought to reform the system, but he was stymied at every turn. He clashed with The Citadel's powerful Board of Visitors, an eleven-member committee of alumni that sets school policy. The Board of Visitors overruled his expulsion of a senior cadet who had reportedly been threatening freshmen with a pistol. A year into his presidency, Stockdale submitted his resignation. After he left, the board reinstated an avenging friend of the senior cadet who, according to Stockdale, had attempted to break into his house one evening. (The then chairman of the Board of Visitors maintains that the cadet was drunk and looking for the barracks.)

"They thought they were helping people into manhood," Stockdale recalled, from a more serene post in Palo Alto, California, where he is a scholar at Stanford's Hoover Institution on War, Revolution, and Peace. "But they had no idea what that meant—or who they were."

After Watts became president, in 1989, some faculty members began to observe a creeping militarization imposed by the administration upon the Corps's already drill-heavy regimen. Four special military days were added to the academic year. At the beginning of one semester, President Watts held a faculty meeting in a room above the mess hall. "Watts had these soldiers standing around the room with their hands behind them," Gardel Feurtado, a political-science professor and one of only two African-American professors, recalled. Watts, he said, lectured the faculty for about three hours. "He didn't talk about academics or educational goals. He just talked about cadets' training, and he showed us a film of it," Feurtado told me. According to Feurtado, Watts told the faculty to line up in groups behind the soldiers for a tour of the barracks.

"I said, 'Enough of this,' and I started to walk out. And this soldier stopped me and said, 'Where do you think you're going, sir?' and I said, 'You do realize that I am not in the military?'" Feurtado had to push by him to leave.

When Michael Lake looked back on the abuse he suffered during his abbreviated knob year of '91, he could now see before him, like the emergence of invisible ink on what appeared to be a blank piece of paper, the faint outlines of another struggle. What he saw was a submerged gender battle, a bitter but definitely fixed contest between the sexes, con-

Illustration by Mark Zingarelli, originally published in *The New Yorker*. © Mark Zingarelli/House of Zing

cealed from view by the fact that men played both parts. The beaten knobs were the women, "stripped" and humiliated, and the predatory upperclassmen were the men, who bullied and pillaged. If they couldn't re-create a male-dominant society in the real world, they could restage the drama by casting male knobs in all the subservient feminine roles.

"They called you a 'pussy' all the time," Lake recalled. "Or a 'fucking little girl.'" It started the very first day they had their heads shaved, when the upperclassmen stood around and taunted. "Oh, you going to get your little girlie locks cut off?" When they learned that Lake would be playing soccer that fall, their first response was "What is that, a girl's sport?" Another former cadet said that he had withstood "continual abuse," until he found himself thinking about jumping out the fourth-story window of the barracks—and quit. He reported an experience similar to Lake's. Virtually every taunt equated him with a woman: whenever he showed fear, they would say, "You look like you're having an abortion," or "Are you menstruating?" The knobs even experienced a version of domestic violence. The upperclassmen, this cadet recalled, "would go out and get drunk and they would come home and haze, and you just hoped they didn't come into your room."

"According to the Citadel creed of the cadet," Lake said, "women are objects, they're things that you can do with whatever you want to." In order to maintain this world-view, the campus has to be free of women whose status might challenge it—a policy that, of course, is rarely enunciated. The acknowledged policy is that women are to be kept at a distance so they can be "respected" as ladies. Several months before Faulkner's lawsuit came to trial, I was sitting in the less than Spartan air-conditioned quarters of the senior regimental commander, Norman Doucet, the highest-ranking cadet, who commanded the barracks. Doucet, who was to be The Citadel's star witness at the Faulkner trial, was explaining to me how excluding women had enhanced his gentlemanly perception of the opposite sex. "The absence of women makes us understand them better," Doucet said. "In an aesthetic kind of way, we appreciate them more—because they are not there."

Women at less of a remove fare less well. In The Citadel's great chain of being, the "waitees"—as many students call that all-black, all-female mess-hall staff—rate as the bottom link. Some upperclassmen have patted them on their rear ends, tried to trip them as they pass the tables, or hurled food at their retreating backs. Cadets have summoned them with "Come here, bitch," or addressed one who dropped a plate or forgot an order as "you stupid whore." The pages of the *Brigadier*, the school's newspaper, bear witness to the cadets' contempt for these women. Gary Brown, now the editor-in-chief of the *Brigadier*, once advised fellow-cadets to beware of "waitee" food contamination—"the germ-filled hands, the hair follicles, and other unknown horrors." Not only was he dismayed by "wavy little follicles in my food" but he found the women insufficiently obedient. "Duty is certainly not the sublimest word in the Waitee language," he wrote. In a letter to the editor, Jason S. Pausman, class of '94, urged fellow-cadets to demand "waitees without chronic diseases that involve sneezing, coughing or wiping of body parts ... The reality is simple, we CANNOT sit by and let the waitees of this school control us."

Some women faculty members report similarly resentful responses to their presence, despite—or because of—their positions of authority. Angry messages on a professor's door are one tactic. When Jane Bishop recently posted on her office door a photocopy of a *New York Times* editorial supporting women's admission to the Corps of Cadets, she found it annotated with heated rejoinders in a matter of days. "Dr. Bishop, you are a prime example of why women should not be allowed here," one scribble read. Another comment: "Women will destroy the world."

The Citadel men's approach to women seems to toggle between extremes of gentility and fury. "First, they will be charming to the women to get their way," Linda Ross said. "But if that doesn't work they don't know any other way. So then they will get angry." It's a pattern that is particularly evident in some cadets' reaction to younger faculty women.

December Green joined The Citadel's Political Science Department in 1988, the first woman that the department had ever hired for a tenure-track position. She was twenty-six and attractive—"someone the cadets might fantasize about," a colleague recalled. They were less enchanted, however, by her left-leaning politics. She soon found herself getting obscene phone calls in the middle of the night. Then obscenities began appearing on her office door. "Pussy" is the one that sticks in her mind.

Though Green's work at The Citadel was highly praised—she received an award for teaching, research, and service—she said that no one in the administration tried to stop her when she left in 1992 in despair over her inability to contain the cadets' fury. Nor, apparently, had anyone responded to her appeals to correct the situation. "A lot of terrible things happened to me there," Green, who is now teaching in Ohio, said, reluctant to revisit them. The hostility ranged from glowering group stares in the hallway to death threats—some of which appeared on the cadets' teacher-evaluation forms. The male faculty offered little support. Green recalls the department chairman instructing her to "be more

The legendary Citadel elder known as the Boo, who oversaw racial integration at The Citadel in the sixties, says, "With women, there's going to be sexual harassment." His wife, Margaret, counters, "Oh, honey, those cadets are harassing each other right now." "That's different," he says. "That's standard operating procedure." Illustration by Mark Zingarelli, originally published in *The New Yorker*. © Mark Zingarelli/House of Zing

maternal toward the students" when a cadet lodged a complaint about her (she had challenged his essay in which he praised apartheid). And a professor who stood by one day while his students harassed her and another woman informed her, "You get what you provoke."

Green said she eventually had to get an unlisted number to stop the obscene calls, and also moved, in part out of fear of the cadets' vengeance. The last straw, however, came when she submitted the written threats she had received to her chairman, who passed them on to the dean of undergraduate studies, in hopes of remedial action. The dean, she said, did nothing for some months, and then, after she inquired, said he had "misplaced" the offending documents.

The dean, Colonel Isaac (Spike) Metts, Jr., told me he didn't recall saying he misplaced the documents but "I might have said it's not on my desk at that time and I don't know where it is." He added that Green was a "very valuable" professor. "I don't know what else we could've done," Metts said. In any event, soon after submitting the threatening notes to the dean, Green gave up. At her exit interview, she recalled, President Watts told her he didn't understand why she had been upset by the cadet harassment. "It's just a bunch of kid stuff," another male colleague said. (Lewis Spearman, the assistant to the president, said that, because of federal privacy law, Watts would have no response to Green's version of events.)

The remaining category of women that cadets have to deal with is "the dates," as the young women they socialize with are generally called. (There are no wives; Citadel policy forbids cadets to marry, and violators are expelled.) In some respects, these young women are the greatest challenge to the cadet's sense of gender hierarchy. While the "waitees" can be cast as household servants and the female teachers as surrogate mothers, the dates are more difficult to place. Young women their age are often college students, with the same aspirations as the cadets, or even greater ones. The cadets deal with young women's rising ambitions in a number of ways. One is simply to date high-school girls, an option selected by a number of cadets. Another strategy, facilitated by The Citadel, is to cast the young women who are invited on campus into the homecoming-queen mold. The college holds a Miss Citadel contest each year, and Anne Poole, whose husband, Roger, is the vice-president of academic affairs and the dean of the college, has sat on the judging panel. Each cadet company elects a young woman mascot from a photograph competition, and their faces appear in the yearbook.

The school also sends its young men to an in-house etiquette-training seminar, in which the Citadel "hostess," a pleasant woman in her forties named Susan Bowers, gives them a lecture on how "to act gentlemanly with the girls." She arms cadets with *The Art of Good Taste*, a do's-and-don'ts manual with a chapter entitled "Helping the Ladies." The guidebook outlines the "correct way of offering an arm to a lady ... to help her down the steps," and the best method for assisting "a lady in distress." (The example of distress provided involves an elderly woman trying to open a door when her arms are full of shopping bags.) Such pointers are illustrated with pictures of fifties-style coeds sporting Barbie-doll hair flips and clinging to the arms of their cadets, who are escorting them to "the Hop." The manual's preface states emphatically, "At all times [ladies] must be sheltered and protected not only from the elements and physical harm but also from embarrassment, crudity, or coarseness of any sort."

Susan Bowers explained the duties of her office: "At the beginning of the year, we do 'situation cards' for the freshmen. And we'll bring in cheerleaders and use them as props....We show cadets how to go through the receiving line, how to introduce your date, and what to say to them. In the past, we didn't have the cheerleaders to use, so they dressed up some of the guys as girls." Bowers said she felt bad for the cadets, who often come to her seeking maternal consolation. "They are very timid—afraid, almost," she said. "They are so lost, and they need a shoulder."

The Art of Good Taste is silent on the subject of proper etiquette toward women who require neither deference nor rescue. And, as Linda Ross observed, when the gentlemanly approach fails them, cadets seem to have only one fallback—aggression. Numerous cadets spoke to me of classmates who claimed to have "knocked around" uncompliant girlfriends. Some of those classmates, no doubt, were embellishing to impress a male audience, but not always. "I know lots of stories where cadets are violent toward women," a 1991 Citadel graduate named Ron Vergnolle said. He had witnessed cadets hitting their girlfriends at a number of Citadel parties—and observed one party incident in which two cadets held down a young woman while a third drunken cadet leaned over and vomited on her. Vergnolle, a magna cum laude graduate of the Citadel class of '91, recounted several such stories to me, and added that bragging about humiliating an ex-girlfriend is a common practice—and the more outrageous the humiliation, the better the story, as far as many cadets are concerned. Two such cadet storytellers, for example, proudly spread the word of their exploits on Dog Day, a big outdoor party sponsored by The Citadel's senior class. The two cadets told about the time they became enraged with their dates, followed them to the Portosans, and, after the women had entered, pushed the latrines over so they landed on the doors, trapping the occupants. The cadets left them there. Another cadet told Vergnolle that he had tacked a live hamster to a young woman's door. There was also the cadet who boasted widely that, as vengeance against an uncooperative young woman, he smashed the head of her cat against a window as she watched in horror. "The cat story," Vergnolle noted, "that was this guy's calling card."

Something of these attitudes shows up even in the ditties the cadets chant during their daily runs. Many of the chants are the usual military "jodies," well known for their misogynistic lyrics. But some are vintage Citadel and include lyrics about gouging out a woman's eyes, lopping off body parts, and evisceration. A cadence remembered by one Citadel cadet, sung to the tune of "The Candy Man," begins, "Who can take two jumper cables/Clip 'em to her tit/ Turn on the battery and watch the bitch twitch." Another verse starts with "Who can take an ice pick..." and so on.

The day after last Thanksgiving, the phone rang at one-thirty in the morning in the home of Sandy and Ed Faulkner in Powdersville, South Carolina, a tiny community on the outskirts of Greenville. The caller was a neighbor. They had better come outside, he said—a car had been circling their block. Sandy and Ed, the parents of Shannon Faulkner, went out on their front lawn and looked around. At first, they saw nothing. Then, as they turned back to the house, they saw that across the white porch columns and along the siding of the house, painted in gigantic and what Sandy later recalled as "blood-red" letters, were the words, "Bitch," "Dyke," "Whore," and "Lesbo." Ed got up again at 6 A.M. and, armed with a bucket of white paint, hurried to conceal the message from his daughter.

A few days after the judge ordered The Citadel to admit Faulkner to the Corps of Cadets, morning rush-hour drivers in Charleston passed by a huge portable sign that read "Die Shannon." At least this threat wasn't home delivered. In the past year, instances of vandalism and harassment have mounted at the Faulkner home. Someone crawled under the house and opened the emergency exhaust valve on the water heater. The gas tank on Sandy's car was pried open. Someone driving a Ford Bronco mowed down the mailbox. Another motorist "did figure-eights through my flower bed," Sandy said. "This year, I didn't even plant flowers because I knew they would just tear them up." And someone with access to Southern Bell's voice-mail system managed, twice, to tap into their voice mail and change their greeting, both times to a recording featuring rap lyrics about a "bitch" with a "big butt." Callers phoned in the middle of the night with threatening messages. Sandy called the county sheriff's department about the vandalism, but in Anderson County, which has been home to many Citadel graduates, the deputy who arrived was not particularly helpful. He told them, Sandy recalled, "Well, if you're going to mess with The Citadel, you're just going to have to expect that."

Every trial has its rare moments of clarity, when the bramble of admissibility arguments and technicalities is cut away and we see the actual issue in dispute. One such moment came toward the end of the Faulkner-Citadel trial, when Alexander Astin, the director of the Higher Education Research Institute at the University of California at Los Angeles, took the stand. Astin, who is widely viewed as a leading surveyor of college-student performance and attitudes, found no negative effects on male students in nineteen all-male colleges he had studied which had gone coeducational.

"Can you tell me what kind of woman you would think would want to attend a coeducational Citadel?" Robert Patterson, the Citadel attorney who had previously represented V.M.I., asked Astin, his voice full of unflattering insinuation about the kind of woman he imagined her to be.

ASTIN: I suppose the same as the kind of men who want to go there.

PATTERSON: Would it be a woman that would not be all that different from men?

ASTIN: Yes.

To Patterson, this was a triumphant moment, and he closed on it: he had forced the government's witness to admit that a woman like Shannon Faulkner would have to be a mannish aberration from her gender. But in fact Astin's testimony expressed the precise point that the plaintiff's side had been trying to make all along, and that The Citadel strenuously resisted: that the sexes were, in the end, not all that different.

"I was considered the bitch of the band," Shannon Faulkner said, without embarrassment, of her four years in her high school's marching band—just stating a fact. She was lounging on the couch in her parents' living room, comfortable in an old T-shirt and shorts, one leg swung over an arm of the couch. "That's because I was the one who was mean and got it done." The phone rang, for the millionth time—another media call. "I'm not giving statements to the press right now," she said efficiently into the phone and hung up. She did not apologize for her brusqueness, as I was half expecting her to do, after she put down the receiver. There is nothing of the good girl about her. Not that she is disagreeable; Shannon Faulkner just doesn't see the point in false deference. "I never let anyone push me around, male or female," Faulkner said, and that fact had been exasperatingly obvious to reporters who covered the trial: they found that all the wheedling and cheap flatteries that usually prompt subjects to say more than they should didn't work with Faulkner.

One could scrounge around in Faulkner's childhood for the key to what made her take on The Citadel. You could say that it was because she was born six weeks premature, and her fierce struggle to live forged a "survivor." You could cite her memory that as a small child she preferred playing outside with the boys to playing with certain girls whom she deemed "too prissy." You could point to her sports career in high school and junior high: she lettered in softball for four years and kept stats for three of the schools' four basketball teams. You could note her ability to juggle tasks: she edited the yearbook, wrote for the school paper, and graduated with a 3.48 grade-point average. And you could certainly credit the sturdy backbone and outspokenness of both her mother and her maternal grandmother; this is a family where the women talk and the men keep a low profile. Her father, Ed, owns a small fence-building business. At thirty, a few years after Shannon's birth, Sandy returned to college to get her degree, a double major in psychology and education, and became a high-school teacher of psychology, sociology, United States history, and minority cultures. When a male professor had complained about certain "older women" in his class who asked "too many questions," Sandy hurled one of her wedge-heeled sandals at him. "I said, 'I'm paying for this class, and don't you ever tell me what I can ask.'" Shannon's maternal grandmother, sixty-seven-year-old Evelyn Richey, was orphaned at six and worked most of her life in textile factories, where, she noted, "women could do the job and men got the pay." Of her granddaughter's suit she said, "Women have got to come ahead. I say, let's get on with the show."

But there's little point in a detailed inspection of family history because there's no real mystery here. What is most striking about Shannon herself is that she's not particularly unusual. She reads novels by Tom Clancy and John Grisham, has worked in a local day-care center, is partial to places like Bennigan's. She wants a college education so she can support herself and have a career as a teacher or a journalist—she hasn't yet decided which. She might do a stint in the military, she might not. She is in many ways representative of the average striving lower-middle-class teenage girl, circa 1994, who intends to better herself and does not intend to achieve that betterment through a man—in fact, she has not for a moment entertained such a possibility.

Throughout the trial, cadets and Citadel alumni spoke of a feminist plot: she is "a pawn" of the National Organization for Women, or—a theory repeatedly posited to me by cadets—"Her mother put her up to it." Two Citadel alumni asked me in all seriousness if feminist organizations were paying Shannon Faulkner to take the stand. In truth, Shannon makes an unlikely feminist poster girl. She prefers to call herself "an individualist" and seems almost indifferent to feminist affairs; when I mentioned Gloria Steinem's name once in conversation, Shannon asked me, "Who's that?" After the judge issued his decision to admit her to the Corps, she told the *New York Times* that she didn't consider the ruling a victory "just for women"—only a confirmation of her belief that if you want something, "go for it." Shannon Faulkner's determination to enter The Citadel's Corps of Cadets was fuelled not so much by a desire to trailblaze as by a sense of amazement and indignation that this trail was barricaded in the first place. She had never, she told the court, encountered such a roadblock in all her nineteen years—a remark that perhaps only a young woman of her fortunate generation could make without perjuring herself.

Shannon Faulkner got the idea of attending The Citadel back in December of 1992. She was taking a preparatory education course at Wren High School, the local public school. Mike Hazel, the teacher, passed out articles for them to read and discuss, and Faulkner picked the article in *Sports Illustrated* about hazing at The Citadel. "It was almost as accidental as Rosa Parks," Hazel recalled. "I just held up *Sports Illustrated* and asked, 'Who wants to do this?'"

Faulkner told me she'd selected the article because "I had missed that issue." During the ensuing discussion, the class wandered off the subject of hazing and onto the question of what, exactly, a public state institution was doing barring women from its classrooms. After a while, Faulkner got up and went down to the counselor's office and returned with an application form from The Citadel. "I said, 'Hey, it doesn't even say 'Male/Female,'" she recalled. While she was sitting in class, she filled it out. "I didn't really make a big to-do about it."

Two weeks after Faulkner received her acceptance letter, The Citadel got word she was a woman and revoked her admission, and in August of 1993 she went off to spend a semester at the University of South Carolina at Spartanburg while the courts thrashed out the next move. As the lawyers filed papers, The Citadel's defenders delivered their own increasingly agitated personal beliefs to the plaintiff herself. Faulkner worked evenings as a waitress in a local bar called Chiefs Wings and Firewater until the nightly tirades from the many drunk Citadel graduate customers got to be too much. Actually, Faulkner said, she wouldn't have quit if some of her male college friends hadn't felt the need to defend her honor. "I didn't want them getting hurt," she said. Her manner of dealing with the Citadel crowd was more good-humored. One day at the bar, she recalled, "a guy came up to me. 'Are you Shannon Faulkner?' he asked, and I said, 'Why?'—very casual. Then he got real huffy-puffy, madder and madder." Finally, she said, he stuck his ring in her face, then slammed his hand down on the table. "You will never wear *that!*" he yelled. Shannon saw him a few times in the bar after that, scowling at her from a far table. To lighten the mood, she once had the bartender send him a beer. He wouldn't drink it.

"I never show my true emotions in public," Shannon said. "I consider that weak." She can laugh at the cadets' threats, even when they turn ugly, because she doesn't see the reason for all the fuss. Whenever she is asked to sign the latest T-shirt inspired by the controversy, which depicts a group of male bulldogs (The Citadel's mascot) in cadet uniforms and one female bulldog in a red dress, above the caption "1,952 Bulldogs and 1 Bitch," Faulkner told me, "I always sign under the 'Bitch' part."

The first day that Shannon Faulkner attended classes, in January 1994, the cadets who had lined up by the academic building told the media the same thing over and over. "We were trained to be gentlemen, and that's what we'll be." But in Shannon's first class, biology, all three cadets assigned to sit in her row changed their seats. The teacher, Philippe Ross, had to threaten to mark them absent to get them to return to their places. (More than twenty unexcused absences a semester is grounds for failure.) Shortly thereafter, a rumor began to circulate that Faulkner was using a fake I.D. in the local bars. This summer, talk of a plot against Faulkner surfaced—to frame her, perhaps by planting drugs in her belongings. The threat seemed real enough for Faulkner to quit her summer job, in the Charleston area, and return home.

The *Brigadier's* column "Scarlet Pimpernel" took up the anti-Shannon cause with a vengeance. The columnist dubbed her "the divine bovine," likening her to a plastic revolving cow at a nearby mall (the mounting of which is a cadet tradition). The "Pimpernel" comments on an incident that occurred on Faulkner's first day were particularly memorable. An African-American cadet named Von Mickle dared to shake her hand in front of the media and say, "It's time for women," and compared the exclusion of women to that of blacks. For this lone act, he was not only physically threatened by classmates but derided in the "Pimpernel." "The PIMP doth long to tame the PLASTIC COW on this most wondrous of nights," the anonymous author wrote, with the column's usual antique-English flourishes and coded references. "But it seems that we will have a live specimen, a home grown DAIRY QUEEN from the stables of Powdersville. Perhaps NON DICKLE will be the first to saddle up. He is DIVINE BOVINE's best friend after all."

More disturbing were cadet writings on Faulkner that were not for public consumption. Tom Lucas, a graduate student in The Citadel's evening program, told me about some "very harsh" graffiti that he'd found all over one of the men's rooms in The Citadel's academic building. The inscription that most stuck in his mind: "Let her in—then fuck her to death."

On the whole, The Citadel administrators to whom I spoke were defensive, evasive, or dismissive of the cadets' hostile words and deeds toward Faulkner. When I asked Citadel officials to respond to reports of barracks violence, harassment of women on staff, or verbal abuse of Faulkner, the responses were dismaying. Cases of violence and abuse were "aberrations"; cadets who spoke up were either "troublemakers" or "mama's boys"; and each complaint by a female faculty member was deemed a "private personnel matter" that could not be discussed further.

Certainly the administrators and trustees themselves are less than enthusiastic about Faulkner's arrival. William F. Prioleau, Jr., until recently a member of the Board of Visitors, implied on a radio talk show that abortions would go up as a result of the female invasion, as he claimed had happened at West Point. Meanwhile, in The Citadel's Math Department, all that was going up as a result of Shannon Faulkner's presence was the grade-point average. Faulkner's highest mark at the semester's end was in calculus, where she earned an A (prompting a surprised Dean Poole to comment to her that she was "certainly not the stereotypical woman"). The Math Department has in recent years invited A students to an annual party. But rather than include Faulkner, the department limited the guest list to math majors. Math professor David Trautman, who was in charge of invitations to the party, explained in an e-mail message to colleagues, "Her presence would put a damper on the evening."

Linda Ross, then a professor at The Citadel, was speaking one day with a seventy-six-year-old alumnus, and the talk turned to Faulkner's lawsuit. He asked her if she thought it possible that this young woman might prevail. "Well, it's probably an inevitable turning of the tide," Ross said, shrugging. To her amazement, the alumnus began to cry.

"I have the worst chance in society of getting a job, because I'm a white male," William H. Barnes, the senior platoon leader, shouted at me over the din in The Citadel's mess hall, a din created by the upperclassmen's tradition of berating knobs at mealtime. "And that's the major difference between me and my father." In a society where, at least since the Second World War, surpassing one's father has been an expected benchmark of American manhood, Barnes's point is a plangent one. But it's hard to say which Citadel generation is more undone by the loss of white male privilege—the young men who will never partake of a dreamed world of masculine advantage or the older men who are seeing that lived world split apart, shattered.

"I was in Vietnam in '63, and I'll defy you or Shannon or anyone else to hike through the rice paddies," the usually genial Colonel Harvey Dick, sixty-seven, a Board of Visitors member, an ex-marine, and an Army lieutenant colonel, was practically shouting from his recliner armchair in his Charleston home. He popped a Tums in his mouth. "There's just no way you can do that.... You can't pick up a ninety-five-pound projectile. There are certain things out there that are differences." On the wall above his head were seven bayonets. He was wearing his blue Citadel T-shirt, which matched the Citadel mementos that overwhelmed his den—Citadel mugs, hats, footballs, ceramic bulldogs. It was a room known in the Dick household as "Harvey's 'I Love Me' Room." Dick treated it as his command post—whenever the phone rang, he whipped it off the cradle and barked "Colonel Dick!"—but what he was commanding was unclear; he retired in 1993 from a sixteen-year stint as The Citadel's assistant commandant. Still, he at least knew that he was once in charge, that he once enjoyed lifetime job security as a career military man. This was something his son couldn't say: Harvey Dick II, a nuclear pipe fitter, had recently been laid off at the Charleston Naval Shipyard.

Colonel Dick wanted it known that he wasn't "one of those male-chauvinist pigs"; in fact, he believes that women are smarter than men. "Women used to let the men dominate," he said. "Maybe we need a male movement, since evidently we're coming out second on everything." He slipped another Tums from an almost empty roll. The sun was dropping as we spoke, and shadows fell across the Citadel hats and figurines in his room. "Go back and look at your Greek and Roman empires and why they fell," he said.

His wife cleared her throat. "This doesn't have anything to do with male-female," she said.

"I see a decline in this great nation of ours," Dick said. He crossed his arms and stared into the gathering darkness of the late summer afternoon. After a while, he said, "I guess I sound like a buffoon."

Unlike the cadets, the older male Citadel officials often have to face dissent from wives or daughters whose views and professional aspirations or accomplishments challenge their stand on women's proper place. Lewis Spearman, the assistant to the president, recently remarried, and his wife is a feminist paralegal who is now getting her master's degree in psychology. She says she engaged for more than a year in "shriekfests" with him over the Shannon Faulkner question before she halfheartedly came around to The Citadel party line on barring women. And, while the wife of Dean Poole may have sat on the Miss Citadel judging panel, their daughter, Mindy, had loftier ambitions. Despite the fact that she suffered from cystic fibrosis, she was an ardent skier, horseback rider, and college athlete, rising at 5 A.M. daily with her crew-team members at the University of Virginia. And, despite a double lung transplant during her junior year, she graduated in 1991 with honors and won a graduate fellowship. "She was an outstanding young lady," Poole said. "I was very proud of her." His eyes clouding over at the memory, he recalled that she had made him promise to take her to the big Corps Day parade on The Citadel's sesquicentennial. The day the father and daughter were to attend the parade was the day she died. "Sort of an interesting footnote," he said, wiping at his moist eyes. What if she had wanted to go to The Citadel? Well, actually, Poole said, she had talked about it. If she had persisted he would have tried to change her mind, he said, but he added, "I would never have stopped her from doing something she wanted to do."

One of the biggest spousal battles over Shannon Faulkner is waged nightly at the home of a man who might seem the least likely figure at The Citadel to wind up with a feminist wife. Probably The Citadel's most legendary elder, thanks to Pat Conroy's thinly veiled and admiring portrait of him in *The Lords of Discipline*, is Lieutenant Colonel T. Nugent Courvoisie, who, as an assistant commandant in the sixties, oversaw the admission of the first African-American cadet to The Citadel. A gravelly voiced and cigar-chomping tender tyrant, Courvoisie—or the Boo, as he is known, for obscure reasons—was a fixture at the school for more than two decades. There are two Citadel scholarships in his family name, and his visage peers down from two portraits on campus.

A courtly man, and still dapper at seventy-seven, the Boo, who has since given up cigars, insisted on picking me up at my hotel and driving me to his home, though I had a rental car sitting in the parking lot. On the drive over, he ticked off the differences between the sexes that he believed made it impossible for The Citadel to admit women—differences such as that "the average female is not as proficient athletically as the average male." When we were settled in the living room, the Boo on his recliner and his second wife, Margaret, who is also seventy-seven, in a straight-back chair, the subject of Shannon Faulkner was revisited. The first words out of Margaret's mouth were "The Citadel wants to chop the head off women." A low growl emanated from the Boo's corner. He lowered the recliner a notch. "We don't talk about it here," Margaret said—an obvious untruth. "We haven't come to blows yet, but—"

The Boo interrupted, "I have the correct view."

She retorted, "No one has the *correct* view." She turned and addressed me. "You have to understand him," she said of her husband of nine years. "This is a man who went to military prep schools and a church that was male-dominated, naturally."

The Boo interrupted. "J.C. picked twelve *men* as his disciples," he said.

Margaret rolled her eyes. "See? He even takes it into the church—and he's on such familiar ground with Christ he calls him J.C."

The Boo said, "J.C. never picked a woman, except his mother."

Margaret said, "Oh God, see, this is why we don't go into it."

But, as usual, go into it they did. As the words got batted back and forth, with Margaret doing most of the batting, the Boo levered his recliner progressively lower, until all I could see of him were the soles of his shoes.

MARGARET: You had plenty of good women soldiers in Saudi Arabia.

BOO: Plenty of pregnant ones....

MARGARET: What, do you think [the cadets] didn't get girls pregnant before? There've been plenty of abortions. And I know of a number of cases that, by the time [a cadet] graduated, there were four or five kids.

BOO: That's an exaggeration. Maybe two or three ... With women, there's going to be sexual harassment.

MARGARET: Oh, honey, those cadets are harassing each other right now, all the time.

BOO: That's different. That's standard operating procedure.

In the nineteen-sixties, Margaret worked in the library at The Citadel, where she would often see Charles Foster, the first African-American cadet (who died a few years ago), alone at one of the library desks. "He would just come to the library and sit there a lot. It's hard to be the only one, to be the groundbreaker. That's why I admire this girl."

Boo's voice boomed from the depths of his recliner: "But there's no need for her. She's ruining a good thing."

Margaret gave a mock groan. "This is the last vestige of male bastionship," she said, "and it's going to kill 'em when it crumbles." Boo raised his chair halfway back up and considered Margaret. "She has a good mind," he told me after a while.

Margaret smiled. "I'm a new experience for him. He's always been military. People didn't disagree with him."

The Boo showed the way upstairs, to the attic, where he has his own "Citadel room"—a collection of Citadel memorabilia vaster than but almost identical to Dick's. Around the house, there were sketches of Boo at various points in his Citadel career. He told me that, before he retired, the cadets commissioned a portrait of him that hangs in Jenkins Hall. "Man, I looked good in that," he said. "Like a man. A leader."

Margaret didn't think so. "No, it was horrible," she said. "It didn't look like you."

"If Shannon were in my class, I'd be fired by March for sexual harassment," Colonel James Rembert, an English professor, was saying as we headed toward his classroom. He had a ramrod bearing and a certain resemblance to Ted Turner (who, it happens, sent all three of his sons to The Citadel—Beau Turner among them—and donated twenty-five million dollars to the school earlier this year). The Colonel identifies himself as one of "the last white Remberts" in South Carolina, the Remberts being a Huguenot family of sufficiently ancient lineage to gain him admission to the St. John's Hunting Club of South Carolina—an all-male society chaired by a Citadel alumnus. Rembert, who has a Cambridge University doctorate and wrote a book on Jonathan Swift, said he preferred the company of men, in leisure and in learning. "I've dealt with young men all my life," he went on. "I know how to play with them. I have the freedom here to imply things I couldn't with women. I don't want to have to watch what I say."

The literary work under discussion that day was *Beowulf*, and the cadets agreed that it was all about "brotherhood loyalty" and, in the words of one student, "the most important characteristics of a man—glory and eternal fame." Then they turned to their papers on the topic.

"Mr. Rice," Rembert said in mock horror. "You turned in a single-spaced paper." This was a no-no. Rembert instructed him to take a pencil and "pen-e-trate"—Rembert drew the syllables out—the paper with the point. He shook his head. "What a pansy!" Rembert said. "Can't catch, can't throw, can't write." Another student was chastised for the use of the passive voice. "Never use the passive voice—it leads to effeminacy and homosexuality," Rembert told the class. "So next time you use the passive voice I'm going to make you lift up your limp wrist." Literary pointers concluded, Rembert floated the subject of Shannon Faulkner. The usual objections were raised. But then the class wandered into more interesting territory, provoked by a cadet's comment that "she would change the relationship between the men here." Just what is the nature of that relationship?

"When we are in the showers, it's very intimate," a senior cadet said. "We're one mass, naked together, and it makes us closer…. You're shaved, you're naked, you're afraid together. You can cry." Robert Butcher, another senior, said that the men take care of each classmate. "They'll help dress him, tuck in his shirt, shine his shoes." "You mean like a mother-child relationship?" I asked.

"That *is* what it is," another cadet said. "It's a family, even the way we eat—family style." A fourth cadet said, "Maybe it's a Freudian thing, but males feel more affection with each other when women are not around. Maybe we're all homosexuals."

The class groaned. "Speak for yourself, buddy," a number of cadets said, almost in a chorus.

Rembert said, "With no women, we can hug each other. There's nothing so nurturing as an infantry platoon."

The hooted-down cadet weighed in again: "When I used to wrestle in high school, we had this great tradition. Right before the game, the coach, he'd slap us really hard on the butt."

Rembert, a onetime paratrooper, said he and his skydiving buddies did that, too, right before they jumped. "First man out gets a pat right there."

Over lunch, Rembert returned to the theme of manly nurturance among Citadel men. "We hug each other," he said. One of his colleagues "always kisses me on the cheek," he went on. "It's like a true marriage. There's an affectionate intimacy that you will find between cadets. With this security they can, without being defensive, project tenderness to each other."

Months later, I was sitting in court watching Norman Doucet, the cadet regimental commander, testify. He was showing the judge a video of the Citadel experience and explaining the various scenes. First we were shown "one of the great parts" of a knob's first day—the mothers looking weepy at the gate as their sons were led away. Doucet lingered over the head-shaving scene. "This is what does it, right here," he said. "Mothers can't even tell their sons apart after

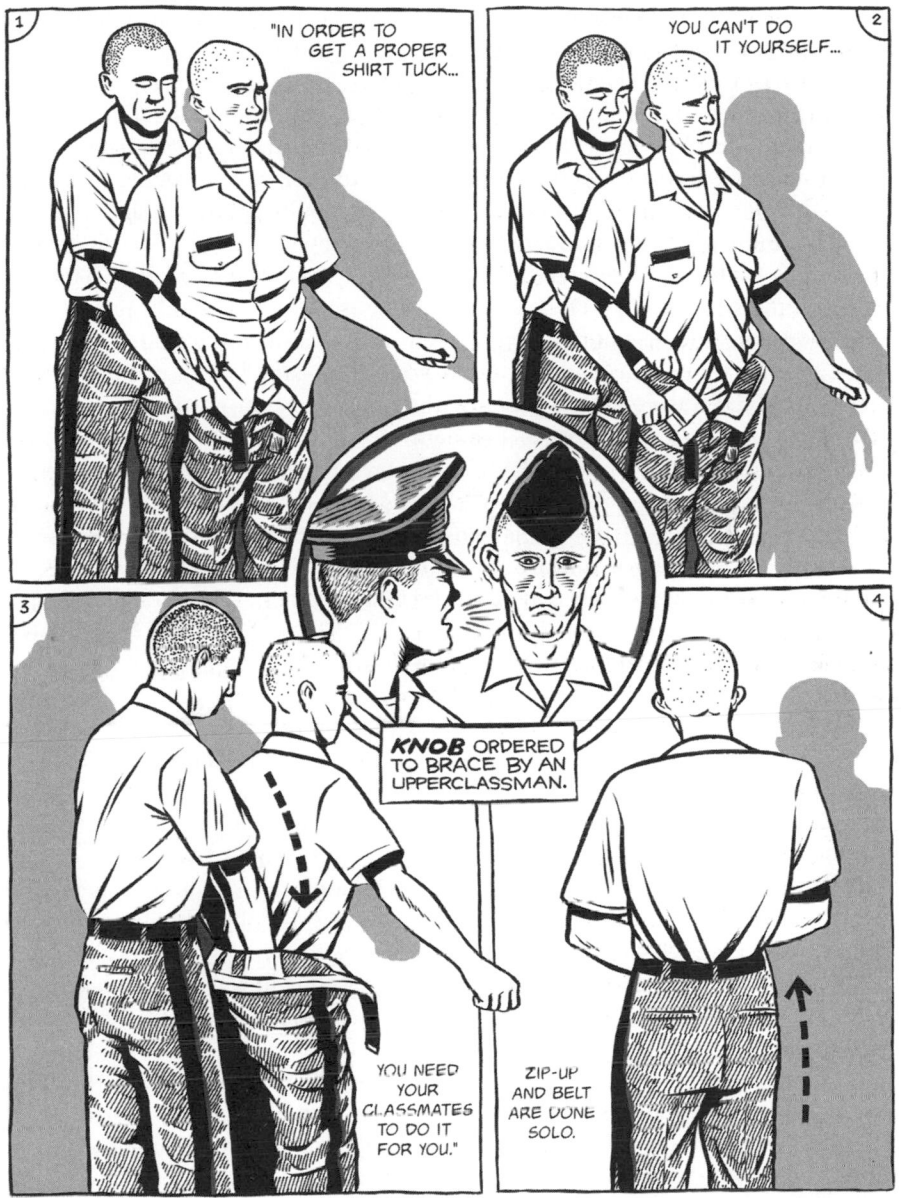

Dependency is a main theme in cadet relationships. Colonel James Rembert says that the cadets' intimate bond is "like a true marriage." Illustration by Mark Zingarelli, originally published in *The New Yorker*. © Mark Zingarelli/House of Zing

this." Thus shielded from the prying maternal eye, the cadets began their new life, and the video action shifted to a typical day in the life of the Corps. But the editing made it a day as heavy on early-morning domestic chores as it was on martial activity. Much of the film was devoted to housekeeping: scenes of cadets making beds, dressing each other, sweeping, taking out the trash, all of which Doucet described as "like some kind of a ballet or a dance that's going on." This is a dance where the most important moves took place before the show, in the dressing room. "What they are doing here is the Citadel shirt tuck," Doucet said. The tuck requires that a cadet unzip his pants halfway and fold down his waistband, then stand still while his helper approaches him from the back, puts his arms around the cadet's waist, pulls the loose shirt material firmly to the back, jams it as far down in the pants as he can, and then pulls the cadet's pants up. "If you watch closely right here, this is what the fourth-class system is all about," Doucet continued. "In order to get a proper shirt tuck, you can't do it yourself—you need your classmates to do it for you. There's really a lot of dependence upon your classmates." But, as Doucet's account suggested, cadets can experience that dependence only in concealment, away from mothers, away from all women.

When a Citadel attorney asked Doucet why female cadets would pose a problem on the campus, the only issue he raised was the humiliation that cadets feel if women observe the cadets' on-campus interactions. He spoke of the shame that knobs feel when, on occasion, a woman happened to be on the parade ground while upperclassmen were disciplining them. The cadets observing in the courtroom nodded in agreement.

It may seem almost paradoxical that the fourth-class system should be so solicitous of the emotional vulnerability of its wards—the same wards it subjects to such rigors. And yet the making of Whole Men evidently requires an initial stage of infantilization. Indeed, the objective of recapitulating childhood development is plainly spelled out in The Citadel's yearbook, known as "the Sphinx." The 1990 "Sphinx" explained, "As a freshman enters, he begins to release his childhood and takes the first steps to becoming a 'Citadel Man.'... As a 'knob,' every aspect of life is taught, a new way to walk.... Knobs are told how, where, and when to walk." Reentrance into manhood for the toddling knobs occurs on Recognition Day, when the upperclassmen force the knobs to do calisthenics until they drop, then gently lift up their charges and nurse them with cups of water. At that moment, for the first time in nine months, the older cadets call the knobs by their first names and embrace them.

The relationship between knobs and upperclassmen following Recognition Day, as they are integrated into the Corps, shifts from maternal to matrimonial. The yearbooks of the last several years picture Citadel men spending a lot of time embracing and kissing. Of course, this impulse, when it is captured on film, is always carefully disarmed with a jokey caption.

One afternoon, a group of cadets recounted for me the campus's many "nudity rituals," as they jokingly called them. There's "Senior Rip-Off Day," a spring rite in which three hundred seniors literally rip each other's clothes off, burn them in a bonfire, and hug and wrestle on the ground. There's "Nude Platoon," in which a group of juniors, unclad except for their cross-webbing, run around the quad yelling, "We love the Nude Platoon!" And there's the birthday ritual, in which the birthday boy is stripped, tied to a chair, and covered with shaving cream, while his groin is coated in liquid shoe polish.

During the fall semester before graduation, the seniors receive their "band of gold" (as it is called) in the Ring Ceremony. The chaplain blesses each class ring. (Receiving the ring, which I was constantly reminded is "the biggest class ring of any college," is a near-sacrament, and the yearbooks are filled with pictures of young men holding up their rings in fervor, as if clutching a crucifix before a vampire.) Then each senior walks through a ten-foot replica of the class ring with his mother on one arm and his "date" on the other. In a sort of reverse marriage ceremony, the mother gives the cadet away. Mother and date accompany him through the towering ring; then he kisses Mother farewell and marches under the arched swords of the Junior Sword Drill, a new bride of the Corps. Several cadets and alumni told me that when a Citadel graduate marries, it is a tradition to slide the class ring over the wedding band. Indeed, I saw such an ordering of priorities on the fingers of a number of Citadel men in the courtroom.

In the late-twentieth-century setting of The Citadel, in a time when extreme insecurity and confusion about masculinity's standing run rampant, the Corps of Cadets once again seeks to obscure a domestic male paradise with an intensifying of virile showmanship and violence. The result is a ruthless intimacy, in which physical abuse stands in for physical affection, and every display of affection must be counterbalanced by a display of sadism. Knobs told me that they were forced to run through the showers while the upperclassmen "guards" knocked the soap out of their hands and, when the knobs leaned over to retrieve it the upperclassmen would unzip their pants and yell, "Don't pick it up, don't pick it up! We'll use you like we used those girls!" A former Citadel Halloween tradition of upperclassmen dressing up—mostly in diapers and women's clothes—and collecting candy treats from knobs, has given way to "tricks" of considerable violence. (One upperclassman told me of cadets who knocked dressers over on candy-dispensing cadets and then walked on top of them.) The administration tried, unsuccessfully, to put a stop to the whole affair; too many freshmen were getting injured. And the playful pat on the butt that served to usher cadets into the brotherhood has degenerated into more invasive acts. According to a recent graduate, one company of cadets recently devised a regimen in which the older cadets tested sophomores nightly with increasingly painful treatments—beatings and stompings and so forth. The process, which they dubbed "Bananarama," culminated on a night in which an unpeeled banana was produced—and shoved into a cadet's anus.

Given this precarious dynamic, it is not surprising that in the past few years at The Citadel social rage has been directed toward any men who were perceived to be gay. Several young men who were suspected of homosexual inclinations were hounded out of the school. One cadet, Herbert Parker, who said that he was falsely accused of having a sexual encounter with a male janitor, recalled a year of total isolation—cadets refused to sit near him in the mess hall or in classes—and terror: incessant threatening phone calls and death threats. The cadets and the administration—which had responded to the report of his encounter by sending out a campus-security police car with lights flashing to question him—acted "like I had murdered someone."

The scapegoating reached such brutal proportions that the counseling center recently set up a sort of group-therapy session for the targeted young men, who are known as It, as in the game of tag.

One evening after the trial, I went over to the Treehouse, a "mixed" bar in Charleston, with an upstairs gay bar and nightly drag shows on the weekends. My intention was to ask about cadet violence against gay men. I presumed that on a campus where every second epithet was "faggot" such hate crimes were all but inevitable. There were indeed a few such cases, I learned, but the circumstances were different from what I had imagined. Nor were those cases the essence of my findings that evening.

"The proper terminology for The Citadel," a customer at the bar named Chris said, "is The Closet." Up and down the bar, heads bobbed in agreement. "They love faggots like me." What he meant by "like me," however, was not that he was gay. That night, he looked like a male model—sleek black hair and a handsome, chiseled face. But on the nights he was dressed for a performance he could pass for a woman. Arching an eyebrow, Chris said, "The cadets go for the drag queens."

Chris's observation was echoed in ensuing conversations in the bar. There are thousands of cadets, presumably, who have not dated drag queens, but in two visits to the Treehouse I could find only two drag queens, out of maybe a dozen, who did not tell me of dating a cadet—and that was only because these two found Citadel men "too emotional." Cadets can also occasionally be dangerous, Chris told me. "You can get the ones who are violent. They think they want it, then afterwards they turn on you, like you made them do it." Nonetheless, a drag queen who called himself Holly had been happily involved with a cadet for three years now. Marissa, another drag queen, the reigning "Miss Treehouse 1993–94," had gone out with one cadet, broken up, and was now in the throes of a budding romance with another. A third drag queen, who asked to be identified as Tiffany, was known to be a favorite of cadets.

As Chris and I were talking that first night, a drag queen called Lownie wandered in and settled on a bar stool. Lownie delighted in the Corps of Cadets pageantry—especially the Friday dress parades. "The parades are a big thing with the queers in Charleston," he said. "We'll have a cocktail party and go over and watch the boys. It's a very Southern-'lady' thing to do." Years ago, Lownie had been a student at the College of Charleston when he met *his* Citadel lover, and they had begun covert assignations—communicating through notes slipped in little-used books in the Citadel library. The only drawback, Lownie said, was dealing with his lover's constant emotional anxiety over making the grade at The Citadel. He was, in fact, a model macho cadet: a Junior Sword Drill member, a regimental officer, and a "hang king," who could dangle interminably from a closet rack by his fingertips. Lownie, who found such records more amusing than impressive, grinned, and said, "I used to make him wear his shako"—The Citadel's military cap—"when we were having sex. It's manhood at its most."

Lownie said he could begin to fathom his cadet's intense attachment to The Citadel—an emotion that he likened to a love affair—because he himself had spent four years in the Air Force. "The day-to-day aspect of being in a military environment is that you run around in a little bit of clothing and you are being judged as to how good a man you are by doing women's work—pressing pants, sewing, polishing shoes. You are a *better* man if you have mastery of womanly arts.... The camaraderie doesn't get any stronger than when you are in the barracks, sitting around at the end of the day in your briefs and T's and dogtags—like a bunch of hausfraus, talking and gossiping." The military stage set offers a false front and a welcome trapdoor—an escape hatch from the social burdens of traditional masculinity. Behind the martial backdrop, Lownie said, "you don't have to be a breadwinner. You don't have to be a leader. You can play back seat. It's a great relief. You can act like a human being and not have to act like a man."

"You know what the [cadet] I'm seeing now said to me?" Tiffany said. We were sitting in the dressing room a couple of hours before the night's performance, and as Tiffany spoke he peered into an elaborate mirror set illuminated with miniature movie-star lights, applying layer after layer of mascara and eyeliner with expert precision. "He said, 'You're more of a woman than a woman is.' And that's an exact quote." Tiffany stood up and struck a Southern belle pose by way of illustration. "I overexemplify everything a female is—my breasts, my hair, the way I hold myself." And who could better complete the hoopskirts picture than a fantasy gentleman in uniform?

Marissa, Miss Treehouse, looked up from his labors, painting row after row of fake nails with pink polish. "I love how they wear their caps slung low so you can't quite see their eyes," he said. "It's like all of us are female illusionists and they are male illusionists. A man in a uniform is a kind of dream."

Tiffany said, "For Halloween, you know what my cadet boyfriend wanted to dress as? A cadet."

The dressing-room scene before me, of a group of men tenderly helping each other get ready for the evening—an elaborate process of pinning and binding and stuffing—was not very different, in its way, from the footage in Norman Doucet's video of the cadets tucking in each other's shirts. As the drag queens conversed, they tossed stockings and Ace bandages and cosmetic bags back and forth. "Has anyone seen my mascara wand?" "O.K., who has the blush?" There was a homey comfort that reminded me of slumber parties when I was a girl, where we would put big pink spongy rollers in each other's hair and screech with laughter at the results. And suddenly it became obvious to me what was generating that void, that yearning, in the cadets' lives—and maybe in the lives of many American men. What was going on here was play—a kind of freedom and spontaneity that, in this culture, only women are permitted.

No wonder men found their Citadels, their Treehouses, where the rules of gender could be bent or escaped. For the drag queens of the Treehouse, the distinctions between the sexes are a goof, to be endlessly manipulated with fun-house-mirror glee. For cadets, despite the play set of The Citadel and the dress-up braids and ribbons, the guarding of their treehouse is a dead-serious business. Still, undercover at The Citadel, the cadets have managed to create for themselves a world in which they get half the equation that Lownie described: they can "act like human beings" in the safety of the daily domestic life of the barracks. But, in return, the institution demands that they never cease to "act like a man"—a man of cold and rigid bearing, a man no more male than Tiffany's Southern belle is female, a man that no one, humanly, can be. That they must defend their inner humanity with outer brutality may say as much about the world outside The Citadel walls as about the world within them. The cadets feel called to defend those walls. Never mind that their true ideal may not be the vaunted one of martial masculinity, just as their true enemy is not Shannon Faulkner. The cadets at The Citadel feel that something about their life and routine is worthy on its merits and is endangered from without. And in that they may be right.

QUESTIONS FOR MAKING CONNECTIONS
WITHIN THE READING

1. In "The Naked Citadel," Susan Faludi provides a series of vignettes that describe life at the military school. Why does she present the vignettes in the order she does? Why does she start her article in Jane Bishop's classroom? Why does she then move to the courtroom? Make a chart that tracks the organization of Faludi's essay. What is the argument that Faludi is making by telling these vignettes in this order?

2. The sociologist Erving Goffman coined the term "total institutions" to describe places that become almost entirely self-enclosed and self-referential in their values and behaviors. Goffman's principal example was the mental asylum. Can we describe The Citadel accurately as a "total institution"? Are its values the product of its isolation, or does Faludi's account furnish evidence that the attitudes holding sway in The Citadel also persist outside the institution as well? Is The Citadel just an aberration, or does it tell us certain truths about our own society?

3. Faludi offers this overview of The Citadel:

    > In the late-twentieth-century setting of The Citadel, in a time
    > when extreme insecurity and confusion about masculinity's standing
    > run rampant, the Corps of Cadets once again seeks to obscure a
    > domestic male paradise with an intensifying of virile showmanship
    > and violence. The result is a ruthless intimacy, in which physical
    > abuse stands in for physical affection, and every display of affection
    > must be counterbalanced by a display of sadism.

    On the basis of the evidence Faludi provides, is this a fair assessment of the culture of The Citadel? What evidence confirms this assessment? What evidence might be said to complicate or even contradict it? What other explanations might we offer for events at The Citadel? Does masculinity have to occupy the central place in our analysis, or might other factors be more important?

QUESTIONS FOR WRITING

1. In what sense is Susan Faludi a feminist? If we define a feminist as someone who is specifically concerned with defending the rights of women, does she qualify? Does she regard the rights of women as practically or theoretically distinct from the rights of men? How about the needs and aspirations of women? Are these fundamentally different from the needs and aspirations of men? Does Faludi see men as "oppressors of women"? Does she imply that our society systematically empowers men while systematically disempowering women, or does disempowerment cross gender lines?

2. "The Naked Citadel" might be described as a case study of the relations between sexuality and social structures. In what ways do social structures shape sexuality at The Citadel? Does Faludi's account call into question the belief in a single, natural form of male sexual expression? Is the problem with The Citadel that natural sexuality has been perverted by linking it to relations of power? Can sexuality and power ever be separated?

QUESTIONS FOR MAKING CONNECTIONS
BETWEEN READINGS

1. In "Immune to Reality," Daniel Gilbert sets out to create a theory of happiness, one that explains why humans, in general, are so unprepared to predict what things and accomplishments will lead to happiness. Does Gilbert's theory shed new light on the choices and the actions of the cadets at The Citadel? Would Gilbert's explanation for why The Citadel continues to attract students—male and female—reinforce, extend, or contradict Faludi's understanding? Write an essay about the degree to which happiness, as Gilbert defines it, plays a role in education inside and outside The Citadel.

2. In "When I Woke Up Tuesday Morning, It was Friday," from *The Myth of Sanity*, Martha Stout explores the psychological dynamics of dissociation. According to Stout, the experience of trauma "changes the brain itself." Under conditions of extreme pain or distress, the brain becomes unable to organize experience "usefully" or to integrate new experience with other, prior memories. Does it seem possible that dissociation plays a role in the training of cadets at The Citadel? What circumstantial evidence can you find to support this claim, or to dispute it? Does Stout's account of dissociation help to explain why so few cadets rebel against the treatment they receive? Is it possible that certain institutions use dissociation intentionally to weaken bonds sustained by affection and shared values? How might our society protect itself against the use of dissociation as a political instrument?

CAROLINE FRASER

One key to Caroline Fraser's work is the problem of isolation, not only from other human beings but also from the natural world. Born into a family of Christian Scientists, she was taught that matter is illusory—that the world in its true form is purely spiritual and subject to the power of faith through prayer, which can cure all illness if only we believe ardently enough. Once Fraser started high school, however, and encountered different ways of seeing, she began to distance herself from the religion of her parents. After receiving a B.A. from UCLA she went on to earn a Ph.D. in English and American Literature at Harvard. She then began a successful career as a poet, journalist, and freelance writer.

Education and experience helped Fraser overcome the sense of separateness that accompanied growing up in a minority faith, but the two books she has published so far might both be read as profound accounts of isolation in American life. *God's Perfect Child* (1999), her first book, explores the hidden world of Christian Science, which places an enormous emphasis on spiritual self-reliance. The book's title comes from Fraser's own experience. "When I was little and got carsick," she recalls, "I prayed frantically, saying over and over to myself, 'I am God's perfect child, I am God's perfect child'.... I was afraid to admit to feeling ill." Because Christian Science equates disease with a lack of faith, conventional medical treatment is discouraged—an outlook that has led, in several highly publicized cases, to the deaths of children. Beyond its function as an exposé, *God's Perfect Child* calls attention to the ways that our beliefs can isolate us, not only from those we love the most, but even from the needs of our own bodies.

At first glance Fraser's second book, *Rewilding the World*, might seem far removed from the first. But here again isolation is a major theme. The isolation she describes this time is a matter of geography—the confinement of unspoiled nature to "island communities" in parks and reserves, where many species simply fade away for lack of a large enough habitat. Unless we can find an alternative, and do so rather quickly, we will see the greatest mass extinction since the disappearance of the dinosaurs, a development that could potentially push humans toward extinction as well. The solution that some biologists propose is greater

Fraser, Caroline. *Rewilding the World: Dispatches from the Conservation Revolution* (New York: Metropolitan Books, 2009), 17–42.

The quotation in paragraph two is drawn from http://www.theatlantic.com/past/unbound/flashbks/xsci/suffer.htm. Other biographical information comes from http://carolinefraser.net/.

connectivity: the building of corridors to create a wilderness network within the heart of what we call "civilization." And yet geography may not be our greatest obstacle: instead it may be our standard ways of thinking. Perhaps the most important corridor we need to create is one "in people's minds" after all.

■ ■

Rewilding North America

Pluie

THE PROOF WAS A WOLF. IN JUNE OF 1991, A FIVE-YEAR-OLD alpha female, perhaps searching for new territory, embarked on a two-year foray, roaming over five hundred miles through the Rockies, an area of around 40,000 square miles, twelve times larger than Yellowstone National Park. As scientists were learning, this is what wolves do.[1]

She was wearing a radio collar fitted with a satellite transmitter, and Paul Paquet, a Canadian zoologist studying wolf movement for the World Wildlife Fund, was watching her. Paquet found and collared her in the rain, so he named her Pluie. He and a colleague, biologist Diane Boyd, tracked her with growing amazement as she inscribed an enormous circle, starting near Banff National Park in Alberta, Canada, heading south into Montana, skirting the southern boundary of Glacier National Park, swinging past Coeur d'Alene, Idaho, and Spokane, Washington, and then trekking north into British Columbia, making another pass at Banff. Paquet told a reporter, "We thought she was on a pickup truck for a while, she was moving so fast."[2]

Pluie's journey provided key evidence substantiating the theories on which rewilding is based. In the early 1990s, rewilding as a conservation method was still in its formative stages, but Pluie helped move it from a collection of hypotheses to a specific set of recommendations. A perfect illustration of the cores-corridors-carnivores idea, Pluie's traverse showed a top predator traveling from one core area to another, using wilderness corridors to do it. Her journey made national parks look minuscule, highlighting their inadequate size, isolation, and fragmentation. Although Pluie utilized parks such as Banff and Glacier, she clearly needed a space many times their size, a space a dozen times the size of Yellowstone.

The corridors she used were passageways of remaining forest linking large wilderness areas. Some—particularly in the Bow Valleys—were bisected by major highways and railroads, forming dangerous bottlenecks or breaks.

Pluie's travels let scientists identify the movement corridors, which, once located, could potentially be protected or restored by fencing off highways and providing safe overpasses for wildlife.

Pluie's journey, Paquet told me later, "made very clear what kind of geographic scale we should be thinking of. We were able to show pretty definitively that these theoretical corridors that we imagined were *actually* there and being used."[3] Now that scientists could watch elusive species like wolves traveling across the landscape, they could begin planning to manage, maintain, and even restore the necessary cores and corridors.

Pluie also demonstrated the contribution of "umbrella species," as biologists called wide-ranging animals: protecting the vast spaces they required could provide shelter for countless additional species.[4] If conservationists were able to put in place a series of big enough protected areas linked by corridors, they would be protecting not only wolves but everything else under that umbrella.

In 1993, Pluie lost her collar, which was found with a bullet hole in it. The wolf herself was shot dead two years later, along with her mate and several pups. Her fate matched that of most wolves, bears, and other large animals in today's West: shot or hit by cars, trucks, or freight trains. She was lucky to have survived as long as she did. One of Paquet's graduate students enumerated the toll that traffic on the Trans-Canada Highway and the Canadian Pacific Railway near Banff National Park had taken on wolves:

> In the last 15 years or so, 27-percent of the known wolf deaths have been from the railway, and 60-percent were on the highway. Just 5-percent were natural.... The Bow Valley used to have three packs. Now it has one. In 1996, three of the four pups born to this pack were lost to the highway. The next year, none of the five pups born survived, and we know at least one was hit on the railway. During 1998, the pack had no pups and was down to three members.[5]

Such figures—the rapidity with which an entire population of wolves can become roadkill—suggested the urgency of the need to find a way around these bottlenecks. Almost as soon as Pluie had run her course, the data gathered about the places she went and the routes she took were pressed into service to design a wilderness network. Most importantly, Pluie's movements inspired the first major rewilding project designed around cores, corridors, and carnivores, the Yellowstone to Yukon Conservation Initiative. Pluie's story, Paquet later said, "was the founding story of Y2Y. Really, the whole idea evolved out of it."[6]

But we get ahead of ourselves. Before the projects, before Pluie, before the proof, there was a theory. Like Newton's falling apple, Pluie acted as inspiration and demonstration, but scientific journeys begin with questions, not answers. The origins of rewilding—the conservation method designed to slow a wave of human-caused extinctions—are rooted in the most important ecological theory of the twentieth century, a theory that examines the forces governing extinction, the theory of island biogeography.

The Trouble with Islands

Nature is not a closed system. Since 1930, when a British botanist coined the term *ecosystem* to define the complex interrelationships between plants, animals, and microorganisms and the physical elements they interact with—rocks, soil, water, air—scientists began to recognize that wilderness cannot be preserved by sealing it off. To seal off is to interrupt processes that make life possible: natural selection, predation, competition. Because ecosystems contain such an extraordinary diversity of interactive species and processes, because they are not static, they have proved notoriously difficult to classify and study. Wrenched by larger environmental events—climate change, storms, fires, floods—they are capable of shifting, changing, evolving, and disappearing. Only within the past century have we begun to understand the laws that govern the evolution and transformation of ecosystems.

A momentous advance in understanding such systems came in 1967, when Robert H. MacArthur and Edward O. Wilson published *The Theory of Island Biogeography*. Wilson was thirty-seven when this epochal work appeared and would eventually become the most impassioned elder statesman of conservation, writing Pulitzer Prize–winning volumes about natural history and the need to protect biodiversity; indeed, his books popularized the term, a compression of "biological diversity." But in his early thirties, he was still a young Harvard biologist, albeit the world's greatest taxonomic expert on several subfamilies of ants in Melanesia, having spent years collecting in New Guinea and the islands of Fiji, as well as in Australia and South America. Over the years, he had noticed a pattern: the number of different ant species on any given island seemed to correlate to its size.[7]

As told in Wilson's autobiography, *Naturalist*, and David Quammen's history *The Song of the Dodo: Island Biogeography in an Age of Extinctions*, Wilson discussed this pattern and other issues in the emerging, genetics-driven field of population biology with MacArthur, a young University of Pennsylvania mathematician and ecologist legendary for his ability to discern patterns from masses of data and to construct sophisticated mathematical models illustrating general principles. The theory Wilson and MacArthur shaped is an explanation of how natural forces act to control the number of species populating a given area. Paradoxically, the theory that launched a worldwide movement to protect enormous continental areas was inspired by the smallest of land units, the island.

As MacArthur and Wilson noted at the outset, an island "is certainly an intrinsically appealing study object. It is simpler than a continent or an ocean, a visibly discrete object that can be labelled with a name and its resident populations identified thereby. In the science of biogeography, the island is the first unit that the mind can pick out and begin to comprehend."[8] But as they intuited, islands also provided useful information about the conditions that humanity was creating everywhere, even within continents. Islands were not only land masses surrounded by water; they were also isolated habitats surrounded by development. The principles of insularity—reduction and fragmentation—were going to apply "to an accelerating extent in the future" as habitats were "broken up by the encroachment of civilization."[9]

To understand why size and distance were related to the number of species populating an area, the authors examined two crucial ways in which species rise or fall on an island: immigration and extinction. Using data on ants and other species, they worked out that, as new species arrived, a similar number of established species was becoming locally extinct, in a process of turnover. They set forth a mathematical model illustrating how an island's area and its distance from other islands or mainlands regulated the balance between arrivals and displacement. Their model allowed calculation of a number representing equilibrium—predictable and stable—that was based on those factors of area and distance. If the key factors changed, so did the equilibrium. According to the mathematical model, altering the factors of area and/or distance would cause the number representing equilibrium to reset. If a theoretical island grew smaller or more distant, the number reset downward; if it grew larger or closer to other land masses, the number reset upward. Although I have drastically simplified this explanation, leaving out discussion of additional factors (climate, location relative to ocean currents, initial species composition, etc.), the essence is this: the smaller the island and the more distant from other places, the fewer species it supports. As a rule, a 90-percent decrease in the area of an island results in a 50-percent decrease in diversity.

Equilibrium itself, and the species it represented, could vanish when an island or fragment became so small and isolated that immigration stopped occurring. This was known as "ecosystem decay" and could be seen in one illustrative example: MacArthur and Wilson reproduced a series of maps showing the reduction and fragmentation of a woodland in Wisconsin between 1831 and 1950; the maps clearly showed the progressive diminution of wooded remnants to tiny scraps that could support little variety of flora or fauna.[10] As evidence supporting their theory, the authors looked at the famous volcanic eruption of Krakatau Island in 1883, which snuffed out all life under a sterilizing layer of searing pumice and ash. Although there were no comprehensive data on the flora and fauna prior to the eruption, there were for the subsequent "recolonization episode," in which insects, birds, and mammals returned to an island that had lost two-thirds of its total area. MacArthur and Wilson calculated that the number representing equilibrium for bird species, based on its new area and distance from other islands, should have settled at roughly thirty species within forty years. The historical data on recolonization seemed to confirm their calculation.[11]

The last chapter of *The Theory of Island Biogeography* described how further testing might be done by reproducing "miniature 'Krakataus'"—eliminating all species or all of a particular class of organisms (insects, fish) from a series of small islands or lakes, either "manually or by poisoning," and monitoring their return.[12] Wilson and one of his graduate students, Daniel Simberloff, re-created the sterile island experiment, performing an exacting census of all species of insects on several tiny mangrove islands in the Florida Keys, then hiring exterminators to tent and fumigate them. Over the following year, Simberloff monitored their return. "To my absolute delight," Wilson later told Quammen, "we watched the numbers of species rise to what was obviously equilibrium within about a year."[13] The experiment confirmed the theory as it related not only to area but also to distance: the most remote of the experimental islands was the slowest to return to equilibrium, and with the lowest number of species.

The havoc that equilibrium would play in small, remote protected areas was immediately obvious to biologists. By extrapolation, the smaller and more isolated an area is, the farther it is from the nearest wild area—the more *islandlike* it is—the more likely it will exhibit the characteristics of an island, including reduced diversity of species and a higher rate of extinction. Quammen distilled the issue of scale to a single, unforgettable metaphor. What do you get when you take a beautiful Persian carpet, he asked, and cut it into thirty-six pieces? Thirty-six separate carpets? Or thirty-six worthless, fraying scraps? Substitute ecosystems for carpet, he suggested, and you begin to see the problem.[14]

In a 1972 paper inspired by the equilibrium theory, the ornithologist Jared Diamond, who had done extensive fieldwork in New Guinea, directly addressed how equilibrium would affect protected areas that were too small and too island-like. He observed that the government of that country was in the process of setting aside small rain forest "tracts" as preserves. While the intentions were good, Diamond wrote, the outcome was likely to be the opposite of what they planned. The governments of New Guinea and other tropical countries were creating islands within islands, surrounded by "a 'sea' of open country in which forest species cannot live."[15] Diamond argued that the diminution and fragmentation would cause a "relaxation to equilibrium." The size of the preserves would inevitably trim the number of species they protected to a lower number than the forests initially held, undercutting their very purpose. In yet another paper, Diamond set forth initial suggestions for the size and design of nature reserves, the first to be based on the equilibrium theory. Large is better than small, he argued, and reserves grouped together or, better yet, connected to one another would support more species.

Given the evidence already available, many biologists were quick to agree that when it comes to preserving ecosystems, large is better than small, connected is better than isolated, and whole is better than fragmented. But some were resistant, arguing against a rush to judgment, suggesting that protected areas in the real world might prove vastly more complex, each with unique characteristics that might affect the outcome. The intellectual debate over the subject became so vituperatively colorful that David Quammen made it a central focus of *The Song of the Dodo*. The arguments were heated, he explained, because what was at stake was nothing less than saving the planet: "At a time when humanity was cutting forests and plowing savannas at a rapid pace, when habitat everywhere was becoming fragmented and insularized, the equilibrium theory embodied minatory truths. It was not just an interesting set of ideas—it was goddamned important. If heeded and applied, it might help save species from extinction."[16]

The most prolonged and violent debate to come out of island biogeography, a veritable "pissing match," as one biologist put it, was the debate over "SLOSS": "single large or several small."[17] Are single large protected areas better than several small ones? Jared Diamond strongly defended the idea that a single large reserve would tend to preserve more species. Large reserves, he argued, would preserve large carnivores, which need more space; they would provide more protection in the event of extreme climate change. Others thought that the theory had yet to be proved and ... the most adamant critic of the "single large" camp was Daniel Simberloff. He pointed to cases in which officials in Costa Rica and Israel, in a position to make decisions about conservation, nearly threw out plans for reserves that seemed too small and therefore—or *so they* thought—useless. Small parks might target hot spots of endemism; the conviction that big is better, Simberloff said, is "a cocktail-party idea" with the "trappings of science."[18]

The SLOSS debate eventually wound down, as more and more scientists and conservationists moved toward the big-is-better-than-small hypothesis. Looking around, they could see that national parks, protected areas, and reserves in the United States and around the world were small, fragmented, isolated. As anyone who has driven to Yosemite or Yellowstone knows, parks have indeed become islands of protected land in a sea of development—motels, shops, restaurants, malls, homes, roads—that washes right up to the entrance gates. In addition, many were poorly placed to preserve biological diversity. "National parks," conservation biologists argued, "are essentially square. Few conform to watersheds, mountain ranges, or other ... features that define natural regions. Most parks are too small."[19] Moreover, those dating back to the nineteenth century revealed the tastes of their creators in their emphasis on aesthetic grandeur—Yosemite's cliffs or Glacier's peaks—a criterion now derided by biologists as "rocks and ice," habitat notably short on biodiversity.

But the theory that large protected areas would preserve more species over a longer period of time than smaller ones was not properly tested until 1983, when William Newmark, a graduate student at the University of Michigan, set out in search of data for his doctoral thesis. He drove around the West, sleeping in the back of his Toyota, visiting a couple of dozen national parks in the United States and Canada, researching archival lists of mammal sightings for each one. He compared the record of mammal species present when the parks were founded to their current complement. His study, published in *Nature* in 1987, was a bombshell, the kind of logical observation that seems obvious only in retrospect.

Newmark found that most national parks had lost species since their founding. Mink and black-tailed jackrabbit disappeared from California's Yosemite. Gray wolf, fisher, striped skunk, and lynx disappeared from Washington's Mount Rainier. Caribou disappeared from the Waterton–Glacier parks that lie on the border between Montana and Alberta. The smaller the park, the more likely it was to be affected: river otter, ermine, mink, and spotted skunk vanished from Oregon's Crater Lake (248 square miles); Nuttall's cottontail, fisher, river otter, striped skunk, ringtail, and pronghorn from California's Lassen Volcanic Park (165 square miles); white-tailed jackrabbit, red fox, and spotted skunk from Utah's Bryce Canyon (56 square miles). Only a single protected area—the largest—maintained its original complement of species: the combined area of

were relatively old news: core reserves first appeared in the 1970s as a central feature of UNESCO's "Man and the Biosphere" program, which identified a number of existing parks representing the world's ecosystems as core "biosphere reserves" and urged their protection. MAB also promoted the idea of bolstering core reserves by enveloping them within buffer zones where human activity would be limited to protect and maintain populations of endangered species.

As connectivity became the hot topic of conservation biology, international agencies took notice. Soon corridors appeared in planning conferences and additional treaties and were lauded at the 1992 Rio de Janeiro "Earth Summit." They influenced the resulting Convention on Biological Diversity, a binding treaty requiring ratifying governments to conserve biodiversity through sustainable development. Even the Man and the Biosphere program was revised in 1995 to encourage the planning of corridors between core reserves.

Experts increasingly refined the roles that core reserves, buffer zones, connectivity, and ecological restoration would play in rewilding. Cores were defined as "strictly protected" areas where human access, activities, and particularly roads were limited. In the United States, cores included national parks, wilderness areas on federal lands, some state or provincial parks, and reserves managed by private conservation groups, such as the Nature Conservancy. While cores were familiar from the Man and the Biosphere model, emphasis was now placed on expanding their size substantially.

What would corridors look like? In *Continental Conservation*, Soulé and biologist John Terborgh put it simply: "One size does not fit all."[26] While corridors implied "linear habitats," the definition was expanded to include not just narrow pathways but also wide swaths of habitat permitting daily and seasonal movement, stepping stones, matrixes, mosaics of habitat, or ecological networks combining many forms of connectivity. Any one type could be tweaked to address the spatial scale—big carnivores need more space than rodents—or stretched north or south, or spread into a variety of altitudes to allow species sensitive to climate change to find safe haven.

Corridors linking core areas would allow not only seasonal migration but also dispersal. As animals mature, they leave their home range, looking for their own territory. Mother grizzlies drive off older cubs before mating again; young beavers launch themselves downriver or across forests, seeking places to build new dams and lodges; the young of most species must seek new territories. Dispersal maintains the genetic health of a population, as individuals find mates from distant groups. Confined populations, by contrast, become inbred, susceptible to reduced fertility, genetic disorders, and immune system problems. But so much territory has been altered or destroyed that there is less and less opportunity for dispersal. Corridors would help, permitting movement away from areas under development or degraded by climate change. They would allow recolonization of newly restored habitat. Corridors might be "stopover" mountain meadows where migrating rufous hummingbirds could refuel on their way to Mexico or hedgerows alongside organic strawberry crops in California, providing food and shelter for birds and small mammals. They might be windbreaks of trees in North Dakota, breeding sites for tree-nesting birds. They might be as simple as a repurposed underpass allowing frogs to hop under a highway or as major as a newly fence-free Africa, permitting elephants to resume their stately continental migrations. But all would, as Newmark put it bluntly, "reduce the risk of extinction for many species."[27]

Unlike past environmental campaigns, many of which were based on opposition to dams, construction, or oil drilling, the call for corridors was positive and appealing. Corridors made sense not only to scientists, who could point to a growing body of empirical observations supporting the notion, but to activists, environmentalists, or anyone else concerned about the degradation of local landscapes and parks. Even people without a background in biology or animal behavior could empathize with the need to get from one place to another.

And if connectivity was appealing, restoration was as visionary as science could be, holding out the hope and promise that humanity could heal the environmental damage that had already been done. It was both a radically new conservation tool and an idea with emotional force. In earlier decades, restoration consisted largely of superficial, cosmetic methods employed by mining or logging companies to backfill pits or replant despoiled areas with a scattered remnant of what had been destroyed or removed. Those kinds of rehabilitation rarely rose above disguising aesthetic disasters or forestalling erosion. Now scientists were experimenting with methods of restoring ecosystems on a far more complex and meaningful scale, reintroducing communities of plants and animals, regrowing coral reefs, even replanting tropical forest. They were seeing promising, sometimes astonishing results. Scientists recognized that these methods would be indispensable to continental-scale conservation. So much damage had been done to areas between parks and protected wilderness that it was impossible to imagine enlarging or connecting core reserves without restoring land between them. "Without restoration at large spatial scales," *Continental Conservation* advised, "the goal of protecting all species and ecosystems cannot be achieved."[28]

But restoration was also controversial. For years, the Nature Conservancy, World Wildlife Fund, and other international environmental organizations had based major fund-raising campaigns around the notion that nature, once lost, was lost forever. Ecological restoration contradicted that. Maybe nature wasn't lost forever; maybe ecosystems could be recovered. If so, NGOs wondered, would the public become confused; would donors lose the motivation to give? Would government and industry, real estate developers, oil companies, and agribusiness be emboldened to step up their already voracious consumption of land, arguing that it could be restored later? But the biologists felt that these caveats represented timidity at a time when bold, urgent action was required.

Rewilding was bold, urgent, new, radical. If existing links between parks and reserves could be exploited, fine. But if corridors were not available, they would have to be re-created. If that meant restoring damaged or destroyed forests or grasslands between them or reintroducing carnivores, then that is what had to be done.

With the publication of *Continental Conservation* and a raft of other books and papers explicating connectivity and restoration, the conservation biology community in North America was reaching a consensus, offering a comprehensive show of support for rewilding as a solution, a remedy, a plan. But no one had ever restored a continent before. Where should cores, corridors, and restoration be planned? How should these large-scale networks of protected areas be designed? Who would carry out these projects; how would they be managed? By whom and for how long? Where would the money come from? Rewilding represented an almost infinite number of consequential decisions and tasks. It was a prospect of staggering, overwhelming dimensions. In terms of time, money, scientific expertise, and technological prowess, rewilding made NASA's job of sending a man to the moon look finite and manageable. Every decision made would have real-world consequences affecting land use, water, and wildlife management on a scale never before contemplated. Every decision would also affect an unpredictable and volatile constituency: human communities.

Rewilding in the Real World

In the 1990s, the American environmental landscape presented a discouraging prospect for the new wave of conservation biologists and rewilding activists. Major private conservation organizations, including the Sierra Club, World Wildlife Fund, Nature Conservancy, and Wildlife Conservation Society, had invested decades and millions of dollars in established programs organized around their own priorities, from endangered species protection to buying tracts of private land. Many programs included elements of what would become rewilding, but none were devoted to the promotion of cores, corridors, and carnivores together. It would be difficult to convince such entities to back new, untested, expensive schemes.

Public agencies overseeing environmental issues and land use—the Department of the Interior (including the U.S. Fish and Wildlife Service, the National Park Service, and the Bureau of Land Management) and the Department of Agriculture (which includes the U.S. Forest Service)—were even less promising. Their priorities, altered by successive presidential administrations and appointments, had been highly politicized in recent disputes over the Endangered Species Act and the disposition of logging and grazing rights in the West. For decades they had been heavily influenced by ranching, mining, and logging interests.

So rewilding advocates in North America struck out on their own, creating new groups, essentially seeking to reshape the environmental movement. In 1991, the same year that research on Pluie began, an eclectic group of scientists, activists, and businessmen—including Doug Tompkins, founder of the Esprit and North Face clothing companies; Dave Foreman, a founder of Earth First!; Michael Soulé; Reed Noss; and David Johns, an attorney and environmentalist—banded together to form the Wildlands Project, a group devoted to moving conservation biology from the realm of theory to action. In 1992, the project published a special issue of its magazine, *Wild Earth*, on "Plotting a North American Wilderness Recovery Strategy." The issue was filled with ambitious maps outlining a proposed Adirondack wilderness reserve system, a southern Rockies ecosystem, a southern Appalachian wildlands network sweeping up the Great

Smoky Mountains National Park in a skein of protected areas between Georgia and Virginia. There was also a map of "Paseo Pantera," a plan to create a "Path of the Panther" through the narrow Central American isthmus.[29]

With money from Tompkins, the project distributed seventy-five thousand copies, and Johns remembers seeing it in far-flung locales all over the globe, in the labs and homes of biologists from Europe to Siberia. Throughout the 1990s, the idea of connectivity flew around the world, infiltrating scientific conferences, papers, graduate theses, environmental courses, grassroots meetings. By 1993, conservationists and biologists were debating the steps that should be taken to maintain and restore connectivity in what came to be called Yellowstone to Yukon. The Yellowstone to Yukon Conservation Initiative, formally launched in 1997, promoted a conservation vision for a vast corridor of the northern Rockies, from Canada's Yukon down through the Waterton–Glacier national parks and south into the system of parks, national forests, and wilderness areas that make up what biologists define as the Greater Yellowstone ecoregion. A Canadian environmentalist named Harvey Locke, an early board member of the Wildlands Project who had been captivated by the accounts of Pluie's journey, had an immediate sense of the potential of the Yukon and Yellowstone "myth," as he called it, arising from the romantic wilderness mystique of Robert Service and Jack London.[30] Locke would later say of Y2Y, "I chose those words, 'Yellowstone to Yukon,' because they're deep symbols in people's brains. If I say those words in Stuttgart, Germany, in Toronto, in New York, or in Tokyo, everybody knows what I'm talking about."[31]

Y2Y quickly mobilized environmentalists, mountaineers, and activists in Montana and Wyoming. Rick Bass, Doug Peacock, and Rick Ridgeway wrote essays and gave interviews publicizing it. The Craighead Environmental Research Institute in Bozeman, founded by charismatic twin brothers and grizzly bear biologists Frank Craighead Jr. and John Craighead, whose work on bear territories and behavior predated Paquet's with wolves, began coordinating research projects in the region. Gradually Y2Y seeped out of conservation circles and into the popular culture, championed in catalogs put out by Yvon Chouinard's outdoor clothing company, Patagonia, and discussed on the television drama *The West Wing*. By 2007, there were eight hundred member organizations.

Y2Y was an initiative and a vision. It was not an implementing project and would not carry out or fund corridor or restoration projects on its own. Instead, the initiative would lobby, educate, promote. Much like the Wildlands Project (now Wildlands Network), Y2Y served as a clearinghouse and organizational network, setting up conferences and workshops for joint rewilding projects between conservationists from Canada and the United States. The group facilitated dialogue between the conservation community and members of Native American and First Nation groups, made small grants to research projects, published a sophisticated map of the region that identified priority areas for conservation and potential threats to connectivity, and excelled at promoting the visionary potential of connectivity, maintaining a high profile in features in the *New York Times*, the *Washington Post*, and metropolitan papers in the United States and Canada.[32] While the group was quick to deny that it intended to turn the Y2Y region into

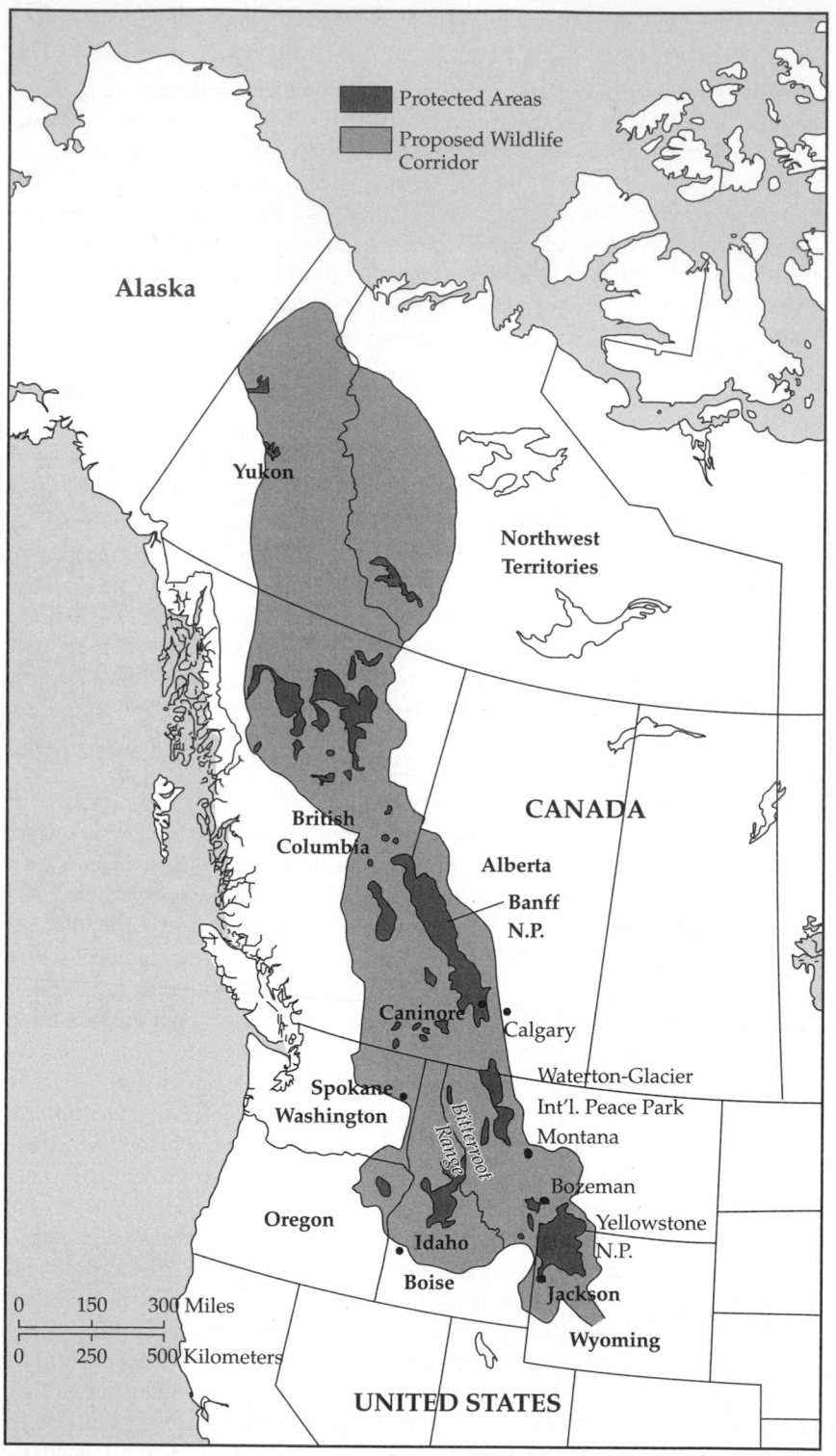

Yellowstone to Yukon: The Yellowstone to Yukon Initiative (Y2Y) aims to forge a single wildlife corridor by connecting isolated parks, national forests, and some of the largest roadless areas left on the continent.

a vast park excluding human use, its promoters intended to influence land management throughout the area by warding off road projects and developments that could interfere with the habitat and movement of wolves, grizzly bears, and their prey.

The most immediate example of Y2Y's influence was its successful lobbying for highway crossing structures for wildlife in the Banff area, which Pluie had so perilously navigated. Widely adopted in Europe for decades, crossing structures are popular not only with conservationists but also with insurance underwriters who value their potential to reduce accidents. In the United States, for example, deer-vehicle collisions alone occur up to one and a half million times each year, costing some two hundred lives and $8.8 billion annually; collisions also imperil the survival of twenty-one endangered and threatened species.

As a result of Y2Y pressure, Canada in the midnineties allocated $3.3 million to build two wildlife bridges and twenty-two underpasses providing passage across the Trans-Canada Highway, the lethal road that cuts the Bow Valley in half. Wolves and grizzlies initially proved reluctant to try the 160-foot-wide bridges, which had been covered in rock, dirt, native trees, and vegetation to replicate a natural crossing. "Not all wolves use them," Paquet told me. "Wolves are like humans. Some are willing, some are not."[33] For the past decade, the Banff Wildlife Crossings Project, a long-running research project supported in part by Y2Y, has monitored that willingness, finding that animal use increased steadily over the years. Grizzly bears utilized the crossings seven times in 1996; in 2006, over a hundred times.[34] Scientists have begun to theorize that grizzly mothers are teaching their cubs to find and use the structures.

To expand their data, Banff Project scientists strung barbed-wire hair snares across the underpasses, a low-cost method of identification for bears, wolves, and other big creatures passing through. Footage from cameras mounted on the underpasses shows bears and mountain lions approaching the wire cautiously, sniffing, and peering around. Then most of them burst over or under the wires, galloping off, leaving samples behind. Using these hair snares, camera footage, and beds raked to reveal tracks, scientists have found that eleven species of large mammals have used the crossings over 104,000 times since 1996. Wildlife collisions have been reduced over 80-percent, and those involving elk and deer by 96-percent. Given that people involved in wildlife collisions end up spending an average of two thousand dollars per accident for repairs, and that many are injured or even killed in such accidents, the Banff crossing structures may have already paid for themselves.

Transportation departments in the United States watched the Banff experiment closely, and highway mitigation projects are now planned throughout the country. In 2008, the Washington State Department of Transportation approved the construction of fourteen wildlife crossing structures on Interstate 90 through the Cascade Mountains: narrow bridges and culverts will be replaced with wider ones to allow wildlife to cross under the highway.[35] Exclusion fences will funnel animals to the crossings and keep them off the road. Two vegetated overpasses will be built. In Montana, forty wildlife crossings were added to a highway reconstruction project on the Flathead Indian Reservation; in Florida, eight alligator underpasses were built on Highway 1 through the Florida Keys. In Arizona, desert bighorn sheep were fitted with radiotelemetry collars that yielded eighty thousand "waypoints," GPS readings indicating where sheep were trying to cross Highway 93 in the Black Mountains near Hoover Dam.[36] The data revealed that bighorns shun underpasses, fearing predators, and prefer high crossings, so state and federal transportation and wildlife officials designed three overpasses that should reunite two groups of the Black Mountains bighorn long separated by the road. Construction began in 2008, and more sheep overpasses are being planned around the country.

Impressed by the success of Y2Y in improving wildlife passages across highways, regional groups took up the mission. In Southern California, the South Coast Wildlands Project launched a campaign to identify threats to connectivity, honing in on Coal Canyon, a critical corridor for mountain lions and bobcats between Anaheim and Riverside. In 2000, the group successfully lobbied the California State Parks agency to purchase a 700-acre tract slated for development and to close and convert an underpass into a wildlife-friendly passage for big cats. "What do you call a freeway interchange ripped up to create a wildlife underpass?" the South Coast Wildlands Project exulted on its Web site. "A good start."[37]

Y2Y led to an explosion of corridor planning across North America and around the world. The Sky Island Alliance scanned the desert southwest of Arizona and New Mexico, focusing on weak or broken connections between mountain ranges. The Algonquin to Adirondack Conservation Initiative (A2A) tackled the corridors of the Great Lakes region compromised by extensive development, researching ways to bolster connectivity in a region anchored by Algonquin Provincial Park in Ontario and Adirondack State Park in upstate New York. Networks of marine reserves were sketched out, including a blueprint of twenty-eight "Marine Priority Conservation Areas" in the coastal Pacific from Baja, California, to the Bering Sea (B2B).[38] As with Y2Y, these cross-border initiatives aimed to engage North American nations in joint conservation planning, to identify species of common concern, and to begin managing and monitoring transportation issues and fisheries collectively.

The North American initiatives were matched and even exceeded by the scale of rewilding projects being planned internationally. With corridors entrenched in international agreements on conservation, large-scale protected areas and transboundary projects proliferated. This was perhaps the greatest effect of Y2Y—altering the scale on which conservation was planned. Y2Y inspired activists to be visionary, ambitious, even Utopian. The new thinking represented a paradigm shift: conservationists were now considering continents and planning for a millenium. One participant said, "We look at things that are too small and we think too short term.... Y2Y has completely changed that whole thinking."[39]

"A Corridor in People's Minds."   But there was just one problem. Many biologists felt that activists had begun advocating for corridors before knowing where to put them. Bill Newmark, for example, believed corridors were a biological necessity. "The issue of whether or not corridors are a wise conservation strategy, I don't think people question that anymore," he told me. But he also thought that there were dozens of questions to be answered before planners could begin to figure out how and where to design potential corridors. When it came to Y2Y, he was dismissive of something that existed, as yet, largely on paper. "It's a corridor in people's minds," he said dryly. "Whether or not animals really use it is another question."[40]

A number of scientists and organizations set out to answer that question and a host of others. Joel Berger, a senior scientist for the Wildlife Conservation Society (WCS) working out of a Teton, Wyoming, field office, focused on the Great Plains ecosystem, leading a team designing a migratory corridor for pronghorn antelope, one of the most important ungulates in North America, with half a million roaming Wyoming alone.

The fastest land animal in the New World, perhaps the fastest long-distance runner on earth, pronghorn migrate astonishing distances, traversing mountain passes and steep canyons, for reasons that are still not completely understood. A population of around two hundred to four hundred pronghorn run an annual marathon from their summer range in Grand Teton National Park, south of Yellowstone, to a winter range to the southeast, in Wyoming's Green River Basin, near the town of Rock Springs, returning in the spring. Sometimes reaching speeds of fifty-five miles an hour, the pronghorn run thirty miles a day without stopping to feed, the longest and most dramatic land migration in the lower forty-eight states. Archaeological evidence shows that the route has been used for some six thousand years, but it has become lethal, blocked and constricted by highways, development, and rampant gas drilling unleashed by the second Bush administration. Berger and his team have seen up to six animals killed at once, in a single vehicle collision. Looking at the historical record, they came to believe that many previous migratory pronghorn routes— one of which went through what is now downtown Jackson Hole—had already been choked off by development. Thus it was all the more important to preserve this last intact route: while the species itself was not technically endangered, although reduced by 95-percent since the 1800s, major impacts to pronghorn migration might spell eventual genetic fragmentation and doom.[41]

Fitting ten pronghorn with radio collars in 2003, the team mapped their journey from the summer to the winter range. The resulting computerized map identified several bottlenecks, including one funnel in midroute only 120 meters wide, which housing developments and parking lots threatened to close completely. Using the data, they designed a plan for the first National Migration Corridor, ninety miles long and a mile wide, virtually all of it on public land managed by the Bureau of Land Management, a federal agency charged with "balancing" energy needs with a responsibility to protect the environment. While the corridor has gained popular support to the north in Jackson Hole and other towns around the Grand Tetons, gas-drilling communities in southern Wyoming oppose it. The state itself lacks statutory authority to manage federal lands, so the nation's first migration corridor is still awaiting a moment when the political and economic stars align in its favor.

In 2006, Jon Beckmann ... filled another data gap, this one in the understanding of carnivore movement. He ran a pack of scat-detector dogs through the Centennial Mountains, near the Idaho-Montana border. The dogs were trained to detect scats of black bear, grizzly, mountain lion, and wolf. Laboring for months, covering two hundred and thirty-two square miles of terrain, the painstaking canines found 660 scats and thirty hair samples. DNA testing showed they achieved 98-percent accuracy in identifying the samples.[42]

The data provided a gold mine of information to determine exactly where carnivore superhighways were located and what kinds of human activities were causing gridlock. The findings persuaded the Bureau of Land Management to close 40-percent of the roads in the western Centennials and helped stop a 1,200-home, eighteen-hole golf course development that had been scheduled to be built right in the fast lane of this busy corridor.

Bill Newmark, too, was gathering information on how to restore connectivity. To identify principles of prey behavior, Newmark used teams of volunteers provided by Earthwatch, an international NGO in the forefront of rewilding research, to study wildlife trails in Idaho's northern mountains. He wanted to know how the landscape influenced the movement of moose, elk, and deer, critical to the survival of carnivores. In Trail Gulch, a historic area on the east side of the north fork of the Salmon River, where Lewis and Clark crossed the Bitterroots and where grazing was permanently prohibited, Newmark deployed his volunteers to complete a vegetation study, and I tagged along. Data on food availability, combined with information on the steepness of slopes and other landscape features, would all contribute to a detailed picture of where ungulates were going and why.

Walking in pairs along transects spaced seventy meters apart, we followed straight lines drawn across a map in order to provide an accurate sampling of vegetation. This meant struggling up and down steep hills and across perpendicular fields of sliding scree. Every ten meters, the volunteers dropped a quadrat, a meter-square measuring device made of PVC pipe, and identified the percentage of food plants (western wheat grass, clover alfalfa, lupine) within it. Newmark himself, a lean, grizzled figure in his fifties, was always first to finish, indifferent to hail, fog, or lightning strikes nearby. Below, vultures and small planes rode the thermals.

One day, he remarked that this place nearly killed Lewis and Clark, whose men hated "these most terrible mountains ... as steep as the roof of a house."[43] Even in an age of four-wheel drive, the mountains remain intimidating, the skyline pierced by jagged peaks. After finishing the transects, it routinely took hours to descend, as the team took the hills at an angle, trying not to fall headfirst.

At another site, equipped with handheld GPS units, the team mapped actual wildlife trails made by elk and deer. Some were barely visible tracks; others looked like highways for the cloven-hoofed. Newmark spent the better part of a day running down one of these major migratory routes with a sophisticated backpack GPS unit, accurate to less than a meter. As he ran, the unit recorded the data, to be downloaded onto a topographical map of the area, yielding a sophisticated visual picture of elk movement. "They're using the same rules we would use," he said later, "taking these steep saddles down to the stream." He was wondering about elk motivation; was saving energy more important during long migrations or was predator avoidance the priority? Understanding their behavior could affect the potential design of functional corridors, which would have to meet the needs of the animals that would actually use them.

Hiking through Trail Gulch, from the trailhead into the mountains and back again, we passed through natural choke points, narrow creek beds where countless deer, elk, and moose had met their end. Predator scat showed that wolves and mountain lions had lain in wait and found their opportunities. The defiles were littered with a chaotic tangle of fallen trees, stumps, skulls, and bones. These corridors, at least, were fully functional and as efficient as an abattoir.

They were also rare. Such glimpses of a healthy balance between predator and prey can be seen only in northern pockets of the West where the wolf is making a comeback. Asked how large predators survived in Africa when many were driven extinct in the Americas, after the arrival of *Homo sapiens*, Newmark stated a simple evolutionary fact. "They evolved with humans," he said, "and they learned, *that's* a nasty predator."

Biologists, for all their carefully calibrated qualifications, excel at this kind of startling bestial insight, stepping outside our species to see how we affect others. And the picture was not a pretty one. Even when Newmark, Berger, and other biologists finished filling in the gaps, they knew they would face resistance from the top predator in this and every ecosystem, one loath to give up any ground.

NOTES

1. "Initiative Inspired by Wandering Wolf," *Connections: Publication of the Yellowstone to Yukon Conservation Initiative* 13 (Winter 2007): 7.

2. Cornelia Dean, "Wandering Wolf Inspires Project," *New York Times*, 23 May 2006.

3. Paul Paquet, telephone interview, 30 July 2007.

4. J. Michael Scott et al., "The Issue of Scale in Selecting and Designing Biological Reserves," in Michael E. Soulé and John Terborgh, eds., *Continental Conservation: Scientific Foundations of Regional Reserve Networks* (Washington: Island Press, 1999), p. 23.

5. Douglas H. Chadwick, *Yellowstone to Yukon* (Washington: National Geographic, 2000), p. 91.

6. Dean, "Wandering Wolf."

7. David Quammen, *The Song of the Dodo: Island Biogeography in an Age of Extinctions* (New York: Scribner, 1996), p. 412.

8. Robert H. MacArthur and Edward O. Wilson, *The Theory of Island Biogeography* (Princeton: Princeton University Press, 1967), p. 3.

9. Ibid.

10. Ibid., p. 4.

11. Ibid., pp. 43–51.

12. Ibid., p. 181.

13. Quammen, *Song of the Dodo*, pp. 428–31.

14. Ibid., p. 11.

15. Jared M. Diamond, "Biogeographic Kinetics: Estimation of Relaxation Time for Avifaunas of Southwest Pacific Islands," *Proceedings of the National Academy of Sciences 69* (Nov. 1972): 3199–203. See also Quammen, *Song of the Dodo*, pp. 442–43.

16. David Quammen, *Song of the Dodo*, p. 444.

17. Ibid., p. 463.

18. Ibid., p. 481.

19. Reed R. Noss and Allen Y. Cooperrider, *Saving Nature's Legacy: Protecting and Restoring Biodiversity* (Washington: Island Press, 1994), p. 132.

20. William D. Newmark, "A Land-Bridge Island Perspective on Mammalian Extinctions in Western North American Parks," *Nature* 325 (29 Jan. 1987): 432. See also William D. Newmark, "Extinction of Mammal Populations in Western North American National Parks," *Conservation Biology 9* (June 1995): 512–26.

21. Aldo Leopold, *A Sand County Almanac* (New York: Oxford University Press, 1949), p. 198.

22. James Gleick, "Species Vanishing from Many Parks," *New York Times*, 3 Feb. 1987.

23. Ibid.

24. Rick Ridgeway, "Paths to Survival," *Patagonia*, Winter 2008, p. 1.

25. Dave Foreman, *Rewilding North America: A Vision for Conservation in the 21st Century* (Washington: Island Press, 2004), p. 117.

26. Michael E. Soulé and John Terborgh, eds., *Continental Conservation: Scientific Foundations of Regional Reserve Networks* (Washington: Island Press, 1999), p. 12.

27. William D. Newmark, *Conserving Biodiversity in East African Forests: A Study of the Eastern Arc Mountains* (Berlin: Springer-Verlag, 2002), p. 137.

28. Daniel J. Simberloff et al., "Regional and Continental Restoration," in Soulé and Terborgh, eds., *Continental Conservation*, p. 70.

29. Susan Marynowski, "Paseo Pantera: The Great American Biotic Interchange," *Wild Earth*, special issue (1992): 71.

30. Charles C. Chester, *Conservation across Borders: Biodiversity in an Interdependent World* (Washington: Island Press, 2006), p. 179.

31. Ibid., p. 177.

32. Ibid., p. 171.

33. Paul Paquet, personal interview, 30 July 2007.

34. Tony Clevenger, "Highways through Habitats: The Banff Wildlife Crossings Project," *TR News* 249 (March–April 2007): 15. For more details on the Banff wildlife crossing structures, see "Ten Quick Facts about Highway Wildlife Crossings in the Park," Banff National Park of Canada, n.d. Web, 14 May 2009.

35. Barbara Christensen, "I-90 Safer for Wildlife and People," *Conservation Northwest*, 2 Sept. 2008. Web, 14 May 2009.

36. "Highway Overpass OK'd for Bighorns," *Tri-State Online*, 8 Jan. 2009. Web, 15 May 2009.

37. Paul Beier et al., "Collaborative, Focal Species Approaches to Linkage Conservation: Lessons from California and Arizona," PowerPoint presentation, p. 36.

38. Lance Morgan et al., *Baja California to the Bering Sea* (Montreal: Commission for Environmental Cooperation of North America and the Marine Conservation Biology Institute, 2005).

39. Chester, *Conservation across Borders*, p. 167.

40. William Newmark, personal interview, 11 June 2005. All subsequent quotations from Newmark in this section are from interviews conducted 11–18 June 2005.

41. For details on Berger's pronghorn studies, see "Preserving a Wild West, for Posterity and for Pronghorn," *Wildlife Conservation Society*, n.d. Web, 14 May 2009. See also Cory Hatch, "Biologist: Protect Pronghorn Migration Route," *Jackson Hole News and Guide*, 24 May 2006.

42. Jon P. Beckmann, "Northern Rockies: Using Scat-Detecting Dogs as a Tool to Model Linkage Zone Functionality for a Suite of Species," Society for Conservation Biology, Chattanooga, 15 July 2008, presentation.

43. Stephen E. Ambrose, *Lewis & Clark: Voyage of Discovery* (Washington, D.C.: National Geographic Society, 1998), pp. 154, 162.

QUESTIONS FOR MAKING CONNECTIONS WITHIN THE READING

1. "Rewilding North America" is not just a story about preservation. It also provides a detailed account of the way that science gets done and how its discoveries can gradually generate profound social change. Using Fraser's narrative as your guide, try to define the stages involved in scientific discovery. As you retrace the process and attempt to represent it step-by-step, you might ask yourself what causes people to rethink well-established knowledge. What are the relations between theory, investigation, and eventual "proof"? Next, try to define the stages in the spread of such new knowledge. How does it make its way into the world? Pay particular attention to the role of institutions that mediate between science and the public sphere.

2. The key to understanding Fraser's argument is the term "connectivity." Re-read the selection in order to take note of all the different forms of connectivity you find, not only in the natural world but also in culture and society. In what ways has greater social connectivity followed from our recent discovery of connectivity in nature? And how have existing institutions—the Sierra Club, for example, or the Department of the Interior—made change in this direction more difficult? Why has nature's connectivity been so hard for us to notice even though it has been there all along?

3. "Nature," Fraser writes, "is not a closed system." But what is a system, and how is nature an *open* system? Noting all the places where systems are described, try to define the principles governing the way systems operate—principles such as equilibrium and interrelatedness. How do these principles

differ from those that govern many human institutions, among them the national parks? Because human institutions often strive for permanence, self-containment, and simplicity (think of the rectangular boundaries of the parks), are they unavoidably at odds with natural systems? Is it possible to design institutions that are flexible enough to accommodate natural processes?

QUESTIONS FOR WRITING

1. How does "Rewilding North America" force us to rethink the relations between the natural world and its human counterpart? For a century we have tried to save the environment by enclosing it in parks and preserves, only to discover that this approach is, in David Quammen's words, like cutting a Persian carpet into little pieces. What assumptions about the way nature works does Fraser call into question—and what assumptions about the proper way for the human community to live? Is there any real alternative to "rewilding"? What might be its implications for the very notion of a "civilization"? How might our civilization benefit from richer connections to the natural world?

2. As we confront the ever-spreading ruin of the natural environment, we can easily conclude that the damage has become irreparable and that all we can do now is watch as the fabric of life on earth unravels. Worse yet, in spite of the urgent need for appropriate action, our institutions can appear to be immovable. Does Fraser's account present an alternative to conclusions of this kind? Might we say that she provides a blueprint for real and far-reaching transformation? In the making of such a transformation, what role does specialized knowledge play? And what is the role of education in conveying knowledge of this kind to society as a whole?

QUESTIONS FOR MAKING CONNECTIONS
BETWEEN THE READINGS

1. In "Selections from Into the Wild," Jon Krakauer tells us that Chris McCandless "went into the wilderness not primarily to ponder nature or the world at large but, rather, to explore the inner country of his own soul." By leaving behind his home and family, McCandless hoped to see what he could do without the support of civilization. But now, as the human population expands and true wilderness becomes more and more remote, we might ask if such an undertaking has become a thing of the past. Is it even possible nowadays to leave civilization behind? (Think about McCandless's books and tools, and his dependence on the bus.) What might rewilding teach us about the "inner country" of our "souls"? If the wilderness is gone,

might we in some way still "rewild" ourselves—reconnecting in a new way with the natural world?

2. In "The Myth of the Ant Queen," Steven Johnson makes an argument about the power of what he calls "self organization." Beginning with a community of ants, he points to the sophistication of their colonies and argues that they did it all without the benefit of any central leader or prearranged plan. From ants he turns to the British city of Manchester, which rose to prominence over several centuries with "no local government to speak of." It was, he writes, "the least planned and most chaotic of cities in the six-thousand year history of urban settlements," and yet it also seemed to possess a "kind of order" that was "wonderful." Ultimately Johnson appears to believe that the best order will arise spontaneously, without any conscious effort or control. Would you say that Fraser confirms Johnson's view? Does the complexity of modern life require less planning, as Johnson suggests, or does it demand much, much more, as Fraser implies?

DANIEL GILBERT

HISTORICALLY, THE STUDY of human psychology has tended to emphasize the negative. Scholars and practitioners of mental health focused on the mysteries of schizophrenia, depression, and other forms of psychological distress. In recent years, however, an interdisciplinary cohort of psychologists and other researchers have directed their attention to what turns out to be an equally misunderstood area: human happiness.

Among the leaders of this movement—sometimes called "positive psychology," or, more informally, "happiness studies"—is Daniel Gilbert, a professor of social psychology at Harvard University. Gilbert pioneered the field of affective forecasting, or the study of the way that people try to predict their future emotional states based on their current situation. In fact, these predictions are often incorrect. Having dropped out of high school to travel and write science fiction, Gilbert is well suited to explore the role that the unexpected can play in our search for happiness. While living in Denver, Colorado, Gilbert tried to enroll in a creative writing course at a local community college. Turned away because of oversubscription, he decided to take the only open course: psychology. Realizing that psychology "wasn't about crazy people" but "about all of us," Gilbert "stumbled" onto the path that brought him to the present.

In his international bestseller *Stumbling on Happiness* (2006), Gilbert argues that people suffer from "illusions of prospection." Through his experimental research, he learned of a remarkable discrepancy: even though few people believe they can predict what the future will bring, many more are convinced they can foresee how they will feel when the future arrives. Yet our predictions are often subject to a high degree of "impact bias," which leads us to overestimate just how intense our feelings will be, whether they are negative or positive.

The chapter from *Stumbling on Happiness* included here, "Immune to Reality," offers just some of Gilbert's counterintuitive discoveries. For example, we meet experimental subjects who fail to predict their level of happiness just minutes into the future. While we might not be surprised by their inability to make these predictions, we probably remain confident that we understand ourselves well enough to avoid the same mistakes. Gilbert also explains the operations of the "psychological immune system," which protects us when we suffer wrenching

Gilbert, Daniel. "Immune to Reality." *Stumbling on Happiness.* New York: Knopf, 2006.

Quotations are drawn from an interview conducted at SXSW available at <http://2006.sxsw.com/bits_n_bytes/pivot/entry.php?id=79#body> and from an interview conducted by Dave Weich of Powell's books at <http://www.powells.com/authors/danielgilbert.html>.

setbacks but not when we try to cope with minor ones, imparting a surprising complacency in the face of significant blows but often leaving us quite helpless when we deal with trivial irritations. Gilbert's conclusions challenge the conventional ways we understand our mental well-being by showing just how poorly these conventions reflect the reality of our emotional lives. Through their work, Gilbert and the other champions of happiness studies are seeking to reshape how we go about the "pursuit of happiness."

Immune to Reality

Upon my back, to defend my belly; upon my wit, to defend my wiles; upon my secrecy, to defend mine honesty; my mask, to defend my beauty.

SHAKESPEARE, *TROILUS AND CRESSIDA*

Albert Einstein may have been the greatest genius of the twentieth century, but few people know that he came *this* close to losing that distinction to a horse. Wilhelm von Osten was a retired schoolteacher who in 1891 claimed that his stallion, whom he called Clever Hans, could answer questions about current events, mathematics, and a host of other topics by tapping the ground with his foreleg. For instance, when Osten would ask Clever Hans to add three and five, the horse would wait until his master had finished asking the question, tap eight times, then stop. Sometimes, instead of *asking* a question, Osten would write it on a card and hold it up for Clever Hans to read, and the horse seemed to understand written language every bit as well as it understood speech. Clever Hans didn't get *every* question right, of course, but he did much better than anyone else with hooves, and his public performances were so impressive that he soon became the toast of Berlin. But in 1904 the director of the Berlin Psychological Institute sent his student, Oskar Pfungst, to look into the matter more carefully, and Pfungst noticed that Clever Hans was much more likely to give the wrong answer when Osten was standing in back of the horse than in front of it, or when Osten himself did not know the answer to the question the horse had been asked. In a series of experiments, Pfungst was able to show that Clever Hans could indeed read—but that what he could read was Osten's body language. When Osten bent slightly, Clever Hans would start tapping, and when Osten straightened up, or tilted his head a bit, or faintly raised an eyebrow, Clever Hans would stop. In other words, Osten was signaling Clever Hans to start and stop tapping at just the right moments to create the illusion of horse sense.

Clever Hans was no genius, but Osten was no fraud. Indeed, he'd spent years patiently talking to his horse about mathematics and world affairs, and he was genuinely shocked and dismayed to learn that he had been fooling himself, as well as everyone else. The deception was elaborate and effective, but it was perpetrated unconsciously, and in this Osten was not unique. When we expose ourselves to favorable facts, notice and remember favorable facts, and hold favorable facts to a fairly low standard of proof, we are generally no more aware of our subterfuge than Osten was of his. We may refer to the processes by which the psychological immune system does its job as "tactics" or "strategies," but these terms—with their inevitable connotations of planning and deliberation—should not cause us to think of people as manipulative schemers who are consciously *trying* to generate positive views of their own experience. On the contrary, research suggests that people are *typically unaware* of the reasons why they are doing what they are doing,[1] but when asked for a reason, they readily supply one.[2] For example, when volunteers watch a computer screen on which words appear for just a few milliseconds, they are unaware of seeing the words and are unable to guess which words they saw. But they are influenced by them. When the word *hostile* is flashed, volunteers judge others negatively.[3] When the word *elderly* is flashed, volunteers walk slowly.[4] When the word *stupid* is flashed, volunteers perform poorly on tests.[5] When these volunteers are later asked to explain *why* they judged, walked, or scored the way they did, two things happen: First, they don't know, and second, they do not say, "I don't know." Instead, their brains quickly consider the facts of which they *are* aware ("I walked slowly") and draw the same kinds of plausible but mistaken inferences about themselves that an observer would probably draw about them ("I'm tired").[6]

When we cook facts, we are similarly unaware of why we are doing it, and this turns out to be a good thing, because *deliberate* attempts to generate positive views ("There must be *something* good about bankruptcy, and I'm not leaving this chair until I discover it") contain the seeds of their own destruction. Volunteers in one study listened to Stravinsky's *Rite of Spring*.[7] Some were told to listen to the music, and others were told to listen to the music while consciously trying to be happy. At the end of the interlude, the volunteers who had tried to be happy were in a *worse* mood than were the volunteers who had simply listened to the music. Why? Two reasons. First, we may be able deliberately to generate positive views of our own experiences if we close our eyes, sit very still, and do nothing else,[8] but research suggests that if we become even slightly distracted, these deliberate attempts tend to backfire and we end up feeling worse than we did before.[9] Second, deliberate attempts to cook the facts are so transparent that they make us feel cheap. Sure, we *want* to believe that we're better off without the fiancée who left us standing at the altar, and we *will* feel better as soon as we begin to discover facts that support this conclusion ("She was never really right for me, was she, Mom?"), but the process by which we discover those facts must *feel* like a discovery and not like a snow job. If we *see* ourselves cooking the facts ("If I phrase the question just this way and ask nobody but Mom, I stand a pretty good chance of having my favored conclusion confirmed"), then the jig is up and *self-deluded* joins *jilted* in our list of pitiful qualities. For positive views to be credible, they must be based on facts that we *believe* we have come upon honestly. We accomplish this by unconsciously cooking the facts and then consciously consuming them. The diner is in the dining room, but the chef is in the basement. The benefit of all this unconscious cookery is that it works, but the cost is that it makes us strangers to ourselves. Let me show you how.

LOOKING FORWARD TO LOOKING BACKWARD

To my knowledge, no one has ever done a systematic study of people who've been left standing at the altar by a cold-footed fiancé. But I'm willing to bet a good bottle of wine that if you rounded up a healthy sample of almost brides and nearly grooms and asked them whether they would describe the incident as "the worst thing that ever happened to me" or "the best thing that ever happened to me," more would endorse the latter description than the former. And I'll bet an entire *case* of that wine that if you found a sample of people who'd never been through this experience and asked them to predict which of all their possible future experiences they are most likely to look back on as "the best thing that ever happened to me," not one of them will list "getting jilted." Like so many things, getting jilted is more painful in prospect and more rosy in retrospect. When we contemplate being hung out to dry this way, we naturally generate the most dreadful possible view of the experience; but once we've actually *been* heartbroken and humiliated in front of our family, friends, and florists, our brains begin shopping for a less dreadful view—and as we've seen, the human brain is one smart shopper. However, because our brains do their shopping unconsciously, we tend not to realize they will do it at all; hence, we blithely assume that the dreadful view we have when we look forward to the event is the dreadful view we'll have when we look back on it. In short, we do not realize that our views will change because we are normally unaware of the processes that change them.

This fact can make it quite difficult to predict one's emotional future. In one study, volunteers were given the opportunity to apply for a good-paying job that involved nothing more than tasting ice cream and making up funny names for it.[10] The application procedure required the volunteer to undergo an on-camera interview. Some of the volunteers were told that their interview would be seen by a judge who had sole discretionary authority to decide whether they would be hired (judge group). Other volunteers were told that their interview would be seen by a jury whose members would vote to decide whether the volunteer should be hired (jury group). Volunteers in the jury group were told that as long as *one* juror voted for them, they would get the job—and thus the only circumstance under which they would *not* get the job was if the jury voted unanimously against them. All of the volunteers then underwent an interview, and all predicted how they would feel if they didn't get the job. A few minutes later, the researcher

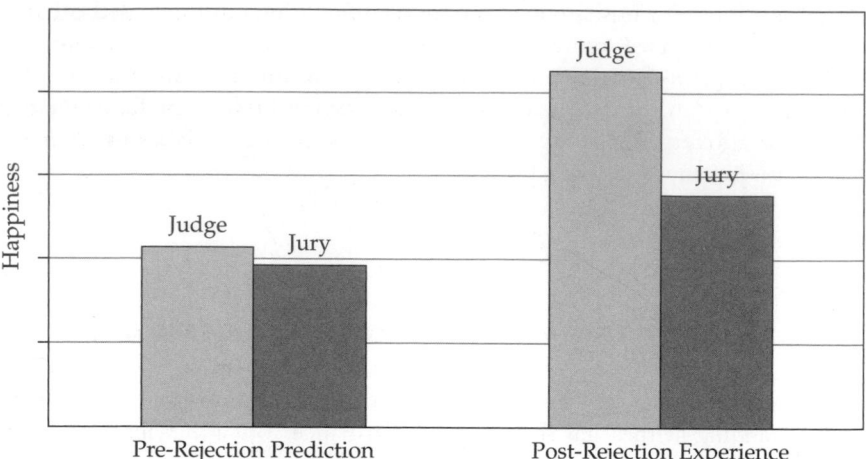

FIGURE Volunteers were happier when they were rejected by a capricious judge than by a unanimous jury (*bars on right*). But they could not foresee this moment before it happened (*bars on left*).

came into the room and explained apologetically that after careful deliberation, the judge or jury had decided that the volunteer just wasn't quite right for the job. The researcher then asked the volunteers to report how they felt.

The results of the study are shown in the figure above. As the bars on the left show, volunteers in the two groups expected to feel equally unhappy. After all, rejection is a major whack on the nose, and we expect it to hurt whether the whacker is a judge, a jury, or a gang of Orthodox rabbis. And yet, as the bars on the right show, the whacks hurt more when they were administered by a jury than by a judge. Why? Well, just imagine that you've applied for a job as a swimsuit model, which requires that you don something skimpy and parade back and forth in front of some gimlet-eyed twit in a three-dollar suit. If the twit looked you over, shook his head, and said, "Sorry, but you're not model material," you'd probably feel bad. For a minute or two. But this is the sort of interpersonal rejection that everyone experiences from time to time, and after a few minutes, most of us get over it and go on with our lives. We do this quickly because our psychological immune systems have no trouble finding ways to exploit the ambiguity of this experience and soften its sting: "The guy wasn't paying attention to my extraordinary pivot," or "He's one of those weirdos who prefers height to weight," or "I'm supposed to take fashion advice from a guy with a suit like *that?*"

But now imagine that you've just modeled the skimpy thing for a whole roomful of people—some men, some women, some old, some young—and they all look you over and shake their heads in unison. You'd probably feel bad. Truly bad. Humiliated, hurt, and confused. You'd probably hurry offstage with a warm feeling in your ears, a tight feeling in your throat, and a wet feeling in your eyes. Being rejected by a large and diverse group of people is a demoralizing experience because it is so thoroughly unambiguous, and hence it is difficult for the psychological immune system to find a way to think about it that is both positive and credible. It's easy to blame failure on the eccentricities of a judge, but it's much more difficult to blame failure on the eccentricities of a unanimous jury. Claims such as "a synchronized mass blink caused ninety-four people to miss my pivot at precisely the same moment" are just not credible. Similarly, volunteers in this study found it easier to blame their rejection on an idiosyncratic judge than on a panel of jurors, which is why they felt worse when they were rejected by a jury.

Now, all this may seem painfully obvious to you as you contemplate the results of this study from the comfort of your sofa, but allow me to suggest that it is painfully obvious only after someone has taken pains to point it out to you. Indeed, if it were really painfully obvious, then why were a bunch of smart volunteers *unable to predict that it would happen just a few minutes before it did*? Why didn't the volunteers realize that they would have more success blaming a judge than a jury? Because when volunteers were asked to predict their emotional reactions to rejection, they imagined its sharp sting. Period. They did not go on to imagine how their brains might try to relieve that sting. Because they were unaware that they would alleviate their suffering by blaming those who caused it, it never occurred to them that they would be more successful if a single person were to blame rather than an entire group. Other studies have confirmed this general finding. For example, people *expect* to feel equally bad when a tragic accident is the result of human negligence as when it is the result of dumb luck, but they *actually* feel worse when luck is dumb and no one is blameworthy.[11]

Ignorance of our psychological immune systems causes us to mispredict the circumstances under which we will blame others, but it also causes us to mispredict the circumstances under which we will blame ourselves.[12] Who can forget the scene at the end of the 1942 film *Casablanca* in which Humphrey Bogart and Ingrid Bergman are standing on the tarmac as she tries to decide whether to stay in Casablanca with the man she loves or board the plane and leave with her husband? Bogey turns to Bergman and says: "Inside we both know you belong with Victor. You're part of his work, the thing that keeps him going. If that plane leaves the ground and you're not with him, you'll regret it. Maybe not today. Maybe not tomorrow. But soon and for the rest of your life."[13]

This thin slice of melodrama is among the most memorable scenes in the history of cinema—not because it is particularly well acted or particularly well written but because most of us have stood on that same runway from time to time. Our most consequential choices—whether to marry, have children, buy a house, enter a profession, move abroad—are often shaped by how we imagine our future regrets ("Oh no, I forgot to have a baby!"). Regret is an emotion we feel when we blame ourselves for unfortunate outcomes that might have been prevented had we only behaved differently in the past, and because that emotion is decidedly unpleasant, our behavior in the present is often designed to preclude it.[14] Indeed, most of us have elaborate theories about when and why people feel regret, and these theories allow us to avoid the experience. For instance, we expect to feel more regret when we learn about alternatives to our choices than when we don't,[15] when we accept bad advice than when we reject good advice,[16] when our bad choices are unusual rather than conventional,[17] and when we fail by a narrow margin rather than by a wide margin.[18]

But sometimes these theories are wrong. Consider this scenario. You own shares in Company A. During the past year you considered switching to stock in Company B but decided against it. You now find that you would have been better off by $1,200 if you had switched to the stock of Company B. You also owned shares in Company C. During the past year you switched to stock in Company D. You now find out that you'd have been better off by $1,200 if you kept your stock in Company C. Which error causes you more regret? Studies show that about nine out of ten people expect to feel more regret when they foolishly switch stocks than when they foolishly fail to switch stocks, because most people think they will regret foolish actions more than foolish inactions.[19] But studies also show that nine out of ten people are wrong. Indeed, in the long run, people of every age and in every walk of life seem to regret *not* having done things much more than they regret things they *did,* which is why the most popular regrets include not going to college, not grasping profitable business opportunities, and not spending enough time with family and friends.[20]

But why do people regret inactions more than actions? One reason is that the psychological immune system has a more difficult time manufacturing positive and credible views of inactions than of actions.[21] When our action causes us to accept a marriage proposal from someone who later becomes an axe murderer, we can console ourselves by thinking of all the things we learned from the experience ("Collecting hatchets is not a healthy hobby"). But when our inaction causes us to reject a marriage proposal from someone who later becomes a movie star, we can't console ourselves by thinking of all the things we learned from the experience because ... well, there wasn't one. The irony is all too clear: Because we do not realize that our psychological immune systems can rationalize an excess of courage more easily than an excess of cowardice, we hedge our bets when we should blunder forward. As students of the silver screen recall, Bogart's admonition about future regret led Bergman to board the plane and fly away with her husband. Had she stayed with Bogey in Casablanca, she would probably have felt just fine. Not right away, perhaps, but soon, and for the rest of her life.

LITTLE TRIGGERS

Civilized people have learned the hard way that a handful of iniquitous individuals can often cause more death and destruction than an invading army. If an enemy were to launch hundreds of airplanes and missiles against the United States, the odds are that none would reach its target because an offensive strike of that magnitude would trigger America's defensive systems, which are presumably adequate to quash the threat. On the other hand, were an enemy to launch seven guys with baggy pants and baseball caps, those men might well reach their targets and detonate bombs, release toxins, or fly hijacked airplanes into tall buildings. Terrorism is a strategy based on the idea that the best offense is the one that fails to trigger the best defense, and small-scale incursions are less likely to set off the alarm bells than are large-scale assaults. Although it is possible to design a defensive system that counters even the smallest threat (e.g., electrified borders, a travel ban, electronic surveillance, random searches), such systems are extraordinarily costly, in terms of both the resources required to run them and the number of false alarms they produce. A system like that would be an exercise in overkill. To be effective, a defensive system must respond to threats; but to be practical, it must respond only to threats that exceed some *critical threshold*—which means that threats that fall short of the critical threshold may have a destructive potential that belies their diminutive size. Unlike large threats, small threats can sneak in under the radar.

The Intensity Trigger

The psychological immune system is a defensive system, and it obeys this same principle. When experiences make us feel sufficiently unhappy, the psychological immune system cooks facts and shifts blame in order to offer us a more positive view. But it doesn't do this *every* time we feel the slightest tingle of sadness, jealousy, anger, or frustration. Failed marriages and lost jobs are the kinds of large-scale assaults on our happiness that trigger our psychological defenses, but these defenses are not triggered by broken pencils, stubbed toes, or slow elevators. Broken pencils may be annoying, but they do not pose a grave threat to our psychological well-being and hence do not trigger our psychological defenses. The paradoxical consequence of this fact is that it is sometimes more difficult to achieve a positive view of a *bad* experience than of a *very bad* experience.

For example, volunteers in one study were students who were invited to join an extracurricular club whose initiation ritual required that they receive three electric shocks.[22] Some of the volunteers had a truly dreadful experience because the shocks they received were quite severe (severe-initiation group), and others had a slightly unpleasant experience because the shocks they received were relatively mild (mild-initiation group). Although you might expect people to dislike anything associated with physical pain, the volunteers in the severe-initiation group actually liked the club more. Because these volunteers suffered greatly, the intensity of their suffering triggered their defensive systems, which immediately began working to help them achieve a credible and positive view of their experience. It isn't easy to find such a view, but it can be done. For example, physical suffering is bad ("Oh my God, that *really* hurt!"), but it isn't *entirely* bad if the thing one suffers for is extremely valuable ("But I'm joining a *very* elite group of *very* special people."). Indeed, research shows that when people are given electric shocks, they actually feel *less pain* when they believe they are suffering for something of great value.[23] The intense shocks were unpleasant enough to trigger the volunteers' psychological defenses, but the mild shocks were not, hence the volunteers valued the club most when its initiation was most painful.[24] If you've managed to forgive your spouse for some egregious transgression but still find yourself miffed about the dent in the garage door or the trail of dirty socks on the staircase, then you have experienced this paradox.

Intense suffering triggers the very processes that eradicate it, while mild suffering does not, and this counterintuitive fact can make it difficult for us to predict our emotional futures. For example, would it be worse if your best friend insulted you or insulted your cousin? As much as you may like your cousin, it's a pretty good bet that you like yourself more, hence you probably think that it would be worse if the epithet were hurled your way. And you're right. It *would* be worse. At first. But if intense suffering triggers the psychological immune system and mild suffering does not, then over time you should be more likely to generate a positive view of an insult that was directed at you ("Felicia called me a pea-brain ... boy, she can really crack me up sometimes") than one that was directed at your cousin ("Felicia called Cousin Dwayne a pea-brain ... I mean, she's *right,* of course, but it wasn't very nice of her to say"). The irony is that you may ultimately feel better when you are the *victim* of an insult than when you are a *bystander* to it.

This possibility was tested in a study in which two volunteers took a personality test and then *one* of them received feedback from a psychologist.[25] The feedback was professional, detailed, and unrelentingly negative. For example, it contained statements such as "You have few qualities that distinguish you from others," and "People like you primarily because you don't threaten their competence." Both of the volunteers read the feedback and then reported how much they liked the psychologist who had written it. Ironically, the volunteer who was the *victim* of the negative feedback liked the psychologist *more* than did the volunteer who was merely a *bystander* to it. Why? Because bystanders were miffed ("Man, that was a really crummy thing to do to the other volunteer."), but they were not devastated, hence their psychological immune systems did nothing to ameliorate their mildly negative feelings. But victims *were* devastated ("Yikes, I'm a certified loser!"), hence their brains quickly went shopping for a positive view of the experience ("But now that I think of it, that test could only provide a small glimpse into my very complex personality, so I rather doubt it means much.") Now here's the important finding: when a new group of volunteers was asked to *predict* how much they would like the psychologist, they predicted that they would like the psychologist *less* if they were victims than if they were bystanders. Apparently, people are not aware of the fact that their defenses are more likely to be triggered by intense rather than mild suffering, thus they mispredict their own emotional reactions to misfortunes of different sizes.

The Inescapability Trigger

Intense suffering is one factor that can trigger our defenses and thus influence our experiences in ways we don't anticipate. But there are others. For example, why do we forgive our siblings for behavior we would never tolerate in a friend? Why aren't we disturbed when the president does something that would have kept us from voting for him had he done it before the election? Why do we overlook an employee's chronic tardiness but refuse to hire a job seeker who is two minutes late for the interview? One possibility is that blood is thicker than water, flags were made to be rallied around, and first impressions matter most.

But another possibility is that we are more likely to look for and find a positive view of the things we're *stuck with* than of the things we're not.[26] Friends come and go, and changing candidates is as easy as changing socks. But siblings and presidents are *ours,* for better or for worse, and there's not much we can do about it once they've been born or elected. When the experience we are having is not the experience we *want* to be having, our first reaction is to go out and have a different one, which is why we return unsatisfactory rental cars, check out of bad hotels, and stop hanging around with people who pick their noses in public. It is only when we cannot *change the experience* that we look for ways to *change our view of the experience,* which is why we love the clunker in the driveway, the shabby cabin that's been in the family for years, and Uncle Sheldon despite his predilection for nasal spelunking. We find silver linings only when we must, which is why people experience an increase in happiness when genetic tests reveal that they *don't* have a dangerous genetic defect, or when the tests reveal that they *do* have a dangerous genetic defect, but *not* when the tests are inconclusive.[27] We just can't make the best of a fate until it is inescapably, inevitably, and irrevocably ours.

Inescapable, inevitable, and irrevocable circumstances trigger the psychological immune system, but, as with the intensity of suffering, people do not always recognize that this will happen. For example, college students in one study signed up for a course in black-and white photography.[28] Each student took a dozen photographs of people and places that were personally meaningful, then reported for a private lesson. In these lessons, the teacher spent an hour or two showing students how to print their two best photographs. When the prints were dry and ready, the teacher said that the student could keep one of the photographs but that the other would be kept on file as an example of student work. Some students (inescapable group) were told that once they had chosen a photograph to take home, they would not be allowed to change their minds. Other students (escapable group) were told that once they had chosen a photograph to take home, they would have several days to change their minds—and if they did, the teacher would gladly swap the photograph they'd taken home for the one they'd left behind. Students made their choices and took one of their photographs home. Several days later, the students responded to a survey asking them (among other things) how much they liked their photographs. The results showed that students in the escapable group liked their photograph *less* than did students in the inescapable group. Interestingly, when a new group of students was asked to *predict* how much they would like their photographs if they were or were not given the opportunity to change their minds, these students predicted that escapability would have no influence whatsoever on their satisfaction with the photograph. Apparently, inescapable circumstances trigger the psychological defenses that enable us to achieve positive views of those circumstances, but we do not anticipate that this will happen.

Our failure to anticipate that inescapability will trigger our psychological immune systems (hence promote our happiness and satisfaction) can cause us to make some painful mistakes. For example, when a new group of photography students was asked whether they would prefer to have or not to have the opportunity to change their minds about which photograph to keep, the vast majority preferred to have that opportunity—that is, the vast majority of students preferred to enroll in a photography course in which they would ultimately be dissatisfied with the photograph they produced. Why would anyone prefer less satisfaction to more? No one does, of course, but most people do seem to prefer more freedom to less. Indeed, when our freedom to make up our minds—or to change our minds once we've made them up—is threatened, we experience a strong impulse to reassert it,[29] which is why retailers sometimes threaten your freedom to own their products with claims such as "Limited stock" or "You must order by midnight tonight."[30] Our fetish for freedom leads us to patronize expensive department stores that allow us to return merchandise rather than attend auctions that don't, to lease cars at a dramatic markup rather than buying them at a bargain, and so on.

Most of us will pay a premium today for the opportunity to change our minds tomorrow, and sometimes it makes sense to do so. A few days spent test-driving a little red roadster tells us a lot about what it might be like to own one, thus it is sometimes wise to pay a modest premium for a contract that includes a short refund period. But if keeping our options open has benefits, it also has costs. Little red roadsters are naturally cramped, and while the committed owner will find positive ways to view that fact ("Wow! It feels like a fighter jet!"), the buyer whose contract includes an escape clause may not ("This car is so tiny. Maybe I should return it."). Committed owners attend to a car's virtues and overlook its flaws, thus cooking the facts to produce a banquet of satisfaction, but the buyer for whom escape is still possible (and whose defenses have not yet been triggered) is likely to evaluate the new car more critically, paying special attention to its imperfections as she tries to decide whether to keep it. The costs and benefits of freedom are clear—but alas, they are not equally clear: We have no trouble anticipating the advantages that freedom may provide, but we seem blind to the joys it can undermine.[31]

EXPLAINING AWAY

If you've ever puked your guts out shortly after eating chili con carne and found yourself unable to eat it again for years, you have a pretty good idea of what it's like to be a fruit fly. No, fruit flies don't eat chili, and no, fruit flies don't puke. But they do associate their best and worst experiences with the circumstances that accompanied and preceded them, which allows them to seek or avoid those circumstances in the future. Expose a fruit fly to the odor of tennis shoes, give it a very tiny electric shock, and for the rest of its very tiny life it will avoid places that smell tennis-shoey. The ability to associate pleasure or pain with its circumstances is so vitally important that nature has installed that ability in every one of her creatures, from *Drosophila melanogaster* to Ivan Pavlov.

But if that ability is necessary for creatures like us, it certainly isn't sufficient because the kind of learning it enables is far too limited. If an organism can do no more than associate particular experiences with particular circumstances, then it can learn only a very small lesson, namely, to seek or avoid those particular circumstances in the future. A well-timed shock may teach a fruit fly to avoid the tennis-shoe smell, but it won't teach it to avoid the smell of snowshoes, ballet slippers, Manolo Blahniks, or a scientist armed with a miniature stun gun. To maximize our pleasures and minimize our pains, we must be able to associate our experiences with the circumstances that produced them, but we must also be able to *explain* how and why those circumstances produced the experiences they did. If we feel nauseous after a few turns on the Ferris wheel and our explanation involves poor equilibrium, then we avoid Ferris wheels in the future—just as a fruit fly would. But unlike a fruit fly, we also avoid some things that are *not* associated with our nauseating experience (such as bungee jumping and sailboats) and we do *not* avoid some things that *are* associated with our nauseating experience (such as hurdy-gurdy music and clowns). Unlike a mere association, an explanation allows us to identify particular aspects of a circumstance (spinning) as the *cause* of our experience, and other aspects (music) as irrelevant. In so doing, we learn more from our upchucks than a fruit fly ever could.

Explanations allow us to make full use of our experiences, but they also change the nature of those experiences. As we have seen, when experiences are unpleasant, we quickly move to explain them in ways that make us feel better ("I didn't get the job because the judge was biased against people who barf on Ferris wheels.") And indeed, studies show that the mere act of explaining an unpleasant event can help to defang it. For example, simply writing about a trauma—such as the death of a loved one or a physical assault—can lead to surprising improvements in both subjective well-being and physical health (e.g., fewer visits to the physician and improved production of viral antibodies).[32] What's more, the people who experience the greatest benefit from these writing exercises are those whose writing contains an *explanation* of the trauma.[33]

But just as explanations ameliorate the impact of *unpleasant* events, so too do they ameliorate the impact of *pleasant* events. For example, college students volunteered for a study in which they believed they were interacting in an online chat room with students from other universities.[34] In fact, they were actually interacting with a sophisticated computer program that simulated the presence of other students. After the simulated students had provided the real student with information about themselves ("Hi, I'm Eva, and I like to do volunteer work."), the researcher pretended to ask the simulated students to decide which of the people in the chat room they liked most, to write a paragraph explaining why, and then to send it to that person. In just a few minutes, something remarkable happened: the real student received e-mail messages from *every one* of the simulated students indicating that they liked the real student best! For example, one simulated message read: "I just felt that something clicked between us when I read your answers. It's too bad we're not at the same school!" Another read: "You stood out as the one I would like the most. I was especially interested in the way you described your interests and values." A third read: "I wish I could talk with you directly because ... I'd ask you if you like being around water (I love water-skiing) and if you like Italian food (it's my favorite)."

Now, here's the catch: Some real students (informed group) received e-mail that allowed them to know *which* simulated student wrote each of the messages, and other real students (uninformed group) received e-mail messages that had been stripped of that identifying information. In other words, every real student received exactly the same e-mail messages indicating that they had won the hearts and minds of all the simulated people in the chat room, but only real students in the informed group knew *which* simulated individual had written each of the messages. Hence, real students in the informed group were able to generate explanations for their good fortune ("Eva appreciates my values because we're both involved with Habitat for Humanity, and it makes sense that Catarina would mention Italian food."), whereas real students in the uninformed group were not ("Someone appreciates my values.... I wonder who? And why would anyone mention Italian food?"). The researchers measured how happy the real students were immediately after receiving these messages and then again fifteen minutes later. Although real students in both groups were initially delighted to have been chosen as everyone's best friend, only the real students in the uninformed group remained delighted fifteen minutes later. If you've ever had a secret admirer, then you understand why real students in the uninformed group remained on cloud nine while real students in the informed group quickly descended to clouds two through five.

Unexplained events have two qualities that amplify and extend their emotional impact. First, they strike us as rare and unusual.[35] If I told you that my brother, my sister, and I were all born on the same day, you'd probably consider that a rare and unusual occurrence. Once I explained that we were triplets, you'd find it considerably less so. In fact, just about *any* explanation I offered ("By *same day* I meant we were all born on a Thursday" or "We were all delivered by cesarean section, so Mom and Dad timed our births for maximum tax benefits") would tend to reduce the amazingness of the coincidence and make the event seem more probable. Explanations allow us to understand how and why an event happened, which immediately allows us to see how and why it might happen again. Indeed, whenever we say that something *can't* happen—for example, mind reading or levitation or a law that limits the power of incumbents—we usually just mean that we'd have no way to explain it if it did. Unexplained events seem rare, and rare events naturally have a greater emotional impact than common events do. We are awed by a solar eclipse but merely impressed by a sunset despite the fact that the latter is by far the more spectacular visual treat.

The second reason why unexplained events have a disproportionate emotional impact is that we are especially likely to keep thinking about them. People spontaneously try to explain events,[36] and studies show that when people do not complete the things they set out to do, they are especially likely to think about and remember their unfinished business.[37] Once we explain an event, we can fold it up like freshly washed laundry, put it away in memory's drawer, and move on to the next one; but if an event defies explanation, it becomes a *mystery* or a *conundrum*—and if there's one thing we all know about mysterious conundrums, it is that they generally refuse to stay in the back of our minds. Filmmakers and novelists often capitalize on this fact by fitting their narratives with mysterious endings, and research shows that people are, in fact, more likely to keep thinking about a movie when they can't explain what happened to the main character. And if they *liked* the movie, this morsel of mystery causes them to remain happy longer.[38]

Explanation robs events of their emotional impact because it makes them seem likely and allows us to stop thinking about them. Oddly enough, an explanation doesn't actually have to *explain* anything to have these effects—it merely needs to *seem* as though it does. For instance, in one study, a researcher approached college students in the university library, handed them one of two cards with a dollar coin attached, then walked away. You'd probably agree that this is a curious event that begs for explanation. Both cards stated that the researcher was a member of the "Smile Society," which was devoted to "random acts of kindness." But one card also contained two extra phrases: "Who are we?" and "Why do we do this?" These empty phrases didn't really provide any new information, of course, but they made students *feel* as though the curious event had been explained ("Aha, *now* I understand why they gave me a dollar!"). About five minutes later, a different researcher approached the student and claimed to be doing a class project on "community thoughts and feelings." The researcher asked the student to complete some survey questions, one of which was "How positive or negative are you feeling right now?" The results showed that those students who had received a card with the pseudo-explanatory phrases felt less happy than those who had received a card without them. Apparently, even a fake explanation can cause us to tuck an event away and move along to the next one.

Uncertainty can preserve and prolong our happiness, thus we might expect people to cherish it. In fact, the opposite is generally the case. When a new group of students was asked which of the two cards [offering a free dollar] would make them happier, 75-percent chose the one with the meaningless explanation. Similarly, when a group of students was asked whether they would prefer to know or not know which of the simulated students had written each of the glowing reports in the online chat-room study, 100-percent chose to know. In both cases, students chose certainty over uncertainty and clarity over mystery—despite the fact that in both cases clarity and certainty had been shown to diminish happiness. The poet John Keats noted that whereas great authors are "capable of being in uncertainties, mysteries, doubts, without any irritable reaching after fact and reason," the rest of us are "incapable of remaining content with half-knowledge."[39] Our relentless desire to explain everything that happens may well distinguish us from fruit flies, but it can also kill our buzz.

ONWARD

The eye and the brain are conspirators, and like most conspiracies, theirs is negotiated behind closed doors, in the back room, outside of our awareness. Because we do not realize that we have generated a positive view of our current experience, we do not realize that we will do so again in the future. Not only does our naïveté cause us to overestimate the intensity and duration of our distress in the face of future adversity, but it also leads us to take actions that may undermine the conspiracy. We are more likely to generate a positive and credible view of an action than an inaction, of a painful experience than of an annoying experience, of an unpleasant situation that we cannot escape than of one we can. And yet, we rarely choose action over inaction, pain over annoyance, and commitment over freedom. The processes by which we generate positive views are many: we pay more attention to favorable information, we surround ourselves with those who provide it, and we accept it uncritically. These tendencies make it easy for us to explain unpleasant experiences in ways that exonerate us and make us feel better. The price we pay for our irrepressible explanatory urge is that we often spoil our most pleasant experiences by making good sense of them.

NOTES

The notes contain references to the scientific research that supports the claims I make in the text. Occasionally they contain some extra information that may be of interest but that is not essential to the argument. If you don't care about sources, aren't interested in nonessentials, and are annoyed by books that make you flip back and forth all the time, then be assured that the only important note in [this chapter] is this one.

1. T. D. Wilson, *Strangers to Ourselves: Discovering the Adaptive Unconscious* (Cambridge, Mass.: Harvard University Press, 2002); and J. A. Bargh and T. L. Chartrand, "The Unbearable Automaticity of Being," *American Psychologist* 54: 462–79 (1999).

2. R. E. Nisbett and T. D. Wilson, "Telling More Than We Can Know: Verbal Reports on Mental Processes," *Psychological Review* 84: 231–59 (1977); D. J. Bem, "Self-Perception Theory," in *Advances in Experimental Social Psychology*, ed. L. Berkowitz, vol. 6 (New York: Academic Press, 1972), 1–62; M. S. Gazzaniga, *The Social Brain* (New York: Basic Books, 1985); and D. M. Wegner, *The Illusion of Conscious Will* (Cambridge, Mass.: MIT Press, 2003).

3. E. T. Higgings, W. S. Rholes, and C. R. Jones, "Category Accessibility and Impression Formation," *Journal of Experimental Social Psychology* 13: 141–54 (1977).

4. J. Bargh, M. Chen, and L. Burrows, "Automaticity of Social Behavior: Direct Effects of Trait Construct and Stereotype Activation on Action," *Journal of Personality and Social Psychology* 71: 230–44 (1996).

5. A. Dijksterhuis and A. van Knippenberg, "The Relation Between Perception and Behavior, or How to Win a Game of Trivial Pursuit," *Journal of Personality and Social Psychology* 74: 865–77 (1998).

6. Nisbett and Wilson, "Telling More Than We Can Know."

7. J. W. Schooler, D. Ariely, and G. Loewenstein, "The Pursuit and Assessment of Happiness Can Be Self-Defeating," in *The Psychology of Economic Decisions: Rationality and Well-Being*, eds. I. Brocas and J. Carillo, vol. 1 (Oxford: Oxford University Press, 2003).

8. K. N. Ochsner et al., "Rethinking Feelings: An fMRI Study of the Cognitive Regulation of Emotion," *Journal of Cognitive Neuroscience* 14: 1215–29 (2002).

9. D. M. Wegner, R. Erber, and S. Zanakos, "Ironic Processes in the Mental Control of Mood and Mood-Related Thought," *Journal of Personality and Social Psychology* 65: 1093–104 (1993); and D. M. Wegner, A. Broome, and S. J. Blumberg, "Ironic Effects of Trying to Relax Under Stress," *Behaviour Research and Therapy* 35: 11–21 (1997).

10. D. T. Gilbert et al., "Immune Neglect: A Source of Durability Bias in Affective Forecasting," *Journal of Personality and Social Psychology* 75: 617–38 (1998).

11. Ibid.

12. D. T. Gilbert et al., "Looking Forward to Looking Backward: The Misprediction of Regret," *Psychological Science* 15: 346–50 (2004).

13. M. Curtiz, *Casablanca*, Warner Bros., 1942.

14. T. Gilovich and V. H. Medvec, "The Experience of Regret: What, When, and Why," *Psychological Review* 102: 379–95 (1995); N. Roese, *If Only: How to Turn Regret into Opportunity* (New York: Random House 2004); G. Loomes and R. Sugden, "Regret Theory: An Alternative Theory of Rational Choice Under Uncertainty," *Economic Journal* 92: 805–24 (1982); and D. Bell, "Regret in Decision Making Under Uncertainty, *Operations Research* 20: 961–81 (1982).

15. I. Ritov and J. Baron, "Outcome Knowledge, Regret, and Omission Bias," *Organizational Behavior and Human Decision Processes* 64: 119–27 (1995); I. Ritov and J. Baron, "Probability of Regret: Anticipation of Uncertainty Resolution in Choice: Outcome Knowledge, Regret, and Omission Bias," *Organizational Behavior and Human Decision Processes* 66: 228–36 (1996); and M. Zeelenberg, "Anticipated Regret, Expected Feedback and Behavioral Decision Making," *Journal of Behavioral Decision Making* 12: 93–106 (1999).

16. M. T. Crawford et al., "Reactance, Compliance, and Anticipated Regret," *Journal of Experimental Social Psychology* 38: 56–63 (2002).

17. I. Simonson, "The Influence of Anticipating Regret and Responsibility on Purchase Decisions," *Journal of Consumer Research* 19: 105–18 (1992).

18. V. H. Medvec, S. F. Madey, and T. Gilovich, "When Less Is More: Counterfactual Thinking and Satisfaction Among Olympic Medalists," *Journal of Personality and Social Psychology* 69: 603–10 (1995); and D. Kahneman and A. Tversky, "Variants of Uncertainty," *Cognition* 11: 143–57 (1982).

19. D. Kahneman and A. Tversky, "The Psychology of Preferences," *Scientific American* 246: 160–73 (1982).

20. Gilovich and Medvec, "The Experience of Regret."

21. T. Gilovich, V. H. Medvec, and S. Chen, "Omission, Commission, and Dissonance Reduction: Overcoming Regret in the Monty Hall Problem," *Personality and Social Psychology Bulletin* 21: 182–90 (1995).

22. H. B. Gerard and G. C. Mathewson, "The Effects of Severity of Initiation on Liking for a Group: A Replication," *Journal of Experimental Social Psychology* 2: 278–87 (1966).

23. P. G. Zimbardo, "Control of Pain Motivation by Cognitive Dissonance," *Science* 151: 217–19 (1966).

24. See also E. Aronson and J. Mills, "The Effect of Severity of Initiation on Liking for a Group," *Journal of Abnormal and Social Psychology* 59: 177–81 (1958); J. L.

Freedman, "Long-Term Behavioral Effects of Cognitive Dissonance," *Journal of Experimental Social Psychology* 1: 145–55 (1965); D. R. Shaffer and C. Hendrick, "Effects of Actual Effort and Anticipated Effort on Task Enhancement," *Journal of Experimental Social Psychology* 7: 435–47 (1971); H. R. Arkes and C. Blumer, "The Psychology of Sunk Cost," *Organizational Behavior and Human Decision Processes* 35: 124–40 (1985); and J. T. Jost et al., "Social Inequality and the Reduction of Ideological Dissonance on Behalf of the System: Evidence of Enhanced System Justification Among the Disadvantaged," *European Journal of Social Psychology* 33: 13–36 (2003).

25. D. T. Gilbert et al., "The Peculiar Longevity of Things Not So Bad," *Psychological Science* 15: 14–19 (2004).

26. D. Frey et al., "Re-evaluation of Decision Alternatives Dependent upon the Reversibility of a Decision and the Passage of Time," *European Journal of Social Psychology* 14: 447–50 (1984); and D. Frey, "Reversible and Irreversible Decisions: Preference for Consonant Information as a Function of Attractiveness of Decision Alternatives," *Personality and Social Psychology Bulletin* 7: 621–26 (1981).

27. S. Wiggins et al., "The Psychological Consequences of Predictive Testing for Huntington's Disease," *New England Journal of Medicine* 327: 1401–5 (1992).

28. D. T. Gilbert and J. E. J. Ebert, "Decisions and Revisions: The Affective Forecasting of Changeable Outcomes," *Journal of Personality and Social Psychology* 82: 503–14 (2002).

29. J. W. Brehm, *A Theory of Psychological Reactance* (New York: Academic Press, 1966).

30. R. B. Cialdini, *Influence: Science and Practice* (Glenview, Ill.: Scott, Foresman, 1985).

31. S. S. Iyengar and M. R. Lepper, "When Choice Is Demotivating: Can One Desire Too Much of a Good Thing?" *Journal of Personality and Social Psychology* 79: 995–1006 (2000); and B. Schwartz, "Self-Determination: The Tyranny of Freedom," *American Psychologist* 55: 79–88 (2000).

32. J. W. Pennebaker, "Writing About Emotional Experiences as a Therapeutic Process," *Psychological Science* 8: 162–66 (1997).

33. J. W. Pennebaker, T. J. Mayne, and M. E. Francis, "Linguistic Predictors of Adaptive Bereavement," *Journal of Personality and Social Psychology* 72: 863–71 (1997).

34. T. D. Wilson et al., "The Pleasures of Uncertainty: Prolonging Positive Moods in Ways People Do Not Anticipate," *Journal of Personality and Social Psychology* 88: 5–21 (2005).

35. B. Fischoff, "Hindsight ≠ foresight: The Effects of Outcome Knowledge on Judgment Under Uncertainty," *Journal of Experimental Psychology: Human Perception and Performance* 1: 288–99 (1975); and C. A. Anderson, M. R. Lepper, and L. Ross, "Perseverance of Social Theories: The Role of Explanation in the Persistence of Discredited Information," *Journal of Personality and Social Psychology* 39: 1037–49 (1980).

36. B. Weiner, "'Spontaneous' Causal Thinking," *Psychological Bulletin* 97: 74–84 (1985); and R. R. Hassin, J. A. Bargh, and J. S. Uleman, "Spontaneous Causal Inferences," *Journal of Experimental Social Psychology* 38: 515–22 (2002).

37. B. Zeigarnik, "Das Behalten erledigter und unerledigter Handlungen," *Psychologische Forschung* 9: 1–85 (1927); and G. W. Boguslavsky, "Interruption and Learning," *Psychological Review* 58: 248–55 (1951).

38. Wilson et al., "Pleasures of Uncertainty."

39. J. Keats, letter to Richard Woodhouse, 27 October 1881, in *Selected Poems and Letters by John Keats*, ed. D. Bush (Boston: Houghton Mifflin, 1959).

QUESTIONS FOR MAKING CONNECTIONS WITHIN THE READING

1. Throughout "Immune to Reality," Gilbert describes mental operations using terms from everyday life: the brain is "one smart shopper"; our brains are "conspirators"; once we come up with an explanation, "we can fold it up like freshly washed laundry, put it away in memory's drawer, and move on to the next one." Obviously, Gilbert is seeking to make his thoughts about human psychology readily accessible, but what exactly is he trying to convey with these descriptions? As you reread the essay, generate a list of the most significant images and analogies Gilbert uses to describe mental operations. What does this list tell you about Gilbert's theory of mind?

2. On the basis of the experiments and studies Gilbert presents, would you say that happiness is fundamentally an illusion? Or is it the *pursuit* of happiness that deserves to be reconsidered? If happiness is not something that we can pursue consciously, then how do we go about becoming happy? Should we be pursuing something other than happiness?

3. What is the meaning of "reality" at the end of Gilbert's discussion of our "psychological immune system"? What exactly is it that this system is designed to protect us from? Is the psychological immune system analogous to our biological immune system, or does it operate according to a different logic? Is the reality from which this system protects us ultimately an illusion? Or are psychological realities fundamentally different from material realities?

QUESTIONS FOR WRITING

1. The Declaration of Independence proclaims that "all men" are "endowed by their Creator with certain unalienable rights," among them "Life, Liberty, and the pursuit of Happiness." What are the *political* implications of the research indicating that the pursuit of happiness is often misdirected because people typically fail to recognize the conditions that will really make them happy? Does Gilbert's work suggest that Thomas Jefferson's thinking in the Declaration was based on a false assumption? Can any government responsibly claim to make happiness available?

2. What are the *economic* implications of Gilbert's argument? If people began to choose "action over inaction, pain over annoyance, and commitment over freedom," would the consumer economy survive? That is, is consumerism dependent upon our collective ignorance about the path to happiness, or is the hope that one's life will be improved by increased purchasing power itself a path to happiness? Is trying to be happy with what one has a form of action or inaction? If Gilbert is right that "explanation robs events of their emotional impact," what role does explanation play in consumer economy?

Is a healthy economy dependent upon consumers who are well informed or consumers who are "immune to reality"?

QUESTIONS FOR MAKING CONNECTIONS
BETWEEN READINGS

1. In "A Life of its Own," Michael Specter heralds the emergence of "synthetic biology"—the deliberate engineering of organic life. One champion of the new field, the physicist Freeman Dyson, even looks forward to a time when school children will play "biotech games" and the creation of new varieties of life will be an "art form" on a par with painting or sculpture. This vision of the future can seem quite exciting, but when we turn to Gilbert's argument, we might begin to have second thoughts. Even if genetic technology can deliver on its bright promises, are the results really likely to be as rewarding as its promoters believe? Might scientists be swayed unconsciously by the "psychological immune system," which conceals the truth from us by "cooking the facts"? Could our tendency to cook the facts make us unaware of the dangers posed by genetic technology?

2. What are the connections between the quest for happiness as Gilbert describes it and the cultivation of wisdom that Robert Thurman outlines? Is the Buddhist experience of nothingness a way of freeing people from the hot states in which we overestimate our own capacity to find satisfaction through changes in external conditions? Or is the notion of wisdom itself an example of the kind of unconscious fact cooking Gilbert describes, which generates happiness only if it feels "like a discovery and not like a snow job"? Is there a way to determine, finally, if another person is happy or wise? Can one know oneself with certainty in either of these systems?

MALCOLM GLADWELL

How do cultures change, and is it possible to control and direct cultural change? These are some of the questions that interest Malcolm Gladwell, author of the best-selling books *The Tipping Point: How Little Things Can Make a Big Difference* (2000), *Blink: The Power of Thinking Without Thinking* (2005), *Outliers: The Story of Success* (2008), and *What the Dog Saw and Other Adventures* (2009). Gladwell first became interested in the notion that ideas might spread through culture like a virus while he was covering the AIDS epidemic for the *Washington Post*. In epidemiology, the "tipping point" is the moment when a virus reaches critical mass; AIDS, as Gladwell learned while doing his research, reached its tipping point in 1982, "when it went from a rare disease affecting a few gay men to a worldwide epidemic." Fascinated by this medical fact, Gladwell found himself wondering whether it also applied to the social world. Is there a specific point where a fad becomes a fashion frenzy, or where delinquency and mischief turn into a crime wave. At what point might repetition lead to change?

The Tipping Point is the result of Gladwell's effort to understand why some ideas catch on and spread like wildfire while others fail to attract widespread attention and wither on the vine. Drawing on psychology, sociology, and epidemiology, Gladwell examines events as diverse as Paul Revere's ride, the success of *Sesame Street* and *Blue's Clues,* and the precipitous decline in the crime rate in New York City, which is discussed in "The Power of Context," the chapter included here. Working across these wide-ranging examples, Gladwell develops an all-encompassing model of how cultural change occurs, a model that highlights the influential role that context plays in shaping and guiding human acts and intentions.

Gladwell returns to the importance of context from a different direction in a later book, *Outliers: The Story of Success.* There he investigates the forces behind the achievements of figures like Bill Gates, Mozart, and the Beatles. Even though many Americans believe that success follows from hard work and genetics, Gladwell paints a much more complicated picture that includes not only practice and education but also social circumstances, timing, culture, and a great deal of luck. A helping hand is often decisive: we might be talented, brilliant, and ambitious, but no one ever makes it to the top without many different kinds of support.

Gladwell, Malcolm. "The Power of Context: Bernie Goetz and the Rise and Fall of New York City Crime," *The Tipping Point: How Little Things Can Make a Big Difference*. Boston: Little, Brown, and Co., 2000. 133–68.

Quotations come from Author Q&A at <http://www.gladwell.com/books2.html> and interview by Toby Lester, *The Atlantic Unbound* <http://www.theatlantic.com/unbound/interviews/ba2000-03-29.htm>.

Gladwell was born in England, grew up in Canada, and graduated with a degree in history from the University of Toronto in 1984. After spending over a decade as a science writer and New York bureau chief for the *Washington Post,* he joined the staff of the *New Yorker* in 1996. In 2007, he received the American Sociological Association's first Award for Excellence in the Reporting of Social Issues. Gladwell sees himself as "a kind of translator between the academic and nonacademic worlds." As he puts it, "There's just all sorts of fantastic stuff out there, but there's not nearly enough time and attention paid to that act of translation. Most people leave college in their early twenties, and that ends their exposure to the academic world. To me that's a tragedy."

The Power of Context

Bernie Goetz and the Rise and Fall of New York City Crime

1. On December 22, 1984, the Saturday before Christmas, Bernhard Goetz left his apartment in Manhattan's Greenwich Village and walked to the IRT subway station at Fourteenth Street and Seventh Avenue. He was a slender man in his late thirties, with sandy-colored hair and glasses, dressed that day in jeans and a windbreaker. At the station, he boarded the number two downtown express train and sat down next to four young black men. There were about twenty people in the car, but most sat at the other end, avoiding the four teenagers, because they were, as eyewitnesses would say later, "horsing around" and "acting rowdy." Goetz seemed oblivious. "How are ya?" one of the four, Troy Canty, said to Goetz, as he walked in. Canty was lying almost prone on one of the subway benches. Canty and another of the teenagers, Barry Allen, walked up to Goetz and asked him for five dollars. A third youth, James Ramseur, gestured toward a suspicious-looking bulge in his pocket, as if he had a gun in there.

"What do you want?" Goetz asked.

"Give me five dollars," Canty repeated.

Goetz looked up and, as he would say later, saw that Canty's "eyes were shiny, and he was enjoying himself.... He had a big smile on his face," and somehow that smile and those eyes set him off. Goetz reached into his pocket and pulled out a chrome-plated, five-shot Smith and Wesson .38, firing at each of the four youths in turn. As the fourth member of the group, Darrell Cabey, lay screaming on the ground, Goetz walked over to him and said, "You seem all right. Here's another," before firing a fifth bullet into Cabey's spinal cord and paralyzing him for life.

In the tumult, someone pulled the emergency brake. The other passengers ran into the next car, except for two women who remained riveted in panic. "Are you all right?" Goetz asked the first, politely. Yes, she said. The second woman was lying on the floor. She wanted Goetz to think she was dead. "Are you all right?" Goetz asked her, twice. She nodded yes. The conductor, now on the scene, asked Goetz if he was a police officer.

"No," said Goetz. "I don't know why I did it." Pause. "They tried to rip me off."

The conductor asked Goetz for his gun. Goetz declined. He walked through the doorway at the front of the car, unhooked the safety chain, and jumped down onto the tracks, disappearing into the dark of the tunnel.

In the days that followed, the shooting on the IRT caused a national sensation. The four youths all turned out to have criminal records. Cabey had been arrested previously for armed robbery, Canty for theft. Three of them had screwdrivers in their pockets. They seemed the embodiment of the kind of young thug feared by nearly all urban-dwellers, and the mysterious gunman who shot them down seemed like an avenging angel. The tabloids dubbed Goetz the "Subway Vigilante" and the "Death Wish Shooter." On radio call-in shows and in the streets, he was treated as a hero, a man who had fulfilled the secret fantasy of every New Yorker who had ever been mugged or intimidated or assaulted on the subway. On New Year's Eve, a week after the shooting, Goetz turned himself in to a police station in New Hampshire. Upon his extradition to New York City, the *New York Post* ran two pictures on its front page: one of Goetz, handcuffed and head bowed, being led into custody, and one of Troy Canty—black, defiant, eyes hooded, arms folded—being released from the hospital. The headline read, "Led Away in Cuffs While Wounded Mugger Walks to Freedom." When the case came to trial, Goetz was easily acquitted on charges of assault and attempted murder. Outside Goetz's apartment building, on the evening of the verdict, there was a raucous, impromptu street party.

2.   The Goetz case has become a symbol of a particular, dark moment in New York City history, the moment when the city's crime problem reached epidemic proportions. During the 1980s, New York City averaged well over 2,000 murders and 600,000 serious felonies a year. Underground, on the subways, conditions could only be described as chaotic. Before Bernie Goetz boarded the number two train that day, he would have waited on a dimly lit platform, surrounded on all sides by dark, damp, graffiti-covered walls. Chances are his train was late, because in 1984 there was a fire somewhere on the New York system every day and a derailment every other week. Pictures of the crime scene, taken by police, show that the car Goetz sat in was filthy, its floor littered with trash, and the walls and ceiling thick with graffiti, but that wasn't unusual because in 1984 every one of the 6,000 cars in the Transit Authority fleet, with the exception of the midtown shuttle, was covered with graffiti—top to bottom, inside and out. In the winter, the cars were cold because few were adequately heated. In the summer, the cars were stiflingly hot because none were air-conditioned. Today, the number two train accelerates to over 40 miles an hour as it rumbles toward the Chambers Street express stop. But it's doubtful Goetz's train went that fast. In 1984, there were 500 "red tape" areas on the system—places where track damage had made it unsafe for trains to go more than 15 miles per hour. Fare-beating was so commonplace that it was costing the Transit Authority as much as $150 million in lost revenue annually. There were about 15,000 felonies on the system a year—a number that would hit 20,000 a year by the end of the decade—and harassment of riders by panhandlers and petty criminals was so pervasive that ridership of the trains had sunk to its lowest level in the history of the subway system. William Bratton, who was later to be a key figure in New York's successful fight against violent crime, writes in his autobiography of riding the New York subways in the 1980s after living in Boston for years and being stunned at what he saw:

> After waiting in a seemingly endless line to buy a token, I tried to put a coin into a turnstile, and found it had been purposely jammed. Unable to pay the fare to get into the system, we had to enter through a slam gate being held open by a scruffy-looking character with his hand out; having disabled the turnstiles, he was now demanding that riders give him their tokens. Meanwhile, one of his cohorts had his mouth on the coin slots, sucking out the jammed coins and leaving his slobber. Most people were too intimidated to take these guys on: Here, take the damned token, what do I care? Other citizens were going over, under, around, or through the stiles for free. It was like going into the transit version of Dante's *Inferno*.

This was New York City in the 1980s, a city in the grip of one of the worst crime epidemics in its history. But then, suddenly and without warning, the epidemic tipped. From a high in 1990, the crime rate went into precipitous decline. Murders dropped by two-thirds. Felonies were cut in half. Other cities saw their crime drop in the same period. But in no place did the level of violence fall farther or faster. On the subways, by the end of the decade, there were 75-percent fewer felonies than there had been at the decade's start. In 1996, when Goetz went to trial a second time, as the defendant in a civil suit brought by Darrell Cabey, the case was all but ignored by the press, and Goetz himself seemed almost an anachronism. At a time when New York had become the safest big city in the country, it seemed hard to remember precisely what it was that Goetz had once symbolized. It was simply inconceivable that someone could pull a gun on someone else on the subway and be called a hero for it.

3.   During the 1990s violent crime declined across the United States for a number of fairly straightforward reasons. The illegal trade in crack cocaine, which had spawned a great deal of violence among gangs and drug dealers, began to decline. The economy's dramatic recovery meant that many people who might have been lured into crime got legitimate jobs instead, and the general aging of the population meant that there were fewer people in the age range—males between eighteen and twenty-four—that is responsible for the majority of all violence. The question of why crime declined in New York City, however, is a little more complicated. In the period when the New York epidemic tipped down, the city's economy hadn't improved. It was still stagnant. In fact, the city's poorest neighborhoods had just been hit hard by the welfare cuts of the early 1990s. The waning of the crack cocaine epidemic in New York was clearly a factor, but then again, it had been in steady decline well before crime dipped. As for the aging of the population, because of heavy immigration to New York in the 1980s, the city was getting younger in the 1990s, not older. In any case, all of these trends are long-term changes that one would expect to have gradual effects. In New York the decline was anything but gradual. Something else clearly played a role in reversing New York's crime epidemic.

The most intriguing candidate for that "something else" is called the Broken Windows Theory. Broken Windows was the brainchild of the criminologists James Q. Wilson and George Kelling. Wilson and Kelling argued that crime is the inevitable result of disorder. If a window is broken and left unrepaired, people walking by will conclude that no one cares and no one is in charge. Soon, more windows will be broken, and the sense of anarchy will spread from the building to the street on which it faces, sending a signal that anything goes. In a city, relatively minor problems like graffiti, public disorder, and aggressive panhandling, they write, are all the equivalent of broken windows, invitations to more serious crimes:

> Muggers and robbers, whether opportunistic or professional, believe
> they reduce their chances of being caught or even identified if they
> operate on streets where potential victims are already intimidated by
> prevailing conditions. If the neighborhood cannot keep a bothersome
> panhandler from annoying passersby, the thief may reason, it is even less
> likely to call the police to identify a potential mugger or to interfere if
> the mugging actually takes place.

This is an epidemic theory of crime. It says that crime is contagious—just as a fashion trend is contagious—that it can start with a broken window and spread to an entire community. The Tipping Point in this epidemic, though, isn't a particular kind of person.... It's something physical like graffiti. The impetus to engage in a certain kind of behavior is not coming from a certain kind of person but from a feature of the environment.

In the mid-1980s Kelling was hired by the New York Transit Authority as a consultant, and he urged them to put the Broken Windows Theory into practice. They obliged, bringing in a new subway director by the name of David Gunn to oversee a multibillion-dollar rebuilding of the subway system. Many subway advocates, at the time, told Gunn not to worry about graffiti, to focus on the larger questions of crime and subway reliability, and it seemed like reasonable advice. Worrying about graffiti at a time when the entire system was close to collapse seems as pointless as scrubbing the decks of the *Titanic* as it headed toward the icebergs. But Gunn insisted. "The graffiti was symbolic of the collapse of the system," he says. "When you looked at the process of rebuilding the organization and morale, you had to win the battle against graffiti. Without winning that battle, all the management reforms and physical changes just weren't going to happen. We were about to put out new trains that were worth about ten million bucks apiece, and unless we did something to protect them, we knew just what would happen. They would last one day and then they would be vandalized."

Gunn drew up a new management structure and a precise set of goals and timetables aimed at cleaning the system line by line, train by train. He started with the number seven train that connects Queens to midtown Manhattan, and began experimenting with new techniques to clean off the paint. On stainless-steel cars, solvents were used. On the painted cars, the graffiti were simply painted over. Gunn made it a rule that there should be no retreat, that once a car was "reclaimed" it should never be allowed to be vandalized again. "We were religious about it," Gunn said. At the end of the number one line in the Bronx, where the trains stop before turning around and going back to Manhattan, Gunn set up a cleaning station. If a car came in with graffiti, the graffiti had to be removed during the changeover, or the car was removed from service. "Dirty" cars, which hadn't yet been cleansed of graffiti, were never to be mixed with "clean" cars. The idea was to send an unambiguous message to the vandals themselves.

"We had a yard up in Harlem on 135th Street where the trains would lay up overnight," Gunn said. "The kids would come the first night and paint the side of the train white. Then they would come the next night, after it was dry, and draw the outline. Then they would come the third night and color it in. It was a three-day job. We knew the kids would be working on one of the dirty trains, and what we would do is wait for them to finish their mural. Then we'd walk over with rollers and paint it over. The kids would be in tears, but we'd just be going up and down, up and down. It was a message to them. If you want to spend three nights of your time vandalizing a train, fine. But it's never going to see the light of day."

Gunn's graffiti cleanup took from 1984 to 1990. At that point, the Transit Authority hired William Bratton to head the transit police, and the second stage of the reclamation of the subway system began. Bratton was, like Gunn, a disciple of Broken Windows. He describes Kelling, in fact, as his intellectual mentor, and so his first step as police chief was as seemingly quixotic as Gunn's. With felonies—serious crimes—on the subway system at an all-time high, Bratton decided to crack down on fare-beating. Why? Because he believed that, like graffiti, fare-beating could be a signal, a small expression of disorder that invited much more serious crimes. An estimated 170,000 people a day were entering the system, by one route or another, without paying a token. Some were kids, who simply jumped over the turnstiles. Others would lean backward on the turnstiles and force their way through. And once one or two or three people began cheating the system, other people—who might never otherwise have considered evading the law—would join in, reasoning that if some people weren't going to pay, they shouldn't either, and the problem would snowball. The problem was exacerbated by the fact fare-beating was not easy to fight. Because there was only $1.25 at stake, the transit police didn't feel it was worth their time to pursue it, particularly when there were plenty of more serious crimes happening down on the platform and in the trains.

Bratton is a colorful, charismatic man, a born leader, and he quickly made his presence felt. His wife stayed behind in Boston, so he was free to work long hours, and he would roam the city on the subway at night, getting a sense of what the problems were and how best to fight them. First, he picked stations where fare-beating was the biggest problem and put as many as ten policemen in plainclothes at the turnstiles. The team would nab fare-beaters one by one, handcuff them, and leave them standing, in a daisy chain, on the platform until they had a "full catch." The idea was to signal, as publicly as possible, that the transit police were now serious about cracking down on fare-beaters. Previously, police officers had been wary of pursuing fare-beaters because the arrest, the trip to the station house, the filling out of necessary forms, and the waiting for those forms to be processed took an entire day—all for a crime that usually merited no more than a slap on the wrist. Bratton retrofitted a city bus and turned it into a rolling station house, with its own fax machines, phones, holding pen, and fingerprinting facilities. Soon the turnaround time on an arrest was down to an hour. Bratton also insisted that a check be run on all those arrested. Sure enough, one out of seven arrestees had an outstanding warrant for a previous crime, and one out of twenty was carrying a weapon of some sort. Suddenly it wasn't hard to convince police officers that tackling fare-beating made sense. "For the cops it was a bonanza," Bratton writes. "Every arrest was like opening a box of Cracker Jack. What kind of toy am I going to get? Got a gun? Got a knife? Got a warrant? Do we have a murderer here?.... After a while the bad guys wised up and began to leave their weapons home and pay their fares." Under Bratton, the number of ejections from subway stations—for drunkenness or improper behavior—tripled within his first few months in office. Arrests for misdemeanors, for the kind of minor offenses that had gone unnoticed in the past, went up fivefold between 1990 and 1994. Bratton turned the transit police into an organization focused on the smallest infractions, on the details of life underground.

After the election of Rudolph Giuliani as mayor of New York in 1994, Bratton was appointed head of the New York City Police Department, and he applied the same strategies to the city at large. He instructed his officers to crack down on quality-of-life crimes: on the "squeegee men" who came up to drivers at New York City intersections and demanded money for washing car windows, for example, and on all the other above-ground equivalents of turnstile-jumping and graffiti. "Previous police administration had been handcuffed by restrictions," Bratton says. "We took the handcuffs off. We stepped up enforcement of the laws against public drunkenness and public urination and arrested repeat violators, including those who threw empty bottles on the street or were involved in even relatively minor damage to property.... If you peed in the street, you were going to jail." When crime began to fall in the city—as quickly and dramatically as it had in the subways—Bratton and Giuliani pointed to the same cause. Minor, seemingly insignificant quality-of-life crimes, they said, were Tipping Points for violent crime.

Broken Windows Theory and the Power of Context are one and the same. They are both based on the premise that an epidemic can be reversed, can be tipped, by tinkering with the smallest details of the immediate environment.

This is, if you think about it, quite a radical idea. Think back, for instance, to the encounter between Bernie Goetz and those four youths on the subway: Allen, Ramseur, Cabey, and Canty. At least two of them, according to some reports, appear to have been on drugs at the time of the incident. They all came from the Claremont Village housing project in one of the worst parts of the South Bronx. Cabey was, at the time, under indictment for armed robbery. Canty had a prior felony arrest for possession of stolen property. Allen had been previously arrested for attempted assault. Allen, Canty, and Ramseur also all had misdemeanor convictions, ranging from criminal mischief to petty larceny. Two years after the Goetz shooting, Ramseur was sentenced to twenty-five years in prison for rape, robbery, sodomy, sexual abuse, assault, criminal use of a firearm, and possession of stolen property. It's hard to be surprised when people like this wind up in the middle of a violent incident.

Then there's Goetz. He did something that is completely anomalous. White professionals do not, as a rule, shoot young black men on the subway. But if you look closely at who he was, he fits the stereotype of the kind of person who ends up in violent situations. His father was a strict disciplinarian with a harsh temper, and Goetz was often the focus of his father's rage. At school, he was the one teased by classmates, the last one picked for school games, a lonely child who would often leave school in tears. He worked, after graduating from college, for Westinghouse, building nuclear submarines. But he didn't last long. He was constantly clashing with his superiors over what he saw as shoddy practices and corner-cutting, and sometimes broke company and union rules by doing work that he was contractually forbidden to do. He took an apartment on Fourteenth Street in Manhattan, near Sixth Avenue, on a stretch of city block that was then heavy with homelessness and drug dealing. One of the doormen in the building, with whom Goetz was close, was beaten badly by muggers. Goetz became obsessed with cleaning up the neighborhood. He complained endlessly about a vacant newsstand near his building, which was used by vagrants as a trash bin and stank of urine. One night, mysteriously, it burned down, and the next day Goetz was out on the street sweeping away the debris. Once at a community meeting, he said, to the shock of others in the room, "The only way we're going to clean up this street is to get rid of the spics and niggers." In 1981, Goetz was mugged by three black youths as he entered the Canal Street station one afternoon. He ran out of the station with the three of them in pursuit. They grabbed the electronics equipment he was carrying, beat him, and threw him up against a plate-glass door, leaving him with permanent damage to his chest. With the help of an off-duty sanitation worker, Goetz managed to subdue one of his three attackers. But the experience left him embittered. He had to spend six hours in the station house, talking to police, while his assailant was released after two hours and charged, in the end, with only a misdemeanor. He applied to the city for a gun permit. He was turned down. In September 1984, his father died. Three months later, he sat down next to four black youths on the subway and started shooting.

Here, in short, was a man with an authority problem, with a strong sense that the system wasn't working, who had been the recent target of humiliation.

Lillian Rubin, Goetz's biographer, writes that his choice to live on Fourteenth Street could hardly have been an accident. "For Bernie," she writes, "there seems to be something seductive about the setting. Precisely because of its deficits and discomforts, it provided him with a comprehensible target for the rage that lives inside him. By focusing it on the external world, he need not deal with his internal one. He rails about the dirt, the noise, the drunks, the crime, the pushers, the junkies. And all with good reason." Goetz's bullets, Rubin concludes, were "aimed at targets that existed as much in his past as in the present."

If you think of what happened on the number two train this way, the shooting begins to feel inevitable. Four hoodlums confront a man with apparent psychological problems. That the shooting took place on the subway seems incidental. Goetz would have shot those four kids if he had been sitting in a Burger King. Most of the formal explanations we use for criminal behavior follow along the same logic. Psychiatrists talk about criminals as people with stunted psychological development, people who have had pathological relationships with their parents, who lack adequate role models. There is a relatively new literature that talks about genes that may or may not dispose certain individuals to crime. On the popular side, there are endless numbers of books by conservatives talking about crime as a consequence of moral failure—of communities and schools and parents who no longer raise children with a respect for right and wrong. All of those theories are essentially ways of saying that the criminal is a personality type—a personality type distinguished by an insensitivity to the norms of normal society. People with stunted psychological development don't understand how to conduct healthy relationships. People with genetic predispositions to violence fly off the handle when normal people keep their cool. People who aren't taught right from wrong are oblivious to what is and what is not appropriate behavior. People who grow up poor, fatherless, and buffeted by racism don't have the same commitment to social norms as those from healthy middle-class homes. Bernie Goetz and those four thugs on the subway were, in this sense, prisoners of their own, dysfunctional world.

But what do Broken Windows and the Power of Context suggest? Exactly the opposite. They say that the criminal—far from being someone who acts for fundamental, intrinsic reasons and who lives in his own world—is actually someone acutely sensitive to his environment, who is alert to all kinds of cues, and who is prompted to commit crimes based on his perception of the world around him. That is an incredibly radical—and in some sense unbelievable—idea. There is an even more radical dimension here. The Power of Context is an environmental argument. It says that behavior is a function of social context. But it is a very strange kind of environmentalism. In the 1960s, liberals made a similar kind of argument, but when they talked about the importance of environment they were talking about the importance of fundamental social factors: crime, they said, was the result of social injustice, of structural economic inequities, of unemployment, of racism, of decades of institutional and social neglect, so that if you wanted to stop crime you had to undertake some fairly heroic steps. But the Power of Context says that what really matters is little things. The Power of

Context says that the showdown on the subway between Bernie Goetz and those four youths had very little to do, in the end, with the tangled psychological pathology of Goetz, and very little as well to do with the background and poverty of the four youths who accosted him, and everything to do with the message sent by the graffiti on the walls and the disorder at the turnstiles. The Power of Context says you don't have to solve the big problems to solve crime. You can prevent crimes just by scrubbing off graffiti and arresting fare-beaters.... This is what I meant when I called the Power of Context a radical theory. Giuliani and Bratton—far from being conservatives, as they are commonly identified—actually represent on the question of crime the most extreme liberal position imaginable, a position so extreme that it is almost impossible to accept. How can it be that what was going on in Bernie Goetz's head doesn't matter? And if it is really true that it doesn't matter, why is that fact so hard to believe?

4. [Elsewhere] I talked about two seemingly counterintuitive aspects of persuasion. One was the study that showed how people who watched Peter Jennings on ABC were more likely to vote Republican than people who watched either Tom Brokaw or Dan Rather because, in some unconscious way, Jennings was able to signal his affection for Republican candidates. The second study showed how people who were charismatic could—without saying anything and with the briefest of exposures—infect others with their emotions. The implications of those two studies go to the heart of the Law of the Few, because they suggest that what we think of as inner states—preferences and emotions—are actually powerfully and imperceptibly influenced by seemingly inconsequential personal influences, by a newscaster we watch for a few minutes a day or by someone we sit next to, in silence, in a two-minute experiment. The essence of the Power of Context is that the same thing is true for certain kinds of environments—that in ways that we don't necessarily appreciate, our inner states are the result of our outer circumstances. The field of psychology is rich with experiments that demonstrate this fact.

In the early 1970s, a group of social scientists at Stanford University, led by Philip Zimbardo, decided to create a mock prison in the basement of the university's psychology building. They took a thirty-five-foot section of corridor and created a cell block with a prefabricated wall. Three small, six-by-nine-foot cells were created from laboratory rooms and given steel-barred, black-painted doors. A closet was turned into a solitary confinement cell. The group then advertised in the local papers for volunteers, men who would agree to participate in the experiment. Seventy-five people applied, and from those Zimbardo and his colleagues picked the twenty-one who appeared the most normal and healthy on psychological tests. Half of the group were chosen, at random, to be guards, and were given uniforms and dark glasses and told that their responsibility was to keep order in the prison. The other half were told that they were to be prisoners. Zimbardo got the Palo Alto Police Department to "arrest" the prisoners in their homes, cuff them, bring them to the station house, charge them with a fictitious crime, fingerprint them, then blindfold them and bring them to the prison Psychology Department basement. Then they were stripped and given a prison uniform to wear, with a number on the front and back that was to serve as their only means of identification for the duration of their incarceration.

The purpose of the experiment was to try to find out why prisons are such nasty places. Was it because prisons are full of nasty people, or was it because prisons are such nasty environments that they make people nasty? In the answer to that question is obviously the answer to the question posed by Bernie Goetz and the subway cleanup, which is how much influence does immediate environment have on the way people behave? What Zimbardo found out shocked him. The guards, some of whom had previously identified themselves as pacifists, fell quickly into the role of hard-bitten disciplinarians. The first night they woke up the prisoners at two in the morning and made them do push-ups, line up against the wall, and perform other arbitrary tasks. On the morning of the second day, the prisoners rebelled. They ripped off their numbers and barricaded themselves in their cells. The guards responded by stripping them, spraying them with fire extinguishers, and throwing the leader of the rebellion into solitary confinement. "There were times when we were pretty abusive, getting right in their faces and yelling at them," one guard remembers. "It was part of the whole atmosphere of terror." As the experiment progressed, the guards got systematically crueler and more sadistic. "What we were unprepared for was the intensity of the change and the speed at which it happened," Zimbardo says. The guards were making the prisoners say to one another they loved each other, and making them march down the hallway, in handcuffs, with paper bags over their heads. "It was completely the opposite from the way I conduct myself now," another guard remembers. "I think I was positively creative in terms of my mental cruelty." After thirty-six hours, one prisoner began to get hysterical, and had to be released. Four more then had to be released because of "extreme emotional depression, crying, rage, and acute anxiety." Zimbardo had originally intended to have the experiment run for two weeks. He called it off after six days. "I realize now," one prisoner said after the experiment was over, "that no matter how together I thought I was inside my head, my prisoner behavior was often less under my control than I realized." Another said: "I began to feel that I was losing my identity, that the person I call ———, the person who volunteered to get me into this prison (because it was a prison to me, it still is a prison to me, I don't regard it as an experiment or a simulation ...) was distant from me, was remote, until finally I wasn't that person. I was 416. I was really my number and 416 was really going to have to decide what to do."

Zimbardo's conclusion was that there are specific situations so powerful that they can overwhelm our inherent predispositions. The key word here is "situation." Zimbardo isn't talking about environment, about the major external influences on all of our lives. He's not denying that how we are raised by our parents affects who we are, or that the kinds of schools we went to, the friends we have, or the neighborhoods we live in affect our behavior. All of these things are undoubtedly important. Nor is he denying that our genes play a role in determining who we are. Most psychologists believe that nature—genetics—accounts for about half of the reason why we tend to act the way we do. His point is simply that there are certain times and places and conditions when much of that can be swept away, that there are instances where you can take normal people from good schools and happy families and good neighborhoods and powerfully affect their behavior merely by changing the immediate details of their situation....

The mistake we make in thinking of character as something unified and all-encompassing is very similar to a kind of blind spot in the way we process information. Psychologists call this tendency the Fundamental Attribution Error (FAE), which is a fancy way of saying that when it comes to interpreting other people's behavior, human beings invariably make the mistake of overestimating the importance of fundamental character traits and underestimating the importance of the situation and context. We will always reach for a "dispositional" explanation for events, as opposed to a contextual explanation. In one experiment, for instance, a group of people are told to watch two sets of similarly talented basketball players, the first of whom are shooting baskets in a well-lighted gym and the second of whom are shooting baskets in a badly lighted gym (and obviously missing a lot of shots). Then they are asked to judge how good the players were. The players in the well-lighted gym were considered superior. In another example, a group of people are brought in for an experiment and told they are going to play a quiz game. They are paired off and they draw lots. One person gets a card that says he or she is going to be the "Contestant." The other is told he or she is going to be the "Questioner." The Questioner is then asked to draw up a list of ten "challenging but not impossible" questions based on areas of particular interest or expertise, so someone who is into Ukrainian folk music might come up with a series of questions based on Ukrainian folk music. The questions are posed to the Contestant, and after the quiz is over, both parties are asked to estimate the level of general knowledge of the other. Invariably, the Contestants rate the Questioners as being a lot smarter than they themselves are.

You can do these kinds of experiments a thousand different ways and the answer almost always comes out the same way. This happens even when you give people a clear and immediate environmental explanation of the behavior they are being asked to evaluate: that the gym, in the first case, has few lights on; that the Contestant is being asked to answer the most impossibly biased and rigged set of questions. In the end, this doesn't make much difference. There is something in all of us that makes us instinctively want to explain the world around us in terms of people's essential attributes: he's a better basketball player, that person is smarter than I am.

We do this because ... we are a lot more attuned to personal cues than contextual cues. The FAE also makes the world a much simpler and more understandable place.... The psychologist Walter Mischel argues that the human mind has a kind of "reducing valve" that "creates and maintains the perception of continuity even in the face of perpetual observed changes in actual behavior." He writes:

> When we observe a woman who seems hostile and fiercely independent some of the time but passive, dependent and feminine on other occasions, our reducing valve usually makes us choose between the two syndromes. We decide that one pattern is in the service of the other, or that both are in the service of a third motive. She must be a really

castrating lady with a façade of passivity—or perhaps she is a warm, passive-dependent woman with a surface defense of aggressiveness. But perhaps nature is bigger than our concepts and it is possible for the lady to be a hostile, fiercely independent, passive, dependent, feminine, aggressive, warm, castrating person all-in-one. Of course which of these she is at any particular moment would not be random or capricious—it would depend on who she is with, when, how, and much, much more. But each of these aspects of her self may be a quite genuine and real aspect of her total being.

Character, then, isn't what we think it is or, rather, what we want it to be. It isn't a stable, easily identifiable set of closely related traits, and it only seems that way because of a glitch in the way our brains are organized. Character is more like a bundle of habits and tendencies and interests, loosely bound together and dependent, at certain times, on circumstance and context. The reason that most of us seem to have a consistent character is that most of us are really good at controlling our environment.

5.   Some years ago two Princeton University psychologists, John Darley and Daniel Batson, decided to conduct a study inspired by the biblical story of the Good Samaritan. As you may recall, that story, from the New Testament Gospel of Luke, tells of a traveler who has been beaten and robbed and left for dead by the side of the road from Jerusalem to Jericho. Both a priest and a Levite—worthy, pious men—came upon the man but did not stop, "passing by on the other side." The only man to help was a Samaritan—the member of a despised minority—who "went up to him and bound up his wounds" and took him to an inn. Darley and Batson decided to replicate that study at the Princeton Theological Seminary. This was an experiment very much in the tradition of the FAE, and it is an important demonstration of how the Power of Context has implications for the way we think about social epidemics of all kinds, not just violent crime.

Darley and Batson met with a group of seminarians, individually, and asked each one to prepare a short, extemporaneous talk on a given biblical theme, then walk over to a nearby building to present it. Along the way to the presentation, each student ran into a man slumped in an alley, head down, eyes closed, coughing and groaning. The question was, who would stop and help? Darley and Batson introduced three variables into the experiment, to make its results more meaningful. First, before the experiment even started, they gave the students a questionnaire about why they had chosen to study theology. Did they see religion as a means of personal and spiritual fulfillment? Or were they looking for a practical tool for finding meaning in everyday life? Then they varied the subject of the theme the students were asked to talk about. Some were asked to speak on the relevance of the professional clergy to the religious vocation. Others were given the parable of the Good Samaritan. Finally, the instructions given by the experimenters to each student varied as well. In some of the cases, as he sent the students on their way, the experimenter would look at his watch and say, "Oh, you're late. They were expecting you a few minutes ago. We'd better get moving." In other cases, he would say, "It will be a few minutes before they're ready for you, but you might as well head over now."

If you ask people to predict which seminarians played the Good Samaritan (and subsequent studies have done just this), their answers are highly consistent. They almost all say that the students who entered the ministry to help people and those reminded of the importance of compassion by having just read the parable of the Good Samaritan will be the most likely to stop. Most of us, I think, would agree with those conclusions. In fact, neither of those factors made any difference. "It is hard to think of a context in which norms concerning helping those in distress are more salient than for a person thinking about the Good Samaritan, and yet it did not significantly increase helping behavior," Darley and Batson concluded. "Indeed, on several occasions, a seminary student going to give his talk on the parable of the Good Samaritan literally stepped over the victim as he hurried on his way." The only thing that really mattered was whether the student was in a rush. Of the group that was, 10-percent stopped to help. Of the group who knew they had a few minutes to spare, 63-percent stopped.

What this study is suggesting, in other words, is that the convictions of your heart and the actual contents of your thoughts are less important, in the end, in guiding your actions than the immediate context of your behavior. The words "Oh, you're late" had the effect of making someone who was ordinarily compassionate into someone who was indifferent to suffering—of turning someone, in that particular moment, into a different person. Epidemics are, at their root, about this very process of transformation. When we are trying to make an idea or attitude or product tip, we're trying to change our audience in some small yet critical respect: we're trying to infect them, sweep them up in our epidemic, convert them from hostility to acceptance. That can be done through the influence of special kinds of people, people of extraordinary personal connection. That's the Law of the Few. It can be done by changing the content of communication, by making a message so memorable that it sticks in someone's mind and compels them to action. That is the Stickiness Factor. I think that both of those laws make intuitive sense. But we need to remember that small changes in context can be just as important in tipping epidemics, even though that fact appears to violate some of our most deeply held assumptions about human nature.

This does not mean that our inner psychological states and personal histories are not important in explaining our behavior. An enormous percentage of those who engage in violent acts, for example, have some kind of psychiatric disorder or come from deeply disturbed backgrounds. But there is a world of difference between being inclined toward violence and actually committing a violent act. A crime is a relatively rare and aberrant event. For a crime to be committed, something extra, something additional, has to happen to tip a troubled person toward violence, and what the Power of Context is saying is that those Tipping Points may be as simple and trivial as everyday signs of disorder like graffiti and fare-beating. The implications of this idea are enormous. The previous notion that disposition is everything—that the cause of violent behavior is always "socio-pathic personality" or "deficient superego" or the inability to delay gratification or some evil in the genes—is, in the end, the most passive and reactive of ideas about crime. It says that once you catch a criminal you can try to help him get better—give him Prozac, put him in therapy, try to rehabilitate him—but there is very little you can do to prevent crime from happening in the first place.

Once you understand that context matters, however, that specific and relatively small elements in the environment can serve as Tipping Points, that defeatism is turned upside down. Environmental Tipping Points are things that we can change: we can fix broken windows and clean up graffiti and change the signals that invite crime in the first place. Crime can be more than understood. It can be prevented. There is a broader dimension to this. Judith Harris has convincingly argued that peer influence and community influence are more important than family influence in determining how children turn out. Studies of juvenile delinquency and high school drop-out rates, for example, demonstrate that a child is better off in a good neighborhood and a troubled family than he or she is in a troubled neighborhood and a good family. We spend so much time celebrating the importance and power of family influence that it may seem, at first blush, that this can't be true. But in reality it is no more than an obvious and common-sensical extension of the Power of Context, because it says simply that children are powerfully shaped by their external environment, that the features of our immediate social and physical world—the streets we walk down, the people we encounter—play a huge role in shaping who we are and how we act. It isn't just serious criminal behavior, in the end, that is sensitive to environmental cues, it is all behavior. Weird as it sounds, if you add up the meaning of the Stanford prison experiment and the New York subway experiment, they suggest that it is possible to be a better person on a clean street or in a clean subway than in one littered with trash and graffiti.

"In a situation like this, you're in a combat situation," Goetz told his neighbor Myra Friedman, in an anguished telephone call just days after the shooting. "You're not thinking in a normal way. Your memory isn't even working normally. You are so hyped up. Your vision actually changes. Your field of view changes. Your capabilities change. What you are capable of changes." He acted, Goetz went on, "viciously and savagely…. If you corner a rat and you are about to butcher it, okay? The way I responded was viciously and savagely, just like that, like a rat."

Of course he did. He was in a rat hole.

QUESTIONS FOR MAKING CONNECTIONS WITHIN
THE READING

1. "The Power of Context" is one of the middle chapters in Malcolm Gladwell's book *The Tipping Point: How Little Things Can Make a Big Difference*. In "The Power of Context," Gladwell refers to the three principles that govern what he calls "the epidemic transmission" of an idea: the Law of the Few, the Stickiness Factor, and the Power of Context. He provides thumbnail sketches of the first two principles in this chapter, along with an elaboration of the Power of Context. What is "the Law of

the Few"? What is "the Stickiness Factor"? How much can you piece together about the first two principles from what Gladwell presents in "The Power of Context"?

2. Gladwell states that the "Broken Windows Theory and the Power of Context are one and the same." What is the "Broken Windows Theory" of crime? How would one go about testing this theory? What other theories are available to explain the cause of crime? Why does it matter which theory one accepts? What real-world consequences followed from the application of a theory in the case of crime prevention in New York? What if some other theory had been applied?

3. Why is it a mistake to think of "character as something unified and all-encompassing"? If we accept the alternative, that character is fragmented and situation specific, what follows? How is Gladwell's argument meant to change its readers' understanding of criminals and their behavior? What about law-abiding citizens and their behavior?

QUESTIONS FOR WRITING

1. Toward the end of "The Power of Context," Gladwell asserts that his discussion of the relationship between criminal activity and local context has implications that "are enormous." Gladwell leaves it to his readers to spell out these implications. How would our social structure, our criminal system, our modes of education have to change if we abandoned what Gladwell terms our "most passive and reactive ideas about crime"?

2. Gladwell argues that "small changes in context" can play a major role in determining whether an idea takes off or disappears without a trace. This fact, he goes on, "appears to violate some of our most deeply held assumptions about human nature." What does "human nature" mean, if one accepts the argument Gladwell makes in "The Power of Context"? Is it possible to create any form of human behavior just by manipulating the contextual background? Does Gladwell's view suggest that humans are more free than previously thought, or that their behavior is more fully determined than previously thought?

QUESTIONS FOR MAKING CONNECTIONS
BETWEEN READINGS

1. Drawing on Darley and Batson's Good Samaritan study, Gladwell finds evidence that "the convictions of your heart and the actual contents of your thoughts are less important, in the end, in guiding your actions than the immediate context of your behavior." The challenge here is defining what

counts as one's "immediate context." Does the generation you belong to count as an immediate context? Explore this possibility and its implications by turning to Jean Twenge's description of the characteristics and qualities of Generation Me. What relationship, if any, is there between the influence of membership in a generation and the Power of Context, as Gladwell describes it?

2. In "The Naked Citadel," Susan Faludi provides a rich description of life in an alternate social structure—the military academy. Does Malcolm Gladwell's account help to explain why Shannon Faulkner wasn't welcomed into the academy? Did Faulkner's appearance cause the academy to "tip"? Does Gladwell's theory have any predictive value? That is, could it tell us, ahead of time, whether the academy would be transformed by being required to admit women?

STEVEN JOHNSON

STEVEN JOHNSON, THE founder and editor of one of the Web's earliest magazines, *Feed,* is the author of many books, including *Emergence: The Connected Lives of Ants, Brains, Cities, and Software* (2001), from which "The Myth of the Ant Queen" is drawn; *Mind Wide Open: Your Brain and the Neuroscience of Everyday Life* (2004); *Everything Bad Is Good for You: How Today's Popular Culture Is Actually Making Us Smarter* (2005); and, *The Invention of Air: A Story of Science, Faith, Revolution, and the Birth of America* (2009).

Johnson's preoccupation in all these books, most controversially in *Everything Bad Is Good for You,* is with reconceiving the nature of intelligence. Although it is common to think of intelligence as located in the individual—the outstanding student, the creative genius, the scientist at work in his lab—Johnson proposes that intelligence is not an attribute of individuals at all, but a property that emerges out of a system working as a whole. To illustrate this new view of intelligence, Johnson looks at complex systems like ant colonies, cities, and software programs, and he argues that in these contexts intelligence emerges in the absence of any central form of leadership or authority. The intelligence of the whole is created by individual agents—ants, people, "subroutines"—following what Johnson terms "local rules." By showing how decentralized, adaptive, self-organizing systems use lower-level thinking to solve higher-order problems, Johnson asks his readers to see the advent of the Internet not simply as an extension of human intelligence, but also as a new frontier where the very nature of human intelligence is being transformed, one hyperlink at a time.

Johnson acknowledges the difficulties involved in imagining intelligence along these lines. When filmmakers try to depict artificial intelligence, for example, they envision a future where cyborgs look and think just like ordinary humans. Johnson predicts, however, that when there is a breakthrough in the effort to create AI, the result "won't quite look like human intelligence. It'll have other properties in it, and it may be hard for us to pick up on the fact that it is intelligent because our criteria [are] different."

Some of Johnson's most recent writing is concerned with the cultural and political implications of his previous work. *The Invention of Air* chronicles the life and achievements of Joseph Priestly, an eighteenth-century scientist who left England for the United States in search of freedom to pursue science and

Johnson, Steven. *Emergence: The Connected Lives of Ants, Brains, Cities, and Software.* New York: Scribner, Simon & Schuster, 2001.
Quotation drawn from <http://www.oreillynet.com/pub/a/network////johnson.html>.

express his liberal, dissenting views on the social issues of the day. If, as Johnson argues, intelligence is indeed an emergent property, then the unhindered exchange of information is clearly an essential element of any healthy civilization.

The Myth of the Ant Queen

It's early fall in Palo Alto, and Deborah Gordon and I are sitting in her office in Stanford's Gilbert Biological Sciences building, where she spends three-quarters of the year studying behavioral ecology. The other quarter is spent doing fieldwork with the native harvester ants of the American Southwest, and when we meet, her face still retains the hint of a tan from her last excursion to the Arizona desert.

I've come here to learn more about the collective intelligence of ant colonies. Gordon, dressed neatly in a white shirt, cheerfully entertains a few borderline-philosophical questions on group behavior and complex systems, but I can tell she's hankering to start with a hands-on display. After a few minutes of casual rumination, she bolts up out of her chair. "Why don't we start with me showing you the ants that we have here," she says. "And then we can talk about what it all means."

She ushers me into a sepulchral room across the hallway, where three long tables are lined up side by side. The initial impression is that of an underpopulated and sterilized pool hall, until I get close enough to one of the tables to make out the miniature civilization that lives within each of them. Closer to a Habitrail than your traditional idea of an ant farm, Gordon's contraptions house an intricate network of plastic tubes connecting a dozen or so plastic boxes, each lined with moist plaster and coated with a thin layer of dirt.

"We cover the nests with red plastic because some species of ants don't see red light," Gordon explains. "That seems to be true of this species, too." For a second, I'm not sure what she means by "this species"—and then my eyes adjust to the scene, and I realize with a start that the dirt coating the plastic boxes is, in fact, thousands of harvester ants, crammed so tightly into their quarters that I had originally mistaken them for an undifferentiated mass. A second later, I can see that the whole simulated colony is wonderfully alive, the clusters of ants pulsing steadily with movement. The tubing and cramped conditions and surging crowds bring one thought immediately to mind: the New York subway system, rush hour.

At the heart of Gordon's work is a mystery about how ant colonies develop, a mystery that has implications extending far beyond the parched earth of the Arizona desert to our cities, our brains, our immune systems—and increasingly, our technology. Gordon's work focuses on the connection between the microbehavior of individual ants and the overall behavior of the colonies themselves, and part of that research involves tracking the life cycles of individual colonies, following them year after year as they scour the desert floor for food, competing with other colonies for territory, and—once a year—mating with them. She is a student, in other words, of a particular kind of emergent, self-organizing system.

Dig up a colony of native harvester ants and you'll almost invariably find that the queen is missing. To track down the colony's matriarch, you need to examine the bottom of the hole you've just dug to excavate the colony: you'll find a narrow, almost invisible passageway that leads another two feet underground, to a tiny vestibule burrowed out of the earth. There you will find the queen. She will have been secreted there by a handful of ladies-in-waiting at the first sign of disturbance. That passageway, in other words, is an emergency escape hatch, not unlike a fallout shelter buried deep below the West Wing.

But despite the Secret Service–like behavior, and the regal nomenclature, there's nothing hierarchical about the way an ant colony does its thinking. "Although *queen* is a term that reminds us of human political systems," Gordon explains, "the queen is not an authority figure. She lays eggs and is fed and cared for by the workers. She does not decide which worker does what. In a harvester ant colony, many feet of intricate tunnels and chambers and thousands of ants separate the queen, surrounded by interior workers, from the ants working outside the nest and using only the chambers near the surface. It would be physically impossible for the queen to direct every worker's decision about which task to perform and when." The harvester ants that carry the queen off to her escape hatch do so not because they've been ordered to by their leader; they do it because the queen ant is responsible for giving birth to all the members of the colony, and so it's in the colony's best interest—and the colony's gene pool—to keep the queen safe. Their genes instruct them to protect their mother, the same way their genes instruct them to forage for food. In other words, the matriarch doesn't train her servants to protect her, evolution does.

Popular culture trades in Stalinist ant stereotypes—witness the authoritarian colony regime in the animated film *Antz*—but in fact, colonies are the exact opposite of command economies. While they are capable of remarkably coordinated feats of task allocation, there are no Five-Year Plans in the ant kingdom. The colonies that Gordon studies display some of nature's most mesmerizing decentralized behavior: intelligence and personality and learning that emerges from the bottom up.

I'm still gazing into the latticework of plastic tubing when Gordon directs my attention to the two expansive white boards attached to the main colony space, one stacked on top of the other and connected by a ramp. (Imagine a two-story parking garage built next to a subway stop.) A handful of ants meander across each plank, some porting crumblike objects on their backs, others apparently just out for a stroll. If this is the Central Park of Gordon's ant metropolis, I think, it must be a workday.

Gordon gestures to the near corner of the top board, four inches from the ramp to the lower level, where a pile of strangely textured dust—littered with tiny shells and husks—presses neatly against the wall. "That's the midden," she says. "It's the town garbage dump." She points to three ants marching up the ramp, each barely visible beneath a comically oversize shell. "These ants are on midden duty: they take the trash that's left over from the food they've collected—in this case, the seeds from stalk grass—and deposit it in the midden pile."

Gordon takes two quick steps down to the other side of the table, at the far end away from the ramp. She points to what looks like another pile of dust. "And this is the cemetery." I look again, startled. She's right: hundreds of ant carcasses are piled atop one another, all carefully wedged against the table's corner. It looks brutal, and yet also strangely methodical.

I know enough about colony behavior to nod in amazement. "So they've somehow collectively decided to utilize these two areas as trash heap and cemetery," I say. No individual ant defined those areas, no central planner zoned one area for trash, the other for the dead. "It just sort of happened, right?"

Gordon smiles, and it's clear that I've missed something. "It's better than that," she says. "Look at what actually happened here: they've built the cemetery at exactly the point that's furthest away from the colony. And the midden is even more interesting: they've put it at precisely the point that maximizes its distance from both the colony and the cemetery. It's like there's a rule they're following: put the dead ants as far away as possible, and put the midden as far away as possible without putting it near the dead ants."

I have to take a few seconds to do the geometry myself, and sure enough, the ants have got it right. I find myself laughing out loud at the thought: it's as though they've solved one of those spatial math tests that appear on standardized tests, conjuring up a solution that's perfectly tailored to their environment, a solution that might easily stump an eight-year-old human. The question is, who's doing the conjuring?

It's a question with a long and august history, one that is scarcely limited to the collective behavior of ant colonies. We know the answer now because we have developed powerful tools for thinking about—and modeling—the emergent intelligence of self-organizing systems, but that answer was not always so clear. We know now that systems like ant colonies don't have real leaders, that the very idea of an ant "queen" is misleading. But the desire to find pacemakers in such systems has always been powerful—in both the group behavior of the social insects, and in the collective human behavior that creates a living city.

Records exist of a Roman fort dating back to A.D. 76 situated at the confluence of the Medlock and Irwell Rivers, on the northwestern edge of modern England, about 150 miles from London. Settlements persisted there for three centuries, before dying out with the rest of the empire around A.D. 400. Historians believe that the site was unoccupied for half a millennium, until a town called Manchester began to take shape there, the name derived from the Roman settlement Mamucium—Latin for "place of the breastlike hill."

Manchester subsisted through most of the millennium as a nondescript northern-England borough: granted a charter in 1301, the town established a college in the early 1400s, but remained secondary to the neighboring town of Salford for hundreds of years. In the 1600s, the Manchester region became a node for the wool trade, its merchants shipping goods to the Continent via the great ports of London. It was impossible to see it at the time, but Manchester— and indeed the entire Lancashire region—had planted itself at the very center of a technological and commercial revolution that would irrevocably alter the future of the planet. Manchester lay at the confluence of several world-historical rivers: the nascent industrial technologies of steam-powered looms; the banking system of commercial London; the global markets and labor pools of the British Empire. The story of that convergence has been told many times, and the debate over its consequences continues to this day. But beyond the epic effects that it had on the global economy, the industrial takeoff that occurred in Manchester between 1700 and 1850 also created a new kind of city, one that literally exploded into existence.

The statistics on population growth alone capture the force of that explosion: a 1773 estimate had 24,000 people living in Manchester; the first official census in 1801 found 70,000. By the midpoint of the century, there were more than 250,000 people in the city proper—a tenfold increase in only seventy-five years. That growth rate was as unprecedented and as violent as the steam engines themselves. In a real sense, the city grew too fast for the authorities to keep up with it. For five hundred years, Manchester had technically been considered a "manor," which meant, in the eyes of the law, it was run like a feudal estate, with no local government to speak of—no city planners, police, or public health authorities. Manchester didn't even send representatives to Parliament until 1832, and it wasn't incorporated for another six years. By the early 1840s, the newly formed borough council finally began to institute public health reforms and urban planning, but the British government didn't officially recognize Manchester as a city until 1853. This constitutes one of the great ironies of the Industrial Revolution, and it captures just how dramatic the rate of change really was: the city that most defined the future of urban life for the first half of the nineteenth century didn't legally become a city until the great explosion had run its course.

The result of that discontinuity was arguably the least planned and most chaotic city in the six-thousand-year history of urban settlements. Noisy, polluted, massively overcrowded, Manchester attracted a steady stream of intellectuals and public figures in the 1830s, traveling north to the industrial magnet in search of the modern world's future. One by one, they returned with stories of abject squalor and sensory overload, their words straining to convey the immensity and uniqueness of the experience. "What I have seen has disgusted and astonished me beyond all measure," Dickens wrote after a visit in the fall of 1838. "I mean to strike the heaviest blow in my power for these unfortunate creatures." Appointed to command the northern districts in the late 1830s, Major General Charles James Napier wrote: "Manchester is the chimney of the world. Rich rascals, poor rogues, drunken ragamuffins and prostitutes form the moral.... What a place! The entrance to hell, realized." De Tocqueville visited Lancashire in 1835 and described the landscape in language that would be echoed throughout the next two centuries: "From this foul drain the greatest stream of human industry flows out to fertilize the whole world. From this filthy sewer pure gold flows. Here humanity attains its most complete development and its most brutish; here civilization works its miracles, and civilized man is turned back almost into a savage."

But Manchester's most celebrated and influential documentarian was a young man named Friedrich Engels, who arrived in 1842 to help oversee the family cotton plant there, and to witness firsthand the engines of history bringing the working class closer to self-awareness. While Engels was very much on the payroll of his father's firm, Ermen and Engels, by the time he arrived in Manchester he was also under the sway of the radical politics associated with the Young Hegelian school. He had befriended Karl Marx a few years before and had been encouraged to visit Manchester by the socialist Moses Hess, whom he'd met in early 1842. His three years in England were thus a kind of scouting mission for the revolution, financed by the capitalist class. The book that Engels eventually wrote, *The Condition of the Working Class in England,* remains to this day one of the classic tracts of urban history and stands as the definitive account of nineteenth-century Manchester life in all its tumult and dynamism. Dickens, Carlyle, and Disraeli had all attempted to capture Manchester in its epic wildness, but their efforts were outpaced by a twenty-four-year-old from Prussia.

But *The Condition* is not, as might be expected, purely a document of Manchester's industrial chaos, a story of all that is solid melting into air, to borrow a phrase Engels's comrade would write several years later. In the midst of the city's insanity, Engels's eye is drawn to a strange kind of order, in a wonderful passage where he leads the reader on a walking tour of the industrial capital, a tour that reveals a kind of politics built into the very topography of the city's streets. It captures Engels's acute powers of observation, but I quote from it at length because it captures something else as well—how difficult it is to think in models of self-organization, to imagine a world without pacemakers.

> The town itself is peculiarly built, so that someone can live in it for years and travel into it and out of it daily without ever coming into contact with a working-class quarter or even with workers—so long, that is to say, as one confines himself to his business affairs or to strolling about for pleasure. This comes about mainly in the circumstances that through an unconscious, tacit agreement as much as through conscious, explicit intention, the working-class districts are most sharply separated from the parts of the city reserved for the middle class....
>
> I know perfectly well that this deceitful manner of building is more or less common to all big cities. I know as well that shopkeepers must in the nature of the business take premises on the main thoroughfares. I know in such streets there are more good houses than bad ones, and that the value of land is higher in their immediate vicinity than in neighborhoods that lie at a distance from them. But at the same time I have never come across so systematic a seclusion of the working class from the main streets as in Manchester. I have never elsewhere seen a

concealment of such fine sensibility of everything that might offend the eyes and nerves of the middle classes. And yet it is precisely Manchester that has been built less according to a plan and less within the limitations of official regulations—and indeed more through accident—than any other town. Still ... I cannot help feeling that the liberal industrialists, the Manchester "bigwigs," are not so altogether innocent of this bashful style of building.

You can almost hear the contradictions thundering against each other in this passage, like the "dark satanic mills" of Manchester itself. The city has built a *cordon sanitaire* to separate the industrialists from the squalor they have unleashed on the world, concealing the demoralization of Manchester's working-class districts—and yet that disappearing act comes into the world without "conscious, explicit intention." The city seems artfully planned to hide its atrocities, and yet it "has been built less according to a plan" than any city in history. As Steven Marcus puts it, in his history of the young Engels's sojourn in Manchester, "The point to be taken is that this astonishing and outrageous arrangement cannot fully be understood as the result of a plot, or even a deliberate design, although those in whose interests it works also control it. It is indeed too huge and too complex a state of organized affairs ever to have been *thought up* in advance, to have preexisted as an idea."

Those broad, glittering avenues, in other words, suggest a Potemkin village without a Potemkin. That mix of order and anarchy is what we now call emergent behavior. Urban critics since Lewis Mumford and Jane Jacobs have known that cities have lives of their own, with neighborhoods clustering into place without any Robert Moses figure dictating the plan from above. But that understanding has entered the intellectual mainstream only in recent years—when Engels paced those Manchester streets in the 1840s, he was left groping blindly, trying to find a culprit for the city's fiendish organization, even as he acknowledged that the city was notoriously unplanned. Like most intellectual histories, the development of that new understanding—the sciences of complexity and self-organization—is a complicated, multithreaded tale, with many agents interacting over its duration. It is probably better to think of it as less a linear narrative and more an interconnected web, growing increasingly dense over the century and a half that separates us from Engels's first visit to Manchester.

Complexity is a word that has frequently appeared in critical accounts of metropolitan space, but there are really two kinds of complexity fundamental to the city, two experiences with very different implications for the individuals trying to make sense of them. There is, first, the more conventional sense of complexity as sensory overload, the city stretching the human nervous system to its very extremes, and in the process teaching it a new series of reflexes—and leading the way for a complementary series of aesthetic values, which develop out like a scab around the original wound. The German cultural critic Walter Benjamin writes in his unfinished masterpiece, *The Arcades Project*:

> Perhaps the daily sight of a moving crowd once presented the eye with a spectacle to which it first had to adapt.... [T]hen the assumption is not

impossible that, having mastered this task, the eye welcomed opportunities to confirm its possession of its new ability. The method of impressionist painting, whereby the picture is assembled through a riot of flecks of color, would then be a reflection of experience with which the eye of a big-city dweller has become familiar.

There's a long tributary of nineteenth- and twentieth-century urban writing that leads into this passage, from the London chapters of Wordsworth's *Prelude* to the ambulatory musings of Joyce's *Dubliners*: the noise and the senselessness somehow transformed into an aesthetic experience. The crowd is something you throw yourself into, for the pure poetry of it all. But complexity is not solely a matter of sensory overload. There is also the sense of complexity as a self-organizing system—more Santa Fe Institute than Frankfurt School. This sort of complexity lives up one level: it describes the system of the city itself, and not its experiential reception by the city dweller. The city is complex because it overwhelms, yes, but also because it has a coherent personality, a personality that self-organizes out of millions of individual decisions, a global order built out of local interactions. This is the "systematic" complexity that Engels glimpsed on the boulevards of Manchester: not the overload and anarchy he documented elsewhere, but instead a strange kind of order, a pattern in the streets that furthered the political values of Manchester's elite without being deliberately planned by them. We know now from computer models and sociological studies—as well as from the studies of comparable systems generated by the social insects, such as Gordon's harvester ants—that larger patterns can emerge out of uncoordinated local actions. But for Engels and his contemporaries, those unplanned urban shapes must have seemed like a haunting. The city appeared to have a life of its own.

A hundred and fifty years later, the same techniques translated into the language of software ... trigger a similar reaction: the eerie sense of something lifelike, something organic forming on the screen. Even those with sophisticated knowledge about self-organizing systems still find these shapes unnerving—in their mix of stability and change, in their capacity for open-ended learning. The impulse to build centralized models to explain that behavior remains almost as strong as it did in Engels's day. When we see repeated shapes and structure emerging out of apparent chaos, we can't help looking for pacemakers.

Understood in the most abstract sense, what Engels observed are *patterns* in the urban landscape, visible because they have a repeated structure that distinguishes them from the pure noise you might naturally associate with an unplanned city. They are patterns of human movement and decision-making that have been etched into the texture of city blocks, patterns that are then fed back to the Manchester residents themselves, altering their subsequent decisions. (In that sense, they are the very opposite of the traditional sense of urban complexity—they are signals emerging where you would otherwise expect only noise.) A city is a kind of pattern-amplifying machine: its neighborhoods are a way of measuring and expressing the repeated behavior of larger collectivities—capturing information about group behavior, and sharing that information with the group. Because those patterns are fed back to the community, small shifts in behavior can quickly escalate into larger movements: upscale shops dominate the main boulevards, while the working class remains clustered invisibly in the alleys and side streets; the artists live on the Left Bank, the investment bankers in the Eighth Arrondissement. You don't need regulations and city planners deliberately creating these structures. All you need are thousands of individuals and a few simple rules of interaction. The bright shop windows attract more bright shop windows and drive the impoverished toward the hidden core. There's no need for a Baron Haussmann in this world, just a few repeating patterns of movement, amplified into larger shapes that last for lifetimes: clusters, slums, neighborhoods.

Not all patterns are visible to every city dweller, though. The history of urbanism is also the story of more muted signs, built by the collective behavior of smaller groups and rarely detected by outsiders. Manchester harbors several such secret clusters, persisting over the course of many generations, like a "standing wave in front of a rock in a fast-moving stream." One of them lies just north of Victoria University, at a point where Oxford Road becomes Oxford Street. There are reports dating back to the mid-nineteenth century of men cruising other men on these blocks, looking for casual sex, more lasting relationships, or even just the camaraderie of shared identity at a time when that identity dared not speak its name. Some historians speculate that Wittgenstein visited these streets during his sojourn in Manchester in 1908. Nearly a hundred years later, the area has christened itself the Gay Village and actively promotes its coffee bars and boutiques as a must-see Manchester tourist destination, like Manhattan's Christopher Street and San Francisco's Castro. The pattern is now broadcast to a wider audience, but it has not lost its shape.

But even at a lower amplitude, that signal was still loud enough to attract the attention of another of Manchester's illustrious immigrants: the British polymath Alan Turing. As part of his heroic contribution to the war effort, Turing had been a student of mathematical patterns, designing the equations and the machines that cracked the "unbreakable" German code of the Enigma device. After a frustrating three-year stint at the National Physical Laboratory in London, Turing moved to Manchester in 1948 to help run the university's embryonic computing lab. It was in Manchester that Turing began to think about the problem of biological development in mathematical terms, leading the way to the "Morphogenesis" paper, published in 1952, that Evelyn Fox Keller would rediscover more than a decade later. Turing's war research had focused on detecting patterns lurking within the apparent chaos of code, but in his Manchester years, his mind gravitated toward a mirror image of the original code-breaking problem: how complex patterns could come into being by following simple rules. How does a seed know how to build a flower?

Turing's paper on morphogenesis—literally, "the beginning of shape"—turned out to be one of his seminal works, ranking up there with his more publicized papers and speculations: his work on Gödel's undecidability problem, the Turing Machine, the Turing Test—not to mention his contributions to the physical design of the modern digital computer. But the morphogenesis paper was only the beginning of a shape—a brilliant mind sensing the outlines of a new problem, but not fully grasping all its intricacies. If Turing had been granted another few decades to explore the powers of self-assembly—not to mention access to the number-crunching horsepower of non-vacuum-tube computers— it's not hard to imagine his mind greatly enhancing our subsequent understanding of emergent behavior. But the work on morphogenesis was tragically cut short by his death in 1954.

Alan Turing was most likely a casualty of the brutally homophobic laws of postwar Britain, but his death also intersected with those discreet patterns of life on Manchester's sidewalks. Turing had known about that stretch of Oxford Road since his arrival in Manchester; on occasion, he would drift down to the neighborhood, meeting other gay men—inviting some of them back to his flat for conversation, and presumably some sort of physical contact. In January of 1952, Turing met a young man named Arnold Murray on those streets, and the two embarked on a brief relationship that quickly turned sour. Murray—or a friend of Murray's—broke into Turing's house and stole a few items. Turing reported the theft to the police and, with his typical forthrightness, made no effort to conceal the affair with Murray when the police visited his flat. Homosexuality was a criminal offense according to British law, punishable by up to two years' imprisonment, and so the police promptly charged both Turing and Murray with "gross indecency."

On February 29, 1952, while the Manchester authorities were preparing their case against him, Turing finished the revisions to his morphogenesis paper, and he argued over its merits with Ilya Prigogine, the visiting Belgian chemist whose work on nonequilibrium thermodynamics would later win him a Nobel prize. In one day, Turing had completed the text that would help engender the discipline of biomathematics and inspire Keller and Segel's slime mold discoveries fifteen years later, and he had enjoyed a spirited exchange with the man who would eventually achieve world fame for his research into self-organizing systems. On that winter day in 1952, there was no mind on the face of the earth better prepared to wrestle with the mysteries of emergence than Alan Turing's. But the world outside that mind was conspiring to destroy it. That very morning, a local paper broke the story that the war-hero savant had been caught in an illicit affair with a nineteen-year-old boy.

Within a few months Turing had been convicted of the crime and placed on a humiliating estrogen treatment to "cure" him of his homosexuality. Hounded by the authorities and denied security clearance for the top-secret British computing projects he had been contributing to, Turing died two years later, an apparent suicide.

Turing's career had already collided several times with the developing web of emergence before those fateful years in Manchester. In the early forties, during the height of the war effort, he had spent several months at the legendary Bell Laboratories on Manhattan's West Street, working on a number of encryption schemes, including an effort to transmit heavily encoded wave forms that could be decoded as human speech with the use of a special key. Early in his visit to Bell Labs, Turing hit upon the idea of using another Bell invention, the Vocoder—later used by rock musicians such as Peter Frampton to combine the sounds of a guitar and the human voice—as a way of encrypting speech. (By early 1943, Turing's ideas had enabled the first secure voice transmission to cross the Atlantic, unintelligible to German eavesdroppers.) Bell Labs was the home base for another genius, Claude Shannon, who would go on to found the influential discipline of information theory, and whose work had explored the boundaries between noise and information. Shannon had been particularly intrigued by the potential for machines to detect and amplify patterns of information in noisy communication channels—a line of inquiry that promised obvious value to a telephone company, but could also save thousands of lives in a war effort that relied so heavily on the sending and breaking of codes. Shannon and Turing immediately recognized that they had been working along parallel tracks: they were both code-breakers by profession at that point, and in their attempts to build automated machines that could recognize patterns in audio signals or numerical sequences, they had both glimpsed a future populated by even more intelligence machines. Shannon and Turing passed many an extended lunchtime at the Bell Labs, trading ideas on an "electronic brain" that might be capable of humanlike feats of pattern recognition.

Turing had imagined his thinking machine primarily in terms of its logical possibilities, its ability to execute an infinite variety of computational routines. But Shannon pushed him to think of the machine as something closer to an actual human brain, capable of recognizing more nuanced patterns. One day over lunch at the lab, Turing exclaimed playfully to his colleagues, "Shannon wants to feed not just data to a brain, but *cultural* things! He wants to play music to it!" Musical notes were patterns, too, Shannon recognized, and if you could train an electronic brain to understand and respond to logical patterns of zeros and ones, then perhaps sometime in the future we could train our machines to appreciate the equivalent patterns of minor chord progressions and arpeggios. The idea seemed fanciful at the time—it was hard enough getting a machine to perform long division, much less savor Beethoven's Ninth. But the pattern recognition that Turing and Shannon envisioned for digital computers has, in recent years, become a central part of our cultural life, with machines both generating music for our entertainment and recommending new artists for us to enjoy. The connection between musical patterns and our neurological wiring would play a central role in one of the founding texts of modern artificial intelligence, Douglas Hofstadter's *Gödel, Escher, Bach*. Our computers still haven't developed a genuine ear for music, but if they ever do, their skill will date back to those lunchtime conversations between Shannon and Turing at Bell Labs. And that learning, too, will be a kind of emergence, a higher-level order forming out of relatively simple component parts.

Five years after his interactions with Turing, Shannon published a long essay in the *Bell System Technical Journal* that was quickly repackaged as a book called *The Mathematical Theory of Communication*. Dense with equations and arcane chapter titles such as "Discrete Noiseless Systems," the book managed to become something of a cult classic, and the discipline it spawned—information theory— had a profound impact on scientific and technological research that followed, on both a theoretical and practical level. *The Mathematical Theory of Communication* contained an elegant, layman's introduction to Shannon's theory, penned by the esteemed scientist Warren Weaver, who had early on grasped the significance of Shannon's work. Weaver had played a leading role in the Natural Sciences division of the Rockefeller Foundation since 1932, and when he retired in the late fifties, he composed a long report for the foundation, looking back at the scientific progress that had been achieved over the preceding quarter century. The occasion suggested a reflective look backward, but the document that Weaver produced (based loosely on a paper he had written for *American Scientist*) was far more prescient, more forward-looking. In many respects, it deserves to be thought of as the founding text of complexity theory—the point at which the study of complex systems began to think of itself as a unified field. Drawing upon research in molecular biology, genetics, physics, computer science, and Shannon's information theory, Weaver divided the last few centuries of scientific inquiry into three broad camps. First, the study of simple systems: two or three variable problems, such as the rotation of planets, or the connection between an electric current and its voltage and resistance. Second, problems of "disorganized complexity": problems characterized by millions or billions of variables that can only be approached by the methods of statistical mechanics and probability theory. These tools helped explain not only the behavior of molecules in a gas, or the patterns of heredity in a gene pool, but also helped life insurance companies turn a profit despite their limited knowledge about any individual human's future health. Thanks to Claude Shannon's work, the statistical approach also helped phone companies deliver more reliable and intelligible long-distance service.

But there was a third phase to this progression, and we were only beginning to understand. "This statistical method of dealing with disorganized complexity, so powerful an advance over the earlier two-variable methods, leaves a great field untouched," Weaver wrote. There was a middle region between two-variable equations and problems that involved billions of variables. Conventionally, this region involved a "moderate" number of variables, but the size of the system was in fact a secondary characteristic:

> Much more important than the mere number of variables is the fact that these variables are all interrelated.... These problems, as contrasted with the disorganized situations with which statistics can cope, *show the essential feature of organization*. We will therefore refer to this group of problems as those of *organized complexity*.

Think of these three categories of problems in terms of [a] billiards table analogy.... A two- or three-variable problem would be an ordinary billiards table, with balls bouncing off one another following simple rules: their velocities, the friction of the table. That would be an example of a "simple system"—and indeed, billiard balls are often used to illustrate basic laws of physics in high school textbooks. A system of disorganized complexity would be that same table enlarged to include a million balls, colliding with one another millions of times a second. Making predictions about the behavior of any individual ball in that mix would be difficult, but you could make some accurate predictions about the overall behavior of the table. Assuming there's enough energy in the system at the outset, the balls will spread to fill the entire table, like gas molecules in a container. It's complex because there are many interacting agents, but it's disorganized because they don't create any higher-level behavior other than broad statistical trends. Organized complexity, on the other hand, is like [a] motorized billiards table, where the balls follow specific rules and through their various interactions create a distinct macrobehavior, arranging themselves in a specific shape, or forming a specific pattern over time. That sort of behavior, for Weaver, suggested a problem of organized complexity, a problem that suddenly seemed omnipresent in nature once you started to look for it:

> What makes an evening primrose open when it does? Why does salt water fail to satisfy thirst? … What is the description of aging in biochemical terms? … What is a gene, and how does the original genetic constitution of a living organism express itself in the developed characteristics of the adult?
>
> All these are certainly complex problems. But they are not problems of disorganized complexity, to which statistical methods hold the key. They are all problems which involve dealing simultaneously with a sizable number of factors which are interrelated into an organic whole.

Tackling such problems required a new approach: "The great central concerns of the biologist … are now being approached not only from *above,* with the broad view of the natural philosopher who scans the whole living world, but also from *underneath,* by the quantitative analyst who measures the underlying facts." This was a genuine shift in the paradigm of research, to use Thomas Kuhn's language—a revolution not so much in the interpretations that science built in its attempt to explain the world, but rather in the types of questions it asked. The paradigm shift was more than just a new mind-set, Weaver recognized; it was also a by-product of new tools that were appearing on the horizon. To solve the problems of organized complexity, you needed a machine capable of churning through thousands, if not millions, of calculations per second—a rate that would have been unimaginable for individual brains running the numbers with the limited calculating machines of the past few centuries. Because of his connection to the Bell Labs group, Weaver had seen early on the promise of digital computing, and he knew that the mysteries of organized complexity would be much easier to tackle once you could model the behavior in close-to-real time. For millennia, humans had used their skills at observation and classification to document the subtle anatomy of flowers, but for the first time they were perched on the brink of answering a more fundamental question, a question that had more to do with patterns developing over time than with static structure: why does an evening primrose open when it does? And how does a simple seed know how to make a primrose in the first place? …

"Organized complexity" proved to be a constructive way of thinking … but … was it possible to model and explain the behavior of self-organizing systems using more rigorous methods? Could the developing technology of digital computing be usefully applied to this problem? Partially thanks to

Shannon's work in the late forties, the biological sciences … made a number of significant breakthroughs in understanding pattern recognition and feedback…. Shortly after his appointment to the Harvard faculty in 1956, the entomologist Edward O. Wilson convincingly proved that ants communicate with one another—and coordinate overall colony behavior—by recognizing patterns in pheromone trails left by fellow ants…. At the Free University of Brussels in the fifties, Ilya Prigogine was making steady advances in his understanding of nonequilibrium thermodynamics, environments where the laws of entropy are temporarily overcome, and higher-level order may spontaneously emerge out of underlying chaos. And at MIT's Lincoln Laboratory, a twenty-five-year-old researcher named Oliver Selfridge was experimenting with a model for teaching a computer how to learn.

There is a world of difference between a computer that passively receives the information you supply and a computer that actively learns on its own. The very first generation of computers such as ENIAC had processed information fed to them by their masters, and they had been capable of performing various calculations with that data, based on the instruction sets programmed into them. This was a startling enough development at a time when "computer" meant a person with a slide rule and an eraser. But even in those early days, the digital visionaries had imagined a machine capable of more open-ended learning. Turing and Shannon had argued over the future musical tastes of the "electronic brain" during lunch hour at Bell Labs, while their colleague Norbert Wiener had written a best-selling paean to the self-regulatory powers of feedback in his 1949 manifesto *Cybernetics*.

"Mostly my participation in all of this is a matter of good luck for me," Selfridge says today, sitting in his cramped, windowless MIT office. Born in England, Selfridge enrolled at Harvard at the age of fifteen and started his doctorate three years later at MIT, where Norbert Wiener was his dissertation adviser. As a precocious twenty-one-year-old, Selfridge suggested a few corrections to a paper that his mentor had published on heart flutters, corrections that Wiener graciously acknowledged in the opening pages of *Cybernetics*. "I think I now have the honor of being one of the few living people mentioned in that book," Selfridge says, laughing.

After a sojourn working on military control projects in New Jersey, Selfridge returned to MIT in the mid-fifties. His return coincided with an explosion of interest in artificial intelligence (AI), a development that introduced him to a then-junior fellow at Harvard named Marvin Minsky. "My concerns in AI," Selfridge says now, "were not so much the actual processing as they were in how systems change, how they evolve—in a word, how they learn." Exploring the possibilities of machine learning brought Selfridge back to memories of his own education in England. "At school in England I had read John Milton's *Paradise Lost*," he says, "and I'd been struck by the image of Pandemonium—it's Greek for 'all the demons.' Then after my second son, Peter, was born, I went over *Paradise Lost* again, and the shrieking of the demons awoke something in me." The pattern recognizer in Selfridge's brain had hit upon a way of teaching a computer to recognize patterns.

"We are proposing here a model of a process which we claim can adaptively improve itself to handle certain pattern-recognition problems which cannot be adequately specified in advance." These were the first words Selfridge delivered at a symposium in late 1958, held at the very same National Physical Laboratory from which Turing had escaped a decade before. Selfridge's presentation had the memorable title "Pandemonium: A Paradigm for Learning," and while it had little impact outside the nascent computer-science community, the ideas Selfridge outlined that day would eventually become part of our everyday life—each time we enter a name in our Palm Pilots or use voice-recognition software to ask for information over the phone. Pandemonium, as Selfridge outlined it in his talk, was not so much a specific piece of software as it was a way of approaching a problem. The problem was an ambitious one, given the limited computational resources of the day: how to teach a computer to recognize patterns that were ill-defined or erratic, like the sound waves that comprise spoken language.

The brilliance of Selfridge's new paradigm lay in the fact that it relied on a distributed, bottom-up intelligence, and not a unified, top-down one. Rather than build a single smart program, Selfridge created a swarm of limited miniprograms, which he called demons. "The idea was, we have a bunch of these demons shrieking up the hierarchy," he explains. "Lower-level demons shrieking to higher-level demons shrieking to higher ones."

To understand what that "shrieking" means, imagine a system with twenty-six individual demons, each trained to recognize a letter of the alphabet. The pool of demons is shown a series of words, and each demon "votes" as to whether each letter displayed represents its chosen letter. If the first letter is *a,* the *a*-recognizing demon reports that it is highly likely that it has recognized a match. Because of the similarities in shape, the *o*-recognizer might report a possible match, while the *b*-recognizer would emphatically declare that the letter wasn't intelligible to it. All the letter-recognizing demons would report to a master demon, who would tally up the votes for each letter and choose the demon that expressed the highest confidence. Then the software would move on to the next letter in the sequence, and the process would begin again. At the end of the transmission, the master demon would have a working interpretation of the text that had been transmitted, based on the assembled votes of the demon democracy.

Of course, the accuracy of that interpretation depended on the accuracy of the letter recognizers. If you were trying to teach a computer how to read, it was cheating to assume from the outset that you could find twenty-six accurate letter recognizers. Selfridge was after a larger goal: how do you teach a machine to recognize letters—or vowel sounds, minor chords, fingerprints—in the first place? The answer involved adding another layer of demons, and a feedback mechanism whereby the various demon guesses could be graded. This lower level was populated by even less sophisticated miniprograms, trained only to recognize raw physical shapes (or sounds, in the case of Morse code or spoken language). Some demons recognized parallel lines, others perpendicular ones. Some demons looked for circles, others for dots. None of these shapes were associated with any particular letter; these bottom-dwelling demons were like two-year-old children—capable of reporting on the shapes they witnessed, but not perceiving them as letters or words.

Using these minimally equipped demons, the system could be trained to recognize letters, without "knowing" anything about the alphabet in advance. The recipe was relatively simple: present the letter *b* to the bottom-level demons, and see which ones respond, and which ones don't. In the case of the letter *b,* the vertical-line recognizers might respond, along with the circle recognizers. Those lower-level demons would report to a letter-recognizer one step higher in the chain. Based on the information gathered from its lieutenants, that recognizer would make a guess as to the letter's identity. Those guesses are then "graded" by the software. If the guess is wrong, the software learns to dissociate those particular lieutenants from the letter in question; if the guess happens to be right, it *strengthens* the connection between the lieutenants and the letter.

The results are close to random at first, but if you repeat the process a thousand times, or ten thousand, the system learns to associate specific assemblies of shape-recognizers with specific letters and soon enough is capable of translating entire sentences with remarkable accuracy. The system doesn't come with any predefined conceptions about the shapes of letters—you train the system to associate letters with specific shapes in the grading phase. (This is why handwriting-recognition software can adapt to so many different types of penmanship, but *can't* adapt to penmanship that changes day to day.) That mix of random beginnings organizing into more complicated results reminded Selfridge of another process, whose own underlying code was just then being deciphered in the form of DNA. "The scheme sketched is really a natural selection on the processing demons," Selfridge explained. "If they serve a useful function they survive and perhaps are even the source for other subdemons who are themselves judged on their merits. It is perfectly reasonable to conceive of this taking place on a broader scale.... [I]nstead of having but one Pandemonium we might have some crowd of them, all fairly similarly constructed, and employ natural selection on the crowd of them."

The system Selfridge described—with its bottom-up learning, and its evaluating feedback loops—belongs in the history books as the first practical description of an emergent software program. The world now swarms with millions of his demons.

QUESTIONS FOR MAKING CONNECTIONS
WITHIN THE READING

1. Do you accept Johnson's analogy between the behavior of harvester ants and the emergence of cities like Manchester? Does Johnson mean that instinct guides human builders in much the same way as it guides the ants? Does he mean that in both cases an order has emerged entirely by accident? Or does he mean that there is something about "systems" in general—ant colonies as well as sprawling conurbations—that makes them self-organizing? What exactly is

a self-organizing system, and how do both the ant colony and the city qualify as equally appropriate examples? How does each system organize itself?

2. The idea of self-organizing systems might seem to suggest that order automatically and smoothly arises as ants and human beings go about their private business. Can Manchester in the nineteenth century, when Napier, Dickens, and Engels each observed it, be described as orderly? Was there an order behind the apparent disorder? How can we distinguish between a self-organizing system and results that are produced entirely by chance?

3. One could say that there are three different parts to "The Myth of the Ant Queen." The first deals with the colony of harvester ants. The second deals with the city of Manchester. The third deals with the emergence of complexity theory. In what ways are these three parts connected? Why doesn't Johnson make the connections more explicit—why does he leave them for the reader to work out? Could the structure of his chapter in some way reflect the nature of his argument about self-organization?

QUESTIONS FOR WRITING

1. What role does intelligence play in self-organizing systems? This question might be more complex than it seems at first because intelligence may exist on multiple levels. The intelligence demonstrated by an ant colony may be much greater than the intelligence of an individual ant. On any particular day during the 1880s, life in Manchester must have seemed to many people very close to absolute chaos, but could it be said that the city as a whole possessed a certain intelligence? Does Johnson mean to suggest that the ideas and aspirations of individuals do not matter? Are we, from the standpoint of complexity theory, intelligent beings? What is intelligence, anyway?

2. Families, communities, schools, religious groups, circles of friends, political parties, public service organizations—all of these qualify as social institutions, and there are many others. Choose one institution and, drawing on Johnson's chapter, decide whether it qualifies as truly self-organizing. If it does not, can you imagine how it might be reorganized in a bottom-up fashion? In what ways do our customs and traditions encourage or discourage self-organization? What do you conclude from the importance of kings, presidents, generals, CEOs, bosses, coaches, principals, and other leaders in our culture?

QUESTIONS FOR MAKING CONNECTIONS
BETWEEN READINGS

1. Do self-organizing systems manage, as time goes on, to insulate themselves from the influence of chance? Does chance continue to play a role, or does

it actually become even more important? To explore these questions, you might consider the examples that Johnson provides—the ant colony, the city, and the development of the science of complexity. But you might also consider Edward Tenner's discussion of technology and unintended consequences. Although technology appears to make life safer and more stable, it also exposes us to "revenge effects." Does self-organization protect us from these effects, or might it make them more likely?

2. At first glance, Robert Thurman's claim that we have no permanent or essential self may seem like sheer nonsense, since, clearly, each of us is a self or has one. But does "the self," as we call it, actually represent a self-organizing system, more like an ant colony than a single ant, or more like a city than a single neighborhood? As you work through this question, you should move beyond the two texts to consider your own experience. Are you always the same person from one moment to the next? To what degree is your identity at any particular time shaped by your interactions with others? Can you accurately predict what you will be like ten years from now? Ten months? Ten days?

CHRISTINE KENNEALLY

SOME ASPECTS OF what it means to be human are relatively easy to track throughout history. The archaeological excavation of bones and tools allows us to trace the development of our ancestors as they took the physical form and developed the cultural habits that we now consider to be distinctly human. Other aspects of human culture are much more obscure, however, and foremost among these is language. While there exists a scattered and incomplete history of the written word, the origins of spoken language have long evaded anthropologists, evolutionary psychologists, linguists, and other scholars.

Journalist Christine Kenneally takes on this challenge in *The First Word: The Search for the Origins of Language* (2007). A native Australian, Kenneally earned her bachelor's degree in English and linguistics at Melbourne University and her doctorate in linguistics at Cambridge University, and then moved to the United States to become a freelance writer. Before turning her attention to the historical investigation of language, she wrote widely for the *New Yorker*, the *New York Times, Discover, Slate,* and *Salon,* among other publications, on subjects ranging from Alex the talking African grey parrot to hemispherectomies—operations involving the removal of half of a human brain.

The First Word follows two narratives. The first is an evolutionary story, exploring the possible random adaptations that led to the emergence of *Homo loquens,* the talking human. The second traces the politics of scientific research, asking why the study of linguistic evolution was a taboo subject for so long, "formally banned by the Linguistics Society of Paris" in an interdiction that was never officially relaxed. In her research, Kenneally discovers that "the platforms of language were built over thousands of millennia and we share many of these with very different animals." The following chapter from her book, entitled "You Have Gestures," traces some of these shared communicative habits. Weaving together different strands of research to offer a holistic view of how language evolves, Kenneally forces into the light of day the uncomfortable issues that led some scholarly groups to ban the study of linguistic evolution in the first place. Just how exceptional is human expression? How are we to interpret the many forms of language-based expression (foremost among these literature) if language is simply an evolutionary quirk? By bringing these questions back into the conversation about language, Kenneally offers new ways to understand our world and our words.

Kenneally, Christine. "You Have Gestures." *The First Word*. New York: Viking Penguin, 2007.

The quotation is drawn from "A Path to Language," an original essay by Kenneally available at the Powell's Books Web site <http://www.powells.com/essays/kenneally.html>.

You Have Gestures

Picture the house in which you grew up. Think about the rooms, the hallways, the stairs, visualize where they all are. Where was the front door? The back door? What color was the roof? Did you have wall-to-wall carpeting or were rugs spread all over the place? If you turned now and attempted to describe the house to someone nearby, it's highly likely that you'd gesture as you spoke. In fact, even if you just imagine a person and then describe the house aloud to her, you'll probably gesture as well. Gesture experts say that it is almost impossible to talk about space without gesturing. Gesture is spontaneous, and as integral to individual expression as it is to communication. Even though you probably won't gesture as much if you are talking on the phone, you will still wave your arms about. Blind people gesture when they speak in the same way that seeing people do.

Gesture may be integral to human expression, but it is not uniquely human. At the Gestural Communication in Nonhuman and Human Primates Conference in 2004, Mike Tomasello of the Max Planck Institute in Leipzig, Germany, and his associates presented a huge compilation of gestures that they had observed in monkeys, gibbons, gorillas, chimpanzees, bonobos, and orangutans. Many of them had been observed at the spectacular ape exhibit at the Leipzig City Zoo, where a leafy path leads to the center of a big ring. Radiating out from the central space are walks that divide all the great ape species from one another. In one section are the gorillas, sitting impassively. In another are the bonobos—only three of them, a reflection of their dwindling numbers worldwide. In the third section are the orangutans. The male sits near the viewing window looking profoundly deflated, while his orange cage mate hangs upside down from a tree stump and stretches. In the fourth section are the chimpanzees. There are more than a dozen chimps in the compound, and they make a lively community. Some recline sensuously, others fly through the air on ropes or trunks. Some busily work at boxes, inserting sticks into various holes. The exhibit is climate-controlled; it feels like a light summer day. Tomasello has a number of testing rooms installed at the zoo for his various experiments.

Gestures play a large role in primate communication, Tomasello explained, and as is the case with humans, these gestures are learned, flexible, and under voluntary control. Most primates, humans included, gesture communicatively with their right hands, suggesting that the dominance of one side of the brain for vocal and gestural communication could be as old as thirty million years. Just as with human gestures, ape gestures can involve touch, noise, or vision. Apes wait until they have the attention of another ape before making visual gestures, and often if their visual or auditory gestures are unacknowledged, they will go over to the ape they want to communicate with and make some kind of touching gesture instead. Apes also repeat gestures that don't get the desired response. Like human gestures, ape gestures seem to be holistic: a series of gestures doesn't break down cleanly into meaningful components. Moreover, a set of different gestures may mean just one thing, while a single gesture may be used to convey many meanings.

Tomasello and his group divide ape gestures into two types: attention getters and intention movements. Attention getters, said Tomasello, slapping the podium, do just what they say—they call attention to the ape making the gesture. Chimpanzees will hit the ground, clap their hands, and stamp their feet for this purpose. They also lay their arms on other chimps, tug on their hair, or poke them. Once the observer pays attention to the gesturing ape, said Tomasello, what is required becomes clear. To illustrate this, Tomasello showed a video of a chimpanzee who walks over to another chimp and starts jumping up and down on the spot. When the second chimp finally notices the display, the first one turns around and sits down. The message is obvious—groom me, and that's what the second ape starts to do.

Intention movements are the beginnings of an actual movement, like a raised fist to indicate a threat in humans.

The process by which these gestures evolve in individuals, Tomasello explained, goes like this: "I'm really doing something, you come to anticipate it, I notice your anticipation so I only make the beginnings of the movement." Male chimpanzees, for example, make a penis-offer gesture to propose sex. They sit back on their haunches and repeatedly thrust their pelvis, pushing their erect penis in the direction of another chimpanzee. "In papers we call it the penis offer," Tomasello said. "Between ourselves, it's called 'dirty dancing.'"

Mimicking another intention movement, Tomasello rolled his arms over his head, like a chimp barrel-hitting a companion. The move is reminiscent of the way that humans feint at each other to make a point without actually following through. Cats and dogs make a similar movement when they raise their paws and bat them, as if they are about to strike another animal, so the gesture is not restricted to primates. "It's typical mammalian play," Tomasello explained. "Remember," he said, invoking the tree of life, "it's not a ladder; it's a tree. It's not a ladder; it's a tree."

Another gesture researcher, Joanna Blake at York University in Canada, directly compared the gestures that infants make when they are learning language with the gestures made by apes, which have a lot in common. Both apes and children make a lot of request gestures—begging for food, raising their arms to be picked up and carried—and they extend their whole hand to point. Children and apes likewise make the same gestures of protest, pushing someone away or turning away themselves while shaking their heads. They also emote in the same ways, stamping their feet, flapping their arms, and rocking, and when they want someone to do something, both take a person's or an ape's hand and place it on the object to be manipulated, or they proffer objects that they want someone to manipulate. Clearly there is a close family relationship between human and ape gesture, confirming that it is an ancient trait that precedes the existence of modern humans and of language.

Janette Wallis, who has been watching primates since she was an undergraduate at the University of Oklahoma, is drawn to the more subtle aspects of primate communication. She used hidden cameras to capture evidence of a baboon gesture she calls the muzzle wipe—a quick pass across the bridge of the nose with the hand. The muzzle wipe typically occurs in situations in which a baboon may be nervous or conflicted for some reason. As with many human gestures, there's no evidence that the wipe is intentional, but it's likely that other animals read it as a signal that reveals information about the wiper.[1]

Wallis presented videos of the muzzle wipe at the Leipzig gesture conference. Although most early studies of baboons, she said, hardly mention the gesture, her films showed baboons doing it in captivity and in the wild. The gesture rarely lasts longer than a few seconds, so it is not easy to see, yet once Wallis told the audience what to look for, the muzzle wipe was clearly evident. Nervous baboons could be seen constantly putting their hands to their faces in difficult situations. She noted that monkeys make a similar move and that a chimpanzee will often put its wrist to its forehead in similar contexts. Could this overlooked gesture be some kind of precursor to comparable gestures in humans? asked Wallis. Humans do put their hand to their face when nervous, and indeed, as she pointed out, psychiatrists and law enforcement officials often interpret a hand-to-face gesture as evidence of uncertainty or even deception.

Once Wallis convinced the audience that the muzzle wipe existed, she showed a video of George H. W. Bush. The ex-president was speaking at a press conference about his son the president of the United States. He discussed what was at the time headline news— George W. Bush's having been arrested in his youth on a drunk-driving charge. "Unlike some," said the older Bush in a tone of complete confidence, "he accepts responsibility." He then raised his hand to the bridge of his nose and scratched it.[2]

Only ten years ago researchers were unanimous in their agreement that pointing was unique to humans. Even now many stand by that claim. In fact, apes and many species of monkeys that are much more distantly related to humans do point as well, though they typically do so with their whole hand.[3] (Scholars of gesture complain that pointing with the hand has been treated as a second-class kind of pointing, even though it is common in many human groups.) Usually, apes make this gesture only for humans, not between themselves. They point at objects and alternate their gaze between the object that is pointed at and the human they are pointing for. The animals learn how to point without explicit training, and simply pick it up from humans.

Although there is only one anecdotal report of a bonobo's pointing with its index finger in the wild, some apes have been shown to do so in captivity. William D. Hopkins, a researcher at the Yerkes National Primate Research Center at Emory University, and his colleague David Leavens, a professor of psychology at the University of Sussex, showed a videotape at the gesture conference of a chimpanzee pointing. In the video, Leavens is in a white lab coat and a surgical mask while a chimpanzee stands eating on the other side of a wall of wire mesh. When the ape drops some food through the mesh, it points its index finger through the wire to indicate the food and looks at Leavens, who picks it up and returns it. "I submit," Leavens said, "that there is a well-trained primate in this video, but it is not the chimpanzee."

At the Leipzig conference Tomasello was skeptical that apes could point and, if they did, that it actually meant anything. But he began to wonder about it and later said, "Many of the aspects of language that make it such a uniquely powerful form of human cognition and communication are already present in the humble act of pointing."

Tomasello had already established in previous experiments that apes know what other apes are seeing, and it was clear that they gesture easily and creatively for one another. More recent experiments have shown that chimpanzees will cooperate with one another in situations where collective help is needed (in order to get food, for example), and in quite simple tasks they'll also assist without the prospect of a reward—like picking up a dropped object and handing it to someone. While the Hopkins and Leavens video showed they are capable of pointing, why, Tomasello asked, do apes point only for humans and not one another? The answer he arrived at is both simple and far-reaching: it is because humans respond. Apes don't point referentially for other apes, because they will be ignored.

Human children learn to point at a very young age. Tomasello and his colleagues have videotaped many instances of children spontaneously pointing in a helpful manner. In one experimental setup, a very young child was placed on her mother's lap. Mother and child sat across a desk from a woman stapling papers together. The woman left the room for a moment, and while she was away a man entered, took the stapler, and placed it on a cupboard behind the desk. When the woman returned, she made a great show of looking for the stapler. The infant watched her for a while, and then, unprompted, pointed to where the stapler had been moved so the woman could find it. In other examples, a child and adult played together until for some reason (the ball dropped, the toy fell) the game stopped. Without prompting, the child looked at the adult and pointed to the problem, clearly requesting that the game begin again. In other cases, the child pointed at an object or proffered it merely to show it to the adult in order to elicit a reaction.

Tomasello first started to consider how much this kind of shared, cooperative attention mattered at dinner in a restaurant one night. He was watching a mother and child play together. The mother blew a raspberry on the child's arm, then the roles were reversed, and the baby followed suit. Why did it happen this way? wondered Tomasello. Why did the child reciprocate the gesture rather than simply imitating the action on himself?

The answer, he believes, is that humans are particularly cooperative in the way they communicate.[4] Reciprocation is fundamental to the interactions of our species. Offering is not instinctive for humans, but is taught by parents to children, who learn it very easily. And crucially, we offer not only food and other objects but information and experiences as well. Children, says Tomasello, want you to look at what they are looking at and to emote in response. In many theories of evolution, human altruism is treated as an anomaly. But Tomasello thinks of it as an evolutionary strategy that has served us incredibly well.

Chimps don't spontaneously point in this fashion, and Tomasello believes it is due to a fundamental difference in the balance of cooperation and competition within the species. Chimpanzees lack the set of skills and motivations that underlie our pointing. Tomasello conducted an experiment with Brian Hare, then a doctoral student, in which two barrels were set up in a room. Food was placed in one, while the other was left empty. Hare stood on one side of the barrels as a chimpanzee entered the room. In one run-through, Hare pointed helpfully at the barrel with the food in it. But, said Tomasello, the chimpanzee would look at the finger, and then look at the barrel, and then look at the other barrel, and then it would choose completely randomly between them. It did not comprehend that Hare was being helpful and telling it where the food was located. In another run-through of the experiment, the chimpanzee would come into the room, and instead of pointing to the food, Hare would reach for the barrel, as if to grab it and the food in it. The chimpanzee understood this gesture without any problem, and it would head for the appropriate barrel. The movement Hare made was essentially the same in each case—a basic arm extension—but his intention was clearly cooperative in the first instance and competitive in the second.[5]

Tomasello and his colleagues' gesture work demonstrates both a continuum that connects human and ape communication and significant differences between them. In our evolutionary history some individuals must have been born with a greater inclination and ability to collaborate than our common ancestor with chimpanzees. These individuals were more successful and bred more offspring with those characteristics, Tomasello said. What we have evolved into now is a species for whom an experience means little if it's not shared. Chimpanzees took a different path. In their communication, there is never just plain showing, where the goal is simply to share attention. While they do share and collaborate and understand different kinds of intentions, they don't have communicative intentions. We do, said Tomasello, and it's in this shared space that the symbolic communication of language lies.

Tomasello's conclusions resonate deeply with observations made by Sue Savage-Rumbaugh. Before Kanzi, Savage-Rumbaugh worked with two apes called Sherman and Austin. The apes had successfully acquired many signs and used them effectively. There didn't seem to be anything odd about their language use until one day they were asked to talk to each other. What resulted was a sign-shouting match; neither ape was willing to listen. Language, wrote Savage-Rumbaugh, "coordinates behaviors between individuals by a complex process of exchanging behaviors that are punctuated by speech."[6]

At its most fundamental, language is an act of shared attention, and without the fundamentally *human* willingness to listen to what another person is saying, language would not work. Symbols like words, said Tomasello, are devices that coordinate attention, just as pointing does. They presuppose a general give-and-take that chimpanzees don't seem to have. For this reason, Tomasello explained, "asking why only humans use language is like asking why only humans build skyscrapers, when the fact is that only humans, among primates, build free-standing shelters at all…. At our current level of understanding, asking why apes do not have language may not be our most productive question. A much more productive question, and one that can currently lead us to much more interesting lines of empirical research, is asking why apes do not even point."

Whether you are human or another kind of ape, one of the ways that gesture becomes ritualized and communicative is in being passed on by learning. As humans, we observe a gesture, and then we reproduce it by imitation. Imitation is crucial to the learning process, and we are not the only imitators in the animal world. Lori Marino, one of the researchers who explored the ability of dolphins to recognize themselves in mirrors, said that "imitation is an everyday behavior with dolphins." They are very good at shadowing, imitation in real time. "If you make certain hand gestures in front of the tank in a captive facility, they will be able to follow your hand, even when you're moving your hand back and forth in different ways. They also seem able to pick up patterns very well and anticipate patterns, so if you set up a certain pattern going and then you stop, they seem to anticipate what the next step in the pattern is."

Frans de Waal speaks of the difficulties of measuring fleeting and ephemeral behaviors like imitation. "A lot of the cognition studies are on technical cognition, like: Can they count? How do they use tools? Do they understand gravity? Social intelligence is more difficult," he said.

Particular difficulties arise with imitation studies, as de Waal explained:

> What people do, for example, in these imitation studies is they put an experiment in front of the chimpanzee and they show how to do something, and then they see the chimp imitate. But I think imitation also requires that you identify with the person and that you like the person actually. If you look at humans who imitate, children who imitate, they imitate the people they know and they like, and they want to be like Mom or they want to be like Dad or their big brother or whatever. They're not imitating a random person. It's very selective. I think the scientists who have failed to come up with these social learning tasks on chimpanzees, to some degree, have worked with the wrong paradigm. They put a human in front of the animal, which is already a different species, and the human may not have much of a relationship with them [sic]. I think we can only resolve these issues by focusing on behavior among animals themselves.

De Waal has been studying the ways that capuchins imitate one another. The experimenters train one capuchin to perform a task, and while other monkeys watch it, they attempt to determine if any imitation is taking place. De Waal is also probing the relevance of who gets imitated—if a capuchin is more likely to imitate its mother, for example, than an unrelated male.

Sue Savage-Rumbaugh's experiences with Kanzi back up de Waal's observation about laboratory experiments. She noted that Kanzi's mother, Matata, had two other children who never got the amount of attention from human caretakers that Kanzi did. She believes it was the significant relationships with humans in the period in which Kanzi was most sensitive to acquiring language that enabled him to pick it up.[7]

Other research suggests that imitation can be affected by who the original performer is. One recent study described the way a population of dolphins off the coast of western Australia passed on a tradition of tool use. These dolphins learned from adults in the pod to use sponges to forage on the ocean floor. But they didn't just acquire the skill from any of the adults: the tradition seemed to be passed down solely from mother to daughter.

The combination of gestural communication and imitation can be as powerful as vocal communication. In human hunter-gatherer groups, such as the Ngatatjara of western Australia and the northern Déné of the Canadian subarctic, the transmission of knowledge about the environment and how to survive in it is achieved by observation and experimentation rather than by verbal explanation. Moreover, studies have shown that a group learning how to manufacture a stone flake (such as those used by Stone Age societies) from a teacher who only gestured took no longer at the task than, and were as good at it as, a group in which the teacher gave precise verbal instructions on how to make the flake.[8]

In modern humans gestures come in a variety of types. There is here-and-now pointing (this book, right here!), action gestures (she picked it up with one hand!), abstract pointing (and another thing!), and metaphorical gestures that make symbolic reference to people, events, space, motion, action. Most gestures are initiated with the right hand. They typically occur slightly before or at the same time as speech.

Gestures that accompany speech typically amplify the meaning conveyed by the speaker. Sometimes, gesture communicates information that isn't explicitly stated in the verbal message it accompanies. For example, a speaker may move his fingers stepwise in a spiral while saying, "I ran all the way upstairs." The listener can infer that the staircase was spiral even though the fact was not stated.[9] While gesture doesn't break up into wordlike segments, there are rules about the way gestures can be combined. And as obvious as the meaning of many gestures is when they are used by people while they are talking, listeners can usually guess at the meaning of a gesture without sound only 50 to 60-percent of the time. (Think about gesturing while saying, "I had a big ball," and "The guy had a huge hot dog.")

For a long time gesture was more or less ignored in linguistics, and elsewhere it received little attention. Researchers considered it paralinguistic, meaning that it was merely supplementary to language, perhaps useful in terms of emphasis but ultimately a secondary and unimportant phenomenon. People assumed that gesture was only for the benefit of the listener and justified removing it from serious consideration for the simple reason that it could be removed. It is possible, after all, to hear and understand someone even if you don't look at him. (In the same way, structure in language has been treated as separate from meaning, because you can go a long way analyzing both of them without reference to the other. Similarly, intonation has been largely ignored within Chomskyan linguistics.) The assumption was that because you could separate them in analysis, they worked independently in the body and they therefore evolved independently of each other. But even though you can discover much about speech and language without worrying about gesture, the fact is they usually occur together in the real world. Speech is disembodied only on the phone or radio, and in evolutionary time these types of communication have not been around very long.

Today, like the study of language evolution itself, the field of gesture studies is undergoing a small revolution. More and more people are engaging in experimental studies of gesture, and researchers are discovering how complicated and interesting it can be. Conference organizers in the last few years have been surprised at the number of scholars who want to attend meetings about gesture. This mini-boom is part of the general trend to reconsider what used to be called the epiphenomena of language. In a relatively short amount of time, researchers have shown that speech and gesture, as well as gesture and thought, interact as language is being learned and even after it has been fully acquired.

Traditionally, developmental psychologists thought that children gestured simply because they saw their parents do so. They believed that infants acquired language separate from any gesturing and in a predictable pattern. There was a one-word stage, followed by a two-word stage, and once a child crossed a critical threshold into a three-word stage, her three words very rapidly became many structured sentences. Seen this way, language acquisition was quite miraculous: children went from one word to many in the space of two years.

Experts now agree the picture is more complicated. Strictly speaking, there is no one-word stage. The first sign of language is usually a gesture, which infants will make at about ten months. The best way to think about this process is that it begins with a one-element stage, and that element may be a word or a gesture, such as pointing. If you have ever seen a baby sit and whack his high chair table imperiously, demanding his lunch, you have witnessed the origins of language in the individual. Following the first one-element stage, there is a two-element stage, when word and gesture appear together. This combination can function like a sentence, as when a child says "eat" and points at a banana at the same time. Gesture-and-speech combinations increase between fourteen and twenty-two months. Children also show a three-element stage using both gesture and speech before producing three-elements in speech alone.[10] Following this stage, speech starts to emerge as the prime method of communication.

These findings suggest that gesture doesn't simply precede language but is fundamentally tied to it.[11] In fact gesture and speech are so integral to each other in children that researchers are able to predict a child's language ability at three years of age based on its gesturing at one year. They can also diagnose delays or problems that children might be having with language by examining their gestures.

For a long time the trend was to regard infants, much like animals, as mute and unthinking. Until they learned their first few words, it was thought that not a lot was going on inside their heads. And certainly, if you removed gesture from the language acquisition picture, children did seem eventually to pull language out of thin air. But when you take gesture into account, you can see the preliminary scaffolding of language even before a child has spoken a word, and the acquisition of language, while still incredible, looks a little less mysterious.

Developmental psychologists now talk about the cross-modality of language, meaning that language is expressed in various ways. Instead of the image of a brain issuing language to a mouth, from which it emerges as imperfect speech, think, rather, of language emerging in the child as an expression of its entire body, articulating both limbs and mouth at the same time.

Before the teaching of sign language became widespread, and more recently the use of cochlear implants, the fate of deaf children was contingent on their family situation. Most children who are born without hearing now receive systematic education in schools designed to help them, but there are still rare cases where children who are born deaf do not receive sign language instruction. Whether the reasons are socioeconomic or otherwise, these children are generally spoken to by their parents using normal language and gesture, and they must invent their own ways to express what they want. Susan Goldin-Meadow, who investigates gesture at her laboratory in Chicago, has studied a number of these children. The gestural language they invent is called homesign. Goldin-Meadow's work on homesign and other gestures reveals a great deal about the way the ancient platform of gesture works in modern humans.

The versions of homesign used by each of these children share a number of traits, including the fact that they generally feature a stable list of words and a kind of syntax. Certain words will appear in a particular spot in a sentence depending on the role they take. There is structure in homesign words, as well as in homesign sentences. The symbols that homesigning children invent are not specific to a particular situation or time. For example, they might use a "twist" gesture to ask someone to open a jar, or to indicate that a jar has been twisted open, or to observe that it is possible to twist a jar open. Homesign symbols are also like words in that the number that can be invented appears to be limitless, as well as stable.[12] Even though these children are exposed to a normal combination of gesture and speech by their parents, their own homesign doesn't resemble their parents' gesturing. Children who develop homesign pass through stages of development similar to those of hearing children who are learning speech. Moreover, the linear ordering of elements in a homesign utterance appears to be universal, regardless of the language community the children are born into. Interestingly, if hearing people gesture without speaking, their gestures start to look like the signs of homesigners.

How is it possible that these homesign children who are spoken to (even if they can't hear the words) and gestured at end up gesturing communicatively in the absence of a sign education? Where does this facility for structure and words come from? Goldin-Meadow believes that sentence- and word-level structure are inherent.

Altogether, Goldin-Meadow's studies show that gesture is highly versatile. It is used both with speech and without, and it differs depending on whether it is used with the spoken word. It takes a backseat when it accompanies language, and it becomes much more mimetic when it is used alone. When gesture carries the full burden of communication, says Goldin-Meadow, it becomes much more segmented. She likens it to beads on a string.

Homesign may represent an extreme example of the way that gesture and speech interact, but other recent experiments have demonstrated how speech and gesture can depend on each other. It's been shown that adults will gesture differently depending on the language they are speaking and the way that their language encodes specific concepts, like action. For example, experimenters have compared the idiosyncratic way that Turkish and English speakers describe a cartoon that depicts a character rolling down a hill. Asli Özyürek, a research associate at the Max Planck Institute for Psycholinguistics, compared the performance of children and adults in this task. She showed that initially children produce the same kinds of gestures regardless of the language they are speaking. It takes a while for gesture to take on the characteristic forms of a specific language. When it does, people change their gestures depending on the syntax of the language they are speaking. At this stage, instead of gesture's providing occasional, supplementary meaning to speech without being connected to it in any real way, language and gesture appear to interact online in expression.

In another experiment Goldin-Meadow asked children and adults to solve a particular type of math problem.[13] After they completed the task, the participants were asked to remember a list of words (for the children) and letters (for the adults). Subjects were then asked to explain at a blackboard how they had solved the problem. Goldin-Meadow and her colleagues found that when the experimental subjects gestured during their explanation, they later remembered more from the word list than when they did not gesture. She noted that while people tend to think of gesturing as reflecting an individual's mental state, it appears that gesture contributes to shaping that state. In the case of her subjects, their gesturing somehow lightened the mental load, allowing them to devote more resources to memory.

Gesture interacts with thought and language in other complicated ways. In another experiment Goldin-Meadow asked a group of children to solve a different kind of problem.[14] She then videotaped them describing the solution and noted the way they gestured as they answered. In one case, the children were asked if the amount of water in two identical glasses was the same. (It was.) One of the glasses was then poured into a low and wide dish. The children were asked again if the amount of water was the same. They said it wasn't. They justified their response by describing the height of the water, explaining it's different because this one is taller than that one. As they spoke, some of the children produced what Goldin-Meadow calls a gesture-speech match; that is, they said the amounts of water in the glass and the bowl were unequal, and as they did, they indicated the different heights of the water with their gesture (one hand at one height, the other hand at the other height). Other children who got the problem wrong showed an interesting mismatch between their gesture and their speech. Although these children also said that the amount of the water was different because the height was different, gesturally they indicated the width of the dishes. "This information," said Goldin-Meadow, "when integrated with the information in speech, hints at the correct answer—the water may be higher but it's also skinnier."

The mismatch children suggested by their hand movements that they knew unconsciously what the correct response was. And it turned out that when these children were taught what the relationship between the two amounts of water was after the initial experiment, they were much closer to comprehension than those whose verbal and gestural answers matched—and were wrong.

Gestures also affect listeners. In another experiment children were shown a picture of a character and later asked what he had been wearing. As the researcher posed the question, she made a hat gesture above her head. The children said that the character was wearing a hat even though he wasn't.

Such complicated dependencies and interactions demonstrate that speech and gesture are part of the same system, say Goldin-Meadow and other specialists. Moreover, this system, made up of the two semi-independent subsystems of speech and gesture, is also closely connected to systems of thought. Perhaps we should designate another word entirely for intentional communication that includes gesture and speech. Whatever it should be, Goldin-Meadow and others have demonstrated that this communication is fundamentally embodied.[15]

The most important effect of this research is that it makes it impossible to engage with the evolution of modern language without also considering the evolution of human gesture. Precisely how gesture and speech may have interacted since we split from our common ancestors with chimpanzees is still debated. Michael Corballis, who wrote *From Hand to Mouth: The Origins of Language,* has suggested that quite complicated manual, and possibly facial, gesture may have preceded speech by a significant margin, arising two million years ago when the brains of our ancestors underwent a dramatic burst in size. The transition to independent speech from this gesture language would have occurred gradually as a result of its many benefits, such as communication over long distances and the ability to use hands for other tasks, before the final shift to autonomous spoken language. Other researchers stress how integral gesture is to speech today, arguing that even as the balance of speech and gesture may have shifted within human communication, it is unlikely that gesture would have evolved first without any form of speech. David McNeill, head of the well-known McNeill Laboratory Center for Gesture and Speech Research at the University of Chicago, and his colleagues propose that from the very beginning it is the combination of speech and gestures that were selected in evolution.

NOTES

1. Baboons have a rich repertoire of gestures in addition to the muzzle wipe. The adult males exchange complicated greetings, where they make particular facial expressions, assume certain postures, embrace each other, and briefly handle one another's genitals—kind of like a handshake but with the most vulnerable part of the body.

2. Wallis was introduced by Josep Call, a highly experienced researcher, and afterward, Call showed a video of chimpanzees in the wild, mentioning that he hadn't noticed any muzzle-wipe behavior in the animals. On the spot, Wallis got him to replay

some frames of his video. She pointed out at least five examples of a movement that looked like a muzzle wipe. Call was visibly startled to see the gesture, then he laughed and turned to the audience: he recounted yet another time that Wallis was told by a primatologist that he had never seen the gesture she was talking about. Then, too, Wallis got the primatologist to replay some of his own footage, and she pointed out what he had missed. Some make the case that we've been observing chimpanzees and other animals for so long now—fifty years—we are not going to find anything that would surprise us. And yet until Wallis showed her videos of the baboons' muzzle wipe, it could have been said that there was no evidence for this gesture—despite the fact that it exists and is ubiquitous. Wallis was the only one to see it and take it seriously, and her experience shows how easy it is for experts to miss what is right before their eyes.

Ideally, science would be based on observations of all reality, but it is not like this, and animal science is even less so. Instead, the picture is blotchy. Each researcher who announces findings about animal behavior has made choices along the way about what observations are possible, what they have time for, and what they have money for. For instance, if the available spot to observe a gesturing gorilla is four meters away, the researcher may not be able to note the animal's facial expressions because the faces of gorillas are very dark and hard to see. With a lighter-faced animal, like a chimpanzee, four meters would be no problem. In some cases, this partial gathering of information won't matter, but it's possible the facial expressions accompanying the gestures would alter the conclusions. There are other practical considerations as well. Tomasello observed that it would be interesting to study throwing in chimpanzees, but it's not something that any researcher is willing to do—if they reward throwing behavior, the chimpanzees will start throwing their feces at the researchers.

3. D. A. Leavens and W. D. Hopkins, "The Whole-Hand Point."

4. Orangutans are quite cooperative, as are bonobos, which raises the possibility that we didn't evolve to become cooperative from being noncooperative, but that chimpanzees evolved away from this trait.

5. Tomasello and Hare also ran the experiment with dogs, and the canines had no problem interpreting the cooperative pointing. The researchers attribute the dogs' sensitivity to the human-behavior agenda to their domestication.

6. E. S. Savage-Rumbaugh, "Why Are We Afraid of Apes with Languages?"

7. E. S. Savage-Rumbaugh, S. Shanker, and T. J. Taylor, *Apes, Language, and the Human Mind*.

8. T. M. Pearce, "Did They Talk Their Way Out of Africa?"

9. S. Goldin-Meadow et al., "Explaining Math: Gesturing Lightens the Load."

10. S. Özçaliskan and S. Goldin-Meadow, "Gesture Is at the Cutting Edge of Early Language Development."

11. J. M. Iverson and S. Goldin-Meadow, "Gesture Paves the Way for Language Development."

12. S. Goldin-Meadow, "What Language Creation in the Manual Modality Tells Us About the Foundations of Language."

13. The children were asked to solve problems like $4 + 5 + 3 = ? + 3$. The adults were asked to solve problems like $x^2 - 5x + 6 = (\_)(\_)$. S. Goldin-Meadow et al., "Explaining Math: Gesturing Lightens the Load."

14. S. Goldin-Meadow and S. M. Wagner, "How Our Hands Help Us Learn."

15. In recent years, linguists have studied two very interesting cases where small deaf communities invented a sign language, the first in Nicaragua and the second among the Al-Sayyid Bedouin group in Israel. In both cases, the inception of the language has been pinpointed in time, and the codification of grammar in ensuing generations has been traced. The resulting syntactic conventions are taken as evidence of innate linguistic structure. These investigations are fascinating and important, but whether they reveal innate properties of language is considered controversial. The most salient criticism is that the deaf individuals are communicating with people who already have language. Surely the success or failure of the interpretations made by listeners who are not deaf (including, in the case of the Al-Sayyid Bedouin group, all of the deaf individuals' parents) guides the way the sign language evolves. These issues, which also relate to the investigation of homesign, are yet to be resolved.

REFERENCES

Goldin-Meadow, S., "What Language Creation in the Manual Modality Tells Us About the Foundations of Language," *The Linguistic Review* 22 (2005): 199–225.

Goldin-Meadow, S., H. Nusbaum, S. D. Kelly, and S. Wagner, "Explaining Math: Gesturing Lightens the Load," *Psychological Science* 12 (2001): 516–22.

Goldin-Meadow, S., and S. M. Wagner, "How Our Hands Help Us Learn," *Trends in Cognitive Science* 9 (2006): 234–41.

Iverson, Jana M., and S. Goldin-Meadow, "Gesture Paves the Way for Language Development," *Psychological Science* 16 (2005): 367–71.

Leavens, D. A., and W. D. Hopkins, "The Whole-Hand Point: The Structure and Function of Pointing from a Comparative Perspective," *Journal of Comparative Psychology* 113 (1999): 417–25.

Özçalişkan, S., and S. Goldin-Meadow, "Gesture Is at the Cutting Edge of Early Language Development," *Cognition* 96 (2005): B101–13.

Pearce, T. M., "Did They Talk Their Way Out of Africa?" *Behavioral and Brain Sciences* 26 (2003): 235–36.

Savage-Rumbaugh, E. S., "Why Are We Afraid of Apes with Language?" in Arnold B. Scheibel and J. William Schopf, eds., *The Origin and Evolution of Intelligence* (Boston: Jones and Bartlett, 1997), pp. 43–69.

Savage-Rumbaugh, E. S., S. Shanker, and T. J. Taylor, *Apes, Language, and the Human Mind* (New York: Oxford University Press, 1998).

QUESTIONS FOR MAKING CONNECTIONS WITHIN THE READING

1. Kenneally's article begins with a thought experiment: Imagine describing the house you grew up in to another person. Kenneally asserts that it is "highly likely" that you would see yourself gesturing during your description; she

says, as well, that it is "almost impossible to talk about space without gesturing." Without any mention of gesturing, ask some of your friends and acquaintances to describe places they've lived. What do you notice? Is Kenneally right?

2. At a pivotal point in her article, Kenneally cites Mike Tomasello on the importance of moving beyond questions about why primates don't have language: "A much more productive question, and one that can currently lead us to much more interesting lines of empirical research, is asking why apes do not even point." Why is exploring the absence of certain intentional gestures in primates a better way to go? What does this question make visible that remained unnoticed while researchers were focusing on language alone?

3. Kenneally lists two categories of gestures: attention getters and intention movements. At the end of her article, she notes recent research that unsettles the commonplace understanding of "gesture as reflecting an individual's mental state," suggesting instead that "gesture contributes to that state." Drawing on examples of gestures that Kenneally provides and others from your own experience, fill out the hypothesis that gesture is not simply reflective of a mental state, but also constitutive of it. Do we think before we gesture, or do our gestures enable us to think?

QUESTIONS FOR WRITING

1. After arguing that both speech and gesture "are part of the same system," Kenneally calls for a new word or phrase to designate intentional communication, one emphasizing that such communication "is fundamentally embodied." Both writing and reading surely qualify as intentional communication, and yet it is not immediately evident what role embodiment plays in either one. Like gesture and speech, writing might be said to "coordinate attention," but writing seems uniquely "mental," not physical. And yet if writing is truly disembodied, why does reading sometimes seem to produce powerful physical effects—anger, excitement, titillation, shock?

2. The dominant version of Darwin's theory of evolution focuses on competition and the "survival of the fittest." The research on gesture that Kenneally discusses, however, highlights the importance and the centrality of reciprocation, cooperation, and altruism. "Language," Kenneally states, "is an act of shared attention." Language can obviously be used in the service of aggression and hostility as well as cooperation and altruism, so what is gained by defining language as "an act of shared attention"? How does this differ from saying that language is a means of communication, for example, or a means of persuasion?

QUESTIONS FOR MAKING CONNECTIONS
BETWEEN READINGS

1. Language might be understood as a technology—a tool, in other words, allowing us to act on our surroundings in some manner. Consider, for example, the ways language helps to coordinate the collective actions necessary for social life in its many different forms. But if language is indeed a technology, has it produced "revenge effects" of the sort described by Edward Tenner in "Another Look Back, and a Look Ahead"? Think about the ways that language in our time can be used to deceive and distract—on television, the Web, and in print. In his discussion of revenge effects, Tenner argues that one effective approach is reducing "intensity." What would that mean in the case of language? Right now we are rapidly multiplying avenues of communication. Should we being taking in the opposite tack by using language more sparingly?

2. "Language," Kenneally states, "is an act of shared attention, and without the fundamentally *human* willingness to listen to what another person is saying, language would not work." In what ways might Kenneally's definition expand the range of what we understand as "language"? Drawing on Juhani Pallasmaa's *The Eyes of the Skin*, consider the ways in which buildings might be said to be acts of "shared attention." How might our overemphasis on vision prevent us from recognizing everything that buildings are designed to communicate? If architecture really is a language, and if it addresses all five senses at once, then is it possible for language to include touch, taste, and smell as well as sound and sight?

JON KRAKAUER

Jon Krakauer, a regular contributor to *Outside Magazine,* rose to national prominence with the publication of *Into the Wild,* his investigative account of the life and death of Chris McCandless, a young man who disappeared after graduating from college in Georgia in the early 1990s and whose body was discovered two years later in an abandoned school bus in the wilds of Alaska. The book became the object of renewed interest in the fall of 2007, when Sean Penn adapted it for the screen. In an interview, Krakauer explained why he was driven to pursue McCandless's story in such detail:

> I was haunted by the particulars of the boy's starvation and by vague, unsettling parallels between events in his life and those in my own. Unwilling to let McCandless go, I spent more than a year retracing the convoluted path that led to his death in the Alaskan taiga, chasing down details of his peregrinations with an interest that bordered on obsession. In trying to understand McCandless, I inevitably came to reflect on other, larger subjects as well: the grip wilderness has on the American imagination, the allure high-risk activities hold for young men of a certain mind, the complicated, highly charged bond that exists between fathers and sons.

Retracing McCandless's journey, Krakauer meditates not only on what it now means to be a man but also on the increasingly marginal place of nature in the contemporary world.

After completing *Into the Wild,* Krakauer turned his attention to the tourist industry's trendy guided climbs up Mount Everest. *Into Thin Air,* which also became an instant bestseller, is Krakauer's firsthand account of his experiences on a disastrous trip up Mount Everest that left nine climbers dead after a storm. That this tragedy could have been avoided by staying off the mountain did not escape Krakauer's attention: "When I got back from Everest, I couldn't help but think that maybe I'd devoted my life to something that isn't just selfish and vainglorious and pointless, but actually wrong. There's no way to defend it, even to yourself, once you've been involved in something like this disaster. And yet I've continued to climb."

Why do people choose to put their lives at risk under extreme conditions? This question informs Krakauer's more recent work as well. *Under the Banner of*

Krakauer, Jon. *Into the Wild*. New York: Villard Books, Random House, 1996.

Quotations come from Krakauer's "Everest a Year Later: Lessons in Futility," *Outside,* May 1997 <http://www.outside mag.com/magazine/0597/9705krakauer.html> and Krakauer's author introduction, *Outside* <http://www.outsidemag. com/disc/guest/krakauer/bookintro.html>.

Heaven: A Story of Violent Faith (2003) looks critically at violence and religious revelation in the history of Mormon fundamentalism. In *Where Men Win Glory* (2009), Kraukauer takes on the saga of Pat Tillman, an unconventional NFL star who left his career behind to serve in Iraq—only to get killed by friendly fire, and then to become the subject of a massive government cover-up.

∎ ∎

Selections from
Into the Wild

The Alaska Interior

I wished to acquire the simplicity, native feelings, and virtues of savage life; to divest myself of the factitious habits, prejudices and imperfections of civilization; ... and to find, amidst the solitude and grandeur of the western wilds, more correct views of human nature and of the true interests of man. The season of snows was preferred, that I might experience the pleasure of suffering, and the novelty of danger.

—ESTWICK EVANS
A Pedestrious Tour, of Four Thousand Miles,
Through the Western States and Territories,
During the Winter and Spring of 1818

Wilderness appealed to those bored or disgusted with man and his works. It not only offered an escape from society but also was an ideal stage for the Romantic individual to exercise the cult that he frequently made of his own soul. The solitude and total freedom of the wilderness created a perfect setting for either melancholy or exultation.

—RODERICK NASH
Wilderness and the American Mind

On April 15, 1992, Chris McCandless departed Carthage, South Dakota, in the cab of a Mack truck hauling a load of sunflower seeds. His "great Alaskan odyssey" was under way. Three days later he crossed the Canadian border at Roosville, British Columbia, and thumbed north through Skookumchuck and Radium Junction, Lake Louise and Jasper, Prince George and Dawson Creek—where, in the town center, he took a snapshot of the signpost marking the official start of the Alaska Highway. MILE "0," the sign reads, FAIRBANKS 1,523 MILES.

Hitchhiking tends to be difficult on the Alaska Highway. It's not unusual, on the outskirts of Dawson Creek, to see a dozen or more doleful-looking men and women standing along the shoulder with extended thumbs. Some of them may wait a week or more between rides. But McCandless experienced no such delay. On April 21, just six days out of Carthage, he arrived at Liard River Hotsprings, at the threshold of the Yukon Territory.

There is a public campground at Liard River, from which a boardwalk leads half a mile across a marsh to a series of natural thermal pools. It is the most popular way-stop on the Alaska Highway, and McCandless decided to pause there for a soak in the soothing waters. When he finished bathing and attempted to catch another ride north, however, he discovered that his luck had changed. Nobody would pick him up. Two days after arriving, he was still at Liard River, impatiently going nowhere.

At six-thirty on a brisk Thursday morning, the ground still frozen hard, Gaylord Stuckey walked out on the boardwalk to the largest of the pools, expecting to have the place to himself. He was surprised, therefore, to find someone already in the steaming water, a young man who introduced himself as Alex.

Stuckey—bald and cheerful, a ham-faced sixty-three-year-old Hoosier—was en route from Indiana to Alaska to deliver a new motor home to a Fairbanks RV dealer, a part-time line of work in which he'd dabbled since retiring after forty years in the restaurant business. When he told McCandless his destination, the boy exclaimed, "Hey, that's where I'm going, too! But I've been stuck here for a couple of days now, trying to get a lift. You mind if I ride with you?"

"Oh, jiminy," Stuckey replied. "I'd love to, son, but I can't. The company I work for has a strict rule against picking up hitchhikers. It could get me canned." As he chatted with McCandless through the sulfurous mist, though, Stuckey began to reconsider: "Alex was clean-shaven and had short hair, and I could tell by the language he used that he was a real sharp fella. He wasn't what you'd call a typical hitchhiker. I'm usually leery of 'em. I figure there's probably something wrong with a guy if he can't even afford a bus ticket. So anyway, after about half an hour I said, 'I tell you what, Alex: Liard is a thousand miles from Fairbanks. I'll take you five hundred miles, as far as Whitehorse; you'll be able to get a ride the rest of the way from there.'"

A day and a half later, however, when they arrived in Whitehorse—the capital of the Yukon Territory and the largest, most cosmopolitan town on the Alaska Highway—Stuckey had come to enjoy McCandless's company so much that he changed his mind and agreed to drive the boy the entire distance. "Alex didn't come out and say too much at first," Stuckey reports. "But it's a long, slow drive. We spent a total of three days together on those washboard roads, and by the end he kind of let his guard down. I tell you what: he was a dandy kid. Real courteous, and he didn't cuss or use a lot of that there slang. You could tell he came from a nice family. Mostly he talked about his sister. He didn't get along with his folks too good, I guess. Told me his dad was a genius, a NASA rocket scientist, but he'd been a bigamist at one time—and that kind of went against Alex's grain. Said he hadn't seen his parents in a couple of years, since his college graduation."

McCandless was candid with Stuckey about his intent to spend the summer alone in the bush, living off the land. "He said it was something he'd wanted to do since he was little," says Stuckey. "Said he didn't want to see a single person, no airplanes, no sign of civilization. He wanted to prove to himself that he could make it on his own, without anybody else's help."

Stuckey and McCandless arrived in Fairbanks on the afternoon of April 25. The older man took the boy to a grocery store, where he bought a big bag of rice, "and then Alex said he wanted to go out to the university to study up on what kind of plants he could eat. Berries and things like that. I told him, 'Alex, you're too early. There's still two foot, three foot of snow on the ground. There's nothing growing yet.' But his mind was pretty well made up. He was chomping at the bit to get out there and start hiking." Stuckey drove to the University of Alaska campus, on the west end of Fairbanks, and dropped McCandless off at 5:30 P.M.

"Before I let him out," Stuckey says, "I told him, 'Alex, I've driven you a thousand miles. I've fed you and fed you for three straight days. The least you can do is send me a letter when you get back from Alaska.' And he promised he would.

"I also begged and pleaded with him to call his parents. I can't imagine anything worse than having a son out there and not knowing where he's at for years and years, not knowing whether he's living or dead. 'Here's my credit card number,' I told him. '*Please* call them!' But all he said was 'Maybe I will and maybe I won't.' After he left, I thought, 'Oh, why didn't I get his parents' phone number and call them myself?' But everything just kind of happened so quick."

After dropping McCandless at the university, Stuckey drove into town to deliver the RV to the appointed dealer, only to be told that the person responsible for checking in new vehicles had already gone home for the day and wouldn't be back until Monday morning, leaving Stuckey with two days to kill in Fairbanks before he could fly home to Indiana. On Sunday morning, with time on his hands, he returned to the campus. "I hoped to find Alex and spend another day with him, take him sightseeing or something. I looked for a couple of hours, drove all over the place, but didn't see hide or hair of him. He was already gone."

After taking his leave of Stuckey on Saturday evening, McCandless spent two days and three nights in the vicinity of Fairbanks, mostly at the university. In the campus bookstore, tucked away on the bottom shelf of the Alaska section, he came across a scholarly, exhaustively researched field guide to the region's edible plants, *Tanaina Plantlore/Dena'ina K'et'una: An Ethnobotany of the Dena'ina Indians of Southcentral Alaska* by Priscilla Russell Kari. From a postcard rack near the cash register, he picked out two cards of a polar bear, on which he sent his final messages to Wayne Westerberg and Jan Burres from the university post office.

Perusing the classified ads, McCandless found a used gun to buy, a semiautomatic .22-caliber Remington with a 4x20 scope and a plastic stock. A model called the Nylon 66, no longer in production, it was a favorite of Alaska trappers because of its light weight and reliability. He closed the deal in a parking lot, probably paying about $125 for the weapon, and then purchased four one-hundred-round boxes of hollow-point long-rifle shells from a nearby gun shop.

At the conclusion of his preparations in Fairbanks, McCandless loaded up his pack and started hiking west from the university. Leaving the campus, he walked past the Geophysical Institute, a tall glass-and-concrete building capped with a large satellite dish. The dish, one of the most distinctive landmarks on the Fairbanks skyline, had been erected to collect data from satellites equipped with synthetic aperture radar of Walt McCandless's design. Walt had in fact visited Fairbanks during the start-up of the receiving station and had written some of the software crucial to its operation. If the Geophysical Institute prompted Chris to think of his father as he tramped by, the boy left no record of it.

Four miles west of town, in the evening's deepening chill, McCandless pitched his tent on a patch of hard-frozen ground surrounded by birch trees, not far from the crest of a bluff overlooking Gold Hill Gas & Liquor. Fifty yards from his camp was the terraced road cut of the George Parks Highway, the road that would take him to the Stampede Trail. He woke early on the morning of April 28, walked down to the highway in the predawn gloaming, and was pleasantly surprised when the first vehicle to come along pulled over to give him a lift. It was a gray Ford pickup with a bumper sticker on the back that declared, I FISH THEREFORE I AM. PETERSBURG, ALASKA. The driver of the truck, an electrician on his way to Anchorage, wasn't much older than McCandless. He said his name was Jim Gallien.

Three hours later Gallien turned his truck west off the highway and drove as far as he could down an unplowed side road. When he dropped McCandless off on the Stampede Trail, the temperature was in the low thirties—it would drop into the low teens at night—and a foot and a half of crusty spring snow covered the ground. The boy could hardly contain his excitement. He was, at long last, about to be alone in the vast Alaska wilds.

As he trudged expectantly down the trail in a fake-fur parka, his rifle slung over one shoulder, the only food McCandless carried was a ten-pound bag of long-grained rice—and the two sandwiches and bag of corn chips that Gallien had contributed. A year earlier he'd subsisted for more than a month beside the Gulf of California on five pounds of rice and a bounty of fish caught with a cheap rod and reel, an experience that made him confident he could harvest enough food to survive an extended stay in the Alaska wilderness, too.

The heaviest item in McCandless's half-full backpack was his library: nine or ten paperbound books, most of which had been given to him by Jan Burres in Niland. Among these volumes were titles by Thoreau and Tolstoy and Gogol, but McCandless was no literary snob: he simply carried what he thought he might enjoy reading, including mass-market books by Michael Crichton, Robert Pirsig, and Louis L'Amour. Having neglected to pack writing paper, he began a laconic journal on some blank pages in the back of *Tanaina Plantlore*.

The Healy terminus of the Stampede Trail is traveled by a handful of dog mushers, ski tourers, and snow-machine enthusiasts during the winter months, but only until the frozen rivers begin to break up, in late March or early April. By the time McCandless headed into the bush, there was open water flowing on most of the larger streams, and nobody had been very far down the trail for two or three weeks; only the faint remnants of a packed snow-machine track remained for him to follow.

McCandless reached the Teklanika River his second day out. Although the banks were lined with a jagged shelf of frozen overflow, no ice bridges spanned the channel of open water, so he was forced to wade. There had been a big thaw in early April, and breakup had come early in 1992, but the weather had turned cold again, so the river's volume was quite low when McCandless crossed—probably thigh-deep at most—allowing him to splash to the other side without difficulty. He never suspected that in so doing, he was crossing his Rubicon. To McCandless's inexperienced eye, there was nothing to suggest that two months hence, as the glaciers and snowfields at the Teklanika's headwater thawed in the summer heat, its discharge would multiply nine or ten times in volume, transforming the river into a deep, violent torrent that bore no resemblance to the gentle brook he'd blithely waded across in April.

From his journal we know that on April 29, McCandless fell through the ice somewhere. It probably happened as he traversed a series of melting beaver ponds just beyond the Teklanika's western bank, but there is nothing to indicate that he suffered any harm in the mishap. A day later, as the trail crested a ridge, he got his first glimpse of Mt. McKinley's high, blinding-white bulwarks, and a day after that, May 1, some twenty miles down the trail from where he was dropped by Gallien, he stumbled upon the old bus beside the Sushana River. It was outfitted with a bunk and a barrel stove, and previous visitors had left the improvised shelter stocked with matches, bug dope, and other essentials. "Magic Bus Day," he wrote in his journal. He decided to lay over for a while in the vehicle and take advantage of its crude comforts.

He was elated to be there. Inside the bus, on a sheet of weathered plywood spanning a broken window, McCandless scrawled an exultant declaration of independence:

TWO YEARS HE WALKS THE EARTH. NO PHONE, NO POOL, NO PETS, NO CIGARETTES. ULTIMATE FREEDOM. AN EXTREMIST. AN AESTHETIC VOYAGER WHOSE HOME IS <u>THE ROAD</u>. ESCAPED FROM ATLANTA. THOU SHALT NOT RETURN, 'CAUSE "THE WEST <u>IS</u> THE BEST." AND NOW AFTER TWO RAMBLING YEARS COMES THE FINAL AND GREATEST ADVENTURE. THE CLIMACTIC BATTLE TO KILL THE FALSE BEING WITHIN AND VICTORIOUSLY CONCLUDE THE SPIRITUAL PILGRIMAGE. TEN DAYS AND NIGHTS OF FREIGHT TRAINS AND HITCHHIKING BRING HIM TO THE GREAT WHITE NORTH. NO LONGER TO BE POISONED BY CIVILIZATION HE FLEES, AND WALKS ALONE UPON THE LAND TO BECOME LOST <u>IN THE WILD</u>.

—ALEXANDER SUPERTRAMP
May 1992

Reality, however, was quick to intrude on McCandless's reverie. He had difficulty killing game, and the daily journal entries during his first week in the bush include "Weakness," "Snowed in," and "Disaster." He saw but did not shoot a grizzly on May 2, shot at but missed some ducks on May 4, and finally killed and ate a spruce grouse on May 5; but he didn't shoot anything else until May 9, when he bagged a single small squirrel, by which point he'd written "4th day famine" in the journal.

But soon thereafter his fortunes took a sharp turn for the better. By mid-May the sun was circling high in the heavens, flooding the taiga with light. The sun dipped below the northern horizon for fewer than four hours out of every twenty-four, and at midnight the sky was still bright enough to read by. Everywhere but on the north-facing slopes and in the shadowy ravines, the snowpack had melted down to bare ground, exposing the previous season's rose hips and lingonberries, which McCandless gathered and ate in great quantity.

He also became much more successful at hunting game and for the next six weeks feasted regularly on squirrel, spruce grouse, duck, goose, and porcupine. On May 22, a crown fell off one of his molars, but the event didn't seem to dampen his spirits much, because the following day he scrambled up the nameless, humplike, three-thousand-foot butte that rises directly north of the bus, giving him a view of the whole icy sweep of the Alaska Range and mile after mile of uninhabited country. His journal entry for the day is characteristically terse but unmistakably joyous: "CLIMB MOUNTAIN!"

McCandless had told Gallien that he intended to remain on the move during his stay in the bush. "I'm just going to take off and keep walking west," he'd said. "I might walk all the way to the Bering Sea." On May 5, after pausing for four days at the bus, he resumed his perambulation. From the snapshots recovered with his Minolta, it appears that McCandless lost (or intentionally left) the by now indistinct Stampede Trail and headed west and north through the hills above the Sushana River, hunting game as he went.

It was slow going. In order to feed himself, he had to devote a large part of each day to stalking animals. Moreover, as the ground thawed, his route turned into a gauntlet of boggy muskeg and impenetrable alder, and McCandless belatedly came to appreciate one of the fundamental (if counterintuitive) axioms of the North: winter, not summer, is the preferred season for traveling overland through the bush.

Faced with the obvious folly of his original ambition, to walk five hundred miles to tidewater, he reconsidered his plans. On May 19, having traveled no farther west than the Toklat River—less than fifteen miles beyond the bus—he turned around. A week later he was back at the derelict vehicle, apparently without regret. He'd decided that the Sushana drainage was plenty wild to suit his purposes and that Fairbanks bus 142 would make a fine base camp for the remainder of the summer.

Ironically, the wilderness surrounding the bus—the patch of overgrown country where McCandless was determined "to become lost in the wild"— scarcely qualifies as wilderness by Alaska standards. Less than thirty miles to the east is a major thoroughfare, the George Parks Highway. Just sixteen miles to the north, beyond an escarpment of the Outer Range, hundreds of tourists rumble daily into Denali Park over a road patrolled by the National Park Service. And unbeknownst to the Aesthetic Voyager, scattered within a six-mile radius of the bus are four cabins (although none happened to be occupied during the summer of 1992).

But despite the relative proximity of the bus to civilization, for all practical purposes McCandless was cut off from the rest of the world. He spent nearly four months in the bush all told, and during that period he didn't encounter another living soul. In the end the Sushana River site was sufficiently remote to cost him his life.

In the last week of May, after moving his few possessions into the bus, McCandless wrote a list of housekeeping chores on a parchmentlike strip of birch bark: collect and store ice from the river for refrigerating meat, cover the vehicle's missing windows with plastic, lay in a supply of firewood, clean the accumulation of old ash from the stove. And under the heading "LONG TERM" he drew up a list of more ambitious tasks: map the area, improvise a bathtub, collect skins and feathers to sew into clothing, construct a bridge across a nearby creek, repair mess kit, blaze a network of hunting trails.

The diary entries following his return to the bus catalog a bounty of wild meat. May 28: "Gourmet Duck!" June 1: "5 Squirrel." June 2: "Porcupine, Ptarmigan, 4 Squirrel, Grey Bird." June 3: "Another Porcupine! 4 Squirrel, 2 Grey Bird, Ash Bird." June 4: "A THIRD PORCUPINE! Squirrel, Grey Bird." On June 5, he shot a Canada goose as big as a Christmas turkey. Then, on June 9, he bagged the biggest prize of all: "MOOSE!" he recorded in the journal. Overjoyed, the proud hunter took a photograph of himself kneeling over his trophy, rifle thrust triumphantly overhead, his features distorted in a rictus of ecstasy and amazement, like some unemployed janitor who'd gone to Reno and won a million-dollar jackpot.

Although McCandless was enough of a realist to know that hunting game was an unavoidable component of living off the land, he had always been ambivalent about killing animals. That ambivalence turned to remorse soon after he shot the moose. It was relatively small, weighing perhaps six hundred or seven hundred pounds, but it nevertheless amounted to a huge quantity of meat. Believing that it was morally indefensible to waste any part of an animal that has been shot for food, McCandless spent six days toiling to preserve what he had killed before it spoiled. He butchered the carcass under a thick cloud of flies and mosquitoes, boiled the organs into a stew, and then laboriously excavated a burrow in the face of the rocky stream bank directly below the bus, in which he tried to cure, by smoking, the immense slabs of purple flesh.

Alaskan hunters know that the easiest way to preserve meat in the bush is to slice it into thin strips and then air-dry it on a makeshift rack. But McCandless, in his naïveté, relied on the advice of hunters he'd consulted in South Dakota, who advised him to smoke his meat, not an easy task under the circumstances. "Butchering extremely difficult," he wrote in the journal on June 10. "Fly and mosquito hordes. Remove intestines, liver, kidneys, one lung, steaks. Get hindquarters and leg to stream."

June 11: "Remove heart and other lung. Two front legs and head. Get rest to stream. Haul near cave. Try to protect with smoker."

June 12: "Remove half rib-cage and steaks. Can only work nights. Keep smokers going."

June 13: "Get remainder of rib-cage, shoulder and neck to cave. Start smoking."

June 14: "Maggots already! Smoking appears ineffective. Don't know, looks like disaster. I now wish I had never shot the moose. One of the greatest tragedies of my life."

At that point he gave up on preserving the bulk of the meat and abandoned the carcass to the wolves. Although he castigated himself severely for this waste of a life he'd taken, a day later McCandless appeared to regain some perspective, for his journal notes, "henceforth will learn to accept my errors, however great they be."

Shortly after the moose episode, McCandless began to read Thoreau's *Walden*. In the chapter titled "Higher Laws," in which Thoreau ruminates on the morality of eating, McCandless highlighted, "when I had caught and cleaned and cooked and eaten my fish, they seemed not to have fed me essentially. It was insignificant and unnecessary, and cost more than it came to."

"THE MOOSE," McCandless wrote in the margin. And in the same passage he marked,

> *The repugnance to animal food is not the effect of experience, but is an instinct. It appeared more beautiful to live low and fare hard in many respects; and though I never did so, I went far enough to please my imagination. I believe that every man who has ever been earnest to preserve his higher or poetic faculties in the best condition has been particularly inclined to abstain from animal food, and from much food of any kind....*
>
> *It is hard to provide and cook so simple and clean a diet as will not offend the imagination; but this, I think, is to be fed when we feed the body; they should both sit down at the same table. Yet perhaps this may be done. The fruits eaten temperately need not make us ashamed of our appetites, nor interrupt the worthiest pursuits. But put an extra condiment into your dish, and it will poison you.*

"YES," wrote McCandless and, two pages later, "*Consciousness* of food. Eat and cook with *concentration*.... Holy Food." On the back pages of the book that served as his journal, he declared:

> *I am reborn. This is my dawn. Real life has just begun.*
>
> *Deliberate Living*: *Conscious attention to the basics of life, and a constant attention to your immediate environment and its concerns, example → A job, a task, a book; anything requiring efficient concentration (Circumstance has no value. It is how one relates to a situation that has value. All true meaning resides in the personal relationship to a phenomenon, what it means to you).*
>
> *The Great Holiness of* **FOOD,** *the Vital Heat.*
> *Positivism, the Insurpassable Joy of the Life Aesthetic.*
> *Absolute Truth and Honesty.*
> *Reality.*
> *Independence.*
> *Finality—Stability—Consistency.*

As McCandless gradually stopped rebuking himself for the waste of the moose, the contentment that began in mid-May resumed and seemed to continue through early July. Then, in the midst of this idyll, came the first of two pivotal setbacks.

Satisfied, apparently, with what he had learned during his two months of solitary life in the wild, McCandless decided to return to civilization: it was time to bring his "final and greatest adventure" to a close and get himself back to the world of men and women, where he could chug a beer, talk philosophy, enthrall strangers with tales of what he'd done. He seemed to have moved beyond his need to assert so adamantly his autonomy, his need to separate himself from his parents. Maybe he was prepared to forgive their imperfections; maybe he was even prepared to forgive some of his own. McCandless seemed ready, perhaps, to go home.

Or maybe not; we can do no more than speculate about what he intended to do after he walked out of the bush. There is no question, however, that he intended to walk out.

Writing on a piece of birch bark, he made a list of things to do before he departed: "Patch Jeans, Shave!, Organize pack...." Shortly thereafter he propped his Minolta on an empty oil drum and took a snapshot of himself brandishing a yellow disposable razor and grinning at the camera, clean-shaven, with new patches cut from an army blanket stitched onto the knees of his filthy jeans. He looks healthy but alarmingly gaunt. Already his cheeks are sunken. The tendons in his neck stand out like taut cables.

On July 2, McCandless finished reading Tolstoy's "Family Happiness," having marked several passages that moved him:

> IIe was right in saying that the only certain happiness in life is to live for others....
>
> I have lived through much, and now I think I have found what is needed for happiness. A quiet secluded life in the country, with the possibility of being useful to people to whom it is easy to do good, and who are not accustomed to have it done to them; then work which one hopes may be of some use; then rest, nature, books, music, love for one's neighbor—such is my idea of happiness. And then, on top of all that, you for a mate, and children, perhaps—what more can the heart of a man desire?

Then, on July 3, he shouldered his backpack and began the twenty-mile hike to the improved road. Two days later, halfway there, he arrived in heavy rain at the beaver ponds that blocked access to the west bank of the Teklanika River. In April they'd been frozen over and hadn't presented an obstacle. Now he must have been alarmed to find a three-acre lake covering the trail. To avoid having to wade through the murky chest-deep water, he scrambled up a steep hillside, bypassed the ponds on the north, and then dropped back down to the river at the mouth of the gorge.

When he'd first crossed the river, sixty-seven days earlier in the freezing temperatures of April, it had been an icy but gentle knee-deep creek, and he'd simply strolled across it. On July 5, however, the Teklanika was at full flood, swollen with rain and snowmelt from glaciers high in the Alaska Range, running cold and fast.

If he could reach the far shore, the remainder of the hike to the highway would be easy, but to get there he would have to negotiate a channel some one hundred feet wide. The water, opaque with glacial sediment and only a few degrees warmer than the ice it had so recently been, was the color of wet concrete. Too deep to wade, it rumbled like a freight train. The powerful current would quickly knock him off his feet and carry him away.

McCandless was a weak swimmer and had confessed to several people that he was in fact afraid of the water. Attempting to swim the numbingly cold torrent or even to paddle some sort of improvised raft across seemed too risky to consider. Just downstream from where the trail met the river, the Teklanika erupted into a chaos of boiling whitewater as it accelerated through the narrow gorge. Long before he could swim or paddle to the far shore, he'd be pulled into these rapids and drowned.

In his journal he now wrote, "Disaster.... Rained in. River look impossible. Lonely, scared." He concluded, correctly, that he would probably be swept to his death if he attempted to cross the Teklanika at that place, in those conditions. It would be suicidal; it was simply not an option.

If McCandless had walked a mile or so upstream, he would have discovered that the river broadened into a maze of braided channels. If he'd scouted carefully, by trial and error he might have found a place where these braids were only chest-deep. As strong as the current was running, it would have certainly knocked him off his feet, but by dog-paddling and hopping along the bottom as he drifted downstream, he could conceivably have made it across before being carried into the gorge or succumbing to hypothermia.

But it would still have been a very risky proposition, and at that point McCandless had no reason to take such a risk. He'd been fending for himself quite nicely in the country. He probably understood that if he was patient and waited, the river would eventually drop to a level where it could be safely forded. After weighing his options, therefore, he settled on the most prudent course. He turned around and began walking to the west, back toward the bus, back into the fickle heart of the bush.

The Stampede Trail

Nature was here something savage and awful, though beautiful. I looked with awe at the ground I trod on, to see what the Powers had made there, the form and fashion and material of their work. This was that Earth of which we have heard, made out of Chaos and Old Night. Here was no man's garden, but the unhandselled globe. It was not lawn, nor pasture, nor mead, nor woodland, nor lea, nor arable, nor waste land. It was the fresh and natural surface of the planet Earth, as it was made forever and ever,—to be the dwelling of man, we say,—so Nature made it, and man may use it if he can. Man was not to be associated with it. It was Matter, vast, terrific,—not his Mother Earth that we have heard of, not for him to tread on, or to be buried in,—no, it were being too familiar even to let his bones lie there,—the home, this, of Necessity and Fate. There was clearly felt the presence of a force not bound to be kind to man. It was a place of heathenism and superstitious rites,—to be inhabited by men nearer of kin to the rocks and to wild animals than we.... What is it to be admitted to a museum, to see a myriad of particular things, compared with being shown some star's surface, some hard matter in its home! I stand in awe of my body, this matter to which I am bound has become so strange to me. I fear not spirits, ghosts, of which I am one,—that my body might,—but I fear bodies, I tremble to meet them. What is this Titan that has possession of me? Talk of mysteries! Think of our life in nature,—daily to be shown matter, to come in contact with it,—rocks, trees, wind on our cheeks! the solid earth! the actual world! the common sense! Contact! Contact! Who are we? where are we?

—HENRY DAVID THOREAU
"Ktaadn"

A year and a week after Chris McCandless decided not to attempt to cross the Teklanika River, I stand on the opposite bank—the eastern side, the highway side—and gaze into the churning water. I, too, hope to cross the river. I want to visit the bus. I want to see where McCandless died, to better understand why.

It is a hot, humid afternoon, and the river is livid with runoff from the fast-melting snowpack that still blankets the glaciers in the higher elevations of the Alaska Range. Today the water looks considerably lower than it looks in the photographs McCandless took twelve months ago, but to try to ford the river here, in thundering midsummer flood, is nevertheless unthinkable. The water is too deep, too cold, too fast. As I stare into the Teklanika, I can hear rocks the size of bowling balls grinding along the bottom, rolled downstream by the powerful current. I'd be swept from my feet within a few yards of leaving the bank and pushed into the canyon immediately below, which pinches the river into a boil of rapids that continues without interruption for the next five miles.

Unlike McCandless, however, I have in my backpack a 1:63,360-scale topographic map (that is, a map on which one inch represents one mile). Exquisitely detailed, it indicates that half a mile downstream, in the throat of the canyon, is a gauging station that was built by the U.S. Geological Survey. Unlike McCandless, too, I am here with three companions: Alaskans Roman Dial and Dan Solie and a friend of Roman's from California, Andrew Liske. The gauging station can't be seen from where the Stampede Trail comes down to the river, but after twenty minutes of fighting our way through a snarl of spruce and dwarf birch, Roman shouts, "I see it! There! A hundred yards farther."

We arrive to find an inch-thick steel cable spanning the gorge, stretched between a fifteen-foot tower on our side of the river and an outcrop on the far shore, four hundred feet away. The cable was erected in 1970 to chart the Teklanika's seasonal fluctuations; hydrologists traveled back and forth above the river by means of an aluminum basket that is suspended from the cable with pulleys. From the basket they would drop a weighted plumb line to measure the river's depth. The station was decommissioned nine years ago for lack of funds, at which time the basket was supposed to be chained and locked to the tower on our side—the highway side—of the river. When we climbed to the top of the tower, however, the basket wasn't there. Looking across the rushing water, I could see it over on the distant shore—the bus side—of the canyon.

Some local hunters, it turns out, had cut the chain, ridden the basket across, and secured it to the far side in order to make it harder for outsiders to cross the Teklanika and trespass on their turf. When McCandless tried to walk out of the bush one year ago the previous week, the basket was in the same place it is now, on his side of the canyon. If he'd known about it, crossing the Teklanika to safety would have been a trivial matter. Because he had no topographic map, however, he had no way of conceiving that salvation was so close at hand.

Andy Horowitz, one of McCandless's friends on the Woodson High cross-country team, had mused that Chris "was born into the wrong century. He was looking for more adventure and freedom than today's society gives people." In coming to Alaska, McCandless yearned to wander uncharted country, to find a blank spot on the map. In 1992, however, there were no more blank spots on the map—not in Alaska, not anywhere. But Chris, with his idiosyncratic logic, came up with an elegant solution to this dilemma: he simply got rid of the map. In his own mind, if nowhere else, the *terra* would thereby remain *incognita*.

Because he lacked a good map, the cable spanning the river also remained in-cognito. Studying the Teklanika's violent flow, McCandless thus mistakenly con-cluded that it was impossible to reach the eastern shore. Thinking that his escape route had been cut off, he returned to the bus—a reasonable course of action, given his topographical ignorance. But why did he then stay at the bus and starve? Why, come August, didn't he try once more to cross the Teklanika, when it would have been running significantly lower, when it would have been safe to ford?

Puzzled by these questions, and troubled, I am hoping that the rusting hulk of Fairbanks bus 142 will yield some clues. But to reach the bus, I, too, need to cross the river, and the aluminum tram is still chained to the far shore.

Standing atop the tower anchoring the eastern end of the span, I attach my-self to the cable with rock-climbing hardware and begin to pull myself across, hand over hand, executing what mountaineers call a Tyrolean traverse. This turns out to be a more strenuous proposition than I had anticipated. Twenty minutes after starting out, I finally haul myself onto the outcrop on the other side, completely spent, so wasted I can barely raise my arms. After at last catching my breath, I climb into the basket—a rectangular aluminum car two feet wide by four feet long—disconnect the chain, and head back to the eastern side of the canyon to ferry my companions across.

The cable sags noticeably over the middle of the river; so when I cut loose from the outcrop, the car accelerates quickly under its own weight, rolling faster and faster along the steel strand, seeking the lowest point. It's a thrilling ride. Zipping over the rapids at twenty or thirty miles per hour, I hear an involuntary bark of fright leap from my throat before I realize that I'm in no danger and regain my composure.

After all four of us are on the western side of the gorge, thirty minutes of rough bushwhacking returns us to the Stampede Trail. The ten miles of trail we have already covered—the section between our parked vehicles and the river—were gentle, well marked, and relatively heavily traveled. But the ten miles to come have an utterly different character.

Because so few people cross the Teklanika during the spring and summer months, much of the route is indistinct and overgrown with brush. Immediately past the river the trail curves to the southwest, up the bed of a fast-flowing creek. And because beavers have built a network of elaborate dams across this creek, the route leads directly through a three-acre expanse of standing water. The beaver ponds are never more than chest deep, but the water is cold, and as we slosh forward, our feet churn the muck on the bottom into a foul-smelling miasma of decomposing slime.

The trail climbs a hill beyond the uppermost pond, then rejoins the twisting, rocky creek bed before ascending again into a jungle of scrubby vegetation. The going never gets exceedingly difficult, but the fifteen-foot-high tangle of alder pressing in from both sides is gloomy, claustrophobic, oppressive. Clouds of mosquitoes materialize out of the sticky heat. Every few minutes the insects' piercing whine is supplanted by the boom of distant thunder, rumbling over the taiga from a wall of thunderheads rearing darkly on the horizon.

Thickets of buckbrush leave a crosshatch of bloody lacerations on my shins. Piles of bear scat on the trail and, at one point, a set of fresh grizzly tracks—each print half again as long as a size-nine boot print—put me on edge. None of us has a gun. "Hey, Griz!" I yell at the undergrowth, hoping to avoid a surprise encounter. "Hey, bear! Just passing through! No reason to get riled!"

I have been to Alaska some twenty times during the past twenty years—to climb mountains, to work as a carpenter and a commercial salmon fisherman and a journalist, to goof off, to poke around. I've spent a lot of time alone in the country over the course of my many visits and usually relish it. Indeed, I had intended to make this trip to the bus by myself, and when my friend Roman invited himself and two others along, I was annoyed. Now, however, I am grateful for their company. There is something disquieting about this Gothic, overgrown landscape. It feels more malevolent than other, more remote corners of the state I know—the tundra-wrapped slopes of the Brooks Range, the cloud forests of the Alexander Archipelago, even the frozen, gale-swept heights of the Denali massif. I'm happy as hell that I'm not here alone.

At 9:00 P.M. we round a bend in the trail, and there, at the edge of a small clearing, is the bus. Pink bunches of fireweed choke the vehicle's wheel wells, growing higher than the axles. Fairbanks bus 142 is parked beside a coppice of aspen, ten yards back from the brow of a modest cliff, on a shank of high ground overlooking the confluence of the Sushana River and a smaller tributary. It's an appealing setting, open and filled with light. It's easy to see why McCandless decided to make this his base camp.

We pause some distance away from the bus and stare at it for a while in silence. Its paint is chalky and peeling. Several windows are missing. Hundreds of delicate bones litter the clearing around the vehicle, scattered among thousands of porcupine quills: the remains of the small game that made up the bulk of McCandless's diet. And at the perimeter of this boneyard lies one much larger skeleton: that of the moose he shot, and subsequently agonized over.

When I'd questioned Gordon Samel and Ken Thompson shortly after they'd discovered McCandless's body, both men insisted—adamantly and unequivocally— that the big skeleton was the remains of a caribou, and they derided the greenhorn's ignorance in mistaking the animal he killed for a moose. "Wolves had scattered the bones some," Thompson had told me, "but it was obvious that the animal was a caribou. The kid didn't know what the hell he was doing up here."

"It was definitely a caribou," Samel had scornfully piped in. "When I read in the paper that he thought he'd shot a moose, that told me right there he wasn't no Alaskan. There's a big difference between a moose and a caribou. A real big difference. You'd have to be pretty stupid not to be able to tell them apart."

Trusting Samel and Thompson, veteran Alaskan hunters who've killed many moose and caribou between them, I duly reported McCandless's mistake in the article I wrote for *Outside,* thereby confirming the opinion of countless readers that McCandless was ridiculously ill prepared, that he had no business heading into any wilderness, let alone into the big-league wilds of the Last Frontier. Not only did McCandless die because he was stupid, one Alaska correspondent observed, but "the scope of his self-styled adventure was so small as to ring pathetic—squatting in a wrecked bus a few miles out of Healy, potting jays and squirrels, mistaking a caribou for a moose (pretty hard to do).... Only one word for the guy: incompetent."

Among the letters lambasting McCandless, virtually all those I received mentioned his misidentification of the caribou as proof that he didn't know the first thing about surviving in the back country. What the angry letter writers didn't know, however, was that the ungulate McCandless shot was exactly what he'd said it was. Contrary to what I reported in *Outside,* the animal was a moose, as a close examination of the beast's remains now indicated and several of McCandless's photographs of the kill later confirmed beyond all doubt. The boy made some mistakes on the Stampede Trail, but confusing a caribou with a moose wasn't among them.

Walking past the moose bones, I approach the vehicle and step through an emergency exit at the back. Immediately inside the door is the torn mattress, stained and moldering, on which McCandless expired. For some reason I am taken aback to find a collection of his possessions spread across its ticking: a green plastic canteen; a tiny bottle of water-purification tablets; a used-up cylinder of Chap Stick; a pair of insulated flight pants of the type sold in military-surplus stores; a paperback copy of the bestseller *0 Jerusalem!,* its spine broken; wool mittens; a bottle of Muskol insect repellent; a full box of matches; and a pair of brown rubber work boots with the name Gallien written across the cuffs in faint black ink.

Despite the missing windows, the air inside the cavernous vehicle is stale and musty. "Wow," Roman remarks. "It smells like dead birds in here." A moment later I come across the source of the odor: a plastic garbage bag filled with feathers, down, and the severed wings of several birds. It appears that McCandless was saving them to insulate his clothing or perhaps to make a feather pillow.

Toward the front of the bus, McCandless's pots and dishes are stacked on a makeshift plywood table beside a kerosene lamp. A long leather scabbard is expertly tooled with the initials R. F.: the sheath for the machete Ronald Franz gave McCandless when he left Salton City.

The boy's blue toothbrush rests next to a half-empty tube of Colgate, a packet of dental floss, and the gold molar crown that, according to his journal, fell off his tooth three weeks into his sojourn. A few inches away sits a skull the size of a watermelon, thick ivory fangs jutting from its bleached maxillae. It is a bear skull, the remains of a grizzly shot by someone who visited the bus years before McCandless's tenure. A message scratched in Chris's tidy hand brackets a cranial bullet hole: ALL HAIL THE PHANTOM BEAR, THE BEST WITHIN US ALL. ALEXANDER SUPERTRAMP, MAY 1992.

Looking up, I notice that the sheet-metal walls of the vehicle are covered with graffiti left by numerous visitors over the years. Roman points out a message he wrote when he stayed in the bus four years ago, during a traverse of the Alaska Range: NOODLE EATERS EN ROUTE TO LAKE CLARK 8/89. Like Roman, most people scrawled little more than their names and a date. The longest, most eloquent graffito is one of several inscribed by McCandless, the proclamation of joy that begins with a nod to his favorite Roger Miller song: TWO YEARS HE WALKS THE EARTH, NO PHONE, NO POOL, NO PETS, NO CIGARETTES. ULTIMATE FREEDOM. AN EXTREMIST. AN AESTHETIC VOYAGER WHOSE NAME IS THE ROAD....

Immediately below this manifesto squats the stove, fabricated from a rusty oil drum. A twelve-foot section of a spruce trunk is jammed into its open doorway, and across the log are draped two pairs of torn Levi's, laid out as if to dry. One pair of jeans—waist thirty, inseam thirty-two—is patched crudely with silver duct tape; the other pair has been repaired more carefully, with scraps from a faded bedspread stitched over gaping holes in the knees and seat. This latter pair also sports a belt fashioned from a strip of blanket. McCandless, it occurs to me, must have been forced to make the belt after growing so thin that his pants wouldn't stay up without it.

Sitting down on a steel cot across from the stove to mull over this eerie tableau, I encounter evidence of McCandless's presence wherever my vision rests. Here are his toenail clippers, over there his green nylon tent spread over a missing window in the front door. His Kmart hiking boots are arranged neatly beneath the stove, as though he'd soon be returning to lace them up and hit the trail. I feel uncomfortable, as if I were intruding, a voyeur who has slipped into McCandless's bedroom while he is momentarily away. Suddenly queasy, I stumble out of the bus to walk along the river and breathe some fresh air.

An hour later we build a fire outside in the fading light. The rain squalls, now past, have rinsed the haze from the atmosphere, and distant, backlit hills stand out in crisp detail. A stripe of incandescent sky burns beneath the cloud base on the northwestern horizon. Roman unwraps some steaks from a moose he shot in the Alaska Range last September and lays them across the fire on a blackened grill, the grill McCandless used for broiling his game. Moose fat pops and sizzles into the coals. Eating the gristly meat with our fingers, we slap at mosquitoes and talk about this peculiar person whom none of us ever met, trying to get a handle on how he came to grief, trying to understand why some people seem to despise him so intensely for having died here.

By design McCandless came into the country with insufficient provisions, and he lacked certain pieces of equipment deemed essential by many Alaskans: a large-caliber rifle, map and compass, an ax. This has been regarded as evidence not just of stupidity but of the even greater sin of arrogance. Some critics have even drawn parallels between McCandless and the Arctic's most infamous tragic figure, Sir John Franklin, a nineteenth-century British naval officer whose smugness and hauteur contributed to some 140 deaths, including his own.

In 1819, the Admiralty assigned Franklin to lead an expedition into the wilderness of northwestern Canada. Two years out of England, winter overtook his small party as they plodded across an expanse of tundra so vast and empty that they christened it the Barrens, the name by which it is still known. Their food ran out. Game was scarce, forcing Franklin and his men to subsist on lichens scraped from boulders, singed deer hide, scavenged animal bones, their own boot leather, and finally one another's flesh. Before the ordeal was over, at least two men had been murdered and eaten, the suspected murderer had been summarily executed, and eight others were dead from sickness and starvation. Franklin was himself within a day or two of expiring when he and the other survivors were rescued by a band of métis.

An affable Victorian gentleman, Franklin was said to be a good-natured bumbler, dogged and clueless, with the naïve ideals of a child and a disdain for acquiring backcountry skills. He had been woefully unprepared to lead an Arctic expedition, and upon returning to England, he was known as the Man Who Ate His Shoes—yet the sobriquet was uttered more often with awe than with ridicule. He was hailed as a national hero, promoted to the rank of captain by the Admiralty, paid handsomely to write an account of his ordeal, and, in 1825, given command of a second Arctic expedition.

That trip was relatively uneventful, but in 1845, hoping finally to discover the fabled Northwest Passage, Franklin made the mistake of returning to the Arctic for a third time. He and the 128 men under his command were never heard from again. Evidence unearthed by the forty-odd expeditions sent to search for them eventually established that all had perished, the victims of scurvy, starvation, and unspeakable suffering.

When McCandless turned up dead, he was likened to Franklin not simply because both men starved but also because both were perceived to have lacked a requisite humility; both were thought to have possessed insufficient respect for the land. A century after Franklin's death, the eminent explorer Vilhjalmur Stefansson pointed out that the English explorer had never taken the trouble to learn the survival skills practiced by the Indians and the Eskimos—peoples who had managed to flourish "for generations, bringing up their children and taking care of their aged" in the same harsh country that killed Franklin. (Stefansson conveniently neglected to mention that many, many Indians and Eskimos have starved in the northern latitudes, as well.)

McCandless's arrogance was not of the same strain as Franklin's, however. Franklin regarded nature as an antagonist that would inevitably submit to force, good breeding, and Victorian discipline. Instead of living in concert with the land, instead of relying on the country for sustenance as the natives did, he attempted to insulate himself from the northern environment with ill-suited military tools and traditions. McCandless, on the other hand, went too far in the opposite direction. He tried to live entirely off the country—and he tried to do it without bothering to master beforehand the full repertoire of crucial skills.

It probably misses the point, though, to castigate McCandless for being ill prepared. He was green, and he overestimated his resilience, but he was sufficiently skilled to last for sixteen weeks on little more than his wits and ten pounds of rice. And he was fully aware when he entered the bush that he had given himself a perilously slim margin for error. He knew precisely what was at stake.

It is hardly unusual for a young man to be drawn to a pursuit considered reckless by his elders; engaging in risky behavior is a rite of passage in our culture no less than in most others. Danger has always held a certain allure. That, in large part, is why so many teenagers drive too fast and drink too much and take too many drugs, why it has always been so easy for nations to recruit young men to go to war. It can be argued that youthful derring-do is in fact evolutionarily adaptive, a behavior encoded in our genes. McCandless, in his fashion, merely took risk-taking to its logical extreme.

He had a need to test himself in ways, as he was fond of saying, "that mattered." He possessed grand—some would say grandiose—spiritual ambitions. According to the moral absolutism that characterizes McCandless's beliefs, a challenge in which a successful outcome is assured isn't a challenge at all.

It is not merely the young, of course, who are drawn to hazardous undertakings. John Muir is remembered primarily as a no-nonsense conservationist and the founding president of the Sierra Club, but he was also a bold adventurer, a fearless scrambler of peaks, glaciers, and waterfalls whose best-known essay includes a riveting account of nearly falling to his death, in 1872, while ascending California's Mt. Ritter. In another essay Muir rapturously describes riding out a ferocious Sierra gale, by choice, in the uppermost branches of a one-hundred-foot Douglas fir:

> [N]ever before did I enjoy so noble an exhilaration of motion. *The slender tops fairly flapped and swished in the passionate torrent, bending and swirling backward and forward, round and round, tracing indescribable combinations of vertical and horizontal curves, while I clung with muscles firm braced, like a bobolink on a reed.*

He was thirty-six years old at the time. One suspects that Muir wouldn't have thought McCandless terribly odd or incomprehensible.

Even staid, prissy Thoreau, who famously declared that it was enough to have "traveled a good deal in Concord," felt compelled to visit the more fearsome wilds of nineteenth-century Maine and climb Mt. Katahdin. His ascent of the peak's "savage and awful, though beautiful" ramparts shocked and frightened him, but it also induced a giddy sort of awe. The disquietude he felt on Katahdin's granite heights inspired some of his most powerful writing and profoundly colored the way he thought thereafter about the earth in its coarse, undomesticated state.

Unlike Muir and Thoreau, McCandless went into the wilderness not primarily to ponder nature or the world at large but, rather, to explore the inner country of his own soul. He soon discovered, however, what Muir and Thoreau already knew: an extended stay in the wilderness inevitably directs one's attention outward as much as inward, and it is impossible to live off the land without developing both a subtle understanding of, and a strong emotional bond with, that land and all it holds.

The entries in McCandless's journal contain few abstractions about wilderness or, for that matter, few ruminations of any kind. There is scant mention of the surrounding scenery. Indeed, as Roman's friend Andrew Liske points out upon reading a photocopy of the journal, "These entries are almost entirely about what he ate. He wrote about hardly anything except food."

Andrew is not exaggerating: the journal is little more than a tally of plants foraged and game killed. It would probably be a mistake, however, to conclude thereby that McCandless failed to appreciate the beauty of the country around him, that he was unmoved by the power of the landscape. As cultural ecologist Paul Shepard has observed,

> *The nomadic Bedouin does not dote on scenery, paint landscapes, or compile a nonutilitarian natural history.... [H]is life is so profoundly in transaction with nature that there is no place for abstraction or esthetics or a "nature philosophy" which can be separated from the rest of his life.... Nature and his relationship to it are a deadly serious matter, prescribed by convention, mystery, and danger. His personal leisure is aimed away from idle amusement or detached tampering with nature's processes. But built into his life is awareness of that presence, of the terrain, of the unpredictable weather, of the narrow margin by which he is sustained.*

Much the same could be said of McCandless during the months he spent beside the Sushana River.

It would be easy to stereotype Christopher McCandless as another boy who felt too much, a loopy young man who read too many books and lacked even a modicum of common sense. But the stereotype isn't a good fit. McCandless wasn't some feckless slacker, adrift and confused, racked by existential despair. To the contrary: his life hummed with meaning and purpose. But the meaning he wrested from existence lay beyond the comfortable path: McCandless distrusted the value of things that came easily. He demanded much of himself—more, in the end, than he could deliver.

Trying to explain McCandless's unorthodox behavior, some people have made much of the fact that like John Waterman, he was small in stature and may have suffered from a "short man's complex," a fundamental insecurity that drove him to prove his manhood by means of extreme physical challenges. Others have posited that an unresolved Oedipal conflict was at the root of his fatal odyssey. Although there may be some truth in both hypotheses, this sort of posthumous off-the-rack psychoanalysis is a dubious, highly speculative enterprise that inevitably demeans and trivializes the absent analysand. It's not clear that much of value is learned by reducing Chris McCandless's strange spiritual quest to a list of pat psychological disorders.

Roman and Andrew and I stare into the embers and talk about McCandless late into the night. Roman, thirty-two, inquisitive and outspoken, has a doctorate in biology from Stanford and an abiding distrust of conventional wisdom. He spent his adolescence in the same Washington, D.C., suburbs as McCandless and found them every bit as stifling. He first came to Alaska as a nine-year-old to visit a trio of uncles who mined coal at Usibelli, a big strip-mine operation a few miles east of Healy, and immediately fell in love with everything about the North. Over the years that followed, he returned repeatedly to the forty-ninth state. In 1977, after graduating from high school as a sixteen-year-old at the top of his class, he moved to Fairbanks and made Alaska his permanent home.

These days Roman teaches at Alaska Pacific University, in Anchorage, and enjoys statewide renown for a long, brash string of backcountry escapades: he has—among other feats—traveled the entire 1,000-mile length of the Brooks Range by foot and paddle, skied 250 miles across the Arctic National Wildlife Refuge in subzero winter cold, traversed the 700-mile crest of the Alaska Range, and pioneered more than thirty first ascents of northern peaks and crags. And Roman doesn't see a great deal of difference between his own widely respected deeds and McCandless's adventure, except that McCandless had the misfortune to perish.

I bring up McCandless's hubris and the dumb mistakes he made—the two or three readily avoidable blunders that ended up costing him his life. "Sure, he screwed up," Roman answers, "but I admire what he was trying to do. Living completely off the land like that, month after month, is incredibly difficult. I've never done it. And I'd bet you that very few, if any, of the people who call McCandless incompetent have ever done it either, not for more than a week or two. Living in the interior bush for an extended period, subsisting on nothing except what you hunt and gather—most people have no idea how hard that actually is. And McCandless almost pulled it off.

"I guess I just can't help identifying with the guy," Roman allows as he pokes the coals with a stick. "I hate to admit it, but not so many years ago it could easily have been me in the same kind of predicament. When I first started coming to Alaska, I think I was probably a lot like McCandless: just as green, just as eager. And I'm sure there are plenty of other Alaskans who had a lot in common with McCandless when they first got here, too, including many of his critics. Which is maybe why they're so hard on him. Maybe McCandless reminds them a little too much of their former selves."

Roman's observation underscores how difficult it is for those of us preoccupied with the humdrum concerns of adulthood to recall how forcefully we were once buffeted by the passions and longings of youth. As Everett Ruess's father mused years after his twenty-year-old son vanished in the desert, "The older person does not realize the soul-flights of the adolescent. I think we all poorly understood Everett."

Roman, Andrew, and I stay up well past midnight, trying to make sense of McCandless's life and death, yet his essence remains slippery, vague, elusive. Gradually, the conversation lags and falters. When I drift away from the fire to find a place to throw down my sleeping bag, the first faint smear of dawn is already bleaching the rim of the northeastern sky. Although the mosquitoes are thick tonight and the bus would no doubt offer some refuge, I decide not to bed down inside Fairbanks 142. Nor, I note before sinking into a dreamless sleep, do the others.

QUESTIONS FOR MAKING CONNECTIONS WITHIN THE READING

1. Jon Krakauer is telling the story of Chris McCandless, who was interested in, among other things, recording the adventures of "Alexander Supertramp." What is the relationship between McCandless and Supertramp? What does writing under a different name allow McCandless to do that he wouldn't otherwise be able to do?

2. Almost everyone at one time or another has dreamed of getting away from it all. Chris McCandless actually did so. Would he have been able to have the adventure he was looking for if he'd done more research? Would his story be more or less compelling had he brought along a better map? Would it have been more or less compelling if he had survived?

3. One of Krakauer's central concerns in *Into the Wild* is to determine what drove McCandless to embark on such a dangerous journey and to speculate on what McCandless's motives were when he sought to make his way back out of the wild. How does Krakauer go about trying to uncover the answers to these questions? What is his method? What counts as evidence for him? When does Krakauer know—or feel—that he has found what he was looking for?

QUESTIONS FOR WRITING

1. At the end of this reading, Krakauer asserts that one reason adults have so much difficulty understanding McCandless's actions is that they struggle "to recall how forcefully [they] were once buffeted by the passions and longings of youth." What are "the passions and longings of youth," and how are they related to the desire to escape? Does the world that lies ahead for most young adults seem somehow unnatural, contrived, or false? Is the wilderness the best place to look for an alternative? What other places might McCandless have considered?

2. In providing a narrative of McCandless's journey, Krakauer draws on the writings Chris left behind in the blank pages and margins of his books and on the walls of the bus where he spent his final months. What does all this writing tell Krakauer about McCandless's motives for heading off into the wild? Is it possible to escape from civilization in the twenty-first century? Does it make sense to try?

QUESTIONS FOR MAKING CONNECTIONS
BETWEEN READINGS

1. In "The Naked Citadel," Susan Faludi sets out to study how young men are
    turned into soldiers at a military academy and to record how this training
    process was upended when the academy was required to admit young
    women into its ranks. In detailing McCandless's journey into the wild,
    Krakauer provides a glimpse into another ritualized way of "becoming a
    man." Would you argue that McCandless's journey is consistent with The
    Citadel's efforts to create a certain kind of man? Or was McCandless's
    journey an attempt to escape from the masculine ideals embodied by The
    Citadel's students? What, if anything, do these two stories suggest about how
    masculinity might be defined and experienced in the twenty-first century?

2. Toward the end of this reading, Krakauer cites the cultural ecologist Paul
    Shepard's observations about how the nomadic Bedouin relates to the nat-
    ural world. According to Shepard: "The nomadic Bedouin does not dote on
    scenery, paint landscapes, or compile a nonutilitarian natural history....
    [H]is life is so profoundly in transaction with nature that there is no place for
    abstraction or esthetics or a 'nature philosophy' which can be separated from
    the rest of his life." This, Krakauer argues, is the kind of relationship with
    nature that Chris McCandless achieved at the end of his travels. And yet,
    with Leila Ahmed's discussion of Egyptian history in mind, what are we to
    make of the fact that Chris sought to embrace a way of life that the modern
    world has relegated to the very margins of society? Is Chris's retreat from
    civilization essentially self-defeating? Or is it an option only for the privi-
    leged? While the word *Arab* once referred "only to the inhabitants of Arabia
    and to Bedouins of the region's deserts," it has come to define a civilization.
    Are the Arabs that Ahmed describes fleeing the very world that Chris sought
    to embrace?

BETH LOFFREDA

HOW DO THE media decide which stories to cover on any given day? And what gets left out when the stories that are chosen turn into three-minute segments on the nightly news or columns of print in the daily paper? These are some of the issues that Beth Loffreda takes up in *Losing Matt Shepard: Life and Politics in the Aftermath of Anti-Gay Murder*, her book-length study of how the residents of Wyoming responded when Shepard, a young gay student at the university in Laramie, was brutally beaten and left to die by the side of the road in the fall of 1998. Both an ethnographic study and a cultural critique, *Losing Matt Shepard* explores and carefully details the limits of the media's representation of the complexities of life in Wyoming after Shepard's highly publicized murder. In his review of *Losing Matt Shepard* for the *Lambda Book Report*, Malcolm Farley recommended that "[a]nyone who cares about the gay experience in America—or about America in general—should read Loffreda's fiercely intelligent account of the causes and consequences of Matt Shepard's murder."

Beth Loffreda is an associate professor of English and adjunct professor of African-American studies at the University of Wyoming, where she also serves as an adviser to the university's Gay, Lesbian, Bisexual, and Transgender Association. Since the publication of *Losing Matt Shepard,* which was selected as a finalist for the American Library Association's Gay, Lesbian, Bisexual, and Transgendered Round Table Award in 2000, Loffreda has become a national spokesperson in discussions about hate crimes legislation and gay rights. She was also recognized as one of the University of Wyoming's top teachers in 2006, when she received the university's John P. Ellbogen Meritorious Classroom Teaching Award. In the selection from *Losing Matt Shepard* included here, Loffreda shows just how varied the response to Shepard's murder was at the University of Wyoming, in the communities surrounding Laramie, and across the nation. As she does so, she asks her readers to consider the following question: Why is it that, given the high number of murders every year, this one in particular captured the nation's attention?

Loffreda, Beth. Selections from *Losing Matt Shepard*. New York: Columbia University Press, 2000. 1–31.

Biographical information drawn from Beth Loffreda, *Losing Matt Shepard*. New York: Columbia University Press, 2000.

∎ ∎

Selections from
Losing Matt Shepard

Life and Politics in the Aftermath of Anti-Gay Murder

Perhaps the first thing to know about Laramie, Wyoming, is that it is beautiful. On most days the high-altitude light is so precise and clear that Laramie appears some rarefied place without need of an atmosphere. We were having a stretch of days like that in early October 1998, as the news began to trickle in that a man had been found beaten somewhere on the edge of town. We'd later sort out the key facts: that Matt Shepard had encountered Russell Henderson and Aaron McKinney late Tuesday night in the Fireside Bar; that he'd left with them; that they had driven him in a pickup truck to the edge of town; that Henderson had tied him to a fence there and McKinney had beaten him viciously and repeatedly with a .357 Magnum; that they had taken his shoes and wallet and intended to rob his apartment but instead returned to town and got into a fight with two other young men, Jeremy Herrera and Emiliano Morales (McKinney clubbed Morales on the head with the same gun, still covered in Matt's blood; Herrera retaliated by striking McKinney's head with a heavy stick); that the police, responding to the altercation, picked up Henderson McKinney had fled—and saw the gun, Matt's credit card, and his shoes in the truck but didn't yet know the fatal meaning of those objects; that after being released later that night, Henderson and his girlfriend, Chasity Pasley, and McKinney and his girlfriend, Kristen Price, began to hatch their false alibis; and that through all this Matt remained tied to the fence and wouldn't be found until Wednesday evening, after an entire night and most of a day had passed. We'd learn all that, and learn that Matt's sexuality was woven through all of it. Those facts reached us swiftly, but making sense of them took much longer.

Jim Osborn, a recent graduate of the university's education program, was the chair of the Lesbian, Gay, Bisexual, Transgender Association that October, a group that Matt, a freshman, had just recently joined. The LGBTA is the sole gay organization on campus and in Laramie itself. While students make up most of its membership, it welcomes university staff and townspeople as well, although only a few have joined. The group has been active since 1990; before that, another gay campus organization, Gays and Lesbians of Wyoming—GLOW—had an intermittent but vivid life in the 1970s and early 1980s. Women typically outnumber men at LGBTA meetings, although not by a significant margin; altogether, attendance on any given night usually hovers between ten and twenty members. The group's email list, however, reaches far more. There's no single reason for that discrepancy; it most likely arises from a combination of factors, including the familiar reluctance of many college students to join groups and, more specifically in this case, the anxiety some gay or questioning students might feel attending a public meeting.

The LGBTA gathers weekly in a nondescript, carpeted seminar room on the second floor of the university union. It has no office space of its own. (When hundreds of letters arrived after Matt's murder, the group stored them in the corner of the Multicultural Resource Center downstairs.) Meetings are usually hourlong sessions, punctuated by bursts of laughter, during which the group plans upcoming events—speakers, dances, potlucks. The LGBTA juggles numerous, sometimes contradictory roles as it tries to be a public face for gay and lesbian issues on campus (organizing events, running panels about sexuality for many courses) and at the same time create a comfortable, safe space for socializing in a town without a gay bar or bookstore. It also serves as something of a gay news exchange, sharing information about what teachers might be supportive or not, what places in town and elsewhere might be safe or not, what's happening that might not show up in the campus paper, *The Branding Iron*.

That last role mattered on Tuesday, October 6th. As the members handled the last-minute details of Gay Awareness Week, scheduled to begin the following Monday, Jim Osborn warned the group to be careful. The week before, he had been harassed while walking across campus. A young man—Jim thinks he was probably a university student—had come up behind him, said, "You're one of those faggots, aren't you?" and thrown a punch. Jim is a big, strapping white man from northern Wyoming; he blocked the punch and hit his attacker. They then took off in opposite directions. Jim didn't report the attack to the police but did want to alert members of the LGBTA that it had happened. Matt was among those there to hear Jim's story. After the meeting, members of the group, including Matt and Jim, went out for coffee at the College Inn, something of a Tuesday-night LGBTA tradition. Jim remembers that Matt sat at the other end of a crowded table. It was the last Jim would see of him.

Jim can talk an eloquent blue streak and is something of an organizational genius—at LGBTA meetings I've listened to him recall the minutiae of university regulations and budget protocols as if they were fond personal memories. He also has a staggeringly large network of friends and acquaintances. On Thursday morning, he got an email from Tina Labrie, a friend of his and Matt's; she had introduced them in August, when Matt, new to Laramie, wanted to learn about the LGBTA. The message said that Matt had been found near death the evening before and was hospitalized in Fort Collins, Colorado. (Matt had initially been taken to Ivinson Memorial Hospital in Laramie and was then transferred to Poudre Valley Hospital's more sophisticated trauma unit. While Matt was being treated in the Ivinson Memorial ER, McKinney was a few curtains down, admitted earlier for the head wound he had received from Herrera; like Matt, McKinney would also be transferred to Poudre Valley.) Horrified, Jim phoned Tina and learned that the police were trying to reconstruct Matt's whereabouts on Tuesday evening. When he called the Laramie Police to tell them what he knew, an officer informed him that Matt wasn't going to make it. Matt was suffering from hypothermia, and there was severe trauma to the brain stem. The officer told Jim that one side of Matt's head had been beaten in several inches and that the neurosurgeon was quite frankly surprised that he was still alive.

Bob Beck, news director for Wyoming Public Radio, also got word of the attack on Thursday. Beck has lived in Laramie since 1984; he's a tall, lanky midwesterner with a serious jones for Chicago Bulls basketball. On the radio he speaks in the sedated tones cultivated by NPR reporters everywhere, but in person he displays a vinegary wit and a likably aggravated demeanor. "It was a strange thing," he told me. "I teach a class, and one of my students called up and told me he needed to miss class that day because one of his friends had got beaten up very badly and was taken to the hospital in Fort Collins." That student was Phil Labrie, Tina's husband. Worried when they couldn't reach Matt, they had called the police on Wednesday, shortly after Matt was found, and learned what had happened. "[Phil] didn't tell me a lot of details because he said the cops had told him not to really tell anyone. But then he said I will know about it later and it will be a big story.... So I right away thought I better follow up on this immediately." He contacted the Albany County Sheriff's Office and learned that a press conference would be held later that day.

Beck attended the press conference that day—typically a routine exercise, but one that in this case would unexpectedly and profoundly shape public reaction to the attack. According to Beck, the sheriff

> indicated that there was a young man who had been very badly beaten, was on life support, had been taken to Poudre Valley Hospital. During the questioning, the sheriff at the time, Gary Puls, indicated that they thought he may have been beaten because he was gay. And when he described this situation to us he told us that [Shepard] was found by a mountain bike rider, tied to a fence like a scarecrow. My recollection is there was discussion of exactly what do you mean, "tied like a scarecrow," and I think every single one of us who were in the room got the impression certainly of being tied up spread-eagled, splayed out.

Matt hadn't actually been tied like a scarecrow; when he was approached first by the mountain biker, Aaron Kreifels, and then by Reggie Fluty, the sheriff's deputy who answered Kreifels's emergency call, Matt lay on his back, head propped against the fence, legs outstretched. His hands were lashed behind him and tied barely four inches off the ground to a fencepost. In dramatic and widely reported testimony, Fluty would later state that at first she thought Matt could have been no older than thirteen, he was so small (Matt was only five feet two inches, barely over one hundred pounds). And when she described Matt's brutally disfigured face, she said that the only spots not covered in blood were the tracks cleansed by his tears—an enduring image that continues to appear in essays, poetry, and songs dedicated to Shepard. It is most likely that Kreifels was the source of Puls's press-conference description. Kreifels told police and reporters that he at first thought Matt was a scarecrow flopped on the ground, maybe some kind of Halloween joke staged a few weeks early. No matter its provenance, the notion that Matt had been strung up in something akin to a crucifixion became the starting point for the reporting and reaction to come.

Beck says, "I know that's how we all reported it, and that was never corrected."[1] The vicious symbolism of that image, combined with Puls's early acknowledgment that the beating might have been an anti-gay hate crime, drew instant attention. Attending the press conference were the Associated Press, members of the Wyoming and Colorado media, Beck, and two friends of Matt, Walt Boulden and Alex Trout. According to press reports, Boulden and Trout, afraid that the attack might go unnoticed, had already begun to alert the media earlier that day. Boulden had had plans with Matt for Tuesday night; Matt had canceled and later, apparently, had decided to head off to the Fireside alone. Boulden was not shy about seizing the attack as a political opportunity, linking the assault to the Wyoming legislature's failure to pass a hate crimes bill: he told reporters that "they said nothing like that happens in Wyoming because someone is gay, but we've always known someone would have to get killed or beaten before they finally listened. I just can't believe it happened to someone I cared so much about." By Friday morning, when the police already had McKinney, Henderson, Price, and Pasley in custody (Beck says "the investigation was one of the better I've seen"), the media interest, spurred by Thursday's press conference, had increased exponentially.

At the same time, Laramie's gay residents were learning what had happened. Stephanie and Lisa, a lesbian couple active in the LGBTA, heard the news from Jim on Thursday evening. Lisa, a striking redhead and a good friend of Jim's, talked to him first: "He told me Matt had been beaten. And I said, well, shit, how badly? Is he okay? And Jim said no—he's in critical condition, had to be airlifted to Poudre Valley." Both Stephanie and Lisa knew Matt only slightly, although Stephanie had expected to have the chance to grow closer. She had just agreed to be Matt's mentor in a program the LGBTA was considering as a way to welcome new students to the gay community. Like Lisa, Steph has an edgy, witty charisma, but it deserted her that night, as she, Lisa, and Jim watched the first TV news reports. "There was this horrifying feeling that we were standing on the brink of learning something really, really awful," she says of that Thursday. "Like the part in the horror movie just before she opens the closet and finds the dead cat. It was that moment. For a day. And then we got the facts ... and everything started happening at this tremendous speed. The next day was the day the story broke. And there were newspaper reporters and cameras all over the place." Steph had called me early that Friday morning, spreading word of the attack and warning people associated with the LGBTA to watch their backs: "I can remember wanting to tell everybody, absolutely everybody, wanting to physically grab people by their lapels and make them listen."

An atmosphere of genuine shock permeated the university; most students and faculty I encountered that day wore stunned and distraught expressions that I imagine mirrored my own; they seemed absorbed simply in trying to understand how something so brutal could have happened within a short walk of their daily lives. Gay and lesbian members of the university that I spoke to felt a wrenching mix of fear and sadness; many, including Stephanie and Lisa, were also immediately and intensely angry. A number of students in my morning American Literature course, after a long discussion in which they sought answers for how to publicly express their repugnance for the crime, decided that the university's homecoming parade, coincidentally scheduled for the following morning, would be an ideal site for that response. Finding like-minded students in the United Multicultural Council, the LGBTA, and the student government, they began printing flyers, making hundreds of armbands, and arranging permits to join the parade.[2] Their unjaded eagerness to publicly involve themselves in the case contrasted sharply with the university administration's first official response, much of which had concerned itself with pointing out that the attack happened off campus and was committed by nonstudents.

On Friday afternoon—as Jim Osborn began to field what would eventually become an overwhelming flood of media requests for interviews—the four accused appeared in court for the first time. Bob Beck attended the initial appearance: "That's where you bring in the people, read them formal charges, and we then get their names, backgrounds—which is important for us." Beck had left for the courthouse a half hour early; initial appearances are typically held in a small room in the courthouse basement, and Beck thought it might be more full than usual. He was right. "It was sold out. It was wall-to-wall cameras." Residents of Laramie—professors and LGBTA members in particular—had also come to witness the proceedings. So many attended that the reading of the charges had to be delayed while everyone moved upstairs to the much larger district court. Beck remembers, "I went in—in fact it was so crowded I got shoved by where the jury box is located—and I stood behind the defendants when they came in. I got a really good look at everybody, and I was actually surprised at how young they looked, how scared they looked, and how little they were." Only Henderson, McKinney, and Chasity Pasley were charged that day; separate proceedings had been arranged for Kristen Price. Pasley wept throughout. She was someone Jim Osborn knew well and liked. She worked in the campus activities center and had helped Jim countless times when the LGBTA needed photocopying or assistance setting up for an event. "She was very supportive of the group," Jim says. Often when he saw her on a Wednesday, she'd ask, "Hey, how'd it go last night?" In the past, he had seen her wearing one of the group's "Straight But Not Narrow" buttons.

I was in the courtroom that afternoon and can remember the professional flatness with which the county judge, Robert Castor, read the charges aloud. Castor had arrived in the courtroom to find a cameraman sitting at the prosecution's table, an early symbol of the persistent media invasion, Bob Beck believes, that frustrated the court and the prosecutor, Cal Rerucha, and led them to sharply limit information about the case thereafter. Castor charged McKinney and Henderson with three identical counts of kidnapping, aggravated robbery, and attempted first-degree murder; Pasley he charged with a count of accessory after the fact to attempted first-degree murder (in addition to providing false alibis for their boyfriends, she and Price had also helped dispose of evidence, including Henderson's bloody clothing). After each count, Castor recited "the essential facts" supporting the charge, in what became a truly grim ritual of repetition. In language I've condensed from the court documents, the essential facts were these: "On or between October 6, 1998, and the early morning hours of

October 7, 1998, Aaron McKinney and Russell Henderson met Matthew Shepard at the Fireside Bar, and after Mr. Shepard confided he was gay, the subjects deceived Mr. Shepard into leaving with them in their vehicle to a remote area near Sherman Hills subdivision in Albany County. En route to said location, Mr. Shepard was struck in the head with a pistol." (McKinney, we'd later learn, had apparently told Matt, "We're not gay, and you just got jacked," before striking him.) "Upon arrival at said location, both subjects tied their victim to a buck fence, robbed him, and tortured him, while beating him with the butt of a pistol. During the incident, the victim was begging for his life. The subjects then left the area, leaving the victim for dead." By the third time Castor read that Matt had begged for his life, the courtroom had become choked with sickness and grief. The true darkness of the crime had become impossible to flee.

The next morning—Saturday—began with the university's homecoming parade. As the parade kicked off, one hundred students, university employees, and townspeople lined up at the end of the long string of floats and marching bands. They had quietly gathered in the morning chill to protest the attack on Matt. The leaders of the march carried a yellow banner painted with green circles, symbols of peace chosen by the UMC. They were followed by a silent crowd wearing matching armbands and holding signs that read "No Hate Crimes in Wyoming," "Is This What Equality Feels Like?" and "Straight But Not Stupid." I walked a few yards from the front, watching Carly Laucomer, a university student holding the middle of the banner, field questions from reporters walking backward a single pace in front of her. Beside me, Cat, another university student, muttered that she wished the marchers weren't so sparse. Cat, like Carly, was then a student in my American Literature course, a smart young woman usually prepared to be disappointed by the world around her. Laramie surprised her. As the march moved west down Ivinson Avenue, spectators began to join, walking off sidewalks into the street. By the time the march reached downtown (where a giant second-story banner proclaimed, "Hate Is Not a Wyoming Value") and circled back toward campus, it had swelled beyond even Cat's demanding expectations; final estimates ranged from five to eight hundred participants. It didn't seem like much—just a bunch of people quietly walking— but it was a genuinely spontaneous, grassroots effort to protest the attack and express the community's profound dismay, and in that sense it was unforgettable.

A very different sort of tribute to Matt appeared in the Colorado State University homecoming parade the same day in the city of Fort Collins. As Matt lay in the hospital just a few miles away, a float in the parade carried a scarecrow draped in anti-gay epithets. While the papers were reluctant to report the full range of insults, I heard that the signs read "I'm Gay" and "Up My Ass." Colorado State University acted quickly to punish the sorority and fraternity responsible for the float (the censured students blamed vandalism committed by an unknown third party), but still it is worth pausing for a moment to consider the degree of dehumanization such an act required, how much those responsible must have felt, however fleetingly or unconsciously, that Matt was not a fellow human being, their age, with his future torn away from him. Fort Collins is home to a visible and energetic community of gay activists, and the float was widely denounced. Still, a week later Fort Collins would vote down, by nearly a two-to-one margin, City Ordinance 22, a proposal to expand the city's antidiscrimination statute to include protections for gays and lesbians.

Later that Saturday, a moment of silence for Matt was held before the University of Wyoming's football game; players wore the UMC's symbols on their helmets. And, impossibly, the media presence continued to grow. Bob Beck, juggling requests for interviews with his own reporting, was in the thick of it and felt a growing frustration at the sloppiness of what he saw around him. "Right away it was horrible. Part of that, in fairness, was that we didn't have all the information we needed. While the sheriff was very up front at first, next thing you know, nobody's talking." City officials, naturally unprepared (in a town with barely a murder a year) for the onslaught, focused their resources on the investigation and, angry that Laramie was being depicted as a hate crimes capital, began to restrict press access. But the media, especially the TV tabloids, Beck says, needed to turn things around quickly, and since they were getting stonewalled by the city and by many Laramie residents, "it seemed like the place they went to interview everybody was in bars. As we all know who are in the media, if you want to get somebody to be very glib, give you a few quick takes, you want to go to a bar. And you certainly are going to meet a segment of our population that will have more interesting things to say." I remember watching for footage of the Saturday morning march later that evening and seeing instead precisely the sort of bar interview Beck describes, a quick and dirty media tactic I heard many residents mock in the coming months.

Beck also remembers one of the first television news reports he saw: "It was this woman reporter outside the Fireside doing what we call a bridge, a stand-up: 'Hate: it's a common word in Wyoming.'" Beck couldn't believe it, but that mirrored precisely the assumptions of most of the media representatives he encountered that week. Journalists who interviewed him began with comments like, "Well, this kind of thing probably happens a lot up there," or, "You have that cowboy mentality in Wyoming, so this was bound to happen." Reporters criticized Laramie, he says, for not having a head trauma unit, not having gay bars, not pushing back homecoming. The tone of the questioning was hostile; Jim Osborn, speaking to journalists from locations as far-flung as Australia and the Netherlands, encountered it, too. Jim says the press he spoke to wanted to hear that this was a hateful, redneck town, that Wyoming was, in the inane rhyming of some commentators, "the hate state." But Jim insisted on what he considered accurate: "Nobody expects murder here—nobody. This is not a place where you kill your neighbor, and we see each other as neighbors. This is a good place."

But the crime, and Laramie, had already begun to take on a second life, a broadcast existence barely tethered to the truths of that night or this place, an existence nourished less by facts and far more by the hyperboles of tabloid emotion. Such a development should be unsurprising to even the most novice of cultural critics, yet to be in the middle of it, to watch rumor become myth, to see the story stitched out of repetition rather than investigation, was something else entirely. Beck told me, "Right away I saw pack journalism like I have not seen pack journalism in a while. It was really something. I remember going to the courthouse, and somebody would say, 'Hey I understand he got burned'— which wasn't true by the way—'where did he get burned?' And somebody would say, 'Oh, on his face,' and they're all taking notes, and they were sources for each other. They would never say where it came from or who had the information—it was just 'there were burns on his face.'" As Beck watched, the mistakes multiplied. One journalist would announce, "'I did an interview with one of the deputies, and he told me this,' and they would all go with it; no one [else] went and interviewed the deputy. Now part of this is that the deputies and other officials weren't available to us ... and the same stuff got continually reported." The lead investigator on the case, Sergeant Rob DeBree of the Sheriff's Office, held a press conference early on in an attempt to correct the errors, but, he told me, it didn't seem to make much of a difference—the media had become a closed loop, feeding off their own energies.

As the fall wore on, the distance between Laramie and its broadcast image would become unbridgeable. The court increasingly limited press access to the case and eventually, in the spring, issued a gag order. In response, the Wyoming Press Association wrangled with the court throughout that year over access to hearings and records, suggesting that the court model its treatment of the media on press access guidelines in the Timothy McVeigh trial. Beck assessed Wyoming Public Radio's own performance for me: "I'm not saying we didn't make any mistakes, because we probably did. But I finally got so weary of it I said, 'You know what? If we can't confirm it ourselves, we don't go with it.' It was just too wild."

As the weekend continued, vigils for Matt were held across the nation. By the end of the week, we'd heard word of vigils in Casper, Cheyenne, and Lander (Wyoming towns), Colorado, Idaho, Montana, Iowa, Arizona, Rhode Island, and Pennsylvania. A memorial in Los Angeles attracted an estimated five thousand participants; a "political funeral" in New York City that ended in civil disobedience and hundreds of arrests, about the same. Several hundred mourners lit candles at a vigil outside Poudre Valley Hospital, and a Web site set up by the hospital to give updates about Matt's condition eventually drew over 815,000 hits from around the world.

In Laramie, we held two vigils of our own Sunday night. Jim spoke at the first, held outside the St. Paul's Newman Catholic Center. Father Roger Schmit, the organizer of the event, had contacted him earlier that weekend and asked him to speak. Jim remembers, "I'm sitting here thinking, 'Catholic Church ... this is not exactly the scene I want to get into.'" But the priest told him, Jim says, "This is such a powerful opportunity—people need to hear from you, and it will help them." Jim thought, "I want to hate him, I want to disagree with him, but I can't." Indeed, such bedfellows would become less strange in the coming months. Matt's death triggered yearlong conversations in several Laramie churches; the Newman Center, the Episcopal church, and the Unitarian–Universalist Fellowship each began discussion groups devoted to questions of sexual orientation and religious doctrine. Father Schmit, the priest Jim regarded with such initial suspicion, would in particular become a vocal advocate for gay tolerance.

I attended that first vigil, which drew nearly one thousand people, a sizable fraction of Laramie's total population. As I crossed Grand Avenue, dodging traffic, the vigil already under way, I was struck by the size and murmurous intensity of the crowd. The speakers included friends of Matt, student leaders, and university officials. Father Schmit had also invited every religious leader in town but found many reluctant to come. The event was genuinely affecting and rightly given over to the desire, as Jim put it, to think of Matt "the person" and not the newly created symbol. While speakers did indeed condemn the homophobia that slid Matt from complicated human being to easy target, others, including Jim, also tried to rehumanize Matt by offering up small details—the nature of his smile, the clothes he liked to wear. The press was there, too, of course, and—perhaps inevitably under such circumstances—a faint odor of PR hung in the air. University president Phil Dubois told the assembled, "Nothing could match the sorrow and revulsion we feel for this attack on Matt. It is almost as sad, however, to see individuals and groups around the country react to this event by stereotyping an entire community, if not an entire state."

Stephanie sensed another trouble, a hypocrisy, at work that night:

> There was a tremendous outpouring of support—the vigils, the parade—
> and a lot of those people—not all of them, not even a substantial portion,
> but some of those people—if they had known that Matt was gay while
> he was alive, would have spit on him. But now it was a cause, and that
> made me upset. Not that I think you can't grieve over this because
> you're straight or anything like that, but I just questioned the sincerity of
> some people. And I grew to be very angry at the vigil Sunday night,
> because it was so like the one I had attended for Steve.

She meant Steve Heyman, a gay man who had been a psychology professor and LGBTA faculty adviser at the university. Heyman was found dead on November 1, 1993, on the edge of Route 70 in Denver. He appeared to have been tossed from a moving car. The case was never solved. To Stephanie, who had known and adored Heyman, the coincidence was unbearable. "It was the same candles, the same fucking hymns. I will never sing 'We are a gentle, angry people' again, because it doesn't change anything. And I'm not going to sing 'We are not afraid today deep in my heart' because I am afraid, and I will always be afraid, and that's what they want, that's why they kill us."

Driven by that anger, Stephanie spoke at the second vigil that night. Much smaller—perhaps one hundred people were in attendance—it was held on the edge of town, at the Unitarian Fellowship. People who went that night tell me it was different from the first. Instead of a lengthy list of official speakers, community members were invited to testify to their mourning, and to their experiences of anti-gay discrimination in Laramie. It was more intense, more ragged, more discomfiting. But both vigils held the same fragile promise of a changed Laramie, a town that—whether it much wanted to or not—would think hard and publicly and not in unison about the gay men and women in its midst, about their safety and comfort and rights.

Later that Sunday night, as the participants in that second vigil left for home, thought about the events of the day, and got ready for bed, Matt Shepard's blood pressure began to drop. He died in the early hours of Monday, October 12th. It was the first day of Gay Awareness Week at the University of Wyoming.

Monday, flags were flown at half-staff on the university campus. Later that week, in Casper, flags were lowered on the day of Matt's funeral to signal a "day of understanding." (According to local newspapers, Wyoming governor Jim Geringer was criticized by the Veterans of Foreign Wars for not following "proper flag etiquette.") That Monday eight hundred people gathered for a memorial service held on Prexy's Pasture, a patch of green in the middle of campus encircled by parking spaces and university buildings and anchored by a statue of "the university family," a happy heterosexual unit of father, mother, and child that one lesbian student, in a letter to the student newspaper, longingly imagined detonating. The memorial service was another exercise in what was becoming a familiar schizophrenia for Laramie residents. Even the layout of the event expressed it: speakers stood in a small clump ringed by sidewalk; spread beyond them was the far larger, shaggy-edged group of listeners. In between the two was an encampment of reporters, flourishing microphones and tape recorders, pivoting cameras back and forth, capturing clips of the speakers and reaction shots of the crowd. It was hard to see past the reporters to the event that had drawn us in the first place, and it was hard to know to a certainty whether we were all there simply to mourn Matt or to make sure that mourning was represented. Not that the second urge was itself necessarily a hypocrisy or a contradiction of the first. It was instead an early manifestation of Laramie's new double consciousness. We didn't simply live here anymore: we were something transmitted, watched, evaluated for symbolic resonance; something available for summary. I suspect a few people naturally sought that televised attention, felt authenticated and confirmed, even thrilled, by the opportunity to be representative; and others seized it, as Walt Boulden had, as a chance to articulate political goals that might otherwise go unheard. Mostly, though, it just pissed people off. As the memorial drew to a close, I walked past satellite vans and the professional autism of TV reporters practicing their opening lines and switching on their solemn expressions and talking to no one in particular.

I was on my way to the first event of Gay Awareness Week. Shortly after the memorial, Leslea Newman, scheduled long before the murder to give the keynote talk, spoke about her gay-themed children's books, which include the oft-censored *Heather Has Two Mommies*. The week's events would be held despite Matt's death, but attendance that evening hadn't necessarily swelled in response—there were maybe seventy folks scattered around in the darkened auditorium. Newman spoke with a bracing, funny, New York brusqueness that scuffed up the audience as she briskly detailed her skirmishes with religious conservatives, and she spoke as well of her sorrow over Matt and her friends' fearful pleading that she cancel her visit to Laramie. They weren't alone in feeling that anxiety; many of the members of the LGBTA were tensed for a backlash as they passed out pro-gay trinkets and "heterosexual questionnaires" at the "Straight But Not Narrow" table in the student union during Awareness Week. They knew the statistics: that anti-gay violence tends to rise sharply in the aftermath of a publicized bashing. But instead, as consoling letters and emails flooded the offices of *The Branding Iron,* the LGBTA, and Wyoming newspapers, supporters flocking to the union tables quickly ran through the association's supplies of buttons and stickers.

As the week dragged on, Laramie residents hung in their windows and cars flyers decrying hate provided by the Wyoming Grassroots Project (a year and a half later, you can still find a few examples around town, stubbornly hanging on). Yellow sashes fluttered from student backpacks; local businesses announced, on signs usually reserved for information about nightly rates, indoor pools, and bargain lunches, their dismay with the crime. The Comfort Inn: "Hate and Violence Are Not Our Way of Life." The University Inn: "Hate Is Not a Laramie Value." Arby's: "Hate and Violence Are Not Wyoming Values 5 Regulars $5.95." Obviously, those signs suggested a typically American arithmetic, promiscuously mixing moral and economic registers. Underneath the sentiment lingered a question: what will his death cost us? But it would be wrong, I think, to see all those gestures as merely cynical calculation, a self-interested weighing of current events against future tourism. We were trying to shape the media summary of Laramie all right, but we were also talking to each other, pained and wondering, through such signs.

Late Monday, about the same time as the Prexy's Pasture memorial, the charges against McKinney, Henderson, and Pasley were upgraded in a closed hearing to reflect Matt's death. Price's charge, the same as Pasley's—accessory after the fact to first-degree murder—was announced at her individual arraignment on Tuesday. In a *20/20* interview that week, Price offered her defense of McKinney and Henderson. She claimed Shepard approached McKinney and Henderson and "said that he was gay and wanted to get with Aaron and Russ." They intended, she said, "to teach a lesson to him not to come on to straight people"—as if torture and murder were reasonable responses to the supposed humiliation of overtures from a gay man. McKinney's father, speaking to the *Denver Post,* argued that no one would care about the crime if his son had killed a heterosexual, which struck me as not exactly on point, even as a media critique. Wyoming's Libertarian gubernatorial candidate (it was an election year) had his own unique twist: he told reporters, "If two gays beat and killed a cowboy, the story would have never been reported by the national media vultures."

Fred Phelps, a defrocked minister, leader of the tiny Kansas Westboro Baptist Church, and author of the Internet site GodHatesFags.com, announced that Monday that he intended to picket Matthew's funeral, scheduled for the coming Friday at St. Mark's Episcopal Church in Casper. His Web site also promised a visit to Laramie on October 19th, but in the end he didn't show. Phelps had made a name for himself in the 1990s as a virulently anti-gay activist, notorious for protesting at the funerals of AIDS victims. Never one to shy from media attention, Phelps faxed reporters images of the signs he and his followers intended to carry at the funeral: "Fag Matt in Hell," "God Hates Fags," "No Tears for

Queers." On his Web site, Phelps wrote that "the parents of Matt Shepard did not bring him up in the nature and admonition of the Lord, or he would not have been trolling for perverted sex partners in a cheap Laramie bar." He also, to the bitter laughter of members of the LGBTA, deemed the University of Wyoming "very militantly pro-gay." "The militant homosexual agenda is vigorously pursued" at the university, he proclaimed. At the time of Phelps's statement, the university's equal employment and civil rights regulations did not include sexual orientation as a protected category, nor did the university offer insurance benefits to same-sex partners. President Dubois and the board of trustees, in response to Matt's death, eventually rectified the former failure in September 1999; the latter still remains true to this day. Apparently none of that mattered much in Phelps's estimation, and he would become a familiar figure in Laramie in the months to come.

The Westboro Church's announcement was only one manifestation of the murder's parallel national life, its transmutation into political and religious currency. Matt himself might have been dead, but his image was resurrected by Phelps as well as by his antagonists, and those resurrections, while not invariably hypocritical or grotesque, nevertheless struck me as always risky. Not because we shouldn't talk about Matt, about the murder, looking hard at the facts of it, as well as at its contexts. The risk, it seemed to me, lay in what his image was so often used for in the coming months—the rallying of quick and photogenic outrage, sundered from the hard, slow work for local justice.

On Wednesday, October 14th, the national gay organization the Human Rights Campaign held a candlelight vigil on the steps of the U.S. Capitol, noteworthy if only for the incongruity of an event that paired the likes of Ted Kennedy and Ellen DeGeneres. Jim Osborn was also there—Cathy Renna, a member of GLAAD (Gay and Lesbian Alliance Against Defamation), who had arrived in Laramie the previous weekend to monitor events for her organization, had asked Jim to participate and taken him to Washington. That night, DeGeneres declared that "this is what she was trying to stop" with her television sitcom *Ellen*. The proportions of that statement—the belief that a sitcom could breathe in the same sentence as the brutal vortex of murder—seemed out of kilter to say the least, but it is the age of celebrity politics, after all: Elton John would send flowers to Matt's funeral, Barbra Streisand would phone the Albany County Sheriff's office to demand quick action on the case, and Madonna would call up an assistant to UW president Dubois to complain about what had happened to Matt. Jim Osborn remembers standing next to Dan Butler, an actor on *Frasier,* during the vigil; later, he spotted Kristen Johnston (of *Third Rock from the Sun*) smoking backstage. Attended by numerous federal legislators, the vigil was skipped by Wyoming's two senators, who had announced their sorrow and condemned intolerance in press releases the previous day. The disconnect worked both ways: the Human Rights Campaign, for all its sustained rallying on the national level, never, according to Jim, sent a representative to Laramie until the following summer.

Back in Laramie, on the same day as the D.C. vigil, the university initiated a three-day series of teach-ins on "prejudice, intolerance, and violence" to begin, according to the announcement, "the healing process." The ideas expressed that day were valuable, the sympathies genuine, but I remember feeling overloaded by premature talk of closure. It may have seemed easy for straight mourners to move so quickly, but as Stephanie told me that week, she'd barely begun to realize the extent of her anger. In the face of that, the swiftness of the official move to "healing" seemed at best a well-intended deafness, and indeed, in their outrage by proxy, denunciations of hatred, and exhortations for tolerance, most of the speakers seemed to be talking implicitly and exclusively to straight members of the audience who already agreed.

Many professors on campus also made time in their classes that week to let their students talk about Matt; the university provided a list of teachers willing to facilitate such discussions if individual faculty were uncomfortable raising such an emotionally fraught issue. It was indeed, as Jim Osborn put it, a "teachable moment," and those conversations undoubtedly did real good. One student, who spoke to me on the condition I didn't use his name, told me that before Matt's death he "straight-up hated fags." It hadn't occurred to him that there actually were any gays or lesbians around (a surprisingly common assumption at the university, not to mention in Wyoming generally)—"fag" was a word handy mainly for demeaning other guys in his dorm for "being pussy" (a typical but still depressing conflation of slurs). After seeing students cry in one of his classes as they discussed Matt's death, he had what he called, with a defensive grin, a real breakthrough: he felt a little sick, he told me, that he had thought things about gays that the two killers had probably been thinking about Shepard.

It's impossible to quantify such changes in attitude, but clearly they were happening in many classrooms around campus. Those developments were heartening, but it would be wrong to imply that the changes were immediate or seismic; several students in the coming weeks would describe to me overhearing others saying Matt "got what he deserved." One woman told me that during a class devoted to discussing the murder, "There was a really ugly incident with a couple of guys in the back who were like 'I hate gays and I'm not changing my opinion.'" "People really think that way here," she finished with a resigned expression. In the coming year students and faculty checking out books on gay topics sometimes found them defaced, and in the spring of 1999 vandals defecated on the university's copies of *The Advocate,* a gay magazine.

It would be wrong, too, to imply that the faculty were perfectly equipped to handle the events of October. When Matt died, there was only one openly gay faculty member on the university campus—Cathy Connelly, a professor of sociology. Since her arrival in 1991, Professor Connelly had periodically taught graduate courses on gay and lesbian issues, but other than Connelly and the small Safe Zone diversity-training group, the university had few resources in place to respond to what had happened. Troubling as well were the reactions of more than one professor I spoke to that week, whose primary responses were to comment on their own uselessness, their own irrelevance—as scholars of obscure fields of inquiry—to such primal issues of life and death. Academics tend to be fairly skilled at self-lacerating narcissism, but it seemed to me at the time an appalling luxury, an indulgence in a kind of intellectual self-pity at a moment when the basic skills of education—critical thinking, articulation, self-reflection—could be so concretely valuable. I wondered about that, and I wondered, too, when we'd stop talking about how we felt and begin talking about what to do.

Not that public political gestures are always more meaningful than private, emotional ones. On October 15th, the day before Shepard's funeral, the U.S. House of Representatives approved a resolution condemning the murder. Sponsored by Wyoming's sole representative, Barbara Cubin, it struck me as an essentially empty gesture. The nonbinding resolution stated that the House would "do everything in its power" to fight intolerance, and Cubin herself announced that "our country must come together to condemn these types of brutal, nonsensical acts of violence. We cannot lie down, we cannot bury our heads, and we cannot sit on our hands." Stirring stuff, but she also told reporters that day that she opposes federal hate crimes legislation and suggested such things be left up to individual states. So much for "our country coming together." Cubin was not alone, of course, in her contradictory patriotic embrace of Matt; flags were lowered, resolutions passed, in a nation otherwise happy to express its loathing of gays by closeting them in the military, refusing them antidiscrimination protection in most cities and states, repressing their presence in school curricula, faculty, and clubs, and denouncing them in churches. Meanwhile, back in Wyoming that afternoon, a bewildered and frustrated Casper City Council grappled with more concrete resolutions than those that faced the United States Congress. At an emergency meeting to address Phelps's intended picketing of Matt's funeral, the council decided that protesters must stay at least fifty feet from the church. Casper's SWAT team and the Street Drug Unit would be in attendance outside St. Mark's. Streets would be closed nearby the church, the Casper *Star-Tribune* reported, to allow "media satellite vehicles to position themselves."

The funeral on Friday unfurled as a heavy, wet snow fell on Casper. The storm ripped down power lines, cutting electricity in and around Casper; hundreds of cottonwoods and elms lost their branches. Phelps and his handful of protesters (along with another anti-gay protester, W. N. Orwell of Enterprise, Texas) were penned inside black plastic barricades, taunting the huge crowd of mourners, which included strangers, gay and straight alike, drawn to the scene from Cheyenne, Denver, Laramie, and elsewhere. As Charles Levendosky put it a few days later in the *Star-Tribune,* "One thousand others from Wyoming and surrounding states flew or drove into Wyoming to mourn for Matt Shepard, the symbol." While a few mourners engaged in heated debate with the picketers— one carrying a sign reading "Get Back in Your Damn Closet"—most turned their backs to them, the umbrellas pulled out for the snow acting as a fortuitous blockade. To protect the Shepard family from hearing Phelps, the assembled crowd sang "Amazing Grace" to drown out his anti-gay preaching. (The family's loss would intensify that day—Shepard's great uncle suffered what would be a fatal heart attack in the church shortly before the service began.) The funeral inside St. Mark's remained restricted to friends and family of Matt, but a live audio feed carried the service to the First Presbyterian Church nearby. Outside St. Mark's, more mourners ("some wearing black leather," the *Star-Tribune* observed) listened to a KTWO radio broadcast of the service. At the funeral, Matt's cousin Ann Kirch, a minister in Poughkeepsie, New York, delivered the sermon. Emphasizing Matt's gentleness and desire "to help, to nurture, to bring joy to others," she echoed a statement made by Matt's father earlier in the day at a press conference outside city hall: "A person as caring and loving as our son Matt would be overwhelmed by what this incident has done to the hearts and souls of people around the world."

Three days later, the university held yet another memorial service. Around one thousand people heard songs by a multicultural chorus, psalms read by Geneva Perry of the university's Office of Minority Affairs, and statements by Tina Labrie, Jim Osborn, and Trudy McCraken, Laramie's mayor. Rounding out the service was university president Dubois, who made a passionate, personal plea for hate crimes legislation—the political issue that had already, only one week after his death, come to dominate discussions of Matt's murder. "No hate crime statute, even had it existed, would have saved Matt," Dubois read. "But Matt Shepard was not merely robbed, and kidnapped, and murdered. This was a crime of humiliation. This crime was all about being gay…. We must find a way to commemorate this awful week in a way that will say to the entire state and nation that we will not forget what happened here."

On Tuesday, October 20th, the Wyoming Lodging and Restaurant Association offered one such response to the nation by passing a resolution in favor of hate crimes legislation. The association was up front about its motivations: to curry favor among tourists who might seek recreation elsewhere. The director was quoted in the Casper *Star-Tribune*: "We want them to know this was an isolated case and could happen anywhere."

Could happen anywhere indeed. While that oft-repeated phrase was the quick defense offered by many who felt Laramie was being unfairly vilified, it also bumped up against an undeniable truth: in the late 1990s, homosexuality and vehement opposition to it were everywhere in American public culture and politics. Gays in the military, gays in the schools, gays in church, gays in marriage— the place of gay men and lesbians in American culture seemed to be debated in every way possible. For example, on October 14th, two days before Matt's funeral, the Supreme Court upheld a Cincinnati ordinance that denied gays and lesbians legal protection from discrimination in housing, employment, and other public accommodations. Later that autumn Ohio hosted a conference, organized by Focus on the Family, on how to prevent childhood homosexuality; one speaker there, John Paulk, became notorious during the summer of 1998 when he posed with his wife for national newspaper ads announcing that they were former homosexuals "cured" by their faith in God. About the same time the Supreme Court ruled on the city ordinance, the Roman Catholic Archdiocese of Cincinnati announced a deeply contradictory attempt to "reconcile church teachings that denounce homosexual sex as immoral but encourage the loving acceptance of gays." As long as they're celibate, that is—as long as they "live chaste lives." "Hate the sin, love the sinner"—that idea was invoked again and again in Laramie, in church congregations and letters to the editor. But it seems to me that in such visions sexuality slides so intimately close to identity itself that in the end such exhortations call for moral acrobatics requiring an impossible and fundamentally hypocritical kind of dexterity.

Religious justifications were everywhere, of course, in the attacks on homosexuality. Senate Majority Leader Trent Lott, in June 1998, said he learned from the Bible that "you should try to show them a way to deal with [homosexuality] just like alcohol ... or sex addiction ... or kleptomaniacs." Pat Robertson announced that "the acceptance of homosexuality is the last step in the decline of Gentile civilization." Bob Jones University in South Carolina instituted a rule banning gay alumni from returning to campus. The religious right boycotted Disney and American Airlines for having policies that refused to discriminate against gays and lesbians. Salt Lake City banned all student clubs rather than allow a gay-straight alliance to continue at one public high school. The Mormon Church donated roughly half a million dollars to supporters of Alaska's Proposition 2, an initiative banning same-sex marriage that succeeded in the fall of 1998. Bans on gay marriage would also pass in Hawaii, California, and West Virginia in the next year and a half. Vermont, with its legalization of gay "civil unions" early in 2000, would be one of the few bright spots.

That Matt's death occurred in the midst of such pervasive anxiety and upheaval might begin to explain why the nation paid attention, but it doesn't stretch very far—his was only one of thirty-three anti-gay murders that year, followed by, in the first months of 1999, a beheading in Virginia and a vicious beating in Georgia. Here in Laramie, we asked a version of that question, too: why Matt, when no one in the media seemed to take a second glance at the other truly awful recent murders we had the grim distinction of claiming? Why Matt, and not Daphne Sulk, a fifteen-year-old pregnant girl stabbed seventeen times and dumped in the snow far from town? Why Matt, and not Kristin Lamb, an eight-year-old Laramie girl who was kidnapped while visiting family elsewhere in Wyoming and then raped, murdered, and thrown in a landfill? Governor Geringer asked those very questions in an October 9th press release, and we asked them, too, in Laramie—in letters to the editor, in private conversation. But we didn't always mean the same thing. To some, the media attention to Matt seemed to imply that his death was somehow worse than the deaths of the two girls, and such an implication was genuinely offensive. To some, like Val Pexton, a graduate student in creative writing, it had something to do with the politics of gender: "What happened to [Lamb] was certainly as violent, as hateful, as horrible; and I guess one of my first thoughts was, if [Henderson and McKinney] had done that to a woman, would this have made it into the news outside of Laramie, outside of Wyoming?" And to some, like Jim Osborn, the comparison of Matt to Kristin and Daphne sometimes masked a hostility to gays: "They became incensed—why didn't Kristin Lamb get this kind of coverage, why didn't Daphne Sulk get this kind of coverage? That was the way people could lash out who very much wanted to say, fuck, it was just a gay guy. But they couldn't say it was just a gay guy, so they said, what about these two girls?"

In some ways, it's easy to understand why the media industry seized upon Matt, and why so many responded to the image it broadcast (Judy Shepard, Matt's mother, told *The Advocate* magazine in March 1999 that the family had received "about 10,000 letters and 70,000 emails," as well as gifts, stuffed animals, blankets, and food). Matt was young (and looked younger), small, attractive; he had been murdered in a particularly brutal fashion. The mistaken belief that he had been strung up on the fence provided a rich, obvious source of symbolism: religious leaders, journalists, and everyday people saw in it a haunting image of the Crucifixion, and at the memorial services and vigils for Matt here and elsewhere, that comparison was often drawn. And while Matt had not in reality been put on display in that fashion, the idea that he had been resonated deeply with America's bitter history of ritual, public violence against minorities—many, including *Time* magazine, compared the attack to a lynching. But Matt seemed to provide a source of intense, almost obsessive interest whose explanation lies well beyond these considerations. Perhaps it was merely the insistent repetition of his image in those early days. In the few snapshots that circulated in the press, Matt appeared boyish, pensive, sweet, charmingly vulnerable in oversized wool sweaters—a boy who still wore braces when he died, a boy who looked innocent of sex, a boy who died because he was gay but whose unthreatening image allowed his sexuality to remain an abstraction for many. In my darker moods, I wonder, too, if Matt invited such sympathy and political outrage precisely because he was dead—if, for many of the straight people who sincerely mourned his murder, he would nevertheless have been at best invisible while alive. To Jim Osborn, the explanation was less dark and more simple: Matt was "someone we can identify with. Matt was the boy next door. He looked like everybody's brother and everybody's neighbor. He looked like he could have been anyone's son."

"He was the nuclear son of the nuclear family." Jay, a Shoshone-Northern Arapahoe-Navajo American Indian born on the Wind River Reservation in the center of Wyoming, is talking to me about the limits of identification. "If that was me hung on the fence, they'd just say, oh, another drunk Indian. No one would have paid much attention." Jay is gay (he uses the Navajo term *nádleeh*—which he translates as "one who loves his own kind"—to describe himself), and while he feels sympathy for Matt, he doesn't feel much kinship. To Jay, the reason why the nation seized upon Matt is just as simple as Jim Osborn's reason but radically different: to Jay, it was as if white, middle-class America finally had its own tragedy. His argument makes some undeniable sense: in a media culture consecrated to repetition, to the endless recopying of the supposed center of American life—white, moneyed, male—Matt did indeed fit the bill, did suit the recycled homogeneities of a still-myopic national culture. For Jay, the tremendous public outpouring of grief, no matter how sincere, remained essentially alienating. When I ask him how people he knows back on the reservation reacted to the murder, he sums up what he describes as a common response, which he himself shared: "Well, at least now one of them"—whites—"knows what we live through every day." Matt learned it, he says. "And one mother now knows, for a little while anyway, what our lives have always been." As he speaks, defiance, resignation, bitterness, and pride mingle in his voice. "Now people might know what our lives are like," what forms of violence—physical, political, cultural—native people experience in the still-hostile territories of the American West.

Jay's home on the reservation was without running water or electricity, but that never felt like deprivation or unusual circumstance to him—"It's just the way it was." When he was nine, Jay moved to Laramie with his family. They arrived after dark. "Laramie looked so beautiful—all these lights spread out—[it] seemed huge to me." He laughs as he describes how he has learned to love the materialism of life off the reservation—"I really, really like having things now," he admits in simultaneous mockery of himself and Anglo consumerism. When I ask him what white residents here don't know about their town, he replies that "Laramie's a nice town"—he likes life here fine—with a pointed caveat: "White people always say there's no bias in Laramie, no racism, but they just don't want to see." Jay has long black hair pulled back in a braid and a round, lived-in face; he's frequently mistaken for Hispanic. As a child, it didn't take him long to stumble across the racial fault lines he describes. In his first year in Laramie, as he walked home from school near the university campus, a college-aged man spit on him. And on the day we talked, a white woman hissed "spic" at Jay minutes before we met. A student at the university, Jay says there is a reason why the October vigils held for Matt were mostly attended by whites: when Matt died and then later, during the legal proceedings against Henderson and McKinney, Jay observes, "you never saw a minority alone on campus—they either left town, or stayed home, or walked in pairs or groups." They were, he and others say, afraid of a backlash—if "someone got killed for being gay, then someone might get killed for being black or Hispanic or native—that's how we felt." In Jay's opinion, the surprise and horror expressed at the vigils—not to mention simply attending them— was almost something of a white luxury: "They felt shock," Jay says, but "I wasn't shocked—I knew this was coming, since I was in high school, seeing the white and Hispanic kids fight. I knew sooner or later someone was going to die." To Jay, risk, the risk of visible difference, didn't seem all that unfamiliar.

Other minority students on campus confirm Jay's point, however melodramatic it might seem to some. Carina Evans, a young woman of Latino and African-American heritage, told me that when the minority community on campus heard that two Latino teenagers had also been attacked by Henderson and McKinney that night, "the immediate response was, oh my God, what about my safety? How safe am I here? And I think our way of dealing with it was just to not talk about it, because I think we figured the less we drew attention to ourselves, the less the chance that something else was going to happen. Which was a sorry response, but a lot of people left town, just did not feel safe, went away for the week or the weekend."[3] She and others thought, "I'm not going to make myself a target—I'm going to get out of here." No such retaliation was ever reported, but the fact that minority members of the community so feared its possibility that it felt logical to leave town—at the same time that so many white residents could unquestionably consider the attack an isolated incident—reveals something about the complexities of daily life in Laramie.

The divides that run through Jay's and Carina's lives became harder for many in Laramie to ignore in the aftermath of Matt's death. But it was nevertheless a town made defensive by such half-unearthed truths. "Hate is not a Wyoming value," residents kept telling each other, telling visitors, telling the press. "We really take care of each other here," a woman told me one day in a coffee shop, echoing a dearly held ethos I've heard from many in Laramie and that strikes me as generally true. That defensiveness intensified as it encountered the first, clumsy journalistic attempts to offer sociological explanations for the roots of Henderson and McKinney's violence, attempts that implied—to us here, anyway—that Laramie was to blame. Perhaps the most locally reviled version was an article written by Todd Lewan and Steven K. Paulson for the Associated Press that appeared in October, an occasionally persuasive attempt at class analysis hamstrung by bad facts and a love affair with the thuddingly clichéd symbolic density of the railroad tracks that cut through town. Here is their Laramie:

> On the east side is the University of Wyoming's ivy-clad main campus, where students drive sports cars or stroll and bike along oak-shaded sidewalks. On the opposite side of town, a bridge spans railroad tracks to another reality, of treeless trailer parks baking in the heavy sun, fenced-off half-acre lots, stray dogs picking for scraps among broken stoves, refrigerators, and junked pickups. Unlike the university students, youths on the west side have little in the way of entertainment: no malls, no organized dance troupes, no theater or playing fields.

Blowing holes in this picture is still a local sport, more than a year after the murder. Bob Beck, for example, takes fairly comprehensive aim at the story:

> They decided that the reason a murder like this happened was because those of us, including me, who live in west Laramie, the "other side of the tracks," are underprivileged, don't have benefits, all this stuff. Because we're over there, we're obviously looking to get even with the good side of the tracks and are going to commit a crime like this. [They] basically blamed the fact that some of us who live in west Laramie don't have a mall (meanwhile there isn't a mall on the east side either); so we don't have a mall, we don't have paved streets, apparently don't have trees. And this is the reason for all this violence? That was one of the most damaging stories in retrospect, because it got picked up by just about every major paper. A lot of people got their impressions of the case from that.

The list of mistakes could continue: Henderson and McKinney didn't even live in west Laramie; oaks rarely grow at seven thousand feet; and few university students drive fancy sports cars—more likely, like many of the students I've encountered, they're working fifteen to thirty hours a week to pay their tuition, maybe at the same Taco Bell where Henderson worked as a teenager. It's hard to choose, but my personal favorite is the anguished handwringing over west Laramie's lack of organized dance troupes. Organized dance troupes?

Plenty of folks I've spoken to volunteer that they live on the west side and are quick to say they're "not trash," that they like the rustic character of west Laramie's unpaved streets, that they don't necessarily feel excluded from "Laramie proper," despite, for example, the west side's usual lack of representation on the city council. And I've found few residents who weren't offended by such shallow press characterizations of Laramie, who didn't argue that status doesn't matter much here, that Laramie is friendly and easygoing and safe, that most folks don't even bother to lock their doors. All their points of rebuttal are well taken, and indeed they're reasons why many love to live here. But nevertheless I think the eager rapidity with which so many of us rejected such examples of journalistic ineptitude masked at times a certain unease—and sometimes a hardworking amnesia—about the subtle realities of class, sexuality, and race here in Laramie. Those realities may be too complicated to sum up through the convenient shorthand of railroad tracks and trailer parks, but they still flow, hushed yet turbulent, beneath daily life in this town.

NOTES

1. Melanie Thernstrom's essay on the murder in the March 1999 issue of *Vanity Fair* notes that Matt was not strung up, but only in a parenthetical remark near the end of the piece, and the article itself has the title "The Crucifixion of Matthew Shepard." JoAnn Wypijewski's tough-minded essay "A Boy's Life," which appeared in the September 1999 issue of *Harper's Magazine,* was the first thorough demystification of this myth in the national media, but many people still believe it. For example, Melissa Etheridge's song "Scarecrow" on her 1999 album *Breakdown* relies on it, as well as on other early misstatements of fact, including the false report that Shepard had been burned by his killers.

2. While the United Multicultural Council did good work that day, and while some strong connections have been made between the UMC and the LGBTA since Matt's death, it would be wrong to imply that those ties have been built without friction. Carina Evans, a university student who worked in the Minority Affairs Office that year, observed that at the time some members of the "diversity clubs" represented by the UMC "would not deal with the gay issue. The United Multicultural Council had no representation from the LGBTA, had no representation of openly gay students—and I think that's not at all multicultural. But they don't want to handle that. It's not like they're hostile about it, but they just don't encourage it." The tension flows both ways: Jay, a gay American Indian now active in the UMC, told me that some gay students of color he knows are uncomfortable attending LGBTA meetings because they feel that some members are not sensitive to racial differences.

3. A Mexican-American student, Lindsey Gonzales, spoke to me as well about the attack on Morales and Herrera. Lindsey knew Morales quite well (they'd hung out together in the past). She thinks neither the media nor the public cared much about the attack on Morales and Herrera compared to Matt because "they didn't die." But if they had, she speculates, people probably wouldn't have cared much more. When I ask her why, she says she's not sure, but she speculates that racial prejudice is simply more "familiar," something with a longer and better-known history in America, whereas "we're all just getting used to" homosexuality right now, and "that made it a big deal."

QUESTIONS FOR MAKING CONNECTIONS WITHIN THE READING

1. As Beth Loffreda works to unpack the significance of Matt Shepard's murder, she finds herself confronting a wide array of prejudices, not only about gays, but about Wyoming, the West, and Native Americans. Create a chart that details all of the prejudices that Loffreda uncovers. What are the relationships among these prejudices? Does Loffreda have any prejudices, or is her view unbiased?

2. In detailing the responses to Shepard's murder, Loffreda refers to many different individuals by name. Who are the most important people in the story that Loffreda has to tell? Which responses had more weight at the time of the murder? Which responses have the most weight with Loffreda? With you?

3. How is this selection from *Losing Matt Shepard* organized? Is it a series of observations or an argument? Does it build to a point? Does it have a structure? How does the structure that Loffreda has chosen influence what she has to say?

QUESTIONS FOR WRITING

1. One of Loffreda's arguments in *Losing Matt Shepard* is that Matt Shepard, the individual, got lost in the media frenzy that followed his murder. Part of the shock of Shepard's death, Loffreda reports, was "to watch rumor become myth, to see the story stitched out of repetition rather than investigation." If the media got Shepard's murder wrong, what are we to make of how and why they got it wrong? What would it take to provide "better coverage" of such tragedies? Are the print and visual media capable of providing nuanced understandings of unfolding events?

2. In describing how her colleagues at the University of Wyoming responded to Shepard's death, Loffreda records her own frustration at hearing teachers speak of their own "uselessness" and "irrelevance" in the face of such a tragedy. Such remarks struck Loffreda as "an appalling luxury, an indulgence in a kind of intellectual self-pity at a moment when the basic skills of education—critical thinking, articulation, self-reflection—could be so concretely valuable. I wondered about that, and I wondered, too, when we'd stop talking about how we felt and begin talking about what to do." What is it that teachers can or should do at such times? What role should secular institutions play in trying to shape the way their students see and understand the world?

QUESTIONS FOR MAKING CONNECTIONS
BETWEEN READINGS

1. This selection from *Losing Matt Shepard* closes with Loffreda's discussion of
    what she terms "the limits of identification," starting with her account of
    Jay, an American Indian student at the university. In a sense, Susan Faludi's
    "The Naked Citadel" could also be described as a piece centrally concerned
    with "the limits of identification"—including identification based on gender.
    What are the limits Loffreda has in mind, and what limits do you find at The
    Citadel? How are these limits discovered by people in both communities?
    Do you see evidence of change?

2. Both Leila Ahmed and Beth Loffreda could be said to be autoethnographers—
    writers who make sense of cultures of which they themselves are members.
    Both are concerned with violence, incomprehension, and change. Beyond
    these similarities, would you say that there is a method to this kind of work?
    Is there a way to assess the results of such studies—to tell good work from
    bad? Is objectivity a goal in autoethnography? A necessity? An impossibility?
    Write a paper that draws on Ahmed and Loffreda to explore the dynamics
    and demands of studying one's own culture.

AZAR NAFISI

Azar Nafisi Rose to international prominence in 2003 with the publication of her critically acclaimed bestseller, *Reading Lolita in Tehran: A Memoir in Books*. A professor of aesthetics, culture, and literature, Dr. Nafisi was expelled from the University of Tehran in 1981 for refusing to comply with the Ayatollah Khomeini's mandate that women wear the *chador,* or Islamic veil. Nafisi resumed teaching in 1987, but resigned eight years later in protest over the Iranian government's increasingly harsh treatment of women. *Reading Lolita in Tehran* provides an account of the seminar that Nafisi then went on to hold in her home from 1995 to 1997, in which seven of her best students joined her to discuss some of the classic texts of Western literature. Nafisi saw the change in her circumstances as an opportunity to fulfill a dream of working with "a group of students who just love literature, who are in it not for the grades, not just to graduate and get a job but just want to read Nabokov and Austen." That Nafisi and her students persisted in this activity, despite the obvious dangers it posed, has come to symbolize for readers around the world how the struggle against totalitarianism is waged on the level of everyday human experience.

Currently the Executive Director of Cultural Conversations and a Professorial Lecturer at the Foreign Policy Institute of the Johns Hopkins University's School of Advanced International Studies (SAIS) in Washington, D.C., Nafisi directs the Dialogue Project, "a multiyear initiative designed to promote—in a primarily cultural context—the development of democracy and human rights in the Muslim world." At the same time, the Dialogue Project is also engaged in a program of education and outreach designed to provide knowledge about the Muslim world to Western policymakers, scholars, development professionals, media workers, and citizens.

For Nafisi, the freedom to talk and think together in small groups, in a context where the ideas raised and the topics of conversation are not determined in advance, is the litmus test for a true democracy. To engage in this act, she believes, is to embrace a shared humanity that extends beyond the boundaries of national and religious differences. More recently, Nafisi has begun to explore tyranny of another kind—not in a totalitarian state but in the habits of self-censorship and repression that are taught by the family. In *Things I Have Been Silent About: Memories of a Prodigal Daughter* (2008), she explores her complicated struggles with a mother whose overwhelming expectations virtually ensured that her daughter's future life would be successful but unhappy.

Nafisi, Azar. Excerpt from *Reading Lolita in Tehran: A Memoir in Books*. New York: Random House, 2003. 3–26.

Biographical information comes from Azar Nafisi's home page at <http://dialogueproject.sais-jhu.edu/anafisi.php>; quotation about the Dialogue Project comes from <http://dialogueproject.sais-jhu.edu/aboutDP.php>.

■ ■   ■

Selections from
Reading Lolita in Tehran

A Memoir in Books

1.   In the fall of 1995, after resigning from my last academic post, I decided to indulge myself and fulfill a dream. I chose seven of my best and most committed students and invited them to come to my home every Thursday morning to discuss literature. They were all women—to teach a mixed class in the privacy of my home was too risky, even if we were discussing harmless works of fiction. One persistent male student, although barred from our class, insisted on his rights. So he, Nima, read the assigned material, and on special days he would come to my house to talk about the books we were reading.

I often teasingly reminded my students of Muriel Spark's *The Prime of Miss Jean Brodie* and asked, Which one of you will finally betray me? For I am a pessimist by nature and I was sure at least one would turn against me. Nassrin once responded mischievously, You yourself told us that in the final analysis we are our own betrayers, playing Judas to our own Christ. Manna pointed out that I was no Miss Brodie, and they, well, they were what they were. She reminded me of a warning I was fond of repeating: *do not,* under *any* circumstances, belittle a work of fiction by trying to turn it into a carbon copy of real life; what we search for in fiction is not so much reality but the epiphany of truth. Yet I suppose that if I were to go against my own recommendation and choose a work of fiction that would most resonate with our lives in the Islamic Republic of Iran, it would not be *The Prime of Miss Jean Brodie* or even *1984* but perhaps Nabokov's *Invitation to a Beheading* or better yet, *Lolita*.

A couple of years after we had begun our Thursday-morning seminars, on the last night I was in Tehran, a few friends and students came to say good-bye and to help me pack. When we had deprived the house of all its items, when the objects had vanished and the colors had faded into eight gray suitcases, like errant genies evaporating into their bottles, my students and I stood against the bare white wall of the dining room and took two photographs.

I have the two photographs in front of me now. In the first there are seven women, standing against a white wall. They are, according to the law of the land, dressed in black robes and head scarves, covered except for the oval of their faces and their hands. In the second photograph the same group, in the same position, stands against the same wall. Only they have taken off their coverings. Splashes of color separate one from the next. Each has become distinct through the color and style of her clothes, the color and the length of her hair; not even the two who are still wearing their head scarves look the same.

The one to the far right in the second photograph is our poet, Manna, in a white T-shirt and jeans. She made poetry out of things most people cast aside. The photograph does not reflect the peculiar opacity of Manna's dark eyes, a testament to her withdrawn and private nature.

Next to Manna is Mahshid, whose long black scarf clashes with her delicate features and retreating smile. Mahshid was good at many things, but she had a certain daintiness about her and we took to calling her "my lady." Nassrin used to say that more than defining Mahshid, we had managed to add another dimension to the word *lady*. Mahshid is very sensitive. She's like porcelain, Yassi once told me, easy to crack. That's why she appears fragile to those who don't know her too well; but woe to whoever offends her. As for me, Yassi continued good-naturedly, I'm like good old plastic; I won't crack no matter what you do with me.

Yassi was the youngest in our group. She is the one in yellow, bending forward and bursting with laughter. We used to teasingly call her our comedian. Yassi was shy by nature, but certain things excited her and made her lose her inhibitions. She had a tone of voice that gently mocked and questioned not just others but herself as well.

I am the one in brown, standing next to Yassi, with one arm around her shoulders. Directly behind me stands Azin, my tallest student, with her long blond hair and a pink T-shirt. She is laughing like the rest of us. Azin's smiles never looked like smiles; they appeared more like preludes to an irrepressible and nervous hilarity. She beamed in that peculiar fashion even when she was describing her latest trouble with her husband. Always outrageous and outspoken, Azin relished the shock value of her actions and comments, and often clashed with Mahshid and Manna. We nicknamed her the wild one.

On my other side is Mitra, who was perhaps the calmest among us. Like the pastel colors of her paintings, she seemed to recede and fade into a paler register. Her beauty was saved from predictability by a pair of miraculous dimples, which she could and did use to manipulate many an unsuspecting victim into bending to her will.

Sanaz, who, pressured by family and society, vacillated between her desire for independence and her need for approval, is holding on to Mitra's arm. We are all laughing. And Nima, Manna's husband and my one true literary critic—if only he had had the perseverance to finish the brilliant essays he started to write—is our invisible partner, the photographer.

There was one more: Nassrin. She is not in the photographs—she didn't make it to the end. Yet my tale would be incomplete without those who could not or did not remain with us. Their absences persist, like an acute pain that seems to have no physical source. This is Tehran for me: its absences were more real than its presences.

When I see Nassrin in my mind's eye, she's slightly out of focus, blurred, somehow distant. I've combed through the photographs my students took with me over the years and Nassrin is in many of them, but always hidden behind something—a person, a tree. In one, I am standing with eight of my students in the small garden facing our faculty building, the scene of so many farewell photographs over the years. In the background stands a sheltering willow tree. We are laughing, and in one corner, from behind the tallest student, Nassrin peers out, like an imp intruding roguishly on a scene it was not invited to. In another I can barely make out her face in the small V space behind two other girls' shoulders. In this one she looks absentminded; she is frowning, as if unaware that she is being photographed.

How can I describe Nassrin? I once called her the Cheshire cat, appearing and disappearing at unexpected turns in my academic life. The truth is I can't describe her: she was her own definition. One can only say that Nassrin was Nassrin.

For nearly two years, almost every Thursday morning, rain or shine, they came to my house, and almost every time, I could not get over the shock of seeing them shed their mandatory veils and robes and burst into color. When my students came into that room, they took off more than their scarves and robes. Gradually, each one gained an outline and a shape, becoming her own inimitable self. Our world in that living room with its window framing my beloved Elburz Mountains became our sanctuary, our self-contained universe, mocking the reality of black-scarved, timid faces in the city that sprawled below.

The theme of the class was the relation between fiction and reality. We read Persian classical literature, such as the tales of our own lady of fiction, Scheherazade, from *A Thousand and One Nights,* along with Western classics— *Pride and Prejudice, Madame Bovary, Daisy Miller, The Dean's December* and, yes, *Lolita.* As I write the title of each book, memories whirl in with the wind to disturb the quiet of this fall day in another room in another country.

Here and now in that other world that cropped up so many times in our discussions, I sit and reimagine myself and my students, my girls as I came to call them, reading *Lolita* in a deceptively sunny room in Tehran. But to steal the words from Humbert, the poet/criminal of *Lolita,* I need you, the reader, to imagine us, for we won't really exist if you don't. Against the tyranny of time and politics, imagine us the way we sometimes didn't dare to imagine ourselves: in our most private and secret moments, in the most extraordinarily ordinary instances of life, listening to music, falling in love, walking down the shady streets or reading *Lolita* in Tehran. And then imagine us again with all this confiscated, driven underground, taken away from us.

If I write about Nabokov today, it is to celebrate our reading of Nabokov in Tehran, against all odds. Of all his novels I choose the one I taught last, and the one that is connected to so many memories. It is of *Lolita* that I want to write, but right now there is no way I can write about that novel without also writing about Tehran. This, then, is the story of *Lolita* in Tehran, how *Lolita* gave a different color to Tehran, and how Tehran helped redefine Nabokov's novel, turning it into this *Lolita,* our *Lolita.*

2. And so it happened that one Thursday in early September we gathered in my living room for our first meeting. Here they come, one more time. First I hear the bell, a pause, and the closing of the street door. Then I hear footsteps coming up the winding staircase and past my mother's apartment. As I move towards the front door, I register a piece of sky through the side window. Each girl, as soon as she reaches the door, takes off her robe and scarf, sometimes shaking her head from side to side. She pauses before entering the room. Only there is no room, just the teasing void of memory.

More than any other place in our home, the living room was symbolic of my nomadic and borrowed life. Vagrant pieces of furniture from different times and places were thrown together, partly out of financial necessity, and partly because of my eclectic taste. Oddly, these incongruous ingredients created a symmetry that the other, more deliberately furnished rooms in the apartment lacked.

My mother would go crazy each time she saw the paintings leaning against the wall and the vases of flowers on the floor and the curtainless windows, which I refused to dress until I was finally reminded that this was an Islamic country and windows needed to be dressed. I don't know if you really belong to me, she would lament. Didn't I raise you to be orderly and organized? Her tone was serious, but she had repeated the same complaint for so many years that by now it was an almost tender ritual. Azi—that was my nickname—Azi, she would say, you are a grown-up lady now; act like one. Yet there was something in her tone that kept me young and fragile and obstinate, and still, when in memory I hear her voice, I know I never lived up to her expectations. I never did become the lady she tried to will me into being.

That room, which I never paid much attention to at that time, has gained a different status in my mind's eye now that it has become the precious object of memory. It was a spacious room, sparsely furnished and decorated. At one corner was the fireplace, a fanciful creation of my husband, Bijan. There was a love seat against one wall, over which I had thrown a lace cover, my mother's gift from long ago. A pale peach couch faced the window, accompanied by two matching chairs and a big square glass-topped iron table.

My place was always in the chair with its back to the window, which opened onto a wide cul-de-sac called Azar. Opposite the window was the former American Hospital, once small and exclusive, now a noisy, overcrowded medical facility for wounded and disabled veterans of the war. On "weekends"—Thursdays and Fridays in Iran—the small street was crowded with hospital visitors who came as if for a picnic, with sandwiches and children. The neighbor's front yard, his pride and joy, was the main victim of their assaults, especially in summer, when they helped themselves to his beloved roses. We could hear the sound of children shouting, crying and laughing, and, mingled in, their mothers' voices, also shouting, calling out their children's names and threatening them with punishments. Sometimes a child or two would ring our doorbell and run away, repeating their perilous exercise at intervals.

From our second-story apartment—my mother occupied the first floor, and my brother's apartment, on the third floor, was often empty, since he had left for England—we could see the upper branches of a generous tree and, in the distance, over the buildings, the Elburz Mountains. The street, the hospital and its visitors were censored out of sight. We felt their presence only through the disembodied noises emanating from below.

I could not see my favorite mountains from where I sat, but opposite my chair, on the far wall of the dining room, was an antique oval mirror, a gift from my father, and in its reflection, I could see the mountains capped with snow, even in summer, and watch the trees change color. That censored view intensified my impression that the noise came not from the street below but from some far-off place, a place whose persistent hum was our only link to the world we refused, for those few hours, to acknowledge.

That room, for all of us, became a place of transgression. What a wonderland it was! Sitting around the large coffee table covered with bouquets of flowers, we moved in and out of the novels we read. Looking back, I am amazed at how much we learned without even noticing it. We were, to borrow from Nabokov, to experience how the ordinary pebble of ordinary life could be transformed into a jewel through the magic eye of fiction.

3.   Six A.M.: the first day of class. I was already up. Too excited to eat breakfast, I put the coffee on and then took a long, leisurely shower. The water caressed my neck, my back, my legs, and I stood there both rooted and light. For the first time in many years, I felt a sense of anticipation that was not marred by tension: I would not need to go through the torturous rituals that had marked my days when I taught at the university—rituals governing what I was forced to wear, how I was expected to act, the gestures I had to remember to control. For this class, I would prepare differently.

Life in the Islamic Republic was as capricious as the month of April, when short periods of sunshine would suddenly give way to showers and storms. It was unpredictable: the regime would go through cycles of some tolerance, followed by a crackdown. Now, after a period of relative calm and so-called liberalization, we had again entered a time of hardships. Universities had once more become the targets of attack by the cultural purists who were busy imposing stricter sets of laws, going so far as to segregate men and women in classes and punishing disobedient professors.

The University of Allameh Tabatabai, where I had been teaching since 1987, had been singled out as the most liberal university in Iran. It was rumored that someone in the Ministry of Higher Education had asked, rhetorically, if the faculty at Allameh thought they lived in Switzerland. *Switzerland* had somehow become a byword for Western laxity: any program or action that was deemed un-Islamic was reproached with a mocking reminder that Iran was by no means Switzerland.

The pressure was hardest on the students. I felt helpless as I listened to their endless tales of woe. Female students were being penalized for running up the stairs when they were late for classes, for laughing in the hallways, for talking to members of the opposite sex. One day Sanaz had barged into class near the end of the session, crying. In between bursts of tears, she explained that she was late because the female guards at the door, finding a blush in her bag, had tried to send her home with a reprimand.

Why did I stop teaching so suddenly? I had asked myself this question many times. Was it the declining quality of the university? The ever-increasing indifference among the remaining faculty and students? The daily struggle against arbitrary rules and restrictions?

I smiled as I rubbed the coarse loofah over my skin, remembering the reaction of the university officials to my letter of resignation. They had harassed and limited me in all manner of ways, monitoring my visitors, controlling my actions, refusing a long-overdue tenure; and when I resigned, they infuriated me by suddenly commiserating and by refusing to accept my resignation. The students had threatened to boycott classes, and it was of some satisfaction to me to find out later that despite threats of reprisals, they in fact did boycott my replacement. Everyone thought I would break down and eventually return.

It took two more years before they finally accepted my resignation. I remember a friend told me, You don't understand their mentality. They won't accept your resignation because they don't think you have the right to quit. *They* are the ones who decide how long you should stay and when you should be dispensed with. More than anything else, it was this arbitrariness that had become unbearable.

What will you do? my friends had asked. Will you just stay home now? Well, I could write another book, I would tell them. But in truth I had no definite plans. I was still dealing with the aftershocks of a book on Nabokov I had just published, and only vague ideas, like vapors, formed when I turned to consider the shape of my next book. I could, for a while at least, continue the pleasant task of studying Persian classics, but one particular project, a notion I had been nurturing for years, was uppermost in my mind. For a long time I had dreamt of creating a special class, one that would give me the freedoms denied me in the classes I taught in the Islamic Republic. I wanted to teach a handful of selected students wholly committed to the study of literature, students who were not handpicked by the government, who had not chosen English literature simply because they had not been accepted in other fields or because they thought an English degree would be a good career move.

Teaching in the Islamic Republic, like any other vocation, was subservient to politics and subject to arbitrary rules. Always, the joy of teaching was marred by diversions and considerations forced on us by the regime—how well could one teach when the main concern of university officials was not the quality of one's work but the color of one's lips, the subversive potential of a single strand of hair? Could one really concentrate on one's job when what preoccupied the faculty was how to excise the word *wine* from a Hemingway story, when they decided not to teach Brontë because she appeared to condone adultery?

I was reminded of a painter friend who had started her career by depicting scenes from life, mainly deserted rooms, abandoned houses, and discarded photographs of women. Gradually, her work became more abstract, and in her last exhibition, her paintings were splashes of rebellious color, like the two in my living room, dark patches with little droplets of blue. I asked about her progress from modern realism to abstraction. Reality has become so intolerable, she said, so bleak, that all I can paint now are the colors of my dreams.

The colors of my dreams, I repeated to myself, stepping out of the shower and onto the cool tiles. I liked that. How many people get a chance to paint the colors of their dreams? I put on my oversize bathrobe—it felt good to move from the security of the embracing water to the protective cover of a bathrobe wrapped around my body. I walked barefoot into the kitchen, poured some coffee into my favorite mug, the one with red strawberries, and sat down forgetfully on the divan in the hall.

This class was the color of my dreams. It entailed an active withdrawal from a reality that had turned hostile. I wanted very badly to hold on to my rare mood of jubilance and optimism. For in the back of my mind, I didn't know what awaited me at the end of this project. You are aware, a friend had said, that you are more and more withdrawing into yourself, and now that you have cut your relations with the university, your whole contact with the outside world will be mainly restricted to one room. Where will you go from here? he had asked. Withdrawal into one's dreams could be dangerous, I reflected, padding into the bedroom to change; this I had learned from Nabokov's crazy dreamers, like Kinbote and Humbert.

In selecting my students, I did not take into consideration their ideological or religious backgrounds. Later, I would count it as the class's great achievement that such a mixed group, with different and at times conflicting backgrounds, personal as well as religious and social, remained so loyal to its goals and ideals.

One reason for my choice of these particular girls was the peculiar mixture of fragility and courage I sensed in them. They were what you would call loners, who did not belong to any particular group or sect. I admired their ability to survive not despite but in some ways because of their solitary lives. We can call the class "a space of our own," Manna had suggested, a sort of communal version of Virginia Woolf's room of her own.

I spent longer than usual choosing my clothes that first morning, trying on different outfits, until I finally settled on a red-striped shirt and black corduroy jeans. I applied my makeup with care and put on bright red lipstick. As I fastened my small gold earrings, I suddenly panicked. What if it doesn't work? What if they won't come?

Don't, don't do that! Suspend all fears for the next five or six hours at least. Please, please, I pleaded with myself, putting on my shoes and going into the kitchen.

4.   I was making tea when the doorbell rang. I was so preoccupied with my thoughts that I didn't hear it the first time. I opened the door to Mahshid. I thought you weren't home, she said, handing me a bouquet of white and yellow daffodils. As she was taking off her black robe, I told her, There are no men in the house—you can take that off, too. She hesitated before uncoiling her long black scarf. Mahshid and Yassi both observed the veil, but Yassi of late had become more relaxed in the way she wore her scarf. She tied it with a loose knot under her throat, her dark brown hair, untidily parted in the middle, peeping out from underneath. Mahshid's hair, however, was meticulously styled and curled under. Her short bangs gave her a strangely old-fashioned look that struck me as more European than Iranian. She wore a deep blue jacket over her white shirt, with a huge yellow butterfly embroidered on its right side. I pointed to the butterfly: did you wear this in honor of Nabokov?

I no longer remember when Mahshid first began to take my classes at the university. Somehow, it seems as if she had always been there. Her father, a devout Muslim, had been an ardent supporter of the revolution. She wore the scarf even before the revolution, and in her class diary, she wrote about the lonely mornings when she went to a fashionable girls' college, where she felt neglected and ignored—ironically, because of her then-conspicuous attire. After the revolution, she was jailed for five years because of her affiliation with a dissident religious organization and banned from continuing her education for two years after she was out of jail.

I imagine her in those pre-revolutionary days, walking along the uphill street leading to the college on countless sunny mornings. I see her walking alone, her head to the ground. Then, as now, she did not enjoy the day's brilliance. I say "then, as now" because the revolution that imposed the scarf on others did not relieve Mahshid of her loneliness. Before the revolution, she could in a sense take pride in her isolation. At that time, she had worn the scarf as a testament to her faith. Her decision was a voluntary act. When the revolution forced the scarf on others, her action became meaningless.

Mahshid is proper in the true sense of the word: she has grace and a certain dignity. Her skin is the color of moonlight, and she has almond-shaped eyes and jet-black hair. She wears pastel colors and is soft-spoken. Her pious background should have shielded her, but it didn't. I cannot imagine her in jail.

Over the many years I have known Mahshid, she has rarely alluded to her jail experiences, which left her with a permanently impaired kidney. One day in class, as we were talking about our daily terrors and nightmares, she mentioned that her jail memories visited her from time to time and that she had still not found a way to articulate them. But, she added, everyday life does not have fewer horrors than prison.

I asked Mahshid if she wanted some tea. Always considerate, she said she'd rather wait for the others and apologized for being a little early. Can I help? she asked. There's really nothing to help with. Make yourself at home, I told her as I stepped into the kitchen with the flowers and searched for a vase. The bell rang again. I'll get it, Mahshid cried out from the living room. I heard laughter; Manna and Yassi had arrived.

Manna came into the kitchen holding a small bouquet of roses. It's from Nima, she said. He wants to make you feel bad about excluding him from the class. He says he'll carry a bouquet of roses and march in front of your house during class hours, in protest. She was beaming; a few brief sparkles flashed in her eyes and died down again.

Putting the pastries onto a large tray, I asked Manna if she envisioned the words to her poems in colors. Nabokov writes in his autobiography that he and his mother saw the letters of the alphabet in color, I explained. He says of himself that he is a painterly writer.

The Islamic Republic coarsened my taste in colors, Manna said, fingering the discarded leaves of her roses. I want to wear outrageous colors, like shocking pink or tomato red. I feel too greedy for colors to see them in carefully chosen words of poetry. Manna was one of those people who would experience ecstasy but not happiness. Come here, I want to show you something, I said, leading her into our bedroom. When I was very young, I was obsessed with the colors of places and things my father told me about in his nightly stories. I wanted to know the color of Scheherazade's dress, her bedcover, the color of the genie and the magic lamp, and once I asked him about the color of paradise. He said it could be any color I wanted it to be. That was not enough. Then one day when we had guests and I was eating my soup in the dining room, my eyes fell on a painting I had seen on the wall ever since I could remember, and I instantly knew the color of my paradise. And here it is, I said, proudly pointing to a small oil painting in an old wooden frame: a green landscape of lush, leathery leaves with two birds, two deep red apples, a golden pear and a touch of blue.

My paradise is swimming-pool blue! Manna shot in, her eyes still glued to the painting. We lived in a large garden that belonged to my grandparents, she said, turning to me. You know the old Persian gardens, with their fruit trees, peaches, apples, cherries, persimmons and a willow or two. My best memories are of swimming in our huge irregularly shaped swimming pool. I was a swimming champion at our school, a fact my dad was very proud of. About a year after the revolution, my father died of a heart attack, and then the government confiscated our house and our garden and we moved into an apartment. I never swam again. My dream is at the bottom of that pool. I have a recurring dream of diving in to retrieve something of my father's memory and my childhood, she said as we walked to the living room, for the doorbell had rung again.

Azin and Mitra had arrived together. Azin was taking off her black kimonolike robe—Japanese-style robes were all the rage at the time—revealing a white peasant blouse that made no pretense of covering her shoulders, big golden earrings and pink lipstick. She had a branch of small yellow orchids—from Mitra and myself, she said in that special tone of hers that I can only describe as a flirtatious pout.

Nassrin came in next. She had brought two boxes of nougats: presents from Isfahan, she declared. She was dressed in her usual uniform—navy robe, navy scarf and black heelless shoes. When I had last seen her in class, she was wearing a huge black chador, revealing only the oval of her face and two restless hands, which, when she was not writing or doodling, were constantly in motion, as if trying to escape the confines of the thick black cloth. More recently, she had exchanged the chador for long, shapeless robes in navy, black or dark brown, with thick matching scarves that hid her hair and framed her face. She had a small, pale face, skin so transparent you could count the veins, full eyebrows, long lashes, lively eyes (brown), a small straight nose and an angry mouth: an unfinished miniature by some master who had suddenly been called away from his job and left the meticulously drawn face imprisoned in a careless splash of dark color.

We heard the sound of screeching tires and sudden brakes. I looked out the window: a small old Renault, cream-colored, had pulled up on the curb. Behind the wheel, a young man with fashionable sunglasses and a defiant profile rested his black-sleeved arm on the curve of the open window and gave the impression that he was driving a Porsche. He was staring straight in front of him as he talked to the woman beside him. Only once did he turn his head to his right, with what I could guess was a cross expression, and that was when the woman got out of the car and he angrily slammed the door behind her. As she walked to our front door, he threw his head out and shouted a few words, but she did not turn back to answer. The old Renault was Sanaz's; she had bought it with money saved from her job.

I turned towards the room, blushing for Sanaz. That must be the obnoxious brother, I thought. Seconds later the doorbell rang and I heard Sanaz's hurried steps and opened the door to her. She looked harassed, as if she had been running from a stalker or a thief. As soon as she saw me, she adjusted her face into a smile and said breathlessly: I hope I am not too late?

There were two very important men dominating Sanaz's life at the time. The first was her brother. He was nineteen years old and had not yet finished high school and was the darling of their parents, who, after two girls, one of whom had died at the age of three, had finally been blessed with a son. He was spoiled, and his one obsession in life was Sanaz. He had taken to proving his masculinity by spying on her, listening to her phone conversations, driving her car around, and monitoring her actions. Her parents had tried to appease Sanaz and begged her, as the older sister, to be patient and understanding, to use her motherly instincts to see him through this difficult period.

The other was her childhood sweetheart, a boy she had known since she was eleven. Their parents were best friends, and their families spent most of their time and vacations together. Sanaz and Ali seemed to have been in love forever. Their parents encouraged this union and called it a match made in heaven. When Ali went away to England six years ago, his mother took to calling Sanaz his bride. They wrote to each other, sent photographs, and recently, when the number of Sanaz's suitors increased, there were talks of engagement and a reunion in Turkey, where Iranians did not require entrance visas. Any day now it might happen, an event Sanaz looked forward to with some fear and trepidation.

I had never seen Sanaz without her uniform, and stood there almost transfixed as she took off her robe and scarf. She was wearing an orange T-shirt tucked into tight jeans and brown boots, yet the most radical transformation was the mass of shimmering dark brown hair that now framed her face. She shook her magnificent hair from side to side, a gesture that I later noticed was a habit with her; she would toss her head and run her fingers through her hair every once in a while, as if making sure that her most prized possession was still there. Her features looked softer and more radiant—the black scarf she wore in public made her small face look emaciated and almost hard.

I'm sorry I'm a little late, she said breathlessly, running her fingers through her hair. My brother insisted on driving me, and he refused to wake up on time. He never gets up before ten, but he wanted to know where I was going. I might be off on some secret tryst, you know, a date or something.

I have been worrying in case any of you would get into trouble for this class, I said, inviting them all to take their seats around the table in the living room. I hope your parents and spouses feel comfortable with our arrangement.

Nassrin, who was wandering around the room, inspecting the paintings as if seeing them for the first time, paused to say offhandedly, I mentioned the idea very casually to my father, just to test his reaction, and he vehemently disapproved.

How did you convince him to let you come? I asked. I lied, she said. You lied? What else can one do with a person who's so dictatorial he won't let his daughter, at *this age,* go to an all-female literature class? Besides, isn't this how we treat the regime? Can we tell the Revolutionary Guards the truth? We lie to them; we hide our satellite dishes. We tell them we don't have illegal books and alcohol in our houses. Even my venerable father lies to them when the safety of his family is at stake, Nassrin added defiantly.

What if he calls me to check on you? I said, half teasingly. He won't. I gave a brilliant alibi. I said Mahshid and I had volunteered to help translate Islamic texts into English. And he believed you? Well, he had no reason not to. I hadn't lied to him before—not really—and it was what he wanted to believe. And he trusts Mahshid completely.

So if he calls me, I should lie to him? I persisted. It's up to you, Nassrin said after a pause, looking down at her twisting hands. Do *you* think you should tell him? By now I could hear a note of desperation in her voice. Am I getting you into trouble?

Nassrin always acted so confident that sometimes I forgot how vulnerable she really was under that tough-girl act. Of course I would respect your confidence, I said more gently. As you said, you are a big girl. You know what you're doing.

I had settled into my usual chair, opposite the mirror, where the mountains had come to stay. It is strange to look into a mirror and see not yourself but a view so distant from you. Mahshid, after some hesitation, had taken the chair to my right. On the couch, Manna settled to the far right and Azin to the far left; they instinctively kept their distance. Sanaz and Mitra were perched on the love seat, their heads close together as they whispered and giggled.

At this point Yassi and Nassrin came in and looked around for seats. Azin patted the empty part of the couch, inviting Yassi with her hand. Yassi hesitated for a moment and then slid between Azin and Manna. She slumped into place and seemed to leave little room for her two companions, who sat upright and a little stiff in their respective corners. Without her robe, she looked a little overweight, as if she had not as yet lost her baby fat. Nassrin had gone to the dining room in search of a chair. We can squeeze you in here, said Manna. No, thank you, I actually prefer straight-backed chairs. When she returned, she placed her chair between the couch and Mahshid.

They kept that arrangement, faithfully, to the end. It became representative of their emotional boundaries and personal relations. And so began our first class.

5. "Upsilamba!" I heard Yassi exclaim as I entered the dining room with a tray of tea. Yassi loved playing with words. Once she told us that her obsession with words was pathological. As soon as I discover a new word, I have to use it, she

said, like someone who buys an evening gown and is so eager that she wears it to the movies, or to lunch.

Let me pause and rewind the reel to retrace the events leading us to Yassi's exclamation. This was our first session. All of us had been nervous and inarticulate. We were used to meeting in public, mainly in classrooms and in lecture halls. The girls had their separate relationships with me, but except for Nassrin and Mahshid, who were intimate, and a certain friendship between Mitra and Sanaz, the rest were not close; in many cases, in fact, they would never have chosen to be friends. The collective intimacy made them uncomfortable.

I had explained to them the purpose of the class: to read, discuss, and respond to works of fiction. Each would have a private diary, in which she should record her responses to the novels, as well as ways in which these works and their discussions related to her personal and social experiences. I explained that I had chosen them for this class because they seemed dedicated to the study of literature. I mentioned that one of the criteria for the books I had chosen was their authors' faith in the critical and almost magical power of literature, and reminded them of the nineteen-year-old Nabokov, who, during the Russian Revolution, would not allow himself to be diverted by the sound of bullets. He kept on writing his solitary poems while he heard the guns and saw the bloody fights from his window. Let us see, I said, whether seventy years later our disinterested faith will reward us by transforming the gloomy reality created of this other revolution.

The first work we discussed was *A Thousand and One Nights,* the familiar tale of the cuckolded king who slew successive virgin wives as revenge for his queen's betrayal, and whose murderous hand was finally stayed by the entrancing storyteller Scheherazade. I formulated certain general questions for them to consider, the most central of which was how these great works of imagination could help us in our present trapped situation as women. We were not looking for blueprints, for an easy solution, but we did hope to find a link between the open spaces the novels provided and the closed ones we were confined to. I remember reading to my girls Nabokov's claim that "readers were born free and ought to remain free."

What had most intrigued me about the frame story of *A Thousand and One Nights* were the three kinds of women it portrayed—all victims of a king's unreasonable rule. Before Scheherazade enters the scene, the women in the story are divided into those who betray and then are killed (the queen) and those who are killed before they have a chance to betray (the virgins). The virgins, who, unlike Scheherazade, have no voice in the story, are mostly ignored by the critics. Their silence, however, is significant. They surrender their virginity, and their lives, without resistance or protest. They do not quite exist, because they leave no trace in their anonymous death. The queen's infidelity does not rob the king of his absolute authority; it throws him off balance. Both types of women—the queen and the virgins—tacitly accept the king's public authority by acting within the confines of his domain and by accepting its arbitrary laws.

Scheherazade breaks the cycle of violence by choosing to embrace different terms of engagement. She fashions her universe not through physical force, as does the king, but through imagination and reflection. This gives her the courage to risk her life and sets her apart from the other characters in the tale.

Our edition of *A Thousand and One Nights* came in six volumes. I, luckily, had bought mine before it was banned and sold only on the black market, for exorbitant prices. I divided the volumes among the girls and asked them, for the next session, to classify the tales according to the types of women who played central roles in the stories.

Once I'd given them their assignment, I asked them each to tell the rest of us why they had chosen to spend their Thursday mornings here, discussing Nabokov and Jane Austen. Their answers were brief and forced. In order to break the ice, I suggested the calming distraction of cream puffs and tea.

This brings us to the moment when I enter the dining room with eight glasses of tea on an old and unpolished silver tray. Brewing and serving tea is an aesthetic ritual in Iran, performed several times a day. We serve tea in transparent glasses, small and shapely, the most popular of which is called slim-waisted: round and full at the top, narrow in the middle and round and full at the bottom. The color of the tea and its subtle aroma are an indication of the brewer's skill.

I step into the dining room with eight slim-waisted glasses whose honey-colored liquid trembles seductively. At this point, I hear Yassi shout triumphantly, "Upsilamba!" She throws the word at me like a ball, and I take a mental leap to catch it.

Upsilamba!—the word carries me back to the spring of 1994, when four of my girls and Nima were auditing a class I was teaching on the twentieth-century novel. The class's favorite book was Nabokov's *Invitation to a Beheading*. In this novel, Nabokov differentiates Cincinnatus C., his imaginative and lonely hero, from those around him through his originality in a society where uniformity is not only the norm but also the law. Even as a child, Nabokov tells us, Cincinnatus appreciated the freshness and beauty of language, while other children "understood each other at the first word, since they had no words that would end in an unexpected way, perhaps in some archaic letter, an upsilamba, becoming a bird or catapult with wondrous consequences."

No one in class had bothered to ask what the word meant. No one, that is, who was properly taking the class—for many of my old students just stayed on and sat in on my classes long after their graduation. Often, they were more interested and worked harder than my regular students, who were taking the class for credit. Thus it was that those who audited the class—including Nassrin, Manna, Nima, Mahshid, and Yassi—had one day gathered in my office to discuss this and a number of other questions.

I decided to play a little game with the class, to test their curiosity. On the midterm exam, one of the questions was "Explain the significance of the word *upsilamba* in the context of *Invitation to a Beheading*. What does the word mean, and how does it relate to the main theme of the novel?" Except for four or five students, no one had any idea what I could possibly mean, a point I did not forget to remind them of every once in a while throughout the rest of that term.

The truth was that *upsilamba* was one of Nabokov's fanciful creations, possibly a word he invented out of *upsilon,* the twentieth letter in the Greek alphabet, and *lambda,* the eleventh. So that first day in our private class, we let our minds play again and invented new meanings of our own.

I said I associated *upsilamba* with the impossible joy of a suspended leap. Yassi, who seemed excited for no particular reason, cried out that she always thought it could be the name of a dance—you know, "C'mon, baby, do the Upsilamba with me." I proposed that for the next time, they each write a sentence or two explaining what the word meant to them.

Manna suggested that *upsilamba* evoked the image of small silver fish leaping in and out of a moonlit lake. Nima added in parentheses, Just so you won't forget me, although you have barred me from your class: an upsilamba to you, too! For Azin it was a sound, a melody. Mahshid described an image of three girls jumping rope and shouting "Upsilamba!" with each leap. For Sanaz, the word was a small African boy's secret magical name. Mitra wasn't sure why the word reminded her of the paradox of a blissful sigh. And to Nassrin it was the magic code that opened the door to a secret cave filled with treasures.

Upsilamba became part of our increasing repository of coded words and expressions, a repository that grew over time until gradually we had created a secret language of our own. That word became a symbol, a sign of that vague sense of joy, the tingle in the spine Nabokov expected his readers to feel in the act of reading fiction; it was a sensation that separated the good readers, as he called them, from the ordinary ones. It also became the code word that opened the secret cave of remembrance.

6. In his foreword to the English edition of *Invitation to a Beheading* (1959), Nabokov reminds the reader that his novel does not offer *"tout pour tous."* Nothing of the kind. "It is," he claims, "a violin in the void." And yet, he goes on to say, "I know ... a few readers who will jump up, ruffling their hair." Well, absolutely. The original version, Nabokov tells us, was published in installments in 1935. Almost six decades later, in a world unknown and presumably unknowable to Nabokov, in a forlorn living room with windows looking out towards distant white-capped mountains, time and again I would stand witness to the unlikeliest of readers as they lost themselves in a madness of hair-ruffling.

Invitation to a Beheading begins with the announcement that its fragile hero, Cincinnatus C., has been sentenced to death for the crime of "gnostic turpitude": in a place where all citizens are required to be transparent, he is opaque. The principal characteristic of this world is its arbitrariness; the condemned man's only privilege is to know the time of his death—but the executioners keep even this from him, turning every day into a day of execution. As the story unfolds, the reader discovers with increasing discomfort the artificial texture of this strange place. The moon from the window is fake; so is the spider in the corner, which, according to convention, must become the prisoner's faithful companion. The director of the jail, the jailer, and the defense lawyer are all the same man, and keep changing places. The most important character, the executioner, is first introduced to the prisoner under another name and as a fellow prisoner: M'sieur Pierre. The executioner and the condemned man must learn to love each other and cooperate in the act of execution, which will be celebrated in a gaudy feast. In this staged world, Cincinnatus's only window to another universe is his writing.

The world of the novel is one of empty rituals. Every act is bereft of substance and significance, and even death becomes a spectacle for which the good citizens buy tickets. It is only through these empty rituals that brutality becomes possible. In another Nabokov novel, *The Real Life of Sebastian Knight,* Sebastian's brother discovers two seemingly incongruous pictures in his dead brother's library: a pretty, curly-haired child playing with a dog and a Chinese man in the act of being beheaded. The two pictures remind us of the close relation between banality and brutality. Nabokov had a special Russian term for this: *poshlust.*

Poshlust, Nabokov explains, "is not only the obviously trashy but mainly the falsely important, the falsely beautiful, the falsely clever, the falsely attractive." Yes, there are many examples you can bring from everyday life, from the politicians' sugary speeches to certain writers' proclamations to chickens. Chickens? You know, the ones the street vendors sell nowadays—if you lived in Tehran, you couldn't possibly miss them. The ones they dip in paint—shocking pink, brilliant red, or turquoise blue—in order to make them more attractive. Or the plastic flowers, the bright pink-and-blue artificial gladiolas carted out at the university both for mourning and for celebration.

What Nabokov creates for us in *Invitation to a Beheading* is not the actual physical pain and torture of a totalitarian regime but the nightmarish quality of living in an atmosphere of perpetual dread. Cincinnatus C. is frail, he is passive, he is a hero without knowing or acknowledging it: he fights with his instincts, and his acts of writing are his means of escape. He is a hero because he refuses to become like all the rest.

Unlike in other utopian novels, the forces of evil here are not omnipotent; Nabokov shows us their frailty as well. They are ridiculous and they can be defeated, and this does not lessen the tragedy—the waste. *Invitation to a Beheading* is written from the point of view of the victim, one who ultimately sees the absurd sham of his persecutors and who must retreat into himself in order to survive.

Those of us living in the Islamic Republic of Iran grasped both the tragedy and absurdity of the cruelty to which we were subjected. We had to poke fun at our own misery in order to survive. We also instinctively recognized poshlust—not just in others, but in ourselves. This was one reason that art and literature became so essential to our lives: they were not a luxury but a necessity. What Nabokov captured was the texture of life in a totalitarian society, where you are completely alone in an illusory world full of false promises, where you can no longer differentiate between your savior and your executioner.

We formed a special bond with Nabokov despite the difficulty of his prose. This went deeper than our identification with his themes. His novels are shaped around invisible trapdoors, sudden gaps that constantly pull the carpet from under the reader's feet. They are filled with mistrust of what we call everyday reality, an acute sense of that reality's fickleness and frailty.

There was something, both in his fiction and in his life, that we instinctively related to and grasped, the possibility of a boundless freedom when all options are taken away. I think that was what drove me to create the class. My main link with the outside world had been the university, and now that I had severed that link, there on the brink of the void, I could invent the violin or be devoured by the void.

7. The two photographs should be placed side by side. Both embody the "fragile unreality"—to quote Nabokov on his own state of exile—of our existence in the Islamic Republic of Iran. One cancels the other, and yet without one, the other is incomplete. In the first photograph, standing there in our black robes and scarves, we are as we had been shaped by someone else's dreams. In the second, we appear as we imagined ourselves. In neither could we feel completely at home.

The second photograph belonged to the world inside the living room. But outside, underneath the window that deceptively showcased only the mountains and the tree outside our house, was the other world, where the bad witches and furies were waiting to transform us into the hooded creatures of the first.

The best way I can think of explaining this self-negating and paradoxical inferno is through an anecdote, one that, like similar anecdotes, defies fiction to become its own metaphor.

The chief film censor in Iran, up until 1994, was blind. Well, nearly blind. Before that, he was the censor for theater. One of my playwright friends once described how he would sit in the theater wearing thick glasses that seemed to hide more than they revealed. An assistant who sat by him would explain the action onstage, and he would dictate the parts that needed to be cut.

After 1994, this censor became the head of the new television channel. There, he perfected his methods and demanded that the scriptwriters give him their scripts on audiotape; they were forbidden to make them attractive or dramatize them in any way. He then made his judgments about the scripts based on the tapes. More interesting, however, is the fact that his successor, who was not blind—not physically, that is—nonetheless followed the same system.

Our world under the mullahs' rule was shaped by the colorless lenses of the blind censor. Not just our reality but also our fiction had taken on this curious coloration in a world where the censor was the poet's rival in rearranging and reshaping reality, where we simultaneously invented ourselves and were figments of someone else's imagination.

We lived in a culture that denied any merit to literary works, considering them important only when they were handmaidens to something seemingly more urgent—namely ideology. This was a country where all gestures, even the most private, were interpreted in political terms. The colors of my head scarf or my father's tie were symbols of Western decadence and imperialist tendencies. Not wearing a beard, shaking hands with members of the opposite sex, clapping or whistling in public meetings, were likewise considered Western and therefore decadent, part of the plot by imperialists to bring down our culture.

A few years ago some members of the Iranian Parliament set up an investigative committee to examine the content of national television. The committee issued a lengthy report in which it condemned the showing of *Billy Budd,* because, it claimed, the story promoted homosexuality. Ironically, the

Iranian television programmers had mainly chosen that film because of its lack of female characters. The cartoon version of *Around the World in Eighty Days* was also castigated, because the main character—a lion—was British and the film ended in that bastion of imperialism, London.

Our class was shaped within this context, in an attempt to escape the gaze of the blind censor for a few hours each week. There, in that living room, we rediscovered that we were also living, breathing human beings; and no matter how repressive the state became, no matter how intimidated and frightened we were, like Lolita we tried to escape and to create our own little pockets of freedom. And like Lolita, we took every opportunity to flaunt our insubordination: by showing a little hair from under our scarves, insinuating a little color into the drab uniformity of our appearances, growing our nails, falling in love, and listening to forbidden music.

An absurd fictionality ruled our lives. We tried to live in the open spaces, in the chinks created between that room, which had become our protective cocoon, and the censor's world of witches and goblins outside. Which of these two worlds was more real, and to which did we really belong? We no longer knew the answers. Perhaps one way of finding out the truth was to do what we did: to try to imaginatively articulate these two worlds and, through that process, give shape to our vision and identity.

8.   How can I create this other world outside the room? I have no choice but to appeal once again to your imagination. Let's imagine one of the girls, say Sanaz, leaving my house and let us follow her from there to her final destination. She says her goodbyes and puts on her black robe and scarf over her orange shirt and jeans, coiling her scarf around her neck to cover her huge gold earrings. She directs wayward strands of hair under the scarf, puts her notes into her large bag, straps it on over her shoulder, and walks out into the hall. She pauses a moment on top of the stairs to put on thin lacy black gloves to hide her nail polish.

We follow Sanaz down the stairs, out the door, and into the street. You might notice that her gait and her gestures have changed. It is in her best interest not to be seen, not be heard or noticed. She doesn't walk upright, but bends her head towards the ground and doesn't look at passersby. She walks quickly and with a sense of determination. The streets of Tehran and other Iranian cities are patrolled by militia, who ride in white Toyota patrols, four gun-carrying men and women, sometimes followed by a minibus. They are called the Blood of God. They patrol the streets to make sure that women like Sanaz wear their veils properly, do not wear makeup, do not walk in public with men who are not their fathers, brothers, or husbands. She will pass slogans on the walls, quotations from Khomeini, and a group called the Party of God: MEN WHO WEAR TIES ARE U.S. LACKEYS. VEILING IS A WOMAN'S PROTECTION. Beside the slogan is a charcoal drawing of a woman: her face is featureless and framed by a dark chador. MY SISTER, GUARD YOUR VEIL. MY BROTHER, GUARD YOUR EYES.

If she gets on a bus, the seating is segregated. She must enter through the rear door and sit in the back seats, allocated to women. Yet in taxis, which accept as many as five passengers, men and women are squeezed together like sardines, as the saying goes, and the same goes with minibuses, where so many of my students complain of being harassed by bearded and God-fearing men.

You might well ask, What is Sanaz thinking as she walks the streets of Tehran? How much does this experience affect her? Most probably, she tries to distance her mind as much as possible from her surroundings. Perhaps she is thinking of her brother, or of her distant boyfriend and the time when she will meet him in Turkey. Does she compare her own situation with her mother's when she was the same age? Is she angry that women of her mother's generation could walk the streets freely, enjoy the company of the opposite sex, join the police force, become pilots, live under laws that were among the most progressive in the world regarding women? Does she feel humiliated by the new laws, by the fact that after the revolution, the age of marriage was lowered from eighteen to nine, that stoning became once more the punishment for adultery and prostitution?

In the course of nearly two decades, the streets have been turned into a war zone, where young women who disobey the rules are hurled into patrol cars, taken to jail, flogged, fined, forced to wash the toilets, and humiliated, and as soon as they leave, they go back and do the same thing. Is she aware, Sanaz, of her own power? Does she realize how dangerous she can be when her every stray gesture is a disturbance to public safety? Does she think how vulnerable the Revolutionary Guards are who for over eighteen years have patrolled the streets of Tehran and have had to endure young women like herself, and those of other generations, walking, talking, showing a strand of hair just to remind them that they have not converted?

We have reached Sanaz's house, where we will leave her on her doorstep, perhaps to confront her brother on the other side and to think in her heart of her boyfriend.

These girls, my girls, had both a real history and a fabricated one. Although they came from very different backgrounds, the regime that ruled them had tried to make their personal identities and histories irrelevant. They were never free of the regime's definition of them as Muslim women.

Whoever we were—and it was not really important what religion we belonged to, whether we wished to wear the veil or not, whether we observed certain religious norms or not—we had become the figment of someone else's dreams. A stern ayatollah, a self-proclaimed philosopher-king, had come to rule our land. He had come in the name of a past, a past that, he claimed, had been stolen from him. And he now wanted to re-create us in the image of that illusory past. Was it any consolation, and did we even wish to remember, that what he did to us was what we allowed him to do?

QUESTIONS FOR CONNECTIONS WITHIN THE READING

1. Why does Nafisi spend so much time describing the members of her reading group? What different motives may have brought these readers to Nafisi's apartment? We might normally think of reading as a solitary activity, unlike

watching movies or sports; why was it so important for the women to meet together as a group?

2. Judging from the information that Nafisi provides, why do you think her reading group selected the particular works she mentions: *A Thousand and One Nights,* as well as *Invitation to a Beheading, Lolita,* and other novels by Nabokov? Why might religious authorities, not only in Iran but also in the United States, object to the teaching of such works?

3. Early in Chapter 10 of *Reading Lolita in Tehran,* Nafisi writes, "*Lolita* was *not* a critique of the Islamic Republic, but it went against the grain of all totalitarian perspectives." Without consulting a dictionary, and drawing instead on Nafisi's account, try to define "totalitarian." What social and psychological effects does the totalitarian regime have on Nafisi and her students? In what sense might Lolita or other books you know pose a challenge to totalitarianism? How are literature and the other arts—music, painting, sculpture, dance—inherently liberating? Is it possible for art itself to be totalitarian?

QUESTIONS FOR WRITING

1. Does Nafisi present a theory of interpretation? In other words, what does she see as the "real" or "correct" meaning of a work of art? Does she accept Nabokov's claims that "readers were born free and ought to remain free"? Would Nafisi say a work of art can mean anything we want? What is the value of art if it has no determinate or "correct" meaning? If art has a value, is its value simply personal? Does it also have social, political, and cultural value?

2. Nafisi and her students read Nabokov against the backdrop of the Islamic Republic of Iran. In that setting, what does the experience offer them? Would their reading of the novel provide the same experience if it took place in the United States? Does literature serve a different social function in our society? How might reading a novel in a private group differ from the experience of reading the same novel in an American high school or college classroom?

QUESTIONS FOR MAKING CONNECTIONS
BETWEEN READINGS

1. Nafisi is convinced that reading groups like hers posed a real challenge to the regime. One important part of their effectiveness lay in the ability of art to sustain human connectedness in spite of isolating policies. But taking off the black chador and speaking face-to-face was only the beginning. Still more

powerfully, perhaps, literature gave the members of the reading group permission to become the creators of themselves. Starting with "Is Google Making Us Stupid?," would you say that the Internet poses a challenge to the established order in much the same way as Nabokov's writing did in Iran? Does the Internet help to sustain a sense of face-to-face connectedness, and does it encourage self-creation? Or might it have the opposite effect, making individuals feel invisible and insignificant?

2. Toward the close of his essay "The Mind's Eye," Oliver Sacks asks, "Do any of us, finally, know how we think?" Assuming that the answer to this question is no, what conclusions can we reach about the ways that each of us interprets our individual worlds? If everyone makes things meaningful in his or her own way, what purpose might be served by an activity such as meeting to discuss a work of literature? What does the individual gain from the communal reading of a work of fiction? Do the blind subjects of Sacks's essay have anything in common with Nafisi's students? Do Sacks and Nafisi, taken together, show that there is ultimately only one way to achieve "a rich and full realization" of an inner life?

TIM O'BRIEN

In 1968, DURING the war in Vietnam, Tim O'Brien graduated from college and was served a draft notice. An avowed opponent of the war, he considered fleeing to Canada but ultimately reported for basic training and was stationed near My Lai shortly after the infamous massacre there. O'Brien returned to the United States in 1970, having received injuries that earned him a Purple Heart. Since then he has published dozens of stories and books, both fiction and nonfiction, including the National Book Award–winning *Going After Cacciato* (1978). O'Brien has received many other prestigious awards as well, among them the O. Henry Award, the National Book Critics Circle Award, and the Pulitzer Prize. He is currently a visiting professor and holds an endowed chair at Texas State University in San Marcos, where he teaches in the creative writing program.

"How to Tell a True War Story," which is included in O'Brien's collection *The Things They Carried* (1998), is, paradoxically, a work of fiction. O'Brien's decision to present his narrative in this fashion is a sign of his continued engagement with a puzzle that has shaped his work for almost three decades. For O'Brien, the line between reality and fiction is always a fuzzy one, especially in accounts of war, where the experience outstrips the resources of language. Faced with the complexity of war, O'Brien is not trying to "close the books" on a painful past, but rather to keep the books from ever getting closed by those who might prefer to forget the high price that war always exacts. In O'Brien's work, this high price is not measured just in the loss of life, but also in the permanent loss of moral certainty. In response to a question about why he keeps returning to incidents that took place in the 1960s, O'Brien has said, "The war occurred half a lifetime ago, and yet the remembering makes it now. And sometimes remembering will lead to a story, which makes it forever. That's what stories are for. Stories are for joining the past to the future. Stories are for those late hours in the night when you can't remember how you got from where you were to where you are. Stories are for eternity, when memory is erased, when there is nothing to remember but the story."

O'Brien, Tim. "How to Tell a True War Story." *The Things They Carried*. New York: Broadway Books, 1998. 67–85.

Biographical information comes from http://illyria.com/tob/tobbio.html; quotation comes from http://www.illyria.com/tobhp.html.

■ ■

How to Tell a True War Story

This is true.

I had a buddy in Vietnam. His name was Bob Kiley, but everybody called him Rat.

A friend of his gets killed, so about a week later Rat sits down and writes a letter to the guy's sister. Rat tells her what a great brother she had, how together the guy was, a number one pal and comrade. A real soldier's soldier, Rat says. Then he tells a few stories to make the point, how her brother would always volunteer for stuff nobody else would volunteer for in a million years, dangerous stuff, like doing recon or going out on these really badass night patrols. Stainless steel balls, Rat tells her. The guy was a little crazy, for sure, but crazy in a good way, a real daredevil, because he liked the challenge of it, he liked testing himself, just man against gook. A great, great guy, Rat says.

Anyway, it's a terrific letter, very personal and touching. Rat almost bawls writing it. He gets all teary telling about the good times they had together, how her brother made the war seem almost fun, always raising hell and lighting up villes and bringing smoke to bear every which way. A great sense of humor, too. Like the time at this river when he went fishing with a whole damn crate of hand grenades. Probably the funniest thing in world history, Rat says, all that gore, about twenty zillion dead gook fish. Her brother, he had the right attitude. He knew how to have a good time. On Halloween, this real hot spooky night, the dude paints up his body all different colors and puts on this weird mask and hikes over to a ville and goes trick-or-treating almost stark naked, just boots and balls and an M-16. A tremendous human being, Rat says. Pretty nutso sometimes, but you could trust him with your life.

And then the letter gets very sad and serious. Rat pours his heart out. He says he loved the guy. He says the guy was his best friend in the world. They were like soul mates, he says, like twins or something, they had a whole lot in common. He tells the guy's sister he'll look her up when the war's over.

So what happens?

Rat mails the letter. He waits two months. The dumb cooze never writes back.

A true war story is never moral. It does not instruct, nor encourage virtue, nor suggest models of proper human behavior, nor restrain men from doing the things men have always done. If a story seems moral, do not believe it. If at the end of a war story you feel uplifted, or if you feel that some small bit of rectitude has been salvaged from the larger waste, then you have been made the victim of a very old and terrible lie. There is no rectitude whatsoever. There is no virtue. As a first rule of thumb, therefore, you can tell a true war story by its absolute and uncompromising allegiance to obscenity and evil. Listen to Rat Kiley. Cooze, he says. He does not say bitch. He certainly does not say woman, or girl. He says cooze. Then he spits and stares. He's nineteen years old—it's too much for him—so he looks at you with those big sad gentle killer eyes and says cooze, because his friend is dead, and because it's so incredibly sad and true: she never wrote back.

You can tell a true war story if it embarrasses you. If you don't care for obscenity, you don't care for the truth; if you don't care for the truth, watch how you vote. Send guys to war, they come home talking dirty.

Listen to Rat: "Jesus Christ, man, I write this beautiful fuckin' letter, I slave over it, and what happens? The dumb cooze never writes back."

The dead guy's name was Curt Lemon. What happened was, we crossed a muddy river and marched west into the mountains, and on the third day we took a break along a trail junction in deep jungle. Right away, Lemon and Rat Kiley started goofing. They didn't understand about the spookiness. They were kids; they just didn't know. A nature hike, they thought, not even a war, so they went off into the shade of some giant trees—quadruple canopy, no sunlight at all—and they were giggling and calling each other yellow mother and playing a silly game they'd invented. The game involved smoke grenades, which were harmless unless you did stupid things, and what they did was pull out the pin and stand a few feet apart and play catch under the shade of those huge trees. Whoever chickened out was a yellow mother. And if nobody chickened out, the grenade would make a light popping sound and they'd be covered with smoke and they'd laugh and dance around and then do it again.

It's all exactly true.

It happened, to *me,* nearly twenty years ago, and I still remember that trail junction and those giant trees and a soft dripping sound somewhere beyond the trees. I remember the smell of moss. Up in the canopy there were tiny white blossoms, but no sunlight at all, and I remember the shadows spreading out under the trees where Curt Lemon and Rat Kiley were playing catch with smoke grenades. Mitchell Sanders sat flipping his yo-yo. Norman Bowker and Kiowa and Dave Jensen were dozing, or half dozing, and all around us were those ragged green mountains.

Except for the laughter things were quiet.

At one point, I remember, Mitchell Sanders turned and looked at me, not quite nodding, as if to warn me about something, as if he already *knew,* then after a while he rolled up his yo-yo and moved away.

It's hard to tell you what happened next.

They were just goofing. There was a noise, I suppose, which must've been the detonator, so I glanced behind me and watched Lemon step from the shade into bright sunlight. His face was suddenly brown and shining. A handsome kid, really. Sharp gray eyes, lean and narrow-waisted, and when he died it was almost beautiful, the way the sunlight came around him and lifted him up and sucked him high into a tree full of moss and vines and white blossoms.

In any war story, but especially a true one, it's difficult to separate what happened from what seemed to happen. What seems to happen becomes its own happening and has to be told that way. The angles of vision are skewed. When a booby trap explodes, you close your eyes and duck and float outside yourself. When a guy dies, like Curt Lemon, you look away and then look back for a moment and then look away again. The pictures get jumbled; you tend to miss a lot. And then afterward, when you go to tell about it, there is always that surreal seemingness, which makes the story seem untrue, but which in fact represents the hard and exact truth as it *seemed*.

In many cases a true war story cannot be believed. If you believe it, be skeptical. It's a question of credibility. Often the crazy stuff is true and the normal stuff isn't, because the normal stuff is necessary to make you believe the truly incredible craziness.

In other cases you can't even tell a true war story. Sometimes it's just beyond telling.

I heard this one, for example, from Mitchell Sanders. It was near dusk and we were sitting at my foxhole along a wide muddy river north of Quang Ngai. I remember how peaceful the twilight was. A deep pinkish red spilled out on the river, which moved without sound, and in the morning we would cross the river and march west into the mountains. The occasion was right for a good story.

"God's truth," Mitchell Sanders said. "A six-man patrol goes up into the mountains on a basic listening-post operation. The idea's to spend a week up there, just lie low and listen for enemy movement. They've got a radio along, so if they hear anything suspicious—anything—they're supposed to call in artillery or gunships, whatever it takes. Otherwise they keep strict field discipline. Absolute silence. They just listen."

Sanders glanced at me to make sure I had the scenario. He was playing with his yo-yo, dancing it with short, tight little strokes of the wrist.

His face was blank in the dusk.

"We're talking regulation, by-the-book LP. These six guys, they don't say boo for a solid week. They don't got tongues. *All* ears."

"Right," I said.

"Understand me?"

"Invisible."

Sanders nodded.

"Affirm," he said. "Invisible. So what happens is, these guys get themselves deep in the bush, all camouflaged up, and they lie down and wait and that's all they do, nothing else, they lie there for seven straight days and just listen. And man, I'll tell you—it's spooky. This is mountains. You don't *know* spooky till you been there. Jungle, sort of, except it's way up in the clouds and there's always this fog—like rain, except it's not raining—everything's all wet and swirly and tangled up and you can't see jack, you can't find your own pecker to piss with. Like you don't even have a body. Serious spooky. You just go with the vapors—the fog sort of takes you in.... And the sounds, man. The sounds carry forever. You hear stuff nobody should *ever* hear."

Sanders was quiet for a second, just working the yo-yo, then he smiled at me.

"So after a couple days the guys start hearing this real soft, kind of wacked-out music. Weird echoes and stuff. Like a radio or something, but it's not a radio, it's this strange gook music that comes right out of the rocks. Faraway, sort of, but right up close, too. They try to ignore it. But it's a listening post, right? So they listen. And every night they keep hearing that crazyass gook concert. All kinds of chimes and xylophones. I mean, this is wilderness—no way, it can't be real—but there it *is,* like the mountains are tuned in to Radio fucking Hanoi. Naturally they get nervous. One guy sticks Juicy Fruit in his ears. Another guy almost flips. Thing is, though, they can't report music. They can't get on the horn and call back to base and say, 'Hey, listen, we need some firepower, we got to blow away this weirdo gook rock band.' They can't do that. It wouldn't go down. So they lie there in the fog and keep their mouths shut. And what makes it extra bad, see, is the poor dudes can't horse around like normal. Can't joke it away. Can't even talk to each other except maybe in whispers, all hush-hush, and that just revs up the willies. All they do is listen."

Again there was some silence as Mitchell Sanders looked out on the river. The dark was coming on hard now, and off to the west I could see the mountains rising in silhouette, all the mysteries and unknowns.

"This next part," Sanders said quietly, "you won't believe."

"Probably not," I said.

"You won't. And you know why?" He gave me a long, tired smile. "Because it happened. Because every word is absolutely dead-on true."

Sanders made a sound in his throat, like a sigh, as if to say he didn't care if I believed him or not. But he did care. He wanted me to feel the truth, to believe by the raw force of feeling. He seemed sad, in a way.

"These six guys," he said, "they're pretty fried out by now, and one night they start hearing voices. Like at a cocktail party. That's what it sounds like, this big swank gook cocktail party somewhere out there in the fog. Music and chitchat and stuff. It's crazy, I know, but they hear the champagne corks. They hear the actual martini glasses. Real hoity-toity, all very civilized, except this isn't civilization. This is Nam.

"Anyway, the guys try to be cool. They just lie there and groove, but after a while they start hearing—you won't believe this—they hear chamber music. They hear violins and cellos. They hear this terrific mama-san soprano. Then after a while they hear gook opera and a glee club and the Haiphong Boys Choir and a barbershop quartet and all kinds of weird chanting and Buddha-Buddha stuff. And the whole time, in the background, there's still that cocktail party going on. All these different voices. Not human voices, though. Because it's the mountains. Follow me? The rock—it's *talking.* And the fog, too, and the grass and the goddamn mongooses. Everything talks. The trees talk politics, the monkeys talk religion. The whole country: Vietnam. The place talks. It talks. Understand? Nam—it truly *talks.*

"The guys can't cope. They lose it. They get on the radio and report enemy movement—a whole army, they say—and they order up the firepower. They get arty and gunships. They call in air strikes. And I'll tell you, they fuckin' crash that cocktail party. All night long, they just smoke those mountains. They make jungle juice. They blow away trees and glee clubs and whatever else there is to blow away. Scorch time. They walk napalm up and down the ridges. They bring in the Cobras and F-4s, they use Willie Peter and HE and incendiaries. It's all fire. They make those mountains burn.

"Around dawn things finally get quiet. Like you never even *heard* quiet before. One of those real thick, real misty days—just clouds and fog, they're off in this special zone—and the mountains are absolutely dead-flat silent. Like *Brigadoon*—pure vapor, you know? Everything's all sucked up inside the fog. Not a single sound, except they still *hear* it.

"So they pack up and start humping. They head down the mountain, back to base camp, and when they get there they don't say diddly. They don't talk. Not a word, like they're deaf and dumb. Later on this fat bird colonel comes up and asks what the hell happened out there. What'd they hear? Why all the ordnance? The man's ragged out, he gets down tight on their case. I mean, they spent six trillion dollars on firepower, and this fatass colonel wants answers, he wants to know what the fuckin' story is.

"But the guys don't say zip. They just look at him for a while, sort of funny like, sort of amazed, and the whole war is right there in that stare. It says everything you can't ever say. It says, man, you got *wax* in your ears. It says, poor bastard, you'll never know—wrong frequency—you don't *even* want to hear this. Then they salute the fucker and walk away, because certain stories you don't ever tell."

You can tell a true war story by the way it never seems to end. Not then, not ever. Not when Mitchell Sanders stood up and moved off into the dark.

It all happened.

Even now, at this instant, I remember that yo-yo. In a way, I suppose, you had to be there, you had to hear it, but I could tell how desperately Sanders wanted me to believe him, his frustration at not quite getting the details right, not quite pinning down the final and definitive truth.

And I remember sitting at my foxhole that night, watching the shadows of Quang Ngai, thinking about the coming day and how we would cross the river and march west into the mountains, all the ways I might die, all the things I did not understand.

Late in the night Mitchell Sanders touched my shoulder. "Just came to me," he whispered. "The moral, I mean. Nobody listens. Nobody hears nothin'. Like that fatass colonel. The politicians, all the civilian types. Your girlfriend. My girlfriend. Everybody's sweet little virgin girlfriend. What they need is to go out on LP. The vapors, man. Trees and rocks—you got to *listen* to your enemy."

And then again, in the morning, Sanders came up to me. The platoon was preparing to move out, checking weapons, going through all the little rituals that preceded a day's march. Already the lead squad had crossed the river and was filing off toward the west.

"I got a confession to make," Sanders said. "Last night, man, I had to make up a few things."

"I know that."

"The glee club. There wasn't any glee club."

"Right."

"No opera."

"Forget it, I understand."

"Yeah, but listen, it's still true. Those six guys, they heard wicked sound out there. They heard sound you just plain won't believe."

Sanders pulled on his rucksack, closed his eyes for a moment, then almost smiled at me. I knew what was coming.

"All right," I said, "what's the moral?"

"Forget it."

"No, go ahead."

For a long while he was quiet, looking away, and the silence kept stretching out until it was almost embarrassing. Then he shrugged and gave me a stare that lasted all day.

"Hear that quiet, man?" he said. "That quiet—just listen. There's your moral."

In a true war story, if there's a moral at all, it's like the thread that makes the cloth. You can't tease it out. You can't extract the meaning without unraveling the deeper meaning. And in the end, really, there's nothing much to say about a true war story, except maybe "Oh."

True war stories do not generalize. They do not indulge in abstraction or analysis.

For example: War is hell. As a moral declaration the old truism seems perfectly true, and yet because it abstracts, because it generalizes, I can't believe it with my stomach. Nothing turns inside.

It comes down to gut instinct. A true war story, if truly told, makes the stomach believe.

This one does it for me. I've told it before—many times, many versions—but here's what actually happened.

We crossed that river and marched west into the mountains. On the third day, Curt Lemon stepped on a booby-trapped 105 round. He was playing catch with Rat Kiley, laughing, and then he was dead. The trees were thick; it took nearly an hour to cut an LZ for the dustoff.

Later, higher in the mountains, we came across a baby VC water buffalo. What it was doing there I don't know—no farms or paddies—but we chased it down and got a rope around it and led it along to a deserted village where we set up for the night. After supper Rat Kiley went over and stroked its nose.

He opened up a can of C rations, pork and beans, but the baby buffalo wasn't interested.

Rat shrugged.

He stepped back and shot it through the right front knee. The animal did not make a sound. It went down hard, then got up again, and Rat took careful aim and shot off an ear. He shot it in the hindquarters and in the little hump at its back. He shot it twice in the flanks. It wasn't to kill; it was to hurt. He put the rifle muzzle up against the mouth and shot the mouth away. Nobody said much. The whole platoon stood there watching, feeling all kinds of things, but there wasn't a great deal of pity for the baby water buffalo. Curt Lemon was dead. Rat Kiley had lost his best friend in the world. Later in the week he would write a long personal letter to the guy's sister, who would not write back, but for now it was a question of pain. He shot off the tail. He shot away chunks of meat below the ribs. All around us there was the smell of smoke and filth and deep greenery, and the evening was humid and very hot. Rat went to automatic. He shot randomly, almost casually, quick little spurts in the belly and butt. Then he reloaded, squatted down, and shot it in the left front knee. Again the animal fell hard and tried to get up, but this time it couldn't quite make it. It wobbled and went down sideways. Rat shot it in the nose. He bent forward and whispered something, as if talking to a pet, then he shot it in the throat. All the while the baby buffalo was silent, or almost silent, just a light bubbling sound where the nose had been. It lay very still. Nothing moved except the eyes, which were enormous, the pupils shiny black and dumb.

Rat Kiley was crying. He tried to say something, but then cradled his rifle and went off by himself.

The rest of us stood in a ragged circle around the baby buffalo. For a time no one spoke. We had witnessed something essential, something brand-new and profound, a piece of the world so startling there was not yet a name for it.

Somebody kicked the baby buffalo.

It was still alive, though just barely, just in the eyes.

"Amazing," Dave Jensen said. "My whole life, I never seen anything like it."

"Never?"

"Not hardly. Not once."

Kiowa and Mitchell Sanders picked up the baby buffalo. They hauled it across the open square, hoisted it up, and dumped it in the village well.

Afterward, we sat waiting for Rat to get himself together.

"Amazing," Dave Jensen kept saying. "A new wrinkle. I never seen it before."

Mitchell Sanders took out his yo-yo. "Well, that's Nam," he said. "Garden of Evil. Over here, man, every sin's real fresh and original."

How do you generalize?

War is hell, but that's not the half of it, because war is also mystery and terror and adventure and courage and discovery and holiness and pity and despair and longing and love. War is nasty; war is fun. War is thrilling; war is drudgery. War makes you a man; war makes you dead.

The truths are contradictory. It can be argued, for instance, that war is grotesque. But in truth war is also beauty. For all its horror, you can't help but gape at the awful majesty of combat. You stare out at tracer rounds unwinding through the dark like brilliant red ribbons. You crouch in ambush as a cool, impassive moon rises over the nighttime paddies. You admire the fluid symmetries of troops on the move, the harmonies of sound and shape and proportion, the great sheets of metal-fire streaming down from a gunship, the illumination rounds, the white phosphorus, the purply orange glow of napalm, the rocket's red glare. It's not pretty, exactly. It's astonishing. It fills the eye. It commands you. You hate it, yes, but your eyes do not. Like a killer forest fire, like cancer under a microscope, any battle or bombing raid or artillery barrage has the aesthetic purity of absolute moral indifference—a powerful, implacable beauty—and a true war story will tell the truth about this, though the truth is ugly.

To generalize about war is like generalizing about peace. Almost everything is true. Almost nothing is true. At its core, perhaps, war is just another name for death, and yet any soldier will tell you, if he tells the truth, that proximity to death brings with it a corresponding proximity to life. After a firefight, there is always the immense pleasure of aliveness. The trees are alive. The grass, the soil—everything. All around you things are purely living, and you among them, and the aliveness makes you tremble. You feel an intense, out-of-the-skin awareness of your living self—your truest self, the human being you want to be and then become by the force of wanting it. In the midst of evil you want to be a good man. You want decency. You want justice and courtesy and human concord, things you never knew you wanted. There is a kind of largeness to it, a kind of godliness. Though it's odd, you're never more alive than when you're almost dead. You recognize what's valuable. Freshly, as if for the first time, you love what's best in yourself and in the world, all that might be lost. At the hour of dusk you sit at your foxhole and look out on a wide river turning pinkish red, and at the mountains beyond, and although in the morning you must cross the river and go into the mountains and do terrible things and maybe die, even so, you find yourself studying the fine colors on the river, you feel wonder and awe at the setting of the sun, and you are filled with a hard, aching love for how the world could be and always should be, but now is not.

Mitchell Sanders was right. For the common soldier, at least, war has the feel—the spiritual texture—of a great ghostly fog, thick and permanent. There is no clarity. Everything swirls. The old rules are no longer binding, the old truths no longer true. Right spills over into wrong. Order blends into chaos, love into hate, ugliness into beauty, law into anarchy, civility into savagery. The vapors suck you in. You can't tell where you are, or why you're there, and the only certainty is overwhelming ambiguity.

In war you lose your sense of the definite, hence your sense of truth itself, and therefore it's safe to say that in a true war story nothing is ever absolutely true.

Often in a true war story there is not even a point, or else the point doesn't hit you until twenty years later, in your sleep, and you wake up and shake your wife and start telling the story to her, except when you get to the end you've forgotten the point again. And then for a long time you lie there watching the story happen in your head. You listen to your wife's breathing. The war's over. You close your eyes. You smile and think, Christ, what's the *point?*

This one wakes me up.

In the mountains that day, I watched Lemon turn sideways. He laughed and said *something* to Rat Kiley. Then he took a peculiar half step, moving from shade into bright sunlight, and the booby-trapped 105 round blew him into a tree. The parts were just hanging there, so Dave Jensen and I were ordered to shinny up and peel him off. I remember the white bone of an arm. I remember pieces of skin and something wet and yellow that must've been the intestines. The gore was horrible, and stays with me. But what wakes me up twenty years later is Dave Jensen singing "Lemon Tree" as we threw down the parts.

You can tell a true war story by the questions you ask. Somebody tells a story, let's say, and afterward you ask, "Is it true?" and if the answer matters, you've got your answer.

For example, we've all heard this one. Four guys go down a trail. A grenade sails out. One guy jumps on it and takes the blast and saves his three buddies.

Is it true?

The answer matters.

You'd feel cheated if it never happened. Without the grounding reality, it's just a trite bit of puffery, pure Hollywood, untrue in the way all such stories are untrue. Yet even if it did happen—and maybe it did, anything's possible—even then you know it can't be true, because a true war story does not depend upon that kind of truth. Absolute occurrence is irrelevant. A thing may happen and be a total lie; another thing may not happen and be truer than the truth. For example: Four guys go down a trail. A grenade sails out. One guy jumps on it and takes the blast, but it's a killer grenade and everybody dies anyway. Before they die, though, one of the dead guys says, "The fuck you do *that* for?" and the jumper says, "Story of my life, man," and the other guy starts to smile but he's dead.

That's a true story that never happened.

Twenty years later, I can still see the sunlight on Lemon's face. I can see him turning, looking back at Rat Kiley, then he laughed and took that curious half step from shade into sunlight, his face suddenly brown and shining, and when his foot touched down, in that instant, he must've thought it was the sunlight that was killing him. It was not the sunlight. It was a rigged 105 round. But if I could ever get the story right, how the sun seemed to gather around him and pick him up and lift him high into a tree, if I could somehow re-create the fatal whiteness of that light, the quick glare, the obvious cause and effect, then you would believe the last thing Curt Lemon believed, which for him must've been the final truth.

Now and then, when I tell this story, someone will come up to me afterward and say she liked it. It's always a woman. Usually it's an older woman of kindly temperament and humane politics. She'll explain that as a rule she hates war stories; she can't understand why people want to wallow in all the blood and gore. But this one she liked. The poor baby buffalo, it made her sad. Sometimes, even, there are little tears. What I should do, she'll say, is put it all behind me. Find new stories to tell.

I won't say it but I'll think it.

I'll picture Rat Kiley's face, his grief, and I'll think, *You dumb cooze.*

Because she wasn't listening.

It *wasn't* a war story. It was a *love* story.

But you can't say that. All you can do is tell it one more time, patiently, adding and subtracting, making up a few things to get at the real truth. No Mitchell Sanders, you tell her. No Lemon, no Rat Kiley. No trail junction. No baby buffalo. No vines or moss or white blossoms. Beginning to end, you tell her, it's all made up. Every goddamn detail—the mountains and the river and especially that poor dumb baby buffalo. None of it happened. *None* of it. And even if it did happen, it didn't happen in the mountains, it happened in this little village on the Batangan Peninsula, and it was raining like crazy, and one night a guy named Stink Harris woke up screaming with a leech on his tongue. You can tell a true war story if you just keep on telling it.

And in the end, of course, a true war story is never about war. It's about sunlight. It's about the special way that dawn spreads out on a river when you know you must cross the river and march into the mountains and do things you are afraid to do. It's about love and memory. It's about sorrow. It's about sisters who never write back and people who never listen.

QUESTIONS FOR MAKING CONNECTIONS WITHIN THE READING

1. Tim O'Brien's "How to Tell a True War Story" is part of a collection of stories by the author entitled *The Things They Carried*. Although the ostensible subject of this particular short story is a series of events that may have actually happened, the subtitle of the entire collection is "A Work of Fiction." "How to Tell a True War Story" begins with the explicit statement "This is true," but what sort of truth does it manage to convey? As you consider possible answers, please remember that the narrator warns us, "In many cases a true war story cannot be believed. If you believe it, be skeptical." Why is the issue of truth so important to a story about what happens in war? Does O'Brien really mean that there is no such thing as truth when we are talking about war? If everything about war is subjective, is it ever possible for one person to judge another person's military conduct?

2. Why does Rat Kiley write a letter to Curt Lemon's sister? What do you make of the details of his letter? Conventionally, such a letter would praise a fallen fellow combatant as a "hero," someone of exemplary character who had chosen to make the "ultimate sacrifice." Instead, Rat writes about the times he and Curt were "raising hell and lighting up villes and bringing smoke to bear every which way." Is Rat trying to insult the sister? Seduce her? Destroy her positive memories of her brother? When she fails to write back to him, why does Rat refer to her as a "dumb cooze"? For that matter, why does he refer to the Vietnamese as "gooks"? Is this simply an example of crude prejudice? If Rat thought of the Vietnamese as people, much like his own family back home, how would such a change influence his behavior? If he thought of Lemon's sister as nothing more than a "cooze," why did he bother to write to her at all?

3. Why does Rat Kiley kill the baby water buffalo? And why is it that "the whole platoon stood there watching, feeling all kinds of things, but [not] a great deal of pity for the baby water buffalo"? How do you explain the reaction of Mitchell Sanders: "Well, that's Nam. Garden of Evil. Over here ... every sin's fresh and original"? If the men view Rat's killing of the buffalo as a "sin," why do they make no effort to stop him? Why do they appear to feel no remorse afterward? Do they displace onto the buffalo their desire to get back at the Vietnamese, or is their behavior even more

complicated? When they kill the buffalo, are they killing something in themselves? What part of themselves might they be killing, and why might they want to do so?

QUESTIONS FOR WRITING

1. Readers might perceive O'Brien's story to be a powerfully realistic evocation of war as people actually live it. On the other hand, in spite of its realistic qualities, the story sometimes becomes highly poetic, as in passages like this one:

    > Twenty years later, I can still see the sunlight on Lemon's face. I can see him turning, looking back at Rat Kiley, then he laughed and took the curious half step from shade into sunlight, his face suddenly brown and shining, and when his foot touched down, in that instant, he must've thought it was the sunlight that was killing him.

    Is O'Brien guilty of aestheticizing war—that is, of making it seem more beautiful, romantic, or exotic than it really is? Do you think that your reading of his account has made you less likely or more likely to regard war as necessary and noble? Has O'Brien's account made it less likely or more likely that you will think of war as a natural and even indispensable part of life as a human being?

2. What is the connection in O'Brien's short story between experience and language? Does he believe that our language predetermines the nature of our experience, or does he suggest, instead, that our experience is often more complex than our language can accommodate? Toward the end of the story, the narrator describes the kind of exchange he has, after reading his short stories in public, often with "an older woman of kindly temperament and humane politics." What sense can you make of the narrator's remarks about this exchange? Is it ever possible to describe our experience to others? Would listeners who had served in Vietnam be more likely to understand the narrator's account than those who had never been there? How about someone who had served in a different war? How much experience must people share in order to understand one another?

QUESTIONS FOR MAKING CONNECTIONS
BETWEEN READINGS

1. Would O'Brien's narrator be comfortable at The Citadel as described by Susan Faludi? Does the form of camaraderie we find at The Citadel correspond to the "love" felt by the men who served with the narrator of

O'Brien's story? Can we understand the rituals performed at The Citadel as forging bonds similar to those forged by war, or do you see significant differences? In what ways does O'Brien's story suggest that the culture of The Citadel is likely to prove more enduring than Faludi suggests? Is the culture of The Citadel really the culture of war itself? If you think so, then why have some distinguished military leaders tried to reform that institution?

2. Would Christopher McCandless, as described by Jon Krakauer, have fit in with the soldiers O'Brien describes? Would they have valued the same things? Were they looking for the same forms of satisfaction? In what ways might the soldiers' experience of war have been shaped by attitudes and outlooks they already held as Americans even before they arrived in Vietnam—attitudes and outlooks expressed by Chris McCandless's journey "into the wild"? Did Vietnam become the "wilderness" for the American soldiers there? In what ways might the values we sometimes think of as closest to nature—values like independence and toughness—be the product of centuries of war? Is there really such a thing as "wilderness"? How is wilderness different from a battlefield? Is the real wilderness inside us?

JUHANI PALLASMAA

The architect Juhani Pallasmaa began his career as a "constructivist" in keeping with the dominant aesthetic of Finnish architecture in the 1960s. This aesthetic emphasized the self-consciously "modern" rationality and standardization championed by great theorists such as Ludwig Mies van der Rohe, Walter Gropius, and Le Corbusier, who famously remarked that houses should be designed as "machines for living." Although Pallasmaa grew quite accomplished in this austere functionalism, his fascination with Japanese culture, together with new insights gleaned from a trip to Africa, gradually produced a profound change in the way he thought about buildings. During this same period he immersed himself in Continental phenomenology, a branch of philosophy that regards ideas as secondary to direct experience. His engagement with phenomenology led him to move beyond the modernist aesthetic toward a deeper appreciation of form, no matter what idiom it might assume. He now saw it as the "task of architecture to make visible 'how the world touches us.'"

Architecture, Pallasmaa argues, is never simply a "machine," but is instead an expression of our most elemental physical and spiritual relations to the world. At least as important as the aspect of space is the aspect of time because buildings are meant not only to enclose but also to endure beyond our own lives. Confronted with our physical impermanence, modernism often reacts with terror: it strives for an abstract timelessness that cuts us off from the living world by overemphasizing the sense of sight—the sense most removed from the ceaseless flow of temporal experience. The antidote Pallasmaa prescribes is an architecture that heightens our awareness of being in the here and now by appealing to the full range of our senses. "Materials and surfaces," he writes, "have a language of their own. Stone speaks of its distant geological origins, its durability and inherent symbolism of permanence; brick makes one think of earth and fire, gravity and the ageless traditions of construction; bronze evokes the extreme heat of its manufacture, the ancient processes of casting and the passage of time as measured in

Pallasmaa, Juhani. *The Eyes of the Skin: Architecture and the Senses* (Hoboken, NJ: John Wiley & Sons, 2005), 14–19, 46–60.

Biographical information is drawn from <http://architecture.about.com/od/architectsaz/p/pallasmaa.htm>, <http://www.spiritus-temporis.com/juhani-pallasmaa/a-selection-of-architectural-works-designed-by-juhani-pallasmaa.html>, and <http://www.uiah.fi/opintoasiat/history2/pallas.htm>.

Quotations are taken from Juhani Pallasmaa, "Hapticity and Time: Notes on Fragile Architecture," <http://iris.nyit.edu/~rcody/Thesis/Readings/Pallasmaa %20-%20Hapticity%20and%20Time.pdf>.

its patina.... These are all materials and surfaces that speak pleasurably of time." To "speak pleasurably of time" is to accentuate and savor time's complex dimensions, rather than seeking refuge in simplistic, lifeless perfection.

In addition to his work as a practicing architect, Pallasmaa has served as Director of the Museum of Finnish Architecture (1978–1983), Professor of Architecture at Helsinki University of Technology (1991–97) and also Dean of the Faculty of Architecture (1993–96). He has also taught at various universities in Europe, North and South America, and Africa, and has received a number of important honors, including the Finnish National Architecture Award (1992) and the International Union of Architects' Award for Architectural Criticism (1999). His books are widely admired across a range of disciplines.

Excerpts from
The Eyes of the Skin:
Architecture and the Senses

"The hands want to see, the eyes want to caress."

JOHANN WOLFGANG VON GOETHE[1]

"The dancer has his ear in his toes."

FRIEDRICH NIETZSCHE[2]

"If the body had been easier to understand, nobody would have thought that we had a mind."

RICHARD RORTY[3]

"The taste of the apple ... lies in the contact of the fruit with the palate, not in the fruit itself; in a similar way ... poetry lies in the meeting of poem and reader, not in the lines of symbols printed on the pages of a book. What is essential is the aesthetic act, the thrill, the almost physical emotion that comes with each reading."

JORGE LUIS BORGES[4]

"How would the painter or poet express anything other than his encounter with the world?"

MAURICE MERLEAU-PONTY[5]

Vision and Knowledge

In Western culture, sight has historically been regarded as the noblest of the senses, and thinking itself thought of in terms of seeing. Already in classical Greek thought, certainty was based on vision and visibility. "The eyes are more exact witnesses than the ears," wrote Heraclitus in one of his fragments.[6] Plato regarded vision as humanity's greatest gift,[7] and he insisted that ethical universals must be accessible to "the mind's eye."[8] Aristotle, likewise, considered sight as the most noble of the senses "because it approximates the intellect most closely by virtue of the relative immateriality of its knowing."[9]

Since the Greeks, philosophical writings of all times have abounded with ocular metaphors to the point that knowledge has become analogous with clear vision and light is regarded as the metaphor for truth. Aquinas even applies the notion of sight to other sensory realms as well as to intellectual cognition.

The impact of the sense of vision on philosophy is well summed up by Peter Sloterdijk. "The eyes are the organic prototype of philosophy. Their enigma is that they not only can see but are also able to see themselves seeing. This gives them a prominence among the body's cognitive organs. A good part of philosophical thinking is actually only eye reflex, eye dialectic, seeing-oneself-see."[10] During the Renaissance, the five senses were understood to form a hierarchical system from the highest sense of vision down to touch. The Renaissance system of the senses was related with the image of the cosmic body; vision was correlated to fire and light, hearing to air, smell to vapor, taste to water, and touch to earth.[11]

The invention of perspectival representation made the eye the center point of the perceptual world as well as of the concept of the self. Perspectival representation itself turned into a symbolic form, one which not only describes but also conditions perception.

There is no doubt that our technological culture has ordered and separated the senses even more distinctly. Vision and hearing are now the privileged sociable senses, whereas the other three are considered as archaic sensory remnants with a merely private function, and they are usually suppressed by the code of culture. Only sensations such as the olfactory enjoyment of a meal, fragrance of flowers, and responses to temperature are allowed to draw collective awareness in our ocularcentric and obsessively hygienic code of culture.

The dominance of vision over the other senses—and the consequent bias in cognition—has been observed by many philosophers. A collection of philosophical essays entitled *Modernity and the Hegemony of Vision*[12] argues that "beginning with the ancient Greeks, Western culture has been dominated by an ocularcentric paradigm, a vision-generated, vision-centred interpretation of knowledge, truth, and reality."[13] This thought-provoking book analyzes "historical connections between vision and knowledge, vision and ontology, vision and power, vision and ethics."[14]

As the ocularcentric paradigm of our relation to the world and of our concept of knowledge—the epistemological privileging of vision—has been revealed by philosophers, it is also important to survey critically the role of vision in relation to the other senses in our understanding and practice of the art of architecture. Architecture, as with all art, is fundamentally confronted with questions of human existence in space and time, it expresses and relates man's being in the world. Architecture is deeply engaged in the metaphysical questions of the self and the world, interiority and exteriority, time and duration, life and death. "Aesthetic and cultural practices are peculiarly susceptible to the changing experience of space and time precisely because they entail the construction of spatial representations and artefacts out of the flow of human experience," writes David Harvey.[15] Architecture is our primary instrument in relating us with space and time, and giving those dimensions a human measure. It domesticates limitless space and endless time to be tolerated, inhabited, and understood by humankind. As a consequence of this interdependence of space and time, the dialectics of external and internal space, physical and spiritual, material and mental, unconscious and conscious priorities concerning the senses as well as their relative roles and interactions, have an essential impact on the nature of the arts and architecture.

David Michael Levin motivates the philosophical critique of the dominance of the eye with the following words: "I think it is appropriate to challenge the hegemony of vision—the ocularcentrism of our culture. And I think we need to examine very critically the character of vision that predominates today in our world. We urgently need a diagnosis of the psychosocial pathology of everyday seeing—and a critical understanding of ourselves, as visionary beings."[16]

Levin points out the autonomy-drive and aggressiveness of vision, and "the specters of patriarchal rule" that haunt our ocularcentric culture:

> The will to power is very strong in vision. There is a very strong tendency in vision to grasp and fixate, to reify and totalize: a tendency to dominate, secure, and control, which eventually, because it was so extensively promoted, assumed a certain uncontested hegemony over our culture and its philosophical discourse, establishing, in keeping with the instrumental rationality of our culture and the technological character of our society, an ocularcentric metaphysics of presence.[17]

I believe that many aspects of the pathology of everyday architecture today can likewise be understood through an analysis of the epistemology of the senses, and a critique of the ocular bias of our culture at large, and of architecture in particular. The inhumanity of contemporary architecture and cities can be understood as the consequence of the negligence of the body and the senses, and an imbalance in our sensory system. The growing experiences of alienation, detachment, and solitude in the technological world today, for instance, may be related with a certain pathology of the senses. It is thought-provoking that this sense of estrangement and detachment is often evoked by the technologically most advanced settings, such as hospitals and airports. The dominance of the

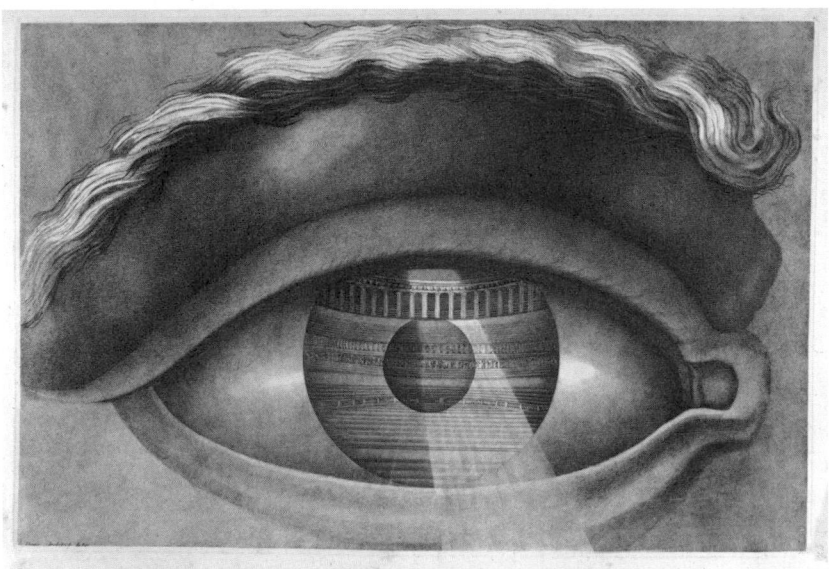

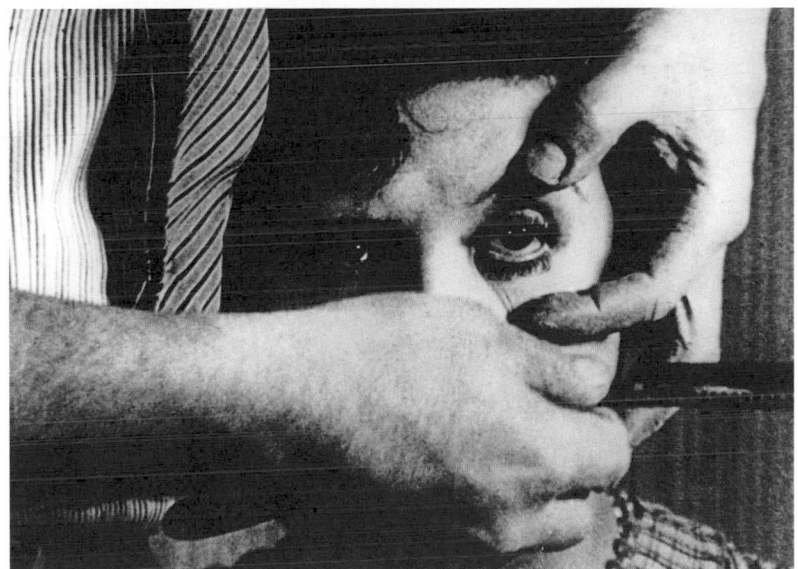

OCULARCENTRISM AND THE VIOLATION OF THE EYE

Architecture has been regarded as an art form of the eye.

Eye Reflecting the Interior of the Theatre of Besançon, engraving after Claude-Nicholas Ledoux. The theatre was built from 1775 to 1784. Detail.

Ledoux, Claude Nicolas (1736–1806) / Bibliotheque des Arts Decoratifs, Paris, France / Archives Charmet / The Bridgeman Art Library.

Vision is regarded as the most noble of the senses, and the loss of eyesight as the ultimate physical loss.

Luis Buñuel and Salvador Dali, *Un Chien Andalou (Andalusian Dog),* 1929. The shocking scene in which the heroine's eye is sliced with a razor blade.

Aito Makinin/Finnish Film Archive.

BUNUEL-DALI / THE KOBAL COLLECTION / Picture Desk.

eye and the suppression of the other senses tend to push us into detachment, isolation, and exteriority. The art of the eye has certainly produced imposing and thought-provoking structures, but it has not facilitated human rootedness in the world. The fact that the modernist idiom has not generally been able to penetrate the surface of popular taste and values seems to be due to its one-sided intellectual and visual emphasis; modernist design at large has housed the intellect and the eye, but it has left the body and the other senses, as well as our memories, imagination, and dreams, homeless.

The Significance of the Shadow

The eye is the organ of distance and separation, whereas touch is the sense of nearness, intimacy, and affection. The eye surveys, controls, and investigates, whereas touch approaches and caresses. During overpowering emotional experiences, we tend to close off the distancing sense of vision; we close the eyes when dreaming, listening to music, or caressing our beloved ones. Deep shadows and darkness are essential, because they dim the sharpness of vision, make depth and distance ambiguous, and invite unconscious peripheral vision and tactile fantasy.

How much more mysterious and inviting is the street of an old town with its alternating realms of darkness and light than are the brightly and evenly lit streets of today! The imagination and daydreaming are stimulated by dim light and shadow. In order to think clearly, the sharpness of vision has to be suppressed, for thoughts travel with an absent-minded and unfocused gaze. Homogenous bright light paralyses the imagination in the same way that homogenization of space weakens the experience of being, and wipes away the sense of place. The human eye is most perfectly tuned for twilight rather than bright daylight.

Mist and twilight awaken the imagination by making visual images unclear and ambiguous; a Chinese painting of a foggy mountain landscape or the raked sand garden of Ryoan-ji Zen Garden give rise to an unfocused way of looking, evoking a trancelike, meditative state. The absent-minded gaze penetrates the surface of the physical image and focuses in infinity.

In his book *In Praise of Shadows,* Junichiro Tanizaki points out that even Japanese cooking depends upon shadows, and that it is inseparable from darkness: "And when *Than* is served in a lacquer dish, it is as if the darkness of the room were melting on your tongue."[18] The writer reminds us that, in olden times, the blackened teeth of the geisha and her green-black lips as well as her white painted face were all intended to emphasise the darkness and shadows of the room.

Likewise, the extraordinarily powerful sense of focus and presence in the paintings of Caravaggio and Rembrandt arises from the depth of shadow in which the protagonist is embedded like a precious object on a dark velvet background that absorbs all light. The shadow gives shape and life to the object in light. It also provides the realm from which fantasies and dreams arise. The art of chiaroscuro is a skill of the master architect, too. In great architectural spaces, there is a constant, deep breathing of shadow and light; shadow inhales and illumination exhales light.

In our time, light has turned into a mere quantitative matter and the window has lost its significance as a mediator between two worlds, between enclosed and open, interiority and exteriority, private and public, shadow and light. Having lost its ontological meaning, the window has turned into a mere absence of the wall. "Take ... the use of enormous plate windows ... [T]hey deprive our buildings of intimacy, the effect of shadow and atmosphere. Architects all over the world have been mistaken in the proportions which they have assigned to large plate windows or spaces opening to the outside.... We have lost our sense of intimate life, and have become forced to live public lives, essentially away from home," writes Luis Barragan, the true magician of intimate secrecy, mystery, and shadow in contemporary architecture.[19] Likewise, most contemporary public spaces would become more enjoyable through a lower light intensity and its uneven distribution. The dark womb of the council chamber of Alvar Aalto's Saynatsalo Town Hall recreates a mystical and mythological sense of community; darkness creates a sense of solidarity and strengthens the power of the spoken word.

In emotional states, sense stimuli seem to shift from the more refined senses towards the more archaic, from vision down to hearing, touch and smell, and from light to shadow. A culture that seeks to control its citizens is likely to promote the opposite direction of interaction, away from intimate individuality and identification towards a public and distant detachment. A society of surveillance is necessarily a society of the voyeuristic and sadistic eye. An efficient method of mental torture is the use of a constantly high level of illumination that leaves no space for mental withdrawal or privacy; even the dark interiority of self is exposed and violated.

Acoustic Intimacy

Sight isolates, whereas sound incorporates; vision is directional, whereas sound is omni-directional. The sense of sight implies exteriority, but sound creates an experience of interiority. I regard an object, but sound approaches me; the eye

ARCHITECTURES OF HEARING AND SMELL

In historical towns and spaces, acoustic experiences reinforce and enrich visual experiences.

The early Cistercian Abbey of Le Thoronet, first established at Florielle in 1136, transferred to its present site in 1176.

niceartphoto / Alamy.

In rich and invigorating experiences of places, all sensory realms interact and fuse into the memorable image of the place.

A space of smell: the spice market in Harrar, Ethiopia.

dbimages / Alamy.

reaches, but the ear receives. Buildings do not react to our gaze, but they do return our sounds back to our ears. "The centering action of sound affects man's sense of cosmos," writes Walter Ong. "For oral cultures, the cosmos is an ongoing event with man at its centre. Man is the *umbilicus mundi,* the navel of the world."[20] It is thought-provoking that the mental loss of the sense of center in the contemporary world could be attributed, at least in part, to the disappearance of the integrity of the audible world.

Hearing structures and articulates the experience and understanding of space. We are not normally aware of the significance of hearing in spatial experience, although sound often provides the temporal continuum in which visual impressions are embedded. When the soundtrack is removed from a film, for instance, the scene loses its plasticity and sense of continuity and life. Silent film, indeed, had to compensate for the lack of sound by a demonstrative manner of overacting.

Adrian Stokes, the English painter and essayist, makes perceptive observations about the interaction of space and sound, sound and stone. "Like mothers of men, the buildings are good listeners. Long sounds, distinct or seemingly in bundles, appease the orifices of palaces that lean back gradually from canal or pavement. A long sound with its echo brings consummation to the stone," he writes.[21]

Anyone who has half-woken up to the sound of a train or an ambulance in a nocturnal city, and through his/her sleep experienced the space of the city with its countless inhabitants scattered within its structures, knows the power of sound over the imagination; the nocturnal sound is a reminder of human solitude and mortality, and it makes one conscious of the entire slumbering city. Anyone who has become entranced by the sound of dripping water in the darkness of a ruin can attest to the extraordinary capacity of the ear to carve a volume into the void of darkness. The space traced by the ear in the darkness becomes a cavity sculpted directly in the interior of the mind.

The last chapter of Steen Eiler Rasmussen's seminal book *Experiencing Architecture* is significantly entitled "Hearing Architecture."[22] The writer describes various dimensions of acoustical qualities, and recalls the acoustic percept of the underground tunnels in Vienna in Orson Welles's film *The Third Man*: "Your ear receives the impact of both the length and the cylindrical form of the tunnel."[23]

One can also recall the acoustic harshness of an uninhabited and unfurnished house as compared to the affability of a lived home, in which sound is refracted and softened by the numerous surfaces of objects of personal life. Every building or space has its characteristic sound of intimacy or monumentality, invitation or rejection, hospitality or hostility. A space is understood and appreciated through its echo as much as through its visual shape, but the acoustic percept usually remains as an unconscious background experience.

Sight is the sense of the solitary observer, whereas hearing creates a sense of connection and solidarity; our look wanders lonesomely in the dark depths of a cathedral, but the sound of the organ makes us immediately experience our affinity with the space. We stare alone at the suspense of a circus, but the burst of applause after the relaxation of suspense unites us with the crowd. The sound of church bells echoing through the streets of a town makes us aware of our citizenship. The echo of steps on a paved street has an emotional charge because the sound reverberating from surrounding walls puts us in direct interaction with space; the sound measures space and makes its scale comprehensible. We stroke the boundaries of the space with our ears. The cries of seagulls in the harbor awaken an awareness of the vastness of the ocean and the infiniteness of the horizon.

Every city has its echo which depends on the pattern and scale of its streets and the prevailing architectural styles and materials. The echo of a Renaissance city differs from that of a Baroque city. But our cities have lost their echo altogether. The wide, open spaces of contemporary streets do not return sound, and in the interiors of today's buildings echoes are absorbed and censored. The programmed recorded music of shopping malls and public spaces eliminates the possibility of grasping the acoustic volume of space. Our ears have been blinded.

Silence, Time, and Solitude

The most essential auditory experience created by architecture is tranquillity. Architecture presents the drama of construction silenced into matter, space, and light. Ultimately, architecture is the art of petrified silence. When the clutter of construction work ceases, and the shouting of workers dies away, a building becomes a museum of a waiting, patient silence. In Egyptian temples we encounter the silence that surrounded the pharaohs, in the silence of the Gothic cathedral we are reminded of the last dying note of a Gregorian chant, and the echo of Roman footsteps has just faded away from the walls of the Pantheon. Old houses take us back to the slow time and silence of the past. The silence of architecture is a responsive, remembering silence. A powerful architectural experience silences all external noise; it focuses our attention on our very existence, and as with all art, it makes us aware of our fundamental solitude.

The incredible acceleration of speed during the last century has collapsed time into the flat screen of the present, upon which the simultaneity of the world is projected. As time loses its duration, and its echo in the primordial past, man loses his sense of self as a historical being, and is threatened by the "terror of time."[24] Architecture emancipates us from the embrace of the present and allows us to experience the slow, healing flow of time. Buildings and cities are instruments and museums of time. They enable us to see and understand the passing of history, and to participate in time cycles that surpass individual life.

Architecture connects us with the dead; through buildings we are able to imagine the bustle of the medieval street, and picture a solemn procession approaching the cathedral. The time of architecture is a detained time; in the

SPACES OF INTIMATE WARMTH

Heightened experiences of intimacy, home and protection are sensations of the naked skin.

Pierre Bonnard, *The Nude in the Bath*, 1937. Detail. Musée du Petit-Palais, Paris.

©2010 Artists Rights Society (ARS), New York / ADAGP, Paris / Giraudon / The Bridgeman Art Library.

The fireplace as an intimate and space of warmth.

Antonio Gaudi, Casa Batlló, Barcelona, 1904–06.

Ingolf Pompe 52 / Alamy.

greatest of buildings time stands firmly still. In the Great Peristyle at Karnak time has petrified into an immobile and timeless present. Time and space are eternally locked into each other in the silent spaces between these immense columns; matter, space, and time fuse into one singular elemental experience, the sense of being.

The great works of modernity have forever halted the Utopian time of optimism and hope; even after decades of trying fate they radiate an air of spring and promise. Alvar Aalto's Paimio Sanatorium is heartbreaking in its radiant belief in a humane future and the success of the societal mission of architecture. Le Corbusier's Villa Savoye makes us believe in the union of reason and beauty, ethics and aesthetics. Through periods of dramatic and tragic social and cultural change, Konstantin Melnikov's Melnikov House in Moscow has stood as a silent witness of the will and Utopian spirit that once created it.

Experiencing a work of art is a private dialogue between the work and the viewer, one that excludes other interactions. "Art is memory's *mise en scène,* and Art is made by the alone for the alone," as Cyril Connolly writes in *The Unquiet Grave.* Significantly, these are sentences underlined by Luis Barragan in his copy of this book of poetry.[25] A sense of melancholy lies beneath all moving experiences of art; this is the sorrow of beauty's immaterial temporality. Art projects an unattainable ideal, the ideal of beauty that momentarily touches the eternal.

■   ■

Spaces of Scent

We need only eight molecules of substance to trigger an impulse of smell in a nerve ending, and we can detect more than 10,000 different odors. The most persistent memory of any space is often its smell. I cannot remember the appearance of the door to my grandfather's farmhouse in my early childhood, but I do remember the resistance of its weight and the patina of its wood surface scarred by decades of use, and I recall especially vividly the scent of home that hit my face as an invisible wall behind the door. Every dwelling has its individual smell of home.

A particular smell makes us unknowingly re-enter a space completely forgotten by the retinal memory; the nostrils awaken a forgotten image, and we are enticed to enter a vivid daydream. The nose makes the eyes remember. "Memory and imagination remain associated," as Bachelard writes; "I alone in my memories of another century, can open the deep cupboard that still retains for me alone that unique odor, the odor of raisins, drying on a wicker tray. The odor of raisins! It is an odor that is beyond description, one that it takes a lot of imagination to smell."[26]

What a delight to move from one realm of odor to the next, through the narrow streets of an old town! The scent sphere of a candy store makes one think of the innocence and curiosity of childhood; the dense smell of a shoemaker's workshop makes one imagine horses, saddles, and harness straps and the excitement of riding; the fragrance of a bread shop projects images of health, sustenance, and physical strength, whereas the perfume of a pastry shop makes one think of bourgeois felicity. Fishing towns are especially memorable because of the fusion of the smells of the sea and of the land; the powerful smell of seaweed makes one sense the depth and weight of the sea, and it turns any prosaic harbor town into the image of the lost Atlantis.

A special joy of travel is to acquaint oneself with the geography and microcosm of smells and tastes. Every city has its spectrum of tastes and odors. Sales counters on the streets are appetizing exhibitions of smells: creatures of the ocean that smell of seaweed, vegetables carrying the odour of fertile earth, and fruits that exude the sweet fragrance of sun and moist summer air. The menus displayed outside restaurants make us fantasize the complete course of a dinner; letters read by the eyes turn into oral sensations.

Why do abandoned houses always have the same hollow smell? Is it because the particular smell is stimulated by emptiness observed by the eye? Helen Keller was able to recognize "an old-fashioned country house because it has several levels of odors, left by a succession of families, of plants, of perfumes and draperies."[27]

In *The Notebooks of Malte Laurids Brigge,* Rainer Maria Rilke gives a dramatic description of images of past life in an already demolished house, conveyed by traces imprinted on the wall of its neighboring house:

> There stood the middays and the sicknesses and the exhaled breath and
> the smoke of years, and the sweat that breaks out under armpits and
> makes clothes heavy, and the stale breath of mouths, and the fusel odor
> of sweltering feet. There stood the tang of urine and the burn of soot
> and the grey reek of potatoes, and the heavy, smooth stench of ageing
> grease. The sweet, lingering smell of neglected infants was there, and
> the fearsmell of children who go to school, and the sultriness out of the
> beds of nubile youths.[28]

The retinal images of contemporary architecture certainly appear sterile and lifeless when compared with the emotional and associative power of the poet's olfactory imagery. The poet releases the scent and taste concealed in words. Through his words a great writer is capable of constructing an entire city with all the colors of life. But significant works of architecture also project full images of life. In fact, a great architect releases images of ideal life concealed in spaces and shapes. Le Corbusier's sketch of the suspended garden for a block of flats, with the wife beating a rug on the upper balcony, and the husband hitting a boxing bag below, as well as the fish and the electric fan on the kitchen table of the Villa Stein de Monzie, are examples of a rare sense of life in modern images of architecture. Photographs of the Melnikov House, on the other hand, reveal a dramatic distance between the metaphysical geometry of the iconic house, and the traditionally prosaic realities of life.

■ ■

The Shape of Touch

"[H]ands are a complicated organism, a delta in which life from the most distant sources flows together surging into the great current of action. Hands have histories; they even have their own culture and their own particular beauty. We grant them the right to have their own development, their own wishes, feelings, moods and occupations," writes Rainer Maria Rilke in his essay on Auguste Rodin.[29] The hands are the sculptor's eyes; but they are also organs for thought, as Heidegger suggests: "[the] hand's essence can never be determined, or explained, by its being an organ which can grasp [...] Every motion of the hand in every one of its works carries itself through the element of thinking, every bearing of the hand bears itself in that element...."[30]

The skin reads the texture, weight, density, and temperature of matter. The surface of an old object, polished to perfection by the tool of the craftsman and the assiduous hands of its users, seduces the stroking of the hand. It is pleasurable to press a door handle shining from the thousands of hands that have entered the door before us; the clean shimmer of ageless wear has turned into an image of welcome and hospitality. The door handle is the handshake of the building. The tactile sense connects us with time and tradition: through impressions of touch we shake the hands of countless generations. A pebble polished by waves is pleasurable to the hand, not only because of its soothing shape, but because it expresses the slow process of its formation; a perfect pebble on the palm materializes duration, it is time turned into shape.

When entering the magnificent outdoor space of Louis Kahn's Salk Institute in La Jolla, California, I felt an irresistible temptation to walk directly to the concrete wall and touch the velvety smoothness and temperature of its skin. Our skin traces temperature spaces with unerring precision; the cool and invigorating shadow under a tree, or the caressing sphere of warmth in a spot of sun, turn into experiences of space and place. In my childhood images of the Finnish countryside, I can vividly recall walls against the angle of the sun, walls which multiplied the heat of radiation and melted the snow, allowing the first smell of pregnant soil to announce the approach of summer. These early pockets of spring were identified by the skin and the nose as much as by the eye.

THE SIGNIFICANCE OF SHADOW AND DARKNESS

The face is embedded in darkness as a precious object on a dark surface of velvet. Rembrandt, *Self-Portrait,* 1660. Detail. Musée du Louvre, Paris.
The darkness and shadows of the Finnish peasant's house create a sense of intimacy and silence; light turns into a precious gift. Prado, Madrid, Spain / The Bridgeman Art Library.

The Pertinotsa House from the late 19th century in the Seurasaari Outdoor Museum, Helsinki.
NTPL / Nadia Mackenzie / The National Trust Photolibrary / Alamy.

Gravity is measured by the bottom of the foot; we trace the density and texture of the ground through our soles. Standing barefoot on a smooth glacial rock by the sea at sunset, and sensing the warmth of the sun-heated stone through one's soles, is an extraordinarily healing experience, making one part of the eternal cycle of nature. One senses the slow breathing of the earth.

"In our houses we have nooks and corners in which we like to curl up comfortably. To curl up belongs to the phenomenology of the verb to inhabit, and only those who have learned to do so can inhabit with intensity," writes Bachelard.[31] "And always, in our daydreams, the house is a large cradle," he continues.[32]

There is a strong identity between naked skin and the sensation of home. The experience of home is essentially an experience of intimate warmth. The space of warmth around a fireplace is the space of ultimate intimacy and comfort. Marcel Proust gives a poetic description of such a fireside space, as sensed by the skin: "It is like an immaterial alcove, a warm cave carved into the room itself, a zone of hot weather with floating boundaries."[33] A sense of homecoming has never been stronger for me than when seeing a light in the window of my childhood house in a snow-covered landscape at dusk, the memory of the warm interior gently warming my frozen limbs. Home and the pleasure of the skin turn into a singular sensation.

The Taste of Stone

In his writings, Adrian Stokes was particularly sensitive to the realms of tactile and oral sensations: "In employing smooth and rough as generic terms of architectural dichotomy I am better able to preserve both the oral and the tactile notions that underlie the visual. There is a hunger of the eyes, and doubtless there has been some permeation of the visual sense, as of touch, by the once all-embracing oral impulse."[34] Stokes writes also about the "oral invitation of Veronese marble,"[35] and he quotes a letter of John Ruskin's: "I should like to eat up this Verona touch by touch."[36]

There is a subtle transference between tactile and taste experiences. Vision becomes transferred to taste as well; certain colors and delicate details evoke oral sensations. A delicately colored polished stone surface is subliminally sensed by the tongue. Our sensory experience of the world originates in the interior sensation of the mouth, and the world tends to return to its oral origins. The most archaic origin of architectural space is in the cavity of the mouth.

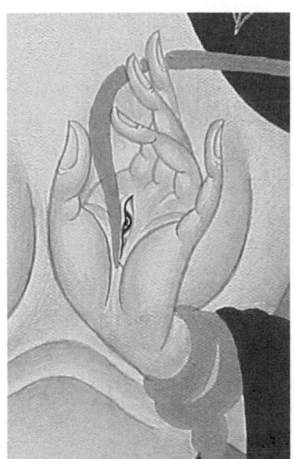

VISION AND HAPTICITY

A tactile ingredient is concealed in vision.

The Buddhist goddess Tara possesses five additional eyes, on the forehead and in her hands and feet. These are considered as signs of enlightenment. Bronze figure from Mongolia, 15th century.

Godong/Robert Harding World Imagery/ Getty Images.

The door pull is the handshake of a building, which can be inviting and courteous, or forbidding and aggressive.

The Iron House/Architect Alvar Aalto. Photo by Heikki Havas, Museum of Finnish Architecture.

Many years ago when visiting the D. L. James Residence in Carmel, California, designed by Charles and Henry Greene, I felt compelled to kneel and touch the delicately shining white marble threshold of the front door with my tongue. The sensuous materials and skilfuly crafted details of Carlo Scarpa's architecture as well as the sensuous colors of Luis Barragan's houses frequently evoke oral experiences. Deliciously colored surfaces of *stucco lustra,* a highly polished color or wood surface, also present themselves to the appreciation of the tongue.

Junichiro Tanizaki describes impressively the spatial qualities of the sense of taste, and the subtle interaction of the senses in the simple act of uncovering a bowl of soup:

> With lacquerware there is a beauty in that moment between removing the lid and lifting the bowl to the mouth when one gazes at the still, silent liquid in the dark depths of the bowl, its color hardly differing from the bowl itself. What lies within the darkness one cannot distinguish, but the palm senses the gentle movements of the liquid, vapor rises from within forming droplets on the rim, and a fragrance carried upon the vapor brings a delicate anticipation.... A moment of mystery, it might almost be called, a moment of trance.[37]

A fine architectural space opens up and presents itself with the same fullness of experience as Tanizaki's bowl of soup. Architectural experience brings the world into a most intimate contact with the body.

NOTES

1. As quoted in *Not Architecture But Evidence That It Exists—Lauretta Vinciarelli: Watercolors,* ed. Brooke Hodge, Harvard University Graduate School of Design (Harvard), 1998, p. 130.

2. Friedrich Nietzsche, *Thus Spake Zarathustra,* Viking Press (New York), 1956, p. 224.

3. Richrd Rorty, *Philosophy and the Mirror of Nature,* Princeton University Press (New Jersey), 1979, p. 239.

4. Jorge Luis Borges, *Selected Poems 1923–1967,* Penguin Books (London), 1985, as quoted in Sören Thurell, *The Shadow of a Thought: The Janus Concept in Architecture,* School of Architecture, The Royal Institute of Technology (Stockholm), 1989, p. 2.

5. As quoted in Richard Kearney, "Maurice Merleau-Ponty," in Richard Kearney, *Modern Movements in European Philosophy,* Manchester University Press (Manchester and New York), 1994, p. 82.

6. Heraclitus, Fragment 101a, as quoted in *Modernity and the Hegemony of Vision,* ed. David Michael Levin, University of California Press (Berkeley and Los Angeles), 1993, p. 1.

7. Plato, *Timaeus,* 47b, as quoted in Martin Jay, *Downcast Eyes: The Denigration of Vision in Twentieth-Century French Thought,* University of California Press (Berkeley and Los Angeles), 1994, p. 27.

8. Georgia Warnke, "Ocularcentrism and Social Criticism," in Levin (1993), p. 287.

9. Thomas R. Flynn, "Foucault and the Eclipse of Vision," in Levin (1993), p. 274.

10. Peter Sloterdijk, *Critique of Cynical Reason*, trans. Michael Eldred, as quoted in Jay (1994), p. 21.

11. As referred to in Steven Pack, "Discovering (Through) the Dark Interstice of Touch," *History and Theory Graduate Studio 1992–1994*, McGill School of Architecture (Montreal), 1994.

12. Levin (1993).

13. Ibid, p. 2.

14. Ibid, p. 3.

15. David Harvey, *The Condition of Postmodernity*, Blackwell (Cambridge), 1992, p. 327.

16. David Michael Levin, "Decline and Fall: Ocularcentrism in Heidegger's Reading of the History of Metaphysics," in Levin (1993), p. 205.

17. Ibid, p. 212.

18. Junichiro Tanizaki, *In Praise of Shadows*, Leete's Island Books (New Haven), 1977, p. 16.

19. Alejandro Ramirez Ugarte, "Interview with Luis Barragan" (1962), in Enrique X de Anda Alanis, *Luis Barragan: Clásico del Silencio*, Colección Somosur (Bogotá), 1989, p. 242.

20. Walter Ong, *Orality and Literacy: The Technologization of the World*, Routledge (London and New York), 191, p. 73

21. Andrian Stokes, "Smooth and Rough," in *The Critical Writings of Adrian Stokes*, Volume II, Thames & Hudson (London), 1978, p. 245.

22. Steen Eiler Rasmussen, *Experiencing Architecture*, MIT Press (Cambridge), 1993.

23. Ibid, p. 225.

24. Karsten Harries, "Building and the Terror of Time," *Perspecta: The Yale Architectural Journal* (New Haven), 19 (1982), pp. 59–69.

25. Quoted in Emilio Ambasz, *The Architecture of Luis Barragan*, The Museum of Modern Art (New York), 1976, p. 108.

26. Gaston Bachelard, *The Poetics of Space*, Beacon Press (Boston), 1969, p. 13.

27. Diane Ackerman, *A Natural History of the Senses*, Vintage Books (New York), 1991, p. 45.

28. Rainer Maria Rilke, *The Notebook of Malte Laurids Brigge*, trans. M. D. Herter, W. W. Norton & Co. (New York and London), 1992, pp. 47–8.

29. Rainer Maria Rilke, *Rodin*, trans. Daniel Slager, Archipelago Books (New York), 2004, p. 45.

30. Martin Heidegger, "What Calls for Thinking," in *Martin Heidegger: Basic Writings*, Harper and Row (New York), 1977, p. 357.

31. Maurice Bachelard, *The Poetics of Reverie*, Beacon Press (Boston), 1971, p. XXXIV.

32. Ibid, p. 7.

33. Marcel Proust, *Kadonnutta aikaa estimässä,Combray* [Remembrance of Things Past, Combray], Otava (Helsinki), 1968, p. 10.

34. Stokes, p. 243.

35. Source unidentified.

36. Stokes, p. 316.

37. Tanizaki, p. 15.

QUESTIONS FOR MAKING CONNECTIONS
WITHIN THE READING

1. Re-read the epigraphs that begin Pallasmaa's selection. What themes, ideas, and implications connect them to one another? Clearly, he is using them to make a point about the senses and experience, but why does he choose five instead of one? What does the activity of putting them together tell us about the way he wants us to read? And how does it prepare us for what follows in the rest of the selection? What is the message of Pallasmaa's *style*—why does his writing often feel more like poetry than ordinary prose?

2. What does Pallasmaa mean when he refers to the "pathology of everyday architecture"? In what ways does that pathology arise from our "ocular-centrism"—our overdependence on the visual? Pallasmaa follows up "Vision and Knowledge" with sections that challenge the "hegemony" of the eye. First, he explores a different way of seeing, one that includes shadows as well as light. Then he considers the experience of sound, of smell, of touch, and even of taste in the built environment. In what ways does each section help to correct the pathology he describes initially?

3. Using Google Images (http://images.google.com), find some examples of the architecture that Pallasmaa celebrates: Luis Barragan's many buildings, Alvar Aalto's Saynatsalo Town Hall or Paimio Sanatorium, the Great Peristyle at Karnak, Le Corbusier's Villa Savoye, Konstantin Melnikov's Melnikov House. How do these structures embody the complexity that Pallasmaa wishes to restore? Were you surprised to see how modern they appear? Do they succeed in nurturing a sense of "human rootedness"? And if so, how do they do it?

QUESTIONS FOR WRITING

1. Pallasmaa writes that architecture "is fundamentally confronted with questions about human existence in space and time, [and] it expresses and relates man's being in the world." What does he mean by "being in the world," and how can a building "express" and "relate" it? In what ways does Pallasmaa challenge the view that architecture is basically all about decorating structures that are much the same except for their surface features? How does architecture shape our experience, and how do our cultural values shape architecture in turn?

2. One crucial aspect of the built environment is the relation between "interiority" and "exteriority." But when Pallasmaa uses those terms he does not mean the inside and outside of a building. Instead, he is referring to the interplay between spaces in the physical world and "the dark interiority of self." In what ways are we "dark" inside ourselves, and how does our enjoyment of space depend on the preservation of this darkness? As you go from building to building today, pay attention to the places that make you feel protected and comfortable. How do these places differ from the ones that seem to leave your interiority "exposed and violated"?

QUESTIONS FOR MAKING CONNECTIONS
BETWEEN READINGS

1. Pallasmaa's book *The Eyes of the Skin,* from which these selections were taken, can be understood as a protest against a loss of depth in our awareness of space, which becomes shallow once we overlook the importance of hearing, smell, touch, and taste. Pallasmaa associates this loss of depth with what he calls the "modernist idiom." "It is thought-provoking," he notes, that a "sense of estrangement and detachment is often evoked by the technologically most advanced settings, such as hospitals and airports." His protest against the modern loss of depth is echoed in a different way by Nicholas Carr in "Is Google Making Us Stupid?" Carr quotes the journalist Bruce Friedman, who complains, "I now have almost totally lost the ability to read and absorb a longish article on the web or in print.... Even a blog post of more than three or four paragraphs is too much to absorb. I skim it." Has the Internet really expanded our world, or has it taken an additional step toward the contraction of consciousness that Pallasmaa warns against? And how might the Internet be transformed to make it more richly sensuous?

2. If Pallasmaa is troubled by the tyranny of sight, Oliver Sacks is intrigued by the experience of blindness (in his essay "The Mind's Eye"). Though an experienced neurologist, Sacks was quite surprised to learn that the blind can adapt their brains to this condition in remarkably different ways. But he was just as surprised to find "huge variations" in the way that those with sight are able to process visual information. As his research continues, he is forced to conclude that the boundary between sight and the other senses is impossible to define with precision. One "can no longer say of one's mental landscape what is visual, what is auditory, what is image, what is language—they are all fused together and imbued with our own individual perspectives and values." Does Sacks lend support to Pallasmaa's argument? How does he contradict or complicate it?"

OLIVER SACKS

WHEN OLIVER SACKS was awarded the Lewis Thomas Prize by Rockefeller University in 2002 for his life's work presenting the case histories of patients with neurological diseases, he was praised for his ability to take his readers into the nearly unimaginable mental worlds of those who have suffered brain damage. "Sacks," the awards committee concluded, "presses us to follow him into uncharted regions of human experience—and compels us to realize, once there, that we are confronting only ourselves." This is an extraordinary claim, given that Sacks has written, most famously, about patients who suffered sleeping sickness for decades, about a man who mistook his wife for a hat, and about what it is like to live with Tourette's syndrome, a disease that drives its victims to spew forth curses in public. It has been Sacks's lifelong project to write about the mentally ill in ways that foreground the humanity of those who are suffering from diseases that generate all manner of strange behavior.

Born and educated in England, Sacks has lived in New York since 1965, where he was for decades a clinical professor of neurology at the Albert Einstein College of Medicine, adjunct professor of neurology at the NYU School of Medicine, and consultant neurologist to the Little Sisters of the Poor. In 2007, he was appointed Professor of Clinical Neurology and Clinical Psychiatry at Columbia University Medical Center; along with this appointment, he was designated Columbia University's first Columbia Artist, granting him close to free rein in working across departments and organizing interdisciplinary programs. Sacks explained in a recent interview that his interest in the brain and in neurology arose from his childhood experience of visual migraines. "I would often lose sight to one side, and sometimes one can lose the idea of one side in a migraine, which can be a very, very strange thing. When I was young I was sort of terrified of these things. I asked my mother, who was a doctor herself and also had visual migraines. She was the first to explain to me that we are not just cameras—we are not just given the visual world. We make it to some extent."

The observation of how patients creatively adapt to the challenges an illness poses has shaped Sacks's own approach to medicine and has led him to create what he has called a "neuroanthropology" of how illness is both perceived and experienced around the world. Most recently he has turned his attention to the nearly universal love of music and its neurological underpinnings. The author of

Sacks, Oliver. "The Mind's Eye." *The New Yorker.* July 28, 2003. 48–59.

Quotations come from the Rockefeller University Web site, http://www.rockefeller.edu/lectures/sacks031802.html, and the Salon.com interview with Sacks, http://www.salon.com/dec96/sacks961223.html.

Awakenings (1973), *The Man Who Mistook His Wife for a Hat* (1985), *An Anthropologist on Mars* (1995), and *Musicophilia: Tales of Music and the Brain* (2007), among other works, Sacks brings together biology and biography in the interest of forging a humane medical practice.

■ ■

The Mind's Eye
What the Blind See

In his last letter, Goethe wrote, "The Ancients said that the animals are taught through their organs; let me add to this, so are men, but they have the advantage of teaching their organs in return." He wrote this in 1832, a time when phrenology was at its height, and the brain was seen as a mosaic of "little organs" subserving everything from language to drawing ability to shyness. Each individual, it was believed, was given a fixed measure of this faculty or that, according to the luck of his birth. Though we no longer pay attention, as the phrenologists did, to the "bumps" on the head (each of which, supposedly, indicated a brain-mind organ beneath), neurology and neuroscience have stayed close to the idea of brain fixity and localization—the notion, in particular, that the highest part of the brain, the cerebral cortex, is effectively programmed from birth: this part to vision and visual processing, that part to hearing, that to touch, and so on.

This would seem to allow individuals little power of choice, of self-determination, let alone of adaptation, in the event of a neurological or perceptual mishap.

But to what extent are we—our experiences, our reactions—shaped, predetermined, by our brains, and to what extent do we shape our own brains? Does the mind run the brain or the brain the mind—or, rather, to what extent does one run the other? To what extent are we the authors, the creators, of our own experiences? The effects of a profound perceptual deprivation such as blindness can cast an unexpected light on this. To become blind, especially later in life, presents one with a huge, potentially overwhelming challenge: to find a new way of living, of ordering one's world, when the old way has been destroyed.

A dozen years ago, I was sent an extraordinary book called *Touching the Rock: An Experience of Blindness*. The author, John Hull, was a professor of religious education who had grown up in Australia and then moved to England. Hull had developed cataracts at the age of thirteen, and became completely blind in his left eye four years later. Vision in his right eye remained reasonable until he was thirty-five or so, and then started to deteriorate. There followed a decade of steadily failing vision, in which Hull needed stronger and stronger magnifying glasses, and had to write with thicker and thicker pens, until, in 1983, at the age of forty-eight, he became completely blind.

Touching the Rock is the journal he dictated in the three years that followed. It is full of piercing insights relating to Hull's life as a blind person, but most striking for me is Hull's description of how, in the years after his loss of sight, he experienced a gradual attenuation of visual imagery and memory, and finally a virtual extinction of them (except in dreams)—a state that he calls "deep blindness."

By this, Hull meant not only the loss of visual images and memories but a loss of the very idea of seeing, so that concepts like "here," "there," and "facing" seemed to lose meaning for him, and even the sense of objects having "appearances," visible characteristics, vanished. At this point, for example, he could no longer imagine how the numeral 3 looked, unless he traced it in the air with his hand. He could construct a "motor" image of a 3, but not a visual one.

Hull, though at first greatly distressed about the fading of visual memories and images—the fact that he could no longer conjure up the faces of his wife or children, or of familiar and loved landscapes and places—then came to accept it with remarkable equanimity; indeed, to regard it as a natural response to a nonvisual world. He seemed to regard this loss of visual imagery as a prerequisite for the full development, the heightening, of his other senses.

Two years after becoming completely blind, Hull had apparently become so nonvisual as to resemble someone who had been blind from birth. Hull's loss of visuality also reminded me of the sort of "cortical blindness" that can happen if the primary visual cortex is damaged, through a stroke or traumatic brain damage—although in Hull's case there was no direct damage to the visual cortex but, rather, a cutting off from any visual stimulation or input.

In a profoundly religious way, and in language sometimes reminiscent of that of St. John of the Cross, Hull enters into this state, surrenders himself, with a sort of acquiescence and joy. And such "deep" blindness he conceives as "an authentic and autonomous world, a place of its own.... Being a whole-body seer is to be in one of the concentrated human conditions."

Being a "whole-body seer," for Hull, means shifting his attention, his center of gravity, to the other senses, and he writes again and again of how these have assumed a new richness and power. Thus he speaks of how the sound of rain, never before accorded much attention, can now delineate a whole landscape for him, for its sound on the garden path is different from its sound as it drums on the lawn, or on the bushes in his garden, or on the fence dividing it from the road. "Rain," he writes, "has a way of bringing out the contours of everything; it throws a coloured blanket over previously invisible things; instead of an intermittent and thus fragmented world, the steadily falling rain creates continuity of acoustic experience ... presents the fullness of an entire situation all at once ... gives a sense of perspective and of the actual relationships of one part of the world to another."

With his new intensity of auditory experience (or attention), along with the sharpening of his other senses, Hull comes to feel a sense of intimacy with nature, an intensity of being-in-the-world, beyond anything he knew when he was sighted. Blindness now becomes for him "a dark, paradoxical gift." This is not just "compensation," he emphasizes, but a whole new order, a new mode of human being. With this he extricates himself from visual nostalgia, from the strain, or falsity, of trying to pass as "normal," and finds a new focus, a new freedom. His teaching at the university expands, becomes more fluent, his writing becomes stronger and deeper; he becomes intellectually and spiritually bolder, more confident. He feels he is on solid ground at last.

What Hull described seemed to me an astounding example of how an individual deprived of one form of perception could totally reshape himself to a new center, a new identity.

It is said that those who see normally as infants but then become blind within the first two years of life retain no memories of seeing, have no visual imagery and no visual elements in their dreams (and, in this way, are comparable to those born blind). It is similar with those who lose hearing before the age of two: they have no sense of having "lost" the world of sound, nor any sense of "silence," as hearing people sometimes imagine. For those who lose sight so early, the very concepts of "sight" or "blindness" soon cease to have meaning, and there is no sense of losing the world of vision, only of living fully in a world constructed by the other senses.

But it seemed extraordinary to me that such an annihilation of visual memory as Hull describes could happen equally to an adult, with decades, an entire lifetime, of rich and richly categorized visual experience to call upon. And yet I could not doubt the authenticity of Hull's account, which he relates with the most scrupulous care and lucidity.

Important studies of adaptation in the brain were begun in the nineteen-seventies by, among others, Helen Neville, a cognitive neuroscientist now working in Oregon. She showed that in prelingually deaf people (that is, those who had been born deaf or become deaf before the age of two or so) the auditory parts of the brain had not degenerated or atrophied. These had remained active and functional, but with an activity and a function that were new: they had been transformed, "reallocated," in Neville's term, for processing visual language. Comparable studies in those born blind, or early blinded, show that the visual areas of the cortex, similarly, may be reallocated in function, and used to process sound and touch.

With the reallocation of the visual cortex to touch and other senses, these can take on a hyperacuity that perhaps no sighted person can imagine. Bernard Morin, the blind mathematician who in the nineteen-sixties had shown how a sphere could be turned inside out, felt that his achievement required a special sort of spatial perception and imagination. And a similar sort of spatial giftedness has been central to the work of Geerat Vermeij, a blind biologist who has been able to delineate many new species of mollusk, based on tiny variations in the shapes and contours of their shells.

Faced with such findings and reports, neurologists began to concede that there might be a certain flexibility or plasticity in the brain, at least in the early years of life. But when this critical period was over, it was assumed, the brain became inflexible, and no further changes of a radical type could occur. The experiences that Hull so carefully recounts give the lie to this. It is clear that his perceptions, his brain, did finally change, in a fundamental way. Indeed, Alvaro Pascual-Leone and his colleagues in Boston have recently shown that, even in adult sighted volunteers, as little as five days of being blindfolded produces marked shifts to nonvisual forms of behavior and cognition, and they have demonstrated the physiological changes in the brain that go along with this. And only last month, Italian researchers published a study showing that sighted volunteers kept in the dark for as little as ninety *minutes* may show a striking enhancement of tactile-spatial sensitivity.

The brain, clearly, is capable of changing even in adulthood, and I assumed that Hull's experience was typical of acquired blindness—the response, sooner or later, of everyone who becomes blind, even in adult life.

So when I came to publish an essay on Hull's book, in 1991, I was taken aback to receive a number of letters from blind people, letters that were often somewhat puzzled, and occasionally indignant, in tone. Many of my correspondents, it seemed, could not identify with Hull's experience, and said that they themselves, even decades after losing their sight, had never lost their visual images or memories. One correspondent, who had lost her sight at fifteen, wrote, "Even though I am totally blind … I consider myself a very visual person. I still 'see' objects in front of me. As I am typing now I can see my hands on the keyboard.… I don't feel comfortable in a new environment until I have a mental picture of its appearance. I need a mental map for my independent moving, too."

Had I been wrong, or at least one-sided, in accepting Hull's experience as a typical response to blindness? Had I been guilty of emphasizing one mode of response too strongly, oblivious to the possibilities of radically different responses?

This feeling came to a head in 1996, when I received a letter from an Australian psychologist named Zoltan Torey. Torey wrote to me not about blindness but about a book he had written on the brain-mind problem and the nature of consciousness. (The book was published by Oxford University Press as *The Crucible of Consciousness,* in 1999.) In his letter Torey also spoke of how he had been blinded in an accident at the age of twenty-one, while working at a chemical factory, and how, although "advised to switch from a visual to an auditory mode of adjustment," he had moved in the opposite direction, and resolved to develop instead his "inner eye," his powers of visual imagery, to their greatest possible extent.

In this, it seemed, he had been extremely successful, developing a remarkable power of generating, holding, and manipulating images in his mind, so much so that he had been able to construct an imagined visual world that seemed almost as real and intense to him as the perceptual one he had lost—and, indeed, sometimes more real, more intense, a sort of controlled dream or hallucination. This imagery, moreover, enabled him to do things that might have seemed scarcely possible for a blind man.

"I replaced the entire roof guttering of my multi-gabled home single-handed," he wrote, "and solely on the strength of the accurate and well-focused manipulation of my now totally pliable and responsive mental space." (Torey later expanded on this episode, mentioning the great alarm of his neighbors at seeing a blind man, alone, on the roof of his house—and, even more terrifying to them, at night, in pitch darkness.)

And it enabled him to think in ways that had not been available to him before, to envisage solutions, models, designs, to project himself to the inside of machines and other systems, and, finally, to grasp by visual thought and simulation (complemented by all the data of neuroscience) the complexities of that ultimate system, the human brain-mind.

When I wrote back to Torey, I suggested that he consider writing another book, a more personal one, exploring how his life had been affected by blindness, and how he had responded to this, in the most improbable and seemingly paradoxical of ways. *Out of Darkness* is the memoir he has now written, and in it Torey describes his early memories with great visual intensity and humor. Scenes are remembered or reconstructed in brief, poetic glimpses of his childhood and youth in Hungary before the Second World War: the sky-blue buses of Budapest, the egg-yellow trams, the lighting of gas lamps, the funicular on the Buda side. He describes a carefree and privileged youth, roaming with his father in the wooded mountains above the Danube, playing games and pranks at school, growing up in a highly intellectual environment of writers, actors, professionals of every sort. Torey's father was the head of a large motion-picture studio and would often give his son scripts to read. "This," Torey writes, "gave me the opportunity to visualize stories, plots, and characters, to work my imagination—a skill that was to become a lifeline and source of strength in the years ahead."

All of this came to a brutal end with the Nazi occupation, the siege of Buda, and then the Soviet occupation. Torey, now an adolescent, found himself passionately drawn to the big questions—the mystery of the universe, of life, and above all the mystery of consciousness, of the mind. In 1948, nineteen years old, and feeling that he needed to immerse himself in biology, engineering, neuroscience, and psychology, but knowing that there was no chance of study, of an intellectual life, in Soviet Hungary, Torey made his escape and eventually found his way to Australia, where, penniless and without connections, he did various manual jobs. In June of 1951, loosening the plug in a vat of acid at the chemical factory where he worked, he had the accident that bisected his life.

"The last thing I saw with complete clarity was a glint of light in the flood of acid that was to engulf my face and change my life. It was a nanosecond of sparkle, framed by the black circle of the drumface, less than a foot away. This was the final scene, the slender thread that ties me to my visual past."

When it became clear that his corneas had been hopelessly damaged and that he would have to live his life as a blind man, he was advised to rebuild his representation of the world on the basis of hearing and touch and to "forget about sight and visualizing altogether." But this was something that Torey could not or would not do. He had emphasized, in his first letter to me, the importance of a most critical choice at this juncture: "I immediately resolved to find out how far a partially sense-deprived brain could go to rebuild a life." Put this way, it sounds abstract, like an experiment. But in his book one senses the tremendous feelings underlying his resolution—the horror of darkness, "the empty darkness," as Torey often calls it, "the grey fog that was engulfing me," and the passionate desire to hold on to light and sight, to maintain, if only in memory and imagination, a vivid and living visual world. The very title of his book says all this, and the note of defiance is sounded from the start.

Hull, who did not use his potential for imagery in a deliberate way, lost it in two or three years, and became unable to remember which way round a 3 went; Torey, on the other hand, soon became able to multiply four-figure numbers by each other, as on a blackboard, visualizing the whole operation in his mind, "painting" the suboperations in different colors.

Well aware that the imagination (or the brain), unrestrained by the usual perceptual input, may run away with itself in a wildly associative or self-serving way—as may happen in deliria, hallucinations, or dreams—Torey maintained a cautious and "scientific" attitude to his own visual imagery, taking pains to check the accuracy of his images by every means available. "I learned," he writes, "to hold the image in a tentative way, conferring credibility and status on it only when some information would tip the balance in its favor." Indeed, he soon gained enough confidence in the reliability of his visual imagery to stake his life upon it, as when he undertook roof repairs by himself. And this confidence extended to other, purely mental projects. He became able "to imagine, to visualize, for example, the inside of a differential gearbox in action as if from inside its casing. I was able to watch the cogs bite, lock, and revolve, distributing the spin as required. I began to play around with this internal view in connection with mechanical and technical problems, visualizing how subcomponents relate in the atom, or in the living cell." This power of imagery was crucial, Torey thought, in enabling him to arrive at a solution of the brain-mind problem by visualizing the brain "as a perpetual juggling act of interacting routines."

In a famous study of creativity, the French mathematician Jacques Hadamard asked many scientists and mathematicians, including Einstein, about their thought processes. Einstein replied, "The physical entities which seem to serve as elements in thought are … more or less clear images which can be 'voluntarily' reproduced and combined. [Some are] of visual and some of muscular type. Conventional words or other signs have to be sought for laboriously only in a secondary stage." Torey cites this, and adds, "Nor was Einstein unique in this respect. Hadamard found that almost all scientists work this way, and this was also the way my project evolved."

Soon after receiving Torey's manuscript, I received the proofs of yet another memoir by a blind person: Sabriye Tenberken's *My Path Leads to Tibet*. While Hull and Torey are thinkers, preoccupied in their different ways by inwardness, states of brain and mind, Tenberken is a doer; she has travelled, often alone, all over Tibet, where for centuries blind people have been treated as less than human and denied education, work, respect, or a role in the community. Virtually single-handed, Tenberken has transformed their situation over the past half-dozen years, devising a form of Tibetan Braille, establishing schools for the blind, and integrating the graduates of these schools into their communities.

Tenberken herself had impaired vision almost from birth but was able to make out faces and landscapes until she was twelve. As a child in Germany, she had a particular predilection for colors, and loved painting, and when she was no longer able to decipher shapes and forms she could still use colors to identify objects. Tenberken has, indeed, an intense synesthesia. "As far back as I can remember," she writes, "numbers and words have instantly triggered colors in me.... The number 4, for example, [is] gold. Five is light green. Nine is vermillion.... Days of the week as well as months have their colors, too. I have them arranged in geometrical formations, in circular sectors, a little like a pie. When I need to recall on which day a particular event happened, the first thing that pops up on my inner screen is the day's color, then its position in the pie." Her synesthesia has persisted and been intensified, it seems, by her blindness.

Though she has been totally blind for twenty years now, Tenberken continues to use all her other senses, along with verbal descriptions, visual memories, and a strong pictorial and synesthetic sensibility, to construct "pictures" of landscapes and rooms, of environments and scenes—pictures so lively and detailed as to astonish her listeners. These images may sometimes be wildly or comically different from reality, as she relates in one incident when she and a companion drove to Nam Co, the great salt lake in Tibet. Turning eagerly toward the lake, Tenberken saw, in her mind's eye, "a beach of crystallized salt shimmering like snow under an evening sun, at the edge of a vast body of turquoise water.... And down below, on the deep green mountain flanks, a few nomads were watching their yaks grazing." But it then turns out that she has been facing in the wrong direction, not "looking" at the lake at all, and that she has been "staring" at rocks and a gray landscape. These disparities don't faze her in the least—she is happy to have so vivid a visual imagination. Hers is essentially an artistic imagination, which can be impressionistic, romantic, not veridical at all, where Torey's imagination is that of an engineer, and has to be factual, accurate down to the last detail.

I had now read three memoirs, strikingly different in their depictions of the visual experience of blinded people: Hull with his acquiescent descent into imageless "deep blindness," Torey with his "compulsive visualization" and meticulous construction of an internal visual world, and Tenberken with her impulsive, almost novelistic, visual freedom, along with her remarkable and specific gift of synesthesia. Was there any such thing, I now wondered, as a "typical" blind experience?

I recently met two other people blinded in adult life who shared their experiences with me.

Dennis Shulman, a clinical psychologist and psychoanalyst who lectures on Biblical topics, is an affable, stocky, bearded man in his fifties who gradually lost his sight in his teens, becoming completely blind by the time he entered college. He immediately confirmed that his experience was unlike Hull's: "I still live in a visual world after thirty-five years of blindness. I have very vivid visual memories and images. My wife, whom I have never seen—I think of her visually. My kids, too. I see myself visually—but it is as I last saw myself, when I was thirteen, though I try hard to update the image. I often give public lectures, and my notes are in Braille; but when I go over them in my mind, I see the Braille notes visually—they are visual images, not tactile."

Arlene Gordon, a charming woman in her seventies, a former social worker, said that things were very similar for her: "If I move my arms back and forth in front of my eyes, I see them, even though I have been blind for more than thirty years." It seemed that moving her arms was immediately translated for her into a visual image. Listening to talking books, she added, made her eyes tire if she listened too long; she seemed to herself to be reading at such times, the sound of the spoken words being transformed to lines of print on a vividly visualized book in front of her. This involved a sort of cognitive exertion (similar perhaps to translating one language into another), and sooner or later this would give her an eye ache.

I was reminded of Amy, a colleague who had been deafened by scarlet fever at the age of nine but was so adept a lipreader that I often forgot she was deaf. Once, when I absent-mindedly turned away from her as I was speaking, she said sharply, "I can no longer hear you."

"You mean you can no longer see me," I said.

"*You* may call it seeing," she answered, "but I experience it as hearing."

Amy, though totally deaf, still constructed the sound of speech in her mind. Both Dennis and Arlene, similarly, spoke not only of a heightening of visual imagery and imagination since losing their eyesight but also of what seemed to be a much readier transference of information from verbal description—or from their own sense of touch, movement, hearing, or smell—into a visual form. On the whole, their experiences seemed quite similar to Torey's, even though they had not systematically exercised their powers of visual imagery in the way that he had, or consciously tried to make an entire virtual world of sight.

There is increasing evidence from neuroscience for the extraordinarily rich interconnectedness and interactions of the sensory areas of the brain, and the difficulty, therefore, of saying that anything is purely visual or purely auditory, or purely anything. This is evident in the very titles of some recent papers—Pascual-Leone and his colleagues at Harvard now write of "The Metamodal Organization of the Brain," and Shinsuke Shimojo and his group at Caltech, who are also exploring intersensory perceptual phenomena, recently published a paper called "What You See Is What You Hear," and stress that sensory modalities can never be considered in isolation. The world of the blind, of the blinded, it seems, can be especially rich in such in-between states—the intersensory, the metamodal—states for which we have no common language.

Arlene, like Dennis, still identifies herself in many ways as a visual person. "I have a very strong sense of color," she said. "I pick out my own clothes. I think, Oh, that will go with this or that, once I have been told the colors." Indeed, she was dressed very smartly, and took obvious pride in her appearance.

"I love travelling," she continued. "I 'saw' Venice when I was there." She explained how her travelling companions would describe places, and she would then construct a visual image from these details, her reading, and her own visual memories. "Sighted people enjoy travelling with me," she said. "I ask them questions, then they look, and see things they wouldn't otherwise. Too often people with sight don't see anything! It's a reciprocal process—we enrich each other's worlds."

If we are sighted, we build our own images, using our eyes, our visual information, so instantly and seamlessly that it seems to us we are experiencing "reality" itself. One may need to see people who are color-blind, or motion-blind, who have lost certain visual capacities from cerebral injury, to realize the enormous act of analysis and synthesis, the dozens of subsystems involved in the subjectively simple act of seeing. But can a visual image be built using *nonvisual* information—information conveyed by the other senses, by memory, or by verbal description?

There have, of course, been many blind poets and writers, from Homer on. Most of these were born with normal vision and lost their sight in boyhood or adulthood (like Milton). I loved reading Prescott's *Conquest of Mexico* and *Conquest of Peru* as a boy, and feel that I first saw these lands through his intensely visual, almost hallucinogenic descriptions, and I was amazed to discover, years later, that Prescott not only had never visited Mexico or Peru but had been virtually blind since the age of eighteen. Did he, like Torey, compensate for his blindness by developing such powers of visual imagery that he could experience a "virtual reality" of sight? Or were his brilliant visual descriptions in a sense simulated, made possible by the evocative and pictorial powers of language? To what extent can language, a picturing in words, provide a substitute for actual seeing, and for the visual, pictorial imagination? Blind children, it has often been noted, tend to be precocious verbally, and may develop such fluency in the verbal description of faces and places as to leave others (and perhaps themselves) uncertain as to whether they are actually blind. Helen Keller's writing, to give a famous example, startles one with its brilliantly visual quality.

When I asked Dennis and Arlene whether they had read John Hull's book, Arlene said, "I was stunned when I read it. His experiences are so unlike mine." Perhaps, she added, Hull had "renounced" his inner vision. Dennis agreed, but said, "We are only two individuals. You are going to have to talk to dozens of people.... But in the meanwhile you should read Jacques Lusseyran's memoir."

Lusseyran was a French Resistance fighter whose memoir, *And There Was Light,* deals mostly with his experiences fighting the Nazis and later in Buchenwald but includes many beautiful descriptions of his early adaptations to blindness. He was blinded in an accident when he was not quite eight years old, an age that he came to feel was "ideal" for such an eventuality, for, while he already had a rich visual experience to call on, "the habits of a boy of eight are not yet formed, either in body or in mind. His body is infinitely supple." And suppleness, agility, indeed came to characterize his response to blindness.

Many of his initial responses were of loss, both of imagery and of interests:

> A very short time after I went blind I forgot the faces of my mother and father and the faces of most of the people I loved.... I stopped caring whether people were dark or fair, with blue eyes or green. I felt that sighted people spent too much time observing these empty things....
> I no longer even thought about them. People no longer seemed to possess them. Sometimes in my mind men and women appeared without heads or fingers.

This is similar to Hull, who writes, "Increasingly, I am no longer even trying to imagine what people look like.... I am finding it more and more difficult to realize that people look like anything, to put any meaning into the idea that they have an appearance."

But then, while relinquishing the actual visual world and many of its values and categories, Lusseyran starts to construct and to use an imaginary visual world more like Torey's.

This started as a sensation of light, a formless, flooding, streaming radiance. Neurological terms are bound to sound reductive in this almost mystical context. Yet one might venture to interpret this as a "release" phenomenon, a spontaneous, almost eruptive arousal of the visual cortex, now deprived of its normal visual input. This is a phenomenon analogous, perhaps, to tinnitus or phantom limbs, though endowed here, by a devout and precociously imaginative little boy, with some element of the supernal. But then, it becomes clear, he does find himself in possession of great powers of visual imagery, and not just a formless luminosity.

The visual cortex, the inner eye, having now been activated, Lusseyran's mind constructed a "screen" upon which whatever he thought or desired was projected and, if need be, manipulated, as on a computer screen. "This screen was not like a blackboard, rectangular or square, which so quickly reaches the edge of its frame," he writes. "My screen was always as big as I needed it to be. Because it was nowhere in space it was everywhere at the same time.... Names, figures, and objects in general did not appear on my screen without shape, nor just in black and white, but in all the colors of the rainbow. Nothing entered my mind without being bathed in a certain amount of light.... In a few months my personal world had turned into a painter's studio."

Great powers of visualization were crucial to the young Lusseyran, even in something as nonvisual (one would think) as learning Braille (he visualizes the Braille dots, as Dennis does), and in his brilliant successes at school. They were no less crucial in the real, outside world. He describes walks with his sighted friend Jean, and how, as they were climbing together up the side of a hill above the Seine Valley, he could say:

> "Just look! This time we're on top.... You'll see the whole bend of the river, unless the sun gets in your eyes!" Jean was startled, opened his eyes wide and cried: "You're right." This little scene was often repeated between us, in a thousand forms.

"Every time someone mentioned an event," Lusseyran relates, "the event immediately projected itself in its place on the screen, which was a kind of inner canvas.... Comparing my world with his, [Jean] found that his held fewer pictures and not nearly as many colors. This made him almost angry. 'When it comes to that,' he used to say, 'which one of us two is blind?'"

It was his supernormal powers of visualization and visual manipulation—visualizing people's position and movement, the topography of any space, visualizing strategies for defense and attack—coupled with his charismatic personality (and seemingly infallible "nose" or "ear" for detecting falsehood, possible traitors), which later made Lusseyran an icon in the French Resistance.

Dennis, earlier, had spoken of how the heightening of his other senses had increased his sensitivity to moods in other people, and to the most delicate nuances in their speech and self-presentation. He could now recognize many of his patients by smell, he said, and he could often pick up states of tension or anxiety which they might not even be aware of. He felt that he had become far more sensitive to others' emotional states since losing his sight, for he was no longer taken in by visual appearances, which most people learn to camouflage. Voices and smells, by contrast, he felt, could reveal people's depths. He had come to think of most sighted people, he joked, as "visually dependent."

In a subsequent essay, Lusseyran inveighs against the "despotism," the "idol worship" of sight, and sees the "task" of blindness as reminding us of our other, deeper modes of perception and their mutuality. "A blind person has a better sense of feeling, of taste, of touch," he writes, and speaks of these as "the gifts of the blind." And all of these, Lusseyran feels, blend into a single fundamental sense, a deep attentiveness, a slow, almost prehensile attention, a sensuous, intimate being at one with the world which sight, with its quick, flicking, facile quality, continually distracts us from. This is very close to Hull's concept of "deep blindness" as infinitely more than mere compensation but a unique form of perception, a precious and special mode of being.

What happens when the visual cortex is no longer limited, or constrained, by any visual input? The simple answer is that, isolated from the outside, the visual cortex becomes hypersensitive to internal stimuli of all sorts: its own autonomous activity; signals from other brain areas—auditory, tactile, and verbal areas; and the thoughts and emotions of the blinded individual. Sometimes, as sight deteriorates, hallucinations occur—of geometrical patterns, or occasionally of silent, moving figures or scenes that appear and disappear spontaneously, without any relation to the contents of consciousness, or intention, or context.

Something perhaps akin to this is described by Hull as occurring almost convulsively as he was losing the last of his sight. "About a year after I was registered blind," he writes, "I began to have such strong images of what people's faces looked like that they were almost like hallucinations."

These imperious images were so engrossing as to preëmpt consciousness: "Sometimes," Hull adds, "I would become so absorbed in gazing upon these images, which seemed to come and go without any intention on my part, that I would entirely lose the thread of what was being said to me. I would come back with a shock ... and I would feel as if I had dropped off to sleep for a few minutes in front of the wireless." Though related to the context of speaking with people, these visions came and went in their own way, without any reference to his intentions, conjured up not by him but by his brain.

The fact that Hull is the only one of the four authors to describe this sort of release phenomenon is perhaps an indication that his visual cortex was starting to escape from his control. One has to wonder whether this signaled its impending demise, at least as an organ of useful visual imagery and memory. Why this should have occurred with him, and how common such a course is, is something one can only speculate on.

Torey, unlike Hull, clearly played a very active role in building up his visual imagery, took control of it the moment the bandages were taken off, and never apparently experienced, or allowed, the sort of involuntary imagery Hull describes. Perhaps this was because he was already very at home with visual imagery, and used to manipulating it in his own way. We know that Torey was very visually inclined before his accident, and skilled from boyhood in creating visual narratives based on the film scripts his father gave him. We have no such information about Hull, for his journal entries start only when he has become blind.

For Lusseyran and Tenberken, there is an added physiological factor: both were attracted to painting, in love with colors, and strongly synesthetic—prone to visualizing numbers, letters, words, music, etc., as shapes and colors—before becoming blind. They already had an overconnectedness, a "cross talk" between the visual cortex and other parts of the brain primarily concerned with language, sound, and music. Given such a neurological situation (synesthesia is congenital, often familial), the persistence of visual imagery and synesthesia, or its heightening, might be almost inevitable in the event of blindness.

Torey required months of intense cognitive discipline dedicated to improving his visual imagery, making it more tenacious, more stable, more malleable, whereas Lusseyran seemed to do this almost effortlessly from the start. Perhaps this was aided by the fact that Lusseyran was not yet eight when blinded (while Torey was twenty-one), and his brain was, accordingly, more plastic, more able to adapt to a new and drastic contingency.

But adaptability does not end with youth. It is clear that Arlene, becoming blind in her forties, was able to adapt in quite radical ways, too, developing not exactly synesthesia but something more flexible and useful: the ability to "see" her hands moving before her, to "see" the words of books read to her, to construct detailed visual images from verbal descriptions. Did she adapt, or did her brain do so? One has a sense that Torey's adaptation was largely shaped by conscious motive, will, and purpose; that Lusseyran's was shaped by overwhelming physiological disposition; and that Arlene's lies somewhere in between. Hull's, meanwhile, remains enigmatic.

There has been much recent work on the neural bases of visual imagery—this can be investigated by brain imaging of various types (PET scanning, functional MRIs, etc.)—and it is now generally accepted that visual imagery activates the cortex in a similar way, and with almost the same intensity, as visual perception itself. And yet studies on the effects of blindness on the human cortex have shown that functional changes may start to occur in a few days, and can become profound as the days stretch into months or years.

Torey, who is well aware of all this research, attributes Hull's loss of visual imagery and memory to the fact that he did not struggle to maintain it, to heighten and systematize and use it, as Torey himself did. (Indeed, Torey expresses horror at what he regards as Hull's passivity, at his letting himself slide into deep blindness.) Perhaps Torey was able to stave off an otherwise inevitable loss of neuronal function in the visual cortex; but perhaps, again, such neural degeneration is quite variable, irrespective of whether or not there is conscious visualization. And, of course, Hull had been losing vision gradually for many years, whereas for Torey blindness was instantaneous and total. It would be of great interest to know the results of brain imaging in the two men, and indeed to look at a large number of people with acquired blindness, to see what correlations, what predictions could be made.

But what if their differences reflect an underlying predisposition independent of blindness? What of visual imagery in the sighted?

I first became conscious that there could be huge variations in visual imagery and visual memory when I was fourteen or so. My mother was a surgeon and comparative anatomist, and I had brought her a lizard's skeleton from school. She gazed at this intently for a minute, turning it round in her hands, then put it down and without looking at it again did a number of drawings of it, rotating it mentally by thirty degrees each time, so that she produced a series, the last drawing exactly the same as the first. I could not imagine how she had done this, and when she said that she could "see" the skeleton in her mind just as clearly and vividly as if she were looking at it, and that she simply rotated the image through a twelfth of a circle each time, I felt bewildered, and very stupid. I could hardly see anything with my mind's eye—at most, faint, evanescent images over which I had no control.

I did have vivid images as I was falling asleep, and in dreams, and once when I had a high fever—but otherwise I saw nothing, or almost nothing, when I tried to visualize, and had great difficulty picturing anybody or anything. Coincidentally or not, I could not draw for toffee.

My mother had hoped I would follow in her footsteps and become a surgeon, but when she realized how lacking in visual powers I was (and how clumsy, lacking in mechanical skill, too) she resigned herself to the idea that I would have to specialize in something else.

I was, however, to get a vivid idea of what mental imagery could be like when, during the nineteen-sixties, I had a period of experimenting with large doses of amphetamines. These can produce striking perceptual changes, including dramatic enhancements of visual imagery and memory (as well as heightenings of the other senses, as I describe in "The Dog Beneath the Skin," a story in *The Man Who Mistook His Wife for a Hat*). For a period of two weeks or so, I found that I could do the most accurate anatomical drawings. I had only to look at a picture or an anatomical specimen, and its image would remain both vivid and stable, and I could easily hold it in my mind for hours. I could mentally project the image onto the paper before me—it was as clear and distinct as if projected by a camera lucida—and trace its outlines with a pencil. My drawings were not elegant, but they were, everyone agreed, very detailed and accurate, and could bear comparison with some of the drawings in our neuroanatomy textbook. This heightening of imagery attached to everything—I had only to think of a face, a place, a picture, a paragraph in a book to see it vividly in my mind. But when the amphetamine-induced state faded, after a couple of weeks, I could no longer visualize, no longer project images, no longer draw—nor have I been able to do so in the decades since.

A few months ago, at a medical conference in Boston, I spoke of Torey's and Hull's experiences of blindness, and of how "enabled" Torey seemed to be by the powers of visualization he had developed, and how "disabled" Hull was—in some ways, at least—by the loss of his powers of visual imagery and memory. After my talk, a man in the audience came up to me and asked how well, in my estimation, *sighted* people could function if they had no visual imagery. He went on to say that he had no visual imagery whatever, at least none that he could deliberately evoke, and that no one in his family had any, either. Indeed, he had assumed this was the case with everyone, until he came to participate in some psychological tests at Harvard and realized that he apparently lacked a mental power that all the other students, in varying degrees, had.

"And what do you do?" I asked him, wondering what this poor man *could* do.

"I am a surgeon," he replied. "A vascular surgeon. An anatomist, too. And I design solar panels."

But how, I asked him, did he recognize what he was seeing?

"It's not a problem," he answered. "I guess there must be representations or models in the brain that get matched up with what I am seeing and doing. But they are not conscious. I cannot evoke them."

This seemed to be at odds with my mother's experience—she, clearly, did have extremely vivid and readily manipulable visual imagery, though (it now seemed) this may have been a bonus, a luxury, and not a prerequisite for her career as a surgeon.

Is this also the case with Torey? Is his greatly developed visual imagery, though clearly a source of much pleasure, not as indispensable as he takes it to be? Might he, in fact, have done everything he did, from carpentry to roof repair to making a model of the mind, without any conscious imagery at all? He himself raises this question.

The role of mental imagery in thinking was explored by Francis Galton, Darwin's irrepressible cousin, who wrote on subjects as various as fingerprints, eugenics, dog whistles, criminality, twins, visionaries, psychometric measures, and hereditary genius. His inquiry into visual imagery took the form of a questionnaire, with such questions as "Can you recall with distinctness the features of all near relations and many other persons? Can you at will cause your mental image ... to sit, stand, or turn slowly around? Can you ... see it with enough distinctness to enable you to sketch it leisurely (supposing yourself able to draw)?" The vascular surgeon would have been hopeless on such tests—indeed, it was questions such as these which had floored him when he was a student at Harvard. And yet, finally, how much had it mattered?

As to the significance of such imagery, Galton is ambiguous and guarded. He suggests, in one breath, that "scientific men, as a class, have feeble powers of visual representation" and, in another, that "a vivid visualizing faculty is of much importance in connection with the higher processes of generalized thoughts." He feels that "it is undoubtedly the fact that mechanicians, engineers, and architects usually possess the faculty of seeing mental images with remarkable clearness and precision," but goes on to say, "I am, however, bound to say, that the missing faculty seems to be replaced so serviceably by other modes of conception ... that men who declare themselves entirely deficient in the power of seeing mental pictures can nevertheless give lifelike descriptions of what they have seen, and can otherwise express themselves as if they were gifted with a vivid visual imagination. They can also become painters of the rank of Royal Academicians." I have a cousin, a professional architect, who maintains that he cannot visualize anything whatever. "How do you think?" I once asked him. He shook his head and said, "I don't know." Do any of us, finally, know how we think?

When I talk to people, blind or sighted, or when I try to think of my own internal representations, I find myself uncertain whether words, symbols, and images of various types are the primary tools of thought or whether there are forms of thought antecedent to all of these, forms of thought essentially amodal. Psychologists have sometimes spoken of "interlingua" or "mentalese," which they conceive to be the brain's own language, and Lev Vygotsky, the great Russian psychologist, used to speak of "thinking in pure meanings." I cannot decide whether this is nonsense or profound truth—it is the sort of reef I end up on when I think about thinking.

Galton's seemingly contradictory statements about imagery—is it antithetical to abstract thinking, or integral to it?—may stem from his failure to distinguish between fundamentally different levels of imagery. Simple visual imagery such as he describes may suffice for the design of a screw, an engine, or a surgical operation, and it may be relatively easy to model these essentially reproductive forms of imagery or to simulate them by constructing video games or virtual realities of various sorts. Such powers may be invaluable, but there is something passive and mechanical and impersonal about them, which makes them utterly different from the higher and more personal powers of the imagination, where there is a continual struggle for concepts and form and meaning, a calling upon all the powers of the self. Imagination dissolves and transforms, unifies and creates, while drawing upon the "lower" powers of memory and association. It is by such imagination, such "vision," that we create or construct our individual worlds.

At this level, one can no longer say of one's mental landscapes what is visual, what is auditory, what is image, what is language, what is intellectual, what is emotional—they are all fused together and imbued with our own individual perspectives and values. Such a unified vision shines out from Hull's memoir no less than from Torey's, despite the fact that one has become "nonvisual" and the other "hypervisual." What seems at first to be so decisive a difference between the two men is not, finally, a radical one, so far as personal development and sensibility go. Even though the paths they have followed might seem irreconcilable, both men have "used" blindness (if one can employ such a term for processes which are deeply mysterious, and far below, or above, the level of consciousness and voluntary control) to release their own creative capacities and emotional selves, and both have achieved a rich and full realization of their own individual worlds.

QUESTIONS FOR MAKING CONNECTIONS
WITHIN THE READING

1. Early in his essay, Sacks poses this question: "Does the mind run the brain or the brain the mind—or, rather, to what extent does one run the other?" Most of the discussion that follows this question, however, concerns the experience of blindness. Instead of providing an extended analysis of mental processing or brain chemistry, Sacks gives us details about people who have lost their vision and then adapted in different ways. How do these accounts of blindness connect to the debate about mind and brain?

2. To what extent are the different responses of the people Sacks discusses attributable to their individual ways of "being in the world"? Do you see any evidence of a continuity in the behavior of his subjects before and after the onset of their blindness? What are the larger implications of their adaptations? Would you say that the world is what we make it, or are there limits to the power of imagination, intelligence, and determination? What does Sacks appear to believe?

3. At one point in his essay, Sacks recalls a period in his life when he was "experimenting with large doses of amphetamines":

> For a period of two weeks or so, I found that I could do the most accurate anatomical drawings. I had only to look at a picture or an anatomical specimen, and its image would remain both vivid and stable, and I could easily hold it in my mind for hours. I could mentally project the image onto the paper before me—it was as clear and distinct as if projected by a camera lucida—and trace its outlines with a pencil.... But when the amphetamine-induced state faded, ... I could no longer visualize, no longer project images, no longer draw—nor have I been able to do so in the decades since.

Why does Sacks include this vignette? What point does he make, and how does the passage extend the argument he develops in the previous pages? Does it matter that the story he tells is personal?

QUESTIONS FOR WRITING

1. Do the discoveries of neuroscience undermine our assumptions about such issues as free will, the uniqueness of each individual, and the importance of creativity? Ordinarily, we might think that if we can explain an emotion like love or the experience of beauty as the product of the brain's hardwiring, something important will be lost. But will it? Is human behavior in any way diminished or degraded by our knowledge of brain science? In what ways might an understanding of neuroscience foster greater understanding and a tolerance for diversity—and uniformity—in human behavior?

2. For the last century or so, thinkers have debated the relative influence of "nature" and "nurture" over human behavior. By "nature," people ordinarily mean biology, chemistry, genetics, and neuroscience. By "nurture," they mean custom, culture, and education. What does Sacks's essay contribute to this debate? Can he be accused of perpetuating "reductionism"— in other words, does he oversimplify the complexities of human life by reducing everything to one explanation? In other words, does he oversimplify the complexities of human life by reducing everything to one explanation?

3. On the basis of the evidence that Sacks provides, can we ever say that human behavior is entirely "hardwired"? Can we argue, in other words, that how we act is predetermined by the structure and functioning of our brains? Or are we entitled to say that the brain is flexible enough to adapt to an event like the loss of sight in ways that are infinitely varied? Do the adaptations vary infinitely, or are there biological limits? Are there commonalities among all the different adaptations that Sacks discusses? Do you think that these commonalities have their origin in the brain, or can they be explained in some other way?

QUESTIONS FOR MAKING CONNECTIONS
BETWEEN READINGS

1. Sacks's account of people who lose their sight is, in part, a story about hope—about the power of human beings to create rich and satisfying new worlds when their old worlds fall apart. One element of their success is the adaptability of the human brain. But does this adaptability also mean that people can transform themselves in ways quite far removed from the positive examples that fill the pages of Sacks account? Consider what happens to the cadets in Susan Faludi's "The Naked Citadel." If the brain is highly adaptable, as Sacks's narrative suggests, is there any natural limit to the way that people can behave? Can we count on "human nature" to prevent individuals from self-deception and destructiveness? Or do we still see in Sacks's account some limits to the ability of human beings to transform themselves and their ways of life?

2. Sacks suggests that the human brain is actually quite flexible in its adaptations to the world. Charles Siebert finds evidence of a similar adaptability in the brains of elephants. This seeming similarity poses a problem, though. If the brains of all mammals can adapt to trauma, what is the role of choice in the process? Is it possible that human consciousness has evolved through trial and error in much the same way as different species have evolved? Or do humans merely project their own mental states onto the rest of the world, discovering trauma in elephants when, in fact, there is no evidence that these animals have consciousness or that they can be traumatized? Drawing on Sacks and Siebert, discuss the relationships among choice, consciousness, and trauma.

CHARLES SIEBERT

HAVING CLAIMED DOMINANCE over the planet for centuries, human beings have, by and large, made use of the earth without much consideration for the environmental and social needs of other animals. As a result, the areas in which animals are free to move about without danger from humans have steadily declined both in size and number. Overall, most of the animal kingdom has acquiesced without substantial resistance. But what happens when an animal community responds to the destruction of its natural habitat by turning against people, other species, and themselves? Charles Siebert addresses these questions in "An Elephant Crackup?,"an article that appeared in the *New York Times Magazine.*

An essayist, novelist, and a poet, Siebert has published numerous articles in the *New York Times Magazine,* the *New Yorker, Harpers,* and other periodicals. He has published four books, *A Man After His Own Heart* (2004), a meditation on the human heart (literally); *Angus: A Novel* (2000), an account of the inner life of a Jack Russell terrier; *Wickerby: An Urban Pastoral* (1998), which explores the fluid relationship between the urban and the rural worlds; and *The Wauchula Woods Accord: Toward a New Understanding of Animals* (2009).

"An Elephant Crackup?" is a further example of the sympathy for the emotional lives of animals that Siebert first explored in *Angus.* Here, he conducts research across Africa, India, and parts of southeastern Asia on the new phenomenon called "Human-Elephant Conflict," which has resulted in hundreds of human deaths since the year 2000. This is especially troubling, Siebert feels, because elephants possess "a highly developed sensibility" and "a deep-rooted sense of family" that is nowhere in evidence during these violent rampages. Drawing on research into the social fabric of animal society and the similarities between the emotional brains of elephants and the emotional brains of humans, Siebert weaves a compelling narrative of conflict between a species that once enjoyed dominance over its territory and the species that has the upper hand now.

If "An Elephant Crackup?" explores the surprisingly "human" psychology of elephants in distress, *The Wauchula Woods Accord* looks at our ambivalence toward animals because we fear the animal in ourselves. As Siebert said in a recent interview, "The degree to which we humans will finally stop abusing other creatures,

Siebert, Charles. "An Elephant Crackup?" *New York Times Magazine.* October 8, 2006. 42–71. Final quotation drawn from "An Interview with Writer Charles Siebert about his New Book *The Wauchula Woods Accord.*"

http://animalinventory.net/2009/06/22/an-interview-with-writer-charles-siebert-about-his-new-book-the-wauchula-woods-accord/.

and for that matter, one another, will be measured by the degree to which we come to understand how integral a part of us all other creatures actually are."

■ ■

An Elephant Crackup?

"We're not going anywhere," my driver, Nelson Okello, whispered to me one morning this past June, the two of us sitting in the front seat of a jeep just after dawn in Queen Elizabeth National Park in southwestern Uganda. We'd originally stopped to observe what appeared to be a lone bull elephant grazing in a patch of tall savanna grasses off to our left. More than one "rogue" crossed our path that morning—a young male elephant that has made an overly strong power play against the dominant male of his herd and been banished, sometimes permanently. This elephant, however, soon proved to be not a rogue but part of a cast of at least thirty. The ground vibrations registered just before the emergence of the herd from the surrounding trees and brush. We sat there watching the elephants cross the road before us, seeming, for all their heft, so light on their feet, soundlessly playing the wind-swept savanna grasses like land whales adrift above the floor of an ancient, waterless sea.

Then, from behind a thicket of acacia trees directly off our front left bumper, a huge female emerged—"the matriarch," Okello said softly. There was a small calf beneath her, freely foraging and knocking about within the secure cribbing of four massive legs. Acacia leaves are an elephant's favorite food, and as the calf set to work on some low branches, the matriarch stood guard, her vast back flank blocking the road, the rest of the herd milling about in the brush a short distance away.

After fifteen minutes or so, Okello started inching the jeep forward, revving the engine, trying to make us sound as beastly as possible. The matriarch, however, was having none of it, holding her ground, the fierce white of her eyes as bright as that of her tusks. Although I pretty much knew the answer, I asked Okello if he was considering trying to drive around. "No," he said, raising an index finger for emphasis. "She'll charge. We should stay right here."

I'd have considered it a wise policy even at a more peaceable juncture in the course of human-elephant relations. In recent years, however, those relations have become markedly more bellicose. Just two days before I arrived, a woman was killed by an elephant in Kazinga, a fishing village nearby. Two months earlier, a man was fatally gored by a young male elephant at the northern edge of

the park, near the village of Katwe. African elephants use their long tusks to forage through dense jungle brush. They've also been known to wield them, however, with the ceremonious flash and precision of gladiators, pinning down a
victim with one knee in order to deliver the decisive thrust. Okello told me
that a young Indian tourist was killed in this fashion two years ago in Murchison
Falls National Park, just north of where we were.

These were not isolated incidents. All across Africa, India, and parts of
Southeast Asia, from within and around whatever patches and corridors of their
natural habitat remain, elephants have been striking out, destroying villages and
crops, attacking and killing human beings. In fact, these attacks have become so
commonplace that a whole new statistical category, known as Human-Elephant
Conflict, or HEC, was created by elephant researchers in the mid-1990s to
monitor the problem. In the Indian state Jharkhand near the western border of
Bangladesh, 300 people were killed by elephants between 2000 and 2004. In the
past twelve years, elephants have killed 605 people in Assam, a state in northeastern India, 239 of them since 2001; 265 elephants have died in that same period, the majority of them as a result of retaliation by angry villagers, who have
used everything from poison-tipped arrows to laced food to exact their revenge.
In Africa, reports of human-elephant conflicts appear almost daily, from Zambia
to Tanzania, from Uganda to Sierra Leone, where 300 villagers evacuated their
homes last year because of unprovoked elephant attacks.

Still, it is not only the increasing number of these incidents that is causing
alarm but also the singular perversity—for want of a less anthropocentric term—
of recent elephant aggression. Since the early 1990s, for example, young male
elephants in Pilanesberg National Park and the Hluhluwe-Umfolozi Game
Reserve in South Africa have been raping and killing rhinoceroses; this abnormal
behavior, according to a 2001 study in the journal *Pachyderm,* has been reported in
"a number of reserves" in the region. In July of last year, officials in Pilanesberg
shot three young male elephants who were responsible for the killings of sixty-
three rhinos, as well as attacks on people in safari vehicles. In Addo Elephant
National Park, also in South Africa, up to ninety percent of male elephant deaths
are now attributable to other male elephants, compared with a rate of six percent
in more stable elephant communities.

In a coming book on this phenomenon, Gay Bradshaw, a psychologist at the
environmental sciences program at Oregon State University, notes that in India,
where the elephant has long been regarded as a deity, a recent headline in
a leading newspaper warned, "To Avoid Confrontation, Don't Worship
Elephants." "Everybody pretty much agrees that the relationship between elephants and people has dramatically changed," Bradshaw told me recently.
"What we are seeing today is extraordinary. Where for centuries humans and
elephants lived in relative peaceful coexistence, there is now hostility and violence. Now, I use the term 'violence' because of the intentionality associated
with it, both in the aggression of humans and, at times, the recently observed
behavior of elephants."

For a number of biologists and ethologists who have spent their careers
studying elephant behavior, the attacks have become so abnormal in both

number and kind that they can no longer be attributed entirely to the customary factors. Typically, elephant researchers have cited, as a cause of aggression, the high levels of testosterone in newly matured male elephants or the competition for land and resources between elephants and humans. But in "Elephant Breakdown," a 2005 essay in the journal *Nature,* Bradshaw and several colleagues argued that today's elephant populations are suffering from a form of chronic stress, a kind of species-wide trauma. Decades of poaching and culling and habitat loss, they claim, have so disrupted the intricate web of familial and societal relations by which young elephants have traditionally been raised in the wild, and by which established elephant herds are governed, that what we are now witnessing is nothing less than a precipitous collapse of elephant culture.

It has long been apparent that every large, land-based animal on this planet is ultimately fighting a losing battle with humankind. And yet entirely befitting of an animal with such a highly developed sensibility, a deep-rooted sense of family and, yes, such a good long-term memory, the elephant is not going out quietly. It is not leaving without making some kind of statement, one to which scientists from a variety of disciplines, including human psychology, are now beginning to pay close attention.

Once the matriarch and her calf were a comfortable distance from us that morning, Okello and I made the twenty-minute drive to Kyambura, a village at the far southeastern edge of the park. Back in 2003, Kyambura was reportedly the site of the very sort of sudden, unprovoked elephant attack I'd been hearing about. According to an account of the event in the magazine *New Scientist,* a number of huts and fields were trampled, and the townspeople were afraid to venture out to surrounding villages, either by foot or on their bikes, because elephants were regularly blocking the road and charging out at those who tried to pass.

Park officials from the Uganda Wildlife Authority with whom I tried to discuss the incident were reluctant to talk about it or any of the recent killings by elephants in the area. Ecotourism is one of Uganda's major sources of income, and the elephant and other wildlife stocks of Queen Elizabeth National Park are only just now beginning to recover from years of virtually unchecked poaching and habitat destruction. Tom Okello, the chief game warden at the park (and no relation to my driver), and Margaret Driciru, Queen Elizabeth's chief veterinarian, each told me that they weren't aware of the attack in Kyambura. When I mentioned it to the executive director of the wildlife authority, Moses Mapesa, upon my initial arrival in the capital city, Kampala, he eventually admitted that it did happen, but he claimed that it was not nearly as recent as reported. "That was fourteen years ago," he said. "We have seen aggressive behavior from elephants, but that's a story of the past."

Kyambura did look, upon our arrival, much like every other small Ugandan farming community I'd passed through on my visit. Lush fields of banana trees, millet, and maize framed a small town center of pastel-colored, single-story cement buildings with corrugated-tin roofs. People sat on stoops out front in the available shade. Bicyclers bore preposterously outsize loads of bananas, firewood, and five-gallon water jugs on their fenders and handlebars. Contrary to what I had read, the bicycle traffic along the road in and out of Kyambura didn't seem impaired in the slightest.

But when Okello and I asked a shopkeeper named Ibrah Byamukama about elephant attacks, he immediately nodded and pointed to a patch of maize and millet fields just up the road, along the edges of the surrounding Maramagambo Forest. He confirmed that a small group of elephants charged out one morning two years earlier, trampled the fields and nearby gardens, knocked down a few huts, and then left. He then pointed to a long orange gash in the earth between the planted fields and the forest: a fifteen-foot-deep, twenty-five-foot-wide trench that had been dug by the wildlife authority around the perimeter of Kyambura in an attempt to keep the elephants at bay. On the way out of town, Okello and I took a closer look at the trench. It was filled with stacks of thorny shrubs for good measure.

"The people are still worried," Byamukama said, shaking his head. "The elephants are just becoming more destructive. I don't know why."

Three years ago, Gay Bradshaw, then working on her graduate degree in psychology at the Pacifica Graduate Institute outside Santa Barbara, California, began wondering much the same thing: was the extraordinary behavior of elephants in Africa and Asia signaling a breaking point? With the assistance of several established African-elephant researchers, including Daphne Sheldrick and Cynthia Moss, and with the help of Allan Schore, an expert on human trauma disorders at the department of psychiatry and biobehavioral sciences at UCLA, Bradshaw sought to combine traditional research into elephant behavior with insights about trauma drawn from human neuroscience. Using the few remaining relatively stable elephant herds in places like Amboseli National Park in Kenya as control groups, Bradshaw and her colleagues analyzed the far more fractious populations found in places like Pilanesberg in South Africa and Queen Elizabeth National Park in Uganda. What emerged was a portrait of pervasive pachyderm dysfunction.

Elephants, when left to their own devices, are profoundly social creatures. A herd of them is, in essence, one incomprehensibly massive elephant: a somewhat loosely bound and yet intricately interconnected, tensile organism. Young elephants are raised within an extended, multitiered network of doting female caregivers that includes the birth mother, grandmothers, aunts, and friends. These relations are maintained over a life span as long as seventy years. Studies of established herds have shown that young elephants stay within fifteen feet of their mothers for nearly all of their first eight years of life, after which young females are socialized into the matriarchal network, while young males go off for a time into an all-male social group before coming back into the fold as mature adults.

When an elephant dies, its family members engage in intense mourning and burial rituals, conducting weeklong vigils over the body, carefully covering it with earth and brush, revisiting the bones for years afterward, caressing the bones with their trunks, often taking turns rubbing their trunks along the teeth of a skull's lower jaw, the way living elephants do in greeting. If harm comes to a member of an elephant group, all the other elephants are aware of it. This sense of cohesion is further enforced by the elaborate communication system that elephants use. In close proximity they employ a range of vocalizations, from low-frequency rumbles to higher-pitched screams and trumpets, along with a variety of visual signals, from the waving of their trunks to subtle anglings of the head, body, feet, and tail. When communicating over long distances—in order to pass along, for example, news about imminent threats, a sudden change of plans or, of the utmost importance to elephants, the death of a community member—they use patterns of subsonic vibrations that are felt as far as several miles away by exquisitely tuned sensors in the padding of their feet.

This fabric of elephant society, Bradshaw and her colleagues concluded, had effectively been frayed by years of habitat loss and poaching, along with systematic culling by government agencies to control elephant numbers and translocations of herds to different habitats. The number of older matriarchs and female caregivers (or "allomothers") had drastically fallen, as had the number of elder bulls, who play a significant role in keeping younger males in line. In parts of Zambia and Tanzania, a number of the elephant groups studied contained no adult females whatsoever. In Uganda, herds were often found to be "semipermanent aggregations," as a paper written by Bradshaw describes them, with many females between the ages of fifteen and twenty-five having no familial associations.

As a result of such social upheaval, calves are now being born to and raised by ever younger and inexperienced mothers. Young orphaned elephants, meanwhile, that have witnessed the death of a parent at the hands of poachers are coming of age in the absence of the support system that defines traditional elephant life. "The loss of elephants' elders," Bradshaw told me, "and the traumatic experience of witnessing the massacres of their family, impairs normal brain and behavior development in young elephants."

What Bradshaw and her colleagues describe would seem to be an extreme form of anthropocentric conjecture if the evidence that they've compiled from various elephant researchers, even on the strictly observational level, wasn't so compelling. The elephants of decimated herds, especially orphans who've watched the death of their parents and elders from poaching and culling, exhibit behavior typically associated with post-traumatic stress disorder and other trauma-related disorders in humans: abnormal startle response, unpredictable asocial behavior, inattentive mothering, and hyperaggression. Studies of the various assaults on the rhinos in South Africa, meanwhile, have determined that the perpetrators were in all cases adolescent males that had witnessed their families being shot down in cullings. It was common for these elephants to have been tethered to the bodies of their dead and dying relatives until they could be rounded up for translocation to, as Bradshaw and Schore describe them, "locales lacking traditional social hierarchy of older bulls and intact natal family structures."

In fact, even the relatively few attempts that park officials have made to restore parts of the social fabric of elephant society have lent substance to the elephant-breakdown theory. When South African park rangers recently introduced a number of older bull elephants into several destabilized elephant herds in Pilanesburg and Addo, the wayward behavior—including unusually premature hormonal changes among the adolescent elephants—abated.

But according to Bradshaw and her colleagues, the various pieces of the elephant-trauma puzzle really come together at the level of neuroscience, or what might be called the physiology of psychology, by which scientists can now map the marred neuronal fields, snapped synaptic bridges, and crooked chemical streams of an embattled psyche. Though most scientific knowledge of trauma is still understood through research on human subjects, neural studies of elephants are now under way. (The first functional MRI scan of an elephant brain, taken this year, revealed, perhaps not surprisingly, a huge hippocampus, a seat of memory in the mammalian brain, as well as a prominent structure in the limbic system, which processes emotions.) Allan Schore, the UCLA psychologist and neuroscientist who for the past fifteen years has focused his research on early human brain development and the negative impact of trauma on it, recently wrote two articles with Bradshaw on the stress-related neurobiological underpinnings of current abnormal elephant behavior.

"We know that these mechanisms cut across species," Schore told me. "In the first years of humans as well as elephants, development of the emotional brain is impacted by these attachment mechanisms, by the interaction that the infant has with the primary caregiver, especially the mother. When these early experiences go in a positive way, it leads to greater resilience in things like affect regulation, stress regulation, social communication, and empathy. But when these early experiences go awry in cases of abuse and neglect, there is a literal thinning down of the essential circuits in the brain, especially in the emotion-processing areas."

For Bradshaw, these continuities between human and elephant brains resonate far outside the field of neuroscience. "Elephants are suffering and behaving in the same ways that we recognize in ourselves as a result of violence," she told me. "Elephant behavior is entirely congruent with what we know about humans and other mammals. Except perhaps for a few specific features, brain organization and early development of elephants and humans are extremely similar. That's not news. What is news is when you start asking, What does this mean beyond the science? How do we respond to the fact that we are causing other species like elephants to psychologically break down? In a way, it's not so much a cognitive or imaginative leap anymore as it is a political one."

Eve Abe says that in her mind, she made that leap before she ever left her mother's womb. An animal ethologist and wildlife-management consultant now based in London, Abe (pronounced AH-bay) grew up in northern Uganda. After several years of studying elephants in Queen Elizabeth National Park, where decades of poaching had drastically reduced the herds, Abe received her doctorate at Cambridge University in 1994 for work detailing the parallels she saw between the plight of Uganda's orphaned male elephants and the young male orphans of her own people, the Acholi, whose families and villages have been decimated by years of civil war. It's work she proudly proclaims to be not only "the ultimate act of anthropomorphism" but also what she was destined to do.

"My very first encounter with an elephant was a fetal one," Abe told me in June in London as the two of us sipped tea at a cafe in Paddington Station. I was given Abe's contact numbers earlier in the spring by Bradshaw, who is currently working with Abe to build a community center in Uganda to help both elephants and humans in their recovery from violence. For more than a month before my departure from New York, I had been trying without luck to arrange with the British Home Office for Abe, who is still waiting for permanent residence status in England, to travel with me to Uganda as my guide through Queen Elizabeth National Park without fear of her being denied re-entry to England. She was to accompany me that day right up to the departure gate at Heathrow, the two of us hoping (in vain, as it turned out) for a last-minute call that would have given her leave to use the ticket I was holding for her in my bag.

"My dad was a conservationist and a teacher," explained Abe, a tall, elegant woman with a trilling, nearly girlish voice. "He was always out in the parks. One of my aunts tells this story about us passing through Murchison Park one day. My dad was driving. My uncle was in the front seat. In the back were my aunt and my mom, who was very pregnant with me. They suddenly came upon this huge herd of elephants on the road, and the elephants just stopped. So my dad stopped. He knew about animals. The elephants just stood there, then they started walking around the car, and looking into the car. Finally, they walked off. But my father didn't start the car then. He waited there. After an hour or more, a huge female came back out onto the road, right in front of the car. It reared up and trumpeted so loudly, then followed the rest of the herd back into the bush. A few days later, when my mom got home, I was born."

Abe began her studies in Queen Elizabeth National Park in 1982, as an undergraduate at Makerere University in Kampala, shortly after she and her family, who'd been living for years as refugees in Kenya to escape the brutal violence in Uganda under the dictatorship of Idi Amin, returned home in the wake of Amin's ouster in 1979. Abe told me that when she first arrived at the park, there were fewer than 150 elephants remaining from an original population of nearly 4,000. The bulk of the decimation occurred during the war with Tanzania that led to Amin's overthrow: soldiers from both armies grabbed all the ivory they could get their hands on—and did so with such cravenness that the word "poaching" seems woefully inadequate. "Normally when you say 'poaching,'" Abe said, "you think of people shooting one or two and going off. But this was war. They'd just throw hand grenades at the elephants, bring whole families down, and cut out the ivory. I call that mass destruction."

The last elephant survivors of Queen Elizabeth National Park, Abe said, never left one another's side. They kept in a tight bunch, moving as one. Only one elderly female remained; Abe estimated her to be at least sixty-two. It was this matriarch who first gathered the survivors together from their various hideouts on the park's forested fringes and then led them back out as one group into open savanna. Until her death in the early 90s, the old female held the group together, the population all the while slowly beginning to rebound. In her yet-to-be-completed memoir, *My Elephants and My People,* Abe writes of the prominence of the matriarch in Acholi society; she named the park's matriarchal elephant savior Lady Irene, after her own mother. "It took that core group of survivors in the park about five or six years," Abe told me, "before I started seeing whole new family units emerge and begin to split off and go their own way."

In 1986, Abe's family was forced to flee the country again. Violence against Uganda's people and elephants never completely abated after Amin's regime collapsed, and it drastically worsened in the course of the full-fledged war that developed between government forces and the rebel Lord's Resistance Army. For years, that army's leader, Joseph Kony, routinely "recruited" from Acholi villages, killing the parents of young males before their eyes, or sometimes having them do the killings themselves, before pressing them into service as child soldiers. The Lord's Resistance Army has by now been largely defeated, but Kony, who is wanted by the International Criminal Court for numerous crimes against humanity, has hidden with what remains of his army in the mountains of Murchison Falls National Park, and more recently in Garamba National Park in northern Congo, where poaching by the Lord's Resistance Army has continued to orphan more elephants.

"I started looking again at what has happened among the Acholi and the elephants," Abe told me. "I saw that it is an absolute coincidence between the two. You know we used to have villages. We still don't have villages. There are over 200 displaced people's camps in present-day northern Uganda. Everybody lives now within these camps, and there are no more elders. The elders were systematically eliminated. The first batch of elimination was during Amin's time, and that set the stage for the later destruction of northern Uganda. We are among the lucky few, because my mom and dad managed to escape. But the families there are just broken. I know many of them. Displaced people are living in our home now. My mother said let them have it. All these kids who have grown up with their parents killed—no fathers, no mothers, only children looking after them. They don't go to schools. They have no schools, no hospitals. No infrastructure. They form these roaming, violent, destructive bands. It's the same thing that happens with the elephants. Just like the male war orphans, they are wild, completely lost."

On the ride from Paddington that afternoon out to Heathrow, where I would catch a flight to Uganda, Abe told me that the parallel between the plight of Ugandans and their elephants was in many ways too close for her to see at first. It was only after she moved to London that she had what was, in a sense, her first full, adult recognition of the entwinement between human and elephant that she says she long ago felt in her mother's womb.

"I remember when I first was working on my doctorate," she said. "I mentioned that I was doing this parallel once to a prominent scientist in Kenya. He looked amazed. He said, 'How come nobody has made this connection before?' I told him because it hadn't happened this way to anyone else's tribe before. To me it's something I see so clearly. Most people are scared of showing that kind of anthropomorphism. But coming from me it doesn't sound like I'm inventing something. It's there. People know it's there. Some might think that the way I describe the elephant attacks makes the animals look like people. But people are animals."

Shortly after my return from Uganda, I went to visit the Elephant Sanctuary in Tennessee, a 2,700-acre rehabilitation center and retirement facility situated in the state's verdant, low-rolling southern hill country. The sanctuary is a kind of asylum for some of the more emotionally and psychologically disturbed former zoo and circus elephants in the United States—cases so bad that the people who profited from them were eager to let them go. Given that elephants in the wild are now exhibiting aberrant behaviors that were long observed in captive elephants, it perhaps follows that a positive working model for how to ameliorate the effects of elephant breakdown can be found in captivity.

Of the nineteen current residents of the sanctuary, perhaps the biggest hard-luck story was that of a forty-year-old, five-ton Asian elephant named Misty. Originally captured as a calf in India in 1966, Misty spent her first decade in captivity with a number of American circuses and finally ended up in the early 80s at a wild-animal attraction known as Lion Country Safari in Irvine, California. It was there, on the afternoon of July 25, 1983, that Misty, one of four performing elephants at Lion Country Safari that summer, somehow managed to break free of her chains and began madly dashing about the park, looking to make an escape. When one of the park's zoologists tried to corner and contain her, Misty killed him with one swipe of her trunk.

There are, in the long, checkered history of human-elephant relations, countless stories of lethal elephantine assaults, and almost invariably of some gruesomely outsize, animalistic form of retribution exacted by us. It was in the very state of Tennessee, back in September 1916, that another five-ton Asian circus elephant, Mary, was impounded by a local sheriff for the killing of a young hotel janitor who'd been hired to mind Mary during a stopover in the northeast Tennessee town of Kingsport. The janitor had apparently taken Mary for a swim at a local pond, where, according to witnesses, he poked her behind the left ear with a metal hook just as she was reaching for a piece of floating watermelon rind. Enraged, Mary turned, swiftly snatched him up with her trunk, dashed him against a refreshment stand, and then smashed his head with her foot.

With cries from the townspeople to "Kill the elephant!" and threats from nearby town leaders to bar the circus if "Murderous Mary," as newspapers quickly dubbed her, remained a part of the show, the circus's owner, Charlie Sparks, knew he had to do something to appease the public's blood lust and save his business. Among the penalties he is said to have contemplated was electrocution, a ghastly precedent for which had been set thirteen years earlier, on the grounds of the nearly completed Luna Park in Coney Island. A longtime circus elephant named Topsy, who'd killed three trainers in as many years—the last one after he tried to feed her a lighted cigarette—would become the largest and most prominent victim of Thomas Edison, the father of direct-current electricity, who had publicly electrocuted a number of animals at that time using his rival George Westinghouse's alternating current, in hopes of discrediting it as being too dangerous.

Sparks ultimately decided to have Mary hanged and shipped her by train to the nearby town of Erwin, Tennessee, where more than 2,500 people gathered at the local rail yard for her execution. Dozens of children are said to have run off screaming in terror when the chain that was suspended from a huge industrial crane snapped, leaving Mary writhing on the ground with a broken hip. A local rail worker promptly clambered up Mary's bulk and secured a heavier chain for a second, successful hoisting.

Misty's fate in the early 80s, by contrast, seems a triumph of modern humanism. Banished, after the Lion Safari killing, to the Hawthorn Corporation, a company in Illinois that trains and leases elephants and tigers to circuses, she would continue to lash out at a number of her trainers over the years. But when Hawthorn was convicted of numerous violations of the Animal Welfare Act in 2003, the company agreed to relinquish custody of Misty to the Elephant Sanctuary. She was loaded onto a trailer transport on the morning of November 17, 2004, and even then managed to get away with one final shot at the last in her long line of captors.

"The details are kind of sketchy," Carol Buckley, a founder of the Elephant Sanctuary, said to me one afternoon in July, the two of us pulling up on her all-terrain four-wheeler to a large grassy enclosure where an extremely docile and contented-looking Misty, trunk high, ears flapping, waited to greet us. "Hawthorn's owner was trying to get her to stretch out so he could remove her leg chains before loading her on the trailer. At one point he prodded her with a bull hook, and she just knocked him down with a swipe of her trunk. But we've seen none of that since she's been here. She's as sweet as can be. You'd never know that this elephant killed anybody."

In the course of her nearly two years at the Elephant Sanctuary—much of it spent in quarantine while undergoing daily treatment for tuberculosis—Misty has also been in therapy, as in psychotherapy. Wild-caught elephants often witness as young calves the slaughter of their parents, just about the only way, shy of a far more costly tranquilization procedure, to wrest a calf from elephant parents, especially the mothers. The young captives are then dispatched to a foreign environment to work either as performers or laborers, all the while being kept in relative confinement and isolation, a kind of living death for an animal as socially developed and dependent as we now know elephants to be.

And yet just as we now understand that elephants hurt like us, we're learning that they can heal like us as well. Indeed, Misty has become a testament to the Elephant Sanctuary's signature "passive control" system, a therapy tailored in many ways along the lines of those used to treat human sufferers of post-traumatic stress disorder. Passive control, as a sanctuary newsletter describes it, depends upon "knowledge of how elephants process information and respond to stress" as well as specific knowledge of each elephant's past response to stress. Under this so-called nondominance system, there is no discipline, retaliation, or withholding of food, water, and treats, which are all common tactics of elephant trainers. Great pains are taken, meanwhile, to afford the elephants both a sense of safety and freedom of choice—two mainstays of human trauma therapy—as well as continual social interaction.

Upon her arrival at the Elephant Sanctuary, Misty seemed to sense straight off the different vibe of her new home. When Scott Blais of the sanctuary went to free Misty's still-chained leg a mere day after she'd arrived, she stood peaceably by, practically offering her leg up to him. Over her many months of quarantine, meanwhile, with only humans acting as a kind of surrogate elephant family, she has consistently gone through the daily rigors of her tuberculosis treatments—involving two caregivers, a team of veterinarians, and the use of a restraining chute in which harnesses are secured about her chest and tail—without any coaxing or pressure. "We'll shower her with praise in the barn afterwards," Buckley told me as Misty stood by, chomping on a mouthful of hay, "and she actually purrs with pleasure. The whole barn vibrates."

Of course, Misty's road to recovery—when viewed in light of her history and that of all the other captive elephants, past and present—is as harrowing as it is heartening. She and the others have suffered, we now understand, not simply because of us, but because they are, by and large, us. If as recently as the end of the Vietnam War people were still balking at the idea that a soldier, for example, could be physically disabled by a psychological harm—the idea, in other words, that the mind is not an entity apart from the body and therefore just as woundable as any limb—we now find ourselves having to make an equally profound and, for many, even more difficult leap: that a fellow creature as ostensibly unlike us in every way as an elephant is as precisely and intricately woundable as we are. And while such knowledge naturally places an added burden upon us, the keepers, that burden is now being greatly compounded by the fact that sudden violent outbursts like Misty's can no longer be dismissed as the inevitable isolated revolts of a restless few against the constraints and abuses of captivity.

They have no future without us. The question we are now forced to grapple with is whether we would mind a future without them, among the more mindful creatures on this earth and, in many ways, the most devoted. Indeed, the manner of the elephants' continued keeping, their restoration and conservation, both in civil confines and what's left of wild ones, is now drawing the attention of everyone from naturalists to neuroscientists. Too much about elephants, in the end—their desires and devotions, their vulnerability and tremendous resilience—reminds us of ourselves to dismiss out of hand this revolt they're currently staging against their own dismissal. And while our concern may ultimately be rooted in that most human of impulses—the preservation of our own self-image—the great paradox about this particular moment in our history with elephants is that saving them will require finally getting past ourselves; it will demand the ultimate act of deep, interspecies empathy.

On a more immediate, practical level, as Gay Bradshaw sees it, this involves taking what has been learned about elephant society, psychology, and emotion and inculcating that knowledge into the conservation schemes of researchers and park rangers. This includes doing things like expanding elephant habitat to what it used to be historically and avoiding the use of culling and translocations as conservation tools. "If we want elephants around," Bradshaw told me, "then what we need to do is simple: learn how to live with elephants. In other words, in addition to conservation, we need to educate people how to live with wild animals like humans used to do, and to create conditions whereby people can live on their land and live with elephants without it being this life-and-death situation."

The other part of our newly emerging compact with elephants, however, is far more difficult to codify. It requires nothing less than a fundamental shift in the way we look at animals and, by extension, ourselves. It requires what Bradshaw somewhat whimsically refers to as a new "trans-species psyche," a commitment to move beyond an anthropocentric frame of reference and, in effect, be elephants. Two years ago, Bradshaw wrote a paper for the journal *Society and Animals,* focusing on the work of the David Sheldrick Wildlife Trust in Kenya, a sanctuary for orphaned and traumatized wild elephants—more or less the wilderness-based complement to Carol Buckley's trauma therapy at the Elephant Sanctuary in Tennessee. The trust's human caregivers essentially serve as surrogate mothers to young orphan elephants, gradually restoring their psychological and emotional well-being to the point at which they can be reintroduced into existing wild herds. The human "allomothers" stay by their adopted young orphans' sides, even sleeping with them at night in stables. The caregivers make sure, however, to rotate from one elephant to the next so that the orphans grow fond of all the keepers. Otherwise an elephant would form such a strong bond with one keeper that whenever he or she was absent, that elephant would grieve as if over the loss of another family member, often becoming physically ill itself.

To date, the Sheldrick Trust has successfully rehabilitated more than sixty elephants and reintroduced them into wild herds. A number of them have periodically returned to the sanctuary with their own wild-born calves in order to reunite with their human allomothers and to introduce their offspring to what— out on this uncharted frontier of the new "trans-species psyche"—is now being recognized, at least by the elephants, it seems, as a whole new subspecies: the human allograndmother. "Traditionally, nature has served as a source of healing for humans," Bradshaw told me. "Now humans can participate actively in the healing of both themselves and nonhuman animals. The trust and the sanctuary are the beginnings of a mutually benefiting interspecies culture."

On my way back to New York via London, I contacted Felicity de Zulueta, a psychiatrist at Maudsley Hospital in London, who treats victims of extreme trauma, among them former child soldiers from the Lord's Resistance Army. De Zulueta, an acquaintance of Eve Abe's, grew up in Uganda in the early 1960s on the outskirts of Queen Elizabeth National Park, near where her father, a malaria doctor, had set up camp as part of a malaria-eradication program. For a time she had her own elephant, orphaned by poaching, that local villagers had given to her father, who brought it home to the family garage, where it immediately bonded with an orphan antelope and dog already residing there.

"He was doing fine," de Zulueta told me of the pet elephant. "My mother was loving it and feeding it, and then my parents realized, How can we keep this elephant that is going to grow bigger than the garage? So they gave it to who they thought were the experts. They sent him to the Entebbe Zoo, and although they gave him all the right food and everything, he was a lonely little elephant, and he died. He had no attachment."

For de Zulueta, the parallel that Abe draws between the plight of war orphans, human and elephant, is painfully apt, yet also provides some cause for hope, given the often startling capacity of both animals for recovery. She told me that one Ugandan war orphan she is currently treating lost all the members of his family except for two older brothers. Remarkably, one of those brothers, while serving in the Ugandan Army, rescued the younger sibling from the Lord's Resistance Army; the older brother's unit had captured the rebel battalion in which his younger brother had been forced to fight.

The two brothers eventually made their way to London, and for the past two years, the younger brother has been going through a gradual process of recovery in the care of Maudsley Hospital. Much of the rehabilitation, according to de Zulueta, especially in the early stages, relies on the basic human trauma therapy principles now being applied to elephants: providing decent living quarters, establishing a sense of safety and of attachment to a larger community, and allowing freedom of choice. After that have come the more complex treatments tailored to the human brain's particular cognitive capacities: things like reliving the original traumatic experience and being taught to modulate feelings through early detection of hyperarousal and through breathing techniques. And the healing of trauma, as de Zulueta describes it, turns out to have physical correlatives in the brain just as its wounding does.

"What I say is, we find bypass," she explained. "We bypass the wounded areas using various techniques. Some of the wounds are not healable. Their scars remain. But there is hope because the brain is an enormous computer, and you can learn to bypass its wounds by finding different methods of approaching life. Of course there may be moments when something happens and the old wound becomes unbearable. Still, people do recover. The boy I've been telling you about is eighteen now, and he has survived very well in terms of his emotional health and capacities. He's a lovely, lovely man. And he's a poet. He writes beautiful poetry."

On the afternoon in July that I left the Elephant Sanctuary in Tennessee, Carol Buckley and Scott Blais seemed in particularly good spirits. Misty was only weeks away from the end of her quarantine, and she would soon be able to socialize with some of her old cohorts from the Hawthorn Corporation: eight female Asians that had been given over to the sanctuary. I would meet the lot of them that day, driving from one to the next on the back of Buckley's four-wheeler across the sanctuary's savannalike stretches. Buckley and Blais refer to them collectively as the Divas.

Buckley and Blais told me that they got word not long ago of a significant breakthrough in a campaign of theirs to get elephants out of entertainment and zoos: the Bronx Zoo, one of the oldest and most formidable zoos in the country, had announced that upon the death of the zoo's three current elephant inhabitants, Patty, Maxine, and Happy, it would phase out its elephant exhibit on social-behavioral grounds—an acknowledgment of a new awareness of the elephant's very particular sensibility and needs. "They're really taking the lead," Buckley told me. "Zoos don't want to concede the inappropriateness of keeping elephants in such confines. But if we as a society determine that an animal like this suffers in captivity, if the information shows us that they do, hey, we are the stewards. You'd think we'd want to do the right thing."

Four days later, I received an e-mail message from Gay Bradshaw, who consults with Buckley and Blais on their various stress-therapy strategies. She wrote that one of the sanctuary's elephants, an Asian named Winkie, had just killed a thirty-six-year-old female assistant caretaker and critically injured the male caretaker who'd tried to save her.

People who work with animals on a daily basis can tell you all kinds of stories about their distinct personalities and natures. I'd gotten, in fact, an elaborate breakdown from Buckley and Blais on the various elephants at the sanctuary and their sociopolitical maneuverings within the sanctuary's distinct elephant culture, and I went to my notebook to get a fix again on Winkie. A forty-year-old, 7,600-pound female from Burma, she came to the sanctuary in 2000 from the Henry Vilas Zoo in Madison, Wisconsin, where she had a reputation for lashing out at keepers. When Winkie first arrived at the sanctuary, Buckley told me, she used to jump merely upon being touched and then would wait for a confrontation. But when it never came, she slowly calmed down. "Has never lashed out at primary keepers," my last note on Winkie reads, "but has at secondary ones."

Bradshaw's e-mail message concludes: "A stunning illustration of trauma in elephants. The indelible etching."

I thought back to a moment in Queen Elizabeth National Park this past June. As Nelson Okello and I sat waiting for the matriarch and her calf to pass, he mentioned to me an odd little detail about the killing two months earlier of the man from the village of Katwe, something that, the more I thought about it, seemed to capture this particularly fraught moment we've arrived at with the elephants. Okello said that after the man's killing, the elephant herd buried him as it would one of its own, carefully covering the body with earth and brush and then standing vigil over it.

Even as we're forcing them out, it seems, the elephants are going out of their way to put us, the keepers, in an ever more discomfiting place, challenging us to preserve someplace for them, the ones who in many ways seem to regard the matter of life and death more devoutly than we. In fact, elephant culture could be considered the precursor of our own, the first permanent human settlements having sprung up around the desire of wandering tribes to stay by the graves of their dead. "The city of the dead," as Lewis Mumford once wrote, "antedates the city of the living."

When a group of villagers from Katwe went out to reclaim the man's body for his family's funeral rites, the elephants refused to budge. Human remains, a number of researchers have observed, are the only other ones that elephants will treat as they do their own. In the end, the villagers resorted to a tactic that has long been etched in the elephant's collective memory, firing volleys of gunfire into the air at close range, finally scaring the mourning herd away.

QUESTIONS FOR MAKING CONNECTIONS
WITHIN THE READING

1. What evidence does Siebert provide to support the claim there is such a thing as an "elephant culture"? In making this claim is Siebert guilty of anthropomorphism? That is, does he ascribe to animals the thoughts and

emotions that only humans have? Or is he guilty of the opposite mistake, the error of anthropocentrism—treating human beings as the standard by which all other species should be measured? Is it possible that these "mistakes" are really not mistakes at all, especially because we *Homo sapiens* are in fact animals, too? Would you agree that understanding other minds— human or otherwise—requires us to start with what we know about own mental processes? Can we even prove that our fellow human beings have thoughts and emotions like our own?

2. As Siebert's discussion unfolds, he describes elephants who experience acute trauma and then become deliberately aggressive. He also shows that they respond to psychotherapies that were initially developed to assist human beings. Do you find these developments surprising? Is Siebert seeking to establish that humans and elephants are part of a continuum? Does he mean to imply that the minds of the two species are identical? Or does he see them on parallel paths?

3. Siebert's essay ends with two acts of violence: a caretaker killed by an elephant in captivity, and a villager killed and buried by an elephant herd. Why does he structure the piece in this way? Since he also began by describing violence, has Siebert come full circle? Or has he put his readers in a better position to understand the violence?

QUESTIONS FOR WRITING

1. Throughout "An Elephant Crackup?" Siebert gestures towards modes of consciousness that differ significantly from the model of an individual thinking. He describes a herd of elephants as, "in essence, one incomprehensibly massive elephant." He observes that saving elephants from extinction "will demand the ultimate act of deep, interspecies empathy." And he cites Gay Bradshaw's call for the development of a "trans-species psyche" that will allow humans to "be elephants." How would one go about creating these new modes of consciousness? Does Siebert's narrative provide any hints about how the two species might begin to share the same conceptual world?

2. Siebert notes that those who are concerned with the effects of trauma on the elephant population are now focusing on the "physiology of psychology"— that is, on the neurological foundation for psychological development. Based on the preliminary results of these studies, would you say that the turn to neurology provides cause for optimism about the possibilities of overcoming trauma? Or does the fact that trauma during the formative years results in "a literal thinning down of the essential circuits in the brain" mean that there's no saving young victims of trauma, be they elephant or human?

QUESTIONS FOR MAKING CONNECTIONS
BETWEEN READINGS

1. "Language," as Christine Kenneally defines it, "is an act of shared attention, and without the fundamentally *human* willingness to listen to what another person is saying, language would not work." Throughout "An Elephant Crackup?" Siebert casts humans and elephants as being in communication with one another. Is the kind of communication that concerns Siebert what Kenneally means by "language"? Or would Kenneally reject the idea of an interspecies language? In tracing the evolution of language through the primates, has Kenneally overlooked essential evidence elsewhere in the animal kingdom? Or is animal communication simply an anthropocentric projection onto creatures we can never understand?

2. In "Meat and Milk Factories," Peter Singer and Jim Mason describe in detail the practices of the pork industry. Should the interspecies empathy that Siebert calls for extend to pigs? Or does the brutality described by Singer and Mason suggest that such empathy is simply not part of human nature? That is, couldn't one argue that the human ingenuity that has gone into creating the pork industry shows that humans are predisposed to the domination of other life forms? If one develops a "trans-species psyche," does this lead to a concern for the fate only of elephants, or of other species as well?

PETER SINGER AND JIM MASON

PETER SINGER IS controversial. When he first joined the Princeton University Center for Human Values faculty in 1999 after teaching for over two decades at Monash University in Australia, campus protests led to multiple arrests. Yet even his opponents respect him. One of these opponents, the disability rights lawyer Harriet McBryde Johnson, concedes that many consider Singer "the most influential philosopher of our time."

Singer is best known for his work in applied ethics, a style of philosophy that brings theoretical ethical constructs to bear on real-life situations. In the over forty books he has written or edited, the most influential being *Practical Ethics* (1979), Singer returns repeatedly to questions of responsibility. What responsibility does a person have with respect to another person? To a less privileged person? To members of other species? To the environment? Singer's work is so controversial because he challenges the conventional understanding of what it means to be a person, arguing that disability and other factors that influence an individual's self-realization over time can make someone more or less of a person and thus more or less entitled to various rights and privileges.

Though in recent years he has drawn the most criticism for his contentions about the nature of humanity, Singer rose to international prominence for his passionate defense of animals, first outlined in *Animal Liberation* (1975). He condemns "speciesism," or discrimination based on morally irrelevant physical details, and calls for changing the relationship between humans and other animal species. He considers the claim that animals have less intelligence or self-awareness invalid, arguing that some developmentally disabled humans are less mentally capable than some animals, yet they are still afforded privileged treatment as a result of their membership in the human species. Thus, our ethical responsibility to reduce suffering applies beyond the confines of our species to any being capable of experiencing suffering.

In an immediate, practical sense, this means attending to the animals we see only after their suffering is over: the ones we eat. With Jim Mason, an attorney who grew up on a Missouri farm, Singer has co-authored two books that address this issue, *Animal Factories* (1980) and *The Ethics of What We Eat: Why Our*

Singer, Peter, and Jim Mason. "Meat and Milk Factories," *The Ethics of What We Eat: Why Our Food Choices Matter.* New York: Rodale Books, 2006. 42–68.

Details in the first paragraph come from Harriet McBryde Johnson, "Unspeakable Conversations," *The New York Times Magazine,* February 16, 2003 <http://query.nytimes.com/gst/fullpage.html?res=9401EFDC113BF935A25751C0A9659 C8B63&sec=health&spon=&pagewanted=all>.

Food Choices Matter (2006). "Meat and Milk Factories," a chapter drawn from the latter of these two books, is an inside look into the industrial practices of America's pork, dairy, and beef producers. Drawing on the visits they and others have paid to massive farms, as well as on research into the conditions that are optimal for the animals themselves, Singer and Mason make clear the differences between the conditions in which the animals are forced to live and the conditions under which they could live comfortably. They point out case after case in which the profit motive supersedes ethical responsibility. By emphasizing the richness of the animals' cognitive and emotional lives when treated well, Singer and Mason compel us to wonder why we have allowed industrial-scale farming.

Meat and Milk Factories

The average American eats more than 200 pounds of red meat, poultry, and fish per year. That's an increase of 23 pounds over 1970, and it would be difficult for anyone to maintain that Americans in 1970 were not eating enough of these foods. In the last thirty-five years, the amount of beef eaten has fallen, but that has been outweighed by the near doubling of chicken consumption. Pork comes in third, at 51 pounds per person, behind chicken and beef. More than 60 percent of the pork eaten by Americans is bought already processed, as bacon, ham, lunch meats, hot dogs, or sausage.[1]

The Oscar Mayer bacon that Jake bought is in this category. We wanted to trace it back to the farms that raised the pigs, but that proved impossible. Oscar Mayer is now owned by Kraft Foods, the largest food and beverage company in North America and the second largest in the world (only Nestlé is bigger).[2] After numerous phone calls that involved working our way through seemingly endless menu options, we spoke to Consumer Services' Renee Zahery, who told us that "information about our procurement and processing of our product is considered proprietary in nature" and suggested we take up these questions with "a great source," Janet Riley, senior vice president at the American Meat Institute.[3]

When we talked with Riley, she told us only that Oscar Mayer probably has contracts with suppliers such as Tyson, Smithfield, and some of the lesser known, vertically integrated pork producing companies. So although we could not identify any of the specific farms that produce pigs for Oscar Mayer, it seems a fair assumption that their bacon comes from a cross section of today's intensive pork industry. What is that industry like?

The Poop on Pigs

When Peter first wrote about factory farming in America in 1975, there were more than 660,000 pig farms producing just under 69 million pigs a year.[4] Over the next 30 years, nearly 90 percent of those pig farms vanished, so that by 2004 there were only 69,000. But these farms will produce 103 million pigs a year.[5] Across the country, the family pig farmer has been replaced by Smithfield, ConAgra, ContiGroup, and the Seaboard Corporation. Most pigs raised today come from factory farms.

The boom in mega-piggeries has caused environmental problems even more acute than those caused by intensive chicken production. An adult pig produces about four times the amount of feces of a human, so a large confinement operation with, say, fifty thousand pigs, creates half a million pounds of pig urine and excrement every day. That's as much waste as a medium-sized town—but remember that human sewage is elaborately treated before being released into the environment and factory farm waste is not.

The summer of 1995 was wetter than usual in North Carolina. During the preceding 15 years, pig production in that state had boomed, making the state the second largest pork producer in the United States. Its pigs were producing 19 million tons of waste per year—or 2.5 tons of feces and urine for every citizen in the state.[6] During that wet summer, spilled animal waste killed ten million fish in North Carolina. In one of the most dramatic incidents, an 8-acre waste pond—the industry term is "lagoon" but that word conjures up images of blue water around a coral island, not a vast outdoor cesspool—burst, releasing 25 million gallons of liquid pig excrement into the New River, killing thousands of fish and polluting the river for miles downstream. Regulations in North Carolina were tightened, but spills continue to happen from time to time across the country. Even when there is no major spill, there is often seepage from the waste pond and run-off into the creeks when the manure is sprayed onto nearby farmland.[7]

Pig-factory farms are, if anything, even worse neighbors than chicken-factory farms. Carolyn Johnsen, a reporter for the Nebraska Public Radio Network, covered the controversial growth of mega-piggeries in that state. She attended heated public meetings, divided between those who saw economic opportunities in the new industry and those angry at the contamination of their air and water and concerned about the fate of the family farm. She spoke to people like Janie Mullinex, who lives south of Imperial, Nebraska, about a mile away from 48,000 pigs confined in 24 large barns. The owner had claimed, before putting up the confinement operation, that he had new technology and it would not smell. But Mullinex claimed that was not the case. "It comes in the house—even with the windows shut, it comes in with a strong south wind," Mullinex says. "It gives my seven-year-old diarrhea if we have it all day and it makes me sick. I don't vomit, but I'm nauseous and I have a tremendous headache." The Mullinex family has new storm windows and new siding and they have insulated their house, but it hasn't stopped the smell from coming in.

Johnsen also visited Mabel Bernard, who has lived and raised her family on her property near Enders, Nebraska, since 1926. Her enjoyment of her home has been spoiled by the construction of sheds holding 36,000 pigs about a mile north. When the wind comes from that direction, the stench wakes her up at night, burning her eyes and making her feel sick.[8] One Nebraska pig producer gave implicit support to those who don't want pig farms nearby when he won a 30-percent property tax reduction on his house by arguing that its value was decreased because it was located near a pig farm—his own.[9]

But big pig farms are more than a nuisance. They are also a public-health risk, according to the American Public Health Association, the largest body of public-health professionals in the United States. In 2003, citing a host of human diseases linked to farm animal waste and antibiotic use, the APHA passed a resolution urging government officials to adopt a moratorium on the construction of new factory farms.[10]

A Pig's Life

Pigs are affectionate, inquisitive animals. The film *Babe* was on solid scientific ground when it made its hero capable of doing everything a dog can do in the way of herding sheep. In fact, Professor Stanley Curtis thinks that the sheepdog's job would be a "pushover" for pigs he has investigated. Curtis is a hard-nosed scientist who worked for many years in the Department of Animal Sciences at the University of Illinois and received a Distinguished Service Award from the National Pork Producers Council in 2001. He conceived the idea of making it possible for pigs to tell producers what kind of conditions they prefer, and to that end, trained them to operate joystick-controlled video games. They learned quickly, and Curtis discovered that "there is much more going on in terms of thinking and observing by these pigs than we would ever have guessed."[11] The big problem, in fact, is not getting pigs to tell us what they prefer, but persuading the producers to give it to them.

To keep a dog locked up for life in a crate too narrow for her to turn around or walk more than a step or two forwards or backwards would be cruel and illegal. Yet when it comes to how pigs are kept in the U.S., here are two startling and critical, facts:

1. There is no federal law governing the welfare of farmed animals on the farm. Literally, nothing. In the U.S., federal law begins only when animals are transported or arrive at the slaughterhouse. (And even then, there is no law regarding the slaughter of chickens or other birds, who make up 95 percent of all land animals slaughtered in the U.S.) This is not because there is any constitutional barrier to covering the welfare of animals on farms, but simply because Congress has never chosen to enact any such law.

2. Most states with major animal industries have written into their anti-cruelty laws exemptions for "common farming practices." Effectively, then, cruelty is legal as long as it is done by most farmers, and you can't prosecute anyone for it.

Together, these two points mean that, as lawyer and author David Wolfson puts it, "farmed animals in such states are literally beyond the law and any common practice, no matter how horrifying, is legal."[12]

More than 90 percent of pigs raised for meat today are raised indoors in crowded pens of concrete and steel. They never get to go outside or root around in pasture and don't even have straw to bed down in.[13] The most tightly confined of all are the breeding sows. Under the factory's rigid production schedule, they are made to produce litter after litter as quickly as possible, which means that they are pregnant for most of their lives. During their pregnancies, which last about 16 weeks, most American sows are confined in "gestation crates"—steel-barred crates or stalls just a foot or so longer than their bodies, and so narrow that the sows cannot even turn around. Of the 1.8 million sows used for breeding by America's ten biggest pig producers, about 90 percent are kept in this manner, and for the industry as a whole, the figure is around 80 percent.[14]

In these conditions, apart from the brief period when they are eating, these sensitive, intelligent, and highly social animals have nothing to do all day. They cannot walk around or socialize with other sows. All they can do is stand up or lie down on the bare concrete floor. When the time comes to give birth, they are also confined in what producers call a farrowing crate. (Is it part of the gulf we draw between ourselves and other animals that leads farmers to talk of animals as "farrowing" rather than "giving birth," "feeding" rather than "eating," and "gestating" rather than "being pregnant"?) The farrowing crate keeps the sow in position, with her teats always exposed to her piglets. She is unable to roll over—and this, the defenders of the crate say, ensures that she will not roll on top of, and perhaps smother, her piglets.

In Europe, widespread public concern about the close confinement of sows led to the European Union asking its scientific veterinary advisory committee to investigate the impact of gestation crates—or sow stalls, as they are known there—on the welfare of the sows. The investigation found that sow stalls had "major disadvantages" for welfare. Pigs like to forage and explore their environment. In natural conditions they will spend up to three-quarters of their waking hours doing this. In stalls, of course, they cannot. When a sow is first put into a stall, she typically tries to escape and may push against or attack the bars. After a time, she gives up, and often becomes quite inactive and unresponsive. This, the scientific veterinary committee says, indicates clinical depression. Other sows in stalls carry out meaningless, repetitive motions, like biting the bars of the stall, chewing the air, shaking their heads from side to side, nosing around repeatedly in the empty feed trough. These pointless movements are signs of stress, similar to the endless back and forth pacing of tigers and other big cats when kept in the traditional sterile cages of old-fashioned zoos. Fortunately, many zoos have become more enlightened and no longer keep their animals in such cages. No doubt public disapproval helped persuade them to make the change. Sows in factory farms are actually worse off than the big cats in zoos used to be, because they can't even pace back and forth. But they are invisible to the public.

In addition to psychological stress, sows in crates are also less healthy than sows able to walk around. (That shouldn't be a surprise to anyone who knows that it is healthy to get some exercise.) Sows in crates frequently become lame and develop foot injuries from standing on concrete for every moment when they are not lying down. They also get more urinary-tract infections.

In sum, the scientific veterinary committee concluded, "sows should preferably be kept in groups."[15] After considering this report, the European Union passed a law phasing out sow crates by the end of 2012, except for the first four weeks after mating, and requiring that sows be given straw or similar materials that they can play around with, to reduce the stress of boredom. This law will apply to all 25 countries of the European Union, which together slaughter more than twice as many pigs as the United States.[16] Even before the new law comes into effect, Britain and Sweden acted to ban sow stalls. All of the 600,000 breeding sows in Britain now have, at least, room to turn around and can interact with other pigs.

"Wayne Bradley," Iowa Pig Producer

As we mentioned when discussing how agribusiness corporations refused our requests to see how they keep their animals, one Iowa pig producer was more open than all the rest. In his view, "education is the best defense against the animal rights attack on the livestock industry." He felt he had an obligation to show people around his farm, he told us, because many years ago he had become "unglued" by a television show about farming. His wife told him: 'I'm not going to listen to this. Next time somebody calls out here for an interview … you better talk to them. Either that or just shut up." He's been talking ever since. He talked to us several times—by telephone and in person when we toured his farm. Everything went well until we sent him what we had written and asked him to check it for any inaccuracies. At that point he suddenly asked us to not use his real name or say anything that might identify his farm and location. He had worries about "animal-rights people," he said, "doing damage to things." In what follows, therefore, everything is as it happened, but we have changed the farmer's name.

The Bradley farmhouse and main buildings stand near the intersection of two county roads. Like many farmsteads in Iowa, it is sheltered from the winter winds by rows of lush cedar trees along the north and west. There is a big white house, a wide yard, silos, and an old barn. But these emblems of an older way of farming are overwhelmed by those of the new. The driveway opens up on an array of tractors, trucks, and machinery and, farther down, rows of low metal pig-confinement buildings. A complex of metal grain bins, augers, and pipes towers over everything. Wayne Bradley greets us in the driveway. He is a big, hefty man, 50-something, full of energy, friendly and talkative. We walk to a small office in the corner of one of the pig buildings and sit down. Things are a bit tense at first, but grow easier as he tells us about his family and farm. He farms the land of his father and grandfather—Bradleys have been farming here since 1875. His son, Alex, farms with him and runs a herd of cattle on land of his own. It is a family farm, he says, but also a corporation because of financial advantages that incorporation offers. He farms 2,600 acres, much of it land rented from neighbors "scattered around about 9 miles." The Bradleys have 500 sows, and they sell between 10,000 and 12,000 pigs a year.

As we chat, he is eager to make a few points right away. He emphatically opposes the claim that pigs in confinement are abused. "When it's thirty below zero, my hogs are laying out comfortable in a 70-degree building—granted, it's not bedded, but they're clean and they're just laying there grunting and oblivious to the blizzard that's going on outside. That's as opposed to when we used to raise them out in open sheds and we spent the day bedding them and they'd have frozen ears and frozen tails and those types of things."

Wayne wants us to understand the economics that have driven his decisions. "We've had to specialize to a certain degree," he says. His other major concern is government regulation, primarily of waste handling. He feels that his farm is "under intense regulation and intense scrutiny all the time." He believes it is unfair because he collects manure and wastes in a concrete basin and can use the nutrients on the fields as weather permits. "Our capability of handling wastes now is so much better than before. Our chances of polluting are so much less because we inject it." Many pig producers mix the manure with water and spray it onto fields. That just leaves it on the surface where it can easily run off into creeks when it rains. Wayne has a liquid manure injector, which he pulls behind a tractor. Essentially a large tank on wheels, it pumps liquid manure down on the ground where discs cover it with about 2 inches of topsoil.

Wayne obviously feels caught in the middle—being squeezed between those who promote organic or pasture-raised pork and the giant corporations that now dominate pig production. "I'll defend confinement. I'm not going to defend Smithfield Foods because I think it's taking it to the extreme. They had 250,000 sows and then they went to 500,000 and now they're up to 700,000 sows. I don't think that's economically healthy…. The packers are getting more power and control than they need."

Making Bacon

The Bradleys' pigs are in what's known as "total confinement"—none of them ever go outdoors. He begins the tour by taking us into one of his four farrowing rooms, where his sows give birth and then feed their piglets. These were his first confinement buildings, which he built himself in 1975. He tells us, "I was so happy when we got the hogs in here. I could get them in out of the cold." We are in a large room maybe 20 by about 40 feet. It stinks inside, of course, but not as badly as some units we've been in over the years. A concrete walkway runs down the length of the building between two rows of farrowing crates containing sows and baby pigs. The crate has two parts: a taller metal framework to hold the large sow and a lower "creep" area to one side where the baby pigs sleep when they are not nursing. The sow's part is about 2 feet by 6 feet; her body nearly fills the space. She can stand up and lie down to sleep or nurse her piglets. She cannot turn around or do much else.

In some crates, the "floors" are steel slats; in others, large-gauge wire mesh coated in plastic. There is no straw or other soft bedding material. Pig wastes pass through the openings and fall into a shallow pit below. A system of cables and scrapers periodically sweeps the wastes down to a pipe and they flow into a covered pit outside.

Each sow stays in her farrowing crate for about 20 days. Wayne tells us that the crate offers the piglets a safe area away from the sow when she lies down to sleep or nurse them. We look down on a sow with a litter of baby pigs all piled up like puppies and fast asleep and say something about how cute they are. "Do they look like they're abused?" he asks. No, they certainly don't, we tell him. But what about the various mutilations that we had heard are routinely carried out on pigs kept in confinement: cutting off their tails and clipping their "needle teeth" and castrating them without an anesthetic? There are reasons for each of them, Wayne explains. The pigs' needle teeth can cut their mother's nipples and they can cut each other in fighting over nipples. "Tail docking" prevents pigs from biting and chewing on each other's tails. We press him further: Isn't it only pigs in confinement who bite each other's tails? Don't they do this because they are bored, spending all their time crowded together in a sterile environment with nothing to do all day long? "I guess I would have to agree with that to a point. But we used to raise pigs out in large pens like cattle lots and we had tail-biting then too. So we've been docking tails for quite a number of years." We've seen cattle lots, and we would not be surprised if the pigs were bored there, too. But we keep that thought to ourselves.

Wayne castrates his male pigs at ten days after birth. Consumer demand drives that, Wayne says. Meat from male pigs with testicles has a distinctive gamy taste called "boar taint" that consumers, apparently, don't like. If the pigs are killed at an earlier age, as happens in some other countries, this isn't a problem. But the U.S. consumer likes large cuts of meat that can only come from a more mature pig, and then the taint becomes more noticeable.

Why are these painful procedures done without any anesthetic? Again, Wayne is disarmingly candid: "I guess I don't have a good answer for that." We ask if it is the expense involved. "Well, it would be an expense. Obviously it is going to cost money. I have no idea. I can't sit here and say, 'Well it's going to cost me a dollar a pig.' Because if it was a dollar a pig, I mean there's not a dollar a pig to throw away. If it was a nickel or a penny or something like that, there would be no reason that we couldn't. But I doubt that it would be that inexpensive." We ask Wayne if he has ever heard of anyone using a local anesthetic for these procedures: "I never have. It's obviously a question to be asked." He hesitates before continuing: "You know, maybe farm folks are more ... I don't know if I'd say immune to that or not. I mean until I was 22 years old my dentist never used novocaine. I went to the dentist and I grabbed ahold of the chair and he drilled and it was over."

We're thinking that we would have made a different choice—and perhaps the pigs would, too, if they could—when Wayne turns the conversation back to the sow with her piglets in the farrowing crate in front of us. "Another advantage to this versus a pasture farrowing situation is that we can do a better job of keeping an eye on the sow and the pigs. If there's a problem, you're right here. It's very easy to give her a shot if she's not feeling well."

Wayne's piglets are weaned when they are two weeks and a few days old. In more natural environments, piglets nurse from their mothers for at least nine weeks, and sometimes longer,[17] but nursing would prevent the sow becoming pregnant again during that period, thereby reducing her productivity. So the piglets are removed from their mother and she goes back to the breeding area, while they are placed together with other litters in a "nursery" building on a nearby farm. The breeding area is part of the gestation room, and that is where Wayne takes us next. At one end stand three huge, hairy boars, one to a stall. Wayne explains that they stay in these stalls about half the time, spending the other half in a resting pen where they do have room to walk around. They rotate the boars back and forth, he says, because "overuse" lowers semen quality. The boars are rough and wild-looking.

A sow will be made pregnant again as soon as she comes into estrus. Wayne uses a combination of "live mating"—a boar is allowed to mount the sow—and "AI," or artificial insemination. Wayne's pregnant sows live in group pens instead of the narrow crates that are typical of the big corporate pig factories. Each of the three pens here holds up to forty sows. Each pen has an automated self-feeder in the center; it looks like another kind of crate but with gates on each end. It holds one sow at a time. Wayne explains how it works: "The sows are all tagged with an electronic chip. When one goes in there, that machine reads the chip and it tells whether or not she's had her feed for the day. They're allowed so many pounds. They can go through there until they've eaten their daily quota." The purpose, he says, is to make sure that every sow gets to eat her ration at her own speed.

We move on past the pens of pregnant sows and down a corridor. We stop at a steel door with a small window. Wayne motions for us to take a look. It's the room where the herd manager collects semen from the boar. We ask the obvious question: "How do you collect sperm from the boar?" Wayne is all business: "We use a steel dummy." He leads us a few steps to a dusty, windowless cubby hole just off the corridor. It is about 7 or 8 feet square and empty except for a low steel bench with a rubber mat under it. "There's the dummy. Some of the boars will jump right on that and ride it and ejaculate. And others won't. You have to use a sow. The herdsman catches the semen in a thermos with a gloved hand. He'll extend the semen so that one ejaculation can make about twenty doses of semen. Once again, it's an economic thing. It gives us more use of that one boar, instead of having to feed so many boars. But it goes beyond that. We can change our genetics faster than we could if we had a stable of twenty or twenty-five boars. It's better to have one really good boar and use his semen."

Next stop is the nursery—that's the industry term for a place where early-weaned pigs are given special feed to enable them to survive the stress of separation and weaning. Each of the pens contains a few dozen small pigs. We ask him how the pigs handle the stress of weaning. "Oh, there really isn't much that happens. The first day they just kind of lay around. Whenever you come in the building, they grunt and make a lot of noise because they are used to having mama around."

We get back in the truck and go to another farm where Wayne has a finishing building, where the pigs are grown to market weight. Along the way, we talk about the changes in farming we've both seen over the years. He mentions the loss of middle-income people in the rural areas around him. Now, he says, "We've got a bunch of people that are looking for $150-a-month houses to move into. They're making meth and they're making trouble. The rural countryside has changed dramatically." (Making methamphetamine, in Iowa? At the time, we thought Wayne must have been exaggerating, but when we checked it out, we found that Iowa has the second highest number of meth labs and the fourth highest level of meth use in the nation.[18] Is that a consequence of the loss of family farmers, too, we wondered?)

The conversation drifts to the price of corn and subsidies. Wayne thinks that years of government subsidies have kept corn artificially cheap for livestock producers. "We've been producing grain below the cost of production for so many years that it's just a given. It's a guarantee. If we'd gotten corn prices up to where they ought to be, a lot of this livestock thing never would have happened. It's been on the back of cheap grain. I don't know how you change that."

We have reached the finishing building. It's open on both sides. Running the length of the building on each side is a plastic curtain he can roll up and down to adjust temperature and ventilation. "Let's open the door just to give you a whiff of the air quality." We step through to the pens. On this mild spring day, a breeze is blowing over the pens full of pigs. It is total confinement, but with a breath of semi-fresh air. "If it's thirty below zero outside, these curtains will be closed and the furnace will be running a bit. These old pigs here'll be all stretched out and as comfortable as if they were in the Bahamas."

We ask him about drugs and medications administered to these pigs. He says that this is "one of those deals that gets misrepresented. People think we're feeding a lot of antibiotics out here. Our whole goal is not to feed a lot of them because they cost us money." He explains that when he first brings pigs into a finishing building he gives them a dose of the antibiotic tetracycline in their feed "just to give them something for the stress in moving them." Then he puts them on "a growth promotant called BMD, bacitracin something something. I can't tell you what all is in it. It helps them grow faster and that's the name of the game." (He's referring to bacitracin methylene disalicylate, another antibiotic.) If the pigs develop diarrhea or "a cough or a problem," they give them an antibiotic or other medication, usually in the water. "A pig will drink when they won't eat," he explains.

Our tour is over and it's time to leave. We're sitting in Wayne's pickup truck in the driveway back at his home. He emphasizes again how he wants to get the right story out there. "What really concerns us in animal agriculture is that we've been made out to be the bad guys. We're working hard to produce a quality product and we're treated like we're just ... well, terrible people. It doesn't go down well in the ag community."

We don't think he's a bad guy. He worked hard to buy the farm from his parents and brothers—a farm that had been in the family for a century—and he found a way to keep it going when most family pig farms were going out of business. We like the fact that he doesn't keep his pregnant sows in crates—probably the least defensible aspect of standard pig-confinement practices in America. We particularly admire his openness about what he is doing, a refreshing contrast to all the other intensive pig producers we contacted. His method of disposing of his manure seems more responsible than that of many pig producers. We appreciate that his buildings keep his pigs warm in the cold Iowa winters. But we wondered if there couldn't be a way of keeping them warm and giving them a better life than they can have living in an environment as barren and restrictive as his total-confinement buildings.

When we sent Wayne what we had written about our visit, in addition to asking not to be identified and making a few other minor suggestions, he and Mrs. Bradley wrote that they thought our final sentence—the one you have just read—made "no sense." Instead they suggested a different way of ending our account of our visit to their farm. Here it is, with their original underlining. You be the judge.

> Raising pigs today is so much improved over methods used by our great-grandparents, and the meat that we consume is so much leaner and healthier for us to eat! The highest-quality standard of 'the other white meat' is the goal of USA pork production in the 21st century. Let's thank the American farmer for a solid science-based industry that includes good animal care while being good stewards of the environment. Let's enjoy that pork chop hot off the grill, or that pork roast with potatoes and carrots, because there's no safer food source than USA-raised pigs for the pork consumers in the USA and other countries which import our pork!

Profitability and Animal Welfare

The real ethical issue about factory farming's treatment of animals isn't whether the producers are good or bad guys, but that the system seems to recognize animal suffering only when it interferes with profitability. The animal industry always says that producers take care of their animals because what is good for the animals is good for the producer. Professor Bernard Rollin, who has taught veterinary ethics at Colorado State University for almost 30 years, has given a graphic example of how profitability and animal welfare can pull in opposite directions. A veterinarian was visiting a 500-sow, "farrow to finish" swine operation with three full-time employees and a manager. He noticed that one of the sows in the gestation crates had a hind leg sticking out at an odd angle. When he inquired, he was told "She broke her leg yesterday, and she's due to farrow next week. We'll let her farrow in here, and then we'll shoot her and foster off her pigs." The vet was troubled by the idea of leaving the sow for a week with a broken leg and offered to put the leg in a splint, charging only the cost of his materials. He was told that the operation could not afford the manpower involved in separating and caring for the sow. At this point, the vet, who had been brought up on a family pig farm where the animals had names and were treated as individuals, realized that "confinement agriculture had gone too far."[19]

Is this an extreme case, or common practice? The cost calculations that Wayne made when discussing the possible use of a local anesthetic to reduce the pain of operations like castration—"there's not a dollar a pig to throw away"—show that this kind of thinking is built into intensive animal raising. As long as the market provides no incentive for reducing the pigs' pain, the pig producer cannot afford to spend more than a penny, or perhaps a nickel, for that purpose. If he does, someone else who won't spend anything to reduce pain will produce cheaper pigs and put him out of business. That is why the way that factory farming treats animals is not so much a problem of gratuitous cruelty or sadism, and the main problem is not a matter of preventing isolated incidents of animal abuse. The core issue is the commercial pressures that exist in a competitive market system in which animals are items of property, and the conditions in which they are kept are not regulated by federal or state animal-welfare law.

Tracking Down Jake's Milk

Jake thought that she was buying milk from local farms because Coleman Dairy, the brand she bought at Wal-Mart, is an Arkansas-based corporation. When we called and asked if we could see their cows, however, Walt Coleman told us that they hadn't had any cows since 1935. They buy their milk from Dairy Farmers of America, a big dairy cooperative, and although some of their milk comes from Arkansas, it can also come from Texas or New Mexico. Coleman wasn't willing to help us any further in our quest to see the source of Jake's milk.

Milk and cheese production enjoy a better reputation than other forms of intensive farming, and the dairy industry is keen to keep it that way. In advertisements for dairy products, it's common to see cows enjoying acres of rolling green pasture, often with their calves nearby. The impression many consumers get is that dairy cows lead natural lives, and we humans merely take the surplus milk that the calf does not require. People also think that cows are placid animals without much of an emotional life. Both are misconceptions. Cows have strong emotional lives. They form friendships with two, three, or four other cows, and, if permitted, will spend most of their time together, often licking and grooming each other. On the other hand, they can form dislikes to other cows and bear grudges for months or even years.

More remarkably still, cows can get excited when they solve intellectual challenges. Donald Broom, professor of animal welfare at Cambridge University, set cows a problem—to work out how to open a door to get some food—while measuring their brainwave patterns. When the cows solved the problem, Broom reported, "Their brainwaves showed their excitement; their heartbeat went up and some even jumped into the air. We called it their eureka moment."[20]

Peter Lovenheim is a writer who lives in Rochester, New York. He was standing in line at McDonald's one day when he decided that he'd like to know more about how a hamburger is produced. He bought three newborn calves and had them raised in the usual way until it was time to slaughter them. Because Rochester is close to many of New York State's dairy farms—and New York is the third largest dairying state in the U.S., after Wisconsin and California—Lovenheim bought male calves from a nearby dairy farm. Most males born to dairy calves are raised for veal, or slaughtered immediately for pet food, but a few of the stronger ones are raised for beef. Thanks to Andrew and Sue Smith, who were remarkably open about what they do, Lovenheim was able to spend a lot of time at Lawnel Farm, and the following account draws on his description of Lawnel when he was there in 2000.[21]

With about 900 cows being milked—that doesn't include young cows who were not yet giving milk, nor cows who were temporarily not lactating—Lawnel was a medium-sized dairy operation, larger than some of the organic farms we will describe in Part II but small compared to, say, Bill Braum's dairy near Tuttle, Oklahoma, which milks over 10,000 cows, or Threemile Canyon in Oregon, which milks 18,000 cows.[22] A Cornell University study expects the number of dairy farms in the United States to decline from 105,000 in 2000 to 16,000 in 2020, while the number of cows per farm and the total milk production both increase.[23]

At Lawnel, the cows were kept indoors, in barns. Unlike many dairy farms, they were free to walk around inside the barn— they were not in "tie-stalls" that confine cows, for most of the year, to a single stall where they are fed and milked. In the western United States, dairy cows are more likely to be kept outside, but even then they are just in dirt lots. Very few dairy cows in the U.S. get to graze in the grassy meadows typical of dairy-industry advertising—the exceptions are mostly cows producing milk certified "organic," but, as we shall see, even some of them are not on pasture.

The modern dairy cow has been bred to produce as much milk as possible and now produces more than three times as much milk as a typical dairy cow did 50 years ago.[24] The result is considerable stress on the cow's body. To increase milk production still further, the Smiths gave their cows injections, every other week, of BST, or bovine somatotrophin, a genetically engineered growth hormone. BST is banned in Canada and in the European Union because of concerns for the health and welfare of dairy cows, but it is widely used in the United States. It increases milk production by about 10 percent, but the site of the injection may become swollen and tender. BST can also increase problems with mastitis, a painful udder infection that afflicts about one in six U.S. dairy cows.[25] Sue Smith said she didn't like giving the injections, but "[i]f we're making more milk and it's profitable, it's something we should be doing."[26]

Like human females, dairy cows do not give milk until they have given birth, and their milk production will begin to decline some six months after the birth. So after they reach maturity they are made pregnant by artificial insemination roughly every year. Normally a calf would suckle from its mother for six months, and the bond between mother and child would remain strong during that period, but dairy farms are in business to sell milk, not give it to calves. At Lawnel Farms, Lovenheim watched a cow give birth and begin to lick her calf, but forty minutes later a farmhand came and took the calf away. The cow sniffed the straw where the calf had been, bellowed, and began to pace around. Hours later she was sticking her nose under the gate to the barn in which she was confined, bellowing continuously. Meanwhile her calf was in another part of the farm, lying shivering on a concrete floor. Within a few days he was dead, and his body was lying on the farm's compost pile.[27]

Oliver Sacks, who writes about people with unusual neurological conditions, spent some time with Temple Grandin, the livestock consultant McDonald's has employed to advise them on animal-welfare issues. Sacks was more interested in Grandin's autism than in her work with animals, but he accompanied her on a visit to a dairy farm. As Sacks describes it: "We saw one cow outside the stockade, roaming, looking for her calf, and bellowing. 'That's not a happy cow,' Temple said. 'That's one sad, unhappy, upset cow. She wants her baby. Bellowing for it, hunting for it. She'll forget for a while, then start again. It's like grieving, mourning—not much written about it. People don't like to allow them thoughts or feelings.'"[28] John Avizienius, the senior scientific officer in the Farm Animals Department of the RSPCA in Britain, says that he "remembers one particular cow who appeared to be deeply affected by the separation from her calf for a period of at least six weeks. When the calf was first removed, she was in acute grief; she stood outside the pen where she had last seen her calf and bellowed for her offspring for hours. She would only move when forced to do so. Even after six weeks, the mother would gaze at the pen where she last saw her calf and sometimes wait momentarily outside of the pen. It was almost as if her spirit had been broken and all she could do was to make token gestures to see if her calf would still be there."[29]

Female dairy calves may be reared as replacements for the "culled" cows who get sent to slaughter. Although the natural lifespan of a cow is around 20 years, dairy cows are usually killed at between five and seven years of age, because they cannot sustain the unnaturally high rate of milk production. Male calves who survive are sent to auction at an age when they can barely walk. Temple Grandin has strong views about that, too: "Worst thing you can do is put a bawling baby on a trailer. It's just an awful thing to do."[30]

The usual options for these male dairy calves are, as already mentioned, to be slaughtered immediately or to be raised for "milk-fed" veal. From the calf's point of view, immediate slaughter is the better fate, for it spares him 16 weeks of confinement in semi-darkness, in a bare wooden crate too narrow to turn around. He will be tied at the neck, further restricting his movements. Already stressed by separation from his mother and unable to mingle with others of his kind, he will be fed only "milk replacer," a liquid mixture of dried milk products, starch, fats, sugar, antibiotics, and other additives. This diet is deliberately so low in iron that he will develop subclinical anemia. That's what the veal producer wants, because it means that the calf's flesh, instead of becoming the normal healthy red color of a 16-week-old calf on pasture, will retain the pale pink color and soft texture of "prime veal." Bought mostly by expensive restaurants catering to gourmet tastes, that kind of veal fetches the highest price. For the same reason, the calf will be denied hay or straw for bedding—if he had it, his desire for roughage and something to chew on would cause him to eat it, and since it contains iron, that too would change the color of his flesh. The wooden stalls and neck tether are part of the same plan. If the stall had iron fittings, he would lick them, and if he were able to turn around, he would lick his own urine—again, in order to satisfy his craving for iron.

Apart from the separation of cows from their calves and the way the new-born male calves are treated, the most disturbing passages in Lovenheim's description of Lawnel Farm portray the treatment of "downers"—cows who, through illness or accident, are no longer able to stand. On one occasion Lovenheim saw Sue Smith trying to raise a downed cow, No. 4482. She started by coaxing her with gentle words, but when that didn't work she twisted the stump of the cow's tail, then jabbed her knee into the cow's side and screamed into her ear. When that met with no success she twisted the cow's ear and jabbed her several times in the ribs with an electric prod. That didn't work either. If a downed cow can't be raised, she is dragged out. So they called Bill, a renderer, to take the cow away. Lovenheim describes what happened next: "Andrew gets on a small tractor and backs it through the barn door while Bill ties a sling around 4482's front right hoof. When the sling is attached to the tractor, Andrew reverses direction, dragging the downed cow 30 or 40 feet across the barn door, her useless back feet spread wide, her left front hoof kind of paddling along to keep up." (While this was going on, Andrew and Bill discussed what crops the farm had planted that season.) Once out of the barn, Bill winched the cow up a steeply inclined ramp into the back of a truck that took her to the slaughterhouse. After watching this, Lovenheim asked Sue if she had ever considered euthanizing downed animals on the farm. She told him that they'd done that once, but the procedure was expensive.[31]

Manure from dairies, like that from chicken and pig factory farms, pollutes rivers, kills fish, and ruins the homes of nearby residents. Another pollution problem, more specific to cows, is often treated as a joke. When cows ruminate, or "chew the cud," they produce gases called "volatile organic compounds." (For those who like anatomical details, most is generated in burps rather than farts.) When there are a lot of cows, that makes for a lot of gas and can cease to be a joke. The San Joaquin Valley, part of California's Central Valley and one of the world's richest agricultural regions, ranks alongside Houston and Los Angeles as having the worst air pollution in the United States. Over the last six years, the valley has violated the federal limit on ozone smog over an eight-hour period more often than any other region in the country. Officials from the San Joaquin Valley Air Pollution Control District believe that the valley's 2.5 million dairy cows are the biggest single source of a major smog-causing pollutant and are trying to force the dairy industry to do something about it. Other gases are emitted by cow manure and the lagoons in which it is stored. The dairy industry is resisting proposals for change. Tom Frantz, who says he has developed asthma as a result of dairy farms moving near to him, heads a group called the Association of Irritated Residents that is calling for stricter regulation. Frantz says: "Ag hasn't been regulated in the past, but times are changing. Our lungs will not become an agricultural subsidy."[32]

The problem isn't only one for local residents, either. The gases contain methane, which contributes significantly to global warming. In that respect we are all subsidizing agriculture.

The Beef Industry

By a curious coincidence, about the same time that Peter Lovenheim in New York was buying calves in order to follow the process of turning a calf into a hamburger, Michael Pollan, another writer, was doing much the same thing in the Midwest. Lovenheim's calves were byproducts of the dairy industry and were raised by a dairy farmworker and his wife who kept about a dozen cattle on the side. Pollan bought a young steer—a castrated male—from a ranch in South Dakota and had him fattened alongside 37,000 other cattle on a feedlot in Kansas. The dairy industry that Lovenheim observed is the source of about half of the hamburger meat served at the fast-food restaurants Jake likes to frequent. The beef industry that Pollan portrays is where most of America's 36 million beef cattle are produced every year and is the likely source of the porterhouse steak she buys at Wal-Mart.

Pollan's calf, known as 534, was born in March. The calf remained with his mother for more than six months, part of a herd that had many acres of prairie pasture on which to graze. He wasn't even weaned until October. But it was all downhill from there. The young steer was loaded into a truck and driven 500 miles to Pokey Feeders where, in Pollan's words, "Cattle pens stretch to the horizon, each one home to 150 animals standing dully or lying around in a grayish mud that, it eventually dawns on you, isn't mud at all." When Pollan visited, he could smell a "bus-station–men's-room" odor more than a mile before he got there. Here 534 lived another eight months, until slaughter.[33]

On arrival at the feedlot, 534 was given an implant of a synthetic hormone in the back of his ear—something similar to the muscle-building testosterone surrogates that athletes use. Giving them to cattle is banned in Europe because of concerns about the potential health risk of drug residues, and of course U.S. law prohibits people from self-medicating with steroids. In the U.S., however, giving them to cattle is standard practice. It makes them put on more muscle, which means more money for the growers. When Pollan asked Rich Blair, the rancher from whom he bought 534, what he thought about the hormone implants, Blair said: "I'd love to give up hormones. The cattle could get along better without them. But the market signal's not there, and as long as my competitor's doing it, I've got to do it, too."

Instead of grass, 534 now ate corn kernels, together with a daily dose of antibiotics to enable him to survive on this diet. Dr. Mel Metzen, the staff veterinarian at Pokey Feeders, told Pollan that a great many of the health problems that he and his eight assistants have to deal with stem from the diet. "They're made to eat forage," Metzen says, "and we're making them eat grain." Ruminant animals have a digestive system that has evolved to break down grass. If they don't get enough roughage, they develop lactic acid in their rumens, which creates gas and causes "feedlot bloat," a condition so severe that cattle can suffocate from it. Liver abscesses are also frequent. Putting cattle on a corn-based diet is like putting humans on a diet of candy bars—you can live on it for a while, but eventually you are going to get sick. For the beef producer that doesn't matter, as long as the animal doesn't drop dead before being slaughtered. By feeding antibiotics on a daily basis, the risk of that happening is reduced to manageable proportions—and it is a risk worth taking, because the cattle reach market weight in 14 months, rather than the 18 months to two years they would otherwise take. Without antibiotics, Metzen admitted, it wouldn't be possible to fatten cattle on corn. "Hell, if you gave them lots of grass and space," he joked, "I wouldn't have a job."

Corn isn't the only strange food that cattle are fed. When mad cow disease became a major issue in Europe, the public was surprised to learn that it was caused by cattle eating the remains of sheep who had been infected with a related disease. Since when, people asked, do cattle eat meat? In fact, slaughterhouse leftovers have been going into cattle feed for about 40 years, because they are cheap and add protein to the diet. In the wake of the mad cow disaster, most countries placed restrictions on feeding meat remnants to cattle, but in the U.S. it is still, at the time of writing, permitted for cattle feed to contain beef blood and fat, as well as gelatin, "plate waste" (restaurant leftovers), chicken and pig meat, and chicken litter—which includes fecal matter, dead birds, chicken feathers, and spilled feed. The spilled feed can include the same beef and bone meal that is not allowed to be fed to cattle directly, but can be fed to chickens.

In January 2004 the Food and Drug Administration announced plans to ban blood, plate waste, and chicken litter, and an international review panel convened by the Secretary of Agriculture recommended banning all slaughterhouse remnants; two years later, none of these proposed bans had come into effect. Frustrated at the delay, scientists and McDonald's Corporation told the FDA that stronger steps were needed to stop mad cow disease, which the researchers called "an insidious threat." McDonald's vice president Dick Crawford called on the government "to take further action to reduce this risk."[34]

One of the reasons for the delay, according to Stephen Sundlof, Director of the FDA's Center for Veterinary Medicine, was that the proposed ban on the use of chicken litter generated "huge concern" from chicken producers. No wonder—about a million tons of chicken litter are disposed of by being fed to cattle each year. That means that, on average, each of the 36 million cattle produced in the U.S. has eaten 66 pounds of it. In other words, environmental problems created by the chicken industry are preventing the FDA from taking steps recommended by public health experts to ensure the safety of U.S. beef.

The feedlot system is also an ecological disaster. When we eat ruminants who have been grazing on pasture, we are, in effect, harvesting the free energy of the sun. But feedlots thrive because in the U.S. bulk corn sells for about 4 cents a pound—less than the cost of production, thanks to the billions of taxpayers' dollars the government gives in subsidies to the growers. (Most of the cash goes to people who are already very wealthy.) The corn in turn requires chemical fertilizers, which are made from oil. So a corn-fattened feedlot steer is, as Pollan says, "the very last thing we need: a fossil-fuel machine." Pollan asked David Pimentel, a Cornell ecologist, to calculate how much oil went into fattening 534 to his slaughter weight of 1,250 pounds. Pimentel's answer: 284 gallons.

Then there is the issue of what happens to the run-off from the feedlots. Nebraska is *the* state for big feedlots, with 760 of them authorized to have more than 1,000 head of cattle. The largest, near Broken Bow, is licensed for 85,000 cattle. Alan Kolok, a professor of biology at the University of Nebraska, is studying the impact of feedlots on streams that flow into the Elkhorn River. We met him in Omaha, and he drove us west into Cuming County, one of the nation's top beef-producing counties. Near West Point, we came to a feedlot for about 5,000 cattle—the usual fenced, bare, dirt-and-manure yards with bored-looking cattle standing in the sun. It was June, and although it wasn't especially hot yet, we remarked on the lack of shade, saying to Alan that if any had been provided, most of these cattle would have been standing in it. He said that the weather was going to get hotter. Indeed, by the end of July, much of Nebraska had had 30 days with temperatures above 90 degrees, and several above 100. Roxanne Bergman, who runs a "dead-stock removal" company in Clearwater, said her company alone had hauled out 1,250 dead cattle during a few days of hot weather and could not handle all the calls it was receiving.[35]

Researchers from the Department of Animal Science and Food Technology at Texas Tech University studied the use of shade in feedlots. The study divided cattle into a group that had shade available and one that did not have shade available. The cattle with shade available "used the shade extensively" from 9.00 A.M. to 5.30 P.M., following the shade as the sun moved. Cattle without shade were four times as aggressive to other cattle than those with shade. But the researchers also noted that "in west Texas, shade is generally not used in commercial feedlots because it is not thought to be cost effective."[36] Once again—and not only in west Texas—when better animal welfare costs money, animal welfare loses.

Alan showed us how the feedlot we were looking at had been built right down to the edge of the north fork of Fisher Creek. A holding lagoon built to catch the feedlot run-off, filled with unpleasant-looking brown water, was separated from the creek by an earth embankment. Alan explained that in heavy rain, it was likely that polluted water would run off from the feedlot into the creek, or could seep through the embankment into the creek. We drove on and came to another feedlot on sloping land not far from the Elkhorn River. Here Alan has found local fish, fathead minnows, showing signs of altered sexual features. As compared with fish captured near a wildlife refuge where there are no feedlots, the male minnows had less pronounced masculine features and females had less pronounced feminine features. This phenomenon is known as "endocrine disruption." If fathead minnows are altered, the same could happen to fish used for recreational fishing, like bass and catfish, and the Nebraska Department of Game and Parks is concerned about the problem. Alan and his colleagues have published studies hypothesizing that the most likely explanation is the steroids implanted in the feedlot cattle. The cattle excrete them, and when it rains they wash off into the rivers, where they have a half-life of 6 to 12 months.[37]

Although Nebraska livestock producers say that their state has some of the strictest regulations in the nation, there is very little enforcement of regulations regarding feedlots. In addition to its 4,560 cattle feedlots, Nebraska has thousands of confined pig units, and of course egg and chicken producers as well. In 1999, the Nebraska Department of Environmental Quality stated that there were 25,000 to 30,000 hog and cattle feeding operations in the state, most of which had never applied for permits from the agency, although state law had required permits since 1972. Even if these pig farms and cattle feedlots had applied for permits, the Department simply would not have had the staff to inspect more than a small fraction of them. In 1997, the Department's director testified that he had a staff of five for issuing permits and inspecting livestock-feeding operations and that they "tried" to inspect 225 of the larger operations.[38]

It's not unusual in the U.S. for state departments to lack the resources to monitor water pollution. Idaho, it seems, is in a similar position to Nebraska. Mike Bussell, director of the Environmental Protection Agency's regional office of compliance and enforcement, said that his office was going to have to start inspecting feedlots in Idaho because the Idaho State Department of Agriculture was "never able to accomplish" the basic task of producing an "overall inventory of the regulated community, so we'd know how many operations we were dealing with, and who needs to comply."[39] In Michigan, according to a regional Environmental Protection Agency report, the Department of Environmental Quality "does not conduct inspections to determine compliance by CAFOs (Concentrated Animal Feeding Operations) with permit application and other program requirements."[40]

If the untreated waste from feedlots doesn't flow directly into the streams and rivers, it will be sprayed onto fields through a center-pivot irrigation system. Manure is wet and costly to transport, so it is spread on fields close to the animal feeding operations, often in quantities too great for the soil to absorb, and in heavy rain, it runs off into the creeks. (The method of working it into the soil used by Wayne Bradley in Iowa isn't widespread because it takes more labor.) In 2002, the Nebraska Department of Environmental Quality sampled about 5,000 of the state's more than 16,000 miles of rivers and streams and found that pollution exceeded the standard for uses like recreation, aquatic life, agriculture, and drinking supply in 71 percent—a significant jump on the already alarming 58 percent found to be polluted in 2000.[41] Dennis Schueth, who manages the Upper Elkhorn Natural Resources District, told Nebraska Public Radio Network reporter and author Carolyn Johnsen: "We can be more environmentally sound if we want to pay more for our food."[42] Right. But what mechanism is supposed to bring about that outcome? Even if Jake and Lee were willing to pay more for their meat in order to protect the environment in Nebraska, how could they be sure—or even reasonably hopeful—that the extra dollars they were spending were having this effect?

As we drove back along Route 275 near West Point, Alan pointed out dozens of big containers of anhydrous ammonia—a synthetic nitrogen fertilizer. "Isn't it odd," he asked, "that all this synthetic fertilizer is being used in the midst of a feedlot region, where there is all this much better natural fertilizer available?"

Australian Beef

Raising beef doesn't have to be like this. On a visit to Australia, we met Patrick Francis, the editor of *Australian Farm Journal,* a popular farming magazine. Patrick had heard of our interest in ethical farming and invited us to look at the small beef property—in America it would be called a ranch—that he ran with his wife Anne near Romsey, in Victoria. The property was a delight to stroll around, in part because Patrick and Anne have set aside 20 percent of the land for revegetation, mostly with native eucalyptus. The straightest trees will, in time, be sold for timber, but meanwhile, by storing carbon, they are making a small contribution to mitigating global warming. A recent carbon balance calculation showed that each year the farm was absorbing from the atmosphere 220 tons more carbon dioxide than it was emitting. The plantations also provide a habitat for native animals, including a mob of gray kangaroos who hopped away as we strolled by. Meanwhile, in the open fields, the cattle made a remarkable contrast to the dusty, manure-caked animals we saw in the bare Nebraska feedlots.

It was mid-April, the southern hemisphere's autumn, and there had been little rain for months, but Patrick rotates his cattle around different fields every week or two, a technique that gives the grass time to recover from grazing and ensures healthy soils and well-grassed pastures. This method eliminates the need to conserve fodder—Australian winters are mild and free of snow, and there is enough grass in the fields for the cattle to eat all year round. The rotation makes for thick pastures, which eliminates the need to use pesticides for weed control.

The day we were there coincided with one of those rotations, and we watched as Patrick moved the cattle on to the next field. He has a way of calling his cattle to him, and they follow where he leads. First among them is a particularly affectionate seven-year-old bullock—a term used for an older steer—who Patrick has kept on the farm for his leadership role in showing the newer cattle on the property what to do. (His flesh, by now, would be too tough for anything but hamburger.) The day was pleasant, and the sun had lost the sting it has at the height of summer, but once the cattle had moved into the new pasture, they soon found the shade cast by a row of cypresses, and most of them stood under the trees. Though the youngest calves were six months old, they were still keeping company with their mothers. The lives of these cattle were, it seemed, entirely comfortable. They had what cattle need: plenty of grass, clean water, shade, and their own social group.

Patrick told us that he prefers to sell his cattle direct from the farm to the slaughterhouse, but there are times of the year when he doesn't have enough grass on his pasture to get them ready to market. Then he sells them to a feedlot for short-term fattening. For the Australian domestic market, only about 25 percent of cattle are fattened in feedlots, although that percentage is growing because supermarkets prefer the greater reliability of the quality of the meat. Nevertheless, most Australian cattle are fed for only 70 days, less than half the normal period in feedlots in the U.S. For export markets—predominantly Japan and Korea, with a small amount going to the United States—cattle are generally fed for about 150 days, because consumers there have developed a taste for the marbled, fattier meat that results from fattening cattle largely on grain for a longer period of time.

Slaughter

Mammals killed for food in the U.S.—unlike chickens, ducks, and turkeys—are required by law to be stunned before being killed. No, that's not quite right: the U.S. Department of Agriculture ludicrously classifies rabbits as poultry, although they are mammals, thus allowing producers to avoid the legal requirement to stun them before slaughter. Temple Grandin surveyed American slaughterhouses to find out what percentages of animals are rendered insensible by the first application of the stun-gun. In her first survey, in 1996, only 36 percent of slaughterhouses were able to effectively stun at least 95 percent of animals on the first attempt. Six years later, 94 percent were able to do so. That is a dramatic improvement.

Nevertheless, as a General Accounting Office report to Congress on the enforcement of the Humane Methods of Slaughter Act acknowledges, despite the improvement, setting a standard of only 95 percent of animals being stunned on the first attempt "still indicates that hundreds of thousands of animals were not stunned on the first try.... Thus, there may be undetected instances of inhumane treatment." The report notes that there were "approximately six observations for HMSA compliance per month, or less than two observations per week, for each of the 918 plants that are covered by the act." In other words, with hundreds of animals being killed every hour, the inspectors are rarely present. When they are there, the plant operator knows it, and so what the inspectors observe may not be representative of what happens when they are absent. Even when inspectors are present and do find violations, the report found that enforcement policies were inconsistent and "inspectors often do not take enforcement action when they should."[43]

A video taken by an undercover investigator at AgriProcessors, Inc., in Postville, Iowa, during the summer of 2004 shows what can happen when inspectors are not present. AgriProcessors, Inc., is a kosher slaughterhouse, which means that it kills animals in accordance with orthodox Jewish dietary law, which forbids stunning before slaughter. In theory, in kosher slaughter animals should be killed quickly and cleanly by having their throats cut with a single slash of a sharp knife. Unconsciousness from loss of blood to the brain should follow within a few seconds. In the video, however, cattle who have had their throats cut and their tracheas removed still thrash around for a long time before they die. Some struggle to get to their feet—and even succeed in standing up. While this happens, a worker waits for the animal to collapse so that he can tie a chain around its rear leg and hoist it off the ground. One animal goes so far as to stagger through an opening into a different area of the slaughterhouse before collapsing. Two more cattle come down the killing line and have their throats cut before this one is finally hoisted off its feet and dragged away.[44]

We are not suggesting that these scenes are typical of kosher slaughter, or of American slaughter in general. But it is worth noting that AgriProcessors is the world's largest kosher slaughterhouse, and its owner has stated that "[w]hat you see on the video is not out of the ordinary." Similarly, the Orthodox Union, the world's largest kosher certifier, has defended the plant consistently and has said that the plant meets "the highest standards of Jewish law and tradition" and that its kosher status has never been in jeopardy.[45]

Since inspectors are not assigned to the point of kill in any U.S. slaughterhouses, it is probable that anyone who eats meat will, unknowingly, from time to time be eating meat that comes from an animal who died an agonizing death.

NOTES

1. Christopher G. Davis and Biing-Hwan Lin, "Factors Affecting U.S. Pork Consumption," Economic Research Service, U.S. Department of Agriculture, Outlook Report No. (LDPM13001), May 2005 <www.ers.usda.gov/publications/LDP/may05/ldpm13001/ldpm13001.pdf>.

2. *Corporate Fact Sheet*; Overview, Kraft Foods <http://kraft.com/profile/factsheet.html>.

3. Renee Zahery, telephone message, February 1, 2005.

4. Ronald L. Plain, "Trends in U.S. Swine Industry," paper for U.S. Meat Export Federation Pork Conference, Taipei, Taiwan, September 24, 1997 <www.ssu.missouri.edu/faculty/RPlain/papers/swine.htm>; T. Stout and G. Packer, "National Trends Reflected in Changing Ohio Swine Industry," Ohio State University Extension Research Bulletin, Special Circular 156, Agricultural Economics Department, (n.d.) <http://ohioline.osu.edu/scl56/scl56_48.html>.

5. U.S. Department of Agriculture, National Agricultural Statistics Service, Livestock Slaughter, 2004 Summary, March 2005 <http://usda.mannlib.cornell.edu/reports/nassr/livestock/pls-bban/lsan0305.pdf>. The decline in pig farm numbers averages about 7 percent per year.

6. Environmental Defense, "Factory Hog Farming: The Big Picture," November 2000 <www.environmentaldefense.org/documents/2563_FactoryHogFarmingBigPicture.pdf>.

7. Lynn Bonner, "Critics Say State Must Do More to Protect Rivers," *Raleigh News & Observer*, August 17, 1995; Minority Staff, U.S. Senate Committee on Agriculture, Nutrition and Forestry, "Animal Water Pollution in America: An Emerging National Problem," 105th Congress, 1st session, December 1997, p. 3. We owe these references to Carolyn Johnsen, *Raising a Stink: The Struggle Over Factory Hog Farms in Nebraska*, University of Nebraska Press, Lincoln, 2003, pp. 14–15.

8. Carolyn Johnsen, *Raising a Stink: The Struggle Over Factory Hog Farms in Nebraska*, University of Nebraska Press, Lincoln, 2003, pp. 21–26.

9. Paul Hammel, "Turning Hog Odors into Tax Deductions," *Omaha World-Herald*, March 5, 2002, cited in Carolyn Johnsen *Raising a Stink: The Struggle Over Factory Hog Farms in Nebraska*, University of Nebraska Press, Lincoln, 2003, p. 138.

10. American Public Health Association, "Precautionary Moratorium on New Concentrated Animal Feed Operations," *2003 Policy Statements*, pp. 12–14 <www.apha.org/legislative/policy/2003/2003-007.pdf>.

11. Ross Clark, "If Only Pigs Could Talk," *London Sunday Telegraph*, March 23, 1997; Roger Highfield, "Computer Skills Show Just How Smart Pigs Are," *Ottawa Citizen*, May 29, 1997 (originally published in the *London Daily Telegraph*).

12. David Wolfson, *Beyond the Law: Agribusiness and the Systemic Abuse of Animals Raised for Food or Food Production*, Watkins Glen, NY: Farm Sanctuary, Inc., 1999. See also "COK Talks with David Wolfson, Esq." <www.cok.net/abol/16/04.php>.

13. On the number of pigs kept indoors, see National Animal Health Monitoring System, Animal and Plant Health Inspection Service, U.S. Department of Agriculture, *Swine 2000*, Part I: Reference of Swine Health and Management in the United States, 2000, Washington, DC, 2001, p. 26. Very few total confinement systems in the U.S. use straw or any other form of bedding. <www.aphis.usda.gov/vs/ceah/ncahs/nahms/swine/swine2000/Swine2kPt1.pdf>.

14. On the number of sows in crates in the ten biggest producers, see U.S. Department of Agriculture, Agricultural Research Service, Livestock Issues Research, "Research Project: The Emerging Issue of Sow Housing," 2004 Annual Report. The overall estimate is from Glenn Grimes, professor emeritus of agricultural economics, University of Missouri, interview with Jim Mason, July 5, 2005.

15. See Scientific Veterinary Committee, Animal Welfare Section, The Welfare of Intensively Kept Pigs, 1997, and Clare Druce and Philip Lymbery, "Outlawed in Europe," in Peter Singer, ed., *In Defense of Animals: The Second Wave*, Blackwell, Oxford, 2005.

16. In the European Union, 242 million pigs were slaughtered in 2005, compared to 103 million in the U.S. See "EU Output Data Revised," *Pig International Electronic Newsletter*, June 23, 2005, based on Eurostat information <www.wattnet.com/newsletters/Pig/htm/jun05pigenews.htm>.

17. Per Jensen, "Observations on the Maternal Behaviour of Free-Ranging Domestic Pigs," *Applied Animal Behaviour Science*, vol. 16 (1986), pp. 131–42.

18. Governor's Office of Drug Control Policy, "Iowa, METH Facts," February 23, 2005 <www.state.ia.us/government/odcp/docs/Meth_Other_Drug_Facts_Feb23.pdf>.

19. Bernard Rollin first reported on this case in his column in *Canadian Veterinary Journal*, 32:10 (October 1991), p. 584; the column is reprinted in Bernard Rollin, *Introduction to Veterinary Medical Ethics: Theory and Cases*, Blackwell, Oxford, 1999.

20. Jonathan Leake, "The Secret Lives of Moody Cows," *Sunday Times*, February 27, 2005.

21. Peter Lovenheim, *Portrait of a Burger as a Young Calf*, Three Rivers Press, New York, 2002. We are grateful to Peter Lovenheim for checking our text and clarifying some issues.

22. John Peck, "Dairy Farmer Workers Fight for Their Rights in Oregon," *Z Magazine Online*, vol. 17, no. 12 (December 2004) <http://zmagsite.zmag.org/Dec2004/peckprl204.html>; <www.braums.com/FAQ.asp#9>.

23. Eddy LaDue, Brent Gloy, and Charles Cuykendall, "Future Structure of the Dairy Industry: Historical Trends, Projections and Issues," Cornell University, Ithaca, NY, June 2003 <http://aem.cornell.edu/research/researchpdf/rb0301.pdf>, p. iii.

24. To be precise, the increase is from 665 gallons a year in 1950 to 2,365 gallons per year in 2004, an increase of 355 percent. See Erik Marcus, *Meat Market*, Brio Press, Ithaca, NY, 2005, pp. 10–11, drawing on figures from USDA National Agricultural Statistical Services, and updated from <http//usda.mannlib.cornell.edu/reports/nassr/dairy/pmp-bb/2005/mkpr0105.txt>.

25. USDA, National Animal Health Monitoring System, *Dairy 2002*, Part I: Reference of Dairy Health and Management in the United States, p. 54 <www.aphis.usda.gov/vs/ceah/ncahs/nahms/dairy/dairy02/Dairy02Pt1.Pdf>.

26. Peter Lovenheim, *Portrait of a Burger as a Young Calf*, Three Rivers Press, New York, 2002, p. 87.

27. Peter Lovenheim, *Portrait of a Burger as a Young Calf*, Three Rivers Press, New York, 2002, p. 16.

28. Oliver Sacks, *An Anthropologist on Mars*, Knopf, New York, 1995, p. 267.

29. Quoted from People for the Ethical Treatment of Animals, "Cows Grieve," <www.goveg.com/f-hiddenlivescows_giants.asp>.

30. Jon Bonné, "Can Animals You Eat Be Treated Humanely?" MSNBC News, June 28, 2004 <http://www.msnbc.com/id/5271434/>.

31. Peter Lovenheim, *Portrait of a Burger as a Young Calf*, Three Rivers Press, New York, 2002, pp. 112–113.

32. Miguel Bustillo, "In San Joaquin Valley, Cows Pass Cars as Polluters," *Los Angeles Times*, August 2, 2005.

33. Michael Pollan, "Power Steer," *New York Times Sunday Magazine*, March 31, 2002.

34. "Researchers, McDonald's Say U.S. Govt BSE Defense Not Working," *Cattlenetwork.com*, January 4, 2006 <www.cattlenetwork.com/content.asp?contentid=16082>.

35. Chris Clayton, "More than 1250 Nebraska Cattle Died in Heat Wave," *Omaha World-Herald*, July 27, 2005.

36. F. M. Mitlöhner et al., "Effects of Shade on Heat-Stressed Heifers Housed under Feed-lot Conditions," *Burnett Center Internet Progress Report*, no. 11, February 2001 <www.depts.ttu.edu/liru_afs/pdf/bc11.pdf>; see also F. M. Mitlöhner et al., "Shade Effects on Performance, Carcass Traits, Physiology, and Behavior of Heat-Stressed Feedlot Heifers," *Journal of Animal Science*, vol. 80 (2002), pp. 2043–2050 <http://jas.fass.org/cgi/content/full/80/8/2043>.

37. A. M. Soto et al., "Androgenic and Estrogenic Activity in Cattle Feedlot Effluent Receiving Water Bodies of Eastern Nebraska, USA," *Environmental Health Perspectives*, 112 (2004), pp. 346–352; E. F. Orlando et al., "Endocrine Disrupting Effects of Cattle Feedlot Effluent on an Aquatic Sentinel Species, the Fathead Minnow," *Environmental Health Perspectives*, 112 (2004), pp. 353–358; Janet Raloff, "Hormones: Here's the Beef," *Science News*, vol. 161 (Jan. 5, 2002), p. 10 <www.sciencenews.org/articles/20020105/bob13.asp>.

38. Carolyn Johnsen, *Raising a Stink: The Struggle Over Factory Hog Farms in Nebraska*, University of Nebraska Press, Lincoln, 2003, p. 24.

39. "EPA Says It Will Inspect Idaho Feedlots," *Cow-Calf Weekly* (BEEF), August 5, 2005.

40. U.S. Environmental Protection Agency, Region 5, *Results of an Informal Investigation of the National Pollutant Discharge Elimination System Program for Concentrated Animal Feeding Operations in the State of Michigan*, Interim Report, July 24, 2002; we owe the reference to Tony Dutzik, The State of Environmental Enforcement, CoPIRG Foundation, Denver, 2002 <www.cnvironmentcolorado.org/reports/en-venfco10_02.pdf>, which discusses the problem of lack of state environmental enforcement.

41. Nebraska Department of Environmental Quality, Water Quality Division, 2002 Nebraska Water Quality Report, Lincoln, 2002, cited by Carolyn Johnsen, *Raising a Stink: The Struggle Over Factory Hog Farms in Nebraska*, University of Nebraska Press, Lincoln, 2003, p. 138.

42. Carolyn Johnsen, *Raising a Stink: The Struggle Over Factory Hog Farms in Nebraska*, University of Nebraska Press, Lincoln, 2003, p. 122.

43. U.S. General Accounting Office, *Humane Methods of Slaughter Act*, January 2004 <www.gao.gov/new.items/d04247.pdf>.

44. "AgriProcessors," video available on the Website of People for the Ethical Treatment of Animals <www.petatv.com/inv.html>.

45. Sholem Rubashkin, "Response." Shmais News Service, no date, <www.shmais.com/jnewsdetail.cfm?ID=148>; Department of Public Relations, Orthodox Union, "Orthodox Union Releases Industry Animal Welfare Audit of Agriprocessors," March 7, 2005 <www.ou.org/oupr/2005/agri65.htm>.

QUESTIONS FOR MAKING CONNECTIONS
WITHIN THE READING

1. In "Meat and Milk Factories," Singer and Mason assume that their readers will know what is meant by an "intensive" industry. The beef, chicken, and pork industries are all described as "intensive." What does this term mean? Are each of these industries intensive in the same way?

2. Singer and Mason write that "[t]he real ethical issue about factory farming's treatment of animals isn't whether the producers are good or bad guys, but that the system seems to recognize animal suffering only when it interferes with profitability." What would an ethical system look like? How would it differ from the one in place now? Is the Australian farming system that Singer and Mason describe ethical? Is it not ultimately concerned with profitability?

3. Throughout their piece, Singer and Mason describe farm animals as experiencing maladies that overlap with human experience: the animals experience "clinical depression," "psychological stress," and "the stress of boredom." What evidence do they provide to justify these descriptions? Is there a scientific basis for such descriptions, or are Singer and Mason being metaphorical? Is the impact of their descriptions the result of the evidence they provide or of the stories they tell?

QUESTIONS FOR WRITING

1. Toward the middle of their piece, Singer and Mason pose the following parenthetical question: "Is it part of the gulf we draw between ourselves and other animals that leads farmers to talk of animals as 'farrowing' rather than 'giving birth,' 'feeding' rather than 'eating,' and 'gestating' rather than 'being pregnant'?" What is the answer to this question? If the farmers Singer and Mason describe used a different set of words, would farming practices change? Would the eating habits of American consumers change if the "gulf we draw between ourselves and other animals" were closed?

2. After their visit to "Wayne Bradley's" farm, Singer and Mason share their account of the experience with him and, seeing his words in print, he asks to have his name and location changed. Singer and Mason comply and close their discussion of pork farming by juxtaposing their assessment of the Bradley farm with the Bradleys' self-assessment. What are we to make of the fact that the assessments are diametrically opposed? What would Singer and Mason like the Bradleys to do? Can individuals—producers or consumers— change the system Singer and Mason have described?

QUESTIONS FOR MAKING CONNECTIONS
BETWEEN READINGS

1. In "Another Look Back, and a Look Ahead," Edward Tenner describes what he terms the "revenge effects" of technology and the unintended consequences that follow from these acts of "revenge." Do you think that Tenner would be likely to share Singer and Mason's concerns about the factory farm? What revenge effects might Tenner expect to see follow from intensive farming? On balance, do the benefits of the factory farm outweigh the dangers and the ethical dilemmas posed by the way animals are treated on these farms? Is there an objective way to assess the ethical benefits and costs of this system?

2. Singer and Mason conclude their discussion of the factory farm with gruesome descriptions of the slaughtering process. The last thought they leave their readers with is this: "[I]t is probable that anyone who eats meat will, unknowingly, from time to time be eating meat that comes from an animal who died an agonizing death." It is clear that this fact matters to Singer and Mason, but can they make it matter to all the others whose eating habits fuel the factory farming industries? In "An Army of One: *Me,*" Jean Twenge asserts, "Narcissism is one of the few personality traits that psychologists agree is almost completely negative." Does narcissism play a role in eating habits? Is it fair to say that eating meat evidences a "lack of empathy," or is there an ethical way to be a carnivore?

MICHAEL SPECTER

If any single word could describe the recent work of journalist Michael Specter, it would have to be "controversial." Specter has emerged as a fierce defender of technology against all those who doubt the wisdom of its unimpeded growth. Concerns about the effects of vaccines, bioengineering, and race-based research he attributes to an ignorance of science—made worse, in his view, by a disrespect for expertise as well as established institutions like the pharmaceutical industry. In his book *Denialism* (2009), Specter equates figures like Andrew Weil, a champion of alternative medicine, with people who reject evolution and the reality of climate change. The environmental organizations Greenpeace and Friends of the Earth he portrays as elitist and indifferent to the fate of the world's starving millions. "Fifty years ago," he writes, "we venerated technology." Specter's goal is clearly to restore that veneration, which he sees as more appropriate than ever, given the sheer magnitude of the problems we face.

The pugnacious tone of Specter's current work might surprise those familiar with his distinguished career of balanced reporting. From 1985 to 1991 he covered local news for the *Washington Post,* eventually becoming its national science reporter and, later, its New York bureau chief. After four years as a roving correspondent in Rome, Specter was appointed Moscow Bureau chief for the *New York Times,* and he was one of the first journalists to bring the world's attention to the rebellion in Chechnya. On the staff of the *New Yorker* since 1998, he has written about a wide variety of subjects, from science, technology, and public health to Italian fashion designers. For his coverage of Chechnya he received the Overseas Press Club's Citation for Excellence. He has twice been a recipient of the Global Health Council's Excellence in Media Award, in 2001 for his story on AIDS entitled "India's Plague," and in 2004 for his article "The Devastation," on the testing of HIV vaccines in Africa. For his 2002 article "Rethinking the Brain," he received the AAAS Science Journalism Award.

Even though Specter has become something of a provocateur, often adopting a polemical stance, the questions he poses are some of the most consequential of our time. As he observes of "synthetic biology"—the deliberate engineering of life—"No scientific achievement has promised so much, and none has come with greater risks or clearer possibilities for abuse." While

Specter, Michael. "A Life of Its Own: Where Will Synthetic Biology Lead Us?" *New Yorker*, September 28, 2009: 56, 58–65. The quotation in the first paragraph is drawn from Michael Specter, *Denialism: How Irrational Thinking Hinders Scientific Progress, Harms the Planet, and Threatens Our Lives* (New York: Penguin Press, 2009), 15. Biographical information comes from www.michaelspecter.com.

readily admitting that in the past new technologies were often "oversold," Specter insists that we should press on. Indeed, he describes the engineering of life as unstoppable.

■ ▬ ■

A Life of Its Own

The first time Jay Keasling remembers hearing the word "artemisinin," about a decade ago, he had no idea what it meant. "Not a clue," Keasling, a professor of biochemical engineering at the University of California at Berkeley, recalled. Although artemisinin has become the world's most important malaria medicine, Keasling wasn't an expert on infectious diseases. But he happened to be in the process of creating a new discipline, synthetic biology, which—by combining elements of engineering, chemistry, computer science, and molecular biology—seeks to assemble the biological tools necessary to redesign the living world.

Scientists have been manipulating genes for decades; inserting, deleting, and changing them in various microbes has become a routine function in thousands of labs. Keasling and a rapidly growing number of colleagues around the world have something more radical in mind. By using gene-sequence information and synthetic DNA, they are attempting to reconfigure the metabolic pathways of cells to perform entirely new functions, such as manufacturing chemicals and drugs. Eventually, they intend to construct genes—and new forms of life—from scratch. Keasling and others are putting together a kind of foundry of biological components—BioBricks, as Tom Knight, a senior research scientist at the Massachusetts Institute of Technology, who helped invent the field, has named them. Each BioBrick part, made of standardized pieces of DNA, can be used interchangeably to create and modify living cells.

"When your hard drive dies, you can go to the nearest computer store, buy a new one, and swap it out," Keasling said. "That's because it's a standard part in a machine. The entire electronics industry is based on a plug-and-play mentality. Get a transistor, plug it in, and off you go. What works in one cell phone or laptop should work in another. That is true for almost everything we build: when you go to Home Depot, you don't think about the thread size on the bolts you buy, because they're all made to the same standard. Why shouldn't we use biological parts in the same way?" Keasling and others in the field, who have formed bicoastal clusters in the Bay Area and in Cambridge, Massachusetts, see cells as hardware, and genetic code as the software required to make them run. Synthetic biologists are convinced that, with enough knowledge, they will be able to write programs to control those genetic components, programs that would let them not only alter nature but guide human evolution as well.

No scientific achievement has promised so much, and none has come with greater risks or clearer possibilities for deliberate abuse. The benefits of new technologies—from genetically engineered food to the wonders of pharmaceuticals—often have been oversold. If the tools of synthetic biology succeed, though, they could turn specialized molecules into tiny, self-contained factories, creating cheap drugs, clean fuels, and new organisms to siphon carbon dioxide from the atmosphere.

In 2000, Keasling was looking for a chemical compound that could demonstrate the utility of these biological tools. He settled on a diverse class of organic molecules known as isoprenoids, which are responsible for the scents, flavors, and even colors in many plants: eucalyptus, ginger, and cinnamon, for example, as well as the yellow in sunflowers and the red in tomatoes. "One day, a graduate student stopped by and said, 'Look at this paper that just came out on amorphadiene synthase,'" Keasling told me as we sat in his office in Emeryville, across the Bay Bridge from San Francisco. He had recently been named C.E.O. of the Department of Energy's new Joint BioEnergy Institute, a partnership of three national laboratories and three research universities, led by the Lawrence Berkeley National Laboratory. The consortium's principal goal is to design and manufacture artificial fuels that emit little or no greenhouse gases—one of President Obama's most frequently cited priorities.

Keasling wasn't sure what to tell his student. "'Amorphadiene,' I said. 'What's that?' He told me that it was a precursor to artemisinin, an effective anti-malarial. I had never worked on malaria. So I got to studying and quickly realized that this precursor was in the general class we were planning to investigate. And I thought, Amorphadiene is as good a target as any. Let's work on that."

Malaria infects as many as five hundred million of the world's poorest people every year and kills up to a million, most of whom are children under the age of five. For centuries, the standard treatment was quinine, and then the chemically related compound chloroquine. At ten cents per treatment, chloroquine was cheap and simple to make, and it saved millions of lives. By the early nineties, however, the most virulent malaria parasite—*Plasmodium falciparum*—had grown largely resistant to the drug. Worse, the second line of treatment, sulfadoxine-pyrimethanine, or SP, also failed widely. Artemisinin, when taken in combination with other drugs, has become the only consistently successful treatment that remains. (Reliance on any single drug increases the chances that the malaria parasite will develop resistance.) Known in the West as *Artemisia annua,* or sweet wormwood, the herb that contains artemisinic acid grows wild in many places, but supplies vary widely and so does the price.

Depending so heavily on artemisinin, while unavoidable, has serious drawbacks: combination therapy costs between ten and twenty times as much as chloroquine and, despite increasing assistance from international charities, that is too much money for most Africans or their governments. Artemisinin is not easy to cultivate. Once harvested, the leaves and stems have to be processed rapidly or they will be destroyed by exposure to ultraviolet light. Yields are low, and production is expensive.

Although several thousand Asian and African farmers have begun to plant the herb, the World Health Organization expects that for the next several years the annual demand—as many as five hundred million courses of treatment per year—will far exceed the supply. Should that supply disappear, the impact would be incalculable. "Losing artemisinin would set us back years, if not decades," Kent Campbell, a former chief of the malaria branch at the Centers for Disease Control and Prevention, and director of the Malaria Control Program at the nonprofit health organization PATH, said. "One can envision any number of theoretical public-health disasters in the world. But this is not theoretical. This is real. Without artemisinin, millions of people could die."

Keasling realized that the tools of synthetic biology, if properly deployed, could dispense, with nature entirely, providing an abundant new source of artemisinin. If each cell became its own factory, churning out the chemical required to make the drug, there would be no need for an elaborate and costly manufacturing process either. Why not try to produce it from genetic parts by constructing a cell to manufacture amorphadiene? Keasling and his team would have to dismantle several different organisms, then use parts from nearly a dozen of their genes to cobble together a custom-built package of DNA. They would then need to construct a new metabolic pathway, the chemical circuitry that a cell needs to do its job—one that did not exist in the natural world. "We have got to the point in human history where we simply do not have to accept what nature has given us," he told me.

By 2003, the team reported its first success, publishing a paper in *Nature Biotechnology* that described how the scientists had created that new pathway, by inserting genes from three organisms into E. coli, one of the world's most common bacteria. That research helped Keasling secure a $42.6–million grant from the Bill and Melinda Gates Foundation. Keasling had no interest in simply proving that the science worked; he wanted to do it on a scale that the world could use to fight malaria. "Making a few micrograms of artemisinin would have been a neat scientific trick," he said. "But it doesn't do anybody in Africa any good if all we can do is a cool experiment in a Berkeley lab. We needed to make it on an industrial scale." To translate the science into a product, Keasling helped start a new company, Amyris Biotechnologies, to refine the raw organism, then figure out how to produce it more efficiently. Within a decade, Amyris had increased the amount of artemisinic acid that each cell could produce by a factor of one million, bringing down the cost of the drug from as much as ten dollars for a course of treatment to less than a dollar.

Amyris then joined with the Institute for OneWorld Health, in San Francisco, a nonprofit drugmaker, and, in 2008, they signed an agreement with the Paris–based pharmaceutical company Sanofi–Aventis to make the drug, which they hope to have on the market by 2012. The scientific response has been reverential—their artemisinin has been seen as the first bona-fide product of synthetic biology, proof of a principle that we need not rely on the whims of nature to address the world's most pressing crises. But some people wonder what synthetic artemisinin will mean for the thousands of farmers who have begun to plant the wormwood crop. "What happens to struggling farmers when laboratory vats in California replace farms in Asia and East Africa?" Jim Thomas, a researcher with ETC Group, a technology watchdog based in Canada, asked. Thomas has argued that there has been little discussion of the ethical and cultural implications of altering nature so fundamentally. "Scientists are making strands of DNA that have never existed," Thomas said. "So there is nothing to compare them to. There are no agreed mechanisms for safety, no policies."

Keasling, too, believes that the nation needs to consider the potential impact of this technology, but he is baffled by opposition to what should soon become the world's most reliable source of cheap artemisinin. "Just for a moment, imagine that we replaced artemisinin with a cancer drug," he said. "And let's have the entire Western world rely on some farmers in China and Africa who may or may not plant their crop. And let's have a lot of American children die because of that. Look at the world and tell me we shouldn't be doing this. It's not people in Africa who see malaria who say, Whoa, let's put the brakes on."

Artemisinin is the first step in what Keasling hopes will become a much larger program. "We ought to be able to make any compound produced by a plant inside a microbe," he said. "We ought to have all these metabolic pathways. You need this drug: O.K., we pull this piece, this part, and this one off the shelf. You put them into a microbe, and two weeks later out comes your product."

That's what Amyris has done in its efforts to develop new fuels. "Artemisinin is a hydrocarbon, and we built a microbial platform to produce it," Keasling said. "We can remove a few of the genes to take out artemisinin and put in a different gene, to make biofuels." Amyris, led by John Melo, who spent years as a senior executive at British Petroleum, has already engineered three microbes that can convert sugar to fuel. "We still have lots to learn and lots of problems to solve," Keasling said. "I am well aware that makes some people anxious, and I understand why. Anything so powerful and new is troubling. But I don't think the answer to the future is to race into the past."

For the first four billion years, life on Earth was shaped entirely by nature. Propelled by the forces of selection and chance, the most efficient genes survived, and evolution insured that they would thrive. The long, beautiful Darwinian process of creeping forward by trial and error, struggle and survival, persisted for millennia. Then, about ten thousand years ago, our ancestors began to gather in villages, grow crops, and domesticate animals. That led to stone axes and looms, which in turn led to better crops and a varied food supply that could feed a larger civilization. Breeding of goats and pigs gave way to the fabrication of metal and machines. Throughout it all, new species, built on the power of their collected traits, emerged, while others were cast aside.

By the beginning of the twenty-first century, our ability to modify the smallest components of life through molecular biology had endowed humans with a power that even those who exercise it most proficiently cannot claim to fully comprehend. Human mastery over nature has been predicted for centuries—Bacon insisted on it, Blake feared it profoundly. Little more than a hundred years have passed, however, since Gregor Mendel demonstrated that the defining characteristics of a pea plant—its shape, its size, and the color of the seeds, for example—are transmitted from one generation to the next in ways that can be predicted, repeated, and codified.

Since then, the central project of biology has been to break that code and learn to read it—to understand how DNA creates and perpetuates life. The physiologist Jacques Loeb considered artificial synthesis of life the goal of biology. In 1912, Loeb, one of the founders of modern biochemistry, wrote that there was no evidence that "the artificial production of living matter is beyond the possibilities of science," and declared, "We must either succeed in producing living matter artificially, or we must find the reasons why this is impossible."

In 1946, the Nobel Prize–winning geneticist Hermann J. Muller attempted to do that. By demonstrating that exposure to X-rays can cause mutations in the genes and chromosomes of living cells, he was the first to prove that heredity could be affected by something other than natural selection. He wasn't entirely sure that people would use that information responsibly, though. "If we did attain to any such knowledge or powers there is no doubt in my mind that we would eventually use them," Muller said. "Man is a megalomaniac among animals—if he sees mountains he will try to imitate them by pyramids, and if he sees some grand process like evolution, and thinks it would be at all possible for him to be in on that game, he would irreverently have to have his whack at that too."

The theory of evolution explained that every species on earth is related in some way to every other species; more important, we each carry a record of that history in our body. In 1953, James Watson and Francis Crick began to make it possible to understand why, by explaining how DNA arranges itself. The language of just four chemical letters—adenine, cytosine, guanine, and thymine—comes in the form of enormous chains of nucleotides. When they are joined, the arrangement of their sequences determines how each human differs from all others and from all other living beings.

By the nineteen-seventies, recombinant-DNA technology permitted scientists to cut long, unwieldy molecules of nucleotides into digestible sentences of genetic letters and paste them into other cells. Researchers could suddenly combine the genes of two creatures that would never have been able to mate in nature. As promising as these techniques were, they also made it possible for scientists to transfer viruses—and microbes that cause cancer—from one organism to another. That could create diseases anticipated by no one and for which there would be no natural protection, treatment, or cure. In 1975, scientists from around the world gathered at the Asilomar Conference Center, in Northern California, to discuss the challenges presented by this new technology. They focused primarily on laboratory and environmental safety, and concluded that the field required little regulation. (There was no real discussion of deliberate abuse—at the time, there didn't seem to be any need.)

Looking back nearly thirty years later, one of the conference's organizers, the Nobel laureate Paul Berg, wrote, "This unique conference marked the beginning of an exceptional era for science and for the public discussion of science policy. Its success permitted the then contentious technology of recombinant DNA to emerge and flourish. Now the use of the recombinant DNA technology dominates research in biology. It has altered both the way questions are formulated and the way solutions are sought."

Decoding sequences of DNA was tedious. It could take a scientist a year to complete a stretch that was ten or twelve base pairs long. (Our DNA consists of three billion such pairs.) By the late nineteen-eighties, automated sequencing had simplified the procedure and today machines can process that information in seconds. Another new tool—polymerase chain reaction—completed the merger of the digital and biological worlds. Using PCR, a scientist can take a single DNA molecule and copy it many times, making it easier to read and to manipulate. That permits scientists to treat living cells like complex packages of digital information that happen to be arranged in the most elegant possible way.

Using such techniques, researchers have now resurrected the DNA of the Tasmanian tiger, the world's largest carnivorous marsupial, which has been extinct for more than seventy years. In 2008, scientists from the University of Melbourne and the University of Texas M. D. Anderson Cancer Center, in Houston, extracted DNA from tissue that had been preserved in the Museum Victoria, in Melbourne. They took a fragment of DNA that controlled the production of a collagen gene from the tiger and inserted it into a mouse embryo. The DNA switched on just the right gene, and the embryo began to churn out collagen. That marked the first time that any material from an extinct creature other than a virus has functioned inside a living organism.

It will not be the last. A team from Pennsylvania State University, working with hair samples from two woolly mammoths—one of them sixty thousand years old and the other eighteen thousand—has tentatively figured out how to modify that DNA and place it inside an elephant egg. The mammoth could then be brought to term in an elephant mother. "There is little doubt that it would be fun to see a living, breathing woolly mammoth—a shaggy, elephantine creature with long curved tusks who reminds us more of a very large, cuddly stuffed animal than of a T. Rex.," the *Times* editorialized soon after the discovery was announced. "We're just not sure that it would be all that much fun for the mammoth."

The ultimate goal, however, is to create a synthetic organism made solely from chemical parts and blueprints of DNA. In the mid-nineties, Craig Venter, working at the Institute for Genomic Research, and his colleagues Clyde Hutchison and Hamilton Smith began to wonder whether they could pare life to its most basic components and then use those genes to create such an organism. They began modifying the genome of a tiny bacterium called *Mycoplasma genitaliam,* which contained four hundred and eighty-two genes (humans have about twenty-three thousand) and five hundred and eighty thousand letters of genetic code, arranged on one circular chromosome—the smallest genome of any cell that has been grown in laboratory cultures. Venter and his colleagues then removed genes one by one to find a minimal set that could sustain life.

Venter called the experiment the Minimal Genome Project. By the beginning of 2008, his team had pieced together thousands of chemically synthesized fragments of DNA and assembled a new version of the organism. Then, using nothing but chemicals, they produced from scratch the entire genome of *Mycoplasma genitalium*. "Nothing in our methodology restricts its use to chemically synthesized DNA," Venter noted in the report of his work, which was published in *Science*. "It should be possible to assemble any combination of synthetic and natural DNA segments in any desired order." That may turn out to be one of the most understated asides in the history of science. Next, Venter intends to transplant the artificial chromosome into the walls of another cell and then "boot it up," thereby making a new form of life that would then be able to replicate its own DNA—the first truly artificial organism. (Activists have already named the creation Synthia.) Venter hopes that Synthia and similar products will serve essentially as vessels that can be modified to carry different packages of genes. One package might produce a specific drug, for example, and another could have genes programmed to digest carbon in the atmosphere.

In 2007, the theoretical physicist Freeman Dyson, after having visited both the Philadelphia Flower Show and the Reptile Show in San Diego, wrote an essay in the *New York Review of Books,* noting that "every orchid or rose or lizard or snake is the work of a dedicated and skilled breeder. There are thousands of people, amateurs and professionals, who devote their lives to this business." This, of course, we have been doing in one way or another for millennia. "Now imagine what will happen when the tools of genetic engineering become accessible to these people."

It is only a matter of time before domesticated biotechnology presents us with what Dyson described as an "explosion of diversity of new living creatures.... Designing genomes will be a personal thing, a new art form as creative as painting or sculpture. Few of the new creations will be masterpieces, but a great many will bring joy to their creators and variety to our fauna and flora."

Biotech games, played by children "down to kindergarten age but played with real eggs and seeds," could produce entirely new species—as a lark. "These games will be messy and possibly dangerous," Dyson wrote. "Rules and regulations will be needed to make sure that our kids do not endanger themselves and others. The dangers of biotechnology are real and serious."

Life on Earth proceeds in an arc—one that began with the big bang, and evolved to the point where a smart teenager is capable of inserting a gene from a cold-water fish into a strawberry, to help protect it from the frost. You don't have to be a Luddite—or Prince Charles, who, famously, has foreseen a world reduced to gray goo by avaricious and out-of-control technology—to recognize that synthetic biology, if it truly succeeds, will make it possible to supplant the world created by Darwinian evolution with one created by us.

"Many a technology has at some time or another been deemed an affront to God, but perhaps none invites the accusation as directly as synthetic biology," the editors of *Nature*—who nonetheless support the technology—wrote in 2007. "For the first time, God has competition."

"What if we could liberate ourselves from the tyranny of evolution by being able to design our own offspring?" Drew Endy asked, the first time we met in his office at M.I.T., where, until the summer of 2008, he was assistant professor of biological engineering. (That September, he moved to Stanford.) Endy is among the most compelling evangelists of synthetic biology. He is also perhaps its most disturbing, because, although he displays a childlike eagerness to start engineering new creatures, he insists on discussing both the prospects and the dangers of his emerging discipline in nearly any forum he can find. "I am talking about building the stuff that runs most of the living world," he said. "If this is not a national strategic priority, what possibly could be?"

Endy, who was trained as a civil engineer, spent his youth fabricating worlds out of Lincoln Logs and Legos. Now he would like to build living organisms. Perhaps it was the three well-worn congas sitting in the corner of Endy's office, or the choppy haircut that looked like—something he might have got in a tree house, or the bicycle dangling from his wall—but, when he speaks about putting together new forms of life, it's hard not to think of that boy and his Legos.

Endy made his first mark on the world of biology by nearly failing the course in high school. "I got a D," he said. "And I was lucky to get it." While pursuing an engineering degree at Lehigh University, Endy took a course in molecular genetics. He spent his years in graduate school modeling bacterial viruses, but they are complex, and Endy craved simplicity. That's when he began to think about putting cellular components together.

Never forgetting the secret of Legos—they work because you can take any single part and attach it to any other—in 2005 Endy and colleagues on both coasts started the BioBricks Foundation, a nonprofit organization formed to register and develop standard parts for assembling DNA. Endy is not the only scientist, or even the only synthetic biologist, to translate a youth spent with blocks into a useful scientific vocabulary. "The notion of pieces fitting together—whether those pieces are integrated circuits, microfluidic components, or molecules—guides much of what I do in the laboratory," the physicist and synthetic biologist Rob Carlson writes in his new book, *Biology Is Technology: The Promise, Peril, and Business of Engineering Life.* "Some of my best work has come together in my mind's eye accompanied by what I swear was an audible click."

The BioBricks registry is a physical repository, but it is also an online catalogue. If you want to construct an organism, or engineer it in new ways, you can go to the site as you would one that sells lumber or industrial pipes. The constituent parts of DNA—promoters, ribosome-binding sites, plasmid backbones, and thousands of other components—are catalogued, explained, and discussed. It is a kind of theoretical Wikipedia of future life forms, with the added benefit of actually providing the parts necessary to build them.

I asked Endy why he thought so many people seem to be repelled by the idea of constructing new forms of life. "Because it's scary as hell," he said. "It's the coolest platform science has ever produced, but the questions it raises are the hardest to answer." If you can sequence something properly and you possess the information for describing that organism—whether it's a virus, a dinosaur, or a human being—you will eventually be able to construct an artificial version of it. That gives us an alternate path for propagating living organisms.

The natural path is direct descent from a parent—from one generation to the next. But that process is filled with errors. (In Darwin's world, of course, a certain number of those mutations are necessary.) Endy said, "If you could complement evolution with a secondary path, decode a genome, take it off-line to the level of information"—in other words, break it down to its specific sequences of DNA the way one would break down the code in a software program—"we can then design whatever we want, and recompile it," which could permit scientists to prevent many genetic diseases. "At that point, you can make disposable biological systems that don't have to produce offspring, and you can make much simpler organisms."

Endy stopped long enough for me to digest the fact that he was talking about building our own children. "If you look at human beings as we are today, one would have to ask how much of our own design is constrained by the fact that we have to be able to reproduce," he said. In fact, those constraints are significant. In theory, at least, designing our own offspring could make those constraints disappear. Before speaking about that, however, it would be necessary to ask two essential questions: What sorts of risk does that bring into play, and what sorts of opportunity?

The deeply unpleasant risks associated with synthetic biology are not hard to imagine: Who would control this technology, who would pay for it, and how much would it cost? Would we all have access or, as in the 1997 film *Gattaca*, which envisaged a world where the most successful children were eugenically selected, would there be genetic haves and have-nots and a new type of discrimination—genoism—to accompany it? Moreover, how safe can it be to manipulate and create life? How likely are accidents that would unleash organisms onto a world that is not prepared for them? And will it be an easy technology for people bent on destruction to acquire? "We are talking about things that have never been done before," Endy said. "If the society that powered this technology collapses in some way, we would go extinct pretty quickly. You wouldn't have a chance to revert back to the farm or to the pre-farm. We would just be gone."

Those fears have existed since humans began to transplant genes in crops. They are the central reason that opponents of genetically engineered food invoke the precautionary principle, which argues that potential risks must always be given more weight than possible benefits. That is certainly the approach suggested by people like Jim Thomas, of ETC, who describes Endy as "the alpha Synthusiast." But he also regards Endy as a reflective scientist who doesn't discount the possible risks of his field. "To his credit, I think he's the one who's most engaged with these issues," Thomas said.

The debate over genetically engineered food has often focused on theoretical harm rather than on tangible benefits. "If you build a bridge and it falls down, you are not going to be permitted to design bridges ever again," Endy said. "But that doesn't mean we should never build a new bridge. There we have accepted the fact that risks are inevitable." He believes the same should be true of engineering biology.

We also have to think about our society's basic goals and how this science might help us achieve them. "We have seen an example with artemisinin and malaria," Endy said. "Maybe we could avoid diseases completely. That might require us to go through a transition in medicine akin to what happened in environmental science and engineering after the end of the Second World War. We had industrial problems, and people said, Hey, the river's on fire—let's put it out. And, after the nth time of doing that, people started to say, Maybe we shouldn't make factories that put shit into the river. So let's collect all the waste. That turns out to be really expensive, because then we have to dispose of it. Finally, people said, Let's redesign the factories so that they don't make that crap."

Endy pointed out that we are spending trillions of dollars on health care and that preventing disease is obviously more desirable than treating it. "My guess is that our ultimate solution to the crisis of health-care costs will be to redesign ourselves so that we don't have so many problems to deal with. But note," he stressed, "you can't possibly begin to do something like this if you don't have a value system in place that allows you to map concepts of ethics, beauty, and aesthetics onto our own existence.

"These are powerful choices. Think about what happens when you really can print the genome of your offspring. You could start with your own sequence, of course, and mash it up with your partner, or as many partners as you like. Because computers won't care. And, if you wanted evolution, you can include random-number generators." That would have the effect of introducing the element of chance into synthetic design.

Although Endy speaks with passion about the biological future, he acknowledges how little scientists know. "It is important to unpack some of the hype and expectation around what you can do with biotechnology as a manufacturing platform," he said. "We have not scratched the surface. But how far will we be able to go? That question needs to be discussed openly, because you can't address issues of risk and society unless you have an answer."

Answers, however, are not yet available. The inventor and materials scientist Saul Griffith has estimated that powering our planet requires between fifteen and eighteen terawatts of energy. How much of that could we manufacture with the tools of synthetic biology? Estimates range between five and ninety terawatts. "If it turns out to be the lower figure, we are screwed," Endy said. "Because why would we take this risk if we cannot create much energy? But, if it's the top figure, then we are talking about producing five times the energy we need on this planet and doing it in an environmentally benign way. The benefits in relation to the risks of using this new technology would be unquestioned. But I don't know what the number will be, and I don't think anybody *can* know at this point. At a minimum, then, we ought to acknowledge that we are in the process of figuring that out and the answers won't be easy to provide.

"It's very hard for me to have a conversation about these issues, because people adopt incredibly defensive postures," Endy continued. "The scientists on one side and civil-society organizations on the other. And, to be fair to those groups, science has often proceeded by skipping the dialogue. But some environmental groups will say, Let's not permit any of this work to get out of a laboratory until we are sure it is all safe. And as a practical matter that is not the way science works. We can't come back decades later with an answer. We need to develop solutions by doing them. The potential is great enough, I believe, to convince people it's worth the risk."

I wondered how much of this was science fiction. Endy stood up, "Can I show you something?" he asked, as he walked over to a bookshelf and grabbed four gray bottles. Each one contained about half a cup of sugar, and each had a letter on it A, T, C, or G, for the four nucleotides in our DNA. "You can buy jars of these chemicals that are derived from sugarcane," he said. "And they end up being the four bases of DNA in a form that can be readily assembled. You hook the bottles up to a machine, and into the machine comes information from a computer, a sequence of DNA—like T-A-A-T-A-G-C-A-A. You program in whatever you want to build, and that machine will stitch the genetic material together from scratch. This is the recipe: you take information and the raw chemicals and compile genetic material. Just sit down at your laptop and type the letters and out comes your organism."

We don't have machines that can turn those sugars into entire genomes yet. Endy shrugged. "But I don't see any physical reason why we won't," he said. "It's a question of money. If somebody wants to pay for it, then it will get done." He looked at his watch, apologized, and said, "I'm sorry, we will have to continue this discussion another day, because I have an appointment with some people from the Department of Homeland Security."

I was a little surprised. "They are asking the same questions as you," he said. "They want to know how far is this really going to go."

Scientists skipped a step at the birth of biotechnology, thirty-five years ago, moving immediately to products without first focusing on the tools required to make them. Using standard biological parts, a synthetic biologist or biological engineer can already, to some extent, program living organisms in the same way a computer scientist can program a computer. However, genes work together in ways that are staggeringly complex; proteins produced by one will counteract—or enhance—those made by another. We are far from the point where scientists might yank a few genes off the shelf, mix them together, and produce a variety of products. But the registry is growing rapidly—and so is the knowledge needed to drive the field forward.

Research in Endy's Stanford lab has been largely animated by his fascination with switches that turn genes on and off. He and his students are attempting to create genetically encoded memory systems, and his current goal is to construct a cell that can count to two hundred and fifty-six—a number derived from the mathematics of Basic computer code. Solving the practical challenges will not be easy, since cells that count will need to send reliable signals when they divide and remember that they did.

"If the cells in our bodies had a little memory, think what we could do," Endy said the next time we talked. I wasn't quite sure what he meant. "You have memory in your phone," he explained. "Think of all the information it allows you to store. The phone and the technology on which it is based do not function inside cells. But if we could count to two hundred, using a system that was based on proteins and DNA and RNA—well, now, all of a sudden we would have a tool that gives us access to computing and memory that we just don't have.

"Do you know how we study aging?" Endy continued. "The tools we use today are almost akin to cutting a tree in half and counting the rings. But if the cells had a memory we could count properly. Every time a cell divides, just move the counter by one. Maybe that will let me see them changing with a precision nobody can have today. Then I could give people controllers to start retooling those cells. Or we could say, Wow, this cell has divided two hundred times, it's obviously lost control of itself and become cancer. Kill it. That lets us think about new therapies for all kinds of diseases."

Synthetic biology is changing so rapidly that predictions seem pointless. Even that fact presents people like Endy with a new kind of problem. "Wayne Gretzky once said, 'I skate to where the puck is going to be.' That's what you do to become a great hockey player," Endy told me. "But where do you skate when the puck is accelerating at the speed of a rocket, when the trajectory is impossible to follow? Whom do you hire and what do we ask them to do? Because what preoccupies our finest minds today will be a seventh-grade science project in five years. Or three years.

"We are surfing an exponential now, and, even for people who pay attention, surfing an exponential is a really tricky thing to do. And when the exponential you are surfing has the capacity to impact the world in such a fundamental way, in ways we have never before considered, how do you even talk about that?"

For decades, people have invoked Moore's law: the number of transistors that could fit onto a silicon chip would double every two years, and so would the power of computers. When the I.B.M. 360 computer was released, in 1964, the top model came with eight megabytes of main memory, and cost more than two million dollars. Today, cell phones with a thousand times the memory of that computer can be bought for about a hundred dollars.

In 2001, Rob Carlson, then a research fellow at the Molecular Sciences Institute, in Berkeley, decided to examine a similar phenomenon: the speed at which the capacity to synthesize DNA was growing. He produced what has come to be known as the Carlson curve, and it shows a rate that mirrors Moore's law—and has even begun to exceed it. The automated DNA synthesizers used in thousands of labs cost a hundred thousand dollars a decade ago. Now they cost less than ten thousand dollars, and, most days, at least a dozen used synthesizers are for sale on eBay—for less than a thousand dollars.

Between 1977, when Frederick Sanger published the first paper on automatic DNA sequencing, and 1995, when the Institute for Genomic Research reported the first bacterial-genome sequence, the field moved slowly. It took the next six years to complete the first draft of the immeasurably more complex human genome, and six years after that, in 2007, scientists from around the world began mapping the full genomes of more than a thousand people. The Harvard geneticist George Church's Personal Genome Project now plans to sequence more than a hundred thousand.

In 2003, when Endy was still at M.I.T., he and his colleagues Tom Knight, Randy Rettberg, and Gerald Sussman founded iGEM—the International Genetically Engineered Machine competition—whose purpose is to promote the building of biological systems from standard parts. In 2006, a team of Endy's undergraduate students used BioBrick parts to genetically reprogram E. coli (which normally smells awful) to smell like wintergreen when it grows and like bananas when it is finished growing. They named their project Eau d'E Coli. By 2008, with more than a thousand students from twenty-one countries participating, the winning team—a group from Slovenia—used biological parts that it had designed to create a vaccine for the stomach bug *Helicobacter pylori,* which causes ulcers. There are no such working vaccines for humans. So far, the team has tested its creation on mice, with promising results.

This is open-source biology, where intellectual property is shared. What's available to idealistic students, of course, would also be available to terrorists. Any number of blogs offer advice about everything from how to preserve proteins to the best methods for desalting DNA. Openness like that can be frightening, and there have been calls for tighter control of the technology. Carlson, among many others, believes that strict regulations are unlikely to succeed. Several years ago, with very few tools other than a credit card, he opened his own biotechnology company, Biodesic, in the garage of his Seattle home—a biological version of the do-it-yourself movement that gave birth to so many computer companies, including Apple.

The product that he developed enables the identification of proteins using DNA technology. "It's not complex," Carlson told me, "but I wanted to see what I could accomplish using mail order and synthesis." A great deal, it turned out. Carlson designed the molecule on his laptop, then sent the sequence to a company that synthesizes DNA. Most of the instruments could be bought on eBay (or, occasionally, on LabX, a more specialized site for scientific equipment). All you need is an Internet connection.

"Strict regulation doesn't accomplish its goals," Carlson said. "It's not an exact analogy, but look at Prohibition. What happened when government restricted the production and sale of alcohol? Crime rose dramatically. It became organized and powerful. Legitimate manufacturers could not sell alcohol, but it was easy to make in a garage—or a warehouse."

By 2002, the U.S. government intensified its effort to curtail the sale and production of methamphetamine. Previously, the drug had been manufactured in many mom-and-pop labs throughout the country. Today, production has been professionalized and centralized, and the Drug Enforcement Administration says that less is known about methamphetamine production than before. "The black market is getting blacker," Carlson said. "Crystal-meth use is still rising, and all this despite restrictions." Strict control would not necessarily insure the same fate for synthetic biology, but it might.

Bill Joy, a founder of Sun Microsystems, has frequently called for restrictions on the use of technology. "It is even possible that self-replication be more fundamental than we thought, and hence harder—or even impossible—to control," he wrote in an essay for *Wired* called "Why the Future Doesn't Need Us." "The only realistic alternative I see is relinquishment: to limit development of the technologies that are too dangerous, by limiting our pursuit of certain kinds of knowledge."

Still, censoring the pursuit of knowledge has never really worked, in part because there are no parameters for society to decide who should have information and who should not. The opposite approach might give us better results: accelerate the development of technology and open it to more people and educate them to its purpose. Otherwise, if Carlson's methamphetamine analogy proves accurate, power would flow directly into the hands of the people least likely to use it wisely.

For synthetic biology to accomplish any of its goals, we will also need an education system that encourages skepticism and the study of science. In 2007, students in Singapore, Japan, China, and Hong Kong (which was counted independently) all performed better on an international science exam than American students. The U.S. scores have remained essentially stagnant since 1995, the first year the exam was administered. Adults are even less scientifically literate. Early in 2009, the results of a California Academy of Sciences poll (conducted throughout the nation) revealed that only fifty-three percent of American adults know how long it takes for the Earth to revolve around the sun, and a slightly larger number—fifty-nine percent—are aware that dinosaurs and humans never lived at the same time

Synthetic biologists will have to overcome this ignorance. Optimism prevails only when people are engaged and excited. Why should we bother? Not just to make E. coli smell like chewing gum or fish glow in vibrant colors. The planet is in danger, and nature needs help.

The hydrocarbons we burn for fuel are believed to be nothing more than concentrated sunlight that has been collected by leaves and trees. Organic matter rots, bacteria break it down, and it moves underground, where, after millions of years of pressure, it turns into oil and coal. At that point, we dig it up—at huge expense and with disastrous environmental consequences. Across the globe, on land and sea, we sink wells and lay pipe to ferry our energy to giant refineries. That has been the industrial model of development, and it worked for nearly two centuries. It won't work any longer.

The industrial age is drawing to a close, eventually to be replaced by an era of biological engineering. That won't happen easily (or quickly), and it will never solve every problem we expect it to solve. But what worked for artemisinin can work for many of the products our species will need to survive. "We are going to start doing the same thing that we do with our pets, with bacteria," the genomic futurist Juan Enriquez has said, describing our transition from a world that relied on machines to one that relies on biology. "A house pet is a domesticated parasite," he noted. "It is evolved to have an interaction with human beings. Same thing with corn"—a crop that didn't exist until we created it. "Same thing is going to start happening with energy," he went on. "We are going to start domesticating bacteria to process stuff inside enclosed reactors to produce energy in a far more clean and efficient manner. This is just the beginning stage of being able to program life."

QUESTIONS FOR MAKING CONNECTIONS WITHIN THE READING

1. Throughout Specter's article, the scientists he meets describe synthetic biology using terms borrowed from industry, computer science, and the world of business. Berkeley's Jay Keasling foresees the day when "biological parts" will be standardized, like tools we can buy off the shelf. Craig Venter looks forward to "booting up" new forms of life by transplanting artificial chromosomes. Freeman Dyson, the distinguished physicist, predicts that the children in primary school will play biotech games that might involve competitions to invent the cutest new species. What are some of the potential consequences of this view of nature? Can you think of other ways to talk about nature—and other ways of interacting with it as well?

2. According to Specter, what are some of the potential dangers of bioengineering? What are some of the ethical and philosophical issues that surround it? How much of his article does he devote to questions of this kind? When Drew Endy describes the construction of new life as "scary as hell," do you believe that he is genuinely worried? Does he offer a convincing rationale for taking such enormous risks? And where do you think Specter's loyalties lie? Is he neutral, or would you say that he leans in one direction or the other? Why does he prefer "synthetic biology" to the term "bioengineering"?

3. Can you find "oppositional voices" in Specter's essay—in other words, the voices of those who are suspicious of genetic technology? What arguments do these voices offer for putting the brakes on its development? One of the technology's defenders, John Melo, the founder of Amyris, frames the debate using these terms: "Anything so powerful and new is troubling. But I don't think the answer to the future is to race into the past." In what ways is synthetic biology an "answer to the future"? In what ways might it create new problems instead? Are its opponents actually arguing for a "race into the past"?

QUESTIONS FOR WRITING

1. Many of the people that Specter interviews are not only scientists but entrepreneurs with an enormous financial stake in their new enterprises. Given that most businesses put profits first and that new technologies have outstripped existing legal constraints, should the logic of the marketplace be allowed to replace natural evolution, which has shaped life on earth for billions of years? If the concept of "profit" is a human invention, what goals has natural evolution pursued? How might the logic of natural evolution be more humane in the long run than the logic of the marketplace? Or, might the marketplace be more humane than natural evolution—more responsive to human needs? Do evolutionary principles guide the market itself?

2. Even as he acknowledges the risks of genetic engineering, Specter represents the growth of this new knowledge as virtually unstoppable. In fact, he predicts that by trying to stop it, authorities will only drive it underground, like the thriving illegal industry that produces methamphetamines. Do you find this reasoning persuasive? Could it not be used to justify any activity at all, including slavery and child prostitution, both of which continue even though they are universally condemned? What authority should the citizens of a democracy exercise over technologies that involve large and unpredictable risks? Do these citizens have the right to say "no" to some innovations?

QUESTIONS FOR MAKING CONNECTIONS
BETWEEN READINGS

1. In "Another Look Back, and a Look Ahead," Edward Tenner describes what he calls "revenge effects," the unintended consequences of technological innovation, no matter how carefully designed. Tenner portrays revenge effects as unavoidable, yet he concludes that "the prognosis" for technology in general is primarily "hopeful." He believes that these effects can be kept "under control" because "technology too is evolving and responding." How well does Tenner's argument apply to bioengineering, and why might this be a different case than the ones he considers? Could the costs of error simply prove too high, or does the new technology give us the tools to correct our mistakes in time?

2. In "Rewilding North America," Carolyn Fraser takes us on a tour of a project markedly different from Specter's synthetic biology. Rather than redesign nature to make it more amenable to our lives in a consumer society, rewilding sets out to change the human world in a way that will accommodate more of nature as it has existed for many millions of years. Which approach seems more likely to succeed, and why—changing nature, or changing how we live? Genetic technology would seem to hold the promise of more rapid economic growth, but is economic growth the only way to measure our society's success? How might rewilding offer us a different image of well-being?

MARTHA STOUT

WHAT IS SANITY? Are "normal" people always dependably sane, or could it be said that we experience sanity only as a temporary, fluctuating state? After witnessing a traumatic event, have you ever spent time in a state that is not exactly sane, a state of either frantic agitation or numbness, withdrawal, and distraction? These are the questions that Martha Stout, a clinical psychologist in private practice and the best-selling author of *The Sociopath Next Door* (2005) and *The Paranoia Switch* (2007), pursued in her first book, *The Myth of Sanity: Divided Consciousness and the Promise of Awareness* (2002). Stout taught psychology at Harvard Medical School for 26 years. Drawing on this and her nearly 30 years of clinical experience specializing in treating patients who have suffered psychological trauma, Stout uses her case studies to show that the ability to dissociate from reality, which functions as a life-preserving defense mechanism during times of stress in childhood, can develop into a way of life that leads to emotional detachment and prolonged disengagement with the world. In the most extreme cases, the dissociative behavior can lead individuals to black out for extended periods of time or to develop multiple personalities in order to contend with life's many demands.

In seeking to establish a continuum that extends from the everyday experience of spacing out to the more traumatic experience of being shell-shocked, Stout invites her readers to recognize just how common the experience of dementia, or "self-shifting," can be. The patients Stout focuses on have been forced to come to terms with the extreme forms this dementia can take, and, with her help, they come to see the meaning of their own lives as something they must continually work to construct. In jargonfree prose, Stout tells stories of her patients' struggles for and with sanity, revealing in each case how buried or missing memories of the past serve to disrupt and distort the experience of the present.

Stout, Martha. "When I Woke Up Tuesday Morning, It Was Friday," in *The Myth of Sanity: Divided Consciousness and the Promise of Awareness*. New York: Penguin Books, 2002. 15–43.

Biographical information comes from <http://harvard.com/events/press_release.php?id=1880> and <http://www.huffingtonpost.com/dr-martha-stout/>.

When I Woke Up Tuesday Morning, It Was Friday

"The horror of that moment," the King went on, "I shall never, never forget!"

"You will, though," the Queen said, "if you don't make a memorandum of it."

—LEWIS CARROLL

Imagine that you are in your house—no—you are *locked* in your house, cannot get out. It is the dead of winter. The drifted snow is higher than your windows, blocking the light of both moon and sun. Around the house, the wind moans, night and day.

Now imagine that even though you have plenty of electric lights, and perfectly good central heating, you are almost always in the dark and quite cold, because something is wrong with the old-fashioned fuse box in the basement. Inside this cobwebbed, innocuous-looking box, the fuses keep burning out, and on account of this small malfunction, all the power in the house repeatedly fails. You have replaced so many melted fuses that now your little bag of new ones is empty; there are no more. You sigh in frustration, and regard your frozen breath in the light of the flashlight. Your house, which could be so cozy, is tomblike instead.

In all probability, there is something quirky in the antiquated fuse box; it has developed some kind of needless hair trigger, and is not really reacting to any dangerous electrical overload at all. Should you get some pennies out of your pocket, and use them to replace the burned-out fuses? That would solve the power-outage problem. No more shorts, not with copper coins in there. Using coins would scuttle the safeguard function of the fuse box, but the need for a safeguard right now is questionable, and the box is keeping you cold and in the dark for no good reason. Well, probably for no good reason.

On the other hand, what if the wiring in the house really is overloaded somehow? A fire could result, probably will result eventually. If you do not find the fire soon enough, if you cannot manage to put the fire out, the whole house could go up, with you trapped inside. You know that death by burning is hideous. You know also that your mind is playing tricks, but thinking about fire, you almost imagine there is smoke in your nostrils right now.

So, do you go back upstairs and sit endlessly in a dark living room, defeated, numb from the cold, though you have buried yourself under every blanket in the house? No light to read by, no music, just the wail and rattle of the icy wind outside? Or, in an attempt to feel more human, do you make things warm and comfortable? Is it wise to gamble with calamity and howling pain? If you turn the power back on, will you not smell nonexistent smoke every moment you are awake? And will you not have far too many of these waking moments, for how will you ever risk going to sleep?

Do you sabotage the fuse box?

I believe that most of us cannot know what we would do, trapped in a situation that required such a seemingly no-win decision. But I do know that anyone wanting to recover from psychological trauma must face just this kind of dilemma, made yet more harrowing because her circumstance is not anything so rescuable as being locked in a house, but rather involves a solitary, unlockable confinement inside the limits of her own mind. The person who suffers from a severe trauma disorder must decide between surviving in a barely sublethal misery of numbness and frustration, and taking a chance that may well bring her a better life, but that feels like stupidly issuing an open invitation to the unspeakable horror that waits to consume her alive. And in the manner of the true hero, she must choose to take the risk.

For trauma changes the brain itself. Like the outdated fuse box, the psychologically traumatized brain houses inscrutable eccentricities that cause it to over-react—or more precisely, *mis*react—to the current realities of life. These neurological misreactions become established because trauma has a profound effect upon the secretion of stress-responsive neurohormones such as norepinephrine, and thus an effect upon various areas of the brain involved in memory, particularly the amygdala and the hippocampus.

The amygdala receives sensory information from the five senses, via the thalamus, attaches emotional significance to the input, and then passes along this emotional "evaluation" to the hippocampus. In accordance with the amygdala's "evaluation" of importance, the hippocampus is activated to a greater or lesser degree, and functions to organize the new input, and to integrate it with already existing information about similar sensory events. Under a normal range of conditions, this system works efficiently to consolidate memories according to their emotional priority. However, at the extreme upper end of hormonal stimulation, as in traumatic situations, a breakdown occurs. Overwhelming emotional significance registered by the amygdala actually leads to a *decrease in hippocampal activation,* such that some of the traumatic input is not usefully organized by the hippocampus, or integrated with other memories. The result is that portions of traumatic memory are stored not as parts of a unified whole, but as isolated sensory images and bodily sensations that are not localized in time or even in situation, or integrated with other events.

To make matters still more complex, exposure to trauma may temporarily shut down Broca's area, the region of the left hemisphere of the brain that translates experience into language, the means by which we most often relate our experience to others, and even to ourselves.

A growing body of research indicates that in these ways the brain lays down traumatic memories differently from the way it records regular memories.

Regular memories are formed through adequate hippocampal and cortical input, are integrated as comprehensible wholes, and are subject to meaning-modification by future events, and through language. In contrast, traumatic memories include chaotic fragments that are sealed off from modulation by subsequent experience. Such memory fragments are wordless, placeless, and eternal, and long after the original trauma has receded into the past, the brain's record of it may consist only of isolated and thoroughly anonymous bits of emotion, image, and sensation that ring through the individual like a broken alarm.

Worse yet, later in the individual's life, in situations that are vaguely similar to the trauma—perhaps merely because they are startling, anxiety-provoking, or emotionally arousing—amygdala-mediated memory traces are accessed more readily than are the more complete, less shrill memories that have been integrated and modified by the hippocampus and the cerebral cortex. Even though unified and updated memories would be more judicious in the present, the amygdala memories are more accessible, and so trauma may be "remembered" at inappropriate times, when there is no hazard worthy of such alarm. In reaction to relatively trivial stresses, the person traumatized long ago may truly *feel* that danger is imminent again, be assailed full-force by the emotions, bodily sensations, and perhaps even the images, sounds, smells that once accompanied great threat.

Here is an illustration from everyday life. A woman named Beverly reads a morning newspaper while she sits at a quiet suburban depot and waits for a train. The article, concerning an outrageous local scandal, intrigues her so much that for a few minutes she forgets where she is. Suddenly, there is an earsplitting blast from the train as it signals its arrival. Beverly is painfully startled by the noise; her head snaps up, and she catches her breath. She is amazed that she could have been so lacking in vigilance and relaxed in public. Her heart pounds, and in the instant required to fold the newspaper, she is ambushed by bodily feelings and even a smell that have nothing whatever to do with the depot on this uneventful morning. If she could identify the smell, which she never will, she would call it "chlorine." She feels a sudden rigidity in her chest, as if her lungs had just turned to stone, and has an almost overpowering impulse to get out of there, to run.

In a heartbeat, the present is perceptually and emotionally the past. These fragments of sensation and emotion are the amygdala-mediated memories of an afternoon three decades before, in Beverly's tenth summer, when, walking home from the public swimming pool, she saw her younger sister skip into the street and meet an immediate death in front of a speeding car. At this moment, thirty years later, Beverly *feels* that way again.

Her sensations and feelings are not labeled as belonging to memories of the horrible accident. In fact, they are not labeled as anything at all, because they have always been completely without language. They belong to no narrative, no place or time, no story she can tell about her life; they are free-form and ineffable.

Beverly's brain contains, effectively, a broken warning device in its limbic system, an old fuse box in which the fuses tend to melt for no good reason, emphatically declaring an emergency where none now exists.

Surprisingly, she will probably not wonder about or even remember the intense perceptual and emotional "warnings," because by the next heartbeat, a long-entrenched dissociative reaction to the declared emergency may already have been tripped in her brain, to "protect" her from this "unbearable" childhood memory. She may feel strangely angry, or paranoid, or childishly timid. Or instead she may feel that she has begun to move in an uncomfortably hazy dream world, far away and derealized. Or she may completely depart from her "self" for awhile, continue to act, but without self-awareness. Should this last occur in a minor way, her total experience may be something such as, "Today when I was going to work, the train pulled into the station—the blasted thing is so loud!—and the next thing I remember, it was stopping at my stop." She may even be mildly amused at herself for her spaciness.

Most of us do not notice these experiences very much. They are more or less invisible to us as we go about daily life, and so we do not understand how much of daily life is effectively spent in the past, in reaction to the darkest hours we have known, nor do we comprehend how swampy and vitality-sucking some of our memories really are. Deepening the mire of our divided awareness, in the course of a lifetime such "protective" mental reactions acquire tremendous *habit strength*. These over-exercised muscles can take us away even when traumatic memory fragments have not been evoked. Sometimes dissociation can occur when we are simply confused or frustrated or nervous, whether we recognize our absences or not.

Typically, only those with the most desperate trauma histories are ever driven to discover and perhaps modify their absences from the present. Only the addictions, major depressions, suicide attempts, and general ruination that attend the most severe trauma disorders can sometimes supply motivation sufficiently fierce to run the gauntlet thrown down by insight and permanent change. On account of our neurological wiring, confronting past traumas requires one to re-endure all of their terrors mentally, in their original intensity, to feel as if the worst nightmare had come true and the horrors had returned. All the brain's authoritative warnings against staying present for the memories and the painful emotions, all the faulty fuses, have to be deliberately ignored, and in cases of extreme or chronic past trauma, this process is nothing short of heroic.

It helps to have an awfully good reason to try, such as suffocating depression or some other demonic psychological torment. Perhaps this is a part of the reason why philosophers and theologians through the centuries have observed such a strong connection between unbearable earthly sorrow and spiritual enlightenment, a timeless relationship that psychologists have mysteriously overlooked.

In order to appreciate what psychological trauma can do to the mind, and to a life, let us consider an extreme case of divided awareness, that of a woman whose psyche was mangled by profound trauma in her past, and who came to me for treatment after several serious suicide attempts. Her story is far grimmer than most of us will ever know, and the consequent suffering in her adult life has been nearly unsurvivable. And yet, should one meet her on the street, or know her only casually, she would seem quite normal. In fact, one might easily view her as enviable. Certainly, when looking on from a distance, nothing at all would appear to be wrong, and much would be conspicuously right.

Julia is brilliant. After the *summa cum laude* from Stanford, and the full scholarship at the graduate school in New York, she became an award-winning producer of documentary films. I met her when she was thirty-two, and an intellectual force to be reckoned with. A conversation with her reminds me of the *New York Review of Books,* except that she is funnier, and also a living, breathing human being who wears amethyst jewelry to contrast with her electric auburn hair. Her ultramarine eyes gleam, even when she is depressed, giving one the impression, immediately upon meeting her, that there is something special about her. She is, however, soft-spoken and disarming in the extreme. She does not glorify, does not even seem to notice, either her prodigious intelligence or her beauty.

Those same blue eyes notice everything, instantly, photographically. The first time she walked into my office, she said, "Oh how nice. Did you get that little statue in Haiti? I did a kind of project there once. What a spellbinding place!"

She was referring to a small soapstone figurine, the rounded abstraction of a kneeling man, that I had indeed purchased in Port-au-Prince, and that sat on a shelf parallel to my office door. She had not glanced back in that direction as she came in, and must have captured and processed the image in a microsecond of peripheral perception.

"That's very observant," I said, whereupon she directed at me a smile so sparkling and so warm that, for just the barest moment, her lifelong depression cracked and vanished from the air around her, as if it had been nothing but a bubble. The radiance of her momentary smile caused me to blink, and I knew exactly then, even before the first session began, that if she would let me, I would do everything I could to keep this particular light from going out.

At a moment's notice, Julia can speak entertainingly and at length about film, music, multicultural psychology, African politics, theories of literary criticism, and any number of other subjects. Her memory for detail is beyond exceptional, and she has the storyteller's gift. When she is recounting information, or a story, her own intellectual fascination with it gives her voice the poised and expertly modulated quality of the narrator of a high-budget documentary about some especially wondrous endangered animals, perhaps Tibetan snow leopards. She speaks a few astutely inflected sentences, and then pauses, almost as if she is listening—and expects you to be listening—for the stealthy *crunch-crunch* of paws on the snow's crust.

Curious about this, I once asked her whether she were an actress as well as a filmmaker. She laughed, and replied that she could do first-rate narrative voice-overs, if she did say so herself, but had not a smidgen of real theatrical ability. In fact, she said, sometimes the people she worked with teased her good-naturedly about this minor chink in her armor.

At my first session with her, when I asked her why she had come to therapy, she spent thirty minutes telling me in cinematic detail about her recent attempt to kill herself, by driving to an isolated Massachusetts beach at three A.M. on a

Tuesday in late January, and lying down by the surf. By so doing, she sincerely expected not to be found until well after she had frozen to death. Taking her omniscient narrator tone, intellectually intrigued by the memory, she described the circumstances of her unlikely accidental rescue by a group of drunken college students, and then spent the second thirty minutes of our hour together likening this near-death experience to the strangely impersonal distance from a story one can achieve on film with certain authorial camera moves.

"By then, I was floating above myself, looking down, sort of waiting. And I know I couldn't actually have seen those kids, but I *felt* that I did. Over the sound of the waves, I don't think you can really *hear* footsteps in the sand, but still...."

And I strained to hear the *crunch-crunch*.

Therapy is a frightening thing, and people do not often seek it out because they are only mildly unhappy. In my work, and because of the high-risk individuals who are referred to me, it is not unusual for me to hear stories of attempted suicide from people I have only just met. I have come almost to expect such accounts, in fact.

At our second session, and in exactly the same tone she had used to describe her suicide attempt, Julia began by giving me an interesting account of her new project on the life of a promising writer who had died young, reportedly of a rare blood disease he had contracted in western China. After about fifteen minutes of this, I stopped her, and explained that I wanted to know something about her, about Julia herself, rather than about Julia's work. Seeing the blank expression come over her face, I tried to provide her with some nonthreatening guidance. I asked her some general, factual questions about her childhood.

And at that second session, this is what the articulate, intellectually gifted Julia remembered about her own childhood: An only child, she knew that she had been born in Los Angeles, but she did not know in which hospital. She vaguely remembered that when she was about ten, her parents had moved with her to another neighborhood; but she did not remember anything about the first neighborhood, or even where it was. Though she did not know for sure, she assumed that the move must have taken place because her parents had become more prosperous. She remembered that she had a friend in high school named Barbara (with whom "I must have spent a lot of time"), but she could not remember Barbara's last name, or where Barbara had gone after high school. I asked Julia about her teachers, and she could not remember a single one of them, not from grade school, not from middle school, not from high school. She could not remember whether or not she had gone to her high school prom or her high school graduation. The only thing she seemed to remember vividly from childhood was that when she was about twelve, she had a little terrier dog named Grin, and that her mother had Grin put to sleep when he needed an expensive stomach operation.

And that was all she remembered of her childhood, this successful thirty-two-year-old woman with the cinematic mind. And it took forty-five minutes for her to pull out that much from the dark, silent place that housed her early memories. She could not remember a single holiday or a single birthday. At thirty-two, she could swim, read, drive a car, and play a few songs on the piano. But she could not remember learning any of these skills.

Insufficient memory in the context of an adequate intellect, let alone a gifted one, is the next observation—right after the extraordinary understatement and humor—that causes me to become suspicious about a patient's past.

At our third session, she asked me an astonishing question, but also, really, the obvious question: "Do other people remember those things, about their teachers, and going to their graduation, and learning to drive, and so on?" When I told her that, yes, they usually do remember, at least to a much greater degree than she did, she reverently said, "Wow," and then she was quiet for a few minutes. Finally, she leaned forward a little and asked, "So what's wrong with me?"

Cautiously, because I knew what I had to say might at first sound preposterous or worse to Julia, I said, "I'm wondering about early traumatic experiences in your life. Even when someone's cognitive memory is perfectly good, as yours is, trauma can disrupt the memory in emotional ways."

Julia thought I was way off base; or at least the part of her that collected amethyst jewelry, made award-winning films, and talked about camera angles thought I was way off base. Another part of Julia, the part that kept trying to commit suicide, the part that prevented her from moving back to Los Angeles as her career demanded, the part that sometimes made her so sleepy during the middle of an ordinary day that she had to be driven home, that part kept her coming back to therapy for the next six years. During those six years, step by step, Julia and I cast some light on what had happened to her. She agreed to be hypnotized; she began to remember her dreams; she acknowledged her faint suspicions. She even traveled back to Los Angeles, to talk with distant relatives and old neighbors.

What we eventually discovered was that, when she was a child, Julia had lived in a house of horrors, with monsters jumping out at her without warning and for no apparent reason, except that Julia had come to assume, as abused children do, that she must be a horrible person who deserved these punishments. By the time she was school age, she had learned not to cry, because tears only encouraged her parents to abuse her further. Also, she had lost any inclination whatsoever to let anyone know what was going on. Telling someone and asking for help were concepts foreign to her despairing little soul. The thought that her life might be different had simply stopped occurring to her.

And soon, in a sense, she had stopped telling even herself. When the abuse began, she would "go somewhere else"; she would "not be there." By this, she meant that her mind had learned how to dissociate Julia's self from what was going on around her, how to transport her awareness to a place far enough away that, at most, she felt she was watching the life of a little girl named Julia from a very great distance. A sad little girl named Julia was helpless and could not escape; but psychologically, Julia's self could go "somewhere else," could be psychologically absent.

Simply put, Julia did not remember her childhood because she was not present for it.

All human beings have the capacity to dissociate psychologically, though most of us are unaware of this, and consider "out-of-body" episodes to be far beyond the boundaries of our normal experience. In fact, dissociative experiences happen to everyone, and most of these events are quite ordinary.

Consider a perfectly ordinary person as he walks into a perfectly ordinary movie theater to see a popular movie. He is awake, alert, and oriented to his surroundings. He is aware that his wife is with him and that, as they sit down in their aisle seats, she is to his right. He is aware that he has a box of popcorn on his lap. He knows that the movie he has come to see is entitled *The Fugitive,* and that its star is Harrison Ford, an actor. As he waits for the movie to begin, perhaps he worries about a problem he is having at work.

Then the lights in the theater are lowered, and the movie starts. And within twenty-five minutes, he has utterly lost his grasp on reality. Not only is he no longer worried about work, he no longer realizes that he has a job. If one could read his thoughts, one would discover that he no longer believes he is sitting in a theater, though in reality, he is. He cannot smell his popcorn; some of it tumbles out of the box he now holds slightly askew, because he has forgotten about his own hands. His wife has vanished, though any observer would see that she is still seated four inches to his right.

And without moving from his own seat, he is running, running, running—not with Harrison Ford, the actor—but with the beleaguered fugitive in the movie, with, in other words, a person who does not exist at all, in this moviegoer's real world or anyone else's. His heart races as he dodges a runaway train that does not exist, either.

This perfectly ordinary man is dissociated from reality. Effectively, he is in a trance. We might label his perceptions as psychotic, except for the fact that when the movie is over, he will return to his usual mental status almost instantly. He will see the credits. He will notice that he has spilled some popcorn, although he will not remember doing so. He will look to his right and speak to his wife. More than likely, he will tell her that he liked the movie, as we all tend to enjoy entertainments in which we can become lost. All that really happened is that, for a little while, he took the part of himself that worries about work problems and other "real" things, and separated it from the imaginative part of himself, so that the imaginative part could have dominance. He *dissociated* one part of his consciousness from another part.

When dissociation is illustrated in this way, most people can acknowledge that they have had such interludes from time to time, at a movie or a play, reading a book or hearing a speech, or even just daydreaming. And then the out-of-body may sound a little closer to home. Plainly stated, it is the case that under certain circumstances, ranging from pleasant or unpleasant distraction to fascination to fear to pain to horror, a human being can be psychologically absent from his or her own direct experience. We can go somewhere else. The part of consciousness that we nearly always conceive of as the "self" can be not there for a few moments, for a few hours, and in heinous circumstances, for much longer.

As the result of a daydream, this mental compartmentalization is called distraction. As the result of an involving movie, it is often called escape. As the result of trauma, physical or psychological, it is called a dissociative state. When a hypnotist induces dissociation, by monotony, distraction, relaxation, or any number of other methods, the temporary result is called an hypnotic state, or a trance. The physiological patterns and the primary behavioral results of distraction, escape, dissociative state, and trance are virtually identical, regardless of method. The differences among them seem to result not so much from how consciousness gets divided as from how often and how long one is forced to keep it divided.

Another recognizable example of how consciousness can be split into pieces has to do with the perception of physical pain. On the morning after seeing *The Fugitive,* our moviegoer's wife is working frenetically to pack her briefcase, eat her breakfast, get the kids off to school, and listen to a news report on television, all at the same time. She is very distracted. In the process of all this, she bashes her leg soundly against the corner of a low shelf. Yet the woman is not seemingly aware that she has injured herself. That night, as she is getting ready for bed, she notices that she has a large colorful bruise on her right thigh. She thinks, "Well, now, I wonder how I did that."

In this case, a person was distracted, and the part of her consciousness that would normally have perceived pain was split apart from, and subjugated to, the part of her consciousness that was goal-directed. She was not there for the direct experience of her pain. She was somewhere else (the briefcase, the breakfast, the kids, the news). And because she was not there, she does not remember the accident.

The direct experience of physical pain can be split off in cases of much more serious injury as well. Most of us have heard stories along the lines of the parent who, with a broken leg, goes back to the scene of an accident and wrenches open a mangled car door with her bare hands in order to rescue her child. Less valorous, I myself remember my car being demolished by a speeding limousine. My knee was injured, but I felt no pain just after the crash, was more or less unaware of my body at all. My first thought before being dragged out of my car was to peer into the rearview mirror and inspect my teeth, and to decide that everything must be okay because there were no chips in them. And then there are the war stories about maimed infantrymen who have had to flee from the front line. All such circumstances affect memory in fascinating ways. Note, for example, that when veterans get together, they often laugh and tell war stories as though those times had been the best of their lives.

Agony that is psychological can be dissociated, too. While she was being abused, Julia developed the reaction of standing apart from herself and her situation. She stopped being there. Certainly, some parts of her consciousness must have been there right along. She could watch her parents, even predict their moods. She could run and hide. She could cover her injuries. She could keep her parents' secrets. But the part of her consciousness that she thinks of as her self was not there; it was split off, put aside, and therefore in some sense protected. And because her self had not been there, her self could not remember what had happened to her during much of her childhood.

What does this feel like, not being able to remember whole chapters of one's own life? I have asked many people this question, Julia among them. As usual, her answer was obvious and startling at the same time.

"It doesn't feel like anything," she answered. "I never really thought about it. I guess I just assumed, sort of tacitly assumed, that everyone's memory was like mine, that is to say, kind of blank before the age of twenty or so. I mean, you can't see into someone else's mind, right? All you can do is ask questions, and it never even occurred to me to ask anybody about this. It's like asking, 'What do you see when you see blue?' First of all, you'd never think to ask. And secondly, two people can agree that the clear blue sky is blue, but does the actual color blue look the *same* to both of them? Who knows? How would you even ask that question?

"Of course, every now and then I'd hear people talking about pin-the-tail-on-the-donkey, or some other thing about a little kid's birthday, and I'd wonder how they knew that. But I guess I just figured their memory was especially good, or maybe they'd heard their parents talk about it so much that it seemed like a memory.

"The memories I did have seemed like aberrations, like pinpoints of light in a dark room, so vague that you're not really sure whether you're seeing them or not. Certainly, there was nothing like a continuous thread of memory that linked one part of my life to another.

"Really it wasn't until you started asking me questions about my teachers and so forth that I ever even had any serious questions about my memory. After you started asking, I asked a couple of other people, just out of curiosity, and I began to realize that other people really do have childhood memories, and some of them are pretty vivid. I was surprised.

"What can I tell you? It just never occurred to me to wonder about it before. It felt like ... it felt like nothing."

She shrugged. Most people shrug. They are genuinely surprised, and at a loss.

Now the conspicuous question to ask Julia was, "All this time that you've been so unhappy, all the times you've tried to end your life, what did you think was causing all that misery?"

"I thought I was crazy," she answered.

This is easy enough to understand. Imagine a simple and, relatively speaking, innocuous example. Imagine that someone, call her Alice, leaves work early one day and goes to the oral surgeon to have her two bottom wisdom teeth extracted. The extractions go well; the doctor packs the gums with cotton and sends Alice home. On the way home, for some fictitious reason, let us say magic moonbeams, Alice completely loses her memory of the visit to the oral surgeon. She now assumes that she is driving directly home from work, as she does on most days. After she gets home, she is okay for a while, but gradually the anesthetic wears off, and she begins to experience a considerable amount of pain in her mouth. Soon the pain is too strong to ignore, and she goes to the bathroom mirror to examine the situation. When she looks into her mouth, she discovers that there are wads of cotton in there. And when she takes the cotton out, she discovers that two of her teeth are missing, and she is bleeding!

Alice is now in the twilight zone. The ordinary experience of having her wisdom teeth pulled has turned into a situation that makes her feel insane. One or two more of such experiences, and she would be convinced.

Childhood trauma creates a particularly bewildering picture. Observe normal children at play, and you will realize that children are especially good at dissociating. In the interest of play, a child can, in a heartbeat, leave himself behind, become someone or something else, or several things at once. Reality is even more plastic in childhood. Pretend games are real and wonderful and consuming. It is clear to anyone who really looks that normal children derive unending joy from their superior ability to leap out of their "selves" and go somewhere else, be other things. The snow is not cold. The body is not tired, even when it is on the verge of collapse.

Because children dissociate readily even in ordinary circumstances, when they encounter traumatic situations, they easily split their consciousness into pieces, often for extended periods of time. The self is put aside and hidden. Of course, this reaction is functional for the traumatized child, necessary, even kind. For the traumatized child, a dissociative state, far from being dysfunctional or crazy, may in fact be lifesaving. And thanks be to the normal human mind that it provides the means.

This coping strategy becomes dysfunctional only later, after the child is grown and away from the original trauma. When the original trauma is no longer an ongoing fact of life, prolonged dissociative reactions are no longer necessary. But through the years of intensive use, the self-protective strategy has developed a hair trigger. The adult whom the child has become now experiences dissociative reactions to levels of stress that probably would not cause another person to dissociate.

The events that are most problematic tend to be related in some way to the original trauma. However, human beings are exquisitely symbolic creatures, and "related" can reach unpredictable and often indecipherable levels of abstraction and metaphor. A long shadow from a city streetlight can remind someone of the tall cacti on the Arizona desert where his father used to threaten to "feed" him to the rattlesnakes. An innocent song about the wind in the willow trees can remind someone else of the rice fields that were a part of her childhood's landscape in Cambodia. A car backfiring on Beacon Street in Boston can remind yet another person of that spot on the trail where his eighteen-year-old platoon mate exploded six feet in front of him.

And so for the adult who was traumatized as a child, the present too has a kind of mercurial quality. The present is difficult to hold on to, always getting away.

In Julia's case, though she had not questioned her poverty of memory for the past, she had begun to suspect even before she came into therapy that she was losing time in the present. Probably this is because there are more external reality checks on the present than there are on the past. From other people—and from radio, television, the Internet, date books—there are ongoing reminders of the present time of day, and day of the week. Markers of time in the past are less immediate, and sooner or later most dates and chronologies for the past begin to feel amorphous to us all. It is hardly amazing that one should have forgotten something that happened twenty years ago. But if a person lets on that she has no memory of an important event that occurred this very week, friends and associates are unlikely to let such a lapse go unremarked.

At one of her early sessions with me, Julia announced, "When I woke up Tuesday morning it was Friday."

"Pardon?"

"When I woke up this morning it was Tuesday, and then I discovered that it was Friday for everybody else."

"How do you mean?"

"Well, the last thing I remember before waking up this morning was having dinner Monday night. So I thought it was Tuesday. And then I went in to work, and some sponsors were there that I was supposed to meet with on Friday. So I asked my assistant what was up, and she said, 'You wanted to meet with these people this morning, remember?' And I said, 'No. I wanted to meet with them on Friday.' She looked at me, and said, 'Today is Friday, Julia.'

"I finessed. I laughed and said, 'Of course. That's terrible. No more late nights for me. Pretty soon I'll be forgetting my name. Ha, ha.' But it isn't funny. This happens a lot. I just lose time. Hours, days. They're gone, and I don't know what I've done or where I've been or anything else.

"I've never told anyone this before. It's embarrassing. Actually, it's terrifying.

"I don't understand any of it, but the thing I understand the least is that apparently I go about my business during these times, and nobody notices any difference in me. At least, no one ever says anything. After the meeting this morning, I realized that on Tuesday, Wednesday, and Thursday, I must have done a mountain of editing. There it was, all finished. I did a good job, even. And I don't remember a bloody thing."

During this confession, I saw Julia cry for the first time. Quickly, though, she willed her tears under control, and wanted me to tell her about a word she had heard me use the previous week, "dissociative." She questioned me as if the issue were a strictly academic one for her, which it clearly was not. I gently steered her back to the subject of herself and her week.

"Where did you have dinner Monday night?"

"What? Oh. Dinner Monday night. I had dinner at the Grill 23 with my friend Elaine."

"Was it a nice time?" I continued to question.

"I think so. Yes, I think it was okay."

"What did you and Elaine talk about, do you remember?"

"What did we talk about? Let's see. Well, I think we talked about the film a bit. And we talked about the waiter. Very cute waiter." She grinned. "And we probably spent the longest time talking about Elaine's relationship with this new guy, Peter. Why do you ask?"

"You said the dinner was the last thing you remembered before you woke up this morning. I thought it might be important. What did Elaine say about Peter?"

"Well, she said she's madly in love, and she said she wanted me to meet him because she thought we'd have a lot to talk about. He's from L.A., too."

"You and Peter are both from L.A. What else did you and Elaine say about L.A.?"

Julia looked suddenly blank, and said, "I don't remember. Why? Do you really think something about the place where I grew up scares me enough that just talking about it blasts me into never-never land for three days? That really can't be, though. I mean, I talk about L.A. a lot to people."

"I think it's possible that something during the dinner scared you enough to make you lose yourself for a while, although we'll never know for sure. Obviously, talking about L.A. doesn't always do that, but maybe there was something in that particular conversation that reminded you of something else that triggered something in your mind, something that might seem innocuous to another person, or even to you at another time. But as I say, we'll never know for sure."

"That's frightening. That's awful. It's like I'm in jail in my own head. I don't think I can live this way anymore."

"Yes, it's very frightening. I suspect it's been very frightening for a long time."

"You got that right."

Julia's knowledge of her own life, both past and present, had assumed the airy structure of Swiss cheese, with some solid substance that she and her gifted intellect could use, but riddled with unexplained gaps and hollows. This had its funny side. A few months later, when she had gained a better acceptance of her problem, she came in, sat down, and said in a characteristically charming way, "How do you like my new bracelet?"

"It's beautiful," I replied. "I've always admired your amethyst jewelry. When did you get that piece?"

"Who knows?"

She grinned at me again, and we both laughed.

The somewhat old-fashioned term for Julia's departures from herself during which she would continue to carry out day-to-day activities is "fugue," from the Italian word *fuga,* meaning "flight." A dissociative state that reaches the point of fugue is one of the most dramatic spontaneously occurring examples of the human mind's ability to divide consciousness into parts. In fugue, the person, or the mind of the person, can be subdivided in a manner that allows certain intellectually driven functions to continue—rising at a certain time, conversing with others, following a schedule, even carrying out complex tasks—while the part of consciousness that we usually experience as the "self"—the self-aware center that wishes, dreams, plans, emotes, and remembers—has taken flight, or has perhaps just darkened like a room at night when someone is sleeping.

The departures of fugue are related to certain experiences in ordinary human life that are not generated by trauma. For example, similar is the common experience of the daily commuter by car who realizes that sometimes she or he arrives back at home in the evening without having been aware of the activities of driving. The driving was automatically carried out by some part of the mind, while the self part of the mind was worrying, daydreaming, or listening to the radio. The experience is that of arriving at home without remembering the process of the trip. If one reflects upon the minute and complex decisions and maneuvers involved in driving a car, this ordinary event is really quite remarkable.

Clinical fugue differs from common human experience not so much in kind as in degree. Fugue is terror-driven and complete, while the more recognizable condition is the result of distraction, and relatively transparent. As fugue, the car trip example would involve a driver who failed to remember not just the process of the trip, but also the fact that there had been a trip, and from where. Far beyond distraction, the more remarkable dissociative reaction of fugue would have been set off by something—an event, a conversation, an image, a thought—that was related, though perhaps in some oblique and symbolic way, to trauma.

Not all traumatized individuals exhibit outright fugue. For some people, stressful events trigger a demifugue that is less dramatic but in some ways more agonizing. Another of my patients, Lila, refers to her experience as "my flyaway self":

"I had an argument with the cashier at the Seven-Eleven store. I gave him a twenty and he said I gave him a ten. He wouldn't give me my other ten dollars back. The way he looked at me—it was just the way my stepfather used to, like I was stupid, like I was dirt. I knew he wasn't really my stepfather, but all the feelings were there anyway. After a minute, I just couldn't argue about it. I left without my money, and by the time I got back home, my flyaway self thing had started. Once it starts, it's like there's absolutely nothing I can do about it. I'm gone, and there's nothing I can do about it."

"What does it feel like?"

"Oh boy. I don't know how to describe it. It's just … it's just really awful. I don't know … everything around me gets very small, kind of unreal, you know? It's my flyaway self, I call it. It feels like … my spirit just kind of flies away, and everything else gets very small—people, everything. If it were happening now, for example, you would look very small and far away, and the room would feel kind of unreal. Sometimes even my own body gets small and unreal. It's awful. And when it happens, I can't stop it. I just can't stop it."

What Lila describes as her "flyaway self" is in some respects similar to the derealization that most people have known occasionally, usually under passing conditions of sleep deprivation or physical illness. One temporarily has the sense of looking at the world through the wrong end of a telescope: everything looks small and far away, though one knows intellectually that these same things are just as close and life-sized as ever.

Imagine being forced to live lengthy segments of your life in this state. Imagine that you were falling inexorably into it, to remain there for a week or more at a time, because of events such as an unpleasant argument with a stranger at a convenience store. As bad as this would be, the situation for someone like Lila is incalculably worse, because for her the phenomenon has its origins in trauma.

Another of my patients offered a specific image, and for me an indelible one, to describe the same dissociative condition. Forty-nine-year-old Seth, like Julia, is successful, educated, and visually talented, and his disquieting description reflects his aptitudes. At the beginning of this particular therapy session, he had been telling me about a startling encounter, at a company softball game, with another person lost in the dissociated space with which he himself was all too familiar.

"I knew exactly where she was," said Seth.

"What does it feel like?" I asked. "Can you tell me what it feels like when you're there? How do you change?"

"I don't change. It's not that I change. *Reality* changes. Everything becomes very small, and I exist entirely inside my mind. Even my own body isn't real."

Indicating the two of us and the room around us, he continued, "Right now, this is what's real. You're real. What we're saying is real. But when I'm like that, the office is not real. *You're* not real anymore."

"What is real at those times?" I asked.

"I don't know exactly. It's hard to explain. Only what's going on in my mind is real. I'll tell you what it feels like: I feel like I'm dog-paddling out in the ocean, moving backwards, out to sea. When I'm still close enough to the land, I can sort of look way far away and see the beach. You and the rest of the world are all on the beach somewhere. But I keep drifting backwards, and the beach gets smaller, and the ocean gets bigger and bigger, and when I've drifted out far enough, the beach disappears, and all I can see all around me is the sea. It's so gray—gray on gray on gray."

"Is there anything out in the ocean with you?" I asked.

Seth replied, "No. Not at that point. I'm completely alone, more alone than you can imagine. But if you drift out farther, if you go all the way out to where the bottom of the sea drops off to the real abyss part, then there are awful things, these bloodthirsty sea creatures, sharks and giant eels and things like that. I've always thought that if something in the real world scared me enough, I'd drift out and out to past the dropping-off part, and then I would just be gobbled up, gone—no coming back, ever.

"When I'm floating out in the middle of the sea, everything else is very far away, even time. Time becomes unreal, in a way. An hour could go by that seems like a day to me, or four or five hours could go by, and it seems like only a minute."

Some extreme trauma survivors recognize that they are dissociative, and others do not recognize this. Many times, an individual will realize at some point in adulthood that she or he has had a lifelong pattern of being "away" a grievously large portion of the time.

During the same session, Seth described his own situation in this way:

"Actually, when I was a child, I don't know how much time I spent away like that. I never thought about it. It was probably a lot of the time, maybe even all the time. It just *was*."

"You mean it was your reality, and so of course you never questioned it, any more than any other child questions his reality?"

"Right. That's right. That was when I was a child. And most of the time it still happens automatically, bang, way before I know it's coming; but in here now, sometimes, there's this brief moment when I know I'm about to go away, but I still have time to try to keep it from taking over. Emphasis on *try*."

"How do you do that?" I asked.

"By concentrating. By trying with everything I've got to concentrate on you, and what you're saying, and on the things around me in the office here. But then there's physical pain, too. My eyes hurt, and I know I could make myself feel better if I shut them. But I try not to. And I get this thing in my stomach, which is the hardest thing to fight. There's this pain that feels like I just swallowed a whole pile of burning coals, this torture feeling that beams out from my stomach to the rest of my body; sooner or later, it just takes me over."

He grimaced and put a fist to his breastbone.

When Seth said this about pain in his stomach, I remembered, as I had remembered during descriptions by many, many others, that there is a common Japanese term, *shin pan,* inexactly translated as "agitated heart syndrome," referring to a great pain between the chest and the stomach, just under the solar plexus. *Shin pan,* a condition as real within Eastern medicine as is cataract or ulcer or fractured fibula within Western medicine, is a pain of the heart that does not involve the actual physical organ. In our culture, we consider such a thing—a "heartache," if you will—to be poetry at most. We do not understand that much of the rest of the world considers it to be quite real.

I said to Seth, "It must be frightening to be out in the ocean like that."

"Actually, it's not," he replied. "The abyss part, with the sharks and all, that's frightening. But for most of my life it was really no more frightening than the things that were on the beach, no more frightening than reality, I guess is what I'm saying. So floating in the middle of the ocean was really the best place, even though I guess that sounds strange. Also, being there takes care of the physical pain; there's no more pain when I'm there. It's just that now, I mean lately, the beach, where you are, and everything else, sometimes it makes me wish I could maybe be there instead. I guess you could say that now, at least sometimes, I want to live."

I smiled at him, but he looked away, unsure of what he had just proposed.

Referring back to Seth's softball team acquaintance, whose dissociative episode had begun our discussion, I said, "It must be strange to be with another person when you know she's drifting away in an ocean just like you do sometimes."

"Yes, it's very strange."

"How did you know she was drifting? Did she tell you?"

"No. She didn't tell me. She didn't say anything at all about being dissociated. She was just standing around with us, talking about these incredible things, horrible things from her past, without any emotion, without any reaction to them. She played well that day, actually, but she won't remember any of it, that's for sure."

"You mean," I asked, "another person, besides you, might not have known she was dissociated?"

"Absolutely. I'm sure someone else might not have known at all. It's just that I looked at her, and I saw me. It was like talking to somebody who didn't have a soul."

"You mean her soul was somewhere else?"

"Yes, I guess so. Her soul was somewhere else," Seth said.

After a brief silence, he turned the discussion back to his own life: "The other day, my wife was trying to talk to me about something really important that happened when the twins were born. Doesn't matter what it was; what matters is that I had no idea what she was talking about. I didn't have a clue. It wasn't a dim memory. It wasn't anything. I didn't have that memory because I wasn't there."

"You weren't there, but your wife didn't know that at the time?" I asked.

"No, she didn't know that at all. But you know, most of the time when she and I are making love, and I'm not there, she doesn't know it even then."

"You mean, someone can be that close to you, and still not know?"

"Yes."

At that moment I thought, and then decided to say aloud, "That's so sad."

A single tear skimmed down Seth's cheek. He wiped it quickly with the back of his hand, and said, "I'm sorry, it's just that, well, when I think about it, I realize that, really, I've missed most of my own life."

He stopped and took a deep breath, and I wondered whether he might have to dissociate just to get through this experience in my office.

I asked, "Are you here now, at this moment?"

"Yes, I think so. Yes."

There was another pause, and then with more emotion in his voice than he was usually able to show, he said, "It's so hard, because so much of the time when I'm here, what you're seeing is not what I'm seeing. I feel like such an impostor. I'm out in my ocean, and you don't know that. And I can't tell you what's going on. Sometimes I'd really like to tell you, but I can't. I'm gone."

Seth's description of his inner life makes it wrenchingly clear that the traumatized person is unable to feel completely connected to another person, even a friend, even a spouse. Just as limiting, perhaps even more limiting, is such a person's disconnection from his or her own body. You will recall that Lila's "flyaway self" owned a body that was only "small and unreal," and that when Seth was in his ocean, his mind was separated from his physical self. I began this chapter with Julia, the brilliant producer of documentary films, and as it happens, about a year into her treatment, an event occurred that well illustrates the survivor's trauma-generated dissociation from the body itself, or more accurately, from those aspects of mind that inform one of what is going on in the body.

One morning just after the workday began, Julia's assistant, a gentle young woman who was quite fond of her boss, noticed that Julia was looking extremely pale. She asked how Julia was feeling, and Julia replied that she thought her stomach was a little upset, but other than that she was sure she was fine. Ten minutes later, walking down a corridor, Julia fell to the floor, and by the time the panic-stricken assistant came to her aid, she was unconscious. An ambulance arrived and rushed Julia to the Massachusetts General Hospital, where she underwent an immediate emergency appendectomy. Her life was in danger, and the situation was touch-and-go for a while, because her infected appendix had already ruptured and severe peritonitis had resulted. She survived, however, and during her recovery, when she was well enough to see me again, she recounted a postsurgery conversation with her doctor.

"The doctor kept asking me, 'Didn't you feel anything? Weren't you in pain?' I told her my stomach had been upset that morning, but I didn't remember any real pain. She said, 'Why didn't you call me?' I guess she just couldn't believe that I really hadn't felt any pain. She said that I should have been in agony by the previous night, at the very latest. She kept saying 'agony.' But I didn't feel it. I swear to you I didn't feel any pain, much less agony."

"I believe you," I said to Julia.

"Well, I don't think she did. I guess a ruptured appendix involves a lot of pain for most people."

"Yes. Yes it does," I replied, trying to disguise some of my own astonishment.

"I know I've tried to kill myself intentionally, more than once, so maybe this sounds crazy—but I don't want to die one day just because I'm confused."

"What do you mean?" I asked.

"I don't want to die because I can't feel anything. I don't want to end up dead because I can't feel what's going on in my body, or because I can't tell the difference between that psychosomatic pain I'm always getting in my chest and some honest-to-God heart attack."

Julia said "psychosomatic," but I was thinking *shin pan,* again.

"You know how we talk about my tendency to be dissociative? Well do you think I dissociate from my body, too? Because if that's what I'm doing, then it's the illusion from hell. I mean, if it's supposed to save me, it's not working. In fact, it's going to kill me one day. And even if it doesn't kill me, what's the use of living if I can't feel anything? Why should I be alive when I lose big parts of my life? I mean, really, how can you care about anything if you can't even know the truth about yourself? If you keep losing yourself?"

I said, "I think that's one of the best questions I've ever heard."

"You do? You mean you agree with me about how I can't really care about living if I keep losing myself?"

"I said that's one of the best *questions.* I didn't say I knew the answer."

"Oh boy, you're cagey," she said, and grinned. "So okay, how do I find the answer?"

"Well you know, you could try to remember. We could try hypnosis, for one thing."

I believed that Julia might be ready to bring up the lights in the cold, dark house of her past.

"Yes, so you've said. And the idea scares the hell out of me." There was a substantial pause before she continued. "The idea scares the hell out of me, but I think I have to do it anyway."

"Why do you have to?"

"Because I want to know. Because I want to live."

"So, let's do it?" I asked.

"Let's do it," Julia said.

QUESTIONS FOR MAKING CONNECTIONS
WITHIN THE READING

1. Drawing on the information Stout provides, discuss the relations between the mind—in particular the memory—and the brain. Why are traumatic memories generally inaccessible? When Stout refers to "our divided

awareness," what does she mean? Is it possible for awareness to become undivided? If such a state can be achieved at all, can it ever become permanent, or is "dividedness" an inescapable feature of consciousness itself?

2. Explain the difference between dissociation and ordinary distraction. What is it about Julia's lapses of memory that qualifies them as examples of dissociation? Are there significant differences between Julia's lapses and Seth's? Has Seth devised ways of coping that have proven more successful than Julia's?

3. In her discussion of Seth, Stout makes a reference to the condition known as *shin pan,* a term taken from Asian medicine. Does this reference bring something new to our understanding that the term "heartache" does not? Is Stout just showing off her knowledge of Eastern culture, or is she trying to get us to rethink our own attitudes about the importance of emotions?

QUESTIONS FOR WRITING

1. The title of Stout's book is *The Myth of Sanity: Divided Consciousness and the Promise of Awareness.* Now that you have read one chapter from her book, why do you think she refers to sanity as a "myth"? What does she mean by "the promise of awareness"? How might "awareness" differ from "sanity"?

2. Julia and Seth both qualify as extreme cases of dissociation, but their experiences may also shed some light on ordinary consciousness. Taking Stout's essay as your starting point, and drawing also on your own experience, discuss the nature of consciousness. Does the mind operate like a camcorder, or is awareness more complex and less continuous than the images stored in a camcorder's memory?

3. Can people ever know reality—the world as it actually is—or are we trapped within our own mental worlds? If memory shapes our perceptions from moment to moment, then would you say that experience can ever teach us anything new? If memory is unreliable, then what are the implications for self-knowledge? Is the ancient adage "Know Thyself" actually an invitation to wishful thinking?

QUESTIONS FOR MAKING CONNECTIONS WITHIN
THE READING

1. Could our relation to the natural world be described as "dissociated"? Look again at Caroline Fraser's "Rewilding North America," and ask yourself about the psychology that has shaped our relations to nature. By separating wilderness from ourselves, have we become like Julia and Seth, using numbness as a means of self-protection? Their dissociation has its roots in the experience of trauma. In what ways might contact with the natural world be

traumatic for humans, now or in the past? What dangers might nature pose for us? Does our separation from the natural world create something like *shin pan*? Could rewilding act as a kind of therapy, a way for us to confront our fears and embrace a reality we have been afraid to see? What might that reality entail?

2. In what ways does Oliver Sacks's discussion in "The Mind's Eye" confirm, complicate, or contradict Stout's claims about trauma and its consequences? Although Sacks is concerned with adaptations to blindness and not emotional trauma, both authors explore the ways the mind compensates for losses and injuries of one kind or another. Are Julia and Seth in some ways comparable to the blind men and women Sacks describes?

DEBORAH TANNEN

Deborah Tannen Became interested in cross-cultural communication after she graduated from college in 1966 and taught English in Greece for two years. After earning a master's degree in English from Wayne State University and teaching writing in the United States for a few years, Tannen decided to pursue a doctorate in linguistics at Berkeley. It was just Tannen's luck that the first linguistics institute she attended focused on language in a social context. "Had I gone another summer," Tannen has said, "it's quite likely I would have concluded linguistics was not for me."

Tannen is currently University Professor on the faculty of the linguistics department at Georgetown University. She has published over twenty books and more than one hundred articles and is the recipient of five honorary doctorates. Tannen is probably best known as the author of *You Just Don't Understand: Women and Men in Conversation* (1991), which is credited with bringing gender differences in communication to the forefront of public awareness. This book "was on the *New York Times* bestseller list for nearly four years, including eight months as number one, and has been translated into twenty-nine languages."

More recently Tannen has published *You're Wearing THAT?* (2006) and *You Were Always Mom's Favorite* (2009). Unlike *You Just Don't Understand,* which was focused on gender differences, these two studies provide a fresh look at communication problems that arise exclusively between women—in the first case between mothers and daughters, and in the second case between sisters. Both books challenge simplistic images of life inside families, where genuine affection goes hand in hand with struggles for identity and approval.

"The Roots of Debate in Education and the Hope of Dialogue" is drawn from Tannen's 1998 book *The Argument Culture,* which examines the social, political, and emotional consequences of treating discussions as battles to be won or lost. Tannen's goal in this work is to get her readers to notice "the power of words to frame how you think about things, how you feel about things, how you perceive the world. The tendency in our culture to use war metaphors so pervasively, and to frame everything as a metaphorical battle, influences how we approach each other in our everyday lives."

Tannen, Deborah. "The Roots of Debate in Education and the Hope of Dialogue." *The Argument Culture: Moving from Debate to Dialogue.* New York: Random House, 1998. 256–290.

Biographical information comes from Deborah Tannen's home page, <http://www.georgetown.edu/faculty/tannend/>; quotations come from Harvey Bloom, "Deborah Tannen: A Writer First," *The Boston Book Review* <http://www.bookwire.com/bbr/interviews/amy-tannen.html>.

■ ■

The Roots of Debate in Education and the Hope of Dialogue

The teacher sits at the head of the classroom, feeling pleased with herself and her class. The students are engaged in a heated debate. The very noise level reassures the teacher that the students are participating, taking responsibility for their own learning. Education is going on. The class is a success.

But look again, cautions Patricia Rosof, a high school history teacher who admits to having experienced that wave of satisfaction with herself and the job she is doing. On closer inspection, you notice that only a few students are participating in the debate; the majority of the class is sitting silently, maybe attentive but perhaps either indifferent or actively turned off. And the students who are arguing are not addressing the subtleties, nuances, or complexities of the points they are making or disputing. They do not have that luxury because they want to win the argument—so they must go for the most gross and dramatic statements they can muster. They will not concede an opponent's point, even if they can see its validity, because that would weaken their position. Anyone tempted to synthesize the varying views would not dare to do so because it would look like a "cop-out," an inability to take a stand.

One reason so many teachers use the debate format to promote student involvement is that it is relatively easy to set up and the rewards are quick and obvious: the decibel level of noise, the excitement of those who are taking part. Showing students how to integrate ideas and explore subtleties and complexities is much harder. And the rewards are quieter—but more lasting.

Our schools and universities, our ways of doing science and approaching knowledge, are deeply agonistic. We all pass through our country's educational system, and it is there that the seeds of our adversarial culture are planted. Seeing how these seeds develop, and where they came from, is a key to understanding the argument culture and a necessary foundation for determining what changes we would like to make.

Roots of the Adversarial Approach to Knowledge

The argument culture, with its tendency to approach issues as a polarized debate, and the culture of critique, with its inclination to regard criticism and attack as the best if not the only type of rigorous thinking, are deeply rooted in Western tradition, going back to the ancient Greeks.[1] This point is made by Walter Ong, a Jesuit professor at Saint Louis University, in his book *Fighting for Life*. Ong credits the ancient Greeks[2] with a fascination with adversativeness in language and thought. He also connects the adversarial tradition of educational institutions to their all-male character. To attend the earliest universities, in the Middle Ages, young men were torn from their families and deposited in cloistered environments where corporal, even brutal, punishment was rampant. Their suffering drove them to bond with each other in opposition to their keepers—the teachers who were their symbolic enemies. Similar in many ways to puberty rites in traditional cultures, this secret society to which young men were confined also had a private language, Latin, in which students read about military exploits. Knowledge was gleaned through public oral disputation and tested by combative oral performance, which carried with it the risk of public humiliation. Students at these institutions were trained not to discover the truth but to argue either side of an argument—in other words, to debate. Ong points out that the Latin term for school, *ludus,* also referred to play or games, but it derived from the military sense of the word—training exercises for war.

If debate seems self-evidently the appropriate or even the only path to insight and knowledge, says Ong, consider the Chinese approach. Disputation was rejected in ancient China as "incompatible with the decorum and harmony cultivated by the true sage."[3] During the Classical periods in both China and India, according to Robert T. Oliver, the preferred mode of rhetoric was exposition rather than argument. The aim was to "enlighten an inquirer," not to "overwhelm an opponent." And the preferred style reflected "the earnestness of investigation" rather than "the fervor of conviction." In contrast to Aristotle's trust of logic and mistrust of emotion, in ancient Asia intuitive insight was considered the superior means of perceiving truth. Asian rhetoric was devoted not to devising logical arguments but to explicating widely accepted propositions. Furthermore, the search for abstract truth that we assume is the goal of philosophy, while taken for granted in the West, was not found in the East, where philosophy was concerned with observation and experience.

If Aristotelian philosophy, with its emphasis on formal logic, was based on the assumption that truth is gained by opposition, Chinese philosophy offers an alternative view. With its emphasis on harmony, says anthropologist Linda Young, Chinese philosophy sees a diverse universe in precarious balance that is maintained by talk. This translates into methods of investigation that focus more on integrating ideas and exploring relations among them than on opposing ideas and fighting over them.

Onward, Christian Soldiers

The military-like culture of early universities is also described by historian David Noble, who describes how young men attending medieval universities were like marauding soldiers: the students—all seminarians—roamed the streets bearing arms, assaulting women, and generally creating mayhem. Noble traces the history of Western science and of universities to joint origins in the Christian Church. The scientific revolution, he shows, was created by religious devotees setting up monastery-like institutions devoted to learning. Early universities were seminaries, and early scientists were either clergy or devoutly religious individuals who led monk-like lives. (Until as recently as 1888, fellows at Oxford were expected to be unmarried.)

That Western science is rooted in the Christian Church helps explain why our approach to knowledge tends to be conceived as a metaphorical battle: the Christian Church, Noble shows, has origins and early forms rooted in the military. Many early monks had actually been soldiers before becoming monks.[4] Not only were obedience and strict military-like discipline required, but monks saw themselves as serving "in God's knighthood," warriors in a battle against evil. In later centuries, the Crusades brought actual warrior-monks.

The history of science in the Church holds the key to understanding our tradition of regarding the search for truth as an enterprise of oral disputation in which positions are propounded, defended, and attacked without regard to the debater's personal conviction. It is a notion of truth as objective, best captured by formal logic, that Ong traces to Aristotle. Aristotle regarded logic as the only trustworthy means for human judgment; emotions get in the way: "The man who is to judge would not have his judgment warped by speakers arousing him to anger, jealousy, or compassion. One might as well make a carpenter's tool crooked before using it as a measure."[5]

This assumption explains why Plato wanted to ban poets from education in his ideal community. As a lover of poetry, I can still recall my surprise and distress on reading this in *The Republic* when I was in high school. Not until much later did I understand what it was all about.[6] Poets in ancient Greece were wandering bards who traveled from place to place performing oral poetry that persuaded audiences by moving them emotionally. They were like what we think of as demagogues: people with a dangerous power to persuade others by getting them all worked up. Ong likens this to our discomfort with advertising in schools, which we see as places where children should learn to think logically, not be influenced by "teachers" with ulterior motives who use unfair persuasive tactics.

Sharing Time: Early Training in School

A commitment to formal logic as the truest form of intellectual pursuit remains with us today. Our glorification of opposition as the path to truth is related to the development of formal logic, which encourages thinkers to regard truth seeking as a step-by-step alternation of claims and counterclaims.[7] Truth, in this schema, is an abstract notion that tends to be taken out of context. This formal approach to learning is taught in our schools, often indirectly.

Educational researcher James Wertsch shows that schools place great emphasis on formal representation of knowledge. The common elementary school practice of "sharing time" (or, as it used to be called, "show-and-tell") is a prime arena for such training. Wertsch gives the example of a kindergarten pupil named Danny who took a piece of lava to class.[8] Danny told his classmates, "My mom went to the volcano and got it." When the teacher asked what he wanted to tell about it, he said, "I've always been taking care of it." This placed the rock at the center of his feelings and his family: the rock's connection to his mother, who gave it to him, and the attention and care he has lavished on it. The teacher reframed the children's interest in the rock as informational: "Is it rough or smooth?" "Is it heavy or light?" She also suggested they look up "volcano" and "lava" in the dictionary. This is not to imply that the teacher harmed the child; she built on his personal attachment to the rock to teach him a new way of thinking about it. But the example shows the focus of education on formal rather than relational knowledge—information about the rock that has meaning out of context, rather than information tied to the context: Who got the rock for him? How did she get it? What is his relation to it?

Here's another example of how a teacher uses sharing time to train children to speak and think formally. Sarah Michaels spent time watching and tape-recording in a first-grade classroom. During sharing time, a little girl named Mindy held up two candles and told her classmates, "When I was in day camp we made these candles. And I tried it with different colors with both of them but one just came out, this one just came out blue and I don't know what this color is." The teacher responded, "That's neat-o. Tell the kids how you do it from the very start. Pretend we don't know a thing about candles. Okay, what did you do first? What did you use?" She continued to prompt: "What makes it have a shape?" and "Who knows what the string is for?" By encouraging Mindy to give information in a sequential manner, even if it might not seem the most important to her and if the children might already know some of it, the teacher was training her to talk in a focused, explicit way.

The tendency to value formal, objective knowledge over relational, intuitive knowledge grows out of our notion of education as training for debate. It is a legacy of the agonistic heritage. There are many other traces as well. Many Ph.D. programs still require public "defenses" of dissertations or dissertation proposals, and oral performance of knowledge in comprehensive exams. Throughout our educational system, the most pervasive inheritance is the conviction that issues have two sides, that knowledge is best gained through debate, that ideas should be presented orally to an audience that does its best to poke holes and find weaknesses, and that to get recognition, one has to "stake out a position" in opposition to another.

Integrating Women in the Classroom Army

If Ong is right, the adversarial character of our educational institutions is inseparable from their all-male heritage. I wondered whether teaching techniques still tend to be adversarial today and whether, if they are, this may hold a clue to a dilemma that has received much recent attention: that girls often receive less attention and speak up less in class.[9] One term I taught a large lecture class of 140 students and decided to take advantage of this army (as it were) of researchers to answer these questions. Becoming observers in their own classrooms, my students found plenty of support for Ong's ideas.

I asked the students to note how relatively adversarial the teaching methods were in their other classes and how the students responded. Gabrielle DeRouen-Hawkins's description of a theology class was typical:

> The class is in the format of lecture with class discussion and participation. There are thirteen boys and eleven girls in the class. In a fifty-minute class:
>
> Number of times a male student spoke: 8
>
> Number of times a female student spoke: 3
>
> ... In our readings, theologians present their theories surrounding G-D, life, spirituality, and sacredness. As the professor (a male) outlined the main ideas about the readings, he posed questions like "And what is the fault with Smith's basis that the sacred is individualistic?" The only hands that went up were male. Not one female <u>dared</u> challenge or refute an author's writings. The only questions that the females asked (and all female comments were questions) involved a problem they had with the content of the reading. The males, on the other hand, openly questioned, criticized, and refuted the readings on five separate occasions. The three other times that males spoke involved them saying something like: "/Smith/ is very vague in her theory of XX. Can you explain it further?" They were openly argumentative.[10]

This description raises a number of fascinating issues. First, it gives concrete evidence that at least college classrooms proceed on the assumption that the educational process should be adversarial: the teacher invited students to criticize the reading. (Theology, a required course at Georgetown, was a subject where my students most often found adversarial methods—interestingly, given the background I laid out earlier.) Again, there is nothing inherently wrong with using such methods. Clearly, they are very effective in many ways. However, among the potential liabilities is the risk that women students may be less likely to take part in classroom discussions that are framed as arguments between opposing sides—that is, debate—or as attacks on the authors—that is, critique. (The vast majority of students' observations revealed that men tended to speak more than women in their classes—which is not to say that individual women did not speak more than individual men.)

Gabrielle commented that since class participation counted for 10 percent of students' grades, it might not be fair to women students that the agonistic style is more congenial to men. Not only might women's grades suffer because they speak up less, but they might be evaluated as less intelligent or prepared because when they did speak, they asked questions rather than challenging the readings.

I was intrigued by the student's comment "Smith is very vague in her theory of XX. Can you explain it further?" It could have been phrased "I didn't understand the author's theory. Can you explain it to me?" By beginning "The author is vague in her theory," the questioner blamed the author for *his* failure to understand. A student who asks a question in class risks appearing ignorant. Prefacing the question this way was an excellent way to minimize that risk.

In her description of this class, Gabrielle wrote that not a single woman "dared challenge or refute" an author. She herself underlined the word "dared." But in reading this I wondered whether "dared" was necessarily the right word. It implies that the women in the class wished to challenge the author but did not have the courage. It is possible that not a single woman *cared* to challenge the author. Criticizing or challenging might not be something that appealed to them or seemed worth their efforts. Going back to the childhoods of boys and girls, it seems possible that the boys had had more experiences, from the time they were small, that encouraged them to challenge and argue with authority figures than the girls had.

This is not to say that classrooms are more congenial to boys than girls in every way. Especially in the lowest grades, the requirement that children sit quietly in their seats seems clearly to be easier for girls to fulfill than boys, since many girls frequently sit fairly quietly for long periods of time when they play, while most boys' idea of play involves at least running around, if not also jumping and roughhousing. And researchers have pointed out that some of the extra attention boys receive is aimed at controlling such physical exuberance. The adversarial aspect of educational traditions is just one small piece of the pie, but it seems to reflect boys' experiences and predilections more than girls'.

A colleague commented that he had always taken for granted that the best way to deal with students' comments is to challenge them; he took it to be self-evident that this technique sharpens their minds and helps them develop debating skills. But he noticed that women were relatively silent in his classes. He decided to try beginning discussion with relatively open questions and letting comments go unchallenged. He found, to his amazement and satisfaction, that more women began to speak up in class.

Clearly, women can learn to perform in adversarial ways. Anyone who doubts this need only attend an academic conference in the field of women's studies or feminist studies—or read Duke University professor Jane Tompkins's essay showing how a conference in these fields can be like a Western shoot-out. My point is rather about the roots of the tradition and the tendency of the style to appeal initially to more men than women in the Western cultural context. Ong and Noble show that the adversarial culture of Western science and its exclusion of women were part and parcel of the same historical roots—not that individual women may not learn to practice and enjoy agonistic debate or that individual men may not recoil from it. There are many people, women as well as men, who assume a discussion must be contentious to be interesting. Author Mary Catherine Bateson recalls that when her mother, the anthropologist Margaret Mead, said, "I had an argument with" someone, it was a positive comment. "An argument," to her, meant a spirited intellectual interchange, not a rancorous conflict. The same assumption emerged in an obituary for Diana Trilling, called "one of the very last of the great midcentury New York intellectuals."[11] She and her friends had tried to live what they called "a life of significant contention"—the contention apparently enhancing rather than undercutting the significance.

Learning by Fighting

Although there are patterns that tend to typify women and men in a given culture, there is an even greater range among members of widely divergent cultural backgrounds. In addition to observing adversarial encounters in their current classrooms, many students recalled having spent a junior year in Germany or France and commented that American classrooms seemed very placid compared to what they had experienced abroad. One student, Zach Tyler, described his impressions this way:

> I have very vivid memories of my junior year of high school, which I spent in Germany as an exchange student. The classroom was very debate-oriented and agonistic. One particular instance I remember well was in physics class, when a very confrontational friend of mine had a heated debate with the teacher about solving a problem. My friend ran to the board and scribbled out how he would have solved the problem, completely different from the teacher's, which also gave my friend the right answer and made the teacher wrong.

> STUDENT: "You see! This is how it should be, and you are wrong!"
>
> TEACHER: "No! No! No! You are absolutely wrong in every respect! Just look at how you did this!" (He goes over my friend's solution and shows that it does not work.) "Your solution has no base, as I just showed you!"
>
> STUDENT: "You can't prove that. Mine works just as well!"
>
> TEACHER: "My God, if the world were full of technical idiots like yourself! Look again!" (And he clearly shows how my friend's approach was wrong, after which my friend shut up.)

In Zach's opinion, the teacher encouraged this type of argument. The student learned he was wrong, but he got practice in arguing his point of view.

This incident occurred in high school. But European classrooms can be adversarial even at the elementary school level, according to another student, Megan Smyth, who reported on a videotape she saw in her French class:

> Today in French class we watched an excerpt of a classroom scene of fifth-graders. One at a time, each student was asked to stand up and recite a poem that they were supposed to have memorized. The teacher screamed at the students if they forgot a line or if they didn't speak with enough emotion. They were reprimanded and asked to repeat the task until they did it perfectly and passed the "oral test."

There is probably little question about how Americans would view this way of teaching, but the students put it into words:

> After watching this scene, my French teacher asked the class what our opinion was. The various responses included: French schools are very strict, the professor was "mean" and didn't have respect for the students, and there's too much emphasis on memorization, which is pointless.

If teaching methods can be more openly adversarial in European than American elementary and high schools, academic debate can be more openly adversarial there as well. For example, Alice Kaplan, a professor of French at Duke University, describes a colloquium on the French writer Céline that she attended in Paris:

> After the first speech, people started yelling at each other. "Are you suggesting that Céline was fascist?" "You call that evidence!" "I will not accept ignorance in the place of argument!" I was scared.[12]

These examples dramatize that many individuals can thrive in an adversarial atmosphere. And those who learn to participate effectively in any verbal game eventually enjoy it, if nothing else than for the pleasure of exercising that learned skill. It is important to keep these examples in mind in order to avoid the impression that adversarial tactics are always destructive. Clearly, such tactics sometimes admirably serve the purpose of intellectual inquiry. In addition to individual predilection, cultural learning plays a role in whether or not someone enjoys the game played this way.

Graduate School as Boot Camp

Although the invective Kaplan heard at a scholarly meeting in Paris is more extreme than what is typical at American conferences, the assumption that challenge and attack are the best modes of scholarly inquiry is pervasive in American scholarly communities as well. Graduate education is a training ground not only for teaching but also for scientific research. Many graduate programs are geared to training young scholars in rigorous thinking, defined as the ability to launch and field verbal attacks.

Communications researchers Karen Tracy and Sheryl Baratz tapped into some of the ethics that lead to this atmosphere in a study of weekly symposia attended by faculty and graduate students at a major research university. When they asked participants about the purpose of the symposia, they were told it was to "trade ideas" and "learn things." But it didn't take too much discussion to uncover the participants' deeper concern: to be seen as intellectually competent. And here's the rub: to be seen as competent, a student had to ask "tough and challenging questions."

One faculty member commented, when asked about who participated actively in a symposium,

> Among the graduate students, the people I think about are Jess, Tim, uh, let's see, Felicia will ask a question but it'll be a nice little supportive question.[13]

"A nice little supportive question" diminished the value of Felicia's participation and her intelligence—the sort of judgment a student would wish to avoid. Just as with White House correspondents, there is value placed on asking "tough questions." Those who want to impress their peers and superiors (as most, if not all, do) are motivated to ask the sorts of questions that gain approval.

Valuing attack as a sign of respect is part of the argument culture of academia—our conception of intellectual interchange as a metaphorical battle. As one colleague put it, "In order to play with the big boys, you have to be willing to get into the ring and wrestle with them." Yet many graduate students (and quite a few established scholars) remain ambivalent about this ethic, especially when they are on the receiving rather than the distribution end. Sociolinguist Winnie Or tape-recorded a symposium at which a graduate student presented her fledgling research to other students and graduate faculty. The student later told Or that she left the symposium feeling that a truck had rolled over her. She did not say she regretted having taken part; she felt she had received valuable feedback. But she also mentioned that she had not looked at her research project once since the symposium several weeks before. This is telling. Shouldn't an opportunity to discuss your research with peers and experts fire you up and send you back to the isolation of research renewed and reinspired? Isn't something awry if it leaves you not wanting to face your research project at all?

This young scholar persevered, but others drop out of graduate school, in some cases because they are turned off by the atmosphere of critique. One woman who wrote to me said she had been encouraged to enroll in graduate school by her college professors, but she lasted only one year in a major midwest university's doctoral program in art history. This is how she described her experience and her decision not to continue:

> Grad school was the nightmare I never knew existed.... Into the den of wolves I go, like a lamb to slaughter.... When, at the end of my first year (master's) I was offered a job as a curator for a private collection, I jumped at the chance. I wasn't cut out for academia—better try the "real world."

Reading this I thought, Is it that she was not cut out for academia, or is it that academia as it was practiced in that university is not cut out for people like her? It is cut out for those who enjoy, or can tolerate, a contentious environment.

(These examples remind us again of the gender dynamic. The graduate student who left academia for museum work was a woman. The student who asked a "nice little supportive question" instead of a "tough, challenging one" was a woman. More than one commentator has wondered aloud if part of the reason women drop out of science courses and degree programs is their discomfort with the agonistic culture of Western science. And Lani Guinier has recently shown that discomfort with the agonistic procedures of law school is partly responsible for women's lower grade point averages in law school, since the women arrive at law school with records as strong as the men's.)

The Culture of Critique: Attack in the Academy

The standard way of writing an academic paper is to position your work in opposition to someone else's, which you prove wrong. This creates a need to make others wrong, which is quite a different matter from reading something with an open mind and discovering that you disagree with it. Students are taught that they must disprove others' arguments in order to be original, make a contribution, and demonstrate their intellectual ability. When there is a need to make others wrong, the temptation is great to oversimplify at best, and at worst to distort or even misrepresent others' positions, the better to refute them—to search for the most foolish statement in a generally reasonable treatise, seize upon the weakest examples, ignore facts that support your opponent's views, and focus only on those that support yours. Straw men spring up like scarecrows in a cornfield.

Sometimes it seems as if there is a maxim driving academic discourse that counsels, "If you can't find something bad to say, don't say anything." As a result, any work that gets a lot of attention is immediately opposed. There is an advantage to this approach: weaknesses are exposed, and that is surely good. But another result is that it is difficult for those outside the field (or even inside) to know what is "true." Like two expert witnesses hired by opposing attorneys, academics can seem to be canceling each other out. In the words of policy analysts David Greenberg and Philip Robins:

> The process of scientific inquiry almost ensures that competing sets of results will be obtained.... Once the first set of findings are published, other researchers eager to make a name for themselves must come up with different approaches and results to get their studies published.[14]

How are outsiders (or insiders, for that matter) to know which "side" to believe? As a result, it is extremely difficult for research to influence public policy.

A leading researcher in psychology commented that he knew of two young colleagues who had achieved tenure by writing articles attacking him. One of them told him, in confidence, that he actually agreed with him, but of course he could not get tenure by writing articles simply supporting someone else's work; he had to stake out a position in opposition. Attacking an established scholar has particular appeal because it demonstrates originality and independence of thought without requiring true innovation. After all, the domain of inquiry and the terms of debate have already been established. The critic has only to say, like the child who wants to pick a fight, "Is not!" Younger or less prominent scholars can achieve a level of attention otherwise denied or eluding them by stepping into the ring with someone who has already attracted the spotlight.

The young psychologist who confessed his motives to the established one was unusual, I suspect, only in his self-awareness and willingness to articulate it. More commonly, younger scholars, or less prominent ones, convince themselves that they are fighting for truth, that they are among the few who see that the emperor has no clothes. In the essay mentioned earlier, Jane Tompkins describes how a young scholar-critic can work herself into a passionate conviction that she is morally obligated to attack, because she is fighting on the side of good against the side of evil. Like the reluctant hero in the film *High Noon,* she feels she has no choice but to strap on her holster and shoot. Tompkins recalls that her own career was launched by an essay that

> began with a frontal assault on another woman scholar. When I wrote it I felt the way the hero does in a Western. Not only had this critic argued *a*, *b*, and *c*, she had held *x*, *y*, and *z*! It was a clear case of outrageous provocation.[15]

Because her attack was aimed at someone with an established career ("She was famous and I was not. She was teaching at a prestigious university and I was not. She had published a major book and I had not."), it was a "David and Goliath situation" that made her feel she was "justified in hitting her with everything I had." (This is analogous to what William Safire describes as his philosophy in the sphere of political journalism: "Kick 'em when they're up.")[16]

The claim of objectivity is belied by Tompkins's account of the spirit in which attack is often launched: the many motivations, other than the search for truth, that drive a critic to pick a fight with another scholar. Objectivity would entail a disinterested evaluation of all claims. But there is nothing disinterested about it when scholars set out with the need to make others wrong and transform them not only into opponents but into villains.

In academia, as in other walks of life, anonymity breeds contempt. Some of the nastiest rhetoric shows up in "blind" reviews—of articles submitted to journals or book proposals submitted to publishers. "Peer review" is the cornerstone of academic life. When someone submits an article to a journal, a book to a publisher, or a proposal to a funding institution, the work is sent to established scholars for evaluation. To enable reviewers to be honest, they remain anonymous. But anonymous reviewers often take a tone of derision such as people tend to use only when talking about someone who is not there—after all, the evaluation is not addressed to the author. But authors typically receive copies of the evaluations, especially if their work is rejected. This can be particularly destructive to young scholars just starting out. For example, one sociolinguist wrote her dissertation in a firmly established tradition: she tape-recorded conversations at the company where she worked part-time. Experts in our field believe it is best to examine conversations in which the researcher is a natural participant, because when strangers appear asking to tape-record, people get nervous and may change their behavior. The publisher sent the manuscript to a reviewer who was used to different research methods. In rejecting the proposal, she referred to the young scholar "using the audiotaped detritus from an old job." Ouch. What could justify the sneering term "detritus"? What is added by appending "old" to "job," other than hurting the author? Like Heathcliff, the target hears only the negative and—like Heathcliff—may respond by fleeing the field altogether.

One reason the argument culture is so widespread is that arguing is so easy to do. Lynne Hewitt, Judith Duchan, and Erwin Segal came up with a fascinating finding: speakers with language disabilities who had trouble taking part in other types of verbal interaction were able to participate in arguments. Observing adults with mental retardation who lived in a group home, the researchers found that the residents often engaged in verbal conflicts as a means of prolonging interaction. It was a form of sociability. Most surprising, this was equally true of two residents who had severe language and comprehension disorders yet were able to take part in the verbal disputes, because arguments have a predictable structure.

Academics, too, know that it is easy to ask challenging questions without listening, reading, or thinking very carefully. Critics can always complain about research methods, sample size, and what has been left out. To study anything, a researcher must isolate a piece of the subject and narrow the scope of vision in order to focus. An entire tree cannot be placed under a microscope; a tiny bit has to be separated to be examined closely. This gives critics the handle of a weapon with which to strike an easy blow: they can point out all the bits that were not studied. Like family members or partners in a close relationship, anyone looking for things to pick on will have no trouble finding them.

All of this is not to imply that scholars should not criticize each other or disagree. In the words of poet William Blake, "Without contraries is no progression."[17] The point is to distinguish constructive ways of doing so from nonconstructive ones. Criticizing a colleague on empirical grounds is the beginning of a discussion; if researchers come up with different findings, they can engage in a dialogue: what is it about their methods, data, or means of analysis that explains the different results? In some cases, those who set out to disprove another's claims end up proving them instead—something that is highly unlikely to happen in fields that deal in argumentation alone.

A stunning example in which opponents attempting to disprove a heretical claim ended up proving it involves the cause and treatment of ulcers. It is now widely known and accepted that ulcers are caused by bacteria in the stomach and can be cured by massive doses of antibiotics. For years, however, the cure and treatment of ulcers remained elusive, as all the experts agreed that ulcers were the classic psychogenic illness caused by stress. The stomach, experts further agreed, was a sterile environment: no bacteria could live there. So pathologists did not look for bacteria in the stomachs of ailing or deceased patients, and those who came across them simply ignored them, in effect not seeing what was before their eyes because they did not believe it could be there. When Dr. Barry Marshall, an Australian resident in internal medicine, presented evidence that ulcers are caused by bacteria, no one believed him. His findings were ultimately confirmed by researchers intent on proving him wrong.[18]

The case of ulcers shows that setting out to prove others wrong can be constructive—when it is driven by genuine differences and when it motivates others to undertake new research. But if seeking to prove others wrong becomes a habit, an end in itself, the sole line of inquiry, the results can be far less rewarding.

Believing as Thinking

"The doubting game" is the name English professor Peter Elbow gives to what educators are trained to do. In playing the doubting game, you approach others' work by looking for what's wrong, much as the press corps follows the president hoping to catch him stumble or an attorney pores over an opposing witness's deposition looking for inconsistencies that can be challenged on the stand. It is an attorney's job to discredit opposing witnesses, but is it a scholar's job to approach colleagues like an opposing attorney?

Elbow recommends learning to approach new ideas, and ideas different from your own, in a different spirit—what he calls a "believing game." This does not mean accepting everything anyone says or writes in an unthinking way. That would be just as superficial as rejecting everything without thinking deeply about it. The believing game is still a game. It simply asks you to give it a whirl: read as if you believed, and see where it takes you. Then you can go back and ask whether you want to accept or reject elements in the argument or the whole argument or idea. Elbow is not recommending that we stop doubting altogether. He is telling us to stop doubting exclusively. We need a systematic and respected way to detect and expose strengths, just as we have a systematic and respected way of detecting faults.

Americans need little encouragement to play the doubting game because we regard it as synonymous with intellectual inquiry, a sign of intelligence. In Elbow's words, "We tend to assume that the ability to criticize a claim we disagree with counts as more serious intellectual work than the ability to enter into it and temporarily assent."[19] It is the believing game that needs to be encouraged and recognized as an equally serious intellectual pursuit.

Although criticizing is surely part of critical thinking, it is not synonymous with it. Again, limiting critical response to critique means not doing the other kinds of critical thinking that could be helpful: looking for new insights, new perspectives, new ways of thinking, new knowledge. Critiquing relieves you of the responsibility of doing integrative thinking. It also has the advantage of making the critics feel smart, smarter than the ill-fated author whose work is being picked apart like carrion. But it has the disadvantage of making them less likely to learn from the author's work.

The Socratic Method—Or Is It?

Another scholar who questions the usefulness of opposition as the sole path to truth is philosopher Janice Moulton. Philosophy, she shows, equates logical reasoning with the Adversary Paradigm, a matter of making claims and then trying to find, and argue against, counterexamples to that claim. The result is a debate between adversaries trying to defend their ideas against counterexamples and to come up with counterexamples that refute the opponent's ideas. In this paradigm, the best way to evaluate someone's work is to "subject it to the strongest or most extreme opposition."[20]

But if you parry individual points—a negative and defensive enterprise—you never step back and actively imagine a world in which a different system of ideas could be true—a positive act. And you never ask how larger systems of thought relate to each other. According to Moulton, our devotion to the Adversary Paradigm has led us to misinterpret the type of argumentation that Socrates favored: we think of the Socratic method as systematically leading an opponent into admitting error. This is primarily a way of showing up an adversary as wrong. Moulton shows that the original Socratic method—the elenchus—was designed to convince others, to shake them out of their habitual mode of thought and lead them to new insight. Our version of the Socratic method—an adversarial public debate—is unlikely to result in opponents changing their minds. Someone who loses a debate usually attributes that loss to poor performance or to an adversary's unfair tactics.

Knowledge as Warring Camps

Anne Carolyn Klein, an American woman who spent many years studying Tibetan Buddhism, joined a university program devoted to women's studies in religion. It was her first encounter with contemporary feminist theory, which she quickly learned was divided into two warring camps. In one camp are those who focus on the ways that women are different from men. Among these, some emphasize that women's ways are equally valid and should be respected, while others believe that women's ways are superior and should be more widely adopted. Both these views—called "difference feminism"—contrast with those in the other camp, who claim that women are no different from men by nature, so any noticeable differences result from how society treats women. Those who take this view are called "social constructionists."[21]

Klein saw that separating feminist theory into these two camps reflects the Western tendency to rigid dichotomies. Recalling how Buddhist philosophy tries to integrate disparate forces, she shows that there is much to be gained from both feminist views—and, in any case, both perspectives tend to coexist within individuals. For example, even though the constructionist view of gender has won ascendancy in academic theory (that's why we have the epithet "essentialist" to describe those who hold the view that is in disfavor but no commonly used epithet to sneer at the constructionist view), "feminists still struggle to recognize and name the commonalities among women that justify concern for women's lives around the world and produce political and social alliances." Klein asks, "Why protest current conditions unless the category 'women' is in some way a meaningful one?"[22] She shows, too, that the very inclination to polarize varied views of women and feminism into two opposing camps is in itself essentialist because it reduces complex and varied perspectives to simplified, monolithic representations. This also makes it easy to dismiss—and fight about—others' work rather than think about it.

Reflecting this warring-camps view, journalist Cynthia Gorney asked Gloria Steinem, "Where do you stand in the current debate that the feminist world has divided into 'equity' feminism versus 'difference' feminism—about whether women are to be treated like men or as different from men?" This question bears all the earmarks of the adversarial framework: the term "debate" and the separation of a complex domain of inquiry into two opposed sides. Steinem responded:

> [*Sighs.*] Of course, you understand that I've turned up in every category. So it makes it harder for me to take the divisions with great seriousness, since I don't feel attached to any of them—and also since I don't hear about the division from women who are not academics or in the media.

The idea that there are two "camps" has not been my experience. The mark to me of a constructive argument is one that looks at a specific problem and says, "What shall we do about this?" And a nonconstructive one is one that tries to label people. "Difference" feminist, "gender" feminist—it has no meaning in specific situations.[23]

In this short comment, Steinem puts her finger on several aspects of the argument culture. First, she identifies academics and journalists as two groups that have a habit of—and a stake in—manufacturing polarization and the appearance of conflict. Second, she points out that this view of the world does not describe reality as most people live it. Third, she shows that polarizing issues into "a debate" often goes along with "labeling" the two sides: lumping others together and sticking a label on them makes it easy to ignore the nuances and subtleties of their opinions and beliefs. Individuals are reduced to an oversimplification of their ideas, transformed into the enemy, and demonized.

False dichotomies are often at the heart of discord.

Question the Basic Assumption

My aim is not to put a stop to the adversarial paradigm, the doubting game, debate—but to diversify: like a well-balanced stock portfolio, we need more than one path to the goal we seek. What makes it hard to question whether debate is truly the only or even the most fruitful approach to learning is that we're dealing with assumptions that we and everyone around us take to be self-evident. A prominent dean at a major research university commented to me, "The Chinese cannot make great scientists because they will not debate publicly." Many people would find this remark offensive. They would object because it generalizes about all Chinese scientists, especially since it makes a negative evaluation. But I would also question the assumption that makes the generalization a criticism: the conviction that the only way to test and develop ideas is to debate them publicly. It may well be true that most Chinese scientists are reluctant to engage in public, rancorous debate. I see nothing insulting about such a claim; it derives from the Chinese cultural norms that many Chinese and Western observers have documented. But we also know that many Chinese have indeed been great scientists.[24] The falsity of the dean's statement should lead us to question whether debate is the only path to insight.

Consensus Through Dissension?

The culture of critique driving our search for knowledge in the scientific world of research is akin to what I have described in the domains of politics, journalism, and law. In those three institutions, an increasingly warlike atmosphere has led many people already in those professions to leave, and many who would have considered entering these professions in the past are now choosing other paths. Those who remain are finding it less fun; they don't look forward to getting up and going to work in the same way that they and others used to. And in all these areas, raised voices and tempers are creating a din that is drowning out the perhaps more numerous voices of dialogue and reason. In law, critics of the principle of zealous advocacy object on the grounds of what it does to the souls of those who practice within the system, requiring them to put aside their consciences and natural inclinations toward human compassion—just what some among the press say about what aggression journalism is doing to journalists.

Forces affecting these institutions are intertwined with each other and with others I have not mentioned. For example, the rise of malpractice litigation, while prodding doctors to be more careful and providing deserved recompense to victims, has also made the doctor-patient relationship potentially more adversarial. At the same time, physicians are finding themselves in increasingly adversarial relationships with HMOs and insurance companies—as are the patients themselves, who now need the kind of advice that was offered under the headline "When Your HMO Says No: How to Fight for the Treatment You Need—and Win."[25]

People in business, too, report an increasingly adversarial atmosphere. There are, of course, the hostile takeovers that have become common, along with lawsuits between companies and former employees. But there is also more opposition in the day-to-day doing of business. A man who works at a large computer company in Silicon Valley told me that he sees this daily. Disagreement and verbal attack are encouraged at meetings, under the guise of challenging assumptions and fostering creativity. But in reality, he observes, what is fostered is dissension. In the end, the company's ability to do business can be threatened. He has seen at least one company virtually paralyzed by trying to seek consensus after assiduously stirring up dissension.

Who Will Be Left to Lead?

If this seems to describe an isolated phenomenon in a particular industry, take note: a comparable situation exists in our political life. The culture of critique is threatening our system of governance. Norman Ornstein, a political analyst at the American Enterprise Institute, articulates how.[26]

Ornstein offers some astonishing statistics: between 1975 and 1989, the number of federal officials indicted on charges of public corruption went up by a staggering 1,211 percent. During the same period, the number of nonfederal officials indicted doubled. What are we to make of this? he asks. Does it mean that officials during that decade were far more corrupt than before? Not likely. Every systematic study, as well as all anecdotal evidence, suggests just the opposite: public officials are far less corrupt now; fewer take bribes, get drunk in the middle of their duties, engage in immoral conduct, and so on.

What we have is the culture of critique. The press is poised to pounce on allegations of scandal, giving them primacy over every other kind of news. And the standards by which scandals are judged have declined. Allegations make the news, no matter where they come from, often without proof or even verification. (Remember the ruckus that accompanied reports that planes were forced to circle and travelers were delayed while President Clinton got a haircut on Air Force One in the Los Angeles airport?[27] And that George Bush did not know what a supermarket scanner was? Both turned out to be false.) Political opponents seize on these allegations and use them to punish or bring down opponents. The sad result is that laws designed to improve ethics have not improved ethics at all. Instead, they have made government almost impossible. Allegations trigger long investigations that themselves damage reputations and suggest to the public that terrible things are going on even when they aren't.

Prosecutors, too, are part of the web, Ornstein continues. In the past, an ambitious prosecutor might set out to snare a criminal on the FBI's ten most wanted list. Now the temptation is to go after a senator or cabinet member—or a vice president. That's where attention is paid; that's where the rewards lie.

The threat is not only to those at the highest levels of government but to public servants at every level. I spoke to someone prominent in the arts who was invited to join a federal commission. But first there was a questionnaire to fill out—pages and pages of details requested about the prospective nominee's personal, professional, and financial life. Special request was made for anything that might be embarrassing if it became public. The person in question simply declined the invitation.

The artist I spoke to typified a situation Ornstein described: it is becoming almost impossible to get qualified people to serve in public positions, from the highest executive nominations to part-time or even honorary appointments. Leaving private life for public service has always required personal sacrifice: your family life is disrupted; you take a pay cut. But now those contemplating such a move must be willing to make an even greater sacrifice: putting their personal reputation at risk. Instead of enhancing reputations, going into public services now threatens them, whether or not the officials have done anything to be ashamed of.

Disruption of family life is intensified, too, by the inordinate delay, Ornstein explained. While a nominee waits to be confirmed, life goes on hold: a spouse's job is in limbo; children await a change in schools; houses must—but can't—be found or rented or bought or sold. What is causing the delays to become so much more protracted than they were before? Every step in the process: presidents (and their staffs) must take much more time in choosing potential nominees, to make absolutely sure there is nothing in their lives or backgrounds that could embarrass not just the nominee but the president. Once people are selected, the FBI takes weeks or months longer than it used to for background checks, because it too wants to make sure it is not embarrassed later. Finally, the nomination goes to the Senate, where political opponents of the president or the nominee try to go for the jugular on ethics charges.

The result of all these forces is a much smaller pool of qualified people willing to consider public service, long periods when important posts are left vacant, a climate of suspicion that reinforces public doubts about the ethics of people in government, and real disruption in the running of our country.

We have become obsessed with the appearance of impropriety, as Peter Morgan and Glenn Reynolds show in a book with that title. Meanwhile, real impropriety goes unnoticed. We have to ask, as Ornstein does, whether the price we're paying to have pristine individuals fill every public post is worth what we're getting—and he (like Morgan and Reynolds) doubts that what we're getting is less impropriety.

The Cost in Human Spirit

Whatever the causes of the argument culture—and the many causes I have mentioned are surely not the only ones—the most grievous cost is the price paid in human spirit: contentious public discourse becomes a model for behavior and sets the tone for how individuals experience their relationships to other people and to the society we live in.

Recall the way young boys on Tory Island learned to emulate their elders:

> All around milled little boys imitating their elders, cursing, fluffing, swaggering, threatening. It was particularly fascinating to see how the children learned the whole sequence of behavior. Anything that the men did, they would imitate, shouting the same things, strutting and swaggering.[28]

Tory Island may be an especially ritualized example, but it is not a totally aberrant one. When young men come together in groups, they often engage in symbolic ritual displays of aggression that involve posturing and mock battles. Without pressing the parallel in too literal a way, I couldn't help thinking that this sounds a bit like what journalists and lawyers have observed about their own tribes: that the display of aggression for the benefit of peers is often more important than concrete results.

Consider again law professor Charles Yablon's observation that young litigators learn to value an aggressive stance by listening to their elders' war stories about "the smashing victories they obtained during pretrial discovery in cases which ultimately were settled." Litigators

> derive job satisfaction by recasting minor discovery disputes as titanic struggles. Younger lawyers, convinced that their future careers may hinge on how tough they *seem* while conducting discovery, may conclude that it is more important to look and sound ferocious than act cooperatively, even if all that huffing and puffing does not help (and sometimes harms) their cases.[29]

Against this background, recall too the observations made by journalists that their colleagues feel pressured to ask tough questions to get peer approval. Kenneth Walsh, for example, commented that "it helps your stature in journalism" if you ask challenging questions because that way "you show you're tough and you're independent." Just as litigators trade war stories about how tough they appeared (whether or not that appearance helped their client), Walsh points out that a journalist who dares to challenge the president takes on a heroic aura among his peers. He recalled a specific incident to illustrate this point:

> Remember Brit Hume asking the question ... about the zigzag decision-making process of President Clinton? And of course President Clinton cut off the questions after that one question because he felt it was not appropriate. That's what we all remember about the Ruth Bader Ginsburg period, is that Brit asked that question.[30]

Let's look at the actual exchange that earned Brit Hume the admiration of his peers. President Clinton called the press conference to announce his nomination of Judge Ruth Bader Ginsburg to the Supreme Court. After the president introduced her, Judge Ginsburg spoke movingly about her life, ending with tributes to her family: her children, granddaughter, husband, and, finally, her mother, "the bravest and strongest person I have known, who was taken from me much too soon." Following these remarks, which moved listeners to tears, journalists were invited to ask questions. The first (and, as it turned out, also the last) asked by correspondent Hume was this:

> The withdrawal of the Guinier nomination, sir, and your apparent focus on Judge Breyer and your turn, late, it seems, to Judge Ginsburg, may have created an impression, perhaps unfair, of a certain zigzag quality in the decision-making process here. I wonder, sir, if you could kind of walk us through it and perhaps disabuse us of any notion we might have along those lines. Thank you.

This question reminded everyone—at the very moment of Judge Ginsburg's triumph and honor—that she was not the president's first choice. It broke the spell of her moving remarks by shifting attention from the ceremonial occasion to the political maneuvers that had led up to the nomination—in particular, implying criticism of the president not from the perspective of substance (whether Judge Ginsburg would make a good Supreme Court Justice) but strategy (the decision-making process by which she was chosen). Remarking, "How you could ask a question like that after the statement she just made is beyond me," the president closed the event.

The answer to how Brit Hume could have asked a question like that lies in Walsh's observation that journalists value a display of toughness. In this view, to worry about Judge Ginsburg's feelings—or those of the viewing audience—would be like an attorney worrying about the feelings of a witness about to be cross-examined. But public ceremonies play a role in the emotional lives not only of participants but also of observers, an enormous group in the era of television. Viewers who were moved by Judge Ginsburg's personal statement shared in the ceremony and felt connected to the judge and, by implication, to our judicial system. Such feelings of connection to public figures whose actions affect our lives are a crucial element in individuals' sense of community and their feeling of well-being. Breaking that spell was harmful to this sense of connection, contributing a little bit to what is often called cynicism but which really goes much deeper than that: alienation from the public figures who deeply affect our lives and consequently from the society in which we live.

In this sense, the valuing of the appearance of toughness is related to another theme running through all the domains I discussed: the breakdown in human connections and the rise of anonymity. Lieutenant Colonel Grossman points out that this, too, was one of many ways that the experience of serving in Vietnam was different for American soldiers than was the experience of serving in previous wars. Remember my Uncle Norman, who at the age of eighty-seven was still attending annual reunions of the "boys" he had served with in World War II? This was possible because, as Grossman describes, soldiers in that war trained together, then went to war and served together. Those who were not killed or wounded stayed with the group until they all went home together at the end of the war. No wonder the bonds they forged could last a lifetime. Vietnam, in contrast, was a "lonely war" of individuals assigned to constantly shifting units for yearlong tours of duty (thirteen months for Marines). Grossman's description is graphic and sad:

> In Vietnam most soldiers arrived on the battlefield alone, afraid,
> and without friends. A soldier joined a unit where he was an FNG, a
> "f——ing new guy," whose inexperience and incompetence represented
> a threat to the continued survival of those in the unit. In a few months, for
> a brief period, he became an old hand who was bonded to a few friends
> and able to function well in combat. But then, all too soon, his friends left
> him via death, injury, or the end of their tours. …All but the best of units
> became just a collection of men experiencing endless leavings and arrivals,
> and that sacred process of bonding, which makes it possible for men to do
> what they must do in combat, became a tattered and torn remnant of the
> support structure experienced by veterans of past American wars.[31]

Though this pattern is most painful in this context, it parallels what we have seen in all the other domains of public dialogue. Recall attorney Susan Popik's observation "You don't come up against the same people all the time. That encouraged you to get along with them because you knew that in six months, you would be across the table from them again."[32] Recall journalists' lamenting that the present White House press corps is a large group, often unknown to aides and leaders, kept at a distance from the leaders they are assigned to cover: confined in a small room, in the back of the president's plane, behind ropes at public events. Contrast this with the recollections of those old enough to re-member a small White House press corps that had free run of official buildings and lots of private off-the-record meetings with public officials, including the president and first lady, so that they actually got to know them— as people. And recall departing Senator Heflin's regret about the decline of opportunities for legislators of opposing parties to socialize, which led to friendships developed "across party and ideological lines" that "led to more openness and willingness to discuss issues on a cordial basis" and to finding "common ground." We could add the demise of the family doctor who came to your home, replaced by an overworked internist or family practitioner—if not an anonymous emergency room—and, if you're unlucky enough to need them but lucky enough to get to see them, a cadre of specialists who may not talk to each other or even much to you, or surgeons who may spend hours saving your life or limb but hardly ever see or speak to you afterward.

In all these domains, wonderful progress has been accompanied by more and more anonymity and disconnection, which are damaging to the human spirit and fertile ground for animosity.

Getting Beyond Dualism

At the heart of the argument culture is our habit of seeing issues and ideas as absolute and irreconcilable principles continually at war. To move beyond this static and limiting view, we can remember the Chinese approach to yin and yang. They are two principles, yes, but they are conceived not as irreconcilable polar opposites but as elements that coexist and should be brought into balance as much as possible. As sociolinguist Suzanne Wong Scollon notes, "Yin is always present in and changing into yang and vice versa."[33] How can we translate this abstract idea into daily practice?

To overcome our bias toward dualism, we can make special efforts not to think in twos. Mary Catherine Bateson, an author and anthropologist who teaches at George Mason University, makes a point of having her class compare three cultures, not two.[34] If students compare two cultures, she finds, they are inclined to polarize them, to think of the two as opposite to each other. But if they compare three cultures, they are more likely to think about each on its own terms.

As a goal, we could all try to catch ourselves when we talk about "both sides" of an issue—and talk instead about "all sides." And people in any field can try to resist the temptation to pick on details when they see a chance to score a point. If the detail really does not speak to the main issue, bite your tongue. Draw back and consider the whole picture. After asking "Where is this wrong?" make an effort to ask "What is right about this?"—not necessarily *instead,* but *in addition.*

In the public arena, producers can try to avoid, whenever possible, structuring public discussions as debates. This means avoiding the format of having two guests discuss an issue, pro and con. In some cases three guests—or one—will be more enlightening than two.

An example of the advantage of adding a third guest was an episode of the *Diane Rehm Show* on National Public Radio following the withdrawal of Anthony Lake from nomination as director of central intelligence. White House Communications Director Ann Lewis claimed that the process of confirming presidential appointments has become more partisan and personal.[35] Tony Blankley, former communications director for Newt Gingrich, claimed that the process has always been rancorous. Fortunately for the audience, there was a third guest: historian Michael Beschloss, who provided historical perspective. He explained that during the immediately preceding period of 1940 to 1990, confirmation hearings were indeed more benign than they have been since, but in the 1920s and the latter half of the nineteenth century, he said, they were also "pretty bloody." In this way, a third guest, especially a guest who is not committed to one side, can dispel the audience's frustration when two guests make opposite claims.

Japanese television talk shows provide a window on other possibilities. Sociolinguist Atsuko Honda compared three different current affairs talk shows televised in Japan. Each one presents striking contrasts to what Americans take for granted in that genre. (The very fact that Honda chose to compare three—not two—is instructive.) The Japanese shows were structured in ways that made them less likely to be adversarial. Within each structure, participants vigorously opposed each other's ideas, yet they did so without excessively polarizing the issues.

Consider the formats of the three shows. *Nichiyoo Tooron (Sunday Discussion)* featured a moderator and four guests who discussed the recession for an hour. Only the moderator was a professional news commentator; two guests were associated with research institutes. The two other shows Honda examined concerned Japanese involvement in a peacekeeping mission in Cambodia. *Sunday Project* featured three guests: one magazine editor and two political scientists; the third show was a three-and-a-half-hour discussion involving fourteen panelists sitting around an oval table with a participating studio audience composed of fifty Japanese and Cambodian students. Viewers were also invited to participate by calling or faxing. Among the panelists were a history professor, a military analyst, a movie director, a scholar, a newscaster, and a legislator.

It is standard for American shows to provide balance by featuring two experts who represent contrasting political views: two senators or political consultants (one Republican, one Democrat), two journalist commentators (one on the left, one on the right), or two experts (one pro and one con). These Japanese shows had more than two guests, and the guests were identified by their expertise rather than their political perspectives. Another popular Japanese show that is often compared to ABC's *Nightline* or PBS's *Jim Lehrer News Hour* is called *Close-up Gendai*.[36] Providing thirty minutes of nightly news analysis, the Japanese show uses a format similar to these American TV shows. But it typically features a single guest. Japanese shows, in other words, have a wide range of formats featuring one guest or three or more—anything but two, the number most likely to polarize.

The political talk shows that Honda analyzed included many disagreements and conflicts. But whereas moderators of American and British talk shows often provoke and stoke conflict to make their shows more interesting, the Japanese moderators—and also the other guests—expended effort to modulate conflicts and defuse the spirit of opposition, but not the substance of disagreement. One last example, taken from Honda's study, illustrates how this worked.

In the long discussion among fourteen panelists, a dispute arose between two. Shikata, a former executive of the Japanese Self-Defense Forces, supported sending these forces to Cambodia. He was opposed by Irokawa, a historian who believed that the involvement of these forces violated the Japanese constitution. This exchange comes across as quite rancorous:

SHIKATA: Why is it okay to send troops to the protecting side but not okay to the protected side?

IROKAWA: Because we have the Japanese Constitution.

SHIKATA: Why is it so, if we have the Constitution?

IROKAWA: Well, we have to abide by the Constitution. If you don't want to follow the Constitution, you should get rid of your Japanese nationality and go somewhere else.

These are pretty strong words. And they were accompanied by strong gestures: according to Honda, as Shikata posed his question, he was beating the table with his palms; as Irokawa responded, he was jabbing the air toward Shikata with a pen.

Yet the confrontation did not take on a rancorous tone. The television cameras offered close-ups of both men's faces—smiling. In Japanese and other Asian cultures, smiling has different connotations than it does for Americans and Europeans: it tends to express not amusement but embarrassment. And while Shikata and Irokawa smiled, other panelists rushed to add their voices—and everyone burst out laughing. The laughter served to defuse the confrontation. So did the loud cacophony of voices that erupted as several panelists tried to speak at once. When individual voices finally were distinguished, they did not take one side or the other but tried to mediate the conflict by supporting and criticizing both sides equally. For example, Ohshima, a movie director, said, "I think that both parties overestimate or underestimate the realities for the sake of making a point."

Atsuko Honda found this to be typical of the televised discussions she analyzed: when a conspicuous conflict arose between two parties, other participants frequently moved in with attempts to mediate. In this way, they supported the Japanese ideal of avoiding winners and losers and helped everyone preserve some measure of "face." This mediation did not prevent varying views from being expressed; it resulted in different kinds of views being expressed. If two sides set the terms of debate and subsequent comments support one side or the other, the range of insights offered is circumscribed by the original two sides. If the goal instead is to mediate and defuse polarization, then other panelists are more likely to express a range of perspectives that shed nuanced light on the original two sides or suggest other ways of approaching the issue entirely.

Moving from Debate to Dialogue

Many of the issues I have discussed are also of concern to Amitai Etzioni and other communitarians. In *The New Golden Rule,* Etzioni proposes rules of engagement to make dialogue more constructive between people with differing views. His rules of engagement are designed to reflect—and reinforce—the tenet that people whose ideas conflict are still members of the same community.[37] Among these rules are:

- Don't demonize those with whom you disagree.
- Don't affront their deepest moral commitments.
- Talk less of rights, which are nonnegotiable, and more of needs, wants, and interests.
- Leave some issues out.
- Engage in a dialogue of convictions: don't be so reasonable and conciliatory that you lose touch with a core of belief you feel passionately about.

As I stressed [...] earlier [...], producers putting together television or radio shows and journalists covering stories might consider—in at least some cases—preferring rather than rejecting potential commentators who say they cannot take one side or the other unequivocally. Information shows might do better with only one guest who is given a chance to explore an idea in depth rather than two who will prevent each other from developing either perspective. A producer who feels that two guests with radically opposed views seem truly the most appropriate might begin by asking whether the issue is being framed in the most constructive way. If it is, a third or fourth participant could be invited as well, to temper the "two sides" perspective.

Perhaps it is time to re-examine the assumption that audiences always prefer a fight. In reviewing a book about the history of *National Geographic,* Marina Warner scoffs at the magazine's policy of avoiding attack. She quotes the editor who wrote in 1915, "Only what is of a kindly nature is printed about any country or people, everything unpleasant or unduly critical being avoided."[38] Warner describes this editorial approach condescendingly as a "happy-talk, feel-good philosophy" and concludes that "its deep wish not to offend has often made it dull." But the facts belie this judgment. *National Geographic* is one of the most successful magazines of all time—as reported in the same review, its circulation "stands at over 10 million, and the readership, according to surveys, is four times that number."

Perhaps, too, it is time to question our glorification of debate as the best, if not the only, means of inquiry. The debate format leads us to regard those doing different kinds of research as belonging to warring camps. There is something very appealing about conceptualizing differing approaches in this way, because the dichotomies appeal to our sense of how knowledge should be organized.

Well, what's wrong with that?

What's wrong is that it obscures aspects of disparate work that overlap and can enlighten each other.

What's wrong is that it obscures the complexity of research. Fitting ideas into a particular camp requires you to oversimplify them. Again, disinformation and distortion can result. Less knowledge is gained, not more. And time spent attacking an opponent or defending against attacks is not spent doing something else— like original research.

What's wrong is that it implies that only one framework can apply, when in most cases many can. As a colleague put it, "Most theories are wrong not in what they assert but in what they deny."[39] Clinging to the elephant's leg, they loudly proclaim that the person describing the elephant's tail is wrong. This is not going to help them—or their readers—understand an elephant. Again, there are parallels in personal relationships. I recall a man who had just returned from a weekend human development seminar. Full of enthusiasm, he explained the main lesson he had learned: "I don't have to make others wrong to prove that I'm right." He experienced this revelation as a liberation; it relieved him of the burden of trying to prove others wrong.

If you limit your view of a problem to choosing between two sides, you inevitably reject much that is true, and you narrow your field of vision to the limits of those two sides, making it unlikely you'll pull back, widen your field of vision, and discover the paradigm shift that will permit truly new understanding.

In moving away from a narrow view of debate, we need not give up conflict and criticism altogether. Quite the contrary, we can develop more varied—and more constructive—ways of expressing opposition and negotiating disagreement.

We need to use our imaginations and ingenuity to find different ways to seek truth and gain knowledge, and add them to our arsenal—or, should I say, to the ingredients for our stew. It will take creativity to find ways to blunt the most dangerous blades of the argument culture. It's a challenge we must undertake, because our public and private lives are at stake.

NOTES

1. This does not mean it goes back in an unbroken chain. David Noble, in *A World Without Women,* claims that Aristotle was all but lost to the West during the early Christian era and was rediscovered in the medieval era, when universities were first established. This is significant for his observation that many early Christian monasteries welcomed both women and men who could equally aspire to an androgynous ideal, in contrast to the Middle Ages, when the female was stigmatized, unmarried women were consigned to convents, priests were required to be celibate, and women were excluded from spiritual authority.

2. There is a fascinating parallel in the evolution of the early Christian Church and the Southern Baptist Church: Noble shows that the early Christian Church regarded women as equally beloved of Jesus and equally capable of devoting their lives to religious study, so women comprised a majority of early converts to Christianity, some of them leaving their husbands—or bringing their husbands along—to join monastic communities. It was later, leading up to the medieval period, that the clerical movement gained ascendancy in part by systematically separating women, confining them in either marriage or convents, stigmatizing them, and barring them from positions of power within the church. Christine Leigh Heyrman, in *Southern Cross: The Beginnings of the Bible Belt,* shows that a similar trajectory characterized the Southern Baptist movement. At first, young Baptist and Methodist preachers (in the 1740s to 1830s) preached that both women and blacks were equally God's children, deserving of spiritual authority—with the result that the majority of converts were women and slaves. To counteract this distressing demography, the message was changed: antislavery rhetoric faded, and women's roles were narrowed to domesticity and subservience. With these shifts, the evangelical movement swept the South. At the same time, Heyrman shows, military imagery took over: the ideal man of God was transformed from a "willing martyr" to a "formidable fighter" led by "warrior preachers."

3. Ong, *Fighting for Life,* p. 122. Ong's source, on which I also rely, is Oliver, *Communication and Culture in Ancient India and China.* My own quotations from Oliver are from p. 259.

4. Pachomius, for example, "the father of communal monasticism ... and organizer of the first monastic community, had been a soldier under Constantine" and modeled his community on the military, emphasizing order, efficiency, and military obedience. Cassian, a fourth-century proselytizer, "'likened the monk's discipline to that of the soldier,' and Chrysostom, another great champion of the movement, 'sternly reminded the monks that Christ had armed them to be soldiers in a noble fight'" (Noble, *A World Without Women,* p. 54).

5. Aristotle, quoted in Oliver, *Communication and Culture in Ancient India and China*, p. 259.

6. I came to understand the different meaning of "poet" in Classical Greece from reading Ong and also *Preface to Plato* by Eric Havelock. These insights informed many articles I wrote about oral and literate tradition in Western culture, including "Oral and Literate Strategies in Spoken and Written Narratives" and "The Oral/Literate Continuum in Discourse."

7. Moulton, "A Paradigm of Philosophy"; Ong, *Fighting for Life*.

8. The example of Danny and the lava: Wertsch, *Voices of the Mind,* pp. 113–114.

9. See David and Myra Sadker, *Failing at Fairness*.

10. Although my colleagues and I make efforts to refer to our students—all over the age of eighteen—as "women" and "men" and some students in my classes do the same, the majority refer to each other and themselves as "girls" and "boys" or "girls" and "guys."

11. Jonathan Alter, "The End of the Journey." *Newsweek*, Nov. 4, 1996, p. 61. Trilling died at the age of ninety-one.

12. Kaplan, *French Lessons*, p. 119.

13. Tracy and Baratz, "Intellectual Discussion in the Academy as Situated Discourse," p. 309.

14. Greenberg and Robins, "The Changing Role of Social Experiments in Policy Analysis," p. 350.

15. These and other quotes from Tompkins appear in her essay "Fighting Words," pp. 588–589.

16. Safire is quoted in Howard Kurtz, "Safire Made No Secret of Dislike for Inman," *The Washington Post*, Jan. 19, 1994, p. A6.

17. I've borrowed the William Blake quote from Peter Elbow, who used it to open his book *Embracing Contraries*.

18. Terence Monmaney, "Marshall's Hunch," *New Yorker*, Sept. 20, 1993, pp. 64–72.

19. Elbow, *Embracing Contraries,* p. 258.

20. Moulton, "A Paradigm of Philosophy," p. 153.

21. Social constructionists often deride the ideas of those who focus on differences as "essentialist"—a bit of academic name-calling. It is used only as a way of criticizing someone else's work: "Smith's claims are repugnant because they are essentialist." I have never heard anyone claim, "I am an essentialist," though I have frequently heard elaborate self-defenses: "I am not an essentialist!" Capturing the tendency to use this term as an epithet, *Lingua Franca,* a magazine for academics, describes "essentialist" as "that generic gender studies *j'accuse!*" See Emily Nussbaum, "Inside Publishing," *Lingua Franca,* Dec.–Jan. 1977, pp. 22–24; the quote is from p. 24.

22. Klein, *Meeting the Great Bliss Queen*, pp. 8–9.

23. Cynthia Gorney, "Gloria," *Mother Jones,* Nov.–Dec. 1995, pp. 22–27; the quote is from p. 22.

24. See, for example, Needham, *Science and Civilization in China*.

25. Ellyn E. Spragins, *Newsweek*, July 28, 1997, p. 73.

26. This section is based on an interview with Ornstein. See also Ornstein's article, "Less Seems More."

27. The story behind the haircut story is told by Gina Lubrano, "Now for the Real Haircut Story … ," *San Diego Union-Tribune,* July 12, 1993, p. B7. That the supermarket scanner story was not true was mentioned by George Stephanopoulos at a panel held at Brown University, as reported by Elliot Krieger, "Providence Journal/Brown University Public Affairs Conference," *The Providence Journal-Bulletin,* Mar. 5, 1995, p. 12A.

28. Fox, "The Inherent Rules of Violence," p. 141.

29. Yablon, "Stupid Lawyer Tricks," p. 1639.

30. Kenneth Walsh made this comment on the *Diane Rehm Show,* May 28, 1996.

31. Grossman, *On Killing,* p. 270.

32. Susan Popik made this comment on the *U.S. Business Litigation* panel.

33. Suzanne Wong Scollon: Personal communication.

34. Mary Catherine Bateson: Personal communication.

35. At the time of this show, Ms. Lewis was deputy communications director.

36. Yoshiko Nakano helped me with observations of *Close-up Gendai.*

37. Etzioni, *The New Golden Rule,* pp. 104–106. He attributes the rule "Talk less of rights … and more of needs, wants, and interests" to Mary Ann Glendon.

38. Marina Warner, "High-Minded Pursuit of the Exotic," review of *Reading National Geographic* by Catherine A. Lutz and Jane L. Collins in *The New York Times Book Review,* Sept. 19, 1993, p. 13.

39. I got this from A. L. Becker, who got it from Kenneth Pike, who got it from …

REFERENCES

Elbow, Peter. *Embracing Contraries: Explorations in Learning and Teaching* (New York and Oxford: Oxford University Press, 1986).

Etzioni, Amitai. *The New Golden Rule: Community and Morality in a Democratic Society* (New York: Basic, 1996).

Fox, Robin. "The Inherent Rules of Violence." In *Social Rules and Social Behaviour,* Peter Collet, ed. (Totowa, N.J.: Rowman and Littlefield, 1976), pp. 132–149.

Greenberg, David H., and Philip K. Robins. "The Changing Role of Social Experiments in Policy Analysis." *Journal of Policy Analysis and Management* 5:2(1986), pp. 340–362.

Grossman, Dave. *On Killing: The Psychological Cost of Learning to Kill in War and Society* (Boston: Little, Brown, 1995).

Havelock, Eric A. *Preface to Plato* (Cambridge, Mass.: Belknap Press, Harvard University Press, 1963).

Heyrman, Christine Leigh. *Southern Cross: The Beginnings of the Bible Belt* (New York: Knopf, 1997).

Kaplan, Alice. *French Lessons: A Memoir* (Chicago: University of Chicago Press, 1993).

Klein, Anne Carolyn. *Meeting the Great Bliss Queen: Buddhists, Feminists, and the Art of the Self* (Boston: Beacon Press, 1995).

Kurtz, Howard. *Hot Air: All Talk, All the Time* (New York: Times Books, 1996).

Moulton, Janice. "A Paradigm of Philosophy: The Adversary Method." In *Discovering Reality*, Sandra Harding and Merrill B.Hintikka, eds. (Dordrecht, Holland: Reidel, 1983), pp. 149–164.

Needham, Joseph. *Science and Civilization in China* (Cambridge, England: Cambridge University Press, 1956).

Noble, David. *A World Without Women: The Christian Culture of Western Science* (New York and Oxford: Oxford University Press, 1992).

Oliver, Robert T. *Communication and Culture in Ancient India and China* (Syracuse, N.Y.: Syracuse University Press, 1971).

Ong, Walter J. *Fighting for Life: Contest, Sexuality, and Consciousness* (Ithaca, N.Y.: Cornell University Press, 1981).

Ornstein, Norman J. "Less Seems More: What to Do About Contemporary Political Corruption." *The Responsible Community* 4:1 (Winter 1993–94), pp. 7–22.

Tompkins, Jane. "Fighting Words: Unlearning to Write the Critical Essay." *Georgia Review* 42(1988), pp. 585–590.

Tracy, Karen, and Sheryl Baratz. "Intellectual Discussion in the Academy as Situated Discourse." *Communication Monographs* 60(1993), pp. 300–320.

Wertsch, James V. *Voices of the Mind: A Sociocultural Approach to Mediated Action* (Cambridge, Mass.: Harvard University Press, 1991).

Yablon, Charles. "Stupid Lawyer Tricks: An Essay on Discovery Abuse." *Columbia Law Review* 96(1996), pp. 1618–1644.

QUESTIONS FOR MAKING CONNECTIONS
WITHIN THE READING

1. In the course of her argument Deborah Tannen refers to "our adversarial culture," "the culture of critique," and to maleness, logic, formalism, and polarization. She refers as well to the customs and discourses of Western religion and science, and to contemporary educational practices. Define these terms and explain how they fit together. What is the relation between logic and aggression, between religion and science, and between Ancient Greece and the education offered by our universities?

2. In what ways has the "boot camp" model shaped your own educational experience? In a social setting like a boot camp—marked by inequality and dominance—is the leader the only one who creates the tension, or does everyone collaborate in creating and sustaining an atmosphere of rivalry and violence? How about in the case of schooling: in what ways do the students themselves actively collaborate in making the classroom into a "camp"? In what ways does the system—the culture and the institutions of schooling—reinforce these behaviors?

3. In the section entitled "Getting Beyond Dualism," Tannen describes the dynamics of three Japanese television programs, which she offers as examples

of a less agonistic style of public discussion. What features distinguish these programs from comparable discussions in the U.S. media and in places like the classroom? Does disagreement have a different significance in the context of Japanese culture? When people disagree in Western settings, what might be at stake? What values and outcomes matter the most? In the Japanese context, what values and outcomes are most significant? How might an American misunderstand the Japanese programs?

QUESTIONS FOR WRITING

1. University professors routinely study communities and institutions outside the university, and they are often quite critical of what they discover there, but the university itself is seldom the object of comparable scrutiny. In what ways—if any—does the culture of critique stifle inquiry and thwart constructive change within the university itself? If Tannen is correct in her estimations, would it be fair to say that the advancement of knowledge is only one of the university's many goals and perhaps not even the most important one? What might its other goals be?

2. The university in the United States is a unique institution in many ways. For one thing, all faculty above the level of assistant professor have lifetime employment and cannot be dismissed except for gross dereliction of duty. Most public universities receive automatic funding from state coffers. Many private universities have enormous endowments, sometimes in the billions of dollars. And most professors are shielded from any assessment of their effectiveness as teachers, except through course evaluations. In what ways does the university's unique situation contribute to the persistence of the culture of critique? What about the media? Do the media also contribute to the persistence of this culture?

QUESTIONS FOR MAKING CONNECTIONS
BETWEEN READINGS

1. In "An Elephant Crackup," the psychologist Gary Bradshaw tells the author Charles Siebert, "Everybody pretty much agrees that the relationship between elephants and people has dramatically changed." For centuries, "humans and elephants lived in relative peaceful coexistence," but now there is "hostility and violence." How might the values of the "argument culture," as Tannen describes them, contribute to this deterioration? As societies around the world become increasingly Westernized, are they losing the capacity to interact in less aggressive ways, not only with other people but with the natural world

as well? Do you see evidence in Siebert's account of an emerging dialogue between elephants and humans?

2. How does Malcolm Gladwell's discussion of the dynamics of social change confirm, contradict, or complicate Tannen's argument? Does Gladwell's account suggest that social change is decided by the strongest argument? Does debate even play a significant role? If public debate and rational deliberation have a marginal influence, why does the university place so high a premium on them? Have professors depicted the social world in ways that are flattering to themselves? In what ways is this depiction both accurate and inaccurate?

EDWARD TENNER

EDWARD TENNER HAS been called a "philosopher of everyday technology." His principal concern is the way that human beings interact with the products of technological innovation. In exploring these interactions, Tenner takes an expansive view, and his thinking brings together subjects as diverse as agriculture, antibiotics, automobiles, chairs, shoes, football helmets, and computer software. Tenner's studies of technological development have led him to conclude that innovation often produces—at least in the short term—unintended negative consequences. These negative consequences, which Tenner calls technology's "revenge effects," sometimes actually make life *less* safe, convenient, and efficient than before the inventions came into being. As he puts it, "A small change to solve a minor problem may create a larger one." Moreover, he notes that the risk of technology's revenge effects has only been intensified by the ubiquity of computer software in modern life.

Revenge effects unfold around us everyday—in traffic jams, for example, and as online spam. But Tenner is intrigued and inspired by the way that people have responded with creativity to these problems. Revenge effects are unintended—that much is true—but our efforts to improve the quality of life need not be self-defeating. As Tenner puts it, "human culture, not some inherent will of the machine, has created most revenge effects," and for this reason, he argues that we must not lose sight of our capacity to change and adapt. As the pace of innovation accelerates, Tenner considers one question to be especially important for any reflection on the best course for the future: "How can we break out of ruts and change our thinking?"

Tenner's educational and professional background is eclectic. In addition to *Why Things Bite Back* (1996), he is also the author of *Our Own Devices: How Technology Remakes Humanity* (2003). Tenner is currently a writer, speaker, and technology consultant, and was formerly employed as a science editor at Princeton University Press. He is the recipient of a Guggenheim fellowship and has been affiliated with Princeton's Institute for Advanced Study and the Jerome and Dorothy Lemelson Center for the Study of Invention and Innovation at the Smithsonian.

Tenner, Edward. "Another Look Back, and a Look Ahead." *Why Things Bite Back: Technology and the Revenge of Unintended Consequences*. New York: Knopf, 1996. 254–277.

Biographical information comes from Edward Tenner's home page, <http://www.edwardtenner.com/>. Quotations come from the Princeton University Web site, <http://www.princeton.edu/pr/pwb///a.shtml>, an NPR interview with Tenner, and *Why Things Bite Back*.

Another Look Back, and a Look Ahead

"Doing Better and Feeling Worse." This phrase from a 1970s symposium on health care is more apt than ever, and not only in medicine. We seem to worry more than our ancestors, surrounded though they were by exploding steamboat boilers, raging epidemics, crashing trains, panicked crowds, and flaming theaters. Perhaps this is because the safer life imposes an ever-increasing burden of attention. Not just in the dilemmas of medicine but in the management of natural hazards, in the control of organisms, in the running of offices, and even in the playing of games there are, not necessarily more severe, but more subtle and intractable, problems to deal with.

To investigate why disasters should lead to improvement, and improvement should paradoxically foster discontent, it might help to look at three areas of technology we have not considered before: timekeeping, navigation, and motorization. The automobile first presented an acute problem—collisions—but its success reduced that difficulty while adding to it another, less easily soluble one—congestion. And the recent history of motoring also suggests a paradox of safety, that the better-made and less dangerous motor vehicles become, the greater are the burdens on the operator. The prognosis for revenge effects is hopeful: we will probably keep them under control. By replacing brute force with finesse, concentration with variety, and heavy traditional materials with lighter ones, we are already starting to overcome the thinking and habits that led to many revenge effects. Technology, too, is evolving and responding. The one thing we will not be able to do is avoid the endless rituals of vigilance.

In one example after another, revenge has turned out to be the flip side of intensity. The velocity of twentieth-century transportation and warfare produces trauma on an unprecedented scale, which in turn calls for equally intensive care; but the end result may be chronic brain damage that is beyond medical treatment. Intensive antibiotic therapy has removed the horror of some of the nineteenth century's most feared infections, yet it has also promoted the spread of even more virulent bacteria. Massive shielding of beaches from the energy of waves has deflected their intensity to other shores or robbed these beaches of replenishing sand. Smoke jumpers have suppressed small forest fires but have thereby helped build reservoirs of flammable materials in the understory for more intense ones. Towering smokestacks have propelled particulates at great velocity higher into the atmosphere than ever before—to the dismay of residents over an ever wider radius. Intensive chicken-pig-duck agriculture in China has rushed new influenza virus strains into production, for distribution internationally by the increasingly dense and speedy world network of commercial aircraft. Accelerating processor speed has multiplied computer operations without necessarily reducing costs to programmers, system managers, and end users. Rigid molded ski boots have helped prevent ankle and tibia fractures at the cost of anterior cruciate ligament injuries. And what are so-called pests but intensified life forms? Most of these animals and plants are unusually robust, prolific, and adaptive. The animals are mobile and the plants spread rapidly. Fire ants, Africanized bees, starlings, melaleuca go about their business single-mindedly. Even the dreamy-looking eucalyptus is capable of burning intensely to propagate itself—taking entire neighborhoods with it. And when intensity is a genuine protection against catastrophe, it may fail to address and even complicates persistent low-level problems.

We have learned the limits of intensiveness. What next? In the near time, intensification is still working. Human health and longevity have improved in most places and by most measures. As we have seen, people may feel sicker today because they are more likely to survive with some limitation or chronic illness. But they really are better off. It is hard to disagree with optimists like Leonard Sagan and Aaron Wildavsky when they point to the benefits of growth. Fortunately, every prediction of global famine and misery has failed—so far.

The second argument for optimism is humanity's success in digging deeper and looking harder for old resources and substituting new ones. In the crucible of technological change, shortages produce surpluses and crises yield alternatives. When the biologist Paul Ehrlich lost a bet with the economist Julian Simon on future prices of a bundle of commodities selected by Ehrlich—they dropped between 1980 and 1990, costing Ehrlich $576.06—the transaction seemed to bear out Simon's argument that inexhaustible human ingenuity would find a way around apparent shortages. Market forces appear to impose conservation and encourage discovery more efficiently than legislation generally can. We have seen how the feared hardwood shortage of the early twentieth century never happened, much to the dismay of Jack London and other hopeful eucalyptus growers. Of course, this analysis has revenge effects of its own for market economics: if constraint helps make us so much more clever, why should the state not prod the infinitely creative human mind with more taxes and restrictions? Heavy taxes on fossil fuels should, by the same logic, do wonders for conservation and alternative energy sources.[1]

When it comes to interpreting the last hundred years, the optimists have the upper hand. The future is another matter. Optimists counter projections of global warming, rising sea levels, population growth, and soil depletion with scenarios of gradual adjustment and adaptation. If the crisis of life in the oceans is the problem, then fish farming is the answer. A true optimist sees a silver lining even in the destruction of rain forests and wilderness: there may be much less acreage, but more and more people will be able to travel and see it. In terms of this strange anthropocentric, utilitarian calculus there will actually be more *available* forest and wilderness. As for soil depletion, genetic engineering and new methods of cultivation will presumably let us cope; the world can probably support a population of ten billion or more. (In 1994 it stood at 5.6 billion.) Optimists and pessimists disagree not so much on what is attainable, but on how long it will *be* attainable. What the first group welcomes as a successful adaptation the second belittles as a stopgap. Optimists and pessimists curiously agree that crisis is good for us, but for different reasons. Pessimists welcome emergency as a violent cure for profligacy. Optimists welcome it as an injection of innovatory stimulus.

The Ambiguity of Disaster

One reason for optimism is that disaster is paradoxically creative. It legitimizes and promotes changes in rules—changes that may be resisted as long as the levels of casualties remain "acceptable" prior to a disaster that leads to change. More important, disasters mobilize the kind of ingenuity that technological optimists believe exists in unlimited supply. Of course, new disasters may themselves be unintended consequences of prior solutions. It is uncertain whether, at least in developed countries, the incidence of new catastrophes is gradually declining or not. Should disasters be considered as waves that remain constant in amplitude, damped, or amplified? The unanswerable question about technological revenge effects is whether we are really learning. Even tragedies like Chernobyl and Bhopal are ambiguous as forewarnings. Are they just the most recent in an ongoing series that will strike again in Western Europe and North America, where matters are far less secure than their leaders admit? Or will they spark environmental consciousness and vigilance in the former Soviet bloc and the developing world? It is too soon to say, but there is excellent evidence that great disasters do have long-term reverse revenge effects.

The first great modern stimulus from disaster may have been the defeat of the Spanish Armada in 1588. The economic historian David Landes has speculated that this greatest setback in the history of Spain was what led its king Philip III to offer a perpetual pension of 6,000 ducats to "the discoverer of the longitude" when he ascended the throne ten years later. (Landes is not sure, however, what method would have kept the surviving ships from their fate on the rocks of Ireland and the Orkney Islands.) In France the Duc d'Orléans made a comparable offer. From Galileo to Newton, most of the giants of the scientific revolution of the late sixteenth and seventeenth centuries, with or without prizes in mind, joined the search. None of these thinkers produced a practical astronomical system, yet the shipwrecks and prizes did have other substantial benefits. The sociologist Robert K. Merton has suggested how many advances in mathematics, astronomy, mechanics, and magnetism could be traced to the vast losses that Spain and other maritime powers had suffered.[2]

It took a further disaster to complete the paradoxical work: the wreck of three ships from the fleet of Admiral Sir Cloudesley Shovell in 1707 on the Scilly Isles off the west coast of England, killing almost two thousand sailors. (The admiral reportedly struggled ashore, only to be murdered for his magnificent ring.) Today we know that bad geography, charts, and compasses, and poor navigation, complicated by fog and unpredictable currents, were mainly to blame. To contemporaries, though, the lesson was a new urgency in the search for a way to determine longitude at sea. Of course, a valid method would in turn make possible more accurate printed aids to navigation. The question of longitude was not immediately supported officially; only seven years later, in 1714, was an Act of Parliament passed, offering up to £20,000—at least $1 million in today's purchasing power—for a method of determining longitude on an oceangoing vessel.[3]

Entrepreneurs and cranks had been at work on solutions ever since the wreck, proposing lines of ships somehow "anchored" in mid-ocean, telepathic goats, and even dogs communicating through a "sympathetic powder" said by its promoters to relay sensations from an animal on land to one at sea after having been sprinkled on both. But the prize, after more than another decade had passed, attracted the attention of the gifted clock maker John Harrison, who built a chronometer that met the specifications of the act. The steps and the time it took him to refine his timepiece (along with the fact that he did not secure payment of his claims until 1773, when he was eighty) are not the point here. What matters is that the magnitude of the Scilly Isles wreck eventually justified the great reward offered.

The earlier prizes contributed indirectly to the Act of Parliament. It was Newton, who had long worked on the problem, whose recommendation was essential for the act's passage. Only in hopes of the new prize did Harrison and other leading craftsmen abandon their normal clientele for a largely speculative project that had frustrated the scientific elite of Europe for decades. The search for longitude may represent the first great public high-technology program. In its costs and benefits it became one of the most successful. Anything like it would almost certainly have been long delayed in the absence of a spectacular new disaster.[4]

It took another two hundred years for a single marine disaster to have an international impact comparable to that of the Scilly Isles wreck. This was the sinking of the *Titanic,* pride of the White Star Line, on April 14, 1912. The ship's tragic end was memorialized not only as an enormous loss of life and property—over fifteen hundred passengers and crew perished, including the captain—but also as a cautionary tale. Some of its perceived lessons were social, the image of the frivolous rich fiddling as the world was about to burn, or even escaping in lifeboats as the poor drowned in steerage. Even the failure of other ships to respond to its distress calls has been blamed on the priority given by radio operators to the social cables of their first-class passengers. But in the long run, the dangers of technological pride rather than class conflict seemed to be the message of this disaster. Even more than the loss of the three English ships two centuries earlier, the sinking of the *Titanic* immediately became what risk analysts now call a *signal event*—one that reveals an ominous and previously underestimated kind of danger.[5]

The problem was not mainly in the operation of the ship's systems, useless though some of the lifeboat mechanisms turned out to be. Even though White Star officials never claimed the ship was actually unsinkable, the captain and crew acted with inappropriate confidence, steaming at high speed through waters notorious for sea ice. After the *Titanic* hit the iceberg, the same confidence in the ship's safeguards delayed, with tragic consequences, the implementation of rescue procedures that could have reduced casualties immeasurably. (Her officers doubtless had faith in the owners' stringent design specifications, but marine archaeologists now believe that the vessel's steel plates did not meet these standards.) Belief in the safety of the ship became the greatest single hazard to the survival of its passengers, greater than the icebergs themselves. In fact, crews of other nearby vessels that might have rescued passengers believed the *Titanic's* distress flares could only mean some celebration, not an emergency.

Less known is how important the *Titanic* disaster was in solving what had been a serious problem for international navigation: the prevalence of sea ice in the ocean lanes of the world's most active and lucrative route, the North Atlantic. The wreck had precedents: in the 1880s over fifty passenger ships reported sea ice damage in and around the Grand Banks off the Newfoundland coast where the *Titanic* later went down; fourteen of them had sunk. It was the loss of the *Titanic* that led not only to new regulations requiring lifeboat space for all passengers and crew, but to a series of international conferences on the Safety of Life at Sea (SOLAS) beginning in 1913. The International Ice Patrol, established in 1913, now uses aerial surveillance, satellite images, and radio-equipped oceanographic drifter buoys. The biggest bergs even have their own radio transmitters. Ships possess advanced radar systems. It would require extraordinary negligence for a captain to let an iceberg sink a ship.[6]

At least for passengers embarking in the United States, an ocean cruise now appears extraordinarily safe. From 1970 to 1989, only two of over thirty million passengers died in accidents involving cruise ships operating out of the United States, despite a number of collisions and fires. Each generation of ships meets higher standards. SOLAS now specifies a maximum thirty-minute evacuation time for cruise ships. Only one ship has ever sunk after hitting an iceberg since the *Titanic,* and that was in 1943, when the Ice Patrol was discontinued during the Second World War.[7]

Both tragedies and their consequences illustrate the engineer and historian Henry Petroski's point that a great disaster is often the best stimulus for new engineering ideas. Two things have changed, though, since the early eighteenth century. The growth of engineering as a profession has made a new type of error possible, as Petroski has also shown: overconfidence in the safety of a new design, the defects of which too often remain hidden until some new disaster occurs. But there is also a second type of error: failure to observe the repeated rituals that safe operation of advanced technology entails. The higher potential speed of steamships required (and requires) more rather than less care. The larger number of passengers and crew required (and requires) more careful drills and inspection of equipment. It is still difficult for a prospective passenger to tell how well trained a crew may be to handle an emergency. We know some technology has a built-in demand for care, a maintenance compulsion. But there is always a hidden catch of technological improvement: the need for enhanced vigilance that we have already seen in medicine, in environmental modification, in the translocation of plants and animals, in electronic systems, and even in some aspects of athletics.[8]

At this point in the history of technology we can draw a fundamental lesson from an unexpected source, the law of negligence. In a number of important articles, the legal scholar Mark Grady correlates better and safer technology with the number of lawsuits for malpractice and personal injury. During the centuries when bleeding, purging, and mercury compounds (as we have seen) hastened the deaths of many of the West's elite, legal action against the physicians who pursued these remedies was rare. The public did not hold doctors in awe; neither did they really expect heroic remedies to work. In fact, it was precisely because they doubted the scientific basis of contemporary treatments that a malpractice suit had little point.

According to Grady, "the first negligence explosion occurred during the 1875–1905 period. In that time of industrial revolution, claims increased by fully 800%, and the negligence rule did not change significantly. When machines abound, negligence claims increase. Put differently, a doctor who forgot to perform a modern fetal health procedure could not have been liable in 1960, before the procedure was invented." On this view, a dialysis machine reduces the risk of kidney failure in nature but adds a new risk: that physicians and technicians operating the machines under their supervision may fail to make safe connections, test the hemodialytic solution, or observe all the other precautions of good practice. Anyone who has watched the pilot and copilot of a common two-engine commuter aircraft carry out their extensive preflight procedures, flipping through pages in a printed notebook as they read their scripts, has been struck by the number of precautions that a long-accepted and well-developed technology imposes.[9]

By the standards of its day, the *Titanic* was a ship relatively high in what Grady calls "durable precautions," the safety hardware that popular opinion supposed made it unsinkable. It is true that size, luxury, and speed had higher priority than safety in her design—but she had the latest in communications and damage-containment equipment. Grady's analysis suggests, though, that the very presence of these measures increased the importance of "nondurable precautions"—all the things an officer or crew member must remember to do—in keeping the ship afloat. The flow of messages on the ship's radio demanded constant attention: Did a given message warrant immediate transmission to the bridge? Once the captain was aware of it, did it necessitate a change of speed or course? And with lifeboats come other questions. Have they been inspected regularly? Does each crew member know his or her part in supervising a possible abandonment? If a major marine loss occurs, it is the way an emergency plan is carried out, not physical safeguards alone, that will determine whether or not it becomes a disaster for human life.

Here is where the difference between early and industrial technology becomes telling. The captain of a seventeenth-century oceangoing ship needed excellent navigation skills, and the management of cargo, ballast, and rigging were already arts for specialists. Some captains and pilots of Renaissance and early modern Europe had superb intuition which let them achieve amazing feats of "dead reckoning": the estimation of position from relatively crude measurements of last position, direction, and speed. A gifted mariner could go beyond the limits of the technology of the day. Yet because of the difficulty of measuring longitude, compounded by the other defects of instruments, disaster could happen to the best of seafarers. That is why Sir Cloudesley Shovell still got an overbearing tomb by Grinling Gibbons in Westminster Abbey after his catastrophic end. (On the other hand, Joseph Addison ridiculed it as "the figure of a beau, dressed in a long periwig, and reposing himself upon velvet cushions under a canopy of state," and deplored that it commemorated only his demise and not his victories.) The better and the safer technology becomes, the more we presume human error when something goes seriously wrong. If it is not the error of the captain or crew, it is one of the engineers or designers of equipment, or of executives and their maintenance policies.[10]

The Automobile and Revenge Effects

Intensity—disaster—precaution—vigilance: the cycle appears on land as well as at sea. The rise of motoring shows this more clearly than the transformation of sailing, but in a different way.... [N]ineteenth-century railroad accidents were the first of a new type of technological disaster unknown in the eighteenth century. Historians of technology have long pointed out the importance of indignation over early railroad tragedies in developing the first complex control systems in American business, not to mention safety hardware like signals and air brakes. But there is an equally interesting side to the intensification of transportation by the railroad: the rise of automobile transport. Casualties from car accidents occur as a steady series of small disasters, not the few-but-great wrecks involving trains and steamships. The automobile invited chronic catastrophes. Indignation built more slowly.[11]

The growing capacity of the nation's railroad network had an unforeseen consequence that few scholars have noted—chaos in the horse-drawn city. Nearly every passenger journey or freight shipment began and ended with a horse-drawn vehicle or a horse, at least until cable cars and electric trolleys spread late in the century. Even the physical size of horses increased throughout the nineteenth century, to move the heavier loads and serve the larger populations of European and American cities. By the 1880s, massive Percherons were a familiar sight on American streets. Teamstering already was a crucial trade, and the number of horses for every teamster was growing. Local delivery by horse could cost nearly as much as hundreds of miles by rail. Today's Budweiser Clydesdales, a magnificent public relations asset, are the heritage of yesterday's logistical nightmares.[12]

Herds of horses multiplied. Even after cable and electric power had begun to replace horse traction for streetcars, horses were everywhere. The Fiss, Doerr, and Carroll horse auction mart on East 24th Street in New York drew up to a thousand buyers and boasted its own seven-story, block-long stable. New York City's horses alone produced over 300 million pounds of manure annually; stables accumulated tens of thousands of cubic feet for months at a time. In fact, as we have seen, one imported pest, the English sparrow, thrived on the bounty of grain in horse droppings. Repeated horse epidemics—technically epizootics—paralyzed commerce and interfered with firefighting. Despite limitation of their workdays to four hours, horses died after only a few years of service, usually in the middle of the street, up to fifteen thousand a year in New York. Dust from powdered horse manure helped spread tuberculosis and tetanus. As railroads grew safer, the horse-drawn city became more dangerous.[13]

Less remembered today than the sanitary problems caused by horses were the safety hazards they posed. Horses and horse-drawn vehicles were dangerous, killing more riders, passengers, and pedestrians than is generally appreciated. Horses panicked. In frequent urban traffic snarls, they bit and kicked some who crossed their path. Horse-related accidents were an important part of surgical practice in Victorian England and no doubt in North America as well. In the 1890s in New York, per capita deaths from wagons and carriage accidents nearly doubled. By the end of the century they stood at nearly six per hundred thousand of population. Added to the five or so streetcar deaths, the rate of about 110 per million is close to the rates of motor vehicle deaths in many industrial countries in the 1980s. On the eve of motorization, the urban world was not such a gentle place.[14]

The automobile was an answer to disease and danger. In fact, private internal-combustion transportation was almost utopian. The congested tenements of the center city spread dirt and disease. Dispersing people into the green suburbs was a favorite theme of city reformers. Progressive mayors supported the extension of horsecars and then trolleys. But at least on city stretches, these had an unpleasant intensity of their own. In 1912 the *Los Angeles Record* found their air "a pestilence ... heavy with disease and the emanations from many bodies.... A bishop embraced a stout grandmother, a tender girl touched limbs with a city sport...." And hard-pressed straphangers objected to allegedly high fares, reckless drivers, and rude conductors.[15]

Automobiles may have begun as rich people's toys, but thanks largely to Henry Ford, they soon came to represent independence from the rich: *from* railroad interests, traction (streetcar) companies, center-city landlords. By the 1950s and the 1960s, the automotive industry had come to represent big business at its most arrogant, but motorization won because it rallied so many small businesses. Diffuse interests were its political strength. Motoring did not benefit only car manufacturers and petroleum producers and refiners. It enriched tens of thousands of small businesses: trucking companies, suburban developers, construction contractors, dealers and parts retailers, service station operators. Of course, as Clay McShane and other urban historians before him have documented, road improvement was not really populist, or uniformly popular. It did change the nature of the street, but to the disadvantage of residents. The roadway ceased to be a gathering place and became a thoroughfare. Many neighborhoods resisted asphalt paving, and children even stoned passing cars. Still, motoring showed the political advantages of spreading benefits to many small and medium-sized interests.[16]

In spite of clear damage to urban greenery and space, using roads to help disperse people in private suburban houses remained not just a popular but a politically correct idea for a long time, and not only in America. Franklin D. Roosevelt thought that spreading population would lower the cost of government and directly reduce the expense of urban services. One radical planner,

Carol Aronovici, wrote in 1932: "Let the old cities perish so that we may have great and beautiful cities." Aronovici called for "a thorough emancipation of the suburban communities from the metropolis" that was threatening to "suck their very physical existence into the body politic of decayed and corrupted political organization." (More than sixty years later, these same towns—now aging demographically and economically—are beginning to make common cause with the old central cities against the flight of businesses and residents to the sprawling outer suburbs.)[17]

At virtually the same time a school of Soviet planners called the "disurbanists" were dreaming of dispersing their own overcrowded urban masses into new settlements amid the fields and forests by building new road networks. A distinguished visitor, the French architect Le Corbusier, summed up the mood in his book *La Ville Radieuse* (1930):

> People were encouraged to entertain an idle dream: "The cities will be part of the country; I shall live 30 miles away from my office under a pine tree; my secretary will live 30 miles away from it too, in the other direction, under another pine tree. We shall both have our own car. We shall use up tires, wear out road surfaces and gears, consume oil and gasoline. All of which will necessitate a great deal of work ... enough for all...."[18]

It is almost as though postwar American suburbia was the realized fantasy of Soviet planners. Or, more accurately, the victory of motorization was an unintended consequence of an international decentralizing mood. As Kenneth Jackson has pointed out, even the *Bulletin of the Atomic Scientists* embraced dispersion of cities in a 1951 special issue, "Defense Through Decentralization." It promoted satellite cities and low-density suburbs in which former urbanites could be housed more safely for the duration of the Cold War.[19]

Automobiles and road systems promoted an old technological utopia, the community of private villas. Automobiles also have an immense advantage over railroads and trolleys: they make it possible to go directly from one outlying point to another. America never had an integrated national or even regional transportation network as European countries did. Its trains and even some of its urban transport systems were run by competing corporations. Nostalgic admirers of railroad transportation forget how many trips required completing two sides of a triangle, sometimes with hours of waiting between them. K. H. Schaeffer and Elliot Sclar, transportation analysts, exposed these shortcomings trenchantly in *Access for All*. A trip of fourteen miles from the small town of New Washington, Ohio, to its county seat could take all day by rail, even when train travel was at its peak. And New Washington's two depots were a half mile apart.[20]

Usually, motorization bought space rather than time. Ivan Illich wrote in 1974: "The typical American spends over 1,600 hours a year (or thirty hours a week or four hours a day including Sundays) in his car. This includes the time spent behind the wheel, moving or stopped, the hours of work needed to pay for it and for gasoline, tires, tolls, insurance, fines, and taxes.... For this American it takes 1,600 hours to cover a year total of 6,000 miles, four miles per hour. This is just as fast as a pedestrian and slower than a bicycle."[21]

In fact, the greatest surprise of motoring was the speed at which traffic clogged the roads, including freeways and other limited-access highways built to relieve congestion. When the Washington Beltway was dedicated in 1964, the governor of Maryland, who cut the ribbon on its last segment, called it "a road of opportunity." The federal highway administrator compared it to a wedding ring. The *Washington Post* declared that "the stenographer in Suitland will be able to get to the Pentagon without finding the day ruined almost before it begins." Twenty-two years later, another *Post* correspondent reported: "The dream turned to nightmare. The Great Belt tightened to the point where right now it resembles nothing less than a noose around the communal neck.... We could die on the Beltway and rot until vultures pick clean our bones." London's counterpart, the M25, had already exceeded its projected traffic for the year 2001 by the late 1980s, only three years after completion. Surprisingly, even states like Kentucky, Missouri, Nebraska, South Carolina, Tennessee, and Texas classify more than half their interstate highway mileage as congested. And mature suburbs of large cities have become so traffic-choked that the American Automobile Association itself has moved its headquarters from Fairfax County, Virginia, to Florida.[22]

There are social reasons for this recongestion: not just two-commuter families but the multiple motorized errands that suburban living demands. Saturday afternoons may be the most crowded times of all. Traffic engineers, applied mathematicians, and economists have also discovered that expanding old routes and adding new ones may actually increase travel time. An enlarged bridge will redirect traffic that had been taking a longer route around it, but unless it is substantially larger, it will be just as slow. New highways also may increase total travel time for all travelers when they draw traffic from alternative rail systems. And the ultimate recongesting effect is called Braess's Paradox, in honor of a pioneering investigator of the subject. Where each of two congested routes has a bottleneck, adding what appears to be a shortcut between them may actually increase travel time for everyone. The reason: the new, "direct" road actually funnels traffic through both the old bottlenecks. Thanks to quirks of driver psychology, even common operations like merging traffic can produce equally counterproductive results. Because motorists tend to close up spaces to discourage entering cars from cutting in front of them, especially when these attempt to enter from other roads, mysterious traffic jams can appear a mile or more from the actual merge. Because spaces are tight, a driver decelerating slightly at the head of a clump can unwittingly induce one following motorist after another to brake a bit harder. And when congestion reaches a certain maximum roadway capacity, the flow of cars falls so sharply that traffic engineers recognize (but still can't fully explain) a "breakdown." What appears rational to an individual driver becomes irrational for the motoring population and for society. Recongesting turns out to be a form of recomplicating, of creating a machine of parts coupled in poorly understood ways.[23]

What is interesting technologically about this new congestion is its unexpectedly positive side. It has helped make driving safer than anyone thought it would ever be. Congestion may be a chronic negative side effect of mobility, but safety is a positive outcome of congestion. There is a school of thought that denies that driving or anything else can ever be made safer. This is called risk homeostasis. The phrase means simply that people unconsciously seek a certain level of hazard. They compensate for "dangerous" conditions by driving more cautiously—and offset safety measures by taking more risks. The geographer John G. U. Adams looked into the accident rate of England's "adventure playgrounds," loosely supervised assortments of high wooden ladders and platforms that offer "opportunities to test skills appropriate to chimpanzees." They are visibly more dangerous than "fixed equipment" playgrounds with their smooth surfaces and rubberized matting. Yet insurance companies quote lower liability rates for the adventure playgrounds, and the secretary of the National Playing Fields Association has written that "the accident rate is lower than in orthodox playgrounds since hooliganism which results from boredom is absent." Adams and others (mainly social scientists) have argued conversely that seat belts, by making drivers feel more secure, actually cause more pedestrian casualties even as they reduce motorist injuries.[24]

Few traffic engineers accept risk homeostasis as a principle, or the seat belt as an instance of it. In fact, as Leonard Evans, a physicist and safety researcher, argues, some safety measures save more lives than we might have predicted, but others may actually increase casualties. The fifty-five-mile-per-hour speed limit reduced deaths more than anyone had expected. Seat belts met expectations. Studded tires, improved acceleration, and antilock braking systems (ABS) have a moderate benefit, though there is some evidence that ABS-equipped drivers may have as many crashes as those not similarly equipped, or perhaps even more. New traffic signals seem to have a neutral effect. So do strict inspections. And surprisingly, zebra stripes and flashing lights at crossings actually increase pedestrian injuries significantly. (That does not mean they are useless. As another leading traffic specialist, Frank Haight, has put it, the benefit of some safety measures is fair access rather than safety. They give pedestrians not absolute protection from reckless motorists but the welcome ability to cross roads that would otherwise be almost impassable.) Changing any single piece of hardware, or any law, may or may not have the desired effect.[25]

It isn't only safer equipment, then, that has brought down the rate of deaths per million passenger-miles. In fact, cause and effect might be reversed. Only when drivers start giving up speed and price to protection do manufacturers start selling safer cars. And that seems to depend on the amount of driving. The British mathematician and traffic engineer R. J. Smeed had that most remarkable gift, the ability to point out an obvious pattern that others had missed. In 1949, Smeed began to plot the relationship between fatalities per vehicle and vehicles per capita. What he found then, and what he and others have noticed ever since, is that more driving makes fatal accidents less likely per mile driven.[26]

In the late 1960s, for example, the nations with the highest fatality rates were developing countries with few private automobiles per capita. Even today within Europe, the riskiest countries are those on the periphery, like Portugal, where automobile ownership is still twenty years or more behind England or

Germany. John Adams, while dissenting from Smeed's conclusions about the reasons for greater safety, found that later data supported Smeed's original 1949 paper.[27]

Smeed's observations point to a very complex process: a set of technological, legal, and social changes that more general driving brings. Countries with few roads, wide-open spaces, and few vehicles may be dangerous to motorists' health. A colleague once recalled from her childhood in Iran that on long stretches of country road, chauffeurs raced toward each other in the center, playing a local variation of chicken. Visibility was excellent, but there were no lane-dividing stripes. One driver nearly always turned off; the point was to wait long enough to maintain one's honor. What in the United States are adolescent rites may elsewhere be the serious contests of middle-aged men.

Early motorization's mix of human, animal, and motor power can be equally fatal. In India in the early 1980s, there were seventy-five road deaths a day, half as many as in the United States, which had forty times as many vehicles. Twenty times more people were killed in accidents than in floods. In 1989, more than a thousand died on the Grand Trunk Road from New Delhi to Calcutta alone. Uniquely Indian, or Third World? Not at all. Early in the century, New York also had a mix of animal-drawn vehicles, automobiles, streetcars, bicycles, and pedestrians, and saw casualties double during the earliest driving boom.[28]

Congestion leads to demands for limited-access roads that in turn promote safer high-speed driving. U.S. national statistics also suggest that the most dangerous roads are straight, two-lane desert highways, with the worst being the notorious U.S. 66 near Gallup, New Mexico. One study of motor-vehicle crash mortality found a hundredfold variation; in Esmeralda County, Nevada, the death rate was 558 per 100,000, while in Manhattan it was 2.5.[29] In hilly country with old roads and many new drivers, the results are similar. Whereas the United States had 248 deaths per million vehicles in 1989, Britain 248, and the Netherlands 236, Portugal had 1,163. The Portuguese-based writer Robert D. Kaplan has written of drivers on the twisting and crumbling Sintra–Lisbon highway: "Instead of going slow, they race along ... passing on curves at night, with the ease and tranquillity of a blind person reading Braille."[30] Yet these same people are impeccably courteous pedestrians and have passed stiff written tests requiring a three-month course. The gentle Malaysians, mostly teetotaling Muslims, also reflect the spirit of early motorization. Malaysian drivers "love to pass on blind curves or approaching hills," wrote one visiting American. "They routinely ride up on each other's tails, going 50, 60, 70 miles an hour, then impertinently flash their headlights."[31]

The traffic congestion of highly motorized countries poses a chronic rather than an acute health menace. Road safety statistics do not reflect the health consequences of vehicle emissions. A car that covers ten miles in thirty minutes of rush-hour crawl produces three and a half times the hydrocarbons of one that takes eleven minutes at off-peak hours. Idling engines produce three hundred times as much carbon monoxide as those running freely. While automotive emissions were reduced by 76 to 96 percent from 1967 to 1990, the number of cities with hazardous ground-level ozone increased to over one hundred by the late 1980s. Estimates of the health and agricultural damage done by carbon monoxide and smog range from \$5 billion to \$16 billion per year. All of these are serious chronic consequences, but they don't alter the fact that riding in a motor vehicle has become far safer.[32]

There is an unexpected discipline in the apparently more dangerous congested road. Interstates and other limited-access highways would not be feasible without a minimum traffic volume. Density forces slower and more uniform speeds. It also makes possible greater police supervision, better rescue services, and easier access to emergency treatment facilities. The safest part of the New Jersey Turnpike is the crowded metropolitan portion north of New Brunswick; the more rural South Jersey section has twice its accident rate. And much of the reason is that congestion compels vigilance. The chairman of the Turnpike Authority explained: "[I]n the north ... there is so much going on, you're pumping adrenaline just to stay on top of it. We're keeping you alert up here. Down there you're dozing." In fact, as Albert O. Hirschman has pointed out, proper driving is actually easier in the city than in the country. "The city traffic requires greater technical mastery, but this increase in the difficulty of driving is outweighed by the fact that intense traffic helps [the driver] in the task of focusing his attention."[33]

In spite of countless incidents of violence on the highway, in spite of all our experiences to the contrary, mature motorization seems to engender (relatively) more courteous and disciplined behavior, "collective learning" in Leonard Evans's phrase, or, as the *Washington Post*'s Malcolm Gladwell puts it, "driving under the influence of society."[34]

A spokesman from the Insurance Institute for Highway Safety reports that while safety-related advertising once appeared to harm sales by substituting fear for fantasy, "safety is only second to quality and well ahead of price in the consumer's mind."[35] We are far from the free spirits of early motoring, of Booth Tarkington's George Amberson Miniver, of Kenneth Grahame's Mr. Toad, "the terror, the traffic-queller, the Lord of the lone trail, before whom all must give way or be smitten into nothingness and everlasting night."[36] Or, as the columnist Richard Cohen has written, "Jay Gatsby never dreamed of gridlock."[37]

Conservation of Catastrophe?

Marine navigation and motoring alike seem to argue for optimism, for the idea that intensification can be tamed, in fact that disasters are self-correcting. Society learns. Progress, that long-despised concept, comes in by the back door. The point is not that disasters continue, but that on balance and by most measures, people continue to be better off. Unfortunately for technological optimism, things are not quite so simple.

The *Titanic*'s sinking has been moralized so much that we have to remember the incident would have turned out much differently had her plates not fractured. No one had tested (and possibly no one could have tested) metal for the kind of brittle fracture her hull experienced. Even if the crew had been able to evacuate every passenger safely, the loss of the ship would have been one of the greatest material disasters of peacetime marine history.

The disturbing fact about the accident is that we can never be completely confident of the behavior of any new material as part of a complex system. Splinters from fiber-optic cables, to take just one case, can pose serious health risks for telephone workers (and especially for self-taught laypeople) who have to cut and splice them. Yet it is rare to see this problem mentioned in most discussions of networking.

Software adds another dimension to complexity.... [T]he risk of fatal bugs in life-critical systems can be [very high]. Malfunction in software control of processes is also less likely to produce the warning signals familiar in the mechanical world—heat, noise, color change, vibration. A system crash may be much more sudden. It is harder to achieve what engineers call "graceful degradation."

The historian of science Michael S. Mahoney has observed that computers do not eliminate artisans but reintroduce them in the new guise of programmers. Recomplication has made software so bulky that only teams of programmers can write it, yet talented programmers are individualists who do not usually work efficiently as part of a team. This affects not only operating systems and applications software for desktop computers, but the code that runs everything from aircraft navigation to automotive fuel injection and medical equipment. As John Shore, a software engineer, has pointed out, vigilance works well for mechanical systems; high-rise elevators need constant maintenance, but they rarely injure people. Software requires maintenance, too, but this makes it less rather than more reliable. Every feature that is added and every bug that is fixed adds the possibility of some new and unexpected interaction between parts of the program. A small change to solve a minor problem may create a larger one. The technical writer Lauren Wiener has noted that the repeated paralysis of local and regional telephone systems in 1991 resulted from only a few changed lines in the millions of lines of code that drove call-routing computers. A meaningful test of the revisions would have taken thirteen weeks.[38]

Catastrophic risk will stay with us because more rather than less of life is likely to depend on complex software. Intelligent-vehicle highway systems (IVHS) may someday squeeze more capacity out of existing limited-access roads. Individual vehicles under electronic control would join formations called platoons. These convoys could be spaced more tightly than today's normal traffic. And they could control some of our daily highway nightmares, such as the tailgater, the lane jumper, and the sleepless trucker. But if software or communication or even a lead vehicle's tire failed, the results could be catastrophic. If we add the dependence of government, banking, and commerce on global electronic networks that in turn depend on software, a revival of catastrophic errors cannot be ruled out. (And the critics of IVHS insist that electronically controlled roads will soon be recongested anyway.)[39]

Even more serious than hidden risk may be displaced risk. The safety of one technology has a way of creating danger in another. Our current successes may be preparing us for failures where we least expect them.... [G]ood hygiene left the well-scrubbed children of the middle and upper classes more susceptible to polio than the dirty kids of the poor.... Mirko D. Grmek [has suggested] that success in suppressing bacterial infection indirectly promoted the rise of AIDS and other new viral infections by leaving a niche for virulent pathogens.

If hidden risk is the concern of the liberal, distrustful of corporate assurances of safety through technology, displaced risk is the objection of the conservative to regulation. And conservative skepticism is directed less often at technologies themselves than at attempts to limit, regulate, or impose them. Requiring parents to place their infants in (paid-for) child carrier seats on airlines instead of carrying them on their laps may lead more families to drive instead of fly. Since aircraft are safer than highways, the argument runs, the rule may injure more infants than would have been hurt in the air. Pesticide-free fruit and vegetables at high prices may be more harmful to public health, by reducing consumption by the poor, than cheap produce with pesticide residues would have been. Taking this line of thought to an extreme, one British researcher has even found that male physicians who quit smoking tend to offset their health gains with higher rates of alcoholism, accidents, and suicide. (Not surprisingly, tobacco industry sources supported this study.)[40]

Like hidden risks, displaced risks appear impossible to rule out of any proposed change. The natural and social worlds interact in too many poorly understood ways. Risk analysts call these unexpected effects Type III errors. (A Type I error is an unnecessary preventive step, like evacuating a coastline when storm warnings turn out to be a false alarm, or delaying the approval of a lifesaving drug. A Type II error is a decidedly harmful action like releasing a drug that turns out to have lethal side effects). When strict directives on meat radiation after the Chernobyl meltdown of 1986 destroyed the Lapp reindeer-meat economy, as a recent report of the Royal Society pointed out, the unexpectedness of the result made it a Type III rather than a Type I error. Many market-oriented risk analysts like Aaron Wildavsky urge resilience and gradual responses to unforeseen consequences as they occur, rather than attempts to calculate and balance all possible results. The report of the Royal Society points to clearly organized schools of "anticipationism" and "resilientism." Resilience often turns out to be an excellent policy, provided the phenomena cooperate and appear distinctly and gradually on the horizon.[41]

In the real world, few trends emerge without ambiguity, beyond a reasonable doubt, before precious time is lost. It is now more than 150 years since the eccentric French utopian socialist Charles Fourier predicted that the increasing cultivation of the earth would bring about higher temperatures and eventually a melting of the polar ice cap. While Fourier's scientific credentials were dubious—he thought the northern seas would become "a sort of lemonade" and humanity would move about on "antilions" and get their fish from "antisharks"—he was on to something. In fact, at about the same time, another Frenchman, coincidentally also named Fourier (the physicist Jean-Baptiste), discovered that the earth's atmosphere maintains the planet's warmth by trapping heat. As early as a hundred years ago, the Swedish geochemist Svante Arrhenius speculated on a possible increase of up to 6 degrees Celsius in air temperature if industrial carbon dioxide emissions continued to grow. Yet even now, the science we need most gives us not the precision we want but a set of possible tempos and consequences. We want numbers, but instead our best models give us ranges. We want a truth that will apply to the whole globe, or at least to our own continent, and face the likelihood of patchy local change. We want an idealized eighteenth-century celestial mechanics to rule our world, but we find only probabilistic models.[42]

We can't even count on conditions continuing to drift slowly. As Stephen Jay Gould and others have often reminded us, steep rather than gradual natural change is the norm, and it is extremely hard to predict the future state of a complex system even without the added imponderables of human culture and behavior. Well before climate became an issue, human culture (including technology) set off bizarre chains of cause and effect. The fashion for feathers and entire dead birds on women's hats in the late nineteenth century devastated whole species; but it also drew women and men into bird preservation movements that outlived the fad. The early automobile spread its own nemesis, the puncture weed with its tire-killing spiked seedpods. Decades after safer and puncture-resistant tubeless tires appeared, this technology unexpectedly abetted another pest: the Asian tiger mosquito, a vector for dengue fever, which traveled the Pacific in recycled tires and now enjoys an extended breeding season in water that collects in tire dumps. We have already seen how cleaning up European harbors probably helped spread tenacious zebra mussels to North America. Yet motorization also helped reduce the population of European sparrows.

Anyone correctly predicting these sequences well in advance would have seemed a crank or an alarmist. In fact, most of the greatest changes of the twentieth century simply did not occur to the nineteenth-century imagination. Air war and weapons of mass destruction were outstanding exceptions, and even these were logical extensions of pre-1900 sieges and bombardments. Otherwise the human ability to envision something truly new, good *or* bad, is surprisingly limited. Late-twentieth-century personal computers are radically different not just from nineteenth-century analytical engines and mechanical calculators but even from those (far slower) behemoths, the postwar data processors of the von Neumann era. High European mortality in tropical Asia and Africa did not prepare the Western mind for the emergence of AIDS and other "new" viruses— nor for the influenza epidemic of 1918.

Extrapolation doesn't work, because neither nature nor human society is guaranteed to act reasonably. Some things like computer processor power and data storage get better and cheaper more quickly than the optimists expected; on the other hand, the tasks that they are supposed to perform, like machine translation, turn out to be more difficult than most people had thought. What is almost a constant, though, is that the real benefits usually are not the ones that we expected, and the real perils are not those we feared. What prevail are sets of loosely calculable factors and ranges of outcomes, with no accepted procedure for choosing among them. And since we have seen that it is impossible to rid any computer models of bugs, we have no assurance that reality will not be well beyond our projected range in either direction. Instead of the malice of the isolated object, we face ever more complicated possible linkages among systems of objects.

It is impossible, then, to prove that large-scale disasters will not reassert themselves in North America and the rest of the developed world, that we will not intensify not only our chronic problems but our acute ones. William H.

McNeill has a telling phrase for this possibility: the Conservation of Catastrophe. Just as engineers will continue to explore the bounds of a "safe" bridge design, test pilots will "push the envelope," regional planners will overrate the capacity of roads to evacuate a hurricane zone, and engineers will disregard all they have learned about O-rings. We can even find analogies in the realm of finance: the New Deal's precautions against the bank failures of the Depression created institutions that helped promote the wave of savings-and-loan bankruptcies of the 1980s. International electronic networks for communication and commerce make new kinds of disasters possible, as localized malfunctions now have unprecedented opportunities for spreading. If the postal carriers of one city start hoarding or discarding mail, it is a major problem but no immediate threat to the system's integrity. If a network node were to go wrong in some unforeseen way, worldwide systems could fail before the cause was even identified.

The real question is not whether new disasters will occur. Of course they will. It is whether we gain or lose ground as a result. It is whether our apparent success is part of a long-term and irreversible improvement in the human condition or a deceptive respite in a grim and open-ended Malthusian pressure of human numbers and demands against natural limits. It is whether revenge effects are getting worse or milder. I think, but cannot prove, that in the long run they are going to be good for us. And I would like to suggest why.

Retreating from Intensity

Revenge effects reached their peak in the hundred years between the 1860s and the 1960s, during the very acme of technological optimism. Clobbering nature into submission united North Americans and Europeans, Communists and Republicans. Explosives, heavy machinery, agriculture, and transportation seemed at last to be fulfilling the injunction of Genesis 1:28 to "fill the earth and subdue it." Soviet citizens named their children for Henry Ford and his tractors. Contemporaries thought they were living at the beginning of an era of open-ended change; but it is also clear that few of them reckoned with the tendency of nature to strike back. Although (as the historian Douglas Weiner has documented) Friedrich Engels himself wrote of how nature "avenges" humanity against exploitation, the Eastern Bloc kept subjugating its part of the planet until the bitter end.[43]

The real meaning of Communism's collapse had less to do, in fact, with collectivism than with a fixation on intensity that continued through the Gorbachev years. Officially the regime campaigned to conserve materials. But it also set output goals by weight, not performance. Industrial quotas, meted out in metric tons, were filled with heavy stuff—sometimes incredibly sturdy, more often simply bad. The alleged Soviet boast of producing the world's largest microchips may be apocryphal, but Marshall I. Goldman, an economist who visited the USSR often, noticed an exceptional proportion of office typewriters with unnecessary extra-long carriages.[44]

The Soviet fixation on goals by gross weight and volume was only an extreme case of the pathology of intensity: the single-minded overextension of a good thing. We should keep in mind that the West went through even more serious crises of intensification. Potatoes, a great benefit for the European popular diet, were genetically vulnerable when grown from a single strain and used as a primary source of nutrition by the very poor. Yet terrible as the Irish potato famine of the 1840s was, nothing like it has recurred. The crash of the French raw silk industry in the 1850s, so important for Louis Pasteur's career, also showed how dangerous it could be for so many families to link their economic fate to a single organism.

It is curious how many resource-rich nations and regions have faltered because they relied too strongly on exploiting only one or two sources of natural wealth. The Mississippi Delta, the deserted mining towns of the Rockies, and the desolate coal patches of the Pennsylvania anthracite country all have their counterparts overseas: Sicily, the Ukraine, and Argentina as former world bread-baskets, Romania and Azerbaijan as fabled energy reserves, Zaire and Siberia as gold vaults, the Ruhr as ironworks. The nature of the resource does not seem to matter. Nor do colonialism or foreign rule, though absentee ownership may. It was wealth that became an enemy of a vital diversity. On the other side, resource-poor islands and formerly isolated regions like Switzerland, Japan, Taiwan, and Singapore have become the twentieth century's economic stars.[45]

Of course, it is too optimistic to say that we have overcome the perils of intensity. We have already seen how "rationalized" forestry in England and Scotland has helped turn the familiar ground squirrel of North America into a significant woodland pest. The science writer Matt Ridley has described how even in Tory England, state-promoted conversion of "unproductive" downland to wheat fields and ancient forests to conifer plantations had endangered butterflies and other native wildlife and plants. In Spain and Portugal, the ancient *dehesas* of mixed cork oak and holm oak in a setting of grain and grasslands have also been threatened by clearance for Euro-subsidized crops. Elsewhere, clear-cut forestry and overfishing continue. The greatest risk of any new natural technology, especially a genetic one, is not a superpest. It is an apparently harmless organism or chemical that begins as a stunning success and displaces alternatives in the marketplace. Making anything so hardy and productive is like announcing a huge prize for the first naturally selected pests and parasites. Sooner or later there will be a big winner.[46]

All this hardly means that science or technology has overintensified life, or that traditional agriculture was always environmentally benign. In the Mediterranean and elsewhere, preindustrial agriculture could devastate as well as foster diversity; it is hard to imagine any biologically engineered organism as catastrophic in the wild as the otherwise useful and endearing goat. And technologies can follow a number of alternative paths, depending on the assumptions and interests of those who develop and support them. Technologies can help preserve old genetic resources, evaluate new crops, reduce the quantity of pesticide and herbicide applications, consume less water. In other words, they can diversify and *de*-intensify. This implies a new balance between public and market-driven research, since (as the geneticist Richard C. Lewontin and others have shown) commercial research necessarily neglects natural, nonpatentable varieties of organisms that would be in the public domain after the first sale.

In agriculture, the retreat from intensity means forgoing applications of heavy fertilizer in favor of planting complementary crops in the same fields, increasing both productivity and resilience. In medicine, the retreat from intensity demands a shift away from the heavy reliance on a handful of antibiotics. In business computing, it implies a heavy dose of skepticism about the functional value of "more powerful" new releases of both hardware and software. It also suggests doubts as to whether higher workloads and longer days always yield more profit; sometimes it even calls for deliberately slowing or interrupting the pace of work. In sports, it provokes a harder look at whether stiffer and more powerful equipment necessarily makes for a better game. The retreat from intensification does not necessarily require giving it up; it does mean subjecting it to much greater scrutiny.

It isn't enough, of course, to modify intensity. Reducing revenge effects demands substituting brains for stuff. And the record of human ingenuity in making brainpower do the work of energy and raw materials is impressive. Balloon-frame houses, the invention of anonymous carpenters on the nearly treeless prairies of the nineteenth-century American Midwest, became famous for their durability as well as their economy. In our own time the cheapest electronic computers available today from any discount store can calculate many times faster than the room- and building-size arrays of relays and vacuum tubes of the industry's pioneer days. Steel is lighter and stronger, yet certain plastics are lighter and stronger than steel. Automobiles now weigh less and use less gasoline per mile. A CD weighs a fraction of an LP, and a CD player is lighter and more compact than a conventional turntable. New mathematical algorithms allow the same information to be stored on smaller disks—or more information on the same size disk.

The engineer Robert Herman, the technology analyst Jesse H. Ausubel, and their associates argue that technological change exerts powerful forces both for increasing and for reducing the amount of energy and other resources used. Electronic storage can reduce the consumption of paper, but ... it can also multiply it. Lighter goods may heighten rather than diminish the need for materials if they are marketed or treated as throwaways rather than durables. (Thick, returnable glass bottles may, for example, demand less intense use of energy and other resources than even recyclable aluminum.) In fact, as Herman and Ausubel have suggested, lighter and more efficient automobiles promote resource-consuming if dispersed suburban living and thus materialization. Nuclear power generation begins with low-weight raw materials but ends with vast contaminated structures that probably can never be reused.[47]

What appears to be a technological question—how much of anything we really need—is in the end a social one. It is the size and appearance of a yard or a lawn or a house, the taste for (or repudiation of) meat, and so forth. Often what is most crucial, and most uncertain, is not invention and discovery but taste and preference. The open question, raised during the upheavals of the 1970s and then forgotten during the boom of the 1980s, is whether cultural change can lead to new preferences that will in turn relieve humanity's pressure on the earth's resources. Human culture, not some inherent will of the machine, has created most revenge effects. Without the taste for silk, there would have been no gypsy moths in North America. Without the preference for detached housing, there would still be congestion, perhaps, but more economical congestion. Without the love of oceanside living, shore erosion yes, but no social disruption.

Even more promising than diversification and dematerialization is an attitude that has not yet found its rightful name. It is the substitution of cunning for the frontal attack, and it is not new. It began with immunization against smallpox—as we have seen, a folk practice long before Edward Jenner introduced it to medicine—and continued with the vaccines of the late nineteenth and twentieth centuries.

Finesse means abandoning frontal attacks for solutions that rely on the same kind of latent properties that led to revenge effects in the first place. Sometimes it means ceasing to suppress a symptom. In medicine, finesse suggests closer attention to the evolutionary background of human health and illness, to the positive part that fever plays, for example, in fighting infection. At other times, finesse means living with and even domesticating a problem organism. As we have seen, researchers like Stanley Falkow and Paul Ewald have suggested a kind of evolutionary compromise with what are now lethal bacteria and viruses, turning them into common but harmless companions. In the office, finesse means producing more by taking more frequent breaks and conveying more information by, for example, limiting rather than multiplying color schemes. In construction, finesse means allowing skyscrapers to sway slightly in the wind instead of bracing them to resist it. On the road, finesse means a calmer approach to driving, improving the speed and economy of all drivers by slowing them down at times when impulse would prompt accelerating. It can mean moving more traffic by metering access to some roads and even closing off others. (Some German analysts have written of the "softening," *Besänftigung,* of traffic.) Diversification, dematerialization, and finesse are far from a rejection of science. To the contrary, it is science that points us away from crude reductionism and counterproductive brute force toward technologies that improve human life. But the improvement has a cost.

As the Red Queen said in *Through the Looking-Glass,* we are no longer in the "slow sort of country" where running gets one somewhere: "Now, *here,* you see, it takes all the running you can do, to keep in the same place. If you want to get somewhere else, you must run at least twice as fast as that!" And in fact the alternatives to the intensified, revenge-prone modes of earlier technology seem to take nearly all the running we can do. Even the optimistic report of the Council for Agricultural Science and Technology (CAST) makes clear that most of our agricultural research goes to "maintenance," that is, to keeping the gains we have made: dealing with deteriorating water quality and increasing costs, and offsetting "biological surprises like the appearance of more virulent pests." The same could probably be said of many medical efforts. Similarly, the power of personal computer hardware seems driven by the need to compensate for the way that more elaborate interfaces and features slow the fundamentals of performance.[48]

Technological optimism means in practice the ability to recognize bad surprises early enough to do something about them. And that demands constant monitoring of the globe, for everything from changes in mean temperatures and particulates to traffic in bacteria and viruses. It also requires a second level of vigilance at increasingly porous national borders against the world exchange of problems. But vigilance does not end there. It is everywhere. It is in the random alertness tests that have replaced the "dead man's pedal" for train operators. It is in the rituals of computer backup, the legally mandated testing of everything from elevators to home smoke alarms, routine X-ray screening, securing and loading new computer-virus definitions. It is in the inspection of arriving travelers for products that might harbor pests. Even our alertness in crossing the street, second nature to urbanites now, was generally unnecessary before the eighteenth century. Sometimes vigilance is more of a reassuring ritual than a practical precaution, but with any luck it works. Revenge effects mean in the end that we will move ahead but must always look back just because reality is indeed gaining on us.

NOTES

1. John Tierney, "Betting on the Planet," *New York Times Magazine*, 2 December 1990, 52.

2. David S. Landes, *Revolution in Time: Clocks and the Making of the Modern World* (Cambridge, Mass.: Harvard University Press, 1983), 103–113; Robert K. Merton, *Science, Technology, and Society in Seventeenth-Century England* (New York: Harper Torchbooks, 1970 [1938]), 167–177.

3. Derek Howse, *Greenwich Time and the Discovery of the Longitude* (Oxford: Oxford University Press, 1980), 44–72.

4. David S. Landes, *Revolution in Time: Clocks and the Making of the Modern World* (Cambridge, Mass.: Harvard University Press, 1983), 103–113, 144–157.

5. See Paul Slovic, "Perception of Risk," *Science,* vol. 236, no. 4799 (17 April 1987), 280–285; and Paul Slovic, "Perception of Risk: Reflections on the Psychometric Paradigm," in Sheldon Krimsky and Dominic Golding, eds., *Social Theories of Risk* (Westport, Conn.: Praeger, 1992), 117–152.

6. John P. Eaton and Charles A. Haas, *Titanic: Triumph and Tragedy* (New York: Norton, 1987), 310–311; Edward Bryant, *Natural Hazards* (Cambridge: Cambridge University Press, 1991), 68.

7. James T. Yenckel, "How Safe Is Cruising?," *Washington Post,* 11 August 1991, E6.

8. See Henry Petroski, *To Engineer Is Human: The Role of Failure in Successful Design* (New York: St. Martin's Press, 1985).

9. Mark F. Grady, "Torts: The Best Defense Against Regulation," *Wall Street Journal,* 3 September 1992, A11; Mark F. Grady, "Why Are People Negligent? Technology, Nondurable Precautions, and the Medical Malpractice Explosion," *Northwestern University Law Review,* vol. 82 (Winter 1988), 297–299, 312. See also Grady's review of Paul C. Weiler's *Medical Malpractice on Trial,* "Better Medicine Causes More Lawsuits, and New Administrative Courts Will Not Solve the Problem," *Northwestern University Law Review,* vol. 86 (Summer 1992), 1068–1081.

10. On seventeenth-century navigation, see Landes, *Revolution in Time,* 105–111; Carla Rahn Phillips, *Six Galleons for the King of Spain* (Baltimore: Johns Hopkins University Press, 1986), 129–134. On Shovell's tomb: Margaret Whitney, *Sculpture in Britain, 1530 to 1830* (Baltimore: Penguin, 1964), 58. There is probably more to late-nineteenth and early-twentieth-century litigation than Grady acknowledges: the deference shown by judges and juries of the time toward elite defendants in tort liability cases. To name just three other notorious cases, the industrialists' club that maintained the dam that broke and caused the Johnstown flood in 1889 (2,200 dead), the owners of the *General Slocum,* which caught fire in New York Harbor in 1904 (1,021 dead), and the proprietors of the Triangle Shirtwaist Factory, which burned with 145 dead, escaped civil and criminal action. Even with Astors, Wideners, and Guggenheims among the *Titanic* passengers and the victims' families, the final settlement with the White Star Line was minuscule by late-twentieth-century standards: $663,000 (£136,701) on total claims of $16,804,112 (£3,464,765). See Eaton and Haas, *Titanic,* 277–279.

11. James C. Beniger, *The Control Revolution: Technological and Economic Origins of the Information Society* (Cambridge, Mass.: Harvard University Press, 1986), 221–226 and references.

12. Clay McShane, *Down the Asphalt Path: The Automobile and the American City* (New York: Columbia University Press, 1994), 42–45.

13. Christopher Gray, "Who Holds the Reins of Fate of a 1907 Horse-Auction Mart?" *New York Times,* 8 November 1987, Real Estate, 14; McShane, *Asphalt Path,* 51–54.

14. Daniel Pool, *What Jane Austen Ate and Charles Dickens Knew* (New York: Simon & Schuster, 1993), 250–51; McShane, *Asphalt Path,* 46–50; for a summary of modern fatalities, Leonard Evans, *Traffic Safety and the Driver* (New York: Van Nostrand Reinhold, 1991), 3.

15. Scott L. Bottles, *Los Angeles and the Automobile: The Making of the Modern City* (Berkeley: University of California Press, 1987), 22.

16. On powers and interests in highway building, see Mark H. Rose, *Interstate: Express Highway Politics, 1941–1956* (Lawrence: University Press of Kansas, 1979).

17. Mark S. Foster, *From Streetcar to Superhighway: American City Planners and Urban Transportation, 1900–1940* (Philadelphia: Temple University Press, 1981), 143–145; "Onwards and Outwards," *Economist,* vol. 333, no. 7885 (15 October 1994), 31.

18. Cited in Anatole Kopp, *Town and Revolution: Soviet Architecture and City Planning, 1917–1935* (New York: Braziller, 1970), 173. The Disurbanists (or Deurbanists) actually had in mind the relocation of urban functions along great highways, not the present American suburban pattern.

19. Kenneth Jackson, *Crabgrass Frontier: The Suburbanization of the United States* (New York: Oxford University Press, 1985), 249.

20. K. H. Schaeffer and Elliot Sclar, *Access for All: Transportation and Urban Growth* (Baltimore: Penguin, 1975), 40–44.

21. Ivan Illich, *Energy and Equity* (New York: Harper & Row, 1974), 18–19.

22. Ibid., 95–96; David Remnick, "Berserk on the Beltway," *Washington Post Magazine,* 7 September 1986, 66ff, 95; "Urban Freeways, Interstates in a Jam," *USA Today,* 18 September 1989, 10A; John F. Harris, "Auto Club, Citing Traffic, to Shut Fairfax Office," *Washington Post,* 1 October 1986.

23. Richard Arnott and Kenneth Small, "The Economics of Traffic Congestion," *American Scientist,* vol. 82, no. 5 (September–October 1994), 446–455; Bob Holmes, "When Shock Waves Hit Traffic," *New Scientist,* vol. 142, no. 1931 (25 June 1994), 36–40.

24. "Risk Homeostasis and the Purpose of Safety Regulation," *Ergonomics,* vol. 31, no. 4 (1988), 408–409.

25. Evans, *Traffic Safety,* 287–290; Haight remarks in telephone interview, October 1991.

26. R. J. Smeed and G. O. Jeffcoate, "Effects of Changes in Motorisation in Various Countries on the Number of Road Fatalities," *Traffic Engineering and Control,* vol. 12, no. 3 (July 1970), 150–151.

27. John Adams, "Smeed's Law and the Emperor's New Clothes," in Leonard Evans and Richard C. Schwing, eds., *Human Behavior and Traffic Safety* (New York: Plenum Press, 1985), 195–196, 235–237.

28. William K. Stevens, "When It Comes to Highway Chaos, India is No. 1," *New York Times,* 26 October 1983, A2; Steve Coll, "'Road Kings' Truck Across India," *Washington Post,* 28 October 1989, A1; McShane, *Asphalt Path,* 174–177.

29. "Drivin' My Life Away," *Scientific American,* vol. 257, no. 2 (August 1987), 28, 30; Susan P. Baker, R. A. Whitefield, and Brian O'Neill, "Geographic Variations in Mortality from Motor Vehicle Crashes," *New England Journal of Medicine,* vol. 316, no. 22 (28 May 1987), 1384–1387.

30. "In Portugal, Wheels of Misfortune," *New York Times,* 22 July 1990, Travel, 39.

31. Deborah Fallows, "Malaysia's Mad Motorists," *Washington Post,* 10 July 1988, C5.

32. James J. MacKenzie, Roger C. Dower, and Donald D. T. Chen, *The Going Rate: What It Really Costs to Drive* (Washington: World Resources Institute, 1992), 13.

33. Angus Kress Gillespie and Michael Aaron Rockland, *Looking for America on the New Jersey Turnpike* (New Brunswick, N.J.: Rutgers University Press, 1989), 114–115; Albert O. Hirschman, *The Strategy of Economic Development* (New Haven, Conn.: Yale University Press, 1958), 134, 143–145. Hirschman also points out that "a road that is not traveled is likely to deteriorate sooner than one that has to support heavy traffic: the former will surely be neglected whereas there is some hope that the latter will be maintained." Because bituminous surfaces show deterioration early, they may be more suitable for less-traveled roads in developing countries than gravel would be. They don't degrade gracefully, as electrical engineers put it; they demand attention.

34. "How Driving Under the Influence of Society Affects Traffic Deaths," *Washington Post,* 2 September 1991, A3.

35. Charles Stile, "N.J. Drivers Yielding to Safety," *Trenton Times,* 15 September 1991, A1.

36. Kenneth Grahame, *The Wind in the Willows* (New York: Charles Scribner's Sons, 1961), 121.

37. "Jay Gatsby Never Dreamed of Gridlock," *Trenton Times,* 19 November 1991, A18.

38. Michael S. Mahoney, personal communication; John Shore, "Why I Never Met a Programmer I Could Trust," *Communications of the ACM,* vol. 31, no. 4 (April 1988), 372; Wiener, *Digital Woes,* 99–100.

39. For the most useful recent summary of the vast literature on road issues, see the special issue of *CQ Researcher,* vol. 4, no. 17 (6 May 1994), 385–408.

40. P. N. Lee, "Has the Mortality of Male Doctors Improved with the Reductions in Their Cigarette Smoking?" *British Medical Journal,* 15 December 1979, 1538–1540.

41. *Risk: Analysis, Perception, and Management* (London: Royal Society, 1992), 155–159, 138–142.

42. See Jonathan Beecher, *Charles Fourier: The Visionary and His World* (Berkeley: University of California Press, 1987), 338–341; Spencer Weart, "From the Nuclear Frying Pan into the Global Fire," *Bulletin of the Atomic Scientists,* vol. 48, no. 5 (June 1992), 18–27.

43. See Douglas R. Weiner, *Models of Nature* (Bloomington: University of Indiana Press, 1988), 195, for Engels's article "The Role of Labor in the Transformation from Ape to Man" as a rallying point for Soviet conservationists. Their opponents insisted that Engels meant only abusive capitalist development, not dialectically informed socialist intervention.

44. On early Soviet production quotas and the technological conservatism they encouraged, see Kendall E. Bailes, *Technology and Society Under Lenin and Stalin* (Princeton, N.J.: Princeton University Press, 1978), 350; Marshall I. Goldman, *What Went Wrong with Perestroika* (New York: Norton, 1991), 87; Marshall I. Goldman, *Gorbachev's Challenge* (New York: Norton, 1987), 123–124. Let those who have never used a Pentium computer to compose a yard-sale announcement cast the first stone.

45. The superiority of knowledge and the proper work ethic to wealth in resources became a watchword of 1980s reformers. Nathan Glazer's "Two Inspiring Lessons of the 1980s," *New York Times,* 24 December 1989, Review, 11, even suggests that some resources like the agricultural lands of Europe and Japan with their heavily subsidized surplus crops are becoming "a positive burden to economic success."

46. Matt Ridley, "Butterflies Fall Victim to Man's Interfering Hand," *Sunday Telegraph,* 17 July 1994, 32; Malcolm Smith, "Science: Live the High Life and Save the Wildlife," *Independent,* 30 May 1994, 19.

47. Robert Herman, Siamak A. Ardekani, and Jesse H. Ausubel, "Dematerialization," *Technological Forecasting and Social Change,* vol. 38 (1990), 333–347.

48. Lewis Carroll, *Through the Looking-Glass,* in *The Complete Works of Lewis Carroll* (New York: Modern Library, n.d. [1896 edn.]), 164; "How Much Land Can Ten Billion People Spare for Nature?," Council for Agricultural Science and Technology Task Force Report 121 (February 1994), 26.

QUESTIONS FOR MAKING CONNECTIONS
WITHIN THE READING

1. First, define and explain one of Tenner's key terms, such as "revenge effects," "intensiveness," "technological optimists," "signal event," "homeostasis," "complex system," "recomplication," "extrapolation," "intensity," or "finesse." Next, try to connect the key term that you have chosen with the other key terms. Finally, develop a key term of your own that names an event or process Tenner describes but does not name.

2. On the basis of your reading of "Another Look Back, and a Look Ahead," would you describe Tenner as a "technological optimist"? How can anyone claim to be an optimist about technology if it is, as Tenner concedes,

"extremely hard"—and perhaps even impossible—"to predict the future state of a complex system even without the added imponderables of human culture and behavior"? Is it possible that technological innovation will reach a point of diminishing returns, when the costs of innovation, or the dangers, outweigh the potential benefits? Does Tenner ever consider this possibility?

3. In what ways does Tenner's discussion of new technologies confirm his belief that progress "comes in by the back door"? To what degree does technological change take place in response to people's needs and their conscious choices? To what degree does technology shape those needs and choices? On the basis of Tenner's examples, would it be fair to say that technology has a life of its own that no one can control, or would such a claim be an exaggeration?

QUESTIONS FOR WRITING

1. The last two centuries have brought about technological change on a scale and at a pace that nobody in any prior age could have imagined. In fact, the pace of change has grown so quickly that we expect innovations to outstrip our predictions. Under these conditions, will it ever be possible to say "no" to technology? Many people believe, for example, that the automobile has diminished the quality of American life in many ways— by polluting the air and allowing suburban sprawl to gobble up the countryside, and by depopulating cities and erasing the local cultures of towns and neighborhoods. Perhaps the most remarkable thing about cars is the rapidity of their development—too rapid, perhaps, for anyone to stop and weigh the consequences. If technology now exceeds human control, do we need to rethink the trust we place in it?

2. How has Tenner's account changed the way you think about technology? Ordinarily, we view technology in a number of different lights: as a neutral instrument or tool; as a miraculous gift; as a specialized pursuit, far removed from human feelings; as a form of knowledge synonymous with science; as a Frankenstein-like monster; as an extension of the marketplace. In what ways does Tenner complicate and perhaps even contradict these commonsense ways of viewing technology? Is it naive to think that we have created technology simply to make our lives better and easier? Does technology express an aspect of ourselves we ordinarily overlook? Other than comfort and security, what satisfactions do we derive from its creation?

QUESTIONS FOR MAKING CONNECTIONS
BETWEEN READINGS

1. Tenner assures us that progress, in spite of all the complications, "comes in by the back door." In making this claim, he seems to believe that a self-correcting process will usually operate with "intensity" followed by

"disaster," which produces "precaution" and finally "vigilance." Is this argument confirmed, extended, complicated, or refuted by Charles Siebert's account of the transformation of elephant behavior worldwide? That is, can Tenner's account of how technology advances be used to explain transformations in other areas of human experience? Is human engagement with the animal kingdom a self-correcting system? When technology goes wrong, change follows because humans suffer, but what if we are not the ones who bear the weight of suffering? Will a disaster for elephants stimulate vigilance on our part?

2. Both Tenner and Steven Johnson in his essay, "The Myth of the Ant Queen," ask their readers to reconsider the role of technological innovation in the rise of contemporary society. Would both authors agree that it makes sense to be a "technological optimist"? Or would they say that technological optimism is just an expression of wishful thinking—a hope that things will turn out well when they actually might not? Does it make sense to think that the "emergent systems" Johnson describes tend to find solutions automatically, even when the people or life-forms involved remain blissfully unaware? Or is it essential that we recognize and consciously attempt to solve the problems we have created?

ROBERT THURMAN

ROBERT THURMAN, ONE of the first Americans to be ordained as a Tibetan Buddhist monk, is often considered to be the most prominent and influential expert on Buddhism in the United States today. A scholar, translator, activist, and lecturer (as well as father of the actress Uma Thurman), Thurman began his explorations into Buddhism in his early twenties when he traveled to India on a "vision quest" and ended up becoming a student of the Dalai Lama. Upon returning to the United States, Thurman wanted to continue his studies and become an academic because, in his own words, "[t]he only lay institution in America comparable to monasticism is the university." Thurman is currently the Jey Tsong Khapa Professor of Indo-Tibetan Buddhist Studies at Columbia University and the president of Tibet House, a nonprofit organization dedicated to the study and preservation of Tibetan culture.

Infinite Life (2004), from which "Wisdom" was taken, is one in an impressive series of books that Thurman has written on Buddhism for a Western audience. Chief among his goals in this text is to guide laypeople into their first explorations of the Buddhist concept of selflessness. The ultimate goal of the lessons that Thurman offers his readers is to impart a deeper sense of interconnectedness, a process that is meant to reduce the negative feelings individuals hold about themselves and to increase the positive feelings they have for themselves and others. In doing so, Thurman seeks to show that the happiness America's founders guaranteed "should be ours and that there are methods for discovering which happiness is really reliable and satisfying, and then securing that in an enduring way without depriving others."

Thurman's more recent books are concerned with the relevance of Buddhism to contemporary world problems. He has argued, for example, that pre-invasion Tibet had advanced quite far beyond the militarism that still deforms social life in the modern world. "The fact that a majority of [the] country's single males [were] monks rather than soldiers" is a major lesson for us today. In *Why the Dalai Lama Matters* (2008), Thurman makes the case that the Dalai Lama plays a unique role in global culture precisely because he advocates a new ethics of altruism that can bridge cultural divides.

Thurman, Robert. *Infinite Life: Seven Virtues for Living Well.* New York: Riverhead Books, 2004. Final quotation drawn from Joshua Glenn, "The Nitty Gritty of Nirvana," *Hilobrow*, July 23, 2009 <http://hilobrow.com/2009/07/23/the-nitty-gritty-of-nirvana/>.

■ ■

Wisdom

Preamble: Selflessness

At one point in the early 1970s, after I'd gotten my Ph.D. and started teaching Buddhism, I went back to visit my old teacher, the Mongolian lama Geshe Wangyal. We were working on a project to translate a Buddhist scientific text from the Tibetan. We were six or seven people gathered around a kitchen table, and Geshe-la began to talk about the inner science of Buddhist psychology, the Abhidharma. He was reading us a few verses about the insight of selflessness, the deep release of becoming unbound, when I began to feel a little dizzy, even nauseous. It was a funny feeling. It felt slightly like a vibration spinning in my head. The vibration came not from Geshe-la, but from this ancient tradition. It was as though my habitual mind couldn't quite find traction. I realized that if I fought it, the sensation would only get more nerve-wracking and I would only feel more nauseous. So I didn't fight it. Instead, I let go and relaxed, and soon I was able to orient myself in another way, away from my "self." I felt like I was slowly but surely loosening my self-centered perspective on life and the world. In a useful way, a strengthening way, I was beginning to experience the great Buddhist mystery that is the selflessness of subjects and objects.

The Buddha based his psychology on his discovery of actual and ultimate reality. This he called "selflessness" and "voidness," or "emptiness." Some people love these words from the moment they hear them, but others are frightened by them. People often ask me, "Why did Buddha have to be such a downer? Obviously nirvana is a happy, cheerful state. So why didn't he just call it 'bliss' or something? Why did he have to label the reality he discovered with negative words such as 'voidness,' 'emptiness,' and 'selflessness'?" When people respond negatively to these terms, it's often because they're worried that the words imply they are going to die, disappear, or go crazy in their attempts to seek enlightenment. And that's exactly why the Buddha called reality by those names. He did it on purpose, to liberate you! Why? Because the only thing that's frightened by the word "selflessness" is the artificially constructed, unreal, and unrealistic self. That self is only a pretend self, it lacks reality, it doesn't really exist. That pseudo-self seems to quiver and quake because the habit that makes it seem real wants to keep its hold on you. So if you're seeking happiness and freedom, then you should want to scare the heck out of your "self"—you want to scare it right out of your head!

Actually, *it* is constantly scaring the heck out of *you*. Your "self" is always busy terrorizing you. You have a terrorist in your own brain, coming out of your own instincts and culture, who is pestering you all the time. "Don't relax too much," it is saying, "you'll get stepped on. A bug will bite you. Someone will be nasty to you. You'll get passed by, abused, sick. Don't be honest. Pretend. Because if you're honest, they'll hurt you." And it's ordering you, "Be my slave. Do what I tell you to do. Keep me installed up here at this very superficial level of the brain where I sit in my weird Woody Allen–type cockpit. Because I'm in control." Your falsely perceived, fixated, domineering self is precisely what's getting between you and a fulfilling life.

Early on, some of the Western psychologists who were beginning to learn from the Buddhist tradition—members of the transpersonal and other movements—came up with the idea that the relationship between Buddhist and Western psychology is this: "Western psychology helps somebody who feels they are nobody become somebody, and Buddhist psychology helps somebody who feels they are somebody become nobody." When I first heard this, I was at an Inner Science conference with the Dalai Lama. Everybody laughed, applauded, and thought it was a great insight. The Dalai Lama just looked at me and kind of winked and was too polite to say anything. I started to jump up to make a comment, but he stopped me. He told me to be quiet and let all of them ponder it for a few years until they realized the flaw in their thinking. Because of course that idea is not even remotely correct.

The purpose of realizing your own selflessness is not to feel like you are nobody. After he became enlightened, the Buddha did not sit under a tree drooling and saying, "Oh, wow! I'm nobody!" Think about it: If he just "became nobody," if he escaped from the world through self-obliteration, then he wouldn't have been able to share so many teachings here on earth, to work for the good of all beings for years and years, long after he achieved nirvana. He would've just stayed in his "nobody" state and forgotten about all of us poor humans busy suffering through our miserable lives.

The reason why we sometimes think that the goal of Buddhism is just "to become nobody" is that we don't understand the concept of selflessness. "Selflessness" does not mean that we are nobody. It does not mean that we cease to exist. Not at all. There is no way you can ever "not exist," just as you cannot become "nothing." Even if you go through deep meditation into what is called "the realm of absolute nothingness," you will still exist. Even if you are so freaked out by a tragedy, such as losing your only child, that you try to end your existence completely, you will still exist. I have a healthy respect for tragedy. We do have terrible tragedies. Personally, I don't bear misfortune well; it knocks me out. But there is no way to become nobody. Even if you were to succeed in killing yourself, you will be shocked when you awaken to disembodied awareness, out-of-body but still a somebody, a ghostly wraith who wishes he hadn't just done that. And a terribly unfortunate living person who has been so brutalized that he blanks out who he was in a seemingly impenetrable psychosis is still somebody, as everybody else around him knows.

Our mind is so powerful that it can create a state of absolute nothingness that seems totally concrete. Thousands of yogis in the history of India and a few mystics in the West have entered such a state of nothingness. But no one can stay there forever, and it is not where you want to be.

Have you ever had a minor experience of nothingness? I've had it in the dentist's chair with sodium pentothal, because I used to eat a lot of sweets and not brush my teeth as a youngster so I had to have teeth pulled. They give you this knockout anesthetic, and if you are a hardworking intellectual, you are tired of your mind, so you think, "Oh great, I'm going to be obliterated for a little while." You're really pleased, and you feel this little buzz, and you're just about to get there. You're going to experience nothingness, a little foretaste of the nihilistic notion of nirvana! But suddenly the nurse is shaking you awake saying, "You've been slobbering in that chair long enough. Get out of here." It's over. You started to pass out, wanting to be gone, but now you're suddenly back with no sense of having been gone at all! And that's what it is like in the state of absolute nothingness. It's like being passed out in the dentist's chair. There's no sense of duration of time. But eventually you wake up, totally disoriented with a nasty headache, and you never even got to enjoy the oblivion.

So we can never become nothing, as appealing as that may sound to those who are addicted to the idea of nothingness after death. We are always somebody, even though we are selfless in reality. We are just different sorts of "somebodies" than we used to be. "Realizing your selflessness" does not mean that you become a nobody, it means that you become the type of somebody who is a viable, useful somebody, not a rigid, fixated, I'm-the-center-of-the-universe, isolated-from-others somebody. You become the type of somebody who is over the idea of a conceptually fixated and self-created "self," a pseudo-self that would actually be absolutely weak, because of being unrelated to the reality of your constantly changing nature. You become the type of somebody who is content never to be quite that sure of who you are—always free to be someone new, somebody more.

That's the whole point of selflessness. If you don't know exactly who you are all the time, you're not sick, you're actually in luck, because you're more realistic, more free, and more awake! You're being too intelligent to be stuck inside one frozen mask of personality! You've opened up your wisdom, and you've realized that "knowing who you are" is the trap—an impossible self-objectification. None of us knows who we really are. Facing that and then becoming all that we can be—astonishing, surprising, amazing—always fresh and new, always free to be more, brave enough to become a work in progress, choosing happiness, open-mindedness, and love over certitude, rigidity, and fear—this is realizing selflessness!

I never met the late, great comedian Peter Sellers, except splitting my sides in laughter while watching some of his movies, especially the *Pink Panther* series. I know he had his ups and downs in his personal life, though you can't believe all the things you hear from the tabloids. But I did read a quote from him, or maybe from his psychiatrist, that he was deeply troubled and distressed because he suffered from "not knowing who he really was." He would get into his roles as an actor so totally, he would think he was the person he was playing, and he couldn't find himself easily as his "own" person. So he suffered, feeling himself "out of control" in his life. When I read this, my heart went out to him. I imagined his psychiatrist sternly telling him he had better calm down and track himself down, and put a lid on his ebullient sense of life, leading him on and on in self-absorption in therapy under the guise that he was going to "find himself" once and for all. I, feeling a bit more freed by having awakened to even the tiniest taste of selflessness, wanted to cry out to Peter Sellers, "Stop suffering by thinking your insight is confusion! Don't listen to the misknowing and even fear your freedom! Learn to surf the energy of life that surges through your openness! You have discovered your real self already, your great self of selflessness, and that openness is what enables you to manifest the heart that shines through your work and opens the hearts of your audiences. Your gift is to release them into laughter, itself a taste of freedom! Why be confused and feel your great gift is something wrong?" But I didn't know him so I could not tell him what I'm telling you. But our lives are infinite and I will be telling his ongoing life-form one of these days, whether I recognize him or not!

The Buddha was happy about not knowing who he was in the usual rigid, fixed sense. He called the failure to know who he was "enlightenment." Why? Because he realized that selflessness kindles the sacred fire of compassion. When you become aware of your selflessness, you realize that any way you feel yourself to be at any time is just a relational, changing construction. When that happens, you have a huge inner release of compassion. Your inner creativity about your living self is energized, and your infinite life becomes your ongoing work of art.

You see others caught in the suffering of the terminal self-habit and you feel real compassion. You feel so much better, so highly relieved, that your only concern is helping those constricted other people. You are free to worry about them because, of course, they are having a horrible time trying to know who they are and trying to be who they think they should be! They are busy being ripped apart by the great streams of ignorance, illness, death, and other people's irritating habits. So they suffer. And you, in your boundless, infinitely interconnected, compassionate state, can help them.

This is the other crucial point about selflessness: it does not mean that you are disconnected. Even nirvana is not a state of disconnection from the world. There is no way to become removed from yourself or from other beings. We are ultimately boundless—that is to say, our relative boundaries are permeable. But we are still totally interconnected no matter what we do. You cannot disappear into your own blissful void, because you are part of everyone and they are part of you. If you have no ultimate self, that makes you free to be your relative self, along with other beings. It's as if your hand represents the universe and your fingers represent all beings. Each of your fingers can wiggle on its own, each can operate independently, just as each being has its own identity. And yet your fingers are part of your hand. If your hand did not exist, your fingers would not exist. You are one of many, many fingers on the hand that is all life.

To my surprise and delight, I learned recently that even some Western psychologists are now beginning to study and understand the harm done by self-centered thinking. The psychologist Dr. Larry Scherwitz conducted a study about type A people—the aggressive, loud, annoying types, like me. Scientists used to think that type As died younger because of their fast-paced, stressful lives. But this new study reveals that, in fact, some of us type A people are not going to die of a heart attack that soon after all. The type Bs out there, the mild-mannered, quiet, inward-focused types, might find this worrisome! We may stay around for years bothering them, because it turns out that the type A personality is not a risk factor for coronary heart disease or other stress-related health problems. It turns out that some people, like me, though we freak out all the time, are not always that stressed. Some of us actually enjoy being this way.

What is the real risk factor, then? Scherwitz and his colleagues reanalyzed the data and conducted some new studies. They discovered, by analyzing the speech patterns of type As and type Bs, that the high risk of heart disease and stress-related illness is correlated with the *amount of self-reference* in people's speech—the amount of self-preoccupation, self-centeredness, and narcissism. "Me, me, I, I, my, my, mine, mine. My golf course, my country club, my job, my salary, my way, my family, my religion, my shrine, my guru, my, my, mine." The more "I, me, my, and mine" there is in their speech—"mine" most of all— the more likely they are to succumb to stress, to keel over because their bodies revolt against that pressure of self-involvement. Whereas even though some people can be aggressive, annoying, loud, and seemingly "stressed," if their over- all motivation is altruistic and they don't pay too much attention to themselves, they live longer. And the quiet type Bs who are also more concerned about others, not necessarily out of any altruistic religious inklings, but just naturally not paying much attention to themselves, tend to live longer, too.

I find this study amazing. I was with the Dalai Lama when he heard about the results. He was intrigued and very pleased. "Oh, really?" he said. "Let me see that paper. In Buddhist psychology, we also have this idea that obsessive self-preoccupation—possessiveness and selfishness and self-centeredness—is life's chief demon!"

Let us explore the problems created by this demon of self-preoccupation, the ways in which it causes us suffering. We will then practice a fundamental meditation in which we look for the fixated self and find that it does not, after all, exist. Once we have freed ourselves from the constricting habit of always thinking that we are the center of the universe, we will experience our first taste of the boundless joy and compassion that is infinite life.

Problem: Misknowledge and Self-Preoccupation

One of the hardest things we have to do on a regular basis is to admit that we are wrong. We stubbornly insist that we're right in situations where we're not quite sure if we are, and even when we sense that we've slipped. How much more indignant do we become when we feel certain that we're right and someone has the gall or the stupidity to challenge us? In this case, we feel an absolute imperative to jump up and trumpet our rightness. If we still cannot get others to agree with us, we soon become self-righteous and then outraged.

Believe it or not, the fact that we struggle so much with being wrong is of tremendous importance to our task of awakening to the reality of selflessness. We should examine our habit of needing to be right carefully to see why it feels so good.

Being right means that the world affirms us in what we think we know. "Knowing" something is a way of controlling it, being able to put it in its proper place in relation to us so that we can use it effectively. As Dharmakirti, the seventh-century Indian philosopher, said, "All successful action is preceded by accurate knowledge." So knowledge is power, in the sense that it empowers us to act successfully. Misknowledge, misunderstanding a situation, is weakness, in the sense that our actions may fail in their aim, backfire, or have unintended consequences. Knowledge is security, in that we know our vulnerabilities and can avoid harm. Misknowledge is danger, in that we don't know what others might do to us or what traps may await us. We therefore feel powerful and secure when we're right, weak and vulnerable when we're wrong.

Viewed in this context, being right seems like a struggle for survival, a drive to win. It's natural for us to cling to that feeling, even when we have not investigated the reality around us because we don't really want to know if we are wrong. We think that finding ourselves in the wrong means a loss of power and safety, forgetting that actually *it is the only way* for us to discover what is truly right and truly wrong, thereby gaining real power and real safety. When we pretend, we focus our attention on appearing to be right no matter what the reality, we distract ourselves from being awake to what really is going on, and so place ourselves at a disempowering disadvantage.

In light of this simple analysis, what lies at the center of our constant need to assure our rightness and, therefore, our power and security? Is it not the certainty that "I am"? Does not the strong sense of "I am" seem absolutely right, unquestionable, in fact? Every self-identification, judgment, and impulse beginning with "I am"—"I am me," "I am American," "I am human," "I am male," "I am right," "I am sure," "I am angry"—seems natural, undeniable, imperative. As such, we are habitually driven to obey in feelings, thoughts, words, and deeds whatever comes from within the inexhaustible fountain of I am's, I think's, I want's, I love's, I hate's, and I do's. "I" is the absolute captain of our ship, the agent of our fate, the master of our lives.

When apes or bulls or mountain goats snort and paw the ground and then charge head first at one another, we interpret their behavior as an "I" versus "I" contest, sometimes to the death. Similarly, the imperative issuing from our "I" can be so adamant, so unchallengeable, that we human beings, too, will sacrifice our lives. Just think of the nature of such statements as follows, when the "I" is aligned with country, church, God, family, race, gender, or species: "I am a patriot!" "I am a Protestant!" "I am a Catholic!" "I am a Christian!" "I am a Muslim!" "I am a believer!" "I am an atheist!" "I am white!" "I am a male!" "I am human!" In these situations, the "I" exercises tremendous power over us, and can often lead us to our death.

The "I," the ego-self seemingly absolutely resident in the heart of our being, is the one thing of which we each are absolutely certain, which we will die for, which we will kill for, which we will obey slavishly and unquestioningly throughout our lives. We are so accustomed to our habitual sense of self that we consider even the slightest absence of it—a moment of derangement, a loss of consciousness in fainting or deep sleep, a disorienting distraction of passion or terror, a dizzying state of drunkenness or drug-intoxication, a psychological or neurological disorder—absolutely terrifying. We can't imagine our lives without our "I" as a constant, demanding presence.

What is shocking and difficult for most Westerners to accept is that the Buddha discovered that this most certain knowledge of the "self" is actually "misknowledge"—a fundamental misunderstanding, a delusion. And what's more, he realized that this discovery was the key to liberation, the gateway to enlightenment. When he saw the false nature of the "I," he emitted his "lion's roar," pronouncing the reality of selflessness, identitylessness, voidness. This was his *Eureka!* moment, his scientific breakthrough, his insight into reality, from whence has flowed for thousands of years the whole philosophical, scientific, and religious educational movement that is Buddhism. Identifying this habitual, certain self-knowledge as the core misknowledge allowed the Buddha to give birth to wisdom, truth, and liberating enlightenment.

But the Buddha knew perfectly well that it would do no good to simply order people to accept his declaration of selflessness as dogma and cling to it as a slogan or creed. The instinctual entanglement of human beings within the knot of self-certainty is much too powerful to be dislodged in this way, selflessness at first too counterintuitive to be acknowledged as truth. No, the Buddha realized, people must discover their real nature for themselves. So he made his declaration of selflessness not a statement of fact but rather a challenge to inquiry.

"I have discovered selflessness!" the Buddha announced. "I have seen through the reality of the seemingly solid self that lay at the core of my being. This insight did not destroy me—it only destroyed my suffering. It was my liberation! But you need not believe me. Discover the truth for yourself. Try with all your might to verify this 'self' you feel is in there, to pin it down. If you can do that, fine, tell me I'm wrong and ignore whatever else I may have to say. But if you fail to find it, if each thing you come up with dissolves under further analysis, if you discover, as I did, that there is no atomic, indivisible, durable core 'self,' then do not be afraid. Do not recoil or turn away. Rather, confront that emptiness and recognize it as the doorway to the supreme freedom! See through the 'self' and it will release you. You will discover that you are a part of the infinite web of interconnectedness with all other beings. You will live in bliss from now on as the relative self you always were; free at long last from the struggle of absolute alienation, free to help others find their own blessed freedom and happiness!"

Though in this paraphrase of his core teaching the Buddha offers us much encouragement, the challenge remains its central thrust. "You think you're really you? Don't just accept that blindly! Verify whether or not your 'self' is actually present within you. Turn your focused attention to it and explore it. If it's as solid as it seems, then it should be solidly encounterable. If you can't encounter it, then you must confront your error."

The great philosopher Descartes made a grave error when he thought he discovered in his fixed subjective self the one certain thing about existence. After demolishing the entire universe of observable things with hammer blows of systematic doubt, he was unable to give even a tiny tap to collapse this sense of self! And so he set down as the basis for his entire philosophy the famous proposition, "I think, therefore I am!"

Believe it or not, in his deep exploration for the "self," Descartes almost took another path that would have led him to enlightenment. He got very close to discovering that he could not find the "self" he felt to be so absolutely present. After intensively dissecting appearances, drilling through layer upon layer of seeming certainties, he came out with nothing that he could hold onto as the "self." But then he made the tragic mistake. Instead of accepting his selflessness, he instead said to himself, "Ah! Well, of course I cannot find the self. It is the self that is doing the looking! The 'I' is the subject and so it cannot be an object. Though I cannot find it, still my knowledge that it is the absolute subject cannot be doubted. It confirms its existence by doubting its existence. *Cogito ergo sum!* Of this I can remain absolutely certain."

Why was this mistaken? His logic sounds plausible enough at first. It is, after all, a clever way out of the dilemma of looking for something you are sure is there but cannot find. But what's wrong with it? Let's say that I am looking for a cup. I find it, so I can be certain that the cup exists. I look for my friend and find her, so I can be certain she's there. I look for my glasses, I do not find them—so I proclaim certainty that they are there? No—I go get another pair because I acknowledge I've lost them. I look for my oh-so-familiar "I," and I cannot find it! Why would I think it's there, then? Because I've arbitrarily put it in the category of "things that are there only when I can't find them"? No, when I can't find it, it's rather more sensible that I must give up the sense of certainty that it's there. I feel it's there when I don't look for it, but as soon as I look for it with real effort, it instantly eludes discovery. It seems always to be just around the next corner in my mind, yet each time I turn around to seize it, it disappears. And so I must slowly come to accept the fact that it may not be there after all.

Put another way, imagine that you are walking through the desert when, far off on the horizon, you see an oasis. Yet when you get closer, it disappears. "Aha!" you think to yourself. "A mirage." You walk away. Miles later, you turn around and look back. There's the oasis again! Do you feel certain that the water is there now? No, on the contrary you feel certain that it is only a mirage of water. In the same way, when you look for the "self" and don't find it, you must accept that it is merely a mirage. Your solid self-sense is only an illusion.

Had Descartes persisted and found the door to freedom in his selflessness, as the Buddha did, then instead of proclaiming, "I think, therefore I am," he might have said, "Even though I can find no concrete, fixated 'self,' I still can think. I still seem to be. Therefore I can continue to be myself, selflessly, as a relative, conventional, but ultimately unfindable being."

Whenever you decide to try a particular yoga recommended in this book, the crucial first step is always deciding to make the change. You must begin by accepting the fact that your habitual conceptions could be wrong. If, for example, you live with the delusion that it is just fine to remain addicted to nicotine, that three packs of cigarettes a day puts you in optimal operating condition, then there is no way you will successfully complete a yoga to quit smoking. Likewise, in this crucial quest of the self, the presumed core of your self-addiction, you must first convince yourself through empirical observation that the way you hold your self-identity—the constricted feeling of being wrapped around a solid, independent core—is uncomfortable and disabling.

Why should you even care if the rigid "self" that you believe in so strongly really exists or not? Our self feels most real when we are right and righteous, when we are wrongly or unfairly challenged. And it also seems unique, completely separate from everyone and everything else in the universe. This separateness can feel like freedom and independence when we are in a good mood. But when we are in trouble, lonely or angry, under pressure or dissatisfied, this separateness feels like isolation, alienation, unfair treatment, or deprivation. When we are wholly gripped by fury, the searing energy that wants to attack a target picks our "I" up like a mindless tool and flings us at the other person. It is so disconnected that it even disregards our sense of self-protection, making us take actions that injure us, ignore injuries undergone, and even harm others with no regard for the consequences. There is no more powerful demonstration of our strong sense of being an independent entity than when we give ourselves over completely to anger.

When we look around at others, we see that they are just as alienated from us as we are alienated from them. As we want things from them, they want things from us. As we reject them, they seem to reject us. We don't love them, so how can we expect them to love us? And yet they are endless, while "I" am just one. So I am badly outnumbered. I feel threatened. I can never get enough, have enough, or be enough. I will inevitably lose the me-versus-all-of-them struggle in the long run.

We can, of course, experience moments of unity with other beings, through falling in love, or having a child, for example. When we do, we experience tremendous relief—for a moment, there are two of us teamed up against all the others together. We have an ally. But unfortunately those moments are too rare, and they do not last long before the old self-isolation re-emerges. Even lovers can turn into adversaries, couples often seek divorce, and children recoil from their parents, who in turn reject them.

This alienation caused by the presumed independent, absolute self was why the Buddha saw its illusion as the source of human suffering. The situation of feeling that it's always "the self versus the world," with the self as the long-term loser, is unsatisfactory and untenable. When we recognize the inevitable nonviability of our self-centered reality, it motivates us to engage in the quest for the true nature of the self. It makes it existentially essential for us to pause in our headlong rush through life and turn within, to verify whether the "self" really exists as we feel it does.

We can take great encouragement from the fact that the Buddha told us we could escape from our suffering. Still, we cannot merely accept someone else's report. No one else can do the job of replacing misunderstanding with understanding for us. We must look at reality and verify for ourselves whether our habitual sense of having a fixed self or the Buddha's discovery of selflessness is ultimately true. In this way, we can begin to transform the self-preoccupation that causes chronic suffering into the insightful, gradual opening and letting go of the self that is, paradoxically, so self-fulfilling. We want to be happy, but ironically we can only become happier to the extent that we can develop an unconcern for our "self." This process is long and gradual, though you will experience frequent breakthrough moments that will thrill you and motivate you to continue.

Before we actually engage in the meditation practice used to discover the true nature of the self, we must set up our parameters in practical, clear terms. When we look through a darkened house for a misplaced key, we first remember what the key looks like, and then we search for it carefully, room by room, turning lights on as we go. We use a flashlight to look under beds and in hidden corners. When we have looked everywhere exhaustively and not found it, we decide we've missed it somehow, so we go back and repeat the process. However, after one or two searches of this kind, we come to a decisive conclusion that the key is not in the house. We know we could continue looking endlessly, but that would be impractical. So we decide to proceed accordingly with our lives.

In the case of the quest for the self, we will look through all the processes of our body and mind that we can find and investigate them thoroughly. Our physical systems, sensational feelings, conceptual image bank, emotional energies, and consciousness itself constitute the house through which we will search. There are also various vaguely defined areas such as "spirit" and "soul" that, like a dusty attic or dank cellar, we may feel the need to explore. It is easy to get lost in these murky, dank, and oft-forgotten quarters of the mind. So we must get a clear picture of what we want to find ahead of time. And most important, we must set some limits to the exercise, since practically speaking we cannot continue to search indefinitely.

At this point you should search through the house of your body-mind-spirit a few times with great concentration and systematic thoroughness, with my help and the help of many experts who have guided me through this practice. If, during this process, you find a "self," then enjoy it to the full. If, however, as I suspect will be the case, you do not find what stands up solidly as your "real self" by the end of the process, then you will have to live with the fact that there is no such thing. You will need to make the practical decision to turn from seeking the "self" to explore instead the ramifications of being a relative self without any absolute underpinning.

This commitment to practicality in your quest for the self is of great importance at the outset and will have a significant impact on the success of the endeavor. Once you have made the commitment in your own mind, you may begin.

Practice: Trying to Find Your "I"

You are now prepared to deepen your understanding of your selflessness. You will be looking at yourself introspectively, trying to grasp exactly what your essence is. When you do this practice well, you will begin to feel yourself dissolving, just as I did at my mentor Geshe-la's house many years ago. You will start realizing—gradually and also suddenly, in spurts—that you can't find this mysterious "self." Your strong feeling of having an absolute "I" is maddeningly elusive when you try to pin it down precisely.

… In looking for your "self," start with your body. Ask yourself, "Am I my body?" In order to answer this question, you must define your body. It is composed at least of your five sense organs, right? Your skin and sensitive inner surfaces constitute the touch organ, then you have your eyes for sight, your nose for smell, your ears for hearing, and your tongue for taste. So first let's explore all of your senses together, your sensory system.

Identify the sound sense. What do you hear—a dog barking, a phone ringing, music playing, or perhaps just the sound of your own breathing? Now notice the visual field. You are reading words on the page. What else do you see? What are the images on the edge of your peripheral vision? How about smell? Perhaps you smell the scent of incense burning, or of musty wood. Do you taste anything: something you ate a while ago, tea you drank, or just the taste of your own mouth? The tactile field is everything touching your skin, including other parts of your skin touching your skin. Your hand may be resting on your knee, for example. Your bottom is touching a pillow. Just identify all the sensations, the textures, smells, tastes, sounds, and sights.

Now notice your internal sensations, like the breakfast in your tummy. You might have a slight pain in your back or your knee. Maybe your foot is falling asleep, and you're annoyed because there's a slightly painful sensation there. You might have a pleasurable sensation in some part of you that is feeling good if, for example, you worked out yesterday or had a massage.

Recognize that for each of these sensations you are experiencing, you are receiving data from the outside world. The sensations are not all coming from your own body. So your body is not just inside your skin; your body is both your organs and the field of all incoming sense objects. It's everything you are seeing and hearing and smelling and tasting and touching. It's the chair or pillow you're sitting on. The words you are reading on this page. The incense drifting into your nostrils. If you look at one sensation, you realize that you are sharing your material body with the outside world. Say, for example, you are looking at light bouncing off a table. That light is a part of your shared sensory system, and therefore part of your body, too.

So already you have begun to expand your self-definition, just by looking at your five senses. Suddenly you are not just something that sits there inside your skin. You are your environment as well. Your body interfuses with the outside world that you perceive with your senses. All of our bodies are totally overlapping, all the time. Do you see? And when you think, "this is 'me' over here inside this skin," you are unrealistically thinking that "I" am not connected to others through the sense perceptions that we have in common. But you are connected, even before you talk to them or think anything about them, through your shared environment.

Now you can move to the next level of analysis of the self, which exists at the level of your mind. First is the sensational system, the feelings of pleasure, pain, and numbness associated with sense perceptions of sights, sounds, smells, tastes, textures, and mental sense inner objects. When you experience these six kinds of objects, you react as pleased, irritated, or indifferent. Mentally inventory your sensations at the moment, and notice how you react at this basic feeling level. Notice that this heap of sense-reactions has no self-core within it.

Next is your conceptual system, your ideas, mental maps, and internal images. You have a picture of yourself as you exist in the world. You have a concept of yourself as human, not animal. You have a picture of yourself as male or female. You have a body image, and an image of each part of your body. You have a concept of your identity as a teacher, a manager, a doctor, or whatever. You have a concept of yourself as successful or as a failure. Inventory this mass of ideas and images and notice that you have whole clouds of pictures and concepts. But is this incredibly chaotic mass of images and words and diagrams and maps and so forth that is your conceptual system the real "you"? Your perception of yourself changes all the time, depending on your mood, whom you're with, or what you're doing. Sometimes you think, "I'm a high-powered executive," whereas other times you think, "I'm just a tiny speck on a tiny planet of six billion people." So surely your conceptual system cannot be your "self." The "you" self is not any of these ideas, since it seems to be the entity that is noticing all of them.

At the fourth level of analysis, find your emotional system. You are constantly reacting to all of these images and notions. Right now, you're probably feeling a bit irritated with me. You're thinking to yourself, "Why is he making me do this? Why doesn't he just crack a joke? Let's have some fun. What is this terrible business of exploring the self, 'discovering selflessness'? How is this helping me?" And so on and so forth. You're feeling annoyed and anxious and confused. Or maybe you're just feeling bored. Anyway, your emotions are there in your mind, always functioning, but always changing. You can take a peek at them now, as they swirl around in your heart and head, and you can see that they are not fixed. You are not defined by your emotions. They are not the elusive "self" you're seeking.

Lastly, turn your attention to your consciousness system. It is the most important system of all. You see at once how it is a buzzing, blooming, swirling mass of subtle energies. Nothing is fixed, nothing stable within it. With your mental consciousness, you hop from one sense to another. You analyze your ideas, you focus internally on your emotions and thoughts, and you can even focus on being thought-free. Your consciousness aims itself at being free of thought by the thought of being free of thought. How strange! As you inventory your consciousness, don't allow yourself to rest with a bare awareness, but go a bit deeper—explore further with your analytic attention. Ask yourself, "Who is this supposedly rigid 'self'? Is it the same self right now as the one who woke up grumbling this morning, preparing that cup of coffee, rushing to get ready, quickly brushing its teeth? Is it the same self who was born a tiny, unaware, helpless infant years ago? Who is the 'me' who knows my name, who knows what I want, where I am, and what I'm doing? Who is the 'me' who knows I'm an American, who knows I'm a—whatever: a Buddhist or a Christian or an atheist? Where is that person now? Where is that absolute, unchanging structure?" You can see how your self-consciousness is a buzzing, blooming, swirling mass of confusion—nothing is fixed, nothing stable within it. You can barely remember what you did yesterday morning—I can't remember at all at my age! So how can you possibly have a rigid self? See how releasing these sorts of thoughts can be! ...

The deepest stage of awareness comes when your consciousness begins to turn inward to gaze upon itself. At first it thinks, "I now know that these sensory, mental, and emotional systems looming before me are not the 'self,' they are not 'me.' But the awareness that looks at them, that contemplates and investigates them, that is my 'self.'" And yet you soon discover that you are mistaken even in this conclusion. The moment you begin to examine your own conscious mind, you engage in a whirling, internal dervish-dance where your awareness spins round and round upon itself. This contemplation can be dizzying, nauseating, painful, and even a bit frightening, as the felt "self" disappears and evades its own attention. You can never catch it, even as you become more experienced at this meditation and come back to this place again and again. Time and again you will feel frustrated by your continued failure to come up with a result. Yet you must not lose heart. You must remember that looking for your "self" is the most important thing you can ever do in your evolutionary development. You must keep faith that you are on the brink of a quantum leap; you are so close to awakening.

As you enter into this confusing realm of spinning self-seeking, be careful not to make the mistake Descartes made by withdrawing from it all with some sort of decision about "you" being the subject and therefore not any sort of findable object. Also, be careful not to fall into the nihilistic trap of withdrawing from the spinning by deciding that all is nothing after all and so naturally the self-sense is an illusion. Keep whirling upon your "self" as long as you feel absolutely there is a self to whirl upon, to look at, to catch. Put your full truth-seeking, analytic energy into the drive to find it.

Eventually, you will experience a gradual melting process. The whirling will slowly dissolve without fear: you won't shrink back in terror of falling into an abyss-like void because you are already overcoming your self-addiction. You control the tendency to shrink back in terror of falling into a looming void by your drilling, whirling energy of awareness itself. You dissolve your fearing subject, the object for which you are feeling fear, and the imagined nothingness that only the pseudo-self-addiction wants you to fear. However fully you feel such processes at first, what happens to you is that, as you begin to melt, your drive intensity lessens, you feel buoyed by a floating sensation coming from within your nerves and cells, from within your subjectivity as well as your object-field. At some point, you lose your sense of self entirely, as if you were a field of open space. Like Neo and his colleagues in the movie *The Matrix* when they entered one of the computer-generated training fields, you will find yourself standing in a blank white space—except in your case, in this transcending moment, you break free from your "digital residual self-image." You will be only the blank white space, a bare awareness of yourself as a boundless entity. Dissolving into this space, you'll feel intense bliss, a sense of extreme relief.

When you first melt into the spacious experience of freedom, it is enthralling, like emerging from a dark cave into infinite light. You feel magnificent, vast, and unbound. If you inadvertently fall into this state unprepared by arriving there too quickly, you may be tempted to think that you have arrived at the absolute reality, and this is a bit of a danger. You might think, feeling it nonverbally at this stage, that you've conquered the differentiated universe and realized its true "nothingness," experiencing it as such a profound and liberating release that you never again want any contact with the real world. Remember, however, that nothingness is not your ultimate goal—you are not trying to escape reality, but to embrace it. If you reach this space of release gradually through the repeated whirling of your self turning upon itself, then you'll be able to enjoy the vastness and magnificence without losing awareness that it is only another relational condition. You'll realize that the great emptiness is ultimately empty of itself; it is not reality, either.

Since you *are* the void, you do not need to remain in the void, and your original self-sense slowly reemerges within the universe of persons and things. But you are aware that it is not the same "self" you had before—it is forever different, now become infinite and unbound. You have changed. You now perceive your "self" consciously, living with it yet maintaining an educated distance from it. You are like one of the characters in *The Matrix,* present and active as real being, yet at the same time realizing that the apparent reality that surrounds you is only illusory. All that was apparent becomes transparent.

One of the most significant changes you will notice upon discovering your selflessness is that your sense of being separate from everyone else has now eroded. Your new awareness enables you to perceive others as equal to yourself, a part of you, even. You can see yourself as they see you, and experience empathically how they perceive themselves as locked within themselves. You have arrived at the doorway to universal compassion, and it frees you from being locked away behind a fixed point-of-awareness and opens you to a sort of field awareness wherein others are really just the same as you while simultaneously relationally different. Through the sense of sameness, you feel their pains as if they were your own: when they hurt, you hurt. Yet through the sense of relational difference and balanced responsibility, you naturally feel moved to free them from their pains, just as you move automatically to eliminate your own pains. When your hand is burned by a hot pot handle, you react at once to pull away from the heat, you plunge it into cold water, you rush to find ice. You respond instinctively to remove the pain. You don't consider it a selfless act of compassion for your hand. You just do it through your neural connection to your hand. Your new open awareness feels others' hands through a similar sense of natural connection.

QUESTIONS FOR MAKING CONNECTIONS WITHIN THE READING

1. Choose one important term from Thurman's essay, such as "nirvana," "nothingness," "emptiness," "enlightenment," "meditation," "compassion," "ignorance," "self," "happiness," or "freedom." Then, by tracing Thurman's use of the term throughout the chapter, offer your own explanation of its meaning. While commonplace definitions for all of these terms may be found in a dictionary, here you are being asked to explain the meaning of the term as Thurman uses it. Then you might contrast Thurman's use of the term with more commonplace understandings. "Ignorance," for example,

has a special significance in the context of Buddhist thought. How does it differ from "ignorance" as we normally define it?

2. Instead of discussing the soul, Thurman focuses on the mind. How is "mind" different from "soul"? Where is the mind located, according to Thurman? Is it the same as the brain? What are some of the broader implications of Thurman's attention to the mind instead of the soul? If the mind is transformed, can the essence of the person remain somehow immune to change? Conversely, if a person's mental habits and perceptions remain unchanged, is it possible to imagine that the essence of the person has still been altered somehow? We might ordinarily think of each person as endowed with an individual soul, but is the mind individualized in the same way?

3. Thurman speaks about "enlightenment" instead of "redemption" or "salvation." How does "enlightenment" differ from "salvation"? What are the differences between Thurman's emphasis on the experience of "selflessness" and the famous Greek dictum "Know thyself"? Could selflessness qualify as a form of self-knowledge? Could it qualify as a form of redemption or salvation?

QUESTIONS FOR WRITING

1. Buddhism is often studied on the college level in courses offered by philosophy and religion departments. Judging from Thurman's account, what elements does Buddhism have in common with philosophy? With religion? Or, judging from Thurman's account, would you say that Buddhism has some elements in common with science, which is based on empirical observation? In what ways might Buddhism be closer to a science than to a religion or a philosophy?

2. What are the social and political implications of Thurman's argument? How would the cultivation of "wisdom" as he describes it affect people in a competitive, consumption-oriented society like our own? Is Thurman's brand of meditation compatible with democracy and the idea that all of us are equal? How might the cultivation of wisdom influence the current political climate? Would the climate become less adversarial? Less driven by rigid ideology? Or would people who cultivate wisdom simply wash their hands of politics?

QUESTIONS FOR MAKING CONNECTIONS
BETWEEN READINGS

1. In "When I Woke Up Tuesday Morning, It Was Friday," Martha Stout describes forms of "divided" or "dissociated" consciousness that are produced by severely traumatic events. One of Stout's patients, whom she calls "Julia," becomes so dissociated from the here and now that whole days

never get recorded in Julia's memory. After rereading Stout's analysis of dissociation, decide whether or not the form of meditation that Thurman describes might help someone like Julia. Is it possible that meditation as Thurman describes it could actually *produce* dissociation in healthy people? What aspects of meditation might be most helpful to people like Julia? Is it possible that dissociation is actually more widespread than most people even realize? Is trauma really necessary to produce severely divided consciousness, or do certain features of contemporary life help to produce it—television, commercial radio, video games, and movies?

2. In what ways is reading like the practice of meditation? To explore this question, draw primarily on Azar Nafisi's chapter from *Reading Lolita in Tehran*. At a key moment in her account, Nafisi makes this observation:

    > Whoever we were—and it was not really important what religion we belonged to, whether we wished to wear the veil or not, whether we absorbed certain religious norms or not—we had become the figment of someone else's dreams. A stern ayatollah, a self-proclaimed philosopher-king, had come to rule our land.

    How, according to Nafisi, can the reading of fiction help us throw off the veils—literal and virtual—that others have imposed on us? Does reading as she describes involve its own form of mental cultivation, comparable in some ways to the meditational practice Thurman describes? Does reading allow Nafisi and her students to experience a form of "selflessness"? How can we tell the difference between the veils imposed on us and the persons we really are? Is it possible that "selflessness" allows us to create an identity of our own?

JEAN TWENGE

IN THE SECOND half of the twentieth century, American culture became more and more a celebration of the individual. The shared concerns of the whole society and the language of "us" rather than of "me" fell by the wayside as the self became the primary focus. Many observers, alarmed by this trend, have criticized the last two generations for their sense of entitlement—their unexamined assumption that the world owes them happiness and recognition. But Jean Twenge, a psychologist and associate professor at San Diego State University, adds a new wrinkle to the critique: so much emphasis on the self isn't just bad for society, she argues; it's also bad for the individual.

Twenge's bestselling first book, *Generation Me: Why Today's Young Americans Are More Confident, Assertive, Entitled—and More Miserable than Ever Before* (2006), uses data taken from 1.3 million young people to trace the different perspectives of successive generations on self-esteem, individuality, sexuality, and other issues related to development. In reviewing this data, Twenge sees evidence of an unprecedented shift as both education and culture have come to emphasize selfhood and self-esteem above all other values. Twenge argues that for Baby Boomers, the term "self" was still a novel idea, so novel that that they saw "selfhood" as a difficult goal worth pursuing. However, later generations internalized this idea of the self to the point that young people find it difficult to imagine organizing their lives around anything else.

Twenge's most recent book is a follow-up to *Generation Me. The Narcissism Epidemic: Living in the Age of Entitlement* (2009) co-written with W. Keith Campbell, provides a detailed portrait of a culture defined by "public violence and aggression, self-promotion, and the desire for uniqueness" at the cost of the well-being of others. Even though most young people today are not narcissistic to the degree that it has become debilitating for them, the number who suffer from a clinical disorder is three times greater than a generation ago. And even within mainstream culture, behavior that would have seemed to our grandparents absurdly self-absorbed has become the new normal. Surges in the rates of plastic surgery, credit card debt, and ostentatious consumption all suggest that the celebrity has become the ideal of an age defined by its overconfidence and greed.

Jean, Twenge. Final quotation from "About *The Narcissism Epidemic*: An FAQ on Narcissism," <http://www.narcissism epidemic.com/aboutbook.html>.

An Army of One: *Me*

One day when my mother was driving me to school in 1986, Whitney Houston's hit song "The Greatest Love of All" was warbling out of the weak speakers of our Buick station wagon with wood trim. I asked my mother what she thought the song was about. "The greatest love of all—it has to be about children," she said.

My mother was sweet, but wrong. The song does say that children are the future (always good to begin with a strikingly original thought) and that we should teach them well. About world peace, may be? Or great literature? Nope. Children should be educated about the beauty "inside," the song declares. We all need heroes, Whitney sings, but she never found "anyone to fulfill my needs," so she learned to depend on (wait for it) "me." The chorus then declares, "learning to love yourself is the greatest love of all."

This is a stunning reversal in attitude from previous generations. Back then, respect for others was more important than respect for yourself. The term "self-esteem" wasn't widely used until the late 1960s, and didn't become talk-show and dinner-table conversation until the 1980s. By the 1990s, it was everywhere.

Take, for example, the band Offspring's rockingly irreverent 1994 riff "Self-Esteem." The song describes a guy whose girlfriend "says she wants only me ... Then I wonder why she sleeps with my friends." (Hmmm.) But he's blasé about it—it's OK, really, since he's "just a sucker with no self-esteem."

By the mid-1990s, Offspring could take it for granted that most people knew the term "self-esteem," and knew they were supposed to have it. They also knew how to diagnose themselves when they didn't have it. Offspring's ironic self-parody demonstrates a high level of understanding of the concept, the satire suggesting that this psychological self-examination is rote and can thus be performed with tongue planted firmly in cheek.

In the years since, attention to the topic of self-esteem has rapidly expanded. A search for "self-esteem" in the books section of amazon.com yielded 105,438 entries in July 2005 (sample titles: *The Self-Esteem Workbook, Breaking the Chain of Low Self-Esteem, Ten Days to Self-Esteem, 200 Ways to Raise a Girl's Self-Esteem*). Magazine articles on self-esteem are as common as e-mail spam for Viagra. *Ladies' Home Journal* told readers to "Learn to Love Yourself!" in March 2005,[1] while *Parenting* offered "Proud to Be Me!" (apparently the exclamation point is required) in April, listing "5 simple ways to help your child love who he is."[2] TV and radio talk shows would be immediately shut down by the FCC if "self-esteem" were on the list of banned words. The American Academy of Pediatrics guide to caring for babies and young children uses the word "self-esteem" ten times in the space of seven pages in the first chapter, and that doesn't even count the numerous mentions of self-respect, confidence, and belief in oneself.[3]

How did self-esteem transform from an obscure academic term to a familiar phrase that pops up in everything from women's magazines to song lyrics to celebrity interviews? The story actually begins centuries ago, when humans barely had a concept of a self at all: your marriage was arranged, your profession determined by your parents, your actions dictated by strict religious standards. Slowly over the centuries, social strictures began to loosen and people started to make more choices for themselves. Eventually, we arrived at the modern concept of the individual as an autonomous, free person.

Then came the 1970s, when the ascendance of the self truly exploded into the American consciousness. In contrast to previous ethics of honor and duty, Baby Boomer ideals focused instead on meaning and self-fulfillment. In his 1976 bestseller, *Your Erroneous Zones,* Wayne Dyer suggests that the popular song "You Are the Sunshine of My Life" be retitled "I Am the Sunshine of My Life." Your love for yourself, he says, should be your "first love." The 1970 allegory, *Jonathan Livingston Seagull,* describes a bird bored with going "from shore to food and back again." Instead, he wants to enjoy flying, swooping through the air to follow "a higher meaning, a higher purpose for life," even though his actions get him exiled from his flock. The book, originally rejected by nearly every major publishing house, became a runaway bestseller as Americans came to agree with the idea that life should be fulfilling and focused on the needs of the self. The seagulls in the animated movie *Finding Nemo* were still on message almost twenty-five years later: all that comes out of their beaks is the word "mine."

Boomers and Their "Journey" into the Self

Because the Boomers dominate our culture so much, we have to understand them first so we can see how they differ from the younger Generation Me. Why aren't the Boomers—the Me Generation in the 1970s—the *real* Generation Me? It's about what you explore as a young adult versus what you're born to and take for granted.

For the Boomers, who grew up in the 1950s and 1960s, self-focus was a new concept, individualism an uncharted territory. In his 1981 book *New Rules: Searching for Self-Fulfillment in a World Turned Upside Down,* Daniel Yankelovich describes young Boomers struggling with new questions: How do you make decisions in a marriage with two equal partners? How do you focus on yourself when your parents don't even know what that means? The Boomers in the book sound like people driving around in circles in the dark, desperately searching for something. The world was so new that there were no road signs, no maps to point the way to this new fulfillment and individuality.

That's probably why many Boomers talk about the self using language full of abstraction, introspection, and "growth." New things call for this kind of meticulous thought, and require the idea that the process will take time. Thus Boomers talk about "my journey," "my need to keep growing," or "my unfulfilled potentials." Sixties activist Todd Gitlin called the Boomer quest the "voyage to the interior." Icky as they are to today's young people, these phrases drum with motion and time, portraying self-focus as a continuous project that keeps evolving as Boomers look around for true meaning. In a 1976 *New York Magazine* article, Tom Wolfe described the "new dream" as "remaking, remodeling, elevating and polishing one's very self ... and observing, studying, and doting on it."[4] Sixties radical Jerry Rubin wrote that he tried just about every fad of the 1970s (rolfing, est, yoga, sex therapy, finding his inner child); one of the chapters in his book *Growing (Up) at Thirty-Seven* is called "Searching for Myself."

Such introspection primarily surfaces today in the speech of New Agers, therapists who have read too much Maslow, and over-45 Boomers. When asked what's next in her life, Kim Basinger (born in 1953) replies, "Watching what the rest of my journey is going to be about."[5] In answer to the same question, Sarah Ferguson, Duchess of York (born in 1959) says: "My coming to stay in America for a few months is like my blossoming into my true Sarah, into my true self. And I'm just coming to learn about her myself."[6] Not all Boomers talk this way, of course, but enough do that it's an immediately recognizable generational tic. It's also a guaranteed way to get a young person to roll her eyes. She might also then tell you to lighten up.

Many authors, from William Strauss and Neil Howe in *Generations* to Steve Gillon in *Boomer Nation,* have noted that abstraction and spirituality are the primary hallmarks of the Boomer generation. Gillon describes Boomers as having a "moralistic style" and devotes a chapter to Boomers' "New Fundamentalism."[7] Whether joining traditional churches or exploring meditation or yoga, Boomers have been fascinated with the spiritual for four decades.

Even Boomers who don't adopt New Age language seek higher meaning in the new religion of consumer products—thus the yuppie revolution. In *Bobos in Paradise,* David Brooks demonstrates that upper-class Boomers have poured their wealth into things like cooking equipment, which somehow feels more moral and meaningful than previous money sinks like jewelry or furs. Even food becomes "a barometer of virtue," Brooks says, as 1960s values are "selectively updated.... Gone are the sixties-era things that were fun and of interest to teenagers, like Free Love, and retained are all the things that might be of interest to middle-aged hypochondriacs, like whole grains."[8]

The Boomers' interest in the abstract and spiritual shows up in many different sources. In 1973, 46% of Boomers said they "focused on internal cues."[9] Only 26% of 1990s young people agreed. Thirty percent of Boomers said that "creativity comes from within," versus 18% of young people in the 1990s.[10] Even stronger evidence comes from a national survey of more than 300,000 college freshmen. In 1967, a whopping 86% of incoming college students said that "developing a meaningful philosophy of life" was an essential life goal.[11] Only 42% of GenMe freshmen in 2004 agreed, cutting the Boomer number in half. I'm definitely a member of my generation in this way; despite being an academic, I'm not sure I know what a "meaningful philosophy of life" even is. Jerry Rubin does—if you can understand him. "Instead of seeking with the expectation of finding, I experience my seeking as an end in itself," he writes.

"I become one with my seeking, and merge with the moment."[12] OK, Jerry. Let us know when you've re-entered the Earth's atmosphere.

While up there, maybe Jerry met Aleta St. James, a 57-year-old woman who gave birth to twins in 2004. She explained her unusual actions by saying, "My whole world is about manifesting, so I decided to manifest children."[13] It's not surprising that an enterprising GenMe member put together a list of books on amazon.com titled "Tired of Baby Boomer Self-Righteousness?"

Boomers display another unique and somewhat ironic trait: a strong emphasis on group meetings. Boomers followed in the footsteps of their community-minded elders—they just joined the Weathermen instead of the Elks Lodge. This is one of the many reasons why Boomers are not the true Generation Me—almost everything they did happened in groups: Vietnam protests, marches for feminism, consciousness raising, assertiveness training, discos, even seminars like est. Maybe it felt safer to explore the self within a group—perhaps it felt less radical. No one seemed to catch the irony that it might be difficult to find your own unique direction in a group of other people. Even Boomers' trends and sayings belied their reliance on groups: "Don't trust anyone over 30" groups people by age, as did the long hair many Boomer men adopted in the late 1960s and early 1970s to distinguish themselves from older folks. In a 1970 song, David Crosby says he decided not to cut his hair so he could "let my freak flag fly." If you've got a flag, you're probably a group. Boomers may have thought they invented individualism, but like any inventor, they were followed by those who truly perfected the art.

Boomers took only the first tentative steps in the direction of self-focus, rather than swallowing it whole at birth. Most Boomers never absorbed it at all and settled down early to marry and raise families. Those who adopted the ways of the self as young adults speak the language with an accent: the accent of abstraction and "journeys." They had to reinvent their way of thinking when already grown, and thus see self-focus as a "process." In his book, Rubin quotes a friend who says, "We are the first generation to reincarnate ourselves in our own lifetime."

The Matter-of-Fact Self-Focus of Generation Me

Generation Me had no need to reincarnate ourselves; we were born into a world that already celebrated the individual. The self-focus that blossomed in the 1970s became mundane and commonplace over the next two decades, and GenMe accepts it like a fish accepts water. If Boomers were making their way in the uncharted world of the self, GenMe has printed step-by-step directions from Yahoo! Maps—and most of the time we don't even need them, since the culture of the self is our hometown. We don't have to join groups or talk of journeys, because we're already there. We don't need to "polish" the self, as Wolfe said, because we take for granted that it's already shiny. We don't need to look inward; we already know what we will find. Since we were small children, we were taught to put ourselves first. That's just the way the world works—why dwell on it? Let's go to the mall.

GenMe's focus on the needs of the individual is not necessarily self-absorbed or isolationist; instead, it's a way of moving through the world beholden to few social rules and with the unshakable belief that you're important. It's also not the same as being "spoiled," which implies that we always get what we want; though this probably does describe some kids, it's not the essence of the trend. (GenMe's expectations are so great and our reality so challenging that we will probably get less of what we want than any previous generation). We simply take it for granted that we should all feel good about ourselves, we are all special, and we all deserve to follow our dreams. GenMe is straightforward and unapologetic about our self-focus. In 2004's *Conquering Your Quarterlife Crisis,* Jason, 25, relates how he went through some tough times and decided he needed to change things in his life. His new motto was "Do what's best for Jason. I had to make *me* happy; I had to do what was best for myself in every situation."[14]

Our practical orientation toward the self sometimes leaves us with a distaste for Boomer abstraction. When a character in the 2004 novel *Something Borrowed* watched the 1980s show *thirtysomething* as a teen, she wished the Boomer characters would "stop pondering the meaning of life and start making grocery lists."[15] The matter-of-fact attitude of GenMe appears in everyday language as well—a language that still includes the abstract concept of self, but uses it in a very simple way, perhaps because we learned the language as children. We speak the language of the self as our native tongue. So much of the "common sense" advice that's given these days includes some variation on "self":

- Worried about how to act in a social situation? "Just be yourself."
- What's the good thing about your alcoholism/drug addiction/murder conviction? "I learned a lot about myself."
- Concerned about your performance? "Believe in yourself." (Often followed by "and anything is possible.")
- Should you buy the new pair of shoes, or get the nose ring? "Yes, express yourself."
- Why should you leave the unfulfilling relationship/quit the boring job/tell off your mother-in-law? "You have to respect yourself."
- Trying to get rid of a bad habit? "Be honest with yourself."
- Confused about the best time to date or get married? "You have to love yourself before you can love someone else."
- Should you express your opinion? "Yes, stand up for yourself."

Americans use these phrases so often that we don't even notice them anymore. Dr. Phil, the ultimate in plainspoken, no-nonsense advice, uttered both "respect yourself" and "stop lying to yourself" within seconds of each other on a *Today* show segment on New Year's resolutions.[16] One of his bestselling books is entitled *Self Matters.* We take these phrases and ideas so much for granted, it's as if we learned them in our sleep as children, like the perfectly conditioned citizens in Aldous Huxley's *Brave New World.*

These aphorisms don't seem absurd to us even when, sometimes, they are. We talk about self-improvement as if the self could be given better drywall or a new coat of paint. We read self-help books as if the self could receive

The Self Across the Generations

Baby Boomers	Generation Me
Self-fulfillment	Fun
Journey, potentials, searching	Already there
Change the world	Follow your dreams
Protests and group sessions	Watching TV and surfing the Web
Abstraction	Practicality
Spirituality	Things
Philosophy of life	Feeling good about yourself

tax-deductible donations. The *Self* even has its own magazine. Psychologist Martin Seligman says that the traditional self—responsible, hardworking, stern—has been replaced with the "California self," "a self that chooses, feels pleasure and pain, dictates action and even has things like esteem, efficacy, and confidence."[17] Media outlets promote the self relentlessly; I was amazed at how often I heard the word "self" used in the popular media once I started looking for it. A careful study of news stories published or aired between 1980 and 1999 found a large increase in self-reference words (I, me, mine, and myself) and a marked decrease in collective words (humanity, country, or crowd).[18]

Young people have learned these self-lessons very well. In a letter to her fans in 2004, Britney Spears, 23, listed her priorities as "Myself, my husband, Kevin, and starting a family."[19] If you had to read that twice to get my point, it's because we take it for granted that we should put ourselves first on our list of priorities—it would be blasphemy if you didn't (unless, of course, you have low self-esteem). Twenty-year-old Maria says her mother often reminds her to consider what other people will think. "It doesn't matter what other people think," Maria insists. "What really matters is how I perceive myself. The real person I need to please is myself."

Smart marketers have figured this out, too. In the late 1990s, Prudential replaced its longtime insurance slogan "Get a Piece of the Rock" with the nakedly individualistic "Be Your Own Rock."[20] The United States Army, perhaps the last organization one might expect to focus on the individual instead of the group, has followed suit. Their standard slogan, adopted in 2001, is "An Army of One."

Changes in Self-Esteem: What the Data Say

The data I gathered on self-esteem over time mirror the social trends perfectly. My colleague Keith Campbell and I looked at the responses of 65,965 college students to the Rosenberg Self-Esteem Scale, the most popular measure of general self-esteem among adults.[21] I held my breath when I analyzed these data for the first time, but I needn't have worried: the change was enormous. By the mid-1990s, the average GenMe college man had higher self-esteem than 86%

of college men in 1968. The average mid-1990s college woman had higher self-esteem than 71% of Boomer college women. Between the 1960s and the 1990s, college students were increasingly likely to agree that "I take a positive attitude toward myself" and "On the whole, I am satisfied with myself." Other sources verify this trend. A 1997 survey of teens asked, "In general, how do you feel about yourself?" A stunning 93% answered "good." Of the remainder, 6% said they felt "not very good," and only 1% admitted they felt "bad" about themselves.[22] Another survey found that 91% of teens described themselves as responsible, 74% as physically attractive, and 79% as "very intelligent."[23]

Children's self-esteem scores tell a different but even more intriguing story. We examined the responses of 39,353 children, most ages 9 to 13, on the Coopersmith Self-Esteem Inventory, a scale written specifically for children.[24] During the 1970s—when the nation's children shifted from the late Baby Boom to the early years of GenX—kids' self-esteem declined, probably because of societal instability. Rampant divorce, a wobbly economy, soaring crime rates, and swinging singles culture made the 1970s a difficult time to be a kid. The average child in 1979 scored lower than 81% of kids in the mid-1960s. Over this time, children were less likely to agree with statements like "I'm pretty sure of myself" and "I'm pretty happy" and more likely to agree that "things are all mixed up in my life." The individualism that was so enthralling for teenagers and adults in the 1970s didn't help kids—and, if their parents suddenly discovered self-fulfillment, it might have even hurt them.

But after 1980, when GenMe began to enter the samples, children's self-esteem took a sharp turn upward. More and more during the 1980s and 1990s, children were saying that they were happy with themselves. They agreed that "I'm easy to like" and "I always do the right thing." By the mid-1990s, children's self-esteem scores equaled, and often exceeded, children's scores in the markedly more stable Boomer years before 1970. The average kid in the mid-1990s—right in the heart of GenMe—had higher self-esteem than 73% of kids in 1979, one of the last pre-GenMe years.

This is a bit of a mystery, however. The United States of the 1980s to mid-1990s never approached the kid-friendly stability of the 1950s and early 1960s: violent crime hit record highs, divorce was still at epidemic levels, and the economy had not yet reached its late-1990s boom. So without the calm and prosperity of earlier decades, why did children's self-esteem increase so dramatically during the 1980s and 1990s?

The Self-Esteem Curriculum

The short answer is that they were taught it. In the years after 1980, there was a pervasive, society-wide effort to increase children's self-esteem. The Boomers who now filled the ranks of parents apparently decided that children should always feel good about themselves. Research on programs to boost self-esteem first blossomed in the 1980s, and the number of psychology and education journal articles devoted to self-esteem doubled between the 1970s and the 1980s.[25] Journal articles on self-esteem increased another 52% during the 1990s, and the number of books on

Parents are encouraged to raise their children's self-esteem even when kids are simply coloring. Even the cat has high self-esteem on this coloring book cover. However, the dog lacks a self-esteem boosting ribbon. He probably has low self-esteem—after all, he drinks out of the toilet.

self-esteem doubled over the same time.[26] Generation Me is the first generation raised to believe that everyone should have high self-esteem.

Magazines, television talk shows, and books all emphasize the importance of high self-esteem for children, usually promoting feelings that are actually a lot closer to narcissism (a more negative trait usually defined as excessive self-importance). One children's book, first published in 1991, is called *The Lovables in the Kingdom of Self-Esteem.* "I AM LOVABLE. Hi, lovable friend! My name is Mona Monkey. I live in the Kingdom of Self-Esteem along with my friends the Lovable Team," the book begins.[27] On the next page, children learn that the gates of the kingdom will swing open if you "say these words three times with pride: *I'm lovable! I'm lovable! I'm lovable!*" (If I hear the word "lovable" one more time, I'm going to use my hefty self-esteem to pummel the author of this book).

Another example is the "BE A WINNER Self-Esteem Coloring and Activity Book" pictured in this chapter. Inside, children find activities and pictures designed to boost their self-esteem, including coloring a "poster for your room" that reads "YOU ARE SPECIAL" in yellow, orange, and red letters against a purple background. Another page asks kids to fill in the blanks: "Accept y_ur_e_f. You're a special person. Use p_si_iv_ thinking." A similar coloring book is called "We Are All Special" (though this title seems to suggest that being special isn't so special). All of this probably sounds like Al Franken's *Saturday Night Live* character Stuart Smalley, an insecure, sweater-vest-wearing man who looks in the mirror and unconvincingly repeats, "I'm good enough, I'm smart enough, and doggone it, people like me." It sounds like it because it's exactly the type of thing Franken was parodying. And it's everywhere.

Many school districts across the country have specific programs designed to increase children's self-esteem, most of which actually build self-importance and narcissism. One program is called "Self-Science: The Subject Is Me."[28] (Why bother with biology? *I'm* so much more interesting!) Another program, called "Pumsy in Pursuit of Excellence," uses a dragon character to encourage children to escape the "Mud Mind" they experience when feeling bad about themselves. Instead, they should strive to be in the "Sparkle Mind" and feel good about themselves.[29] The Magic Circle exercise designates one child a day to receive a badge saying "I'm great." The other children then say good things about the chosen child, who later receives a written list of all of the praise. At the end of the exercise, the child must then say something good about him- or herself. Boomer children in the 1950s and 1960s gained self-esteem naturally from a stable, child-friendly society; GenMe's self-esteem has been actively cultivated for its own sake.[30]

One Austin, Texas, father was startled to see his five-year-old daughter wearing a shirt that announced, "I'm lovable and capable." All of the kindergarteners, he learned, recited this phrase before class, and they all wore the shirt to school on Fridays. It seems the school started a bit too young, however, because the child then asked, "Daddy, all the kids are wondering, what does 'capable' mean?"[31]

Some people have wondered if the self-esteem trend waned after schools began to put more emphasis on testing during the late 1990s. It doesn't look that way. Parenting books and magazines stress self-esteem as much as ever, and a large number of schools continue to use self-esteem programs. The mission statements of many schools explicitly announce that they aim to raise students' self-esteem. A Google search for "elementary school mission statement self-esteem" yielded 308,000 Web pages in January 2006. These schools are located across the country, in cities, suburbs, small towns, and rural areas. "Building," "improving," "promoting," or "developing" self-esteem is a stated goal of (among many others) New River Elementary in New River, Arizona; Shady Dell Elementary in Springfield, Missouri; Shettler Elementary in Fruitport, Michigan; Baxter Elementary in Baxter, Tennessee; Rye Elementary in Westchester County, New York; Copeland Elementary in Augusta, Georgia; and Banff Elementary in Banff, Alberta, Canada. Private religious schools are not immune: St. Wendelin Catholic Elementary in Fostoria, Ohio, aims to "develop a feeling of confidence, self-esteem, and self-worth in our students."

Andersen Elementary in Rockledge, Florida, raises the bar, adding that students will "exhibit high self-esteem." So self-esteem must not just be *promoted* by teachers, but must be actively *exhibited* by students.

As John Hewitt points out in *The Myth of Self-Esteem,* the implicit message is that self-esteem can be taught and should be taught. When self-esteem programs are used, Hewitt notes, children are "encouraged to believe that it is acceptable and desirable to be preoccupied with oneself [and] praise oneself." In many cases, he says, it's not just encouraged but required. These exercises make self-importance mandatory, demanding of children that they love themselves. "The child *must* be taught to like himself or herself.... The child *must* take the teacher's attitude himself or herself—'I am somebody!' 'I am capable and loving!'—regardless of what the child thinks."[32]

Most of these programs encourage children to feel good about themselves for no particular reason. In one program, teachers are told to discourage children from saying things like "I'm a good soccer player" or "I'm a good singer."[33] This makes self-esteem contingent on performance, the program authors chide. Instead, "we want to anchor self-esteem firmly to the child ... so that no matter what the performance might be, the self-esteem remains high." In other words, feeling good about yourself is more important than good performance. Children, the guide says, should be taught "that it is who they are, not what they do, that is important." Many programs encourage self-esteem even when things go wrong or the child does something bad. In one activity, children are asked to finish several sentences, including ones beginning "I love myself even though ..." and "I forgive myself for ..."[34]

Teacher training courses often emphasize that a child's self-esteem must be preserved above all else. A sign on the wall of one university's education department says, "We Choose to Feel Special and Worthwhile No Matter What."[35] Perhaps as a result, 60% of teachers and 69% of school counselors agree that self-esteem should be raised by "providing more unconditional validation of students based on who they are rather than how they perform or behave."[36] Unconditional validation, to translate the educational mumbo-jumbo, means feeling good about yourself no matter how you act or whether you learn anything or not. A veteran second-grade teacher in Tennessee disagrees with this practice but sees it everywhere. "We handle children much more delicately," she says. "They feel good about themselves for no reason. We've given them this cotton-candy sense of self with no basis in reality."[37]

Although the self-esteem approach sounds like it might be especially popular in liberal blue-state areas, it's common in red states as well, perhaps because it's very similar to the ideas popularized by fundamentalist Christian churches. For example, the popular Christian children's book *You Are Special* promotes the same unconditional self-esteem emphasized in secular school programs. First published in 1997, the book notes, "The world tells kids, 'You're special if ... you have the brains, the looks, the talent.' God tells them, 'You're special just because. No qualifications necessary.' Every child you know needs to hear this one, reassuring truth." Traditional religion, of course, did have "qualifications" and rules for behavior. Adults hear this message as well.[38] In an article in *Ladies*

Home Journal, Christian author Rick Warren writes, "You can believe what others say about you, or you can believe in yourself as does God, who says you are truly acceptable, lovable, valuable, and capable."[39]

Even programs not specifically focused on self-esteem often place the utmost value on children's self-feelings. Children in some schools sing songs with lyrics like "Who I am makes a difference and all our dreams can come true" and "We are beautiful, magnificent, courageous, outrageous, and great!"[40] Other students pen a "Me Poem" or write a mock TV "commercial" advertising themselves and their good qualities. An elementary school teacher in Alabama makes one child the focus of a "VIP for a week" project.[41] The children's museum in Laramie, Wyoming, has a self-esteem exhibit where children are told to describe themselves using positive adjectives.[42]

Parents often continue the self-esteem lessons their children have learned in school, perhaps because more children are planned and cherished. The debut of the birth control pill in the early 1960s began the trend toward wanted children, which continued in the early 1970s as abortion became legal and cultural values shifted toward children as a choice rather than a duty. In the 1950s, it was considered selfish not to have kids, but by the 1970s it was an individual decision. As a result, more and more children were born to people who really *wanted* to become parents. Parents were able to lavish more attention on each child as the average number of children per family shrank from four to two. Young people often say that their parents believed in building self-esteem. "My mom constantly told me how special I was," said Natalie, 19. "No matter how I did, she would tell me I was the best." Kristen, 22, said her parents had a "wonderful" way of "telling me what a great job I did and repeatedly telling me I was a very special person." Popular media has also promoted this idea endlessly, offering up self-esteem as the cure for just about everything. In one episode of the family drama *7th Heaven,* one young character asks what can be done about war. The father on the show, a minister, says, "We can take a good look in the mirror, and when we see peace, that's when we'll have peace on earth." The rest of the episode featured each character smiling broadly to himself or herself in the mirror. In other words, if we all just loved ourselves enough, it would put an end to war. (Not only is this tripe, but wars, if anything, are usually rooted in too *much* love of self, land, and nation—not too little). But, as TV and movies have taught us, loving yourself is more important than anything else.

These efforts have had their intended impact. Don Tapscott, who interviewed hundreds of people for his book *Growing Up Digital,* notes, "Chat moderators, teachers, parents, and community workers who spend time with [young people] invariably told us that they think this is a confident generation who think highly of themselves."[43] In a CBS News poll, the high school graduates of 2000 were asked, "What makes you feel positive about yourself?" The most popular answer, at 33%, was the tautological "self-esteem." School performance was a distant second at 18%, with popularity third at 13%.[44] Yet this is not surprising: saying that having self-esteem makes you feel positive about yourself—forget any actual reason—is exactly what the self-esteem programs have taught today's young generation since they were in kindergarten.

Yet when everyone wears a shirt that says "I'm Special," as some of the programs encourage, it is a wide-open invitation to parody. The 1997 premiere episode of MTV's animated show *Daria* featured a character named Jane, who cracked, "I like having low self-esteem. It makes me feel special." Later in the episode, the teacher of a "self-esteem class" asks the students to "make a list of ten ways the world would be a sadder place if you weren't in it." "Is that if we'd never been born, or if we died suddenly and unexpectedly?" asks one of the students. Wanting to get out of the rest of the class, Daria and Jane recite the answers to the self-esteem "test": "The next time I start to feel bad about myself [I will] stand before the mirror, look myself in the eye, and say, 'You are special. No one else is like you.'"[45]

By the time GenMe gets to college, these messages are rote. Hewitt, who teaches at the University of Massachusetts, says his students are very excited when they begin discussing self-esteem in his sociology class. But once he begins to question the validity of self-esteem, the students' faces become glum and interest wanes. Hewitt compares it to what might happen in church if a priest suddenly began questioning the existence of God. After all, we worship at the altar of self-esteem and self-focus. "When the importance of self-esteem is challenged, a major part of the contemporary American view of the world is challenged," Hewitt writes.[46]

Girls Are Great

It is no coincidence that the *Daria* episode parodying self-esteem programs features two girls. Feminist Gloria Steinem, who spent the 1970s and 1980s fighting for practical rights like equal pay and maternity leave, spent the early 1990s promoting her book *Revolution from Within: A Book of Self-Esteem.* In 1991, a study by the American Association of University Women (AAUW) announced that girls "lose their self-esteem on the way to adolescence." This study was covered in countless national news outlets and ignited a national conversation about teenage girls and how they feel about themselves. *Reviving Ophelia,* a bestselling book on adolescent girls, popularized this idea further, documenting the feelings of self-doubt girls experience as they move through junior high and high school. Apparently, girls' self-esteem was suffering a severe blow when they became teenagers, and we needed to do something about it.

Before long, programs like the Girl Scouts began to focus on self-esteem through their "Girls Are Great" program. Girls could earn badges like "Being My Best" and "Understanding Yourself and Others." Amanda, 22, says that her Girl Scout troop spent a lot of time on self-esteem. "We did workshops and earned badges based around self-esteem building projects," she says. "We learned that we could do anything we wanted, that it was good to express yourself, and being different is good."

In 2002, the Girl Scout Council paired with corporate sponsor Unilever to launch "Uniquely ME!" a self-esteem program to "address the critical nationwide problem of low self-esteem among adolescent and preadolescent girls." The program includes three booklets for girls ages 8 to 14, each including exercises on "recognizing one's strengths and best attributes" and "identifying core values and personal interests."[47]

However, there is little evidence that girls' self-esteem dives at adolescence. The AAUW study was seriously flawed, relying on unstandardized measures and exaggerating small differences. In 1999, a carefully researched, comprehensive study of sex differences in self-esteem was published in *Psychological Bulletin,* the most prestigious journal in the field. The study statistically summarized 216 previous studies on more than 97,000 people and concluded that the actual difference between adolescent girls' and boys' self-esteem was less than 4%—in other words, extremely small.[48] Exaggerating this difference might be unwise. "We may create a self-fulfilling prophecy for girls by telling them they'll have low self-esteem," said University of Wisconsin professor Janet Hyde, one of the study authors.[49]

When my colleague Keith Campbell and I did a different analysis of 355 studies of 105,318 people, we also found that girls' self-esteem does not fall precipitously at adolescence; it just doesn't rise as fast as boys' self-esteem during the teen years. There was no large drop in girls' self-esteem, and by college the difference between men's and women's self-esteem was very small.[50] Another meta-analysis, by my former student Brenda Dolan-Pascoe, found moderate sex differences in appearance self-esteem, but no sex differences at all in academic self-esteem. Girls also scored *higher* than boys in behavior self-esteem and moral-ethical self-esteem. The achievements of adolescent girls also contradict the idea that they retreat into self-doubt: girls earn higher grades than boys at all school levels, and more go on to college.

In other words, adolescent girls don't have a self-esteem problem—there is no "critical nationwide problem of low self-esteem among adolescent and preadolescent girls" as the Girl Scouts claimed. But in a culture obsessed with feeling good about ourselves, even the hint of a self-esteem deficit is enough to prompt a nationwide outcry. The Girl Scout program premiered three years after the 1999 comprehensive study found a minuscule sex difference in self-esteem. Why let an overwhelming mass of data get in the way of a program that sounded good?

Self-Esteem and Academic Performance

There has also been a movement against "criticizing" children too much. Some schools and teachers don't correct children's mistakes, afraid that this will damage children's self-esteem. One popular method tells teachers not to correct students' spelling or grammar, arguing that kids should be "independent spellers" so they can be treated as "individuals." (Imagine reading a nuespaper wyten useing *that* filosofy.)[51] Teacher education courses emphasize that creating a positive atmosphere is more important than correcting mistakes.[52] In 2005, a British teacher proposed eliminating the word "fail" from education; instead of hearing that they have failed, students should hear that they have "deferred success."[53] In the United States, office stores have started carrying large stocks of purple pens, as some teachers say that red ink is too "scary" for children's papers.[54] Florida elementary schoolteacher Robin Slipakoff said, "Red has a negative connotation, and we want to promote self-confidence."[55]

Grade inflation has also reached record highs. In 2004, 48% of American college freshmen—almost half—reported earning an A average in high school, compared to only 18% in 1968, even though SAT scores decreased over this time period.[56] "Each year we think [the number with an A average] can't inflate anymore. And then it does again. The 'C' grade is almost a thing of the past," noted Andrew Astin, the lead researcher for the study. These higher grades were given out even though students were doing less work.[57] Only 33% of American college freshmen in 2003 reported studying six or more hours a week during their last year of high school, compared to 47% in 1987.[58] So why are they still getting better grades? "Teachers want to raise the self-esteem and feel-good attitudes of students," explains Howard Everson of the College Board.[59] We have become a Lake Wobegon nation: all of our children are above average.

The results of these policies have played out in schools around the country. Emily, 8, came home from school one day proud that she got half of the words right on her spelling test (in other words, a grade of 50). When her mother pointed out that this wasn't very good, Emily replied that her teacher had said it was just fine. At her school near Dallas, Texas, 11-year-old Kayla was invited to the math class pizza party as a reward for making a good grade, even though she had managed only a barely passing 71. The pizza parties used to be only for children who made As, but in recent years the school has invited every child who simply passed.

This basically means that we don't expect children to learn anything. As long as they feel good, that seems to be all that's required. As education professor Maureen Stout notes, many educational psychologists believe that schools should be "places in which children are insulated from the outside world and emotionally—not intellectually—nourished.... My colleagues always referred to the importance of making kids feel good about themselves but rarely, if ever, spoke of achievement, ideals, goals, character, or decency."[60] The future teachers whom Stout was educating believed that "children shouldn't be challenged to try things that others in the class are not ready for, since that would promote competition, and competition is bad for self-esteem. Second, grading should be avoided if at all possible, but, if absolutely necessary, should be done in a way that avoids any indication that Johnny is anything less than a stellar pupil."

Grade inflation and lack of competition may be backfiring: in 2003, 43% of college freshmen reported that they were frequently bored in class during their last year of high school, up from 29% in 1985.[61] This is not surprising: how interesting could school possibly be when everyone gets an A and self-esteem is more important than learning?

Perhaps as a result of all of this self-esteem building, educational psychologist Harold Stevenson found that American children ranked very highly when asked how good they were at math.[62] Of course, their *actual* math performance is merely mediocre, with other countries' youth routinely outranking American children. Every year, news anchors solemnly report how far American kids are falling behind. The emphasis on self-esteem can't be blamed entirely for this, of course, but one could easily argue that children's time might be better spent doing math than hearing that they are special. In 2004, 70% of American college freshmen reported that their "academic ability" was "above average" or "highest 10%," an amusing demonstration of American youths' self-confidence outpacing their ability at math.

What kind of young people does this produce? Many teachers and social observers say it results in kids who can't take criticism. In other words, employers, get ready for a group of easily hurt young workers. Peter Sacks, author of *Generation X Goes to College,* noted the extraordinary thin-skinnedness of the undergraduates he taught, and my experience has been no different. I've learned not to discuss test items that the majority of students missed, as this invariably leads to lots of whiny defensiveness and very little actual learning. The two trends are definitely related: research shows that when people with high self-esteem are criticized, they became unfriendly, rude, and uncooperative, even toward people who had nothing to do with the criticism.[63]

None of this should really surprise us. Students "look and act like what the [self-esteem] theories say they should look and act like," notes Hewitt. "They tend to act as though they believe they have worthy and good inner essences, regardless of what people say or how they behave, that they deserve recognition and attention from others, and their unique individual needs should be considered first and foremost."[64] And, of course, this is exactly what has happened: GenMe takes for granted that the self comes first, and we often believe exactly what we were so carefully taught—that we're special.

But this must have an upside; surely kids who have high self-esteem go on to make better grades and achieve more in school. Actually, they don't. There is a small correlation between self-esteem and grades.[65] However, self-esteem does not cause high grades—instead, high grades cause higher self-esteem. So self-esteem programs clearly put the cart before the horse in trying to increase self-esteem. Even much of the small link from high grades to high self-esteem can be explained by other factors such as income: rich kids, for example, have higher self-esteem and get better grades, but that's because coming from an affluent home causes both of these things, and not because they cause each other. This resembles the horse and the cart being towed on a flatbed truck—neither the cart nor the horse is causing the motion in the other even though they are moving together. As self-esteem programs aren't going to make all kids rich, they won't raise self-esteem this way, either.

Nor does high self-esteem protect against teen pregnancy, juvenile delinquency, alcoholism, drug abuse, or chronic welfare dependency. Several comprehensive reviews of the research literature by different authors have all concluded that self-esteem doesn't cause much of anything.[66] Even the book sponsored by the California Task Force to Promote Self-Esteem and Personal and Social Responsibility, which spent a quarter of a million dollars trying to raise Californians' self-esteem, found that self-esteem isn't linked to academic achievement, good behavior, or any other outcome the Task Force was formed to address.[67]

Are Self-Esteem Programs Good or Bad?

Psychologist Martin Seligman has criticized self-esteem programs as empty and shortsighted. He argues that self-esteem based on nothing does not serve children well in the long run; it's better, he says, for children to develop real skills and feel good about accomplishing something.[68] Roy Baumeister, the lead author of an extensive review of the research on self-esteem, found that self-esteem does not lead to better grades, improved work performance, decreased violence, or less cheating. In fact, people with high self-esteem are often more violent and more likely to cheat. "It is very questionable whether [the few benefits] justify the effort and expense that schools, parents, and therapists have put into raising self-esteem," Baumeister wrote. "After all these years, I'm sorry to say, my recommendation is this: forget about self-esteem and concentrate more on self-control and self-discipline."[69]

I agree with both of these experts. Self-esteem is an outcome, not a cause. In other words, it doesn't do much good to encourage a child to feel good about himself just to feel good; this doesn't mean anything. Children develop true self-esteem from behaving well and accomplishing things. "What the self-esteem movement really says to students is that their achievement is not important and their minds are not worth developing," writes Maureen Stout. It's clearly better for children to value learning rather than simply feeling good.[70]

So should kids feel bad about themselves if they're not good at school or sports? No. They should feel bad if they didn't work hard and try. And even if they don't succeed, sometimes negative feelings can be a motivator. Trying something challenging and learning from the experience is better than feeling good about oneself for no reason.

Also, everyone can do *something* well. Kids who are not athletic or who struggle with school might have another talent, like music or art. Almost all children can develop pride from being a good friend or helping someone. Kids can do many things to feel good about themselves, so self-esteem can be based on something. If a child feels great about himself even when he does nothing, why do anything? Self-esteem without basis encourages laziness rather than hard work. On the other hand, we shouldn't go too far and hinge our self-worth entirely on one external goal, like getting good grades. As psychologist Jennifer Crocker documents, the seesaw of self-esteem this produces can lead to poor physical and mental health.[71] A happy medium is what's called for here: don't feel bad about yourself because you made a bad grade—just don't feel good about yourself if you didn't even study. Use your bad feelings as a motivator to do better next time. True self-confidence comes from honing your talents and learning things, not from being told you're great just because you exist.

The practice of not correcting mistakes, avoiding letter grades, and discouraging competition is also misguided. Competition can help make learning fun; as Stout points out, look at how the disabled kids in the Special Olympics benefit from competing. Many schools now don't publish the honor roll of children who do well in school and generally downplay grades because, they falsely believe, competition isn't good for self-esteem (as some kids won't make the honor roll, and some kids will make Cs). But can you imagine not publishing the scores of a basketball game because it might not be good for the losing team's self-esteem? Can you imagine not keeping score in the game? What fun would that be? The self-esteem movement, Stout argues, is popular because it is sweetly addictive: teachers don't have to criticize, kids don't have to be criticized, and everyone goes home feeling happy. The problem is they also go home ignorant and uneducated.

Kids who don't excel in a certain area should still be encouraged to keep trying. This isn't self-esteem, however: it's self-control. Self-control, or the ability to persevere and keep going, is a much better predictor of life outcomes than self-esteem. Children high in self-control make better grades and finish more years of education, and they're less likely to use drugs or have a teenage pregnancy. Self-control predicts all of those things researchers had hoped self-esteem would, but hasn't.

Cross-cultural studies provide a good example of the benefits of self-control over self-esteem. Asians, for example, have lower self-esteem than Americans.[72] But when Asian students find out that they scored low on a particular task, they want to keep working on that task so they can improve their performance. American students, in contrast, prefer to give up on that task and work on another one.[73] In other words, Americans preserve their self-esteem at the expense of doing better at a difficult task. This goes a long way toward explaining why Asian children perform better at math and at school in general.

Young people who have high self-esteem built on shaky foundations might run into trouble when they encounter the harsh realities of the real world. As Stout argues, kids who are given meaningless As and promoted when they haven't learned the material will later find out in college or the working world that they don't know much at all. And what will *that* do to their self-esteem, or, more important, their careers? Unlike your teacher, your boss isn't going to care much about preserving your high self-esteem. The self-esteem emphasis leaves kids ill prepared for the inevitable criticism and occasional failure that is real life. "There is no self-esteem movement in the work world," points out one father. "If you present a bad report at the office, your boss isn't going to say, 'Hey, I like the color paper you chose.' Setting kids up like this is doing them a tremendous disservice."[74]

In any educational program, one has to consider the trade-off between benefit and risk. Valuing self-esteem over learning and accomplishment is clearly harmful, as children feel great about themselves but are cheated out of the education they need to succeed. Self-esteem programs *might* benefit the small minority of kids who really do feel worthless, but those kids are likely to have bigger problems that self-esteem boosting won't fix. The risk in these programs is in inflating the self-concept of children who already think the world revolves around them. Building up the self-esteem and importance of kids who are already egocentric can bring trouble, as it can lead to narcissism—and maybe it already has.

Changes in Narcissism

Narcissism is one of the few personality traits that psychologists agree is almost completely negative. Narcissists are overly focused on themselves and lack empathy for others, which means they cannot see another person's perspective.[75] (Sound like the last clerk who served you?) They also feel entitled to special privileges and believe that they are superior to other people. As a result, narcissists are bad relationship partners and can be difficult to work with. Narcissists are also more likely to be hostile, feel anxious, compromise their health, and fight with friends and family. Unlike those merely high in self-esteem, narcissists admit that they don't feel close to other people.[76]

All evidence suggests that narcissism is much more common in recent generations. In the early 1950s, only 12% of teens aged 14 to 16 agreed with the statement "I am an important person."[77] By the late 1980s, an incredible 80%—almost seven times as many—claimed they were important. Psychologist Harrison Gough found consistent increases on narcissism items among college students quizzed between the 1960s and the 1990s.[78] GenMe students were more likely to agree that "I would be willing to describe myself as a pretty 'strong' personality" and "I have often met people who were supposed to be experts who were no better than I." In other words, those other people don't know what they're talking about, so everyone should listen to me.

In a 2002 survey of 3,445 people conducted by Joshua Foster, Keith Campbell, and me, younger people scored considerably higher on the Narcissistic Personality Inventory, agreeing with items such as "If I ruled the world it would be a better place," "I am a special person," and "I can live my life any way I want to."[79] (These statements evoke the image of a young man speeding down the highway in the world's biggest SUV, honking his horn, and screaming, "Get out of my way! I'm important!") This study was cross-sectional, though, meaning that it was a one-time sample of people of different ages. For that reason, we cannot be sure if any differences are due to age or to generation; however, the other studies of narcissism mentioned previously suggest that generation plays a role. It is also interesting that narcissism scores were fairly high until around age 35, after which they decreased markedly. This is right around the cutoff between GenMe and previous generations.

Narcissism is the darker side of the focus on the self, and is often confused with self-esteem. Self-esteem is often based on solid relationships with others, whereas narcissism comes from believing that you are special and more important than other people. Many of the school programs designed to raise self-esteem probably raise narcissism instead. Lillian Katz, a professor of early childhood education at the University of Illinois, wrote an article titled "All About Me: Are We Developing Our Children's Self-Esteem or Their Narcissism?" She writes, "Many of the practices advocated in pursuit of [high self-esteem] may instead inadvertently develop narcissism in the form of excessive preoccupation with oneself."[80] Because the school programs emphasize being "special" rather than encouraging friendships, we may be training an army of little narcissists instead of raising kids' self-esteem.

Many young people also display entitlement, a facet of narcissism that involves believing that you deserve and are entitled to more than others. A scale that measures entitlement has items like "Things should go my way," "I demand the best because I'm worth it," and (my favorite) "If I were on the *Titanic,* I would deserve to be on the *first* lifeboat!"[81] A 2005 Associated Press article printed in hundreds of news outlets labeled today's young people "The Entitlement Generation." In the article, employers complained that young employees expected too much too soon and had very high expectations for salary and promotions.[82]

Teachers have seen this attitude for years now. One of my colleagues said his students acted as if grades were something they simply deserved to get no matter what. He joked that their attitude could be summed up by "Where's my A? I distinctly remember ordering an A from the catalog." Stout, the education professor, lists the student statements familiar to teachers everywhere: "I need a better grade," "I deserve an A on this paper," "I *never* get Bs." Stout points out that the self-esteem movement places the student's feelings at the center, so "students learn that they do not need to respect their teachers or even earn their grades, so they begin to believe that they are entitled to grades, respect, or anything else … just for asking!"[83]

Unfortunately, narcissism can lead to outcomes far worse than grade grubbing. Several studies have found that narcissists lash out aggressively when they are insulted or rejected.[84] Eric Harris and Dylan Klebold, the teenage gunmen at Columbine High School, made statements remarkably similar to items on the most popular narcissism questionnaire. On a videotape made before the shootings, Harris picked up a gun, made a shooting noise, and said, "Isn't it fun to get the respect we're going to deserve?"[85] (Chillingly similar to the narcissism item "I insist upon getting the respect that is due me.") Later, Harris said, "I could convince them that I'm going to climb Mount Everest, or I have a twin brother growing out of my back. I can make you believe anything" (virtually identical to the item "I can make anyone believe anything I want them to"). Harris and Klebold then debate which famous movie director will film their story. A few weeks after making the videotapes, Harris and Klebold killed thirteen people and then themselves.

Other examples abound. In a set of lab studies, narcissistic men felt less empathy for rape victims, reported more enjoyment when watching a rape scene in a movie, and were more punitive toward a woman who refused to read a sexually arousing passage out loud to them.[86] Abusive husbands who threaten to kill their wives—and tragically sometimes do—are the ultimate narcissists. They see everyone and everything in terms of fulfilling their needs, and become very angry and aggressive when things don't go exactly their way. Many workplace shootings occur after an employee is fired and decides he'll "show" everyone how powerful he is.

The rise in narcissism has very deep roots. It's not just that we feel better about ourselves, but that we even think to ask the question. We fixate on self-esteem, and unthinkingly build narcissism, because we believe that the needs of the individual are paramount. This will stay with us even if self-esteem programs end up in the dustbin of history.

NOTES

1. Ladies' Home Journal *told readers:* Warren, Rick. "Learn to Love Yourself!" *Ladies' Home Journal*, March 2005; p. 36.

2. *[W]hile Parenting offered:* Lamb, Yanick Rice. "Proud to Be Me!" *Parenting,* April 2005.

3. *The American Academy of Pediatrics guide:* Shelov, Steven, ed. in chief. 1998. *Caring for Your Baby and Young Child: Birth to Age 5.* New York: Bantam.

4. *In a 1976* New York Magazine *article:* Wolfe, Tom. "The Me Decade and the Third Great Awakening." *New York Magazine*, August 23, 1976.

5. *When asked what's next in her life:* "Pop Quiz: Kim Basinger." *People*, September 27, 2004.

6. *In answer to the same question:* Laskas, Jeanne Marie. "Sarah's New Day." *Ladies' Home Journal*, June 2004.

7. *Gillon describes Boomers:* Gillon, Steve. 2004. *Boomer Nation*. New York: Free Press; p. 263.

8. *Even food becomes:* Brooks, David. 2000. *Bobos in Paradise*. New York: Simon & Schuster; p.58.

9. *In 1973, 46% of Boomers:* Smith, J. Walker, and Clurman, Ann. 1997. *Rocking the Ages: The Yankelovich Report on Generational Marketing*. New York: HarperCollins.

10. *Thirty percent of Boomers*: Ibid.

11. *Even stronger evidence:* Astin, A. W., et al. 2002. *The American Freshman: Thirty-Five-Year Trends*. Los Angeles: Higher Education Research Institute, UCLA. Plus 2003 and 2004 supplements.

12. *"Instead of seeking:* Rubin, Jerry. 1976. *Growing (Up) at Thirty-Seven*. New York: Lippincott; p. 175.

13. *Aleta St. James, a 57-year-old woman:* Schienberg, Jonathan. "New Age Mystic to Become Mom at 57." <www.cnn.com>. November 9, 2004.

14. *In 2004's* Conquering Your Quarterlife Crisis: Robbins, Alexandra. 2004. *Conquering Your Quarterlife Crisis*. New York: Perigee; pp. 51–52.

15. *When a character in the 2004 novel:* Giffin, Emily. 2004. *Something Borrowed*. New York: St. Martin's Press; p. 2.

16. *Dr. Phil, the ultimate in plainspoken: Today.* NBC, December 27, 2004.

17. *Psychologist Martin Seligman says:* Seligman, M. E. P. "Boomer Blues." *Psychology Today*, October 1988: pp. 50–53.

18. *A careful study of news stories:* Patterson, Thomas E. 2000. "Doing Well and Doing Good: How Soft News and Critical Journalism Are Shrinking the News Audience and Weakening Democracy—and What News Outlets Can Do About It." Joan Shorenstein Center on the Press, Politics, and Public Policy; p. 5. PDF available for download at <www.ksg.harvard.edu/presspol/ResearchPublications/Reports/>.

19. *In a letter to her fans in 2004:* "The Couples of 2004." *Us Weekly*, January 3, 2005.

20. *In the late 1990s, Prudential:* Hornblower, Margot. "Great Xpectations." *Time*, June 9, 1997.

21. *My colleague Keith Campbell and I looked:* Twenge, J. M., and Campbell, W. K. 2001. Age and Birth Cohort Differences in Self-Esteem: A Cross-Temporal Meta-Analysis. *Personality and Social Psychology Review*, 5: 321–344.

22. *A 1997 survey of teens asked:* "11th Annual Special Teen Report: Teens and Self-Image: Survey Results." *USA Weekend*, May 1–3, 1998.

23. *Another survey found:* Hicks, Rick, and Hicks, Kathy. 1999. *Boomers, Xers, and Other Strangers*. Wheaton, IL: Tyndale; p. 270.

24. *We examined the responses:* Twenge, J. M., and Campbell, W. K. 2001. Age and Birth Cohort Differences in Self-Esteem: A Cross-Temporal Meta-Analysis. *Personality and Social Psychology Review*, 5: 321–344.

25. *Research on programs to boost*: Ibid.

26. *Journal articles on self-esteem:* Hewitt, John. 1998. *The Myth of Self-Esteem.* New York: St. Martin's Press; p. 51.

27. *One children's book:* Loomans, Diane. 1991. *The Lovables in the Kingdom of Self-Esteem.* New York: H. J. Kramer.

28. *One program is called:* Stout, Maureen. 2000. *The Feel-Good Curriculum.* Cambridge, MA: Perseus Books; p. 131.

29. *Another program, called "Pumsy in Pursuit of Excellence":* "Teaching Self-Image Stirs Furor." *New York Times,* October 13, 1993.

30. *The Magic Circle exercise:* <www.globalideasbank.org/site/bank/idea.php?ideaId=573>; and Summerlin, M. L.; Hammett, V. L.; and Payne, M. L. 1983. The Effect of Magic Circle Participation on a Child's Self-Concept. *School Counselor,* 31: 49–52.

31. *One Austin, Texas, father:* Swann, William. 1996. *Self-Traps: The Elusive Quest for Higher Self-Esteem.* New York: W. H. Freeman; p. 4.

32. *When self-esteem programs:* Hewitt, John. 1998. *The Myth of Self-Esteem,* New York: St. Martin's Press; pp. 84–85.

33. *In one program, teachers:* Payne, Lauren Murphy, and Rolhing, Claudia. 1994. *A Leader's Guide to Just Because I Am: A Child's Book of Affirmation.* Minneapolis: Free Spirit Publishing; and Hewitt, John. 1998. *The Myth of Self-Esteem.* New York: St. Martin's Press.

34. *[C]hildren are asked to finish:* Hewitt, John. 1998. *The Myth of Self-Esteem.* New York: St. Martin's Press; p. 79.

35. *A sign on the wall:* Kramer, Rita. 1991. *Ed School Follies: The Miseducation of America's Teachers.* New York: Free Press; p. 33.

36. *Perhaps as a result, 60% of teachers:* Scott, C. G. 1996. Student Self-Esteem and the School System: Perceptions and Implications. *Journal of Educational Research,* 89: 292–297.

37. *A veteran second-grade teacher:* Gibbs, Nancy. "Parents Behaving Badly." *Time,* February 21, 2005.

38. *For example, the popular Christian:* Lucado, Max. 1997. *You Are Special.* Wheaton, IL: Crossway Books.

39. *In an article in Ladies' Home Journal, Christian author:* Warren, Rick. "Learn to Love Yourself!" *Ladies' Home Journal,* March 2005.

40. *Children in some schools:* Lynn Sherr. "Me, Myself and I—The Growing Self-Esteem Movement." 20/20. ABC, March 11, 1994.

41. *An elementary school teacher in Alabama:* Hewitt, John. 1998. *The Myth of Self-Esteem.* New York: St. Martin's Press; p. 81.

42. *The children's museum in Laramie:* Lynn Sherr. "Me, Myself and I—The Growing Self-Esteem Movement." 20/20. ABC, March 11, 1994.

43. *Don Tapscott, who interviewed:* Tapscott, Don. 1998. *Growing Up Digital.* New York: McGraw-Hill; p. 92.

44. *In a CBS News poll:* CBS News. 2001. *The Class of 2000.* Simon & Schuster eBook, available for download, p. 64.

45. *The 1997 premiere episode:* Daria. Episode: "Esteemsters." MTV, March 3, 1997.

46. *Hewitt, who teaches:* Hewitt, John. 1998. *The Myth of Self-Esteem*. New York: St. Martin's Press; pp. 1–3.

47. *In 2002, the Girl Scout Council:* <www.girlscouts.org/program/program_opportunities/leadership/uniquelyme.asp>.

48. *In 1999, a carefully researched:* Kling, K. C., et al. 1999. Gender Differences in Self-Esteem: A Meta-Analysis. *Psychological Bulletin*, 125: 470–500.

49. *"We may create:* <www.news.wisc.edu/wire/i072899/selfesteem.html>.

50. *When my colleague Keith Campbell and I did:* Twenge, J. M., and Campbell, W. K. 2001. Age and Birth Cohort Differences in Self-Esteem: A Cross-Temporal Meta-Analysis. *Personality and Social Psychology Review*, 5: 321–344.

51. *One popular method tells:* Wilde, Sandra. 1989. A Proposal for a New Spelling Curriculum. *Elementary School Journal*, 90: 275–289.

52. *Teacher education courses emphasize:* Kramer, Rita. 1991. *Ed School Follies: The Miseducation of America's Teachers*. New York: Free Press; p. 116.

53. *[A] British teacher proposed:* "Teachers Say No-One Should 'Fail.'" BBC News, July 20, 2005. See <news.bbc.co.uk/1/hi/education/4697461.stm>.

54. *[O]ffice stores have started carrying:* Aoki, Naomi, "Harshness of Red Marks Has Students Seeing Purple." *Boston Globe*, August 23, 2004.

55. *Florida elementary schoolteacher:* Ibid.

56. *In 2004, 48% of American college freshmen:* Astin, A. W., et al. 2002. *The American Freshman: Thirty-Five-Year Trends*. Los Angeles: Higher Education Research Institute, UCLA. Plus 2003 and 2004 supplements.

57. *"Each year we think:* Giegerich, Steve. "College Freshmen Have Worst Study Habits in Years But Less Likely to Drink, Study Finds." Associated Press, January 27, 2003. <www.detnews.com/2003/schools/0301/27/schools-70002.htm>.

58. *Only 33% of American:* Astin, A. W., et al. 2002. *The American Freshman: Thirty-Five Year Trends*. Los Angeles: Higher Education Research Institute, UCLA. Plus 2003 and 2004 supplements.

59. *"Teachers want to raise:* Innerst, Carol. "Wordsmiths on Wane Among U.S. Students." *Washington Times*, August 25, 1994.

60. *As education professor Maureen Stout notes:* Stout, Maureen, 2000. *The Feel-Good Curriculum*. Cambridge, MA: Perseus Books; pp. 3–4.

61. *[I]n 2003, 43% of college freshmen:* Astin, A. W., et al. 2002. *The American Freshman: Thirty-Five-Year Trends*. Los Angeles: Higher Education Research Institute, UCLA. Plus 2003 and 2004 supplements.

62. *[E]ducational psychologist Harold Stevenson:* Stevenson, H. W., et al. 1990. Mathematics Achievement of Children in China and the United States. *Child Development*, 61: 1053–1066.

63. *[R]esearch shows that when people:* Heatherton, T. F., and Vohs, K. D. 2000. Interpersonal Evaluations Following Threats to Self: Role of Self-Esteem. *Journal of Personality and Social Psychology*, 78: 725–736.

64. *Students "look and act like:* Hewitt, John. 1998. *The Myth of Self-Esteem*. New York: St. Martin's Press; p. 84.

65. *There is a small correlation:* Baumeister, R. F., et al. 2003. Does High Self-Esteem Cause Better Performance, Interpersonal Success, Happiness, or Healthier Lifestyles? *Psychological Science in the Public Interest*, 4: 1–44; and Covington, M. V. 1989.

"Self-Esteem and Failure in School." In A. M. Mecca, N. J. Smelser, and J. Vasconcellos, eds. *The Social Importance of Self-Esteem*. Berkeley: University of California Press; p. 79.

66. *Several comprehensive reviews:* Ibid.

67. *Even the book sponsored:* Smelser, N. J. 1989. "Self-esteem and Social Problems." In A. M. Mccca, N. J. Smelser, and J. Vasconcellos, eds. *The Social Importance of Self-Esteem*. Berkeley: University of California Press.

68. *Psychologist Martin Seligman has criticized:* Seligman, Martin. 1996. *The Optimistic Child*. New York: Harper Perennial.

69. *"It is very questionable:* Baumeister, Roy. "The Lowdown on High Self-esteem: Thinking You're Hot Stuff Isn't the Promised Cure-all." *Los Angeles Times*, January 25, 2005.

70. *"What the self-esteem movement:* Stout, Maureen. 2000. *The Feel-Good Curriculum*. Cambridge, MA: Perseus Books; p. 263.

71. *As psychologist Jennifer Crocker documents:* Crocker, J., and Park, L. E.2004. The Costly Pursuit of Self-esteem. *Psychological Bulletin*, 130: 392–414.

72. *Asians, for example, have lower:* Twenge, J. M., and Crocker, J. 2002. Race and Self-Esteem: Meta-Analyses Comparing Whites, Blacks, Hispanics, Asians, and American Indians. *Psychological Bulletin*; 128: 371–408.

73. *But when Asian students find out:* Heine, S. J., et al. 2001. Divergent Consequences of Success and Failure in Japan and North America: An Investigation of Self-improving Motivations and Malleable Selves. *Journal of Personality and Social Psychology*, 81: 599–615.

74. *"There is no self-esteem movement:* Shaw, Robert. 2003. *The Epidemic.* New York: Regan Books; p. 152.

75. *Narcissists are overly focused:* Campbell, W. Keith. 2005. *When You Love a Man Who Loves Himself*. Chicago: Source Books.

76. *Narcissists are also more likely:* Helgeson, V. S., and Fritz, H. L. 1999. Unmitigated Agency and Unmitigated Communion: Distinctions from Agency and Communion. *Journal of Research in Personality*, 33: 131–158.

77. *In the early 1950s, only 12% of teens:* Newsom, C. R., et al. 2003. Changes in Adolescent Response Patterns on the MMPI/MMPI-A Across Four Decades. *Journal of Personality Assessment*, 81: 74–84.

78. *Psychologist Harrison Gough found:* Gough, H. 1991. "Scales and Combinations of Scales: What Do They Tell Us, What Do They Mean?" Paper presented at the 99th Annual Convention of the American Psychological Association, San Francisco, August 1991. Data obtained from Harrison Gough in 2001.

79. *In a 2002 survey of 3,445 people:* Foster, J. D.; Campbell, W. K.; and Twenge, J. M. 2003. Individual Differences in Narcissism: Inflated Self-Views Across the Lifespan and Around the World. *Journal of Research in Personality*, 37: 469–486.

80. *Lillian Katz, a professor:* Stout, Maureen. 2000. *The Feel-Good Curriculum*. Cambridge, MA: Perseus Books; p. 178.

81. *A scale that measures entitlement:* Campbell, W. K., et al. 2004. Psychological Entitlement: Interpersonal Consequences and Validation of a Self-report Measure. *Journal of Personality Assessment*, 83: 29–45.

82. *A 2005 Associated Press article printed:* Irvine, Martha. "Young Labeled 'Entitlement Generation.'" AP, June 26, 2005. <biz.yahoo.com/ap/050626/the_entitlement_ generation. html2.v3>. Also reprinted in many newspapers.

83. *Stout, the education professor, lists:* Stout, Maureen. 2000. *The Feel-Good Curriculum.* Cambridge, MA: Perseus Books; p. 2.

84. *Several studies have found:* Bushman, B. J., and Baumeister, R. F. 1998. Threatened Egotism, Narcissism, Self-esteem, and Direct and Displaced Aggression: Does Self-love or Self-hate Lead to Violence? *Journal of Personality and Social Psychology,* 75: 219–229; and Twenge, J. M., and Campbell, W. K. 2003. "Isn't it fun to get the respect that we're going to deserve?" Narcissism, Social Rejection, and Aggression. *Personality and Social Psychology Bulletin,* 29: 261–272.

85. *Harris picked up a gun:* Gibbs, Nancy, and Roche, Timothy. "The Columbine Tapes." *Time,* December 20, 1999.

86. *In a set of lab studies, narcissistic:* Bushman, B. J., et al. 2003. Narcissism, Sexual Refusal, and Aggression: Testing a Narcissistic Reactance Model of Sexual Coercion. *Journal of Personality and Social Psychology,* 84: 1027–1040.

QUESTION FOR MAKING CONNECTIONS
WITHIN THE READING

1. "An Army of One: *Me*" is written in a lively style, with the author speaking in a number of different voices throughout: objective analyst, insider, and skeptic, to name a few. As you reread, mark the passages where Twenge's voice shifts and identify the voices on both sides of the shift. When you're done, review your markings. Is there a voice or a viewpoint that wins out in the end? Is there a voice that you feel is Twenge's real voice, or are all the voices hers?

2. What kinds of evidence does Twenge use to make her case about Generation Me? After you've generated a complete list, identify the evidence that you feel is the most compelling and the evidence that seems less so. Where would you look to find evidence that would further strengthen Twenge's argument? Is there evidence that could refute Twenge's argument? Can arguments about entire generations be either verified or disproven?

3. Twenge identifies three psychic states: thinking about the self, having self-esteem, and being a narcissist. What is the relationship among these three states? If one is educated and trained in one of these psychic states, is there a way to experience another state of mind? Does Twenge provide any evidence of what causes or enables a shift in perspective?

QUESTIONS FOR WRITING

1. As a member of Generation Me, Twenge is both a source for information about her subject and a translator who provides an inside view of how members of Generation Me interpret the world around them. Given this, how would you characterize Twenge's method? How does she know what she claims to knows about Generation Me? How would you go about

collecting more information to test her hypothesis? Is definitive evidence available?

2. If we grant Twenge's argument about the values and expectations of Generation Me, what follows? Is it possible for this generation to reverse course, or is it too late? Can social change be brought about through conscious effort? Or does the scale of the problem mean that what follows is inevitable? Has Twenge diagnosed a problem for which there is no cure?

QUESTIONS FOR MAKING CONNECTIONS
BETWEEN READINGS

1. Leila Ahmed's "On Becoming an Arab" examines a collective identity— "theArab"— that was forced upon the peoples in the Middle East in a way intended to erase their very real diversity, both as cultures and individuals. By contrast, Twenge tell a story of individualism run amok, an individualism now so extreme that it shades into narcissism. At first glance these two might appear to be polar opposites —a rigid collective identity and an extreme individualism. But are they as different as they seem in their social impact? Is it possible that both have been used to confine people to a very narrow range of possibilities? Between extreme individualism and collective identity, what alternatives might exist? What forms of identity might be most conducive to freedom and fulfillment?

2. Twenge identifies numerous characteristics that define the differences between the way Baby Boomers and Generation Me view the self. Using Tim O'Brien's "How to Tell a True War Story," test out Twenge's theory. Do the characters perform as Twenge's theory predicts? Does O'Brien? Are generations defined by wars? Was Vietnam a Baby Boomer war? Is the Iraq War a Generation Me war? Can O'Brien's "true war story" be true for other generations?

JANINE R. WEDEL

JANINE R. WEDEL is a professor of Public Policy at George Mason University. Typically, specialists in Public Policy are trained in political science, government, law, or history, but Wedel received a Ph.D. in Cultural Anthropology from the University of California at Berkeley. This unique background in human behavior gives her work an originality that has made her one of the keenest observers of the sweeping changes occasioned by the fall of the Soviet Union and the spread of globalization. Wedel's first book, *The Private Poland* (1986), was a study of the everyday lives of Poles living under Communist rule in the former Eastern Bloc. Where some commentators saw only evidence of crushing domination, Wedel describes a complex tableau in which networks of energetic citizens were able to create a functioning society, often with the active but covert support of an inept communist regime. Her next book, *Collision and Collusion* (2001), examined the transition of the Soviet Bloc from communism to something closer to democracy, a transition overseen by representatives from the U.S. and Western Europe. Because the press and many government officials were unwilling to look behind the scenes, the story of progress they told the public could not account for the disasters that ensued: instead of bringing wealth and honest government, the fall of the Soviet Union left many of its member states impoverished and paralyzed by corruption. Wedel lays the lion's share of the blame at the feet of Western advisors—including several distinguished academics—who arrived on the scene hoping to make huge amounts of money for themselves. Out of public view, they could wheel and deal in ways that would have been illegal at home.

Wedel's most recent book, *The Shadow Elite*, picks up where *Collision and Collision* left off. She argues that the wheeler-dealers who could operate with impunity in the old Soviet Bloc have become the model for a new kind of social actor: the flexian. Instead of playing any single role—for example diplomat, entrepreneur, academic, or journalist—flexians play many roles at the same time, using the respectability of public office to mask their self-aggrandizement, or leveraging their apparent neutrality into support for highly partisan policies. Wedel represents the flexian as the embodiment of an emerging social order in which the common good is increasingly sacrificed for private gain.

Wedel's work is often controversial, but her meticulous research has earned the respect of a growing readership. Her writing has appeared in the *New York Times*, the *Financial Times*, the *Washington Post*, the *Wall Street Journal Europe*, the *National*

Wedel, Janine R. *Shadow Elite: How the World's New Power Brokers Undermine Democracy, Government and the Free Market*. (New York: Basic Books, 2009). 1–21. Biographical information is drawn from <http://janinewedel.info/>.

Interest, the *Los Angeles Times*, the *Christian Science Monitor*, the *Boston Globe, Salon*, and *The Nation*.

■ ■

Confidence Men and Their Flex Lives

We live in a world of flexibility. We have flex time, flex workers, flex spending, flex enrollment, flex cars, flex technology, flex perks, mind flex—even flex identities. "Flex" has become an integral part not only of how we live, but of how power and influence are wielded. While influencers flex their roles and representations, organizations, institutions, and states, too, must be flexible in ways they haven't been before. The mover and shaker who serves at one and the same time as business consultant, think-tanker, TV pundit, and government adviser glides in and around the organizations that enlist his services. It is not just his time that is divided. His loyalties, too, are often flexible. Even the short-term consultant doing one project at a time cannot afford to owe too much allegiance to the company or government agency. Such individuals are *in* these organizations (some of the time anyway), but they are seldom *of* them.[1]

Being in, but not of, an organization enables these players to pursue a "coincidence of interests," that is, to interweave and perform overlapping roles that serve their own goals or those of their associates. Because these "non-state" actors working for companies, quasi-governmental organizations, and nongovernmental organizations (NGOs) frequently do work that officials once did, they have privileged access to *official* information—information that they can deploy to their own ends. And they have more opportunities to use this information for purposes that are neither in the public interest nor easily detected, all the while controlling the message to keep their game going.[2]

Take, for instance, Barry R. McCaffrey, retired four-star army general, military analyst for the media, defense industry consultant, president of his own consulting firm, part-time professor, and expert, whose advice on the conduct of the post-9/11 U.S. wars was sought by the George W. Bush administration and Congress. Crucial to McCaffrey's success in these roles was the special access afforded him by the Pentagon and associates still in the military. This included special trips to war zones arranged specifically for him, according to a November 2008 exposé in the *New York Times*. McCaffrey gleaned information from these trips that proved useful in other roles—and not only his part-time professorship at the U.S. Military Academy, which the Pentagon claimed is the umbrella under which his outsider's perspective was sought.

At a time when the administration was trying to convince the American people of the efficacy of U.S. intervention in Iraq, the general appeared frequently as a commentator on the television news—nearly a thousand times on NBC and its affiliates. He was variously introduced as a Gulf War hero, a professor, and a decorated veteran, but not as an unofficial spokesperson for the Pentagon and its positions. He also was oft-quoted in the *New York Times,* the *Wall Street Journal,* and other leading newspapers. Further, in June 2007, according to the *Times,* he signed a consulting contract with one of many defense companies he had relationships with, which sought his services to win a lucrative government contract. Four days later, McCaffrey did the firm's bidding by personally recommending to General David Petraeus, the commanding general in Iraq, that the company supply Iraq with armored vehicles, never mentioning his relationship to it. Nor did he reveal these ties when he appeared on CNBC that same week, during which he praised Petraeus, nor to Congress, where he not only lobbied to have the company supply Iraq with armored vehicles but directly criticized the company's competitor.[3]

Using information and access to link institutions and to leverage influence is what General McCaffrey and other such players were expected to do by an administration seeking public support, media in need of high ratings, industry pursuing profits, and academia in search of superstars. But because only the individual player bridges all these institutions and venues—by, for instance, enlisting access and information available in one to open doors or enhance cachet in another—only he can connect all the dots. Such a game involves a complex, although subtle, system of incentives that must reinforce its players' influential positions and access to knowledge and power. And the players must uphold their end of the bargain. When McCaffrey criticized the conduct of the war on the *Today* show, Secretary of Defense Donald Rumsfeld quickly cut off his invitations to Pentagon special briefings. Tellingly, McCaffrey went back on the air, reiterated the Pentagon's line, and regained entry into those briefings.[4]

McCaffrey owes some of his access to a Pentagon public relations campaign that enrolled retired, high-status military personnel as "message force multipliers" in the media, according to an earlier piece in the *Times.* McCaffrey was among the most high-profile members of the campaign, during which, from 2002 to 2008, the Pentagon provided the seventy-five analysts access to military campaigns and initiatives through private briefings, talking points, and escorted tours. Following the exposé and congressional calls for an investigation, government auditors looked into whether the Pentagon effort "constituted an illegal campaign of propaganda directed at the American public," as the *Times* put it. The Pentagon's inspector general found that Pentagon funds were *not* used inappropriately and that the retired military officers didn't profit unfairly from the arrangement. President Obama's Pentagon later rescinded the inspector general's report, but no new one was issued. Even when they are not whitewashed, such government audits are not designed to capture the reality of today's influencers and the environment in which they operate—a reality that poses potentially much greater harm to a democratic society than a mere drain on taxpayer dollars. While millions of viewers, Congress, and General Petraeus were led to believe that McCaffrey was offering his expert, unbiased opinions, McCaffrey's interlocking roles created incentives for him (and others of his profile) to be a less-than-impartial expert. The *Times* understatedly remarked, "It can be difficult for policy makers and the public to fully understand their interests."[5]

Meanwhile, the official and private organizations in and out of which such movers and shakers glide either just go along to get along or are ill equipped to know what these actors are up to in the various venues in which they operate. In McCaffrey's case, no institution, from the Pentagon to the defense contractor to NBC, had an incentive to be anything but complicit. Operators like the general have surpassed their hosts, speeding past the reach of effective monitoring by states, boards of directors, and shareholders, not to mention voters. And while the players sometimes cause raised eyebrows, they are highly effective in achieving their goals—and often benefit from wide acceptance. Much more than the influence peddlers of the past, these players forge a new system of power and influence—one that profoundly shapes governing and society.

This new breed of players is the product of an unprecedented confluence of four transformational developments that arose in the late twentieth and early twenty-first centuries: the redesign of governing, spawned by the rising tide of government outsourcing and deregulation under a "neoliberal" regime, and the rise of executive power; the end of the Cold War—of relations dominated by two competing alliances—which intensified the first development and created new, sparsely governed, arenas; the advent of ever more complex technologies, especially information and communication technologies; and the embrace of "truthiness," which allows people to play with how they present themselves to the world, regardless of fact or track record. While it may be jarring to mention such seemingly disparate developments in the same breath—and to name "truthiness" as one of them—the changes unleashed by these developments interact as never before.

The proliferation of roles, and the ability of players to construct coincidences of interest by those who perform them, are the natural outcome of these developments. So, for example, increased authority delegated to private players (facilitated by privatization, the close of the Cold War, and new, complex technologies) has enabled them to become guardians of information once resting in the hands of state and international authorities. While supposedly working on behalf of those authorities, such players (working, say, as consultants for states or as special envoys or intermediaries between them) can guard information and use it for their own purposes, all the while eluding monitoring designed for the past order of states and international bodies. And they get away with it. Appearances of the moment have become all-important in today's truthiness society, as comic Jon Stewart expressed in his quip: "You cannot, in today's world, judge a book by its contents."[6] Today's premier influencers deftly elude such judgment. Pursuing their coincidences of interest, they weave new institutional forms of power and influence, in which official and private power and influence are interdependent and even reinforce each other.

The phenomenon I explore is no less than a *systemic* change. A new system has been ushered in—one that undermines the principles that have long defined modern states, free markets, and democracy itself.

Naming the Animal

I call the new breed of influencers "flexians." When such operators work together in long-standing groups, thus multiplying their influence, they are flex nets. Flexians and flex nets operate at one extreme of a continuum in crafting their coincidences of interests.

Performing overlapping roles can be—and often is—not only benign, but can serve the interests of all the organizations involved, as well as the public's. Yet in an international arena that "multiplies the possibilities for double strategies of smugglers ... and brokers ... there are many potential uncertainties and mis-translations surrounding individual positions," as two political-legal scholars point out. Take, for instance, the individual who acts "as a political scientist in one context ... and a lawyer in another; a spokesperson for nationalistic values in one context, a booster of the international rule of law in another." This peripa-tetic political scientist/lawyer is not necessarily engaged in a "double strategy." But his activities on behalf of one organization can be at odds with those on behalf of another—even to the point of undermining the goals of either, or both. Flexians take these coincidences of interest to the *n*th degree. When an individual serves in interdependent roles, and is in the public eye promoting policy prescriptions, *and* when fundamental questions lack straight answers—Who is he? Who funds him? For whom does he work? Where, ultimately, does his allegiance lie?—we have likely encountered a flexian.[7]

To get a sense of flex activity as we could watch it becoming acceptable, let's take a look at Gerhard Schroeder, the Social Democratic chancellor of Germany from 1998 till 2005. While he did not flog a cause as do true flexians, he exhibited certain flex features and *almost* crossed the boundary into flexian-hood. In September 2005, before losing his bid for reelection, Schroeder signed a pact on behalf of his government with Gazprom, the Russian energy giant that commands a quarter of the world's natural gas reserves and represents a murky mix of state and private power. The agreement was to construct a Baltic Sea pipeline to run directly from Russia to Germany and supply gas to Germany and other western European nations. That December, after the election, he accepted a position as the head of Gazprom's shareholders' committee, a post roughly equivalent to board chairman. As the *Washington Post* editorialized, through his actions, Schroeder "catapulted himself into a different league."[8]

Germany paid a political price for the deal. Some Western Europeans warned that the pipeline would saddle Europe with greater dependency on Russian gas. And with the Russian navy ordered to protect the pipeline, critics foresaw new potential for espionage. Moreover, the two countries' central European, Baltic, and Ukrainian neighbors, bypassed by the pipeline's sea route, were outraged at being relegated to nonpartner status. In Poland, the deal unleashed sentiment recalling the Hitler–Stalin pact that had carved up the nation like a side of beef.[9]

Other peculiarities characterized the deal. The pipeline consortium's chief executive is Mathias Warnig, an ex-Stasi captain. As an East German spy, Warnig had worked with Vladimir Putin in the 1980s when the Russian president was overseeing the KGB bureau in Dresden. (The chair, or once deputy chair, of Gazprom's board of directors from 2000 to 2005 was Dmitry Medvedev, a Putin associate from St. Petersburg who became first deputy prime minister in 2005 and took over as president in 2008.) And according to Russian sources, while the German public learned of the pipeline deal in fall 2005, certain elites in Moscow had heard of it a full half year earlier.[10]

In this episode, crudely put, one sovereign state bought the chancellor of another state, one that is not only sovereign but the third largest industrialized nation in the world. Schroeder's arrangement with Gazprom evokes the unregulated deal making of a disintegrating command economy, such as those of 1990s transitional eastern Europe, and the circumvention of the free market by a public officer. During the Cold War, obviously, the deal would have been impossible. The Soviet Union did not have private companies, even ones thoroughly entangled with state power as it does today, to make private pacts with foreign leaders. The idea that the chief representative of a key ally of the United States would strike a deal with its rival that could potentially undermine its own national interest seems unthinkable; and the idea that word of such a deal would be spoken of in Moscow long before Berlin, equally unthinkable. Yet the end of the Cold War has shaken up not only relations among states but also their relations to markets, while creating new opportunities and incentives for the merging of official and private interests and power. Gazprom stands as a monument to what a Russian sociologist has called the "privatization of the state by the state"—a practice that apparently is becoming more acceptable.[11]

The Gazprom–Schroeder covenant challenged previous convention among Western democracies. Even though many people found Schroeder's behavior unacceptable, even scandalous, social pressure or cultural restraint did not deter him. More than four years after he accepted the position with Gazprom, he remained board chairman. If neither public opinion nor available mechanisms of states or international systems can hold Schroeder accountable, then who or what can? What he was able to get away with demonstrates an emerging standard of acceptability in which flexians and almost-flexians operate.[12]

Schroeder's deal with Gazprom does not seem so very different from some of the dealings exposed by the American financial crisis, which have evoked a public outcry about the collusion of high finance and government. Goldman Sachs, the vast investment bank with a wide reach of subsidiaries, investors, and friends—among them Henry Paulson, the former Sachs CEO and secretary of the Treasury who presided over the bailout of the company as the financial crisis came to a head in the fall of 2008—has been called "government Sachs."[13]

The new breed of players, who operate at the nexus of official and private power, cannot only co-opt public policy agendas, crafting policy with their own purposes in mind. They test the time-honored principles of *both* the canons of accountability of the modern state and the codes of competition of the free market. In so doing, they reorganize relations between bureaucracy and business to their advantage, and challenge the walls erected to separate them. As these walls erode, players are better able to use official power and resources without public oversight.

Flexians craft overlapping roles for themselves—coincidences of interest—to promote public policies (and sometimes their personal finances as well). These players, who generally work on more fronts and are more elastic in their dealings than similar operators in the past, both make the new system work and demonstrate how it does so. Consider, for example, Bruce P. Jackson, unofficial envoy, lobbyist, business professional, NGO founder and officer, and Republican Party activist. An operative with longtime ties to prominent neoconservatives Richard Perle and Paul Wolfowitz, as well as to Dick Cheney, Jackson served both in the Department of Defense and as a U.S. Army military intelligence officer from 1979 through the 1980s. After leaving government, he entered the private sector as a strategist for Lockheed Martin, today the largest federal contractor.[14]

In 1996, while Jackson was employed by Lockheed as vice president for strategy and planning, he and other neoconservatives founded the U.S. Committee to Expand NATO (later renamed the U.S. Committee on NATO) to push for the entry of former Eastern Bloc nations into what had been a Cold War defense group. Members of the board included Perle and Wolfowitz. (Jackson was also a project director of the Project for the New American Century, whose signatories included Wolfowitz and Cheney). Jackson served as president of the committee while still working for Lockheed, where, in 1997, he was made responsible for securing fresh international markets for the company after the end of the Cold War. NATO enlargement, of course, would supply that in spades. In 1996 and 2000 he served on and chaired, respectively, Republican Party platform subcommittees responsible for national security and foreign policy. According to journalist John Judis, the efforts of Jackson and the committee proved important to winning Senate approval for expanding NATO to include Poland, Hungary, and the Czech Republic.[15]

With that success in hand, Jackson and his fellows worked to further enlarge NATO and set up a spinoff organization with the same principal officers in the same offices as the U.S. Committee to Expand NATO. In congressional testimony, Jackson credits himself with creating the "Big Bang" concept of NATO expansion that the would-be (second-step) NATO allies largely later adopted. This endeavor meshed nicely with another goal halfway around the world: to overthrow Saddam Hussein via American power. That effort was exemplified by Jackson's creation in 2002 of another neoconservative-powered lobbying group, the Committee for the Liberation of Iraq, which he chaired. During that same year, in which he cut his formal ties to Lockheed, Jackson burnished his profile as a de facto representative for the George W. Bush administration in eastern Europe. Jackson was characterized by the U.S. ambassador to NATO as "an indispensable part of our efforts in reaching out to these [former Soviet bloc] governments" and by Georgia's president as "an official with clout." (The government of Romania also signed Jackson up to facilitate its entry into NATO, according to *Le Monde* and Romanian newspapers, though Jackson denies this.) Jackson's standing as a Bush administration envoy in the eyes of American and eastern European officialdom was indispensable to his efforts to convince the NATO hopefuls to do the administration's bidding—that is, to back the U.S.–crafted invasion of Iraq. Toward that end, Jackson helped draft a declaration supporting the invasion that was signed by the foreign ministers of ten nations then up for NATO membership—later called the Vilnius Ten. This declaration was politically significant, for it came at a time when the administration was eager to show that its "Coalition of the Willing" had substance.[16]

Players like Jackson, ostensibly a private citizen, yet working stealthily for U.S. executive branch masters, peddling and helping to craft policy, are accountable only to their patrons. Such players are not confined by government diplomacy or lobbying rules, yet they routinely perform those functions in a way few diplomats or lobbyists would have the portfolio to do. The whole package that constituted Bruce Jackson—from the exact source(s) of his marching orders, to the source(s) of his funds, to the promises he supposedly made on behalf of the United States to foreign governments, to the fallout from those promises—is saturated with ambiguity.

Jackson's type of brokering has become much more necessary in the post-Cold War world, with its expanded fragmentation of power and frequent relinquishing of information by states to all manner of private players. But such an enterprise is also much more fraught with potential ambiguity, making spies and even double agents look like the simplest of animals. The ability of brokers like Jackson to flex their overlapping roles is made easier when dealing across national, legal, and cultural contexts and in societies in political and legal flux. The reorganizing world has stimulated opportunities for flexians, without establishing balances to check these players' activities. Obtaining reliable information about a player's roles, sources of funds, and actual track record may be difficult, and viable monitoring systems are usually lacking. Flexians can thus continue unchecked to convert their environment into one that is friendly to them.

Now let's turn to a flexian who has championed, mastered, and made acceptable what he calls the "evolving door": Steven Kelman. He is a living example of how the new system has changed the profile of many of today's most successful influencers, moving them beyond the revolving door of the past. In the grand tradition of academics trooping to Washington to put their theories into practice, Kelman was invited by President Bill Clinton in 1993 to come from Harvard's Kennedy School of Government to assume the top contracting job in the federal government, heading the Office of Federal Procurement Policy (OFPP), part of the Office of Management and Budget.[17]

Kelman would perform a lead role in the Clinton administration's efforts at reinventing government. Known for his belief that the rules designed to prevent collusion between government contractors and public officials inhibited more efficient and innovative contracting practices, he set out to reform that system by deregulating the awarding of contracts. While Kelman's reforms did streamline the process, they also encouraged privatization of heretofore officially available information and processes, advanced the partnership idea, and spurred more opportunities for nontransparent deal making between government and contractor officials.[18]

Soon after his departure from government in 1997, Kelman became a member of a Department of Defense (DOD) task force charged with identifying "DOD Policies and Practices that Weaken Health, Competitiveness of U.S.

Defense Industry." One of the stated concerns prompting the formation of this body, according to a DOD press release, was the "beating" that the defense industry was taking on Wall Street at the time. While the task force presented Kelman's credentials as affiliated with Harvard and as a former OFPP administrator, he simultaneously served on the board of directors of, and held an equity interest in, a company with nearly billion-dollar per year average sales, almost all in government contracts.[19]

Kelman also put his punditry skills to work. He began writing a column for a trade publication, *Federal Computer Week,* distributed to nearly 100,000 readers, mostly government personnel involved in IT, contracting, or program management. In his column he has endorsed contractor-friendly policies for more than a decade. To his readers, Kelman is just a former OFPP administrator and Harvard professor promoting "good government"; his industry connections and consulting projects are rarely revealed. And this points to another feature of flexian performance: the tendency to hide behind one's most appealing role. In the world of media and punditry, flexians want to appear objective and devoid of self-interest. There they generally identify themselves to the unsuspecting public in their most honorable, least partisan role, thus concealing or downplaying other agendas. This is strategic: a high-prestige imprimatur like Harvard's enables Kelman and flexians like him to promote views for which they might not get a hearing if they had to fall back on their less neutral roles, such as those of company or industry consultant.[20]

A *Washington Post* news report's use of Kelman's "expert" commentary is one of many such cases. The *Post* article concerned a controversial government financing scheme championed by the Bush II administration, known as Share in Savings contracting. The *Post* quoted Kelman as a Harvard professor and former Clinton procurement policy chief who supported the technique. But he was at the time a registered lobbyist for a government contractor that was one of the largest beneficiaries of such contracting. While the *Post* issued a correction after the matter came to public light, most presentations by flexians are made with impunity and go unnoticed.[21] In an equally revealing incident, Kelman, in a *Post* op-ed, decried inspectors general reports that "generally advocate more checks and controls." Earlier an IG had recommended that a government contractor, in which Kelman held an equity interest and served on the board of directors of, be debarred from receiving federal contracts. "Small wonder he has it in for IGs," commented the Project On Government Oversight, a public interest organization.[22]

All these players, operating in and around diverse organizations and geographical areas, and of diverse ideological persuasions, surge beyond standard roles and responsibilities, as well as beyond standard rules and practices of Western states and international organizations. In the process, their operations swirl in and above the institutions for which they supposedly work—state, corporate, international, or other.

These players also have in common that their activities may sound like a simple litany of questionable ethics. They elicit shock from some: "Wow, did you see what he arranged/did/got away with/accomplished?" Observers are hard pressed to find comparable cases within their own institutional memories.

But, just as often, the response is tolerance—and sometimes downright admiration for the flexians' sheer nerve.

Another common response to the actions of flexians is to label them "conflict of interest" or "corruption." Yet while parties to corrupt activities typically engage in them for profit, the same cannot be said of flexians, who seek influence and to promote their views at least as much as money. And "coincidences of interest" crafted by the players to skirt the letter of the law are often difficult, if not impossible, to pin down as conflicts of interest. When those coincidences span the globe, limited organizational reach and the limited jurisdictions of legal systems can only further empower the players, who seek to derail any mechanisms of accountability that might apply. Flexians are additionally hard to challenge because, while some of their activities are open and appear eminently respectable, others are murky or hidden, often just below the surface.

Thus, while it may be virtually impossible to determine whether flex activity today is statistically on the rise, it does appear to be widely tolerated. Tongues may click in public expression of disapproval but, in the end, passive acceptance and the entrenching system encourage recurrence. The very people who engage in these activities continue to command public respect and influence, sometimes even garnering more. Moreover, national and international governments and organizations are often attracted to, and reward, flexians because they get things done.

Journalists and public interest watchdogs have excavated and published details of activities by all these players, but to little consequence. All of them continue to operate unbridled by institutional constraint or adverse public opinion; their careers—and their likely bank balances—soar ever higher. And the public interest falls by the wayside. But merely exposing certain activities is not enough; framing them is essential.

Evolution of the Species

My longtime focus on central and eastern Europe, studying communism as it really worked and then came undone, was excellent preparation for charting this new phenomenon. For it was there that I observed the sophisticated practices of dealing under the table, reading between the lines, shifting self-presentations, and social networking for survival. These were not only art forms in a society (Poland) where the "authorities" were far removed from the will of the people; they also helped nudge formal bureaucracy and economy away from communism. And when that system unraveled and informal maneuvering was given free rein, self-enfranchising individuals and networks acquired information, resources, and influence heretofore in the hands of communist authorities. These players maneuvered the power vacuums created by crumbling command systems (made obvious by the 1989 fall of the Berlin Wall and the 1991 breakup of the Soviet Union), sometimes joining forces with outside operators as they rushed into the same vacuums.

In late-1980s/early-1990s Poland, as it was sprinting away from communism, a revealing practice attracted my attention. Many officials I was interviewing gave me multiple business cards bearing different job titles. It's hard to count how many times I was given one, two, three, or even more cards by the same official.

This happened first in Poland, then in Hungary, Czechoslovakia, and later in Russia and Ukraine after the Soviet Union fell apart. A deputy minister of privatization, a housing and environmental official, and a key presidential adviser each gave me multiple business cards. In all these countries my interlocutors had established new roles, in fact several roles at once, each to be trotted out as the occasion arose. Typically they knew little about me. As a Western scholar with entrée in the region, they clearly reasoned, I must have potentially useful contacts among Western foundations, businessmen, or aid agencies.

When interviews with officials were winding down or turning more personal, they would hand me their official government card, followed in quick succession by other hot-off-the-press business cards—also theirs. Then they would fill me in on their activities: it seemed that, in addition to their government job, they also headed a consulting firm, a "foundation," or an NGO (often one they or their wives had founded). Sometimes these entities even did business with the government offices these officials supervised.

Those exhibiting flexian features first revealed themselves to me as I observed both native and foreign operators during the so-called transition to democracy, as they facilitated and profited from the changes under way. The edgy players who adapted to the new environment with the most agility and creativity, who tried out novel ways of operating and got away with them, and sometimes were the most ethically challenged, were most rewarded with influence. In the study of foreign aid I undertook in the 1990s, these traits were exhibited in abundance. I saw how the overlapping roles, networks, and sponsors of the actors involved in the aid process were crucial to understanding how certain high-priority aid efforts played out.

Probably nowhere else could flex activity become as integral a part of changes under way and also mingle with global transactions than in the post-Soviet empire. There, legacies of a militarized economy and secret police combined with collapsed command systems, law subordinated to politics, and informal networking, not to mention Western-promoted radical privatization schemes, to accrue spoils to a connected few. There, as well, entire realms of financial practice were created and money laundering reached new heights. Some players who cut their teeth there have taken their skills beyond the region, plying their trade in a global environment where huge sums of money, off the books and largely unmonitored and unregulated by any institution, flow freely and lavishly.

The people I came to call flexians would soon appear on the world stage. Some of them operated across borders in the manner of global elites, international high fliers who ally more comfortably with their fellow global elites than with their own countrymen. In addition to the cross-pollination of practices—and not necessarily "best" ones—among such elites, parallel processes also developed as flexians, transmuting and changing their colors as necessary, carried the tradition of "the fix and the deal" to new levels. Like masterful dancers who push beyond accepted steps and recognized routines, flexians perform on the edge, trying out and inventing new patterns. These players live symbiotically within the system, quietly evading and stretching its rules as they help mediate its transformation. The new system they help fashion blurs the boundaries between the state and private sectors, bureaucratic and market practices, and legal and illegal standing. Ironically perhaps, the formerly communist world and the maneuverings that flowed from its transition away from communism proved an ideal training ground for examining governing, power, and influence in the United States at the dawn of the twenty-first century. There the new era of blurred boundaries is marked by privatization and contracting out, and a resulting fusion (and confusion) of state and private power.

Beyond Old Boys

Flex nets (like flexians) arose to fill a niche that is new. Just as flexians cannot be reduced to mere lobbyists, neither can flex nets be reduced to interest groups, lobbies, old-boy networks, and other such groupings in American society, government, and business. Flex nets are far more complex. Like interest groups and lobbies, flex nets serve a long-established function in the modern state—negotiating between official and private. But while flex nets incorporate *aspects* of these and other such groupings, they also differ from them in crucial ways—and those ways are precisely what make flex nets less visible and less accountable.

Four key features define both flexians as individuals and those influencers who work together as a flex net. Flexians functioning on their own exhibit the modus operandi embodied in all four features discussed below, as does a flex net as a whole. Because members of a flex net benefit from the actions of the collective, pooling resources and dividing labor, not all members of a flex net must exhibit these features individually.

One, *personalizing bureaucracy*. Flexians operate through personalized relations within and across official structures, and act primarily based on loyalty to people, not organizations, to realize their goals. They *use* the formal organizations with which they are affiliated—governmental, corporate, national, or international—but their chief allegiance is to themselves and their networks. Flexians work bureaucracy to their advantage, preferring to operate by means anathema to official, legal, and procedural objectivity—the hallmark of the modern state that harks back to the classic model elucidated by Max Weber, the influential German sociologist.

Members of a flex net, with their loyalty to people over organizations, form an exclusive informal network that serves as *an intricate spine*—the corresponding (first) feature of flex nets. Flex nets draw their membership from a limited circle of players who interact with each other in multiple roles over time, both inside and outside government, to achieve mutual goals. While their roles and environments change, the group provides continuity. For instance, members of what I call the Neocon core, an informal group of a dozen or so members and a successful flex net, have worked with each other in various incarnations for some thirty years to realize their goals for American foreign policy via the assertion of military power. Whereas interest groups promote a political cause or defend the agendas of a particular group, and lobbies offer politicians support and resources in exchange for preference in policies, flex nets are not formal or permanent entities. Their existence is unannounced, and they do not seek to incorporate themselves as such. Moreover, members of flex nets are united by shared activities and interpersonal histories. "Interest groups" and "lobbies" do not convey the ambiguous state–private networks of flex nets, which coordinate power and influence from multiple vantage points—often far removed from public input, knowledge, or potential sanction.[23]

Two, *privatizing information while branding conviction.* Flexians believe—in any event, convincingly assert—that they have complete understanding of the cause that propels them into action. They have a theory. And theory that serves as an organizing catalyst is crucial in times of rapid and intense social change, as Vladimir Lenin famously pointed out. More than the opportunists who have benefited from blurred boundaries and disorder throughout history, flexians operate in today's environment of *perpetual* change. They play on loopholes produced by the four transformational developments. Among them is the vacuum of information left at the end of the Cold War as states could no longer lay exclusive claim to official information. Being frequent gatekeepers of inside access and "knowledge" enables flexians to brand information and control its applications. They are highly skilled at using the media to sell solutions to economic, political, and social ills, sometimes along with their own role in those solutions, so they are also able to convince others of their unique understanding in an uncertain world, one that often takes them on faith. Thus, to keep going on and on (to borrow Celine Dion's phrase), flexians offer easy-to-grasp stories and parables to a public yearning for simple explanations.[24]

When such influencers work together in a flex net, they exhibit *shared conviction and action*—the corresponding second feature of flex nets. Flex nets, like military elites and religious cults, induce obligation and loyalty through shared ideals and ordeals. Their goals as a unit are ideological and political, as well as to varying degrees financial and societal as a unit or a subset thereof. Members of a flex net act as a continuous, self-propelling unit to achieve objectives that are grounded in their common worldview, and to brand that view for the public. For instance, a cornerstone of the Neocon core's success over several decades has been the skill of its members at challenging official U.S. intelligence, creating alternative versions, and branding them as official and definitive for politicians, government, and the media.[25]

As self-sustaining teams with their own agendas, flex nets cut through bureaucracy, connect entities, and streamline decision making. This efficiency can make them attractive to an administration and the public, as was the Neocon core to the Bush II administration, especially in the president's first term. The sense of mission, perseverance, and ready strategy for advancing its goals that can make it an asset to an administration also means it can become a liability if the policies turn out to be unpopular, as did the Neocons'. And while members of a flex net serve "at the pleasure of the president," as does anyone else, they go on and on trying to achieve their goals. They differ from the "Wise Men" of the past such as the influential advisers who refashioned American foreign policy at the end of World War II and John F. Kennedy's "Best and Brightest" who executed the Vietnam War in the 1960s. These men were mainly instruments of the presidents whose policies they pursued.

Three, *juggling roles and representations*. Flexians perform interacting or ambiguous roles to maximize their influence and amass resources. Their repertoire of roles, each with something to offer, affords them more flexibility to wield influence in and across organizations than they would have if they were confined to one role. The juggling of flexians cannot be equated with the "revolving door," in which people move serially between government and the private sector. The revolving door acquired its meaning in an age when the lobbyist and the power holder were the brick and mortar of the influence game. Their roles were defined and confined. The new breed of players is more elastic in its engagement In the United States, for example, where players in policy and governing are just as or more likely to be *outside* formal (federal) government (in, say, consulting firms, think tanks, NGOs, and quasi-government organizations) than in it, players can occupy more roles than in the past and more easily structure their overlap to create a coincidence of interests. The ambiguity inherent in the interconnectedness of flexians' roles that can be kept separate, merged, or played off against each other at will yields not only flexibility but deniability. Ambiguity is not a mere byproduct; it is a defense. It enables flexians to play different sets of constraints off each other, skirting accountability in one venue by claiming they were operating in another. They need not necessarily break the rules; they merely shift around them. In this way, flexians defy scrutiny and public accountability while advancing their own agendas.

The corollary to flexians' juggling roles and representations is that members of a flex net form *a resource pool*—the corresponding third feature of flex nets. The influence of a flex net derives in part from its members' effort to amass and coordinate both material and interpersonal resources. As members parlay their roles and standing into influence opportunities by placing themselves in positions and venues relevant to their goals, the network as a whole can wield far more influence than an individual on his own. The Neocon core, for instance, is an example of how a ready-made network of players with its own private agendas can straddle a state-private seesaw to prescribe and help coordinate government policies of monumental import and impact; sell them to government officials, legislators, the media, and the public; help implement them; and continue this strategy, both to justify what they have done and to influence policies that follow from the course taken. While highly effective, such a group is elusive and more difficult to hold to account than lobbyists, interest groups, and the like.[26]

Four, *relaxing rules* at the interstices of official and private institutions. As flexians inhabit and shift among overlapping roles, they relax rules. They achieve their goals in part by finessing, circumventing, or rewriting *both* bureaucracy's rules of accountability and businesses' codes of competition, thus helping to create many of the choices and structural positions available to them. In (re)organizing relations among official and private institutions, flexians fundamentally change the qualities of each, fashion a new fusion, and give birth to an altogether new beast.

Collectively, members of a flex net help create *a hybrid habitat*—their corresponding fourth feature. A flex net's strength lies in its coordinated ability to reorganize governing processes and bureaucracies to suit the group's purposes. Members of these groups both use and supplant government, as well as establish might-be-official, might-be-unofficial practices to bypass it altogether. Poised to work closely with executive authorities, flex nets eschew legislative and judicial branches of government that may interfere with their activities. The Neocon core did all of these things to help take the United States to war in Iraq. As flex nets infuse governing with their supple, personalized, private-official networks, they transmogrify their environment, whether temporarily or more lastingly. While these groups might call to mind old notions such as conflict of interest, they illustrate why such labels no longer suffice. As a Washington observer sympathetic to the neoconservatives' aims told me, "There is no conflict of interest, because they define the interest."

The rise of flexians and flex nets (and almost flexians and flex nets) illustrates the evolution of the American system of governing. In the old days, when an individual handed someone his business card, there was less doubt about who he represented and what activities he was engaged in. On a collective level, networks within government and political elites that undermine democracy are, of course, nothing new. One study of American political power from the Civil War to the New Deal, for instance, depicts the web of ties among government officials and the threat that those connections pose to the notion of democratic government. Most famously, a half century ago, in his treatise *The Power Elite,* sociologist C. Wright Mills described the interlocking group of government officials, military leaders, and corporate executives at the pinnacle of the nation's establishment, who, he argued, effectively "controlled" major political and social decision making. The rise of flex activity augurs for an even less democratic era. Rather than climbing Mills's pyramid of the political, military, and business establishment, members of flex nets wield influence by forging coincidences of interest among an array of roles across organizations, whose boundaries and purposes often blend. Emergent forms of governing, power, and influence thus play out not in formal organizations or among stable elites, but in social networks that operate within and among organizations at the nexus of official and private power. The players in this system are less stable, less visible, and more global in reach than their forebears. Flex nets are a paradox: more amorphous and less transparent than conventional lobbies and interest groups, yet more coherent and less accountable, as one political scientist has observed. While many activities of flexians, and certainly their views, are public, the full array of their machinations is almost always difficult to detect. And the mechanisms of democratic input and control that could check them are just as difficult to discern.[27]

The new breed of players—today's shadow elite—are as elusive as they are ubiquitous. Agilely evading questions about who funds them, who they work for, or where their loyalties lie, individual flexians as well as those in flex nets benefit from the dust cloud of ambiguity and deniability they leave behind. They are not inherently unethical; in fact they sometimes do good and much-needed works, but they are subject to no greater oversight than their own consciences and the social pressure of their own networks. Their potential "corruption" is so interrelated that mechanisms that might curb their activities have yet to be invented. While charges of corruption may not stick, their activities are potentially more pernicious. They dilute effective monitoring, criticism, and consideration of alternative policies and, wherever they operate, have the potential to reshape governing. The inevitable result is that states, international organizations, companies, and NGOs face a new responsibility of grave proportions: investigating the track records, agendas, sponsors, and allegiances of the movers and shakers who work with them.

Over the past dozen or so years, my attempt to understand and explain the world of players who exhibit flexian behavior has led me to seek out others whose experiences and perspectives can shed light on this phenomenon. One of my many interlocutors has been the irrepressible Jack Blum. A lawyer and longtime observer of U.S. government agencies, he is an expert on money laundering as well as an investigator into Iran–Contra and other lesser-known affairs. In trying to capture the essence of the new breed, he told me one day: "If you're in the academic world, or you're a legal-type focused investigator, you want everything to fit into neat boxes, and none of this stuff fits into neat boxes. It's these multiple roles that these people have. None of these people are neat."[28]

NOTES

1. Anthropologist Aihwa Ong discusses "flexible identities" in Aihwa Ong, *Flexible Citizenship. The Cultural Logics of Transnationality* (Durham and London: Duke University Press, 1999).

2. Intelligence expert Steven Aftergood has employed the term "coincidence of interest" in this meaning, as cited in Tim Shorrock, "Former High-ranking Bush Officials Enjoy War Profits," Salon.com, May 29, 2008, http://www.salon.com/news/excerpt/2008/05/29/spies_for_hire/indexl.html.

3. The *New York Times* article reference is David Barstow, "One Man's Military-Industrial-Media Complex," *New York Times*, November 30, 2008, http://www.nytimes.com/2008/11/30/washington/30generals.html.
   Defense Solutions is the name of the company on whose behalf McCaffrey contacted Petraeus.

4. Ibid.

5. The earlier piece in the *Times* appeared in April 2008. David Barstow, "Behind TV Analysts, Pentagon's Hidden Hand," *New York Times*, April 20, 2008, p. Al, http://www.nytimes.com/2008/04/20/washington/20generals.html. The *Times's* characterization of the call for an investigation is from David Barstow, "Inspector General Sees No Misdeeds in Pentagon's Effort to Make Use of TV Analysts," *New York Times,* January 16, 2009, http://www.nytimes.com/2009/01/17/washington/17military.html.
   The Pentagon's inspector general report is Department of Defense, Office of Inspector General, *Examination of Allegations Involving DOD Public Affairs Outreach Program,* January 14, 2009, Report Number IE-2009–004, http://www.dodig.mil/

Inspections/IE/Reports/ExaminationofAllegationsInvolvingDoDOfficeofPublic
AffairsOutreachProgram.pdf. Responding to the report, the *Times* found striking
factual errors in the DOD's investigation, including that several military analysts
who have easily documented affiliations with defense contractors are listed as
having no such relations. The *Times* also pointed out inherent weaknesses in the
DOD's investigative approach (Barstow, "Inspector General Sees No Misdeeds ...").
For McCaffrey's response to the *Times,* see http://www.reuters.com/article/
pressRelease/idUS70468+17-Jan-2009+PRN20090117, and for response from
McCaffrey's consulting company, as well as a friend, see http://www.mccaffreyas-
sociates.com/pages/news.htm. For response by the *Times'*s ombudsman to these
points, see Clark Hoyt, "The Generals' Second Careers," *New York Times,* January
25, 2009, http://www.newsombudsmen.org/cgi-bin/ono_article.pl?mode=
view&article_id=1232910801.

For information on steps taken (and not taken) by the Obama administration with
regard to the Pentagon Inspector General's report, see Frank Rich, "Obama Can't
Turn the Page on Bush," *New York Times,* May 17, 2009, p. WK12. See also
Glenn Greenwald, "The Ongoing Disgrace of NBC News and Brian Williams,"
Salon.com, November 30, 2008, http://www.salon.com/opinion/greenwald/
2008/ll/30/mccaffrey/ (accessed April 15, 2009), and Glenn Greenwald, "NBC
and McCaffrey's Coordinated Responses to the NYT Story," Salon.com, December
1, 2008, http://www.salon.com/opinion/greenwald/2008/12/01/mccaffrey/
(accessed April 15, 2009). In addition to the Pentagon's inspector general, the
Government Accountability Office and the Federal Communications Commission
also initiated investigations of the Pentagon's program. In July 2009 the GAO found
that the Pentagon did not violate propaganda laws. See: GAO, "Department of
Defense—Retired Military Officers as Media Analysts," July 21, 2009, p. 2, http://
www.gao.gov/decisions/appro/316443.pdf.

6. Jon Stewart's *The Daily Show,* January 26, 2005, http://www.thedailyshow.com/
   video/index.jhtml?videoId=113523&title=headlines-the-rice-storm&byDate=true.

7. The political-legal scholars here quoted are Yves Dezalay and Bryant Garth, *The
   Internationalization of Palace Wars: Lawyers, Economists, and the Contest to Transform
   Latin American States* (Chicago: University of Chicago Press, 2002), pp.11, 10.

8. For mention of Schroeder having negotiated the deal as chancellor and other facts,
   as well as commentary, see: BBC, "Schroeder Attacked over Gas Post," December
   10, 2005, http://news.bbc.co.uk/2/hi/europe/4515914.stm. For *Washington Post*
   editorial, see: Editorial, "Gerhard Schroeder's Sellout," *Washington Post,* December
   13, 2005, p. A26, http://www.washingtonpost.com/wp-dyn/content/article/2005/
   12/12/AR2005121201060.html.

9. See, for instance, Ian Traynor, "Poland Recalls Hitler–Stalin Pact Amid Fears over
   Pipeline," *The Guardian,* May 1, 2006, http://www.guardian.co.uk/world/2006/
   may/01/eu.poland. Information provided by a Russian journalist who heard about
   the deal in April 2005.

10. The Russian sociologist here quoted is Olga Kryshtanovskaya, interviewed by Pavel
    Zhavoronkov, "Proiskhozhdenie VIPov. Bogatstvo v Rossii Ostaetcia Privilegiei
    Nomenklatury" (The Origin of VIPs: Wealth in Russia Remains the Nomenkla-
    tura's Privilege), *Kompania,* May 15, 2003, http://maecenas.ru/doc/2004_5_6.html.

11. Gazprom monopolized (and still monopolizes) the gas sphere, including its
    international aspects conducted in the interest of the Russian state, not a private

corporation. (Gazprom remains a strategic organization of the Kremlin, in which the power of the Kremlin clearly resides. It is in complete control of prospecting, transport, sale, distribution, pricing, and international activities.) Gazprom was born in 1989 in the Soviet Union's dying days when entire resource-rich ministries (in this case, the Ministry of Gas [the official translation is Soviet Ministry of Gas Industry]) were transformed into state enterprises under the personal control of members of the *nomenklatura.* While Gazprom was turned from a state ministry into a so-called private corporation in 1993 (after first being converted into a joint-stock company under the leadership of the prime minister, Viktor Chernomyrdin), the state owns more than 50 percent of its stock. (In November 1992, Russian president Boris Yeltsin signed decree #1333 "On the transformation of the state gas concern Gazprom into Russian joint-stock company 'Gazprom.'" See, for example, Elena Ivanova, "Gazovaia Industriia" [Gas Industry], *Vlast,* no. 47 [November 27, 2001], http://www.kommersant.ru/doc.aspx?DocsID=295883. See also "Theft of the Century: Privatization and the Looting of Russia. An Interview with Paul Webnikov," *The Multinational Monitor* 23, nos. 1, 2 [Jan/Feb 2002], http://multinationalmonitor.org/mm2002/02jan-feb02interviewklebniko.html).

12. For Schroeder's position, see Craig Whilock and Peter Finn, "Schroeder Accepts Russian Pipeline Job," *Washington Post,* December 10, 2005, http://www.washingtonpost.com/wp-dyn/content/article/2005/12/09/AR2005120901755.html.

13. In the fall of 2008, after the failure of Lehman Brothers brought credit markets to their knees, banks found political connections more precious than ever. With American investment banks in free fall, the most politically connected seemed to land on the padded mattress of the TARP program, while their competitors received the concrete blow of forced mergers. Thomas B. Edsell of the *Huffington Post* is among those who have pointed out that it was a Lehman competitor, Goldman Sachs, that benefited most from the bailout of the insurance giant American International Group (AIG). Goldman Sachs was the largest beneficiary of AIG's government sponsored life support—$12.6 billion. The key decision maker on these matters was Treasury Secretary Henry Paulson, the former CEO of Goldman Sachs. In fact, Goldman has taken significant advantage of government funds. As Edsell has written: "On November 25, 2008, Goldman became the first bank in the nation to benefit from the Federal Deposit Insurance Corp.'s Temporary Liquidity Guarantee Program (TLGP) ... All told, Goldman has issued a total of $20 billion in government-guaranteed debt under TLGP. In their dealings with banks, both Treasury and the Fed have been subject to relatively minimal disclosure, in order to protect the proprietary interests of financial institutions, especially to prevent rumors of illiquidity or excessive debt from threatening a bank's viability." Thomas B. Edsell, "AIG Bonus Bombshell Raises New Questions about Goldman Sachs," *Huffington Post,* April 2, 2009, http://www.huffingtonpost.com/2009/03/17/goldman-sachs-goes-for-th_n_175638.html. See also Lila Rajiva, "Three-Card Capitalists: The Financial Disappearing Act of 2008," LewRockwell.com, October 1, 2008, http://www.lewrockwell.com/rajiva/rajiva11.html.

14. Investigative reporter John B. Judis has unearthed many of the facts of Jackson's activities. See John B. Judis, "Minister "Without Portfolio," *The American Prospect, Inc.* 14, no. 5 (April 30, 2003), http://www.prospectorg/cs/articles?artide=minister_without_portfolio. See also Jackson's bio at the Project for the New American Century, http://www.newamericancentury.org/brucejacksonbio.htm. With regard to Lockheed Martin as the largest federal contractor, as of 2006, the

company was the largest defense contractor by revenue (http://www.defensenews.
com/static/features/top100/charts/rank_2007.php?c=FEA&s=TlC) and "the largest
provider of IT services, systems integration, and training to the U.S. Government,"
according to the company (http://www.lockheedmartin.com/aboutus/index.html).
See also Scott Shane and Ron Nixon, "In Washington, Contractors Take on
Biggest Role Ever," *New York Times*, February 4, 2007, p. A1; and Dana Hedgpeth,
"Balancing Defense and the Budget After Eight Boom Years for Spending on
Military Equipment, Contractors Expect a Slowdown," *Washington Post*, October
13, 2008, p.D01, http://www.washingtonpost.com/wp-dyn/content/article/2008/
10/12/AU2008101201724_pf.html. Lockheed Martin's Web site states: "As a global
security and information technology company, the majority of Lockheed Martin's
business is with the U.S. Department of Defense and the U.S. federal government
agencies. The remaining portion of Lockheed Martin's business is comprised of
international government and some commercial sales of our products, services and
platforms." See http://www.lockheedmartin.com/aboutus/index.html.

15. Judis, "Minister Without Portfolio." For perspectives on costs faced by new entrants
    to NATO, see John Laughland, "The Prague Racket," *The Guardian*, November
    22, 2002, http://www.guardian.co.uk/comment/story/0,3604,845129,00.html.
    For signatories of the original (June 3, 1997) statement of principles of the Project
    for the New American Century, see: http://www.newamericancentury.org/
    statementofprinciples.htm. For Jackson's role as project director, see http://www.
    newamericancentury.org/aboutpnac.htm.

16. For Jackson's congressional testimony, see Bruce Pitcairn Jackson, "Testimony
    before the Senate Foreign Relations Committee," April 1, 2003, http://www.
    globalsecurity.org/military/library/congress/2003_hr/jacksontestimony030401.pdf.
    See also F. William Engdahl, "The Emerging Russian Giant Plays its Cards Strate-
    gically," *Geopolitics–Geoeconomics*, http://www.engdahl.oilgeopolitics.net/
    Geopolitics_Eurasia/Russian_Giant/russian_giant.html. The "Vilnius Ten" consisted
    of Albania, Bulgaria, Croatia, Estonia, Latvia, Lithuania, Macedonia, Romania,
    Slovakia, and Slovenia. The text consists of a "Statement of the Vilnius Group
    Countries in Response to the Presentation by the United States Secretary of State to
    the United Nations Security Council Concerning Iraq," February 5, 2003. See
    "Vilnius Group Response to Powell UNSC Presentation on Iraq," America.gov,
    February 7, 2009, http://www.america.gov/st/washfile-english/2003/February/
    200302071732281fenner@pd.state.gov0.5013697.html. The source of Jackson's role
    is Judis, "Minister Without Portfolio." In 2003, Jackson shut the doors of both the
    Iraq and NATO committees. However, in the same set of offices, he and his
    colleagues launched a new undertaking, the Project on Transitional Democracies,
    another neoconservative-sponsored organization. See Engdahl, "The Emerging
    Russian Giant."

17. For Kelman's "evolving door," see, for example, Steven Kelman, "Evolving Door,"
    Government Executive Magazine 36, no. 4 (March 16, 2004), http://www.govexec.
    com/features/0304/0304view.htm. For a profile of Kelman, see Forbes.com,
    "Steven Kelman Profile," http://people.forbes.com/profile/steven-kelman/38757.

18. Kelman also led support for the Federal Acquisition Streamlining Act of 1994 (FASA)
    and the Federal Acquisition Reform Act of 1995 (FARA). See "Steven Kelman,"
    http://www.hks.harvard.edu/about/faculty-staff-directory/steven-kelman.
    For Kelman's views, see, for instance, the front flap of his 1990 book, as follows:
    "Requirements intended to promote competition in contracting have made the

performance of government worse, not better, according to Professor Kelman. Using federal procurement of computer systems as his model, Kelman shows the devastating effects of practices designed to prevent collusion between vendors and officials." Steven Kelman, *Procurement and Public Management: The Fear of Discretion and the Quality of Government Performance* (Washington, DC: American Enterprise Institute Press, 1990).

19. The advisory body Kelman sat on was the Defense Science Board Task Force. The press release is from the Bureau of National Affairs, "Gansler Asks Defense Science Board Group to Identify DOD Policies and Practices That Weaken Health, Competitiveness of U.S. Defense Industry," *Federal Contracts Report* 73, no. 4 (Jan. 25, 2000), p. 105. The board's final briefing is available at Defense Science Board Task Force, "Preserving a Healthy and Competitive U.S. Defense Industry to Ensure our Future National Security," November 2000, http://www.dac.mil/cgi-bin/GetTRDoc?AD=ADA3998658tLoca-tion=U2&doc=GetTRDoc.pdf. The name of the company referred to here is GTSI Corporation. For information about Kelman's role with GTSI, see "Investor Relations—Corporate Governance Biography," http://investor.gtsi.com/phoenix.zhtml?c=116604&p=irol-govBio&ID=58294. According to GTSI's Web site, "GTSI has provided technology products, professional services, and IT infrastructure solutions to federal, state, and local government." For GTSI company information, see "About GTSI," http://www.gtsi.com/cms/aboutgtsi/aboutdefault.aspx?ShopperID=36238be2-88bO-4856-8e7a-64993d5ec6fc. For GTSI's annual sales, see their Securities and Exchange Commission Form 10-K, GTSI Corp. Commission File Number 0-19394, for the fiscal year ending December 31, 2008, Part I, http://www.sec.gov/Archives/edgar/data/850483/000136231009003216/c82046el0vk.hhn#101. See also Forbes.com, "Steven Kelman Profile," http://people.forbes.com/profile/steven-kelman/38757.

20. Information on *Federal Computer Week's* audience and circulation is from its publisher, 1105 Media, Inc., http://certcities.com/pressreleases/release.asp?id=2. Kelman's column, "The Lectern," can be found at http://fcw.com/blogs/lectern/list/blog-list.aspx. For an example of Kelman presenting himself as a Harvard professor and former OFPP administrator, while failing to disclose his paid company connections yet advocating policies that benefit that company, see, for instance, Steve Kelman, "A Pair of Misguided Bills," *Federal Computer Week,* September 18, 2000, http://fcw.com/articles/2000/09/18/a-pair-of-misguided-bills.aspx.

21. Under Share in Savings contracting, contractors finance on behalf of the government certain capital improvements—typically information technology or energy equipment (such as heating or cooling systems)—in return for which the contractor receives a "share of the savings," a largely hypothetical calculation of what the government agency "would have spent" but for the contractors' contributions to capital improvement that led to "savings." Anitha Reddy, "Sharing Savings, and Risk: Special Contracts Appeal to Cash-Strapped Agencies," *Washington Post,* Business section, February 16, 2004, p. E01, http://pqasb.pqarchiver.com/washingtonpost/access/545898301.html?dids=545898301:545898301I&FMT=ABS&FMTS=ABS:FT8dmac=&date=Feb+16%2C+2004&author=Anitha+Reddy&desc=Sharing+Savings%2C+and+Risk. At the time of the *Post* article, Kelman was a registered lobbyist for Accenture Ltd., one of the largest beneficiaries of Share in Savings contracts, as well as a board member of FreeMarkets, Inc. Accenture's primary business model employs Share in Savings techniques (see GAO report, http://www.gao.gov/htext/d03327.html). The *Washington Post's* original article and correction are available at http://www.washingtonpost.com/ac2/wp-dyn/A44259—

2004Feb15?language=printer. Following such incidents and letters to editors demonstrating that Kelman had failed to disclose relevant industry affiliations, he began doing so in his *Federal Computer Week* column.

22. Kelman's op-ed can be found at Steve Kelman, "The IG Ideology," *Washington Post,* April 4, 2007, p. A13. Information from the Project on Government Oversight can be found at "Gutting Government Oversight: The Steve Kelman Ideology," POGO Web site, April 30, 2007, http://pogoblog.typepad.com/pogo/2007/04/gutting_governm.html.

23. With regard to members of flex nets being united by shared activities and interpersonal histories, in social network terms, members have "multiplex" ties vis-à-vis each other, meaning that they play multiple roles vis-à-vis their fellow members. Their ties are also "dense" in that each person in the group knows and can interact with every other person independently of any intermediary. Social network analysis is a long-standing method and theoretical perspective that focuses on social relations among actors, rather than the characteristics of actors. Pioneers in the field were John Barnes, Clyde Mitchell, and Elizabeth Bott, all associated with the Department of Social Anthropology at Manchester University in the 1950s. They saw social structure as networks of relations and focused on "the actual configuration of relations which arose from the exercise of conflict and power." John Scott, *Social Network Analysis: A Handbook* (London, UK: Sage Publications, 1991), p. 27. With respect to interest groups, some scholars have defined them broadly. In his summary analysis of the literature, political scientist Grant Jordan defines "interest groups" (the term typically used by American authors) and "pressure groups" (used by British authors) simply as "organizations that seek to influence public policy." Adam Kuper and Jessica Kuper, eds., *The Social Science Encyclopedia,* 3rd ed., vol. 1: A-K, New York: Routledge, 2004, p. 514. The category typically encompasses labor unions, professional associations, and voluntary associations founded to further a common interest, such as, to name some of the more powerful American groups, the National Organization for Women (NOW), Common Cause, the American Association of Retired Persons (AARP), the American Israel Public Affairs Committee (AIPAC), or the National Rifle Association (NRA).

24. Lenin said: "Without revolutionary theory there can be no revolutionary movement." Vladimir Lenin, quoted in Doug Lorimer, *The Birth of Bolshevism* (Resistance Books, 2005), p. 106, http://books.google.com/books?id=B0q8emwoTncC. Political scientist Theodore J. Lowi elaborates on this point. See Theodore J. Lowi, *The Politics of Disorder* (New York: Basic Books, 1971), especially chapter 2 and pp. 42–47.

25. Ideology and intense interconnectedness in multiple roles and venues distinguish flex nets from "issue networks," as defined by government scholar Hugh Heclo. Heclo coined the concept in 1978 to describe the "partnerships of groups or individuals" who organize around particular policy issues and attempt to influence policy development (James P. Pfiffner, interview with Hugh Heclo, "The Institutionalist: A Conversation with Hugh Heclo," *Public Administration Review,* May/June 2007, p. 421). When it suits their cause, these working groups of individuals form loose alliances with interest groups, nongovernmental organizations, and economic actors (Heclo, "Issue Networks and the Executive Establishment," *The New American Political System* [Washington, DC: American Enterprise Institute, 1978], pp. 87–124). Today, says Heclo, "issue activists are … increasingly important in all aspects of governing and political campaigning" (Pfiffner, "The Institutionalist").
With regard to the crucial role of information, as anthropologist Annelise Riles

points out, information has replaced capital as an organizer of social groups (Annelise Riles, *The Network Inside Out* [Ann Arbor, MI: University of Michigan Press, 2001], especially pp. 92–94).

26. For these reasons, among others, flex nets are not simply cliques, core groups whose members contact one another for multiple purposes and advance their own interests; see Jeremy Boissevain, *Friends of Friends: Networks, Manipulators and Coalition* (Oxford, UK: Basil Blackwell, 1974). Although flex nets can be seen as a *type* of clique (see Jacek Kurczewsld, ed, *Lokalne Wzory Kultury Politycznej* [Warsaw: Wydawnictwo Trio, 2007]), cliques do not typically possess key features of the flex net modus operandi that define its operations. Similarly, flex nets also are not merely political elites. While elites in many contexts exert power and control, as anthropologists (see, for instance, Cris Shore and Stephen Nugent, eds., *Elite Cultures: Anthropological Perspectives* [New York: Routledge, 2002]; and Mattei Dogan, ed., *Elite Configurations at the Apex of Power* [Leiden–Boston: Brill, 2003]) have shown, flex nets—small, mobile, and with a certain modus operandi—mean something much more specific than political elites.

    Flex nets also are not Mafias. While flex nets, like Mafias, work at the interstices of state and private (see Anton Blok, "Mafia," in *International Encyclopedia of the Social and Behavioral Sciences,* vol. 13 [Amsterdam: Elsevier, 2001], p. 9126), pursue common goals, and share rules of behavior, they should not be confused with Mafias (which, in the classic usage, are a type of patronage system, run by family enterprises, that developed in Sicily and Calabria, Italy). Unlike flex nets, which primarily seek to influence policy, Mafias pursue illegal transactions to gain power or wealth and employ violence to achieve their objectives. Federico Varese, "Mafia," *The Concise Oxford Dictionary of Politics,* eds. Iain McLean and Alistair McMillan (Oxford, UK: Oxford University Press, 2003).

27. The political scientist cited here is Simon Reich. See my joint article with Simon Reich, "Conspiracies, Clubs, Competitors, and Cliques: The Changing Character of American Politics," forthcoming. The study cited of American political power from the Civil War to the New Deal is by Philip H. Burch, Jr., *The Civil War to the New Deal* (New York: Holmes & Meier Publishers, Inc., 1981). C. Wright Mills's *The Power Elite* was first published in 1956 (New York: Oxford University Press). Following Mills, G. William Domhoff, in *Who Rules America?* (New York: Prentice-Hall, 1967), asserted that a few rich Americans control the nation. See also Morton Keller's *America's Three Regimes: A New Political History* (New York: Oxford University Press, 2007), which argues that the endurance of American political institutions lies at the heart of its success, and that such endurance depends upon a degree of continuity and exclusivity among political leaders.

28. Author's interview with Jack Blum, November 2, 2004.

QUESTIONS FOR MAKING CONNECTIONS
WITHIN THE TEXT

1. On the basis of Janine Wedel's "Confidence Men and Their Flex Lives," write a job description for a flexian. What kinds of education are probably required, and what kinds of employment? How does a flexian differ from an

ordinary professional, business person, academic specialist, or government bureaucrat? Consider the crucial importance of good communication skills. Why are these skills essential for a flexian's success, and what are the key arenas in which the flexian must communicate? How does a person get started on the road to becoming a flexian, and how do young, prospective flexians begin to create the flexnets within which they operate? In what ways are Barry McCaffrey and Steven Kelman perfect embodiments of the flexian type?

2. One reason that the flexians are hard to recognize, let alone keep track of, is that they move so readily across the boundaries that normally divide government and the public good from business and personal enrichment. A major theme of Wedel's discussion is the persistence of this "ambiguity" in the world of the flexians. What different forms of ambiguity does Wedel describe, and how does each enable the flexians to circumvent public oversight, ethical rules, and, on occasion, even laws? How do "truthiness" and "spin" work to protect flexians from scrutiny? In what ways do the values of a free society, which encourage openness and mobility, allow them to operate out of view?

3. How can we explain the rise of the flexians? Attributing their rise to simple "selfishness" is clearly unsatisfactory because selfishness has been, more or less, a constant throughout human history. What special aspects of social life today have made the flexian modality so appealing and effective? For example, one key element of the flexian life is group loyalty. According to Wedel, "Flex nets, like military elites and religious cults, induce obligation and loyalty through shared ideals and ordeals. Their goals as a group are ideological and political, as well as to varying degrees financial." Why would group loyalty be so important, and also financial advancement? Do flex nets help to compensate for the failure of other institutions which once made people feel secure— neighborhoods, communities, and governments? How might the security that flex nets provide come at the expense of society as a whole?

QUESTIONS FOR WRITING

1. Some readers might object strenuously to Wedel's account of flexians. These readers might argue that the flexians are actually creative and ingenious—in effect, social entrepreneurs. If you agree with this characterization, write a response to Wedel's argument in which you engage with her major points. Look in particular at what she says about their "interlocking roles." Are such interlocking roles an unavoidable consequence of life in a complex society, with many different sectors and layers? Is it possible that in a complex world, existing institutions—such as government and the press—are just too slow and isolated to act effectively?

2. Flexians first made their appearance in the old Soviet Bloc that included Eastern Europe and Russia. "Ironically," Wedel writes, "the formerly communist world and the maneuverings that flowed from its transition away

from communism proved an ideal training ground" for new flexians in Western Europe and the U.S. How does the decline of traditional institutions—government, business, the media, and the university—promote the rise of the flexians? In what ways might that rise be understood as a response to social disintegration, and in what ways do flexians actively contribute to the decay? What effect might their actions have on the credibility of the social order as a whole?

QUESTIONS FOR MAKING CONNECTIONS
BETWEEN READINGS

1. In "An Army of One: Me," Jean Twenge offers an "anatomy" of the Boomers and their offspring, Generation Me. About Generation Me, to which she herself belongs, Twenge makes these observations:

> GenMe's focus on the needs of the individual is not necessarily self-absorbed or isolationist; instead, it's a way of moving through the world beholden to few social rules and with the unshakable belief that you're important.... We simply take it for granted that we should all feel good about ourselves, we are all special, and we all deserve to follow our dreams.... Jason, 25, relates how he went through some tough times and decided he needed to change things in his life. His new motto was "Do what's best for Jason."

In what sense does the worldview of GenMe support the behavior typical of flexians? Consider in particular GenMe's emphasis on individual fulfillment and disregard for "social rules." Are flexians really just the most successful of the Boomers and their children? As you develop your argument, try to find passages that connect with Twenge's observations above.

2. In "A Life of Its Own," Michael Specter introduces his readers to leading figures in the field of "synthetic biology." These figures include Jay Keasling, Tim Knight, and Craig Venter. Even though they are all respected in the world of science, these three and many others in the field also have a financial stake in the research they are conducting, and all three have formed private companies. Do the leading figures whom Specter celebrates qualify as flexians, and if so, what special dangers might arises from their interlocking roles and potentially conflicting loyalties? In what ways might the dangers of bioengineering necessitate greater transparency and more intensive regulation? Are flexians the best people to decide the genetic future of life on earth?

Eight Sample Assignment Sequences

SEQUENCE ONE

Jean Twenge, An Army of One: *Me*
Jon Krakauer, *Selections from* Into the Wild
Caroline Fraser, Rewilding North America

1. We might view the existence of the self as both an objective fact and an unchanging reality, yet Jean Twenge's article strongly suggests that the self has meant different things at different moments in history. Using the details of Twenge's account to support your claims, make an argument responding to the view that the self is actually socially created. In what ways might society create the self, and how do changes in society alter the way people understand their own identity? Could something like a core self exist, independent of culture and history? Building on Twenge's analysis, consider what might be the optimum balance between the self and society as a whole.

2. Look carefully at Twenge's distinctions between Generation Me and the Baby Boomers. While GenMe has an essentially pragmatic orientation to the self, the Boomers' focus is more spiritual and abstract, more a process of self-discovery connected to a vision of a better social life. Then turn to Krakauer's narrative. Are the actions of Chris McCandless consistent with those that Twenge sees as typical of Generation Me? Does he come closer in many ways to the Baby Boomers, or does he seem to fit neither category well? Ultimately, does Krakauer's account confirm, complicate, or contradict Twenge's distinctions between the two generations?

3. The project of "rewilding" as described by Caroline Fraser entails a major re-thinking of the modern separation of wilderness from our cities and suburbs. What we need are not just more parks and preserves but corridors that will bring wilderness back into the heart of the human world. Drawing on Twenge and Krakauer as well as on Fraser, make an argument about the obstacles to re-thinking nature's place. Does GenMe seem to be well prepared to embrace the change that Fraser imagines? Could McCandless offer us a model of how we might overcome those obstacles, or does he represent a wrong turn?

SEQUENCE 2

Azar Nafisi, *Selections from* Reading Nabokov in Tehran
Oliver Sacks, The Mind's Eye
Robert Thurman, Wisdom

1. The members of Nafisi's Thursday morning seminar are all subject to the same policies under the same oppressive government. Yet we can observe subtle differences in the ways they have experienced oppression and in their responses to it. How might the seminar have allowed these and other dif-ferences to emerge? How does it change the young women, and how is Nafisi herself affected? On the basis of Nafisi's account, make an argument about the links between literature, imagination, and the expression of dif-ferences? To what extent do the arts empower people to express themselves? Are literature and, more broadly, the arts inherently liberating, or does the answer depend on the way we use them?

2. Sacks describes people who have lost their sense of sight but then reconstruct their perceptions of the world—and also their own mental processing. Drawing on the evidence that Sacks presents, as well as Nafisi's story of her reading group, make an argument about human creativity and the nature of the real world. Is the real world as fixed and inflexible as people often sup-pose? Is there a single reality at all, or are there many different realities? Are there limits to our ability to reshape the way we experience the real? Is every understanding of the world an act of creativity?

3. In "Wisdom," Thurman advances a surprising claim—that there is no essential self. After considering his reasons, turn your attention once again to Nafisi and Sacks, especially their account of the way that people change themselves and their experience of the world around them. On balance, do their accounts seem to support Thurman's fundamental argument? Or do they imply that an essential self actually seems to exist? If the answer is yes, then how might they respond to Thurman's argument? If the answer is no, then please illustrate, using particular examples from their two accounts.

SEQUENCE 3

Beth Loffreda, *Selections from* Losing Matt Shepard
Leila Ahmed, On Becoming an Arab
Deborah Tannen, Debate and the Hope of Dialogue

1. It is possible to argue that the real subject of "Losing Matt Shepard" is not actually Matt Shepard at all, but the way the media have covered his murder and its complex aftermath? This assignment asks that you explore the images of Matt that the media created, and also the images of the town of Laramie itself, as a community. Would you say the real Matt Shepard disappears in a confusion of representations? What role does Loffreda herself play? And why does it matter if we get the story "right"? Indeed, what would "getting it right" really mean?

2. Both gay people and Arabs occupy an ambivalent position in contemporary Western culture. Relying on the evidence provided by Loffreda and Ahmed, describe the way that personal identity reflects complex relations within the larger society. Ahmed experienced the label of "Arab" as an imposition she continues to resist even to this day. Matt Shepard came out in the open—by joining, for example, the LGBTA—and met with fatal violence. What general conclusion can you reach about identity and society? Does identity always require some degree of struggle, and if so, what does that struggle involve? In what ways do alliances help, and how do those alliances sustain certain kinds of identity against outside pressure?

3. Employ Loffreda's and Ahmed's work to explore the strengths and limits of Tannen's argument. Even though the "argument culture" may indeed have all the defects that Tannen alleges, do you think that dialogue is a viable option if the world is actually the way Loffreda and Ahmed describe it? Instead of deploring the brutality of the argument culture, should we look at it instead as our best response to a violent world? Or does it actually make matters worse by repaying violence with violence?

SEQUENCE 4

Daniel Gilbert, Immune to Reality
Michael Specter, A Life of Its Own
Edward Tenner, Another Look Back, and a Look Ahead

1. In "Immune to Reality" Gilbert marshals a great deal of evidence to support the argument that "people are typically unaware of the reasons why they are doing what they are doing." He maintains that this habit goes unnoticed because we consciously invent reasons that are often far removed from our real, unconscious motives. Is it Gilbert's purpose to demonstrate that reason has no value and should play no part in the conduct of our affairs? Doesn't

Gilbert's own argument qualify as an exercise in reason? Ultimately, what is the value of consciousness and reason in Gilbert's argument?

2. Taking Specter as your guide, explore the motives that might lie behind the growing field of synthetic biology. First of all, what seem to be the conscious motives? Then consider what might be the *unconscious* motives. Look carefully at the things people say about this new program of research, investment, and development. Then, using Gilbert, try to find moments where "cooking the facts" might be taking place. This assignment requires you to look very carefully at what people say—Keasling, Venter, and the others. You should also look carefully at the experiments that Gilbert describes. Finally, try to step back and construct an argument about synthetic biology as a potential path to human happiness. Is it really likely to improve our lives?

3. Tenner begins his selection with the title of a symposium on the effectiveness of health care: "Doing Better and Feeling Worse." He observes a persistent split between the way we understand our situation and a reality that is often much better. Because we are inclined to notice problems first, and because problems are inevitable, we often look with a jaundiced eye on the benefits of progress. Tenner's purpose is to make us think again: even though problems will always arise, he assures us that technology has improved our lives on the whole. But what if Gilbert's argument is correct, and we often cook the facts? How can we be sure that things are really getting better? In the case of a technology like the one that Specter describes, self-deception could be quite dangerous. Using all three authors, make an argument about our ability to control the technology we create. Are we in charge or, in a certain sense, does our technology control us?

SEQUENCE 5

Karen Armstrong, Homo religiosus
Nicholas Carr, Is Google Making Us Stupid?
Juhani Pallasma, *Selections from* The Eyes of the Skin

1. In "Homo religiosus," Armstrong describes religion in a way that we might not even recognize. Rather than focusing her attention on the existence (or nonexistence) of God, personal salvation, and the afterlife, she evokes religious practices that are concerned with self-emptying and the achievement of a deeper, nonverbal connection to the world. Basing your response on Armstrong's account, explore how experiences of this kind could have benefited human beings in the past. What good might have been served, for example, by the experience of *ekstasis*? What value might such experiences have in our own time?

2.   Nicholas Carr is troubled by the possibility that the Internet has narrowed the range of our mental lives—making our reading shallow rather than deep, and contracting our attention spans as we multitask or shift from screen to screen, anxiously surfing for new information. Drawing on Carr's observations, would you say that the new Internet consciousness has important commonalities with the forms of consciousness that Armstrong describes? Or does the Internet create a consciousness different from the ones prevalent in ancient times, and also from the one created by the reading of books? On the basis of these reflections, make an argument about how consciousness has changed, from the Paleolithic era until now.

3.   Using Armstrong, Carr, and Pallasmaa, make an argument about the fate of the sensuous in our time. Pallasmaa's essay is, after all, a protest against the neglect of the senses by modern architecture. When he sets out to retrace the path to our modern predicament, he starts with the Ancient Greeks and the Renaissance, which invented perspectival representation. But the problem may go farther back than that. Does Armstrong's account provide evidence for the conclusion that our ancestors in prehistory were less constrained by "ocularcentrism"? Do you see evidence that they enjoyed sensuous life more fully than we do? And what about the impact of the Internet, as interpreted by Carr? What does "the sensuous" mean today?

SEQUENCE 6

Charles Siebert, An Elephant Crackup?
Jon Krakauer, *Selections from* Into the Wild
Malcolm Gladwell, The Power of Context

1.   In "An Elephant Crackup?," Siebert quotes Gay Bradshaw on the basic changes that humans need to make in order to ensure the survival of healthy elephant populations: "In addition to conservation, we need to educate people about how to live with wild animals like humans used to do, and to create conditions whereby people can live on their land and live with elephants without it being this life-and-death situation." Siebert takes this thinking one step farther by arguing that the elephants' survival depends on humans developing a deeper sense of identification with the natural world. In what ways does Siebert's own essay help to create that sense?

2.   Considering Chris McCandless's experiences in the "wild," what do you think that his story suggests about Siebert's argument for a "deep, interspecies empathy"? Does McCandless's struggle to survive bring him closer to other species, or does it simply reinstate a division between humans and other animals? Might it be the case that people in the modern world—living in cities and relying on sophisticated technology—can develop a greater

empathy precisely because they interact with animals in a less predatory way? Or has modernization made interspecies rivalries more intense?

3. Gladwell demonstrates that social change tends to happen in a nonlinear way. Sometimes small changes can suddenly trigger enormous shifts in the ways that people think and act. Drawing on ideas like the Broken Windows Theory and the Power of Context, make an argument about how we might set the stage for a change in the way people think about the natural world. What Tipping Point might bring about the interspecies understanding Siebert wants to see? What can we learn from Krakauer's account about the difficulties that might arise when we try to live more closely to the natural world?

SEQUENCE 7

Janine Wedel, Confidence Men and Their Flex Lives
Steven Johnson, The Myth of the Ant Queen
Martha Stout, When I Woke Up Tuesday Morning, It Was Friday

1. Normally flexibility is a quality we respect. We praise people who are able to adapt to changing circumstances, and we tend to feel sympathy (or perhaps contempt) for those can't adapt or keep up. On the other hand, we can also feel resentful of people who are so adaptable that we no longer find them worthy of trust, perhaps because their readiness to change threatens the well being of others. In what ways do Wedel's flexians embody certain basic contradictions of a culture that highly values change and adaptability?

2. Johnson's chapter might be understood as a celebration of change that rests on a virtually invincible optimism. No matter how chaotic change might appear, Johnson suggests that an invisible hand will always shape things for the best. In what ways might Wedel's account of flexians complicate Johnson's celebration of change? Is it possible that the forces of change might be taking us to a future where democracy, equality, and honest government have all become distant memories? How can such an outcome be possible if the world operates as Johnson suggests?

3. The focus of Stout's chapter is the experience of dissociation. On the one hand, it has the power to protect us from trauma and violence, but it can also destroy our lives by increasing our isolation from the world and other people, even those we love. Is it possible for whole societies to fall prey to the malady of dissociation that Stout describes? "All human beings," she observes, "have the capacity to dissociate psychologically." If sanity really is a myth, as implied by the title of Stout's book—*The Myth of Sanity*—there could be thousands of Julias, Seths, and Lilas in America today. From the evidence provided by Wedel, Johnson, and Stout, would you say that dissociation has become an important element of social life?

SEQUENCE 8

Christine Kenneally, You Have Gestures
Tim O'Brien, How to Tell a True War Story
Jonathan Boyarin, Waiting for a Jew

1. In "You Have Gestures," Kenneally argues that language has its roots in gesture. Even though we might think of language as distinct from gesture, the two are really part of a single system. At first blush this claim could seem rather unsurprising, but consider the time-honored hierarchy between the mind (language) and the body (gesture). If language really is a form of gesture, and gesture is a kind of language too, then how should we conceive of the relation between the body and the mind? As you respond, take a second look at the examples that Kenneally gives, including those involving animals. When we talk about "mind," do we really mean a special kind of shared attention? Do minds belong to individuals, or to social groups whose members communicate with one another?

2. Look carefully at the examples of nonverbal communication in O'Brien's "How to Tell a True War Story." For example, O'Brien describes the time when Curt Lemon and Rat Kiley "started goofing":

    They went off into the shade … and they were giggling and calling each other yellow mother and playing a silly game they'd invented. The game involved smoke grenades, which were harmless unless you did stupid things, and what they did was pull out the pin and stand a few feet and play catch under the shade of those huge trees.

    Using Kenneally as a guide, explain what the two men might have meant to say with their actions in this passage. Then look at some of the other vignettes and analyze them in the same way. What messages do these vignettes communicate about the experience of war?

3. "Waiting for a Jew" might be understood as a story about what Kenneally calls "shared attention." How is shared attention created by collective activities like reciting the Hebrew alphabet, going to shul on *shabbes*, observing Purim, Rosh Hashanah, and Yom Kippur, wearing teffilin, and so on? In Kenneally's own chapter, language and gesture foster "shared attention" not only among humans, but among other primates, too. And in O'Brien's story, shared attention plays a life-and-death role in circumventing danger while preserving group morale and solidarity. Drawing on Boyarin's narrative as well as Kenneally and O'Brien, make an argument about the links between shared attention and community.

Credits

p. 01 "On Becoming an Arab" from *A Border Passage: Cairo to America—A Woman's Journey* by Leila Ahmed. Copyright © 1999 by Leila Ahmed. Reprinted by permission of Farrar, Straus and Giroux.

p. 21 "Homo religiosus" from *The Case for God* by Karen Armstrong. Copyright © 2009 by Karen Armstrong. Used by permission of Alfred A. Knopf, a division of Random House, Inc.

p. 44 Reprinted from Jonathan Boyarin, "Waiting for a Jew: Marginal Redemption at the Eighth Street Shul," in *Between Two Worlds: Ethnographic Essays on American Jewry,* edited by Jack Kugelmass. Chapter copyright © 1988 by Jonathan Boyarin. Copyright © 1988 by Cornell University. Used by permission of the publisher, Cornell University Press.

p. 66 "Is Google Making Us Stupid?" by Nicholas Carr from THE *ATLANTIC,* July/August 2008. Copyright © 2010 by Nicholas Carr. All Rights Reserved. http://www.theatlantic.com/magazine/archive/2008/07/is-google-making-us-stupid/6868/.

p. 77 "The Naked Citadel" by Susan Faludi. Copyright © 1994 by Susan Faludi. First appeared in The *New Yorker.* Reprinted by permission of the author and the Sandra Dijkstra Literary Agency.

p. 110 "Rewilding North America" by Carolyn Fraser from *Rewilding the World: Dispatches from the Conservation Revolution,* Henry Holt and Company, 2009. Reprinted by permission.

p. 132 "Immune to Reality," from *Stumbling on Happiness* by Daniel Gilbert. Copyright © 2006 by Daniel Gilbert. Used by permission of Alfred A. Knopf, a division of Random House, Inc.

p. 151 From *The Tipping Point: How Little Things Can Make a Big Difference* by Malcolm Gladwell. Copyright © 2000, 2002 by Malcolm Gladwell. By permission of Little, Brown and Company, Inc.

p. 168 Reprinted with the permission of Scribner, an imprint of Simon & Schuster Adult Publishing Group, from *Emergence: The Connected Lives of Ants, Brains, Cities, and Software* by Steven Johnson. Copyright © 2001 by Steven Johnson. All rights reserved.

Author and Title Index

Ahmed, Leila, 1–20
"Another Look Back, and a Look Ahead" (Tenner), 432–458
"Army of One: *Me,* An" (Twenge), 476–501
Armstrong, Karen, 21–43

Boyarin, Jonathan, 44–65

Carr, Nicholas, 66–76
"Confidence Men and Their Flex Lives" (Wedel), 502–525

"Elephant Crackup?, An" (Siebert), 320–336

Faludi, Susan, 77–109
Fraser, Carolyn, 110–131

Gilbert, Daniel, 132–150
Gladwell, Malcolm, 151–167

Homo religiosus (Armstrong), 21–43
"How to Tell a True War Story" (O'Brien), 268–280

"Immune to Reality" (Gilbert), 132–150
"Is Google Making Us Stupid?" (Carr), 66–76

Johnson, Steven, 168–185

Kenneally, Christine, 186–201
Krakauer, Jon, 202–223

Loffreda, Beth, 224–246
"Life of Its Own, A" (Specter), 363–379

Mason, Jim, 337–362
"Meat and Milk Factories" (Singer and Mason), 363–379
"Mind's Eye: What the Blind See, The" (Sacks), 302–319
"Myth of the Ant Queen, The" (Johnson), 168–185

Nafisi, Azar, 247–267
"Naked Citadel, The" (Faludi), 77–109

O'Brien, Tim, 268–280
"On Becoming an Arab" (Ahmed), 1–20

Pallasmaa, Juhani, 281–301
"Power of Context: Bernie Goetz and the Rise and Fall of New York City Crime, The" (Gladwell), 151–167

"Rewilding North America" (Fraser), 110–131
"Roots of Debate in Education and the Hope of Dialogue, The" (Tannen), 401–431

Sacks, Oliver, 302–319
Selections from *Into the Wild* (Krakauer), 202–223
Selections from *Losing Matt Shepard: Life and Politics in the Aftermath of Anti-Gay Murder* (Loffreda), 224–246
Selections from *Reading Lolita in Tehran: A Memoir in Books* (Nafisi), 247–267
Selections from *The Eyes of the Skin* (Pallasmaa), 281–301
Siebert, Charles, 320–336
Singer, Peter, 337–362
Specter, Michael, 363–379
Stout, Martha, 380–400

Tannen, Deborah, 401–431
Tenner, Edward, 432–458
Thurman, Robert, 459–475
Twenge, Jean, 476–501

"Waiting for a Jew: Marginal Redemption at the Eighth Street Shul" (Boyarin), 44–65
Wedel, Janine, 502–525
"When I Woke Up Tuesday Morning, It Was Friday" (Stout), 380–400
"Wisdom" (Thurman), 459–475

"You Have Gestures" (Kenneally), 186–201